Contemporary Democracy

A Bibliography of Periodical Literature, 1974–1994

Contemporary Democracy
A Bibliography of Periodical Literature, 1974–1994

J. J. van Wyk, Ph.D.

Mary C. Custy, J.D., M.A., M.L.S.

Congressional Quarterly Inc.

Washington, D.C.

About the Authors

J. J. van Wyk holds a Ph.D. in political science from the University of Pretoria, South Africa. He is currently a freelance writer and researcher based in Albuquerque, New Mexico. He taught political science at various universities from 1973 to 1994 and served as professor and director of the International Studies Unit at Rhodes University. He is a former editor of *Politikon*. He has published articles in *Journal of Conflict Resolution, Social Science Quarterly, Comparative Strategy, International Studies Notes, Politikon,* and *South African Journal of International Affairs*. He is coauthor of *Basic Political Concepts*.

Mary C. Custy holds a Juris Doctor and master's in international studies from the University of South Carolina as well as a master's of library science from Catholic University of America. She is currently on the faculty of the University of New Mexico School of Law serving as reference librarian and acting associate director. She has published articles in *International Studies Notes, Politikon, South African Journal of International Affairs,* and the *New Mexico Bar Journal*. She is coauthor of *The Jurisprudence of United States Constitutional Interpretation* (forthcoming).

Copyright © 1997 Congressional Quarterly

Printed in the United States of America

Library of Congress Cataloging-in-Publication Data

Van Wyk, J. J., B.A.
    Contemporary democracy : a bibliography of periodical literature,
  1974–1994 / J. J. van Wyk, Mary C. Custy.
      p. cm.
    Includes index.
    ISBN 1-56802-244-1
    1. Democracy—Bibliography.   I. Custy, Mary C.   II. Title.
Z7164.D2V36   1996
[JC423]
016.3209'009'049—dc20   96-44880

To Janie and Jane Custy

Contents

Preface

Contemporary Democracy utilizes a multidisciplinary approach to capture the rich literature on the topic of democracy. Since the mid-1970s, democracy as a form of government has dominated political science literature. Known as the "third wave of democracy," this phenomenon started when countries in southern Europe abandoned dictatorship in favor of more democratic forms of governance. Soon numerous countries in Latin America, Eastern Europe, Asia, and Africa followed suit.

With the process of democratization came efforts to reorganize public life. Governments had to act in a far more accountable manner to the demands and rights of their citizens than ever before. Simultaneously, the effectiveness of established democracies remained an important topic of academic inquiry: various writers noted the obstacles in the processes of democratic governments and the inability of established democracies to solve serious societal ills.

Topics relating to democracy also extended into the workplace, the economy, education, and religion. This broad impact of democracy is reflected in an ever-expanding body of literature as we move into the twenty-first century. Accordingly, the compilation of this work was not driven by any particular definition of democracy. We simply labored to include any article that dealt with democracy in one form or another regardless of the individual author's concept of the term.

Contemporary Democracy is a multidisciplinary reference work designed to access a wide array of literature by offering an extensive collection of journal and periodical citations that specifically focuses on the topics of democracy and democratization. The book is organized in two parts: Bibliography and Subject Index. The parameters of the book are as follows:

A. Topic: Democracy and democratization.
B. Time frame: 1974 to 1994.
C. Resources: More than 1,400 journal and periodical sources.
D. Multidisciplinary focus: Topics of democracy were drawn from the areas of political science, law, business, economics, education, sociology, history, philosophy, public administration, and public policy.
E. Language coverage: English and foreign language citations.

We would like to express our gratitude to the many people who have helped in the preparation of this book. We extend our deep appreciation to the staff of Congressional Quarterly Books for their support and help in preparing the manuscript for publication. In particular, we would like to thank Shana Wagger, Talia Greenberg, Ann O'Malley, and Doris Baker, as well as our anonymous reviewers for their many constructive comments. David Anstine and Susie Marbury, of Computer and Technology Services at the University of New Mexico School of Law, deserve special recognition for their invaluable technological advice and support throughout this project.

User's Guide

Organization: *Contemporary Democracy* is divided into two parts: Bibliography and Subject Index.

Bibliography: The bibliography contains almost 8,000 entries organized in two sections: 7,842 entries arranged alphabetically by first and coauthor's name and 114 entries arranged as a collection of articles.

Each first author entry in the bibliography contains the accession number, author(s), date, article title, journal, volume and number, and page number. An asterisk (*) following an article title denotes a translation.

Example:
304. ASSARSON, J. 1993. The Problem of Intraparty Democracy.* *Statsvetenskaplig Tidskrift* 96(1):39–68.

Subject Index: The subject index is an alphabetical listing of terms related to the study of democracy that includes scholarly terms, persons of theoretic or bibliographic importance, country names, geographical regions, organizations, institutions, government agencies, and events. For each entry in the bibliography there will be one or more terms in the subject index that have been cross-referenced.

The subject index includes three levels of entries. All are related to the theme of democracy.

In the subject index, main terms are capitalized (ECONOMIC DEVELOPMENT). Under each main term there is an alphabetic listing of related terms (democratization). Related terms may be followed by alphabetically arranged terms that furnish more specific information (Latin America).

All subject index entries are followed by at least one accession number that corresponds with accession numbers in the bibliography as outlined above.

Points of Entry: There are three ways of locating an article: By first author's name in the bibliography section; by topic or term in the subject index correlated by accession number to the bibliography entries; and by coauthor's name in the bibliography section.

Examples of searches by author, by topic or term, and by coauthor follow:

Example 1—To search by first author in the bibliography.

To search for articles published by Larry Diamond on democracy, use the following steps:
(1) In the bibliography, search alphabetically for "Diamond, L."
(2) Several article citations will be located ranging from accession numbers 1707 to 1720.

Example 2—To search by topic or term in the subject index.

To search for articles on the "influence of economic development on democratization in Latin America," use the following steps:
(1) Search for main term ECONOMIC DEVELOPMENT in the subject index.
(2) Scan the related terms arranged alphabetically under ECONOMIC DEVELOPMENT until "democratization" is found.
(3) Scan the terms arranged alphabetically under "democratization" to find "Latin America."

(4) Locate the accession numbers following "Latin America," which are 247, 383, 497, 2063, 2528, 6720, 6809, and 6902.

(5) Find accession number 247 in the bibliography for the article citation. The entry reads:

247. Ardito-Barletta, N. June 1990. Democracy and Development. *Washington Quarterly* 13 (3):165–175.

(6) Repeat step 5 for the other article citations listed by accession numbers.

Example 3—To search by coauthor in the bibliography.
(1) In the bibliography, search alphabetically for "Arevalo, J. January 1993."

(2) After the entry is listed a reference to the first author: "*See* Harris, E. (January 1993)."

(3) Find "Harris, E. (January 1993)" listed alphabetically in the bibliography. The entry reads

Harris, E., M. Lopez, J. Arevalo, J. Bellatin, A. Belli, J. Moran, C. Orrego. January 1993. Short Courses on DNA Detection and Amplification for Public Health in Central and South America: The Democratization of Molecular Biology. *Biochemical Education* 21(1):16-22.

(4) Note that "J. Arevalo" is listed as one of many coauthors in the article citation.

List of Sources

Academy of Management Review
Across the Board
Acta Oeconomica
Acta Politica
Acta Psiquiatrica y Psicologica de America Latina
Acta Sociologica
Actes de la Recherche en Sciences Sociales
Administration and Change
Administration and Society
Administrative Change
Administrative Science Quarterly
Adult Education Quarterly
Advances in Nursing Science
Afers Internacionals
Affari Esteri
AFL-CIO American Federationist
Africa
Africa (London)
Africa (Roma)
Africa Quarterly
Africa Report
Africa Spectrum
Africa Today
African Affairs
African Business
African Studies Review
Afrika Spectrum
Afrique Contemporaine
Aggiornamenti Sociali
Air University Review
Akron Business and Economic Review
Albany Law Review
Alberta Law Review
Alternatives
America Latina
America Latina Loy
American Annals of the Deaf
American Anthropologist
American Archivist
American Asian Review
American Bar Association Journal
American Bar Foundation Research Journal
American Behavioral Scientist
American Economic Review

American Educational Research Journal
American Enterprise
American Enterprise Institute Economist
American Historical Review
American Imago
American Journal of Comparative Law
American Journal of Economics and Sociology
American Journal of Education
American Journal of International Law
American Journal of Legal History
American Journal of Political Science
American Journal of Sociology
American Legion Magazine
American Political Quarterly
American Political Science Review
American Politics Quarterly
American Psychologist
American Review of Politics
American Review of Public Administration
American Sociological Review
American Sociologist
American Spectator
American Statistician
American University Journal of International Law and Policy
American-Arab Affairs
Americas
Amicus Journal
Analise Social
Analisis Politico
Annales—Economies Societes Civilisations
Annales Internationales de Criminologie
Annals of Public and Co-operative Economy
Annals of the America Academy of Political and Social Science
Annals of the New York Academy of Sciences
Année Africaine
Annuaire de l'Afrique du Nord

Annuaire de L'URSS et des Pays Socialistes Européen
Annuaire du Tiers Monde
Annuaire Européen
Annuaire Suisse de Science Politique
Annual Review of Sociology
Anthropological Quarterly
Antitrust Bulletin
Antitrust Law and Economic Review
Anuario de Estudios Centroamericanos
Anuario Internacional
Après-Demain
Apuntes
Arab Studies Quarterly
Arabies
Arbor–Ciencia Pensamiento y Cultura
Archipelago
Archiv des Offentlichen Rechts
Archiv für Rechts und Sozialphilosophie
Archives de Philosophie
Archives Europeennes de Sociologie
Arctic
Area
Argument
Armed Forces and Society
ASCI Journal of Management
Asian Affairs
Asian Affairs: An American Review
Asian Affairs (London)
Asian Affairs (New York)
Asian Economies
Asian Forum
Asian Journal of Political Science
Asian Journal of Public Administration
Asian Outlook
Asian Profile
Asian Survey
Asian Thought and Society
Asien, Afrika, Lateinamerika
Association of Comparative Economic Studies Bulletin
Atlanta Economic Review

Atlantic Community Quarterly
Atlantic Papers
Atlas
Aus Politik und Zeitgeschichte
Aussenpolitik
Australian and New Zealand
    Journal of Sociology
Australian Journal of Chinese
    Affairs
Australian Journal of International
    Affairs
Australian Journal of Management
Australian Journal of Political
    Science
Australian Journal of Politics and
    History
Australian Journal of Public
    Administration
Australian Law Journal
Australian Quarterly
Austriaca
Austrian Journal of Public and
    International Law

ð❧

Banker (London)
Baylor Law Review
Behavior & Information
    Technology
Behavioral Psychotherapy
Behavioral Science
Behavioural Sciences and Rural
    Development
Beitraege zur Konfliktforschung
Beleidwetenschap
Berliner Journal für Soziologie
Biblioteca della Liberta
Biochemical Education
Black Law Journal
Black Scholar
Blaetter für Deutsche und
    Internationale Politik
Boletin de Ciencias Politicas y
    Sociales
Boletin Mexicano de Derecho
    Comparado
Boston College Law Review
Boston College Third World Law
    Journal
Boston University International
    Law Journal
Boston University Law Review
Brigham Young University Law
    Review
British Journal of Addiction
British Journal of Criminology

British Journal of Education
    Studies
British Journal of Industrial
    Relations
British Journal of Political Science
British Journal of Sociology
British Journal of Sociology of
    Education
British Medical Journal
British Year Book of International
    Law
Brookings Review
Brooklyn Journal of International
    Law
Buffalo Law Review
Bulletin of Comparative Labour
    Relations
Bulletin of Concerned Asian
    Scholars
Bulletin of Latin American
    Research
Bulletin of Peace Proposals
Bulletin of Science, Technology
    and Society
Bulletin of the American Society
    for Information Science
Bulletin of the Atomic Scientists
Bulletin of the British
    Psychological Society
Bureaucrat
Business and Society Review
Business Forum
Business History Review
Business Horizons
Business Lawyer
Business Quarterly

ð❧

Cadernos de Departamento de
    Ciencia Politica
Cadmos
Cahiers des Ameriques Latines
Cahiers du Communisme
Cahiers du Monde Russe et
    Sovietique
Cahiers Economiques de Bruxelles
Cahiers Internationaux de
    Sociologie
Cahiers Vilfredo Pareto
Calcutta Journal of Political
    Studies
California Business
California Journal
California Law Review
California Management Review
Cambio
Cambridge Journal of Economics

Cambridge Law Journal
Canada's Mental Health
Canadian Business Law Journal
Canadian Journal of
    Administrative Sciences
Canadian Journal of African
    Studies
Canadian Journal of American and
    Caribbean Studies
Canadian Journal of Criminology
Canadian Journal of Development
    Studies
Canadian Journal of Latin
    American and Caribbean
    Studies
Canadian Journal of Political and
    Social Theory
Canadian Journal of Political
    Science
Canadian Journal of Sociology
Canadian Library Journal
Canadian Parliamentary Review
Canadian Public Administration
Canadian Public Policy
Canadian Review of Sociology and
    Anthropology
Canadian Review of Studies in
    Nationalism
Canadian Slavonic Papers
Capital University Law Review
Cardozo Law Review
Caribbean Affairs
Caribbean Review
Caribbean Studies
Caribe Contemporaneo
Carta Mensal
Case Western Reserve Journal of
    International Law
Catholic University Law Review
Cato Journal
Center Magazine
Central European History
Ceskoslovenska Psychologie
Challenge
Change
Chemtech
Chicano-Latino Law Review
China Aktuell
China Information
China Newsletter
China Quarterly
China Report
Chinese Economic Studies
Chinese Law and Government
Chinese Sociology and
    Anthropology
Christianity and Crisis
Cities

Civil Liberties Review
Civil Rights–Civil Liberties Law
  Review
Civilisations
Civilta Cattolica
Civitas
Coexistence
Coleccion Estudios CIENPLAN
College and University
Collegium Antropologicum
Columbia Human Rights Law
  Review
Columbia Journal of Transnational
  Law
Columbia Journal of World
  Business
Columbia Journalism Review
Columbia Law Review
Comer Exterior (Mexico)
Commentaire
Commentary
Commercial Law Journal
Common Ground
Communication
Communication and Cognition
Communication Education
Communication Monographs
Communication Research
Communist and Post-Communist
  Studies
Communist Studies
Community Development Journal
Comparative Communism
Comparative Education
Comparative Education Review
Comparative International
  Development
Comparative Political Studies
Comparative Politics
Comparative Strategy
Comparative Studies in Society
  and History
Comunita
Conflict
Conflict Quarterly
Conflict Studies
Congressional Research Service
  Review
Connaissance Politique
Connecticut Journal of
  International Law
Connecticut Law Review
Constellations
Constitutional Commentary
Constitutional Forum
Constitutional Political Economy
Contemporary Crises
Contemporary Education

Contemporary Marxism
Contemporary Pacific
Contemporary South Asia
Contemporary Southeast Asia
Cooperation and Conflict
Cornell International Law Journal
Cornell Law Review
Corruption and Reform
Cosmopolitiques
Courier
Covert Action
CQ Researcher
Credit Communal de Belgique
Crime and Social Justice
Crime, Law and Social Change
Criminal Law Reform
Criminology
Critica Indixista
Critica Marxistas
Critica y Utopia
Critical Inquiry
Critical Review
Critical Social Policy
Critical Studies in Mass
  Communication
Croissance
Cross-Cultural Research
Crossroads
Cuadernos Americanos
Cuadernos del CLAEH: Rivista
  Uruguaya de Ciencias Sociales
Cuban Studies
Cuestiones Politica
Cultural Anthropology
Cultures et Conflict
Cultures et Développement
Current Contents: Social &
  Behavioral Sciences
Current History
Current Perspectives in Social
  Theory
Current Research on Peace and
  Violence
Current World Leaders
Curriculum Inquiry
Cybernetica

ào

Dados
Dados: Revista de Ciencias Sociais
Daedalus
Dalhousie Review
Deadline
Defense Nationale
Democracy
Democratic Institutions
Democratization

Democrazia e Diritto
Demokratie und Recht
Denver University Law Review
Department of State Bulletin
Der Staat
Desarrollo Economico
Desarrollo Economico: Revista de
  Ciencias Sociales
Deutsche Studien
Deutsche Zeitschrift für
  Philosophie
Deutschland Archiv
Development
Development and Change
Development Policy Review
Dialectical Anthropology
Dialogue
Dickinson Journal of International
  Law
Diogene
Dissent
Dokumente
Duke Environmental Law & Policy
  Forum
Duke Journal of Comparative and
  International Law
Duke Law Journal

ào

Earth Island Journal
East European Politics and
  Societies
East European Quarterly
Eastern European Economics
Economic Analysis (Belgrade)
Economic and Industrial
  Democracy
Economic and Political Weekly
Economic Development and
  Cultural Change
Economic Education Bulletin
Economic Inquiry
Economic Letters
Economic Papers (Australia)
Economic Policy
Economics and Politics
Economie et Humanisme
Economist (London)
Economy and Society
Editorial Research Reports
Education
Education and Urban Society
Education Theory
Educational Administration
  Quarterly
Educational Leadership
Educational Review

Educational Theory
Egypte Monde Arabe
Einheit
Ekistics: The Problems and
 Science of Human Settlement
Ekonomicky Casopis
Ekonomiska Samfundets Tidskrift
Electoral Studies
Emory International Law Review
Employee Responsibilities and
 Rights Journal
Employment Gazette
Encounter
Energy
English Education
English Journal
Entwicklung und Zusammenarbeit
 (E & Z)
Environment and Planning A
Environment and Planning C:
 Government and Planning
Environment and Planning C:
 Government and Policy
Environment and Planning D:
 Society and Space
Environmental Action
Environmental Conservation
Environmental Ethics
Environmental Values
Esprit
Estado y Sociedad
Est-Ouest
Estudios Internacionales
Estudios Latinoamericanos
Estudios Politicos
Estudios Publicos
Estudios Sociales
Estudios Sociales
 Centroamericanos
Ethics
Ethics and International Affairs
Ethnic and Racial Studies
Ethnic Studies
Ethnic Studies Report
Ethnohistory
Ethnology
Etudes
Etudes et Documents (Taipei)
Euromoney
Europa Archiv: Zeitschrift für
 Internationale Politik
Europa Forum
Europa Wehrkunde
Europaeische Rundschau
Europe-Asia Studies
European Economic Review
European Journal of
 Communication

European Journal of Political
 Research
European Law Review
European Politics
European Studies Review
Exchange Organizational Behavior
 Teaching Journal
Explorations in Economic History
Express

ஐ

Federal Bar News and Journal
Feminist Studies
Filosoficky Casopis
Financier
Fletcher Forum of World Affairs
Florida Law Review
Florida State University Law
 Review
Folia Humanistica
Food and Drug Cosmetic Law
 Journal
Food Monitor
Fordham Law Review
Foreign Affairs
Foreign Policy
Foreign Policy Bulletin
Foreign Policy Journal
Foreign Service Journal
Forensic Quarterly
Foro Internacional
Fortune
Forum for Applied Research and
 Public Policy
Frankfurter Hefte
Free Labour World
Free Speech Yearbook
Freedom at Issue
Freedom Review
Frontiers: A Journal of Women's
 Studies
Futures
Futuribles
Futurist

ஐ

Gazette
Gegenwartskunde: Gesellschaft,
 Staat, Erziehung
Gender & Society
Geoforum
Geography
George Washington Law Review
Georgetown Law Journal
Georgetown Law Review
Georgia Journal of International
 and Comparative Law

Georgia Law Review
Geschichte und Gesellschaft
Gewerkschaftliche Monatshefte
Global Affairs
Gosudarstvo I Pravo
Governance
Government and Opposition
Government Information
 Quarterly
Grassroots Development
Growth and Change

ஐ

Habitat International
Hallinnon Tutimus
Hamline Law Review
Harpers
Harriman Institute Forum
Harvard Business Review
Harvard Civil Rights–Civil
 Liberties Law Review
Harvard Educational Review
Harvard Human Rights Journal
Harvard International Law Journal
Harvard International Review
Harvard Journal of Law and Public
 Policy
Harvard Journal on Legislation
Harvard Law Review
Hastings Center Report
Hastings Communications and
 Entertainment Law Journal
Hastings International and
 Comparative Law Review
Hastings Law Journal
Hermes: Zeitschrift für Klassische
 Philologie
High School Behavioral Science
Higher Education
Hispanic American Historical
 Review
Histoire
Historical Journal
Historische Zeitschrift
History and Theory
History of Education Quarterly
History of European Ideas
History of Political Thought
Houston Journal of International
 Law
Houston Law Review
Howard Journal of Criminal
 Justice
Human Context
Human Organization
Human Relations
Human Rights

Jewish Political Studies Review
Journal of African Studies
Journal of Air Law and Commerce
Journal of American History
Journal of Anthropological
  Research
Journal of Applied Behavioral
  Science
Journal of Applied Social
  Psychology
Journal of Arts Management, Law
  and Society
Journal of Asian and African
  Studies
Journal of Asian Studies
Journal of Black Studies
Journal of British Studies
Journal of Business Ethics
Journal of Church and State
Journal of Common Market
  Studies
Journal of Commonwealth &
  Comparative Politics
Journal of Communication
Journal of Communist Studies
Journal of Community Psychology
Journal of Comparative Economics
Journal of Comparative Sociology
Journal of Conflict Resolution
Journal of Constitutional and
  Parliamentary Studies
Journal of Contemporary Asia
Journal of Contemporary China
Journal of Contemporary History
Journal of Corporation Law
Journal of Curriculum Studies
Journal of Democracy
Journal of Developing Areas
Journal of Developing Societies
Journal of Development
  Economics
Journal of Development Studies
Journal of East Asian Affairs
Journal of Economic Behavior &
  Organization
Journal of Economic Education
Journal of Economic History
Journal of Economic Issues
Journal of Economic Perspectives
Journal of Education for Teaching
Journal of Ethnic Studies
Journal of General Management
Journal of Institutional and
  Theoretical Economics
Journal of Interamerican Studies
  and World Affairs
Journal of Interdisciplinary
  History

Journal of Interdisciplinary Studies
Journal of International Affairs
Journal of International
  Development
Journal of International Studies
Journal of International Studies
  and World Affairs
Journal of Islamic Banking and
  Finance
Journal of Japanese Studies
Journal of Labor Research
Journal of Latin American Studies
Journal of Law and Politics
Journal of Law and Society
Journal of Legislation
Journal of Management Studies
Journal of Marriage and the
  Family
Journal of Medicine and
  Philosophy
Journal of Modern African Studies
Journal of Modern History
Journal of Negro Education
Journal of Negro History
Journal of Northeast Asian Studies
Journal of Occupational Behavior
Journal of Palestine Studies
Journal of Peace Research
Journal of Peace Science
Journal of Philosophy
Journal of Policy Modeling
Journal of Political and Military
  Sociology
Journal of Political Economy
Journal of Political Philosophy
Journal of Political Science
Journal of Political Studies
Journal of Politics
Journal of Popular Culture
Journal of Portfolio Management
Journal of Public Administration
  Research and Theory
Journal of Public Economics
Journal of Public Policy
Journal of Religion
Journal of Scientific & Industrial
  Research
Journal of Social History
Journal of Social Issues
Journal of Social Policy
Journal of Social, Political, and
  Economic Studies
Journal of Social Psychology
Journal of Southern African
  Affairs
Journal of Southern African
  Studies
Journal of Soviet Nationalities

Journal of State Government
Journal of Strategic Studies
Journal of Teacher Education
Journal of the American Institute
  of Planners
Journal of the American Medical
  Association
Journal of the American Planning
  Association
Journal of the American Society
  for Information Science
Journal of the History of Ideas
Journal of the History of the
  Behavioral Sciences
Journal of the Institute for
  Socioeconomic Studies
Journal of the Maharaja Sayajirao
  University of Baroda
Journal of Theoretical Politics
Journal of Third World Studies
Journal of Thought
Journal of Urban Affairs
Journal of Urban History
Journal of Value Inquiry
Journal of Voluntary Action and
  Internal Democracy
Journal of Voluntary Action
  Research
Journal of World Trade
Journalism Quarterly
Judges' Journal
Judicature

❧

Kolner Zeitschrift für Soziologie
  und Sozialpsychologie
Korea and World Affairs
Korea Observer
Korean Review
Korean Social Science Journal
Korean Studies
Kritische Justiz
Kyklos
Kyoto University Economic Review

❧

La Nouvel Afrique Asie
La Pensée
La Revue Juridique Themis
La Revue Nouvelle
La Vie Internationale
Labor History
Labor Law Journal
Labor Law Review
Labor Studies Journal
Labour and Society
Labour Monthly

Labour (Rome)
L'Afrique
L'Afrique Contemporaire
L'Afrique et l'Asie Modernes
L'Afrique Politique
Lateinamerika (Hamburg)
Latin American Perspectives
Latin American Research
Latin American Research Review
Law and Contemporary Problems
Law and Philosophy
Law and Policy in International
   Business
Law and Social Inquiry
Law Institute Journal
Law Quarterly Review
Le Debat
Le Mois en Afrique
Le Nouvel Afrique Asie
Le Trimestre du Monde
Legal Economics
Legal Reference Services Quarterly
Legal Studies
Legislative Studies Quarterly
Leisure Sciences
Les Temps Modernes
Leviathan
L'Express
L'Homme et la Societe
Liberal Education
Library Acquisitions—Practice and
   Theory
Library Journal
Libri
Linguistics
Lituanus
Lloyds Bank Review
Local Government Studies
Long Range Planning
Look Japan
Louisiana Law Review
Loyola Los Angeles Law Review
Lusotopie

ɘ

Maghreb Review
Maghreb-Machrek
Management Decision
Management International Review
Manchester School of Economic
   and Social Studies
Mankind Quarterly
Marches Tropicaux et
   Mediterraneens
Marquette Law Review
Maryland Journal of International
   Law and Trade

McGill Law Journal
Media, Culture and Society
Mediaspouvoirs
Mediterranean Quarterly
Melbourne University Law Review
Mental Health and Society
Merkur
Metaphor and Symbolic Activity
Mexican Studies
Michigan Journal of International
   Law
MicroMega
Micropolitics
Mid-American Review of Sociology
Middle East
Middle East Insight
Middle East Journal
Middle East Policy
Middle East Quarterly
Middle East Report
Middle East Research &
   Information Project Reports
Middle East Review
Middle East Studies Association
   Bulletin
Middle Eastern Studies
Midsouth Political Science Journal
Midstream
Midwest Quarterly
Midwest Review of Public
   Administration
Migration World
Milbank Memorial Fund
   Quarterly—Health and Society
Military Review
Millennium
Minerva
Minnesota Law Review
Mirovaia Ekonomika i
   Mezhdunarodnye Otnoshenia
   Nauk
Mitarbeit
Modern Age
Modern Asian Studies
Modern China
Modern Law Review
Monde Arabe Maghreb-Machrek
Monde Diplomatique
Mondes en Developpement
Monthly Labor Review
Monthly Review
Mots
Mouvement Social
Multinational Monitor
Mundo

ɘ

Nation
National Civic Review
National Forum
National Interest
National Journal
Nationalokonomisk Tidsskrift
NATO Review
Nauk Politycznych
Negotiation Journal
Netherlands Journal of Social
   Sciences
Netherlands Journal of Sociology
Neue Ordnung
Neue Politische Literatur
New African
New England Law Review
New Hungarian Quarterly
New Law Journal
New Leader
New Left Review
New Perspectives Quarterly
New Political Science
New Politics
New Republic
New Scientist
New Society
New Times (Moscow)
New Universities Quarterly
New York Law School Journal of
   International and Comparative
   Law
New York Review of Books
New York University Journal of
   International Law and Politics
New York University Law Review
New Zealand Journal of
   Educational Studies
New Zealand University Law
   Review
Nigerian Journal of Policy and
   Strategy
Nomos
Nordish Administrativt Tidsskrift
Nordisk Psykologi
North Carolina Journal of
   International Law and
   Commercial Regulation
North Carolina Law Review
Northwestern University Law
   Review
Notes et Etudes Documentaires
Notes et Etudes Documentaires
   (Problemes Amerique Latine)
Notre Dame Journal of Law, Ethics
   and Public Policy
Notre Dame Law Review

Nouvel Afrique Asie
Nouvel Observateur
Nuestro Tiempo
Nueva Sociedad
Nuevo Proyecto

❧

Observations et Diagnostics
    Economiques
Occasional Papers: Reprints Series
    in Contemporary Asia
Oesterreichische Monatshefte
Oesterreichische Osthefte
Oesterreichische Zeitschrift für
    Aussenpolitik
Oesterreichische Zeitschrift für
    Politikwissenschaft
Oesterreichische Zeitschrift für
    Offentliches Recht und
    Volkerrecht
Ohio Northern University Law
    Review
Ohio State Law Journal
Ohio State Law Review
Opciones
Orbis
Ordo
Organization Studies
Organizational Dynamics
Orient
Orient (Deutsches Orient Institut)
Orientation Scolaire et
    Professionnelle
Osteuropa
Oxford Economic Papers—New
    Series
Oxford Journal of Legal Studies
Oxford Review of Economic Policy
Oxford Review of Education

❧

Pace Yearbook of International
    Law
Pacific Affairs
Pacific Community
Pacific Islands Monthly
Pacific Review
Pacific Sociological Review
Pacific Studies
Padagogische Rundschau
Pakistan Horizon
Pakistan Journal of American
    Studies
Panorama Centroamericano:
    Temas y Documentos de Debate
Panstwo i Pravo
Parameters

Parliamentarian
Parliamentary Affairs
Parolechiave
Passe Present
Paysans
Peabody Journal of Education
Peace Research
Peace Review
Peasant Studies
Pensamiento Iberoamericano
Pensée
Pensiero Politico
Pension World
Personnel Review
Perspectiva Internacional
    Paraguaya
Perspectivas
Perspectives
Perspectives on Political Science
Perspectives Polonaises
Pesquisa e Planejamento
    Economico
Peuples Mediterraneens
Pharmazie
Phi Delta Kappan
Philippine Journal of Public
    Administration
Philosophy and Public Affairs
Philosophy & Social Criticism
Plural Societies
Police Studies
Policy and Politics
Policy Review
Policy Sciences
Policy Studies
Policy Studies Journal
Policy Studies Review
Polish American Studies
Polish Political Science
Polish Political Science Yearbook
Polish Sociological Bulletin
Politeia (Caracas)
Politeia (UNISA)
Politica
Politica (Caracas)
Politica (Santiago, Chile)
Politica del Diritto
Politica Exterior
Politica Internacional (Lisbon)
Politica Internazionale
Political Affairs
Political Behavior
Political Communication
Political Communication and
    Persuasion
Political Geography
Political Geography Quarterly
Political Psychology

Political Quarterly
Political Research Quarterly
Political Science
Political Science and Politics
Political Science Quarterly
Political Science Review
Political Science Reviewer
Political Studies
Political Theory
Politicka Ekonomie
Politicka Misao
Politico
Politics
Politics, Administration, and
    Change
Politics and Society
Politics and the Individual
Politics and the Life Sciences
Politiika
Politik und Zeitgeschichte
Politika
Politikon
Politique
Politique Africaine
Politique Etrangere
Politique Internationale
Politische Bildung
Politische Meinung
Politische Studien
Politische Vierteljahresschrift
Polity
Population
Population and Development
Population and Development
    Review
Post-Soviet Affairs
Pouvoirs
Poznan Studies
Présence Africaine
Presencia (El Salvador)
Presidential Studies Quarterly
Problèmes d'Amerique Latine
Problemi del Socialismo
Problemi dell'Informazione
Problems of Communism
Problems of Economic Transition
Problems of Economics
Proceedings of the Academy of
    Political Science
Proceedings of the American
    Antiquarian Society
Proces
Project
Projet
Prologue—Quarterly of the
    National Archives
Prospects
Prospects and Conditions

Proteus
PS: Political Science & Politics
Psychology Today
Public Administration (London)
Public Administration and
  Development
Public Administration Journal
  (Kathmandu)
Public Administration Review
Public Administration Survey
Public Affairs
Public Affairs Quarterly
Public Choice
Public Culture
Public Finance
Public Finance Quarterly
Public Interest
Public Law
Public Management
Public Manager
Public Money and Management
Public Opinion
Public Opinion (American
  Enterprise Institute)
Public Opinion Quarterly
Publishing Research Quarterly
Publius
Publizistik
Pulp and Paper Canada
Punjab Journal of Politics

੩ঌ

Quaderni di Azione Sociale
Quaderni di Sociologia
Quality & Quantity
Quarterly Journal of Economics
Quarterly Journal of Speech
Quarterly Review of Economics
  and Business
Queen's Quarterly
QueHacer
Questions Actuelles du Socialisme

੩ঌ

R & D Management
Race and Class
Rassegna Italiana di Sociologia
Ratio Juris
Rationality and Society
Real Estate Review
Real Property Probate and Trust
  Journal
Realidad Economica
Reason
Recherche
Recht und Politik
Record

Regards sur l'Actualité
Regional Studies
Relaciones Internacionales
  (Mexico)
Relations Internationales et
  Strategiques
Report on the Americas
Res Publica
Response
Responsive Community
Review (F. Braudel Center)
Review International Commission
  of Jurists
Review of African Political
  Economy
Review of Black Political Economy
Review of Business (St. John's
  University)
Review of International Affairs
Review of International Studies
Review of Politics
Review of Radical Political
  Economics
Review of Social Economy
Review of Social History
Revista (IDOB d'Afers
  Internacionals)
Revista Brasileira de Estudos
  Politicos
Revista de Administracion Publica
Revista de Ciencia Politica
Revista de Ciencia y Cultura
  UNIBE
Revista de Ciencias Sociales
Revista de Ciencias Sociales
  (Uruguay)
Revista de Derecho Politico
Revista de Economia Politica
Revista de Estudios
  Internacionales
Revista de Estudios Politicos
Revista de Estudios Politicos
  (Neuva Epoca)
Revista de Informacao Legislativa
Revista de Instituciones Europeas
Revista de la Facultad de Ciencias
  Juridicas y Politica
Revista Española de Derecho
  Constitucional
Revista Española de
  Investigaciones Sociologicas
Revista Europea Estudios
  Latinoamericanos y del Caribe
Revista Foro
Revista Interamericana de
  Planificacion
Revista Interamericana de
  Sociologia

Revista Mexicana de Ciencias
  Politicas y Sociales
Revista Mexicana de Sociologia
Revista Usem
Revolutionary World
Revue Algérienne des Sciences
  Juridiques, Economiques et
  Politiques
Revue Canadienne d'Etudes du
  Développement
Revue de Droit International de
  Sciences Diplomatiques et
  Politiques
Revue de l'Institut de Sociologie
Revue d'Economie Politique
Revue des Etudes Cooperatives
Revue des Pays de l'Est
Revue d'Etudes Comparatives Est-
  Ouest
Revue du Droit Public et de la
  Science Politique
Revue du Monde Musulman et de
  la Mediterranee
Revue Européenne des Sciences
  Sociales
Revue Française de Droit
  Constitutionnel
Revue Française de Science
  Politique
Revue Française de Sociologie
Revue Française du Marketing
Revue Generale
Revue Internationale d'Action
  Communautaire
Revue Internationale de
  Psychologie Appliquée
Revue Internationale des Sciences
  Administration
Revue Juridique et Politique,
  Independance et Cooperation
Revue Politique et Parlementaire
Revue Roumaine des Sciences
  Sociales (Serie de Sociologie)
Revue Roumaine des Sciences
  Sociales (Serie des Sciences
  Economiques)
RFE/RL Research Report
Risk Analysis
Rivista di Servizio Sociale
Rivista Italiana di Scienza Politica
Rivista Trimestrale di Diritto
  Publico
Round Table
Russian Education and Society
Russian Politics and Law
Russian Review
Rutgers Law Journal

៛

Sage Electoral Studies Yearbook
Sage Professional Papers in
    Comparative Politics
Sage Professional Papers in
    Contemporary Political
    Sociology
SAIS Review
San Diego Law Review
Scandinavian Journal of
    Development Alternatives
Scandinavian Journal of
    Economics
Scandinavian Political Studies
Scandinavian Review
Scholarly Publishing
Schweizer Monatshefte
Schweizer Monatshefte: Zeitschrift
    für Politik, Wirtschaft, Kultur
Science
Science & Society
Science, Technology & Human
    Values
Sciences Sociales (Moscow)
Scientia
Scientist
Scientometrics
Scottish Journal of Sociology
Search
Securities Regulation Law Journal
Security Dialogue
Seminar
Sex Roles
Sintesis
Sintesis (AIETI)
Sistema
Slavic Review
Slavonic and East European
    Review
Small Group Research
SMU Law Review
Social and Economic Studies
Social Choice and Welfare
Social Compass
Social Dynamics
Social Education
Social Forces
Social Justice
Social Philosophy and Policy
Social Policy
Social Politics
Social Problems
Social Research
Social Science & Medicine
Social Science History
Social Science Information
Social Science Journal

Social Science Quarterly
Social Theory and Practice
Socialism and Democracy
Socialisme
Socialismo y Participacion
Socialist Register
Socialist Review
Socialist Revolution
Socialist Thought and Practice
Societas: A Review of Social
    History
Society
Society & Politics
Sociologia
Sociologia Internationalis
Sociological Analysis
Sociological Analysis and Theory
Sociological Forum
Sociological Inquiry
Sociological Perspectives
Sociological Quarterly
Sociological Review
Sociologicky Casopis
Sociologie du Travail
Sociologisk Forskning
Sociology
Sociology of Education
Sociology of Religion
Sociology of Work and
    Occupations
Sociology: The Journal of the
    British Sociological Association
Sojicalizam
Sojourn
Solicitors' Journal
Sotsiologicheskie Issledovaniia
South Africa International
South African Journal of
    Economics
South African Journal of Human
    Rights
South Asia Bulletin
South Atlantic Quarterly
Southeast Asian Affairs
Southeastern Political Review
Southern California Law Review
Southern Economic Journal
Southwestern Law Journal
Sovetskoe Gosudarstvo Pravo
Soviet Economy
Soviet Education
Soviet Law and Government
Soviet Sociology
Soviet Studies
Soviet Studies in Philosophy
Sowjetwissenschaft: Gesellschafts
    Wissenschaftliche Beitrage
Soziale Welt

Special Libraries
Spectrum
Staat und Recht
Stahl und Eisen
Stanford Journal of International
    Law
State and Local Government
    Review
State Government
State Legislatures
Stato e Mercato
Statsvetenskaplig Tidskrift
Storia e Politica
Strategic Analysis
Strategic Review
Studi Storici
Studia Nauk Politycznych
Studies in Comparative
    Communism
Studies in Comparative
    International Development
Studies in Conflict and Terrorism
Studies in East European Thought
Studies in GDR Culture and
    Society
Studies in Philosophy and
    Education
Studies in Political Economy
Studies in Political Economy: A
    Socialist Review
Studies in Soviet Thought
Suedostasien Aktuell
Suedosteuropa
Suedosteuropa-Mitteilungen
Suedosteuropa (Munich)
Survey
Survey of Business
Survival
Sweden Now
Sydney Law Review
Symbolic Interaction
Synthèse
System
Systems Practice

៛

Talking Politics
Teachers College Record
Teaching Political Science
Teaching Politics
Technological Forecasting and
    Social Change
Technology Review
Telecommunication Journal
Telos
Temple Law Quarterly
Temple Law Review

Bibliography

1. Aage, H. (ed.). 1990. Privatization and Democratization in Eastern Europe.*Nationalokonomisk Tidsskrift* 128 (3): 279–295.

2. Aarts, P. March 1993. *See* Beker, M. (March 1993).

3. Aarts, P. October 1993. The Limits of "Political Tribalism": Post-War Kuwait and the Democratization Process. *Monde Arabe Maghreb-Machrek* 141: 61–79.

4. Abadan-Unat, N. 1979. Patterns of Political Modernization and Turkish Democracy. *Turkish Year Book of International Relations* 18: 1–26.

5. Abbott, A., and S. Deviney. June 1992. The Welfare State as Transnational Event: Evidence from Sequences of Policy Adoption. *Social Science History* 16 (2): 245–274.

6. Abdalla, I. S. April 1977. Bringing Democracy into the World Monetary System. *Euromoney* 49–52.

7. Abdallah, A. 1989. The Development of Democracy in Egypt on the Eve of the Twenty-First Century.* *Annuaire de l'Afrique du Nord* 28: 319–333.

8. Abdolani, N. March 1989. *See* Maoz, Z. (March 1989).

9. Abell, P. 1985. Some Theory of Industrial and Economic Democracy. *Economic and Industrial Democracy* 6 (4): 435–460.

10. Abell, P. June 1985. Industrial Democracy, Has It a Future? The West European Experience. *Journal of General Management* 10 (4): 50–62.

11. Abell, P. 1987. Rational Equitarian Democracy, Minimax Class and the Future of Capitalist Society: A Sketch towards a Theory. *Sociology: The Journal of the British Sociological Association* 21 (4): 567–590.

12. Abente, D. March 1988. Constraints and Opportunities: Prospects for Democratization in Paraguay. *Journal of Interamerican Studies and World Affairs* 30 (1): 73–104.

13. Aberbach, J. D. March 1985. *See* Campbell, J. C. (March 1985).

14. Aberbach, J. D., and B. A. Rockman. December 1978. Administrators' Beliefs about the Role of the Public: The Case of American Federal Executives. *Western Political Quarterly* 31 (4): 501–522.

15. Abraham, H. J., B. A. Perry, J. Davison, M. R. Fowler, and J. M. Bunck. 1992. Essays on the Influence of the American Constitution and Legal Institutions on Emerging Democracies. *Albany Law Review* 55: 763–847. 4 essays.

16. Abrahamson, M. A. September 1985. The Public Manager and Excellence. *Bureaucrat* 14 (3): 9–13.

17. Abramowitz, A. I. February 1994. Issue Evolution Reconsidered: Racial Attitudes and Partisanship in the U.S. Electorate. *American Journal of Political Science* 38 (1): 1–24.

18. Abrams, B. A., and K. A. Lewis. December 1993. Human Rights and the Distribution of United States Foreign Aid. *Public Choice* 77 (4): 815–821.

19. Abrams, E. April 1993. Democracy in Nicaragua: Still in Trouble. *American Legion Magazine* 134: 20–21+.

1

20. Abranches, S. H. 1981. Economics, Politics and Democracy: The Logic of State Action.* *Dados: Revista De Ciencias Sociais* 24 (1): 3–23.

21. Abranches, S. H. 1985. Neither Citizens nor Free Men: The Political Predicament of Individuals in the Liberal Democracy.* *Dados: Revista de Ciencias Sociais* 28 (1): 5–25.

22. Abromeit, H. 1989. Majority and Consociational Elements in the Political System of the FRD.* *Oesterreichische Zeitschrift für Politikwissenschaft* 18 (2): 165–180.

23. Abueva, J. V. November 1976. Filipino Democracy and the American Legacy. *Annals of the American Academy of Political and Social Science* 428: 114–133.

24. Abukhalil, A. Winter 1992a. A Viable Partnership: Islam, Democracy and the Arab World. *Harvard International Review* 15 (2): 22–23, 65.

25. Abukhalil, A. Winter 1992b. A New Arab Ideology? The Rejuvenation of Arab Nationalism. *Middle East Journal* 46: 22–36.

26. Abulughod, J. March 1994. Diversity, Democracy, and Self-Determination in an Urban Neighborhood: The East Village of Manhattan. *Social Research* 61 (1): 181–203.

27. Ackerman, B. December 1989. Constitutional Politics, Constitutional Law. *Yale Law Journal* 99 (3): 453–547.

28. Ackerman, B. December 1993. A Credit Card for [U.S.] Voters: A New Start for Financing Electoral Campaigns.* *Politica del Diritto* 24 (4): 647–663.

29. Ackerman, G. February 1994. The Zhirinovsky Card.* *Politica Exterior* 37: 57–65.

30. Ackroyd, S. 1975. Concerns of Industrial Sociology: Some Criticism of Glover on Industrial Democracy. *Sociological Analysis and Theory* 5 (1): 117–124.

31. Adam, B. D. 1988. Neighborhood Democracy in Nicaragua. *Dialectical Anthropology* 13 (1): 5–15.

32. Adam, G. 1979. Democratization of Higher Education through Admission Policy. *Prospects* 9 (1): 54–57.

33. Adam, H. September 1990. Transition to Democracy: South Africa and Eastern Europe. *Telos* 85: 33–55.

34. Adam, H. M. July 1992. Somalia: Militarism, Warlordism or Democracy? *Review of African Political Economy* 19: 11–26.

35. Adam, H. M. March 1994. Formation and Recognition of New States: Somaliland in Contrast to Eritrea. *Review of African Political Economy* 21: 21–38.

36. Adamany, D. W. May 1976. The Sources of Money: An Overview. *Annals of the American Academy of Political and Social Science* 425: 17–32.

37. Adamolekun, L. (ed.). September 1991. Federalism in Nigeria: Toward Federal Democracy. *Publius* 21 (4): 1–188. 13 articles.

38. Adams, D., and A. Goldbard. 1981. Cultural Democracy Versus the Democratization of High Culture. *Social Policy* 12 (1): 52–56.

39. Adams, R. J. March 1992. Efficiency Is Not Enough. *Labor Studies Journal* 17 (1): 18–28.

40. Adams, R. J. June 1992. The Right to Participate. *Employee Responsibilities and Rights Journal* 5 (2): 91–99.

41. Adams, W. E., Jr. June 1994. Pre-election Anti-Gay Ballot Initiative Challenges: Issues of Electoral Fairness, Majoritarian Tyranny, and Direct Democracy. *Ohio State Law Journal* 55: 583–647.

42. Adamson, W. L. 1990. Economic Democracy and the Expediency of Worker Participation. *Political Studies* 38 (1): 56–71.

43. Addi, L. October 1989. De la Democratie en Algeria. *Monde Diplomatique* 36: 9.

44. Addi, L. August 1992. Islam Politique et Democratisation en Algerie. *Esprit:* 143–151.

45. Addi, L. November 1992. Islamicist Utopia and Democracy. *Annals of the American Academy of Political and Social Science* 524: 120–130.

46. Adedeji, A. October 1994. An Alternative for Africa. *Journal of Democracy* 5 (4): 119–132.

47. Adelman, I. June 1980. Economic Development and Political Change in Developing Countries. *Social Research* 47 (2): 213–234.

48. Adelman, I. September 1990. Should There Be a Marshall Plan for Eastern Europe? *Review of Black Political Economy* 19 (2): 17–42.

49. Adelman, K. L. January 1986. The Challenge of Negotiating by Democracies. *Department of State Bulletin* 86: 35–38.

50. Adelman, K. L. March 1986. The Challenge of Negotiations by Democracies. *Presidential Studies Quarterly* 16 (2): 206–212.

51. Adelman, S. September 1994. Accountability and Administrative Law in South Africa's Transition to Democracy. *Journal of Law and Society* 21 (3): 317–328.

52. Adeniras, T. September 1991. The Two-Party System and the Federal Political Process. *Publius* 21 (4): 31–44.

53. Adkin, R. L. June 1991. East European Economic Reform: Are New Institutions Emerging? *Journal of Economic Issues* 25 (2): 589–595.

54. Adler, A. 1977. Construction of Socialism in the Soviet Union and in Democracies of Eastern Europe: From Model to Reality.* *Pensée* (196): 79–98.

55. Adler, G. June 1994. Community Action and Maximum Feasible Participation: An Opportunity Lost but Not Forgotten for Expanding Democracy at Home. *Notre Dame Journal of Law, Ethics and Public Policy* 8: 547–571.

56. Adrogue, G. October 1993. Los Ex Militares en Politica: Bases Sociales y Cambios en los Patrones de Representacion Politica. *Desarrollo Economico* 33: 425–442.

57. Agarwal, A., and S. Narain. September 1992. A Proposal for Global Environmental Democracy. *Earth Island Journal* 7 (4): 31.

58. Agassi, J. 1990. Academic Democracy Threatened: The Case of Boston University. *Interchange* 21 (2): 26–34.

59. Agassi, J. B. 1974. Israeli Experience in Democratization of Work Life. *Sociology of Work and Occupations* 1 (1): 52–81.

60. Agbaje, A. June 1991. *See* Oyediran, O. (June 1991).

61. Agbaje, A. 1992. Adjusting State and Market in Nigeria: The Paradoxes of Orthodoxy. *Afrika Spectrum* 27: 123–137.

62. Agbese, P. O. September 1991. Demilitarization and Prospects for Democracy in Nigeria. *Bulletin of Peace Proposals* 22 (3): 315–327.

63. Agbese, P. O. January 1992. The Autocratic Foundations of Nigeria's Forthcoming Third Republic. *Journal of International Studies* 28: 1–29.

64. Agbese, P. O. March 1992. Sanitizing Democracy in Nigeria. *Transafrica Forum* 9 (1): 41–55.

65. Agbese, P. O. November 1993. *See* Kieh, G. K. (November 1993).

66. Agbese, P. O., and G. K. Kieh. 1992. Military Disengagement from African Politics: The Nigerian Experiment. *Afrika Spectrum* 27 (1): 5–23.

67. Agh, A. November 1990. The Democratic Challenge in Central Europe. *Issues and Studies* 26 (11): 19–32.

68. Agh, A. April 1991. The Transition to Democracy in Central Europe: A Comparative View. *Journal of Public Policy* 11 (2): 133–151.

69. Agh, A. January 1993. Europeanization through Privatization and Pluralization in Hungary. *Journal of Public Policy* 13: 1–35.

70. Agh, A. April 1993. The "Comparative Revolution" and the Transition in Central and Southern Europe. *Journal of Theoretical Politics* 5 (2): 231–252.

71. Agh, A. June 1993. The Premature Senility of the New Democracies: The Hungarian Experience. *PS: Political Science & Politics* 26 (2): 305–307.

72. Agh, A. April 1994. The Hungarian Party System and Party Theory in the Transition of Central Europe. *Journal of Theoretical Politics* 6 (2): 217–238.

73. Agosin, M. May 1993. Democracy for a Ghost Nation. *Human Rights Quarterly* 15 (2): 406–409.

74. Agosta, A. 1979. General Elections of 1977 and the Perspective of the New Democracy in Greece. *Rivista Italiana di Scienza Politica* 9 (1): 97–135.

75. Aguiar, M. A. D., M. Arruda, and P. Flores. 1984. Economic Dictatorship Versus Democracy in Brazil. *Latin American Perspectives* 11 (1): 13–25.

76. Aguila Tejerina, R. January 1982. The Transition to Democracy in Spain: Reform, Break and Consensus.* *Revista de Estudios Politicos* 25: 101–127.

77. Aguilera de Prat, C. R. January 1992. El Uso del Referendum en la Espana Democratica (1976–1986). *Revista de Estudios Politicos* 75: 131–163.

78. Aguilera Peralta, G. January 1993. Guatemala: Transicion sin Ilegar a Ninguna Parte. *Nueva Sociedad* 123: 6–11.

79. Ahikire, J. October 29, 1994. Women, Public Politics, and Organization: Potentialities of Affirmative Action in Uganda. *Economic and Political Weekly* 29 (44): WS77-WS86.

80. Ahluwalia, D. P. November 1993. Democratic Transition in African Politics: The Case of Kenya. *Australian Journal of Political Science* 28 (3): 499–514.

81. Ahmad, A. 1978. Democracy and Dictatorship in Pakistan. *Journal of Contemporary Asia* 8 (4): 477–512.

82. Ahmad, F. April 1985. The Transition to Democracy in Turkey. *Third World Quarterly* 7 (2): 211–226.

83. Ahmed, N. August 1988. Experiments in Local Government Reform in Bangladesh. *Asian Survey* 28 (8): 813–829.

84. Ahn, C. S. December 1991. Economic Development and Democratization in South Korea: An Examination of Economic Change and Empowerment of Civil Society. *Korea and World Affairs* 15 (4): 740–754.

85. Ahn, C. S. December 1993. Democratization and Political Reform in South Korea: Development, Culture, Leadership, and Institutional Change. *Asian Journal of Political Science* 1 (2): 93–109.

86. Ahrari, M. March 1981. Contemporary Constraints on Presidential Leadership. *Presidential Studies Quarterly* 11 (2): 233–243.

87. Aidoo, A. November 1993. Africa: Democracy without Human Rights. *Human Rights Quarterly* 15 (4): 703–715.

88. Airaksinen, T. 1982. Moral Education and Democracy in the School. *Synthese* 51 (1): 117–134.

89. Akashi, Y. December 1992. To Build a New Country: The Task of the UN Transitional Authority in Cambodia. *Harvard International Review* 15 (2): 34–35, 68–69.

90. Ake, C. April 1993. The Unique Case of African Democracy. *International Affairs (London)* 69 (2): 239–244.

91. Akoun, A. January 1993. Democratic Communication.* *Cahiers Internationaux de Sociologie* 94: 51–70.

92. Alam, M. B. March 1986. Democracy in the Third World: Some Problems and Dilemmas. *Indian Journal of Politics* 20 (1–2): 53–68.

93. Alazar, D. J. March 1993. Communal Democracy and Liberal Democracy: An Outside Friend's Look at the Swiss Political Tradition. *Publius* 23 (2): 3–18.

94. Albeda, W. May 1977. Between Harmony and Conflict: Industrial Democracy in the Netherlands. *Annals of the American Academy of Political and Social Science* 431: 74–82.

95. Albert, H. January 1986. Methodological Rules and Democratic Rules. *Biblioteca della Liberta* 92: 63–81.

96. Albrecht, S. L. 1983. Forms of Industrial and Economic Democracy: A Comparison of Prevailing Approaches. *Mid-American Review of Sociology* 8 (2): 43–66.

97. Albrecht, S. L., and S. Deutsch. 1983. The Challenge of Economic Democracy: The Case of Sweden. *Economic and Industrial Democracy* 4 (3): 287–320.

98. Alcantara Saez, M. November 1991. Where Do Latin America's Electoral Democracies Fit In?* *America Latina Loy* 2: 9–13.

99. Alda Fernandez, M., and L. Lopez-Nieto. July 1993. El Parlamento Español 1977–1993: Una Revision de su Papel en la Transicion y en la Consolidacion. *Revista de Estudios Politicos* 80: 241–264.

100. Al-Darwich, K. S. September 1991. La Mauritanie Face à la Democratie. *Arabies* 16–22.

101. Alekseev, S., F. Burlatskii, and S. Shatalin. December 1992. An Alternative to the Break-up of the Forces of the Left: A Movement for Social Democracy. *Soviet Law and Government* 30 (3): 6–20.

102. Alesina, A. April 1989. Politics and Business Cycles in Industrial Democracies. *Economic Policy* 4: 55–98.

103. Alestalo, M. 1979. Patterns of Influence in Research Work: Problems of Autonomy and Democracy. *R & D Management* 9 (1): 221–230.

104. Alexander, A. November 1991. Managing Fragmentation Democracy, Accountability and the Future of Local Government. *Local Government Studies* 17 (6): 63–76.

105. Alexander, A. S. March 1977. Arms Transfers by the United States: Merchant of Death or Arsenal of Democracy. *Vanderbilt Journal of Transnational Law* 10: 249–267.

106. Alexander, D. 1991. Curriculum Turmoil in Liberal Democracies. *Journal of Curriculum Studies* 23 (1): 71–78.

107. Alexander, G. March 1986. African Success Stories: Democracy and Free Enterprise in Five African Nations. *Policy Review* 36: 50–53.

108. Alexander, G. M., and J. C. Loulis. September 1981. The Strategy of the Greek Communist Party 1934–1944: An Analysis of Plenary Decisions. *East European Quarterly* 15 (3): 377–389.

109. Alexander, H. E. May 1976. Rethinking Election Reform. *Annals of the American Academy of Political and Social Science* 425: 1–16.

110. Alexander, J. M. March 1976. A Study of Conflict in Northern Ireland: An Application of Metagame Theory. *Journal of Peace Science* 2 (1): 113–134.

111. Alexander, L. A. 1981. Modern Equal Protection Theories: A Metatheoretical Taxonomy and Critique. *Ohio State Law Review* 42 (1): 3–68.

112. Alexander, L. A. March 1988. Legal Theory and Judicial Accountability: A Comment on Seidman. *Southern California Law Review* 61: 1601–1605.

113. Alexander, R. J. February 1985. Bolivia's Democratic Experience. *Current History* 84 (499): 73–76, 86–87.

114. Alexy, R. July 1994. Basic Rights and Democracy in Jurgen Habermas's Procedural Paradigm of the Law. *Ratio Juris* 7: 227–238.

115. Alfonsin, R. January 1986. The Transition to Democracy in the Third World. *Third World Quarterly* 8 (1): 39–50.

116. Alfonsin, R. R. December 1987. Building Democracy. *Yale Journal of International Law* 12 (1): 121–132.

117. Alford, C. F. June 1985. The "Iron Law of Oligarchy" in the Athenian Polis . . . and Today. *Canadian Journal of Political Science* 18 (2): 295–312.

118. Alford, J. December 1980. Deterrence and Disuse: Some Thoughts on the Problem of Maintaining Volunteer Forces. *Armed Forces and Society* 6 (2): 247–256.

119. Al-Hassan, O. April 1994. Saudi Arabia and the New World Order. *International Relations* 12: 59–70.

120. Al-Hibri, A. Y. December 1992. Islamic Constitutionalism and the Concept of Democracy. *Case Western Reserve Journal of International Law* 24: 1–27.

121. Ali, B. 1987. Pakistan: Is Democracy the Answer? *Economic and Political Weekly* 22 (16): 697–698.

122. Ali, B. 1990. Dismal Prospects for Democracy in Pakistan. *Economic and Political Weekly* 25 (40): 2240–2241.

123. Alisky, M. December 1975. Portugal's Political Tug of War. *Intellect* 104 (2370): 220–222.

124. Alksnis, V. September 1991. Suffering from Self-Determination [in the USSR]. *Foreign Policy* 84: 61–71.

125. Allan, T. R. S. March 1985. Legislative Supremacy and the Rule Of Law: Democracy and Constitutionalism. *Cambridge Law Journal* 44: 111–143.

126. Allardt, E. December 1984. Representative Government in a Bureaucratic Age. *Daedalus* 113 (1): 169–197.

127. Alleman, F. R. 1980. Demokratisiering mit Fragezeichen.* *Schweizer Monatshefte* 60 (4): 289–298.

128. Allen, B. 1991. The Spiral of Silence and Institutional Design: Tocqueville's Analysis of Public Opinion and Democracy. *Polity* 24 (2): 243–267.

129. Allen, C. June 1992. "Goodbye to All That": The Short and Sad Story of Socialism in Benin. *Journal of Communist Studies* 8 (2): 63–81.

130. Allen, C. July 1992. Restructuring an Authoritarian State: "Democratic Renewal" in Benin. *Review of African Political Economy* 19: 42–58.

131. Allen, G. O., and R. Hardin. January 1982. Formal Decision Theory and Majority Rule. *Ethics* 92 (2): 199–210.

132. Allies, P. 1978. Decentralized Democracy, Social Experimentation and Government Reform. *Revue de l'Institut de Sociologie* 4: 389–408.

133. Allison, G. T., and R. P. Beschel, Jr. March 1992. Can the United States Promote Democracy? *Political Science Quarterly* 107 (1): 81–98.

134. Allison, G. T., and R. Blackwill. June 1991. America's Stake in the Soviet Future. *Foreign Affairs* 70 (3): 77–97.

135. Allison, G. T., S. Cohen, and T. Colton. December 1992. Staggering Toward Democracy: Russia's Future Is Far from Certain. *Harvard International Review* 15 (2): 14–17, 60–62.

136. Allison, L. March 1994. On the Gap Between Theories of Democracy and Theories of Democratization. *Democratization* 1 (1): 8–26.

137. Allub, L. April 1974. Industrializacion, Burguesia Dependiente y Democracy en Argentina. *Revista Mexicana de Sociologia* 36: 241–78.

138. Almeida, C. March 1977. Democracy in the Period of Transition from Capitalism to Socialism. *Argument* 19: 223–227.

139. Almond, G. A. September 1991. Capitalism and Democracy. *PS: Political Science & Politics* 24 (3): 467–474.

140. Al-Sayyid, M. K. September 1991. Slow Thaw in the Arab World. *World Policy Journal* 8 (4): 711–738.

141. Al-Sayyid, M. K. March 1993. A Civil Society in Egypt? *Middle East Journal* 47: 228–242.

142. Alshayeji, A. K. May 1992. Kuwait at the Crossroads: The Quest for Democratization. *Middle East Insight* 8: 41–46.

143. Alt, J. E. December 1985. Political Parties, World Demand and Unemployment: Domestic and International Sources of Economic Activity. *American Political Science Review* 79 (4): 1016–1040.

144. Alt, J. E. August 1990. *See* King, G. (August 1990).

145. Alt, J. E., and G. King. July 1994. Transfers of Governmental Power: The Meaning of Time Dependence. *Comparative Political Studies* 27 (2): 190–210.

146. Altbach, P. G. 1992. Higher Education, Democracy, and Development: Implications for Newly Industrialized Countries. *Interchange* 23 (1–2): 143–163.

147. Aluba, S. O. December 1989. Crisis, Repression and the Prospects for Democracy in Nigeria. *Scandinavian Journal of Development Alternatives* 8 (4): 107–122.

148. Alvarez, F. 1988. Notes on Democratization and Counter-Insurgency in El Salvador. *Estudios Sociales Centroamericanos* 47: 51–58.

149. Alvarez, R. M., G. Garrett, and P. Lange. June 1991. Government Partisanship, Labor Organization, and Macroeconomic Performance. *American Political Science Review* 85 (2): 539–556.

150. Alvayay, R., and C. Ruiz (eds.). August 1984. Teoria Contemporanea de la Democracia: Perspectivas Para el Analisis de la Situacion Chilena. *Opciones* 3–197. Special issue.

151. Alves, M. H. M. 1988. Dilemmas of the Consolidation of Democracy from the Top in Brazil: A Political Analysis. *Latin American Perspectives* 15 (3): 47–63.

152. Aly, A. M. S. September 1987. Democratization in Egypt. *American-Arab Affairs* 22: 11–27.

153. Alyushin, A. L. 1992. The Paternalistic Tradition and Russia's Transition to Liberal Democracy. *Democratic Institutions* 1: 1–19.

154. Amacher, R. C., R. D. Tollison, and T. D. Willett. 1975. Budget Size in a Democracy: Review of Arguments. *Public Finance Quarterly* 3 (2): 99–121.

155. Amaggio, V. July 1992. Jacques Maritain and Democracy: Reflections on a Philosophical Itinerary.* *Il Politico* 57 (3): 529–539.

156. Amann, R. July 1990. Soviet Politics in the Gorbachev Era: The End of Hesitant Modernization. *British Journal of Political Science* 20 (3): 289–310.

157. Amato, G. March 1994. Democracy and the European Institutions.* *Il Mulino* 352: 334–339.

158. Amato, T. June 1994. *See* Nadeau, R. (June 1994).

159. Amberg, S. February 1991. Democratic Producerism: Enlisting American Politics for Workplace Flexibility. *Economy and Society* 20 (1): 57–78.

160. Ambler, J. October 1975. Trust in Political and Nonpolitical Authorities in France. *Comparative Politics* 8 (1): 31–58.

161. Ambler, J. S. October 1987. Constraints on Policy Innovation in Education: Thatcher's Britain and Mitterand's France. *Comparative Politics* 20 (1): 85–105.

162. Amdur, R. April 1977. Rawl's Theory of Justice: Domestic and International Perspectives. *World Politics* 29 (3): 438–361.

163. Amenta, E. November 1993. The State-of-the-Art in Welfare State Research on Social Spending Efforts in Capitalist Democracies since 1960. *American Journal of Sociology* 99 (3): 750–763.

164. Ameringer, C. D. March 1982. The Tradition of Democracy in the Caribbean: Betancourt, Figueres, Munoz, and the Democratic Left. *Caribbean Review* 11 (2): 28–31,55–56.

165. Ames Cobian, R. September 1989. The Latin American States between Democracy and Violence: Deadly Mistakes.* *Sintesis* 9: 15–29.

166. Amin, S. October 1987. Democracy and National Strategy in the Periphery. *Third World Quarterly* 9 (4): 1129–1156.

167. Amir, S. January 1991. The Issue of Democracy in the Contemporary Third World. *Socialism and Democracy* 12: 83–104.

168. Anayaoka, E. June 1992. The Commonwealth and the Challenge of Democracy. *Development Policy Review* 10 (2): 99–106.

169. Anbarci, N. April 1993. Strategic Vote Manipulation in a Simple Democracy. *Journal of Economic Behavior & Organization* 20 (3): 319–330.

170. Anckar, D. 1982. Constitutional Change and Democracy: Note on Political Education.* *Politiika* 24 (4): 281–300.

171. Anckar, D. 1982. A Definition of Democracy. *Scandinavian Political Studies* 5 (3): 217–235.

172. Anckar, D. 1994. Finland's Electoral System: A Presentation.* *Statsvetenskaplig Tidskrift* 97 (1): 11–15.

173. Andersen, M. June 1984. Dateline Argentina: Hello, Democracy. *Foreign Policy* (55): 154–172.

174. Andersen, M. E. December 1988. The Military Obstacle to Latin Democracy. *Foreign Policy* (73): 94–113.

175. Anderson, B. 1988. Cacique Democracy in the Philippines: Origins and Dreams. *New Left Review* 169: 3–31.

176. Anderson, B. R. March 1981. Looking Back. *Wilson Quarterly* 5 (2): 112–125.

177. Anderson, C. W. 1993. Recommending a Scheme of Reason: Political Theory, Policy Science, and Democracy. *Policy Sciences* 26 (3): 215–227.

178. Anderson, D. F. December 1982. The Legacy of William Howard Taft. *Presidential Studies Quarterly* 12 (1): 26–33.

179. Anderson, E. S. December 1990. *See* Pildes, R. H. (December 1990).

180. Anderson, G. M. April 1988. Public Finance in Autocratic Process: An Empirical Note. *Public Choice* 57 (1): 25–37.

181. Anderson, C. M., and R. D. Tollison. March 1988. Democracy, Interest Groups and the Price of Votes. *Cato Journal* 8 (1): 53–70.

182. Anderson, J. C. 1978. A Comparative Analysis of Local Union Democracy. *Industrial Relations (Berkeley)* 17 (3): 278–295.

183. Anderson, J. C. 1979. Local Union Democracy: In Search of Criteria. *Industrial Relations* 34 (3): 431–451.

184. Anderson, K. 1994. Women and the Vote in the 1920s: What Happened in Oregon. *Women & Politics* 14 (4): 43–56.

185. Anderson, L. (Leslie) May 1994. Neutrality and Bias in the 1990 Nicaraguan Pre-election Polls: A Comment on Bischoping and Schuman. *American Journal of Political Science* 38 (2): 486–494.

186. Anderson, L. (Lisa) April 1990. Liberalism in Northern Africa. *Current History* 89 (546): 145–148, 174–175.

187. Anderson, L. (Lisa) March 1991. Political Pacts, Liberalism and Democracy: The Tunisian National Pact of 1988. *Government and Opposition* 26 (2): 244–260.

188. Anderson, L. (Lisa) 1992. Remaking the Middle East: The Prospects for Democracy and Stability. *Ethics and International Affairs* 6: 163–178.

189. Anderson, P. 1988. Democracia y Dictadura en America Latina en la Decada del 70. *Revista de Ciencias Sociales* 3: 15–23.

190. Anderson, T. D. March 1987. Progress in the Democratic Revolution in Latin America: Country Assessment 1987. *Journal of Interamerican Studies and World Affairs* 29 (1): 57–71.

191. Anderson, T. P. March 1985. Honduras in Transition. *Current History* 84 (500): 114–117, 132.

192. Andic, F. M. December 1984. Efficiency vs. Equity. *Caribbean Review* 13 (1): 16–19.

193. Andic, F. M., and S. Andic. 1984. The Politics of Redistribution in a Democracy. *International Journal of Social Economics* 11 (1–2): 3–13.

194. Andic, S. 1984. *See* Andic, F. M. (1984).

195. Andorka, R. December 1994. Hungary: Disenchantment after Transition. *World Today* 50 (12): 233–236.

196. Andrain, C. F. December 1984. Capitalism and Democracy Reappraised: A Review Essay. *Western Political Quarterly* 37 (4): 652–664.

197. Andrassy, G., and M. Fulop. 1992. Prospects of a Free and Democratic Society in Hungary. *Journal of Interdisciplinary Studies* 4 (1–2): 121–138.

198. Andreasson, B. 1978. Research on Democracy at the Work Place.* *Nordisk Psykologi* 30 (2): 131–132.

199. Andreev, N. January 1994. Kirgizstan: Grappling with Democracy. *Bulletin of the Atomic Scientists* 50 (1): 52–55.

200. Andreotti, G. 1994. Foreign Policy in the Italian Democracy. *Political Science Quarterly* 109 (3): 529–540.

201. Andrew, C. March 1979. Government and Secret Service: A Historical Perspective. *International Journal* 34 (2): 167–186.

202. Andrews, B. 1980. Criticizing Economic Democracy. *Monthly Review* 32 (1): 19–25.

203. Andrews, R. N. L. December 1980. Value Analysis in Environment Policy. *Policy Studies Journal* 9 (3): 369–378.

204. Andriamirado, S. September 17, 1992. Mali: Dix Chiffres a Combattes. *Jeune Afrique* 32: 35–41.

205. Angell, A. January 1975. Chile One Year after the Coup. *Current History* 68 (401): 11–14,42.

206. Angell, A. October 1993. The Transition to Democracy in Chile: A Model or an Exceptional Case? *Parliamentary Affairs* 46 (4): 563–578.

207. Angell, A., and B. Pollack. 1990. The Chilean Elections of 1989 and the Politics of the Transition to Democracy. *Bulletin of Latin American Research* 9: 1–23.

208. Anghene, M., D. Iliescu, and S. Popescu. 1976. New Aspects of the Citizens' Participation in the Management of Social Life and the State in the Socialist Republic of Romania.* *Annuaire de l'URSS et des Pays Socialistes Europeen* 189–204.

209. Aninkola, A. A. July 1988. Nigeria: The Quest for a Stable Polity: Another Comment. *African Affairs* 348: 441–445.

210. Ankersmit, F. R. July 1991. Tocqueville and the Ambivalence of Democracy. *Rationality and Society* 3 (3): 308–316.

211. Ankersmit, F. R. 1993. Tocqueville and the Sublimity of Democracy. *Tocqueville Review* 14 (2): 173–200.

212. Ankersmit, F. R. January 1993. Stoa, Aesthetics and Democracy. *Acta Politica* 28 (1): 3–17.

213. Annis, S. September 1991. Giving Voice to the Poor. *Foreign Policy* 84: 93–106.

214. Annunziata, L. 1988. Party State Dialectics: Democracy and the Sandinistas. *Nation* 246 (13): 454–456.

215. Ansari, H. February 1987. Egypt: Repression and Liberalization. *Current History* 86 (517): 77–80, 84.

216. Ansolabehere, S., and A. Gerber. November 1994. The Mismeasure of Campaign Spending: Evidence from the 1990 United States House Elections. *Journal of Politics* 56 (4): 1106–1117.

217. Ansolabehere, S., S. Iyengar, A. Simon, and N. Valentino. December 1994. Does Attack Advertising Demobilize the Electorate? *American Political Science Review* 88 (4): 829–838.

218. Ansprenger, F. October 1994. Conflicts in Africa.* *Europa Archiv: Zeitchrift für Internationale Politik* 49 (20): 571–587.

219. Antholis, W. November 1992. *See* Russett, B. (November 1992).

220. Anton, T. J. March 1985. *See* Campbell, J. C. (March 1985).

221. Antonio, R., and D. Kellner. September 1992. Communication, Modernity and Democracy in Habermas and Dewey. *Symbolic Interaction* 15 (3): 277–297.

222. Antonio, R., and T. Knapp. June 1988. Democracy and Abundance: The Declining Liberal and Postliberal Politics. *Telos* 77: 93–114.

223. Antoszewski, A. 1985. The Legislative and Executive Powers in the Bourgeois and Socialist Political Systems.* *Studia Nauk Politycznych* 74: 35–54.

224. Antov, I. 1986. The Aimless Road to Democracy.* *Filosoficky Casopis* 34 (2): 272–280.

225. Antunes, R. December 1994. Recent Strikes in Brazil: The Main Tendencies of the Strike Movement of the 1980s. *Latin American Perspectives* 21 (1): 24–37.

226. Applebaum, A. I. June 1992. Democratic Legitimacy and Official Discretion. *Philosophy and Public Affairs* 21 (3): 240–274.

227. Appleby, J. June 1976. Ideology and Theory: The Tension between Political and Economic Liberalism. *American Historical Review* 81 (3): 499–515.

228. Appleby, J. March 1982. Commercial Farming and the "Agrarian Myth" in the Early Republic. *Journal of American History* 68 (4): 833–849.

229. Apter, D. E. June 1985. The New Myths/Logics and the Specter of Superfluous Man. *Social Research* 52 (2): 269–307.

230. Apter, D. E. August 1991. Institutionalism Reconsidered. *International Social Science Journal* 43 (3): 463–480.

231. Apter, D. E. July 1992. Democracy and Emancipatory Movements: Notes for a Theory of Inversionary Discourse. *Development and Change* 23 (3): 139–173.

232. Aquino, B. A. April 1989. Democracy in the Philippines. *Current History* 88 (537): 181–184, 190.

233. Aragon, M. September 1988. The Legal Efficiency of the Democratic Principle. *Revista Espanola de Derecho Constitucional* 24: 9–45.

234. Arase, D. October 1993. Japanese Policy toward Democracy and Human

Rights in Asia. *Asian Survey* 133 (10): 935–952.

235. Arat, Z. F. September 1986. Human Rights and Democratic Instability in Developing Countries. *Policy Studies Journal* 15 (1): 158–172.

236. Arat, Z. F. October 1988. Democracy and Economic Development: Modernization Theory Revisited. *Comparative Politics* 21 (1): 21–36.

237. Arato, A. December 1985. Some Perspectives of Democratization in East Central Europe. *Journal of International Affairs* 38 (2): 321–335.

238. Arato, A. April 1994. Constitution and Continuity in the East European Transitions. Part I: Continuity and Its Crisis. *Constellations* 1 (1): 92–112.

239. Arato, A., and J. Goldfarb (eds.). December 1983. Democracy: Relationship between the Democratic State and Democratic Society on All Levels. *Social Research* 50: 709–973. Special issue.

240. Arbos, X. March 1987. Central vs. Peripheral Nationalism in Building Democracy: The Case of Spain. *Canadian Review of Studies in Nationalism* 14: 143–160.

241. Arce, L. E. December 1981. In Defense of Restoring Constitutional Order. *Caribbean Review* 10 (1): 35–37.

242. Archamba, D. 1974. Environment, Public Utility and Democracy. *McGill Law Journal* 20 (1): 1–25.

243. Archetti, E. 1989. Culture and Politics: The Lengthy Road to Democracy in Argentina.* *Internasjonal Politikk* (4–6): 215–240.

244. Archibugi, D. 1990. Democracy in the Projects of Perpetual Peace.* *Teoria Politica* 6 (1): 99–133.

245. Archibugi, D. August 1993. The Reform of the UN and Cosmopolitan

Democracy: A Critical Review. *Journal of Peace Research* 30 (3): 301–315.

246. Ardigo, A. September 1980. The Governability of Democracy in Europe: A Sociological Approach. *Sociologia* 14 (3): 3–35.

247. Ardito-Barletta, N. June 1990. Democracy and Development. *Washington Quarterly* 13 (3): 165–175.

248. Arellano, J. P., and R. Cortazar. January 1986. Inflation, Macro Economic Conflict and Democratization in Chile.* *Pensamiento Iberoamericano* 9: 331–354.

249. Arestis, P. September 1986. Post-Keynesian Economic Policies: The Case of Sweden. *Journal of Economic Issues* 20 (3): 709–723.

250. Arevalo, J. January 1993. *See* Harris, E. (January 1993).

251. Argersinger, P. H. June 1989. The Value of the Vote: Political Representation in the Gilded Age. *Journal of American History* 76 (1): 59–90.

252. Argido, A. September 1984. Ethical Dimensions, Social Changes and Problems of Democracy.* *Sociologia* 18 (3): 3–22.

253. Arguedas, L. et al. October 1982. The Possibilities of Democracy in Italy.* *Revista Mexicana de Sociologia* 44 (4): 1119–1162.

254. Arguedas, S. July 1994. Freedom and Liberty: Democracy.* *Revista Mexicana de Ciencias Politicas y Sociales* 157: 143–155.

255. Arian, A. December 1985. Israeli Democracy 1984. *Journal of International Affairs* 38 (2): 259–276.

256. Arian, A., and M. Shamir. December 1993. Two Reversals in Israeli Politics: Why 1992 Was Not 1977. *Electoral Studies* 12 (4): 315–341.

257. Arias, J. May 1994. The Fascination of "Novelty" [in Italy]. *MicroMega* 2: 53–59.

258. Arias-Salgado, R. September 1988. Planning and Improvisation in the Process of Passage to Democracy in Spain.* *Zeitschrift für Parlamentsfragen* 19 (3): 315–322.

259. Arieli, Y. June 1989. The (Israeli) Proclamation of Independence: A Forty Year Perspective. *Jerusalem Quarterly* 51: 48–70.

260. Arienza, M., and C. A. Mallmann. 1985. Argentina on the Road to Democracy: Comparisons with Chile and Uruguay. *International Social Science Journal* 37 (1): 31–46.

261. Ariffin, Y. 1992. Development and Democracy: Macro-Economic Adjustment and Micro-Economic Transformations.* *Le Trimestre du Monde* 17: 61–89.

262. Arinos Demelo Franco, A. June 1984. Contemporary Processes of Constitution Making.* *Revista de Ciencia Politica* 27 (1): 1–32.

263. Arkes, H. 1976. Democracy and European Communism. *Commentary* 61 (5): 38–47.

264. Armand, Y. June 1989. Democracy in Haiti: The Legacy of Anti-Democratic Political and Social Traditions. *International Journal of Politics, Culture and Society* 2 (4): 537–561.

265. Armijo, L. E. 1990. The Resurgence of Political Democracy in Contemporary Latin America. *India International Centre Quarterly* 17 (2): 135–150.

266. Armijo, L. E., T. J. Biersteker, and A. F. Lowenthal. October 1994. The Problem of Simultaneous Transitions. *Journal of Democracy* 5 (4): 161–174.

267. Armingeon, K. 1989. Social Democracy at the End: Development of Power of Social Democratic Parties: An International Survey, 1945–1988.* *Oesterreichische Zeitschrift für Politikwissenschaft* 18 (4): 321–345.

268. Armingeon, K. March 1994. Reasons and Consequences of Declining Electoral Turnout.* *Kolner Zeitschrift für Soziologie und Sozialpsychologie* 46 (1): 43–64.

269. Arneson, R. J. June 1993. Socialism as the Extension of Democracy. *Social Philosophy and Policy* 10 (2): 145–171.

270. Arnhart, L. March 1979. "The God-Like Prince": John Locke, Executive Prerogative, and the American Presidency. *Presidential Studies Quarterly* 9 (2): 121–130.

271. Arnold, R. A., and T. L. Wyrick. 1982. Budgetary Referenda: An Efficient Alternative to Representative Democracy. *Cato Journal* 2 (2): 637–652.

272. Arnot, M. 1991. Equality and Democracy: A Decade of Struggle over Education. *British Journal of Sociology of Education* 12 (4): 447–466.

273. Arnson, C. 1984. *See* Nelson, A. (1984).

274. Arnstine, B. January 1993. *See* Arnstine, D. (January 1993).

275. Arnstine, D., and B. Arnstine. January 1993. Rationality and Democracy: A Critical Appreciation of Israel Scheffler's Philosophy of Education. *Synthese* 94 (1): 25–41.

276. Aro, S. June 22, 1994. *See* Hermanson, T. (June 22, 1994).

277. Arone, L. J. 1992. *See* Entelis, J. P. (1992).

278. Aronson, D. March 1993. Why Africa Stays Poor: And Why It Doesn't Have To. *Humanist* 53: 9–14.

279. Arora, D. March 19, 1994. From State Regulation to Peoples Participation: Case of Forest Management in India. *Economic and Political Weekly* 29 (12): 691–698.

280. Arrington, T. S., and S. Brenner. June 1980. The Advantages of a Plurality Election of the President. *Presidential Studies Quarterly* 10 (3): 476–482.

281. Arrow, K. J. 1978. Capitalism, Socialism, and Democracy. *Commentary* 65 (4): 29–31.

282. Arruda, M. 1984. *See* Aguiar, M. A. D. (1984).

283. Arruda, M. December 1984. *See* De Souza, A. (December 1984).

284. Art, R. J. March 1991. A Defensible Defense: America's Grand Strategy After the Cold War. *International Security* 15 (4): 5–53.

285. Arteaga Zumaran, J. J. September 1987. Notes on Uruguayan Politics.* *Civitas (Roma)* 38 (5): 9–26.

286. Arter, D. March 1980. Social Democracy in a West European Outpost: The Case of the Finnish SDP. *Polity* 12 (3): 363–387.

287. Arter, D. October 1981. Kekkonin's Finland: Enlightened Despotism or Consensual Democracy? *West European Politics* 4: 219–234.

288. Arterton, F. C. June 1988. Political Participation [in the U.S.] and "Teledemocracy." *PS: Political Science & Politics* 21 (3): 620–627.

289. Arutiunian, Y. June 1992. Changing Values of Russians from Brezhnev to Gorbachev. *Journal of Soviet Nationalities* 2: 1–34.

290. Asai, M. 1990. Democracy, an Unintended Victim. *Japan Quarterly* 37 (1): 4–13.

291. Asard, E. 1980. Employee Participation in Sweden 1971–1979: The Issue of Economic Democracy. *Economic and Industrial Democracy* 1 (3): 371–393.

292. Asard, E. 1986. Industrial and Economic Democracy in Sweden: From Consensus to Confrontation. *European Journal of Political Research* 14 (1–2): 207–219.

293. Aschin, G. 1976. Political Pluralism or Elite Democracy.* *Sowjetwissenschaft*:

Gesellschaft Wissenschaftliche Beitrage 29 (2): 180–193.

294. Ascraft, R. September 1977. Economic Metaphors, Behavioralism and Political Theory: Some Observations on the Ideological Uses of Language. *Western Political Quarterly* 30 (3): 313–328.

295. Ashford, D. E. September 1975. Parties and Participation in British Local Government and Some American Parallels. *Urban Affairs Quarterly* 11 (1): 58–81.

296. Ashford, D. E. 1976. Democracy, Decentralization, and Decisions in Subnational Politics. *Sage Professional Papers in Comparative Politics* 5 (105): 5–59.

297. Ashford, D. E. March 1985. *See* Campbell, J. C. (March 1985).

298. Ashley, S. December 1990. Bulgaria. *Electoral Studies* 9 (4): 312–318.

299. Aslund, A. March 1992. Russia's Road from Communism. *Daedalus* 121 (2): 77–95.

300. Aslund, A. October 1994. The Case for Radical Reform. *Journal of Democracy* 5 (4): 63–74.

301. Asmal, K. December 1992. Democracy and Human Rights: Developing a South African Human Rights Culture. *New England Law Review* 27: 287–361.

302. Asmus, R. D. March 1990. A United Germany. *Foreign Affairs* 69 (2): 63–76.

303. Aspin, L. June 1975. The Defense Budget and Foreign Policy: The Role of Congress. *Daedalus* 104 (3): 155–174.

304. Assarson, J. 1993. The Problem of Intra-Party Democracy.* *Statsvetenskaplig Tidskrift* 96 (1): 39–68.

305. Assayag, J. 1986. The Modernization of Castes and the Indianization of Democracy. *Archives Europeennes de Sociologie* 27 (2): 319–352.

306. Assel, H. 1980. Zur Kritik Neomarxistischer Demokratiekritik: Bemerkungen zu einen Aktuellen Problem Politischer Bildung. *Mitarbeit* 29 (2): 97–113.

307. Assies, W. December 1993. Urban Social Movements and Local Democracy in Brazil. *Revista Europea Estudios Latinoamericanos y del Caribe:* 39–58.

308. Athanassakos, A. September 1990. General Fund Financing vs. Earmarked Taxes: An Alternative Model of Budgetary Choice in a Democracy. *Public Choice* 66 (3): 261–278.

309. Atkin, R. S. September 1990. *See* Masters, M. F. (September 1990).

310. Atkinson, M. M., and W. D. Coleman. April 1985. Bureaucrats and Politicians in Canada: An Examination of the Political Administration Model. *Comparative Political Studies* 18 (1): 58–80.

311. Attina, F. July 1992. Parties, Party Systems and Democracy in the European Union. *International Spectator* 27: 67–86.

312. Audi, R. July 1990. The Function of the Press in a Free and Democratic Society. *Public Affairs* 4: 203–215.

313. Audi, R. September 1993. The Place of Religious Argument in a Free and Democratic Society. *San Diego Law Review* 30: 677–702.

314. Austen Smith, D. February 1994. Counteractive Lobbying. *American Journal of Political Science* 38 (1): 25–44.

315. Austin, D. April 1993. Reflections of African Politics: Prospero, Ariel and Caliban. *International Affairs (London)* 69 (2): 203–221.

316. Austin, D., and A. Gupta. April 1994. India: Once More to the Polls. *Round Table* (330): 213–222.

317. Austin, R. March 1993. What Albania Adds to the Balkan Stew. *Orbis* 37: 259–279.

318. Auty, R., and A. Gelb. September 1986. Oil Windfalls in a Small Parliamentary Democracy: Their Impact on Trinidad and Tobago. *World Development* 14 (9): 1161–1175.

319. Avineri, S. 1993. Democracy and Nationalism in the Post-Communist States.* *Europaeische Rundschau* 21 (4): 51–60.

320. Avouyi-Dovi, S. January 1986. Vers un Moindre Poids de l'Etat? Une Evaluation Chiffree des Project de l'Opposition. *Observations et Diagnostics Economiques:* 5–58.

321. Awbrey, K. December 1992. *See* Korzeniewicz, R. P. (December 1992).

322. Ayerbe, L. F. 1991. The Transition to Democracy in Argentina 1984–1989: An Assessment of the Alfonsin Government 1984–1989.* *Perspectivas* 14: 149–171.

323. Azam, J. P. September 1994. Democracy and Development: A Theoretical Framework. *Public Choice* 80 (3–4): 293–305.

324. Azevedo, M. May 1987. The Post-Ahigo Era in Cameroon. *Current History* 86 (520): 217–220, 229–230.

❧

325. Baber, W. F. 1988. Impact Assessment and Democratic Politics. *Policy Studies Review* 8 (1): 172–178.

326. Bachman, D. September 1989. China's Politics: Conservatism Prevails. *Current History* 88 (539): 257–260, 296–297, 320.

327. Bacho, P. April 1987. U.S. Policy Options toward the Philippines. *Asian Survey* 27 (4): 427–441.

328. Bachrach, P. 1983. *See* Botwinick, A. (1983).

329. Bacic, A. 1989. On the Relevance of the Division of Powers Doctrine.* *Politicka Misao* 26 (2): 160–171.

330. Baczko, B. September 1988. The Social Contract of the French: Sieyes and Rousseau. *Journal of Modern History* 60 (Supplement): 98–125.

331. Badaloni, N. March 1982. Theoretical and Practical Considerations on the "Third Way."* *Critica Marxistas* 20 (2): 5–19.

332. Badgley, J. February 1990. *See* Guyot, J. F. (February 1990).

333. Badie, B. 1990. "I Say Western Countries": Democracy and Development: Answers to Six Questions.* *Pouvoirs* 52: 43–53.

334. Badie, B. August 1991. Democracy and Religion: Logics of Culture and Logics of Action. *International Social Science Journal* 43 (3): 511–522.

335. Baechler, J. 1979. On Anticapitalism. *Washington Quarterly* 2 (4): 74–88.

336. Baechler, J. 1980. Origins of Greek Democracy.* *Archives Europeennes de Sociologie* 21 (2): 223–284.

337. Baechler, J. December 1982. Enterprise and Democracy.* *Commentaire* 20: 664–672.

338. Baechler, J. May 1983. The Power of Ideas on Democracy.* *Connaissance Politique* 2: 141–157.

339. Baechler, J. April 1992. Democratic Institutions for Africa.* *Revue Juridique et Politique, Independance et Cooperation* 46 (2): 163–181.

340. Baechler, J. July 1992. Individuals, Groups and Democracy.* *Biblioteca della Liberta* 118: 39–61.

341. Baechler, J. 1993. Federation and Democracy.* *Revue Europeenne des Sciences Sociales* 95: 181–196.

342. Baehr, P. February 1993. *See* Bellamy, R. (February 1993).

343. Bael, I. V. April 1989. Bureaucracy vs. Democracy in the EC: Community Legislation Is Being Shaped by Faceless Technocrats. *International Financial Law Review* 8: 12–14.

344. Baer, M. D. June 1988. Between Evolution and Devolution: Mexican Democracy. *Washington Quarterly* 11 (3): 77–89.

345. Baer, W. 1980. The Collapse of Democracy in Brazil: Comment. *Latin American Research Review* 15 (3): 41–43.

346. Baer, W. (ed.). 1991. Latin America: The Crisis of the Eighties and the Opportunities of the Nineties. *Quarterly Review of Economics and Business* 31: 13–255. 9 articles with comments.

347. Bahgat, G. December 1993. Privatization and Democratization in the Arab World: Is There a Connection? *Journal of Social, Political, and Economic Studies* 18 (4): 427–444.

348. Bahgat, G. January 1994. Democracy in the Middle East: The American Connection. *Studies in Conflict and Terrorism* 17 (1): 87–96.

349. Bahro, H., and J. Zepp. July 1988. Mudanca e Politica de Desenvolvimento Regional no Brasil o Ano 1984. *Revista de Informacao Legislativa* 25: 285–310.

350. Bahry, D., and B. D. Silver. July 1990. Public Perceptions and the Dilemmas of Party Reform in the USSR. *Comparative Political Studies* 23 (2): 171–209.

351. Bahry, D., and B. D. Silver. September 1990. Soviet Citizen Participation on the Eve of Democratization. *American Political Science Review* 84 (3): 821–847.

352. Bailey, M. T. March 1989. *See* Mayer, R. T. (March 1989).

353. Bailin, S. 1992. Culture, Democracy, and the University. *Interchange* 23 (1–2): 63–69.

354. Baily, M. A. July 1994. The Democracy Problem. *Hastings Center Report* 24 (4): 39–42.

355. Bajeux, J. December 1988. The Little Game of January 17th. *Caribbean Review* 16 (2): 7, 27.

356. Bakaty, T. D. 1990. Back to Political Pluralism in Ivory Coast.* *Année Africaine* 161–189.

357. Baker, D. 1976. States Experiment with Anticipatory Democracy. *Futurist* 10 (5): 262+.

358. Baker, E. J. April 1982. Politics in South Korea. *Current History* 81 (474): 173–174, 177–178.

359. Baker, J. A. III. June 1990. CSCE in Copenhagen: An Introduction. *World Affairs* 153 (1): 3–4.

360. Baker, J. W. March 1993. The Convenantal Basis for the Development of Swiss Political Federalism: 1291–1848. *Publius* 23 (2): 19–42.

361. Baker, P. H. May 1990. South Africa on the Move. *Current History* 89 (547): 197–200, 232–233.

362. Baker, P. H. December 1993. Going against the Tide: South Africa's Search for Democracy. *SAIS Review* 13 (1): 13–28.

363. Bakos, G. 1994. Hungarian Transition after Three Years. *Europe-Asia Studies* 46 (7): 1189–1214.

364. Bakunin, J. S. 1976. P. Leroux on Democracy, Socialism and Enlightenment. *Journal of the History of Ideas* 37 (3): 455–474.

365. Bakvis, H. March 1981. Polarization in the Netherlands. *Queen's Quarterly* 88 (1): 74–86.

366. Bakvis, H. April 1984. Toward a Political Economy of Consociationalism: A Commentary on Marxist Views of Pillarization in the Netherlands. *Comparative Politics* 16 (3): 315–334.

367. Bakvis, H. March 1985. Structure and Process in Federal and Consociational Arrangements. *Publius* 15 (2): 57–69.

368. Bakvis, H. July 1994. Intra State Federalism in Australia. *Australian Journal of Political Science* 29 (2): 259–276.

369. Balagopal, K. September 12, 1992. Economic Liberalism and Decline of Democracy: Case of Andra-Pradesh. *Economic and Political Weekly* 27 (37): 1958–1962.

370. Balcerowicz, L. March 1994. Democracy Is No Substitute for Capitalism. *Eastern European Economics* 32 (2): 39–49.

371. Balcerowicz, L. October 1994. Understanding Postcommunist Transitions. *Journal of Democracy* 5 (4): 75–89.

372. Balch, S. H. September 1978. Getting That Extra Edge: Seniority and Early Appointment to the United States Senate. *Polity* 11 (1): 138–146.

373. Balde, T. April 1993. Le Cout des Elections en Afrique. *Jeune Afrique Economie* 38–44.

374. Baldus, B. 1977. Social Control in Capitalist Societies: An Examination of the Problem of Order in Liberal Democracies. *Canadian Journal of Sociology* 2 (3): 247–262.

375. Baldwin, R., and A. F. Westin. November 1977. The ACLU and the FBI: A Conversation between Roger Baldwin and Alan F. Westin. *Civil Liberties Review* 4 (4): 18–25.

376. Balkan, E. M., and K. V. Greene. December 1990. On Democracy and Debt. *Public Choice* 67 (3): 201–211.

377. Balle, F. May 1983. Myths and Reality of Electronic Democracy.* *Connaissance Politique* 2: 106–112.

378. Ballesteros, C. January 1993. The Problem of Democratic Legitimacy and Political Changes.* *Revista Mexicana de Ciencias Politicas y Sociales* 151: 103–116.

379. Ballestrem, K. 1988. "Classical Democratic Theory," Construct or Reality.* *Zeitschrift für Politik* 35 (1): 33–56.

380. Baloyra, E. A. February 1984. Political Change in El Salvador? *Current History* 83 (490): 54–58, 85–87.

381. Baloyra, E. A. December 1985. Dilemmas of Political Transition in El Salvador. *Journal of International Affairs* 38 (2): 221–242.

382. Baloyra, E. A. March 1986. Negotiating War in El Salvador: The Politics of Endgame. *Journal of Interamerican Studies and World Affairs* 28 (1): 123–147.

383. Baloyra, E. A. September 1987. Democracy Despite Development. *World Affairs* 150 (2): 73–92.

384. Baloyra, E. A. April 1992. Salvaging El Salvador. *Journal of Democracy* 3 (2): 70–80.

385. Baloyra, E. A. September 1993. The Salvadoran Elections of 1982–1991. *Studies in Comparative International Development* 28 (3): 3–30.

386. Baltodano, M. P., R. Junghanns, and M. Sommer. 1987. Legal Order in Post-Revolutionary Nicaragua: Claims and Reality.* *Verfassung und Recht in Ubersee* 20 (2): 195–217.

387. Ban, C. November 1991. *See* Thompson, F. J. (November 1991).

388. Banegas, R. 1993. Democratic Transitions: Collective Mobilization and Political Fluidity. *Cultures et Conflict* 12: 105–140.

389. Banerji, A. K. January 1991. Egypt under Mubarak: The Quest for Stability at Home and Normalization Abroad. *Round Table* 317: 7–20.

390. Bang, H. P., and U. Jakobsen. 1994. The Tradition of Democratic Socialism: A Critique of Liberal Realism. *Statsvetenskaplig Tidskrift* 97 (1): 33–61.

391. Bank, H. 1978. Zur Theorie und Realitaet der Beteiligung von Buergern an der Politischen Planung. *Mitarbeit* 27 (3): 203–221.

392. Banner, W. A. June 1980. Distributive Justice and Welfare Claims. *Social Research* 47 (2): 383–398.

393. Bao, H. T. January 5, 1989. Democratization in Vietnam: Renewing the Party for the Sake of the Renewal of Society. *Review of International Affairs* 40: 21–23.

394. Baranczak, S. March 1990. Goodbye, Samizdat. *Wilson Quarterly* 14 (2): 59–66.

395. Barany, Z. D. 1990. On the Road to Democracy: The Hungarian Elections of 1990. *Suedosteuropa* 39 (5): 318–329.

396. Barany, Z. D., and L. Vinton. June 1990. Breakthrough to Democracy: Elections in Poland and Hungary. *Studies in Comparative Communism* 23 (2): 191–212.

397. Barbagallo, F. April 1992. Class, Nation, Democracy: The Left in Italy from 1944 to 1956.* *Studi Storici* 33 (2–3): 479–498.

398. Barber, B. December 1988. Participation and Swiss Democracy. *Government and Opposition* 23 (1): 31–50.

399. Barber, B. R. 1984a. The Conventions: Unconventional Democracy. *Psychology Today* 18 (7): 52–60.

400. Barber, B. R. 1984b. Political Talk and "Strong Democracy." *Dissent* 31 (2): 215–222.

401. Barber, B. R. September 1993. Global Democracy or Global Law: Which Comes First? *Indiana Journal of Global Legal Studies* 1 (1): 119–137.

402. Barbieri, L. April 1984. The Rise and Fall of a Democracy. *Worldview* 27: 5–13.

403. Barbour, I. G. December 1983. Democracy and Expertise in a Technological Society. *National Forum* 63: 3–5.

404. Barcellona, P. January 1987. Complexity and the Problem of Democracy.* *Democrazia e Diritto* 27 (1–2): 7–23.

405. Barcellona, P. March 1990. Constitutional State and Democratic Principle.* *Democrazia e Diritto* 30 (2): 245–264.

406. Barch, C. E. 1979. Thirty Years of Constitution: Justice and Democracy in the Constitution of the Federal Republic of Germany.* *Politische Studien* 30 (245): 239–248.

407. Bardhan, P. June 1993. Symposium on Democracy and Development. *Journal of Economic Perspectives* 7 (3): 45–49.

408. Bareiro-Saguier, R., and F. Navarro. March 1991. Le Paraguay ou les Premices de la Democratie. *Monde Diplomatique* 38: 20.

409. Barenberg, M. April 1994. Democracy and Domination in the Law of Workplace Cooperation: From Bureaucratic to Flexible Production. *Columbia Law Review* 94 (3): 753–983.

410. Baretta, S. R. D. July 1990. *See* Markoff, J. (July 1990).

411. Bargel, T. September 1981. *See* Lind, G. (September 1981).

412. Barkan, J. D. June 1987. *See* Niemi, R. G. (June 1987).

413. Barkenbus, J. March 1991. Can Advanced Technology and Open Democracy Co-Exist? *International Journal on the Unity of the Sciences* 4 (1): 37–57.

414. Barker, A. 1994. The Upturned Stone: Political Scandals and Their Investigation Processes in Twenty Democracies. *Crime, Law and Social Change* 21 (4): 337–374.

415. Barkin, S. 1978. Labor Participation: The Way to Industrial Democracy. *Industrial Relations* 33 (3): 391–405.

416. Barnard, F. M. December 1992. Norms, Procedures, and Democratic Legitimacy. *Political Studies* 40 (4): 659–678.

417. Barnard, J. W. March 1990. Giving Voice to Shareholder Choice: The Drive for Corporate Democracy. *Business and Society Review* 73: 15–17.

418. Barnes, A. 1982. Union Democracy at Stake: What Role for Outsiders? *Nation* 234 (21): 639+.

419. Barnes, F. June 1990. Congressional Despots, Then and Now. *Public Interest* 100: 45–56.

420. Barnes, S. H. August 1984. *See* McDonough, P. (August 1984).

421. Barnes, S. H., P. McDonough, and A. L. Pina. 1985. The Development of Partisanship in New Democracies: The Case of Spain. *American Journal of Political Science* 29 (4): 695–720.

422. Barnet, R. J. 1982. The Future of Democracy. *Yale Review* 72 (1): 19–40.

423. Barnett, G. A. July 1994. *See* Sun, S. L. (July 1994).

424. Barnitz, L. A. December 1990. *See* Said, A. A. (December 1990).

425. Barnum, D. G. May 1982. Decision Making in a Constitutional Democracy: Policy Formation in the Skokie Free Speech Controversy. *Journal of Politics* 44 (2): 480–508.

426. Barnum, D. G. May 1985. The Supreme Court and Public Opinion: Judicial Decision Making in the Post–New Deal Period. *Journal of Politics* 47 (2): 652–666.

427. Barnum, D. G., J. L. Sullivan, and M. Sunkin. 1992. Constitutional and Cultural Underpinnings of Political Freedom in Britain and the United States. *Oxford Journal of Legal Studies* 12: 362–379.

428. Baron, S. March 1982. Morality and Politics in Modern Life: Tocqueville and Solzhenitsyn on the Importance of Religion to Liberty. *Polity* 14 (3): 394–413.

429. Barquin Alvarez, M. January 1986. Government Forms and Latin America's Development.* *Boletin Mexicano de Derecho Comparado* 55: 39–64.

430. Barrett, W. 1978. Capitalism, Socialism, and Democracy. *Commentary* 65 (4): 31–33.

431. Barricelli, L. A. December 1985. Considerations on a Time: Democratic Electoral System. *European Journal of Political Research* 13 (4): 379–386.

432. Barros, E. 1987. Democracy As a Form of Power: A Normative Approach.* *Estudios Publicos* 26: 87–107.

433. Barros, R. June 1986. The Left and Democracy: Recent Debates in Latin America. *Telos* 68: 49–70.

434. Barrow, C. W. December 1988. Charles A. Beard's Social Democracy: A Critique of the Populist-Progressive Style in American Political Thought. *Polity* 21 (2): 253–276.

435. Barrow, D. J. November 1994. *See* Gryski, G. S. (November 1994).

436. Barry, A. June 1993. Television, Truth and Democracy. *Media, Culture and Society* 15 (3): 487–496.

437. Barsh, R. L. February 1992. Democratization and Development. *Human Rights Quarterly* 14 (1): 120–134.

438. Barsotti, F. A. January 1990. The 21st Century: Through a Glass Darkly. *Caribbean Affairs* 3 (1): 1–10.

439. Bar-Tal, D. December 1989. *See* Ichilov, O. (December 1989).

440. Bartel, R. September 1993. Public Auditing As a Means of Political Power Control: An Economic Foundation.* *Politische Vierteljahresschrift* 34 (3): 613–638.

441. Bartlett, D. December 1992. The Political Economy of Privatization: Property Reform and Democracy in Hungary. *East European Politics and Societies* 6 (1): 73–118.

442. Bartlett, W. 1985. Social Services and Local Democracy in Yugoslavia. *Community Development Journal* 20 (1): 18–23.

443. Barton, S. E. December 1983. Property Rights and Human Rights: Efficiency and Democracy as Criteria for Regulatory Reform. *Journal of Economic Issues* 17 (4): 915–930.

444. Barton, T., and H. Dorling. June 1986. The Social and Attitudinal Profile of Social Democratic Party Activists: Note on a Survey of the 1982 Council for Social Democracy. *Political Studies* 34: 296–305.

445. Bartra, R. 1977. From Un-Democratic Mediation to Unmediated Democracy.* *Estudios Sociales Centroamericanos* 6 (16): 45–70.

446. Baruah, S. December 9, 1989. Considerations on Democratic Resurgence. *Economic and Political Weekly* 24 (49): 2725–2727.

447. Barzel, Y. October 1991. *See* Kiser, E. (October 1991).

448. Barzilai, G. 1990. A Jewish Democracy at War: Attitudes of Secular Jewish Political Parties in Israel toward the Question of War (1949–1988). *Comparative Strategy* 9 (3): 179–194.

449. Barzilai, G., and Y. Shain. June 1991. Israeli Democracy at the Crossroads: A Crisis of Non-Governability. *Government and Opposition* 26 (3): 345–367.

450. Barzun, J. 1987. Is Democratic Theory for Export? *Ethics and International Affairs* 1: 53–71.

451. Barzun, J. March 1989. Is Democratic Theory for Export? *Society* 26 (3): 16–23.

452. Basavajah, M. C. October 1989. Towards Multi-Party Democracy in Algeria. *Strategic Analysis* 12 (7): 755–766.

453. Bashevkin, S. B. July 1983. Social Change and Political Partisanship: The Development of Women's Attitudes in Quebec, 1965–1979. *Comparative Political Studies* 16 (2): 147–172.

454. Bass, B. M., and V. J. Shackleton. 1979. Industrial Democracy and Participative Management: A Case for a Synthesis. *Academy of Management Review* 4 (3): 393–404.

455. Bass, B. M., V. J. Shackleton, and E. Rosenstein. 1979. Industrial Democracy and Participative Management: What's the Difference. *Revue Internationale de Psychologie Appliquee* 28 (2): 81–92.

456. Bassin, A. March 1990. *See* Beauregard, R. A. (March 1990).

457. Bata, J. March 27, 1992. Albania's Road to Democracy.* *Aus Politik und Zeitgeschichte* 14: 32–38.

458. Batallon, G. 1984. Military Dictatorship and Political Reversibility in Latin America.* *Passe Present* 4: 115–185.

459. Batbayar, T. January 1994. Mongolia in 1993: A Fragile Democracy. *Asian Survey* 34 (1): 41–45.

460. Bates, R. H. March 1991. The Economics of Transition to Democracy. *PS: Political Science & Politics* 24 (1): 24–27.

461. Bathory, P. D. February 1980. Tocqueville on Citizenship and Faith: A Response to Cushing Strout. *Political Theory* 8 (1): 27–38.

462. Battin, T. July 1993. A Break from the Past: The Labor Party and the Political Economy of Keynesian Social Democracy. *Australian Journal of Political Science* 28 (2): 221–241.

463. Battisti, G. S. 1977. Democracy in Spinoza's Unfinished Tractatus-Politicus. *Journal of the History of Ideas* 38 (4): 623–634.

464. Baubock, R. 1991. Nationalism Versus Democracy.* *Oesterreichische Zeitschrift für Politikwissenschaft* 20 (1): 73–90.

465. Baudson, A. 1980. Democracy, Information, and Telecommunication. *Socialisme* 27 (160): 403–413.

466. Bauer, G. September 1976. Coping with Terrorism: Democracies Must Act Jointly Outside the UN. *Atlas* 23: 11–14.

467. Baum, R. June 1989. Beyond Leninism? Economic Reform and Political Development in Post-Mao China. *Studies in Comparative Communism* 22 (2–3): 111.

468. Baum, R. December 1992. The China Syndrome: Prospects for Democracy in the Middle Kingdom. *Harvard International Review* 15 (2): 32–33, 66.

469. Baumann, H. 1987. The Social and Political Content of Democracy in the Liberated Countries of Asia and Africa.* *Staat und Recht* 36 (9): 740–749.

470. Baumgarten, N. June 1994. Education and Democracy in Frontier St. Louis: The Society of the Sacred Heart. *History of Education Quarterly* 34 (2): 171–192.

471. Bauzon, K. E. 1990. The Multilateral Assistance Initiative and Democratization in the Philippines. *Contemporary Southeast Asia* 12: 120–133.

472. Baxter, C. December 1985. Democracy and Authoritarianism in South Asia. *Journal of International Affairs* 38 (2): 307–319.

473. Baxter, C. December 1989. The Struggle for Development in Bangladesh. *Current History* 88 (542): 437–440, 442–444.

474. Baxter, C. March 1992. Bangladesh: A Parliamentary Democracy, If They Can Keep It. *Current History* 91 (563): 132–136.

475. Bayart, J. F. May 1983. The Democratic Question in Turkey.* *Etudes* 5: 597–605.

476. Bayart, J. F. September 1983. The Revenge of African Societies.* *Politique Africaine* 11: 95–127.

477. Bayat, A. February 1993. Populism, Liberalization and Popular Participation: Industrial Democracy in Egypt. *Economic and Industrial Democracy* 14 (1): 65–87.

478. Baylies, C., and M. Szeftel. July 1992. The Fall and Rise of Multi-Party Politics in Zambia. *Review of African Political Economy* 19: 75–91.

479. Baylis, T. A. September 1980. Collegial Leadership in Advanced Industrial Societies: The Relevance of the Swiss Experience. *Polity* 13 (1): 33–56.

480. Baysinger, B. D. May 1981. *See* Keim, G. D. (May 1981).

481. Beach, S. W. June 1977. Social-Movement Radicalization: The Case of People's Democracy in Northern Ireland. *Sociological Quarterly* 18 (3): 305–318.

482. Beal, F. M. 1994. South Africa's Long Road to Freedom. *Black Scholar* 24 (3): 7–10.

483. Bealy, F. 1987. Stability and Crisis: Fears about Threats to Democracy. *European Journal of Political Research* 15 (6): 687–715.

484. Bealy, F. February 1993. Capitalism and Democracy. *European Journal of Political Research* 23 (2): 203–223.

485. Beam, G. D. June 1980. The Parkinson-Peter Pasquinade. *Bureaucrat* 9 (2): 69–80.

486. Bean, C. July 1988. Class and Party in the Anglo-American Democracies: The Case of New Zealand in Perspective. *British Journal of Political Science* 18: 303–321.

487. Bean, W. 1989. Ruling Canada's North: Democracy in a Frozen State. *Community Development Journal* 24 (1): 19–28.

488. Beattie, K. J. March 1991. Prospects for Democratization in Egypt. *American-Arab Affairs* 36: 31–47.

489. Beatty, D. September 1993. Protecting Constitutional Rights in Japan and Canada. *American Journal of Comparative Law* 41 (4): 535–550.

490. Beauchamp, D. E. 1990. Alcohol and Tobacco as Public Health Challenges in a Democracy. *British Journal of Addiction* 85 (2): 251–254.

491. Beaud, O. 1993. The Sovereign.* *Pouvoirs* 67: 33–45.

492. Beauregard, R. A., R. E. Foglesong, A. Bassin, and M. P. Brooks. March 1990. Counterpoint and Commentary: Bringing the City Back In. *Journal of the American Planning Association* 56 (2): 210–220.

493. Beauvals, E. C. 1978. *See* Fesmire, J. M. (1978).

494. Beazley, K. E. April 1978. Democracy: A Structure of Ethics. *India International Centre Quarterly* 5 (2): 79–91.

495. Bebout, J. E. June 1979. Obligation to Help. *National Civic Review* 68 (6): 283–287, 298.

496. Becker, C. February 1993. Democracy in the Workplace: Union Representation, Elections and Federal Labor Law. *Minnesota Law Review* 77 (3): 495–603.

497. Becker, D. G. 1984. Development, Democracy and Dependency in Latin America: A Post-Imperialist View. *Third World Quarterly* 6 (2): 411–431.

498. Becker, D. G. September 1985. Peru after the "Revolution": Class, Power, and Ideology. *Studies in Comparative International Development* 20 (3): 3–30.

499. Becker, D. G. April 1990. Business Associations in Latin America: The Venezuelan Case. *Comparative Political Studies* 23 (1): 114–138.

500. Becker, D. G., E. Lira, M. I. Castillo, E. Gomez, and J. Kovalskys. September 1990. Therapy with Victims of Political Repression in Chile: The Challenge of Social Reparation. *Journal of Social Issues* 46 (3): 133–149.

501. Becker, T. March 1993. Teledemocracy: Gathering Momentum in State and Local Governance. *Spectrum* 66 (2): 14–19.

502. Becker, U. October 1988. *See* Kersberger, K. (October 1988).

503. Becker, W. 1979. Education and Democracy.* *Padagogische Rundschau* 33 (2): 89–99.

504. Bednar, M. 1993. The Renewal of Czechoslovak Democracy and Czechoslovak Traditions of Political Philosophy. *Filosoficky Casopis* 41 (2): 237–250.

505. Beenstock, M. October 1989. A Democratic Model of the "Rent Sought" Benefit Cycle. *Public Choice* 63 (1): 1–14.

506. Beer, L. W. April 1981. Group Rights and Individual Rights in Japan. *Asian Survey* 21 (4): 437–453.

507. Beer, S. H. March 1978. Federalism, Nationalism, and Democracy in America. *American Political Science Review* 72 (1): 9–21.

508. Beermann, J. M. 1990. Administrative Failure and Local Democracy: The Politics of Deshaney. *Duke Law Journal* (5): 1078–1112.

509. Beetham, D. 1981. Beyond Liberal Democracy. *Socialist Register:* 190-206.

510. Beetham, D. 1992. Liberal Democracy and the Limits of Democratization. *Political Studies* 40: 40–53. Special issue.

511. Beetham, D. February 1993. Four Theorems about the Market and Democracy. *European Journal of Political Research* 23 (2): 187–201.

512. Behm, A. J. October 1991. Terrorism, Violence against the Public, and the Media: The Australian Approach. *Political Communication and Persuasion* 8 (4): 233–246.

513. Behrens, M., and A. M. Rauch. 1991. South Africa on the Road to Democracy. *Aussenpolitik* 42 (4): 402–411.

514. Beilharz, P. September 1989. Australian Laborism, Social Democracy, and Social Justice. *Social Justice* 16 (3): 15–29.

515. Beinart, P. A. September 1989. The Real American Voting Problem. *Polity* 22 (1): 143–156.

516. Beinfield, R. H. 1985. The Hunter Doctrine: An Equal Protection Theory That Threatens Democracy. *Vanderbilt Law Review* 38 (2): 397–430.

517. Beitz, C. R. 1983. Procedural Equality in Democratic Theory: A Preliminary Examination. *Nomos* 25: 69–91.

518. Beitz, C. R. June 1990. The Ethics of Covert Operations. *Bureaucrat* 19 (2): 49–51.

519. Bejararo, A. M. May 1994. Recovering the State So Far as to Reinforce Democracy [in Colombia].* *Analisis Politico* 22: 47–79.

520. Beker, M., and P. Aarts. March 1993. Dilemmas of Development and Democratization in the Arab World. *International Journal of Political Economy* 23 (1): 87–107.

521. Belaunde, D. G. October 1991. Formo de Gobierno en la Constitucion Peruana. *Revista de Estudios Politicos* 74: 615–633.

522. Belcuore, A. F. December 1994. Meeting the Founders: Russians and Kazakhs Work for Democracy. *Law and Policy in International Business* 25: 461–467.

523. Belenkii, V. K., and A. R. Rakhimov. 1978. Current Problems in the Study of Socialist Democracy. *Soviet Sociology* 17 (1): 83–101.

524. Beljajewa, S. S., and M. I. Koser. 1974. New Aspects in the Development of Kolchos Democracy. *Sowjetwissenschaft: Gesellschaft Wissenschaftliche Beitrage* 27 (12): 1316–1325.

525. Bell, G. November 1979. The Concept of Limitation. *International Relations (London)* 6 (4): 694–797.

526. Bell, J. D. December 1990. "Post Communist" Bulgaria. *Current History* 89 (551): 417–420, 427–429.

527. Bell, P. D. September 1985. Democracy and Double Standards: The View from Chile. *World Policy Journal* 2 (4): 711–730.

528. Bell, W. December 1985. Remembrances of a Jamaican Past and Reflections on Its Future. *Caribbean Review* 14 (1): 4–7, 34–36.

529. Bellah, R. N. June 1988. Civil Religion in America. *Daedalus* 117 (3): 97–118.

530. Bellamy, R. 1991. Schumpeter and the Transformation of Capitalism, Liberalism and Democracy. *Government and Opposition* 26 (4): 500–519.

531. Bellamy, R. October 1994. Dethroning Politics: Liberalism, Constitutionalism, and Democracy in the Thought of F. A. Hayek. *British Journal of Political Science* 24 (4): 419–441.

532. Bellamy, R., and P. Baehr. February 1993. Carl Schmitt and the Contradictions of Liberal Democracy. *European Journal of Political Research* 23 (2): 163–185.

533. Bellatin, J. January 1993. *See* Harris, E. (January 1993).

534. Beller, G. E. December 1983. Benevolent Illusions in a Developing Society: The Assertion of Supreme Court Authority in Democratic India. *Western Political Quarterly* 36 (4): 513–532.

535. Belli, A. January 1993. *See* Harris, E. (January 1993).

536. Bello, W. September 1988. USA-Philippine Relations in the Aquino Era. *World Policy Journal* 5 (4): 677–702.

537. Bello, W., and S. Rosenfeld. June 1990. Dragons in Distress: The Crisis of the NICs. *World Policy Journal* 7 (3): 431–468.

538. Bellone C. J., and G. F. Goerl. March 1992. Reconciling Public Entrepreneurship and Democracy. *Public Administration Review* 52 (2): 130–134.

539. Bellows, T. J. February 1990. Singapore in 1989: Progress in a Search for Roots. *Asian Survey* 30 (2): 201–209.

540. Bellue, F. 1986. Sittlichkeit and Democracy in the Young Marx's Articles (February 1842–1843). *Proces* 45–67.

541. Bellush, B., and J. Bellush. May 1985. Participation in Local Politics: District Council 37 in New York. *National Civic Review* 74 (5): 213–230.

542. Bellush, J. May 1985. *See* Bellush, B. (May 1985).

543. Belman, L. S. December 1977. John Dewey's Concept of Communication. *Journal of Communication* 27 (1): 29–37.

544. Beloussow, R. 1976. Socialistic Democracy and Production.* *Sowjetwissenschaft: Gesellschaft Wissenschaftliche Beitrage* 29 (4): 337–347.

545. Beltran, V. R. December 1987. Political Transition in Argentina: 1982 to 1985. *Armed Forces and Society* 13 (2): 215–233.

546. Belyaeva, N. March 1993. Russian Democracy: Crisis as Progress. *Washington Quarterly* 16 (2): 5–17.

547. Ben Yehuda, N. September 1987. *See* Cohen, E. (September 1987).

548. Benard, C. June 1977. Migrant Workers and European Democracy. *Political Science Quarterly* 93 (2): 277–299.

549. Benavente Urbina, A. 1985. La Transicion Politica: Aproximaciones a Una Clasificacion Teorica a Partir del Estudio de Casos. *Politica* 14: 43–79.

550. Benavente Urbina, A. October 1988. Partidos Politicos y Procesos de Transicion en America Latina: La Fase de Crisis Democratica y la Fase Autoritaria. *Politica* 17: 83–106.

551. Benavente Urbina, A., and J. Jaraquemada Roblero. December 1989. Concertacion Social y Consolidacion Democratica: Un Replanteamiento del Corporativismo Socialista. *Politica* 19: 63–93.

552. Bence, G. June 1990. Social Theory in Transition. *Social Research* 57 (2): 245–255.

553. Benedict, M. L. 1981. To Secure These Rights: Rights, Democracy, and Judicial Review in the Anglo-American Constitutional Heritage. *Ohio State Law Journal* 42 (1): 69–86.

554. Benedict, R. C. June 1975. *See* Bone, H. A. (June 1975).

555. Benes, E. 1993. A Revival and Future of the Postwar Democracy.* *Voprosy Istorii* (1): 92–108.

556. Benhabib, S. March 1994. Democracy and Difference: Reflections on the Metapolitics of Lyotard and Derrida. *Journal of Political Philosophy* 2 (1): 1–23.

557. Benhabib, S. April 1994. Deliberate Rationality and Models of Democratic Legitimacy. *Constellations* 1 (1): 26–52.

558. Benitez Manaut, R. July 1987. Democracia y Fuerzas Armadas en Cuba y Nicaragua: Reflexiones en Relacion al Debate Latinoamericano. *Estudios Latinoamericanos* 2: 99–108.

559. Benjamin, G. May 1977. Israel: Too Much Democracy? *Midstream* 28: 3–13.

560. Benn, A. W. 1979. Democracy in the Age of Science. *Political Quarterly* 50 (1): 7–23.

561. Bennett, C. L. June 22, 1994. *See* Hermanson, T. (June 22, 1994).

562. Bennett, D. C., and K. E. Sharpe. June 1982. Capitalism, Bureaucratic Authoritarianism, and Prospects for Democracy in the United States. *International Organization* 36 (3): 633–663.

563. Bennett, D. C., and K. E. Sharpe. June 1984. Is There a Democracy "Overload"? *Dissent* 31 (3): 319–326.

564. Bennett, J. T., and T. J. DiLorenzo. September 1986. Tax-Funded Unionism I: The Unemployment Connection. *Journal of Labor Research* 7 (4): 363–385. Article 1 of 3.

565. Bennett, J. T., and T. J. DiLorenzo. 1987. Tax-Funded Unionism II: The Facade of Culture and Democracy. *Journal of Labor Research* 8 (1): 31–46. Article 2 of 3.

566. Bennett, J. T., and T. J. DiLorenzo. 1987. Tax-Funded Unionism III: Front Organizations. *Journal of Labor Research* 8 (2): 179–189. Article 3 of 3.

567. Bennett, S. E. June 1988. "Know-Nothing" Revisited: The Meaning of Political Ignorance Today. *Social Science Quarterly* 69 (2): 476–490.

568. Bennett, S. E., F. F. Piven, R. A. Cloward, and C. B. Gans. June 1990. The Uses and Abuses of Registration and Turnout Data: An Analysis of Piven and Cloward's Studies of Nonvoting in America. *PS: Political Science & Politics* 23 (2): 166–178.

569. Bennett, S. E., and D. Resnick. August 1990. The Implications of Nonvoting for Democracy in the United States. *American Journal of Political Science* 34 (3): 771–802.

570. Bennett, W. June 1985. Lost Generation: Why America's Children Are Strangers in Their Own Land. *Policy Review* 33: 43–45.

571. Bennett, W. L. December 1992. White Noise: The Perils of Mass Mediated Democracy. *Communication Monographs* 59 (4): 401–406.

572. Bennett, W. L. June 1993. A Policy Research Paradigm for the News Media and Democracy. *Journal of Communication* 43 (3): 180–189.

573. Bennis, W. G. 1990. *See* Slater, P. (1990).

574. Benoit, J. P., and L. A. Kornhauser. March 1994. Social Choice in a Representative Democracy. *American Political Science Review* 88 (1): 185–192.

575. Benomar, J. January 1993. Justice after Transitions. *Journal of Democracy* 4 (1): 3–14.

576. Ben-Porat, A. March 1979. Political Parties and Democracy in the Histadrut. *Industrial Relations* 18 (2): 237–243.

577. Benson, H. W. 1977. Union Democracy, Department of Labor, and the Sadlowski Campaign. *Dissent* 24 (4): 455–464.

578. Benton, G. November 1984. Chinese Communism and Democracy. *New Left Review* 148: 57–73.

579. Benyekhlef, K. April 1993. Democratie et Libertes: Quelques Propos sur le Controle de Constitutionnalite et l'Heteronomie du Droit. *McGill Law Journal* 38: 91–129.

580. Benzler, S. October 1992. Back to Europe? The Transformation Process in East-Central Europe with Special Reference to the Polish Example.* *Blaetter für Deutsche und Internationale Politik* 37 (10): 1222–1232.

581. Berat, L. June 1993. Prosecuting Human Rights Violators from a Predecessor Regime: Guidelines for a Transformed South Africa. *Boston College Third World Law Journal* 13: 199–231.

582. Berat, L., and Y. Shain. January 1991. Interim Governments in Democratic Transition: Lessons from Namibia, Hope for South Africa. *Conflict* 11 (1): 17–39.

583. Berejikian, J. March 1993. *See* Dryzek, J. S. (March 1993).

584. Berg, B. May 1984. Public Choice, Pluralism, and Scarcity: Implications for Bureaucratic Behavior. *Administration and Society* 16 (1): 71–82.

585. Berg, E. March 1986. The Proof of Capitalism: Usher's Celebration of the Status Quo. *Political Studies* 34 (1): 99–119.

586. Bergalli, R. 1989. Poder Politico y Derechos Humanos en America Latina.* *Annales Internationales de Criminologie* 27 (1–2): 153–179.

587. Berger, P. L. 1978. Capitalism, Socialism, and Democracy. *Commentary* 65 (4): 33–34.

588. Berger, P. L. September 1983. Democracy for Everyone? *Commentary* 76 (3): 31–36.

589. Berger, R. 1981. Ely's "Theory of Judicial Review." *Ohio State Law Journal* 42 (1): 87–130.

590. Berger, W. 1978. The Problem in Democratization of Educational Systems.* *Oesterreichische Zeitschrift für Politikwissenschaft* 7 (2): 225–231.

591. Bergesen, A. June 1992. Regime Change in the Semiperiphery: Democratization in Latin America and the Socialist Bloc. *Sociological Perspectives* 35 (2): 405–413.

592. Bergman, T. January 1993. Formation Rules and Minority Governments. *European Journal of Political Research* 23 (1): 55–66.

593. Bergmann, A. E. 1975. Industrial Democracy in Germany: Battle for Power. *Journal of General Management* 2 (4): 20–29.

594. Berg-Schlosser, D. July 1982. Modes and Meaning of Political Participation in Kenya. *Comparative Politics* 14 (4): 397–415.

595. Berg-Schlosser, D. 1985. The Precondition for Democracy in the Third World.* *Politische Vierteljahresschrift* 16: 233–266. Special issue.

596. Berg-Schlosser, D. March 1985. Element of Consociational Democracy in Kenya. *European Journal of Political Research* 13 (1): 95–109.

597. Berg-Schlosser, D., and G. De Meur. April 1994. Conditions of Democracy in Interwar Europe: A Boolean Test of Major Hypothesis. *Comparative Politics* 26 (3): 253–280.

598. Bergstrom, H. July 1991. Sweden's Politics and Party System at the Crossroads. *West European Politics* 14 (3): 8–30.

599. Berhoin, G. March 1989. Democratic Growth or Gridlock? *Washington Quarterly* 12 (2): 183–188.

600. Berkman, M. June 1994. *See* Carmine, E. G. (June 1994).

601. Berlak, H. 1985. Testing in a Democracy. *Educational Leadership* 43 (2): 16–17.

602. Berman, D. February 1984. The $100 Billion Question: Can Brazil's New Democratization Survive the IMF? *Multinational Monitor* 5: 10–15.

603. Bermbach, U. 1974. Citizens Initiatives: Instruments of Direct Democracy.* *Oesterreichische Zeitschrift für Politikwissenschaft* 3 (4): 547–563.

604. Bermbach, U. 1990. Theses on a Theory of Communication-Based Democracy.* *Politicka Misao* 27 (2): 84–91.

605. Bermeo, N. January 1987. Redemocratization and Transition Elections: A Comparison of Spain and Portugal. *Comparative Politics* 19 (2): 213–231.

606. Bermeo, N. April 1992. Democracy and the Lessons of Dictatorship. *Comparative Politics* 24 (3): 273–291.

607. Bermeo, N. March 1994. Democracy in Europe. *Daedalus* 123 (2): 159–178.

608. Bermeo, N. August 1994. Sacrifice, Sequence, and Strength in Successful Dual Transitions: Lessons from Spain. *Journal of Politics* 56 (3): 601–627.

609. Bernas, J. March 1985. *See* Neuhaus, R. J. (March 1985).

610. Bernasconi, R. July 1990. Rousseau and the Supplement to the Social Contract: Deconstruction and the Possibility of Democracy. *Cardozo Law Review* 11: 1539–1564.

611. Bernecker, W. L. December 1990. Spain and Portugal between Regime Transition and Stabilized Democracy.* *Aus Politik und Zeitgeschichte* 51: 15–28.

612. Bernhard, M. H. December 1990. Barriers to Further Political and Economic Change in Poland. *Studies in Comparative Communism* 23 (3–4): 319–339.

613. Bernier, B. L. September 1992. Economic Development in Ravaged Haiti: Is Democracy Really the Answer? *Dickinson Journal of International Law* 11: 49–75.

614. Bernier, B. L. June 1993. Democratization and Economic Development in Haiti: A Review of the Caribbean Basin Initiative. *International Lawyer* 27: 455–470.

615. Bernstein, J., and L. E. Gold. 1982. Union Democracy at Stake: Should the Courts Determine Policy. *Nation* 234 (21): 654–655.

616. Bernstein, M. H. March 1988. Israel: Turbulent Democracy at Forty. *Middle East Journal* 42 (2): 193–201.

617. Bernstein, R. J. March 1990. Rorty's Liberal Utopia. *Social Research* 57 (1): 31–72.

618. Bernstein, R. J., and R. Rorty. November 1987. One Step Forward, Two Steps Backward: Richard Rorty on Liberal Democracy and Philosophy. *Political Theory* 15 (4): 538–580.

619. Bernstorff, D. 1975. Suppression of Indian Democracy. *Politische Studien* 26 (223): 513–516.

620. Berntzen, E. 1993. Democratic Consolidation in Central America: A Qualitative Comparative Approach. *Third World Quarterly* 14 (3): 589–604.

621. Berreau, C. et al. December 1994. Modern Congressional Election Theory Meets the 1992 House Elections. *Political Research Quarterly* 47 (4): 909–922.

622. Berry, C. J. January 1981. Nations and Norms. *Review of Politics* 43 (1): 75–87.

623. Berry, N. O. 1987. The Conflict between United States Intervention and Promoting Democracy in the Third World. *Temple Law Quarterly* 60 (4): 1015–1021.

624. Berry, S., and R. Kiely. October 1993. Is There a Future for Korean Democracy? *Parliamentary Affairs* 46 (4): 594–604.

625. Berselli, E. March 1994. The Bipolar Machine [in Italy].* *Il Mulino* 352: 249–264.

626. Bert, W. November 1990. Chinese Policy toward Democratization Movements: Burma and the Philippines. *Asian Survey* 30 (11): 1066–1083.

627. Bertholome, M. 1981. Party Rule and Social Democracy: An Unavoidable Encounter.* *Socialisme* 28 (167): 437–442.

628. Bertocci, P. J. October 1982. Bangladesh in the Early 1980s: Praetorian Politics in an Intermediate Regime. *Asian Survey* 22 (10): 988–1008.

629. Bertocci, P. J. February 1986. Bangladesh in 1985: Resolute against the Storm. *Asian Survey* 26 (2): 224–234.

630. Bertola, G. February 1981. The Incomplete Democracy in Venezuela.* *Politica Internazionale* 2: 57–66.

631. Berton, G. October 1992. Afrique: L'Etat de la Democratisation. *Croissance* 25–28.

632. Bertram, C. March 1990. The German Question. *Foreign Affairs* 69 (2): 45–62.

633. Bertrand, J., and J. Kauzyo. July 1994. Towards a New Ugandan Constitution.* *Afrique Contemporaine* 171: 17–33.

634. Bertsch, G. K. December 1976. Monitoring the Effects of Governments on Human Dignity: Policy Evaluation in Communist Party States. *International Studies Quarterly* 20 (4): 641–646.

635. Bertschi, C. C. December 1994. Lustration and the Transition to Democracy: The Cases of Poland and Bulgaria. *East European Quarterly* 28 (4): 435–452.

636. Beschel, R. P. , Jr. March 1992. *See* Allison, G. T. (March 1992).

637. Bessis, S. et al. April 7, 1994. Mali Democratie: La Porte Etroite. *Jeune Afrique* 34: 35–49.

638. Beth, L. P. November 1979. Mr. Justice Black and the First Amendment: Comments on the Dilemma of Constitutional Interpretation. *Journal of Politics* 41 (4): 1105–1124.

639. Bethehl, T. March 1983. The Last Civilization of UNESCO. *Policy Review* (24): 19–47.

640. Betten, N. 1976. Polish American Steelworkers: Americanization through Industry and Labor. *Polish American Studies* 32 (2): 31–42.

641. Betz, H. March 1993. Crisis or Change? The Future of Politics in the Post-Industrial Era.* *Politik und Zeitgeschichte* 12: 3–13.

642. Bhalla, K. S. 1983. Nauru: A Central Pacific Parliamentary Democracy. *Parliamentarian* 64 (3): 127–133.

643. Bhatnagar, S. May 1975. Grass Roots Politics in India: A Case Study of the Kanga Valley. *Asian Survey* 15 (5): 440–452.

644. Biagi, M. March 1989. Democracy and Trade Union Action: A Comparative Overview. *Labour (Rome)* 3: 175–185.

645. Bianchi, R. February 1989. Islam and Democracy in Egypt. *Current History* 88 (535): 93–95, 104.

646. Bianchi, R. March 1991. Four Reasons for Optimism. *American-Arab Affairs* 36: 5–6.

647. Biasi, M. (ed.). 1988. Trade Union Democracy and Industrial Relations. *Bulletin of Comparative Labour Relations* (17): 7–206. Conference proceedings.

648. Biberaj, E. September 1991. Albania at the Crossroads. *Problems of Communism* 40 (5): 1–16.

649. Biberaj, E. November 1993. Albania: Road to Democracy. *Current History* 92 (577): 381–385.

650. Bibic, A. July 1992. Some Aspects of the Pluralization of State and Society in Slovenia.* *Teorija in Praksa* 29 (7–9): 703–713.

651. Bidegain, G. 1987. Democracy, Migration and Return: Argentineans, Chileans and Uruguayans in Venezuela. *International Migration* 25 (3): 299–323.

652. Bidegaray, C. 1993. Reflections on the Notion of Democratic Transition in Central and Eastern Europe.* *Pouvoirs* 65: 129–144.

653. Bidwai, P. January 25, 1993. Bringing Down the Temple: Democracy at Risk in India. *Nation* 256 (3): 84–88.

654. Bieber, R., and E. Kopp. December 1992. The EC's Democratic Deficit: Maastricht Is Only a Step in the Right Direction. *Harvard International Review* 15 (2): 18–20, 64–65.

655. Biersteker, T. J. October 1994. *See* Armijo, L. E. (October 1994).

656. Biggart, N. W. December 1984. A Sociological Analysis of the Presidential Staff. *Sociological Quarterly* 25 (1): 27–44.

657. Bigler, R. M. December 1991. From Communism to Democracy: Hungary's Transition Thirty-Five Years after the Revolution. *East European Quarterly* 25 (4): 437–461.

658. Billet, B. L. March 1990. South Korea at the Crossroads: An Evolving Democracy or Authoritarianism Revisited? *Asian Survey* 30 (3): 300–311.

659. Billet, B. L. February 1992. The History and Role of Student Activism in the Republic of Korea: The Politics of Contestation and Conflict Resolution in Fledg-ling Democracy. *Asian Profile* 20 (1): 23–34.

660. Billington, J. H. 1991. The Crisis of Communism and the Future of Freedom. *International Affairs* 5: 87–97.

661. Billington, J. H. 1991. Russia's Fever Break. *Wilson Quarterly* 15 (4): 58–65.

662. Binder, J. March 1974. Vom Wesen und der Wandlungsfaehigkeit der Schweizerischen Demokratie. *Civitas* 29: 385–396.

663. Binford, M. B. December 1983. The Democratic Political Personality: Functions of Attitudes and Styles of Reasoning. *Political Psychology* 4 (4): 663–684.

664. Bingham, J. July 1986. Democracy or Plutocracy: The Case for a Constitutional Amendment to Overturn *Buckley vs. Valeo. Annals of the American Academy of Political and Social Science* 486: 103–114.

665. Bingham, R. D. March 1984. *See* Gibson, J. L. (March 1984).

666. Bingman, C. F. September 1992. Reinventing Government: The Case of Kazakhstan. *Public Manager* 21 (3): 35–38.

667. Binnendijk, H. March 1987. Authoritarian Regimes in Transition. *Washington Quarterly* 10 (2): 153–164.

668. Birle, P. 1991. Democracy and Politics in Argentina: An Assessment of the Years 1983–1990.* *Jahrbuch für Politik* 1 (1): 41–75.

669. Birnbaum, P. August 1991. Catholic Identity and Universal Suffrage: The French Experience. *International Social Science Journal* 43 (3): 571–597.

670. Bischoping, K., and H. Schuman. May 1994. Pens, Polls, and Theories: The 1990 Nicaraguan Election Revisited: A Reply to Anderson. *American Journal of Political Science* 38 (2): 495–499.

671. Bishin, W. R. March 1977. Judicial Review in Democratic Theory. *Southern California Law Review* 50: 1099–1137.

672. Bishirjian, R. J. 1978. Public Philosophy in American Democracy. *Intercollegiate Review* 13 (2): 85–100.

673. Bishop, J. W. 1978. Can Democracy Defend Itself against Terrorism. *Commentary* 65 (5): 55–62.

674. Bissell, R. E. 1990. Who Killed the Third World? *Washington Quarterly* 13 (4): 23–32.

675. Bite, V. April 1992. Parliamentary Developments in the Three Baltic States. *Congressional Research Service Review* 13: 29–30.

676. Bittman, L. June 1990. The Use of Disinformation by Democracies. *International Journal of Intelligence and Counterintelligence* 4: 243–261.

677. Bixby, D. M. March 1981. Roosevelt Court, Democratic Ideology, and Minority Rights: Another Look At *United States vs. Classic. Yale Law Journal* 90: 741–815.

678. Bixler, A. G. 1985. Industrial Democracy and the Managerial Employee Exception to the National Labor Relations Act. *University of Pennsylvania Law Review* 133 (2): 441–468.

679. Bizeau, J. March 1993. Pluralism and Democracy.* *Revue du Droit Public et de la Science Politique* 2: 513–542.

680. Bizzarro, S. February 1978. Rigidity and Restraint in Chile. *Current History* 74 (434): 66–69,83.

681. Bjur, W. E., and G. B. Siegle. June 1977. Voluntary Citizen Participation in Local Government: Cost and Commitment. *Midwest Review of Public Administration* 11 (2): 135–149.

682. Blachman, M. J., and K. E. Sharpe. December 1989. The War on Drugs: American Democracy under Assault. *World Policy Journal* 7: 135–163.

683. Black, C. E., and J. P. Burke. April 1983. Organizational Participation and Public Policy. *World Politics* 35 (3): 393–425.

684. Black, J. K. 1993. Elections and Other Trivial Pursuits: Latin America and the New World Order. *Third World Quarterly* 14 (3): 545–554.

685. Black, L. S. 1978. Shareholder Democracy and Corporate Governance. *Securities Regulation Law Journal* 5 (4): 291–317.

686. Blackburn, J. D. 1981. Worker Participation on Corporate Directories: Is America Ready for Industrial Democracy? *Houston Law Review* 18 (2): 349–370.

687. Blackman, C. N. July 1989. Sir Anthony Lewis and the Agony of the Little Eight Revisited. *Caribbean Affairs* 2 (3): 62–72.

688. Blackwill, R. June 1991. *See* Allison, G. T. (June 1991).

689. Blackwood, L. 1990. Czech and Polish National Democracy at the Dawn of Independent Statehood, 1918–1919. *East European Politics and Societies* 4 (3): 469–488.

690. Blais, A., D. Blake, and S. Dion. February 1993. Do Parties Make a Difference? Parties and the Size of Government in Liberal Democracies. *American Journal of Political Science* 37 (1): 40–62.

691. Blais, A., and E. Gidengil. September 1993. Things Are Not Always What They Seem: French-English Differences and the Problem of Measurement Aquivalence. *Canadian Journal of Political Science* 26: 541–555.

692. Blake, C. H. October 1994. Social Pacts and Inflation Control in New Democracies: The Impact of Wildcat Cooperation in Argentina and Uruguay. *Comparative Political Studies* 27 (3): 381–401.

693. Blake, D. February 1993. *See* Blais, A. (February 1993).

694. Blakeney, A. September 1994. Federalism and Democracy. *Constitutional Forum* 5: 1–9.

695. Blanco, B. 1994. Congo: Corruption and Resistance to Change.* *L'Afrique Politique* 191–198.

696. Blaney, D. L., and M. K. Pasha. March 1993. Civil Society and Democracy in the Third World: Ambiguities and Historical Possibilities. *Studies in Comparative International Development* 28 (1): 3–24.

697. Blank, D. E. February 1980. Oil and Democracy in Venezuela. *Current History* 79 (454): 71–75, 84.

698. Blank, R. H. 1985. Biocracy and Democracy: Comments. *Politics and the Life Sciences* 3 (2): 150–153.

699. Blankart, C. B. March 1993. A Public-Choice View of Swiss Liberty. *Publius* 23 (2): 83–96.

700. Blanke, T. 1986. Autonomy and Democracy.* *Kritische Justiz* 19 (4): 406–422.

701. Blcifuss, J. 1987. Spain: Democracy with Difficulties. *Dissent* 34 (2): 162–167.

702. Blessey, A. July 1978. *See* Blessey, G. (July 1978).

703. Blessey, G., and A. Blessey. July 1978. Teaching and Learning Democratic Government. *Public Administration Survey* 25: 1–4.

704. Blinken, A. J. 1985. Democracy Gets Pushed Around in Seoul: Our Chun, Chum. *New Republic* 192 (10): 13–14.

705. Bloch, J. C. April 1992. Fostering Democracy in Nepal: Helping a Fragile New Order Take Root. *Foreign Service Journal* 69: 31–33.

706. Blomkvist, H., and S. Widmalm. 1992. India's Democratic Paradox.* *Internasjonal Politikk* 50 (4): 421–430.

707. Blommaert, J. M. E. 1991. Nation-building, Democracy, and Pragmatic Leadership in Kenya. *Communication and Cognition* 24 (2): 181–194.

708. Bloomfield, I. June 1984. Managing Technology in the United States and Switzerland: Some Insights from Agriculture. *Policy Studies Journal* 12 (4): 613–626.

709. Bloomfield, L. P. , Jr. 1980. Anarchy in Turkey: The Growing Pains of a Young Democracy. *Conflict* 2 (1): 31–56.

710. Bloomfield, R. J. March 1994. Making the Western Hemisphere Safe for Democracy? The OAS Defense of Democracy Regime. *Washington Quarterly* 17 (2): 157–169.

711. Blum, L. December 1981. The Literacy Campaign. *Caribbean Review* 10 (1): 18–21.

712. Blum, W. 1974. Attack on Our Democracy. *Politische Studien* 25 (216): 427–430.

713. Blumenauer, E. March 1977. The Citizen as Candidate: Challenge of Democracy. *National Civic Review* 66: 122–127.

714. Blumler, J. G. 1983. Communication and Democracy: The Crisis Beyond and the Ferment Within. *Journal of Communication* 33 (3): 166–173.

715. Blumler, J. G., and H. A. Semetko. August 1987. Mass Media and Legislative Campaigns in a Unitary Parliamentary Democracy: The Case of Britain. *Legislative Studies Quarterly* 12 (3): 415–443.

716. Blythe, J. M. October 1986. The Mixed Constitution and the Distinction between Regal and Political Power in the Work of Thomas Aquinas. *Journal of the History of Ideas* 47 (4): 547–565.

717. Blyton, P. 1985. Workplace Democracy, Unemployment and the Reduction of Working Time. *Economic and Industrial Democracy* 6 (1): 113–120.

718. Boaden, N., M. Goldsmith, W. Hampton, and P. Stringer. 1979. Public

Participation in Planning within a Representative Local Democracy. *Policy and Politics* 7 (1): 55–67.

719. Boasberg, T. April 1994. *See* Lee, M. C. M. (April 1994).

720. Bobbio, N. August 1980. Democracy and Invisible Power. *Rivista Italiana di Scienza Politica* 10 (2): 181–203.

721. Bobbio, N. November 1980. Democrazia e Governabilita. *Quaderni di Azione Sociale* 29: 3–19.

722. Bobbio, N. 1981. Democracy and Majority. *Cahiers Vilfredo Pareto* 19 (54–55): 377–388.

723. Bobbio, N. June 1982. Democracy and Invisible Government. *Telos* 52: 41–55.

724. Bobbio, N. September 1984. The Future of Democracy. *Telos* 61: 3–16.

725. Bobbio, N. April 1986. The Future of Democracy.* *Estudios Politicos* 5 (2): 46–58.

726. Boccara, P. November 1981. Basic Forms of the Capitalist State and Development of Their Contradictions.* *La Pensee* 224: 31–41.

727. Bodah, M. M. 1992. Internal Jurisprudence and Trade Union Democracy: The Case of the Auto Workers. *Economic and Industrial Democracy* 13 (1): 45–67.

728. Boehling, R. October 1993. Mothers in Politics: Efforts at American Democratization after 1945: Reply to Rupieper, Hermann, Josef.* *Geschichte und Gesellschaft* 19 (4): 522–529.

729. Boehm, U. March 1980. Social Alternatives: Decentralization and Basic Democracy. *Argument* 22: 208–210.

730. Boehmer, E. June 1994. Election in South Africa. *Journal of Southern African Studies* 20 (2): 163.

731. Boeninger, E. March 1986. The Chilean Road to Democracy. *Foreign Affairs* 64 (4): 812–832.

732. Boesche, R. December 1980. The Prison: Tocqueville's Model for Despotism. *Western Political Quarterly* 33 (4): 550–563.

733. Bognador, V. 1986. The Future of the European Community: Two Models of Democracy. *Government and Opposition* 21 (2): 161–176.

734. Bognador, V. 1989. Direct Elections, Representative Democracy and European Integration. *Electoral Studies* 8 (3): 205–216.

735. Bognador, V. December 1990. Founding Elections and Regime Change. *Electoral Studies* 9 (4): 288–294.

736. Bogner, H. 1991. Jurgen Habermas' Option for Progress, Rationality and Democracy.* *Deutsche Zeitschrift für Philosophie* 39 (3): 245–254.

737. Bogue, A. G., J. M. Clubb, C. R. McKibbin, and S. A. Traugott. September 1976. Members of the House of Representatives and the Processes of Modernization, 1789–1960. *Journal of American History* 63 (2): 275–302.

738. Bogus, C. T. December 1993. Excessive Executive Compensation and the Failure of Corporate Democracy. *Buffalo Law Review* 41 (1): 1–83.

739. Bohlander, G. W. December 1990. *See* Scheck, C. L. (December 1990).

740. Bohman, G. 1981. Democracy and Capitalism in the 1980s.* *Ekonomiska Samfundets Tidskrift* 34 (1): 44–68.

741. Bohman, J. F. March 1990. Communication, Ideology, and Democratic Theory. *American Political Science Review* 84 (1): 93–109.

742. Bohn, D. E. February 1980. Consociational Democracy and the Case of

Switzerland. *Journal of Politics* 42 (1): 165–179.

743. Bohn, D. E. April 1986. The Failure of the Radical Left in Switzerland: A Preliminary Study. *Comparative Political Studies* 19: 71–103.

744. Bohnet, I. March 1993. *See* Frey, B. S. (March 1993).

745. Bohning, D., J. O. Tamayo, and B. Diederich. June 1982. The Springtime of Elections: The Status of Democracy in the Caribbean. *Caribbean Review* 11 (3): 5–7, 40.

746. Bohr, C., and E. Busch. 1983. Protests in Democracy: A Challenge to the Political System of the Federal Republic of Germany. *Beitraege zur Konfliktforschung* 13 (4): 71–96.

747. Boillot, F. 1992. The Catholic Church and the Political Change Process at the Beginning of the 1990s [in Africa].* *Année Africaine* 115–144.

748. Boito, A. , Jr. December 1994. The State and Trade Unionism in Brazil. *Latin American Perspectives* 21 (1): 7–23.

749. Bolanta, K. S. December 1988. Workers' Participation in Industrial Management: Lessons for Nigeria. *Nigerian Journal of Policy and Strategy* 3: 15–53.

750. Bolce, L., G. DeMaio, and D. Muzzio. June 1987. The Equal Rights Amendment, Public Opinion, and American Constitutionalism. *Polity* 19 (4): 551–569.

751. Bolduc, R. 1980. Effects of the Increased Role of the State on Local Democracy.* *Canadian Public Administration* 23 (1): 60–75.

752. Boling, P. November 1991. The Democratic Potential of Mothering. *Political Theory* 19 (4): 606–625.

753. Bollen, K. A. June 1979. Political Democracy and the Timing of Develop-ment. *American Sociological Review* 44 (4): 572–587.

754. Bollen, K. A. June 1980. Issues in the Comparative Measurement of Political Democracy. *American Sociological Review* 45 (3): 370–390.

755. Bollen, K. A. August 1983. World System Position, Dependency, and Democracy. *American Sociological Review* 48 (4): 468–479.

756. Bollen, K. A. March 1990. Political Democracy: Conceptual and Measurement Traps. *Studies in Comparative International Development* 25 (1): 7–24.

757. Bollen, K. A. November 1993. Liberal Democracy: Validity and Method Factors in Cross-National Measures. *American Journal of Political Science* 37 (4): 1207–1230.

758. Bollen, K. A., and B. D. Grandjean. October 1981. The Dimension(s) of Democracy: Further Issues in the Measurement and Effects of Political Democracy. *American Sociological Review* 46 (5): 651–659.

759. Bollen, K. A., and R. W. Jackman. August 1985. Political Democracy and the Size Distribution of Income. *American Sociological Review* 50 (4): 438–457.

760. Bollen, K. A., and R. W. Jackman. August 1989. Democracy, Stability, and Dichotomies. *American Sociological Review* 54 (4): 612–621.

761. Boller, P. F. 1979. William James as an Educator: Individualism and Democracy. *Teachers College Record* 80 (3): 587–601.

762. Bonafede, D. June 29, 1985. Reform of U.S. System of Government Is on the Minds and Agendas of Many. *National Journal* 17: 1521–1524.

763. Bonate, L. 1986. International Democracy: Utopia, Myth or Tragedy.* *Teoria Politica* 2 (2): 33–62.

764. Bonate, L. 1987. Peace or Democracy?* *Teoria Politica* 3 (3): 43–61.

765. Bond, R. D. 1984. Where Democracy Lives. *Wilson Quarterly* 8 (4): 48–62.

766. Bonduki, N. 1987. *See* Kowarich, L. (1987).

767. Bone, H. A., and R. C. Benedict. June 1975. Perspectives on Direct Legislation: Washington State's Experience 1914–1973. *Western Political Quarterly* 28 (2): 330–351.

768. Bonnell, A. G. 1989. The Lassalle Cult in German Social Democracy. *Australian Journal of Politics and History* 35 (1): 50–60.

769. Bonner, Y. March 1992. The New Europe: From Totalitarianism to Democracy. *Queen's Quarterly* 99 (1): 84–90.

770. Bonnio, N. September 1980. Politics between Subjects and Institutions: The Teachings of the Classical Authors. *Democrazia e Diritto* 20 (5): 641–654.

771. Bookman, J. T. March 1992. The Wisdom of the Many: An Analysis of the Arguments of Books III and IV of Aristotle's *Politics*. *History of Political Thought* 13 (1): 1–12.

772. Boorstin, D. J. 1978. Technology and Democracy. *Dialogue* 11 (2): 66–73.

773. Booth, J. A. June 1987. Costa Rican Democracy. *World Affairs* 150 (1): 43–53.

774. Booth, J. A. May 1994. Assessing Candidate Preference Polling and Other Survey Research in Nicaragua, 1989–1990: Comments on Anderson and Bischoping and Schuman. *American Journal of Political Science* 38 (2): 500–513.

775. Booth, R. A. 1985. Self-Regulation in a Democratic Society. *Journal of Air Law and Commerce* 50: 491–512.

776. Boquerat, G. 1992. The Difficult Democratic Itinerary of Southern Asia.* *Le Trimestre du Monde* 17: 145–156.

777. Borde, H. 1989. Khakistocracy: Democratization the Haitian Way.* *Internasjonal Politikk* (4–6): 269–281.

778. Bordo, M., and D. Landau. 1980. The Supply and Demand for Protection: A Positive Theory of Democratic Government. *Statsvetenskaplig Tidskrift* 5: 335–347.

779. Boris, E. 1991. Tenement Homework on Army Uniforms: The Gendering of Industrial Democracy during World War I. *Labor History* 32 (2): 231–252.

780. Bork, R. H. 1986. Judicial Review and Democracy. *Society* 24 (1): 5–8.

781. Boroda, H. November 1993. Ethiopie: Les difficultes de L'Apres-Mengistu. *Nouvel Afrique Asie* 19–20.

782. Boron, A. May 1987. The Dilemmas of Modernization and the Subjects of Democracy.* *Sintesis* 2: 379–392.

783. Borovik, A. September 1991. Waiting for Democracy [in the USSR]. *Foreign Policy* 84: 51–60.

784. Bos, E. May 1993. Can Information Technology Improve the Quality of Democracy. *Behavior & Information Technology* 12 (3): 194–195.

785. Bosch, M. 1978. Notwendigkeit und Chance der Demokratiserung. *Frankfurter Hefte* 33 (4): 89–95.

786. Bose, A. 1984. Democracia y Desarrollo en Asia: La Restriccion Demografica. *Comer Exterior* (*Mexico*) 34 (8): 785–789.

787. Bossanyi, K. 1986. Economy on the Way to Democratization: The Switch Over to Collective Management in Hungarian Industry. *Acta Oeconomica* 37 (3–4): 285–304.

788. Bostrom, M. January 1990. Measuring Political Democracy in Latin America: A Discussion of the Fitzgibbon-Johnson Image-Index. *Statsvetenskaplig Tidskrift* 93 (1): 47–59.

789. Botella, J. July 1989. The Spanish "New" Regions: Territorial and Political

Pluralism. *International Political Science Review* 10 (3): 263–271.

790. Botstein, L. March 1990. Damaged Literacy: Illiteracies and American Democracy. *Daedalus* 119 (2): 55–84.

791. Botwinick, A., and P. Bachrach. 1983. Democracy and Scarcity: Toward a Theory of Participation Democracy. *International Political Science Review* 4 (3): 361–373.

792. Bourmaud, D., and P. J. Quantin (eds.). October 1991. Les Chemins de la Democratie. *Politique Africaine* 3–104. 7 articles.

793. Bourque, S. C., and K. B. Warren. 1989. Democracy without Peace: The Cultural Politics of Terror in Peru. *Latin American Research Review* 24 (1): 7–34.

794. Bouscaren, A. T. May 1981. The Portuguese Labyrinth. *Current History* 80 (466): 205–208, 224–225.

795. Bouvin, A. March 1977. New Swedish Legislation on Democracy at the Workplace. *International Labour Review* 115 (2): 131–143.

796. Bova, R. October 1991. Political Dynamics of the Post-Communist Transition: A Comparative Perspective. *World Politics* 44 (1): 113–137.

797. Boventer, H. August 1980. God, Democracy and Political Education: Are Basic Values Anticonstitutional?* *Aus Politik und Zeitgeschichte* 16 (33–34): 20–30.

798. Bovero, M. 1987. On the Philosophical Foundations of Democracy.* *Teoria Politica* 3 (3): 63–79.

799. Bowers, S. R. September 1988. Pinochet's Plebiscite and the Catholics: The Dual Role of the Chilean Church. *World Affairs* 151 (2): 51–58.

800. Bowler, S., T. Donovan, and T. Happ. June 1992. Ballot Propositions and Information Costs: Direct Democracy and the Fatigued Voter. *Western Political Quarterly* 45 (2): 559–568.

801. Bowles, S., and H. Gintis. May 1978. The Invisible First: Have Capitalism and Democracy Reached a Parting of the Ways? *American Economic Review* 68 (2): 358–363.

802. Bowles, S., and H. Gintis. October 1989. Democratic Demands and Radical Rights. *Socialist Review* 19 (4): 57–72.

803. Bowles, S., D. J. Lanoue, and P. Sovoie. November 1994. Electoral Systems, Party Competition, and the Strength of Partisan Attachment: Evidence from Three Countries. *Journal of Politics* 56 (4): 991–1007.

804. Bowman, A. O., and M. A. Pagano. June 1994. The State of American Federalism. *Publius* 24 (3): 1–22.

805. Bowman, J. H. 1978. *See* McCaffery, J. (1978).

806. Boyce, B. October 1993. The Democratic Deficit of the European Community. *Parliamentary Affairs* 46 (4): 458–477.

807. Boyd, W. I. June 1994. *See* Plank, D. N. (June 1994).

808. Boyer, N. E. 1991. *See* Boyer, W. W. (1991).

809. Boyer, P. December 1988. Plebiscite in a Parliamentary Democracy. *Canadian Parliamentary Review* 11: 2–4.

810. Boyer, W. W. December 1982. *See* Miller, M. J. (December 1982).

811. Boyer, W. W. September 1992. Reflections on Democratization. *PS: Political Science & Politics* 25 (3): 517–522.

812. Boyer, W. W., and N. E. Boyer. 1991. Democratization of South Korea's National Universities. *Korean Studies* 15: 83–98.

813. Boyle, F. A. March 1989. The Hypocrisy and Racism Behind the Formulation of U.S. Human Rights Foreign Policy: In Honor of Clyde Ferguson. *Social Justice* 16 (1): 71–93.

814. Boyle, M. April 1994. Building a Communicative Democracy: The Birth and Death of Citizen Politics in East Germany. *Media, Culture and Society* 16 (2): 183–216.

815. Boyle, P. 1992. Beyond Self-Protection to Prophecy: The Catholic Church and Political Change in Zaire. *Africa Today* 39 (3): 49–96.

816. Boyne, G. A. October 1986. Rate Reform and the Future of Local Democracy. *Political Quarterly* 57 (4): 426–437.

817. Boynton, G. R., and W. H. Kwon. February 1978. An Analysis of Consociational Democracy. *Legislative Studies Quarterly* 3 (1): 11–25.

818. Boyte, H. C. 1978. Beyond Liberalism: Toward a Living Democracy. *Dissent* 25 (3): 270–274.

819. Boyte, H. C. July 1989. Overview: Rethinking Politics. *National Civic Review* 78 (4): 249–254.

820. Boyte, H. C., and F. M. Lappe. September 1990. The Language of Citizen Democracy. *National Civic Review* 79 (5): 417–425.

821. Bozdag, A. 1992. Crisis and Democracy in Kirgizia. *Aussenpolitik* 43 (3): 277–286.

822. Bozdemir, M. June 1984. Military Authoritarianism and Democracy in Turkey.* *Esprit* 6: 110–122.

823. Bozdemir, M. July 1992. Turkey's March toward Democracy. *Peuples Mediterraneens* 60: 9–24.

824. Bozeman, A. B. 1985. U.S. Foreign Policy and the Prospects for Democracy, National Security, and World Peace. *Comparative Strategy* 5 (3): 223–267.

825. Bozeman, A. B. December 1987. American Policy and the Illusion of Congruent Values. *Strategic Review* 15 (1): 11–23.

826. Bozoki, A. 1990. Political Transition and Constitutional Change in Hungary. *Suedosteuropa* 39 (9): 538–549.

827. Bozoki, A. March 1992. Democracy across the Negotiation Table. *New Hungarian Quarterly* 125: 59–78.

828. Bozoki, A. March 1993. Hungary's Road to Systematic Change: The Opposition Round Table. *East European Politics and Societies* 7 (2): 276–308.

829. Bozoki, A. December 1993. Intellectuals and Democratization (in Hungary). *New Hungarian Quarterly* 132: 93–106.

830. Bracher, K. D. 1979. Two German Pasts: The Challenge of Contemporary History.* *Politische Meinung* 187: 8–20.

831. Bracher, K. D. 1980. Experience and Concepts: Between Democracy and Dictatorship. *Government and Opposition* 15 (3–4): 289–296.

832. Bracher, K. D. July 1982. Zwischenstation: Das Problem der Demokratie in der Dritten Welt.* *Politische Meinung* 27: 71–75.

833. Bracher, K. D. January 1985. Political Institutions in Times of Crisis.* *Vierteljahrenreshefte für Zeitgeschichte* 33 (1): 1–27.

834. Bracher, K. D. January 6, 1989. Orientation Problems of Liberal Democracy in [West] Germany.* *Aus Politik und Zeitgeschichte* (1–2): 3–14.

835. Brachet Marquez, V., and D. Davis. 1993. Rethinking Democracy in Mexico. *Cahiers des Ameriques Latines* 16: 69–92.

836. Bradberry, D. September 1992. *See* Smolla, R. A. (September 1992).

837. Bradley, D. August 1990. Radical Principles and the Legal Institution of Marriage: Domestic Relations Law and Social Democracy in Sweden. *International Journal of Law and Family* 4: 154–185.

838. Bradley, K. 1986. Employee Ownership and Economic Decline in Western

Industrial Democracies. *Journal of Management Studies* 23 (1): 51–71.

839. Bradlow, D. A., and M. Silverman. July 1989. Managing the Law Firm: Is Democracy Obsolete? *Legal Economics* 15: 29–32.

840. Bradshaw, L. 1991. Alan Bloom's Defense of Democracy. *Interchange* 22 (1–2): 107–114.

841. Brady, D., and J. Mo. January 1992. Electoral Systems and Institutional Choice: A Case Study of the 1988 Korean Elections. *Comparative Political Studies* 24 (4): 405–429.

842. Brady, J. A. 1986. The Threat of Terrorism to Democracy: A Criminal Justice Response. *Terrorism* 8 (3): 205–211.

843. Braeckman, C. March 1993. L'Impossible Mutation du President Mobutu: Democratisation sous Surveillance au Zaire. *Monde Diplomatique* 40: 20.

844. Braithwaite, J., and V. Braithwaite. 1980. Effects of Income Inequality and Social Democracy on Homicide: A Cross-National Comparison. *British Journal of Criminology* 20 (1): 45–53.

845. Braithwaite, V. 1980. *See* Braithwaite, J. (1980).

846. Brana Shute, G. March 1986. Back to the Barracks? Five Years "Revo" in Suriname. *Journal of Interamerican Studies and World Affairs* 28 (1): 93–121.

847. Brana Shute, G. March 1987. Suriname Surprises: Small Country, Smaller Revolution. *Caribbean Review* 15 (4): 4–7, 26–28.

848. Branberg, D., and S. Holmberg. December 1990. The Berelson Paradox Reconsidered: Intention-Behavior Changers in US and Swedish Election Campaigns. *Public Opinion Quarterly* 54 (4): 530–550.

849. Branco, K. J., and J. B. Williamson. July 1988. Economic Development and Income Distribution: A Cross-National Analysis. *American Journal of Economics and Sociology* 47 (3): 277–297.

850. Brand, D. March 1983. Corporatism, the NRA, and the Oil Industry. *Political Science Quarterly* 98 (1): 99–118.

851. Brand, L. A. March 1991. Democratization in Jordan. *American-Arab Affairs* 36: 21–22.

852. Brandao Cavalcanti, T. October 1978. Political Structure and Characteristics of Democracy in Brazil. *Revista de Ciencia Politica* 21 (4): 3–17.

853. Brandon, D. September 1975. A New Foreign Policy for America. *World Affairs* 138 (2): 83–107.

854. Brandon, D. W. September 1982. A Christian Democratic Party in the United States. *Teaching Political Science* 10 (1): 30–42.

855. Branfman, F. September 1984. Unexplored America: Economic Rebirth in a Post-Industrial World. *World Policy Journal* 2 (1): 33–62.

856. Brann, C. M. B. December 1993. Democratisation of Language Use in Public Domain in Nigeria. *Journal of Modern African Studies* 31 (4): 639–656.

857. Brard, Y., and M. Viou. 1982. La Democratisation des Institutions Politiques de la Cote D'Ivoire. *Revue Juridique et Politique, Independance et Cooperation* 36 (2): 735–758.

858. Bratton, M. April 1992. Zambia Starts Over. *Journal of Democracy* 3 (2): 81–94.

859. Bratton, M. April 1994. Micro-Democracy? The Merger of Farmer Unions in Zimbabwe. *African Studies Review* 37 (1): 9–38.

860. Bratton, M., and N. Van De Walle. July 1992. Popular Protest and Political Reform in Africa. *Comparative Politics* 24 (4): 419–422.

861. Bratton, M., and N. Van De Walle. July 1994. Neo-Patrimonial Regimes and Political Transitions in Africa. *World Politics* 46 (4): 453–489.

862. Braun, D. 1984. *See* Keman, H. (1984).

863. Braungart, R. G. September 1986. Moderate, Extreme, and Left-Right Sources of Youth Politics: A Typology. *Journal of Political and Military Sociology* 14 (2): 199–213.

864. Bray, J. April 1989. Pakistan in 1989: Benazir's Balancing Act. *Round Table* 310: 192–200.

865. Bray, J. April 1991. Nawaz Sharif's New Order in Pakistan. *Round Table* 318: 179–190.

866. Bray, M., and W. Lee. November 1993. Education, Democracy and Colonial Transition: The Case of Hong Kong. *International Review of Education* 39 (6): 541–560.

867. Braybrooke, D. 1983. Can Democracy Be Combined with Federalism or with Liberalism. *Nomos* 25: 109–118.

868. Brazauskas, A. December 1993. Perestroika á la Lituanienne.* *Politique Internationale* 62: 343–350.

869. Breiner, P. November 1989. Democratic Autonomy, Political Ethics, and Moral Luck. *Political Theory* 17 (4): 550–574.

870. Breitman, R. 1976. German Social Democracy and General Schleicher, 1932–33. *Central European History* 9 (4): 352–378.

871. Bremer, S. A. 1993. Democracy and Militarized Interstate Conflict, 1816–1965. *International Interactions* 18 (3): 231–249.

872. Brems, H. 1975. Economic Democracy. *Nationalokonomisk Tidsskrift* 113 (2): 217–229.

873. Brender, Y. June 1993. *See* Vredenburgh, D. (June 1993).

874. Brennan, G. January 1991. Courts, Democracy, and the Law. *Australian Law Journal* 65: 32–42.

875. Brenner, M. J. June 1993. EC: Confidence Lost. *Foreign Policy* 91: 24–43.

876. Brenner, S. June 1980. *See* Arrington, T. S. (June 1980).

877. Bresillon, T. April 1992. Presse Ecrite Algerienne: Intermede Liberal? *Mediaspouvoirs* 54–59.

878. Brest, P. 1981. The Substance of Process. *Ohio State Law Journal* 42 (1): 131–142.

879. Breuning, M. August 1994. *See* Rahn, W. M. (August 1994).

880. Breyer, F., and J. M. G. Von der Schulenburg. November 1990. Family Ties and Social Security in a Democracy. *Public Choice* 67 (2): 155–167.

881. Brice, K. July 1992. Muzzling the Media. *Africa Report* 37: 49–51.

882. Briefs, H. W. 1983. Goetz on Capitalism and Democracy: An Introduction. *Review of Social Economy* 41 (3): 212–227.

883. Brigham, J. September 1990. Bad Attitudes: The Consequences of Survey Research for Constitutional Practice. *Review of Politics* 52 (4): 582–602.

884. Bright, C. September 1990. Neither Dictatorship nor Double Standards: The Reagan Administration's Approach to Human Rights. *World Affairs* 153 (2): 51–80.

885. Brigman, W. E. March 1981. The Executive Branch and the Independent Regulatory Agencies. *Presidential Studies Quarterly* 11 (2): 244–261.

886. Brillantes, A. B. October 1987. The State of Philippine Democracy, 1987. *Philippine Journal of Public Administration* 31 (4): 404–417.

887. Brito, M. N. C. (ed.). 1987. As Mulheres e os Espacos Democraticos na America Latina. *Revista de Ciencias Sociales* 1 (2): 141–304. Papers presented at conference, Universidade Federal do Rio Grande do Sul,1985.

888. Brittan, S. April 1975. The Economic Contradictions of Democracy. *British Journal of Political Science* 5: 129–159.

889. Brittan, S. April 1989. "The Economic Contradictions" Revisited. *Political Quarterly* 60 (2): 190–203.

890. Brocker, M. March 1991. Suffrage and Democracy in John Locke's Political Philosophy.* *Zeitschrift für Politik* 38 (1): 47–63.

891. Brock-Utne, B. September 1990. Listen to Women for a Change. *Peace Review* 2 (4): 32–34.

892. Brodin, E. June 1991. Sweden: No Panacea for Eastern Europeans. *World and I* 6: 84–89.

893. Brodsgaard, K. E. July 1981. The Democracy Movement in China, 1978–1979: Opposition Movements, Wall Poster Campaigns, and Underground Journals. *Asian Survey* 21 (7): 747–774.

894. Broedling, L. A. September 1977. Industrial Democracy and the Future Management of the United States Armed Forces. *Air University Review* 28 (6): 42–52.

895. Broekmeyer, M. J. May 1977. Self-Management in Yugoslavia. *Annals of the American Academy of Political and Social Science* 431: 133–140.

896. Broer, M., and O. Diehl. June 1991. Security of the New Democracies in Europe and NATO.* *Europa Archiv: Zeitschrift für Internationale Politik* 46 (12): 367–376.

897. Brokl, L. 1990. Problems of the Transition to a Pluralistic Democracy.* *Sociologicky Casopis* 26 (4): 249–261.

898. Brokl, L. 1992. Between November 1989 and Democracy: Anatomies of Our Politics.* *Sociologicky Casopis* 28 (2): 150–164.

899. Brokl, L. 1992. Nationalism as an Unintended Consequence of the Democratization of Society: On Nationalism and Post-Totalitarian Mannerism.* *Sociologicky Casopis* 28 (1): 49–57.

900. Bronner, S. E. March 1980. The Socialist Project: In Memory of Rudi Dutschke. *Social Research* 47 (1): 11–35.

901. Bronstein, P. 1986. Intriguing in the Philippines: Can the Aquino Regime Bring Stable Democracy. *Dissent* 33 (4): 505–513.

902. Brooks, A., M. Daniels, G. Kaltoft, E. Kasl, K. Loughlin, and T. Preciphs. September 1993. The Democratization of Knowledge. *Adult Education Quarterly* 44 (1): 43–51.

903. Brooks, J. E. October 1983. Left-Wing Mobilization and Socioeconomic Equality: A Cross-National Analysis of the Developed Democracies. *Comparative Political Studies* 6 (3): 393–416.

904. Brooks, J. E. July 1988. Mediterranean Neo-Democracies and the Opinion-Policy Nexus. *West European Politics* 11 (3): 121–140.

905. Brooks, J. E. July 1992. Abortion Policy in Western Democracies: A Cross-National Analysis. *Governance* 5 (3): 342–357.

906. Brooks, M. P. March 1990. *See* Beauregard, R. A. (March 1990).

907. Brosio, M. 1978. Comments on Eurocommunism and Western Democracy. *Atlantic Community Quarterly* 16 (3): 290–295.

908. Broudy, H. S. May 1983. Federal Interventions in Education: Expectations and Frustrations. *Education and Urban Society* 15 (3): 291–308.

909. Broughton, D., and E. Kirchner. March 1984. Germany: The FDP in Transition Again? *Parliamentary Affairs* 37 (2): 183–198.

910. Brovkin, V. N. October 1990. The Making of Elections to the Congress of People's Deputies (CPD) in March 1989. *Russian Review* 49 (4): 417–442.

911. Brown, A. June 1989. Political Change in the Soviet Union. *World Policy Journal* 6 (3): 469–501.

912. Brown, B. A. January 1992. Poland's Leap to Democracy. *World and I* 7: 180–187.

913. Brown, C. 1988. Chilean Plebiscite: Democracy Versus Fear and Propaganda. *Nation* 247 (8): 257+.

914. Brown, C. R. V. 1977. Cultural Democracy and Cultural Variability in Chicano Literature. *English Education* 8 (2): 83–89.

915. Brown, C. W. J. September 1993. *See* Wilcox, C. (September 1993).

916. Brown, D. March 1987. A Hungarian Connection: Karl Polanyi's Influence on the Budapest School. *Journal of Economic Issues* 21 (1): 339–347.

917. Brown, D. March 1990. Sandinismo and the Problem of Democratic Hegemony. *Latin American Perspectives* 17 (2): 39–61.

918. Brown, J. December 1987. The Military and Politics in Turkey. *Armed Forces and Society* 13 (2): 235–253.

919. Brown, J. February 1988. The Politics of Transition in Turkey. *Current History* 87 (526): 69–72,82–83.

920. Brown, J. L. 1989. When Violence Has a Benevolent Face: The Paradox of Hunger in the World's Wealthiest Democracy. *International Journal of Health Services* 19 (2): 257–277.

921. Brown, L. H. 1985. Democracy in Organizations: Membership Participation and Organizational Characteristics in United States Retail Food Co-operatives. *Organization Studies* 6 (4): 313–334.

922. Brown, L. H. 1989. Locus of Control and Degree of Organizational Democracy. *Economic and Industrial Democracy* 10 (4): 467–498.

923. Brown, R. J. May 1976. The Meaning of Professionalism. *American Behavioral Scientist* 19 (5): 511–522.

924. Browne, E. C. November 1986. *See* Frendreis, J. P. (November 1986).

925. Browne, E. C., J. P. Frendreis, and D. W. Gleiber. July 1984. An "Events" Approach to the Problem of Cabinet Stability. *Comparative Political Studies* 17 (2): 167–198.

926. Browne, E. C., J. P. Frendreis, and D. W. Gleiber. August 1986. The Process of Cabinet Dissolution: An Exponential Model of Duration and Stability in Western Democracies. *American Journal of Political Science* 30 (3): 628–650.

927. Browning, E. K. 1975. Why Social Insurance Budget Is Too Large in a Democracy. *Economic Inquiry* 13 (3): 373–388.

928. Brozmanova, E. 1994. *See* Plichtova, J. (1994).

929. Brubaker, S. C. January 1985. Taking Dworkin Seriously. *Review of Politics* 47 (1): 45–65.

930. Bruckner, P. 1990. Living Without Enemies.* *Politique Internationale* 49: 363–370.

931. Brudney, J. L. June 1984. Local Coproduction of Services and the Analysis of Municipal Productivity. *Urban Affairs Quarterly* 19 (4): 465–484.

932. Bruin, K. 1987. Distinction and Democratization: Royal Decorations in the Netherlands. *Netherlands Journal of Sociology* 23 (1): 17–30.

933. Brulin, G. 1984. Economic Effectiveness, Immigrating Salaried Employees and Economic Democracy.* *Sociologisk Forskning* 21 (1): 68–72.

934. Brulin, G. 1986. Industrial Democracy and Economic Sociology: A Commentary on the Fourth International Conference on the Economics of Self Management.* *Sociologisk Forskning* 23 (1): 93–99.

935. Brumberg, A. June 1986. Nicaragua: The Inner Struggle. Is There Still a Chance for Political Pluralism? *Dissent* 33 (3): 294–303.

936. Brumberg, A. February 1990. Poland: The Demise of Communism. *Foreign Affairs* 69 (1): 70–88.

937. Brumberg, D. March 1991. Prospects for a "Democratic Bargain" in Algeria. *American-Arab Affairs* 36: 23–26.

938. Brundtland, A. O. 1983. It Would Be More Important to Have Effective Diplomacy in Moscow: An Acceptable Democracy in Helsingfors.* *Internasjonal Politikk* (2): 217–219.

939. Bruneau, T. C. April 1974. Continuity and Change in Portuguese Politics: Ten Years after the Revolution. *West European Politics* 7 (2): 72–83.

940. Bruneau, T. C. 1985. Discovering Democracy. *Wilson Quarterly* 9 (1): 67–81.

941. Bruneau, T. C. 1987. Church in the Brazilian Transition.* *Dados* 30 (1): 29–43.

942. Bruneau, T. C. January 1988. *See* Lijphart, A. (January 1988).

943. Bruneau, T. C., and W. E. Hewitt. October 1989. Patterns of Church Influence in Brazil's Political Transition. *Comparative Politics* 22 (1): 39–61.

944. Brunetti, A., and T. Straubhaar. 1991. Internationalization and Direct Democracy.* *Annuaire Suisse de Science Politique* 31: 237–256.

945. Brunk, G. G., G. A. Caldeira, and M. S. Lewis-Beck. 1987. Capitalism, Social-

ism, and Democracy: An Empirical Inquiry. *European Journal of Political Research* 15 (4): 459–470.

946. Brunk, G. G., and T. G. Minehart. August 1984. How Important Is Elite Turnover to Policy Change? *American Journal of Political Science* 28 (3): 559–569.

947. Brunner, J. J. 1989. L'Intelligentsia Chilienne: Cadres Institutionnels et univers Ideologiques. *Notes et Etudes Documentaires* (4): 132–144.

948. Brunner, K. March 1982. Economic Development: Cancun and the Western Democracies. *World Economy* 5 (1): 61–84.

949. Brus, W. December 1993. Marketisation and Democratisation: The Sino-Soviet Divergence. *Cambridge Journal of Economics* 17 (4): 423–440.

950. Bruszt, L. June 1990. The Negotiated Revolution in Hungary. *Social Research* 57 (2): 365–387.

951. Bruszt, L. April 1992. East European Transformation Policies.* *Stato e Mercato* 34: 131–150.

952. Bruszt, L. December 1992. Transformative Politics: Social Costs and Social Peace in East Europe. *East European Politics and Societies* 6 (1): 55–72.

953. Brutti, M. March 1982. Political Democracy and Modernization.* *Democrazia e Diritto* 22 (2): 81–88.

954. Bruzios, C. June 1990. Democratic and Republican Party Activists and Followers: Inter- and Intra-Party Differences. *Polity* 22 (4): 581–601.

955. Bryant, M. N. April 1992. *See* Ronai, I. (April 1992).

956. Brym, R. J. 1977. Democracy and Intellectuals: Test of Karl Mannheim's Thesis. *Scottish Journal of Sociology* 1 (2): 173–182.

957. Brynen, R. March 1992. Economic Crisis and Post-Rentier Democratization in the Arab World: The Case of Jordan.

Canadian Journal of Political Science 25 (1): 67–97.

958. Buchanan, J. H., Jr. July 1989. Civitas: Civic Education to Inform and Involve. *National Civic Review* 78 (4): 279–284.

959. Buchanan, J. M. March 1979. The Potential for Taxpayer Revolt in American Democracy: Implications of the Proposition 13 Vote in California. *Social Science Quarterly* 59 (4): 691–696.

960. Buchanan, J. M., and G. Tullock. September 1977. The Expanding Public Sector: Wagner Squared. *Public Choice* 31: 147–150.

961. Buchanan, P. G. 1989. Plus Ça Change: National Labor Administration and Democracy in Brazil, 1985–1987.* *Dados: Revista de Ciencias Sociais* 32 (1): 75–123.

962. Buchholz, E. 1983. Democracy, Law and Personality Development.* *Deutsche Zeitschrift für Philosophie* 31 (3): 287–299.

963. Buchstein, H., and R. Schmaltzbruns. September 1992. Justice as Democracy: The Political Philosophy of Michael Walzer.* *Politische Vierteljahresschrift* 33 (3): 375–398.

964. Buckley, W. F. 1978. Capitalism, Socialism, and Democracy. *Commentary* 65 (4): 34–36.

965. Buckman, D. December 1993. How Eight Weekly News Magazines Covered Elections in Six Countries. *Journalism Quarterly* 70 (4): 780–792.

966. Budge, I. 1982. Electoral Volatility: Issue Effects and Basic Change in 23 Post-War Democracies. *Electoral Studies* 1 (2): 147–168.

967. Budge, I. September 1985. Party Factions and Government Reshuffles: A General Hypothesis Tested Against Data from 20 Post-War Democracies. *European Journal of Political Research* 13 (3): 327–333.

968. Budge, I. 1989. The Politics of Information Technology: Participation or Authoritarianism?* *Teoria Politica* 5 (1): 67–84.

969. Budge, I. July 1993. *See* Woldendorp, J. (July 1993).

970. Budge, I. May 1994. *See* Strom, K. (May 1994).

971. Budge, I., and H. Keman. April 1990. New Concerns for Coalition Theory: Allocation of Ministries and Sectoral Policy Making: A Comparative Analysis. *Acta Politica* 25 (2): 151–195.

972. Budge, I., and M. Laver. November 1986. Politics, Ideology, and Party Distance: Analysis of Election Programmes in 19 Democracies. *Legislative Studies Quarterly* 11 (4): 607–617.

973. Bueno de Mesquita, B. July 1978. Redistricting and Political Integration in India. *Comparative Political Studies* 11 (2): 279–288.

974. Bueno de Mesquita, B. April 1979. Coalition Payoffs and Electoral Performance in European Democracies. *Comparative Political Studies* 12 (1): 61–81.

975. Bueno de Mesquita, B. (ed.). June 1991. Democracy and Foreign Policy: Community and Constraint. *Journal of Conflict Resolution* 35: 181–381. Special issue.

976. Buergenthal, T. June 1990. Copenhagen: A Democratic Manifesto. *World Affairs* 153 (1): 5–8.

977. Buffett, D. April 1994. Democracy in a Bountiful Setting: The Journey from Pitcairn to the Year 2000. *Parliamentarian* 75 (2): N3-N5.

978. Bugajski, J. December 1990. Poland's Anti-Communist Manifesto. *Orbis* 34 (1): 109–120.

979. Buiks, P. E. J. October 1981. Alexis de Tocqueville and the Ethos of Democracy. *Netherlands Journal of Sociology* 17 (1): 137–150.

980. Buitenschon, N. A. June 1985. Conflict Management in Plural Societies: The Consociational Democracy Formula. *Scandinavian Political Studies* 8 (1–2): 85–103.

981. Bullock, C. S. November 1994. Section 2 of the Voting Rights Act, Districting Formats, and the Election of African Americans. *Journal of Politics* 56 (4): 1098–1105.

982. Bulpitt, J. March 1986. The Discipline of the New Democracy: Mrs. Thatcher's Domestic Statecraft. *Political Studies* 34 (1): 19–39.

983. Bunce, V. June 1990. The Struggle for Liberal Democracy in Eastern Europe. *World Policy Journal* 7 (3): 395–430.

984. Bunce, V. December 1990. A Transition to Liberal Democracy? *Canadian Business Law Journal* 17: 163–172.

985. Bunck, J. M. 1992. *See* Abraham, H. J. (1992).

986. Bundy, W. P. October 1975. Dictatorships and American Foreign Policy. *Foreign Affairs* 54 (1): 51–60.

987. Bunel, J. 1991. Le Syndicalisme Argentine, ou: La Formation d'un Acteur Politique. *Travail et Emploi* 22 (2): 59–74.

988. Bungs, D. September 24, 1993. Elections and Restoring Democracy in the Baltic States. *RFE/RL Research Report* 2: 12–16.

989. Burawoy, M. 1989. Democracy and Production Series: Should We Give Up on Socialism. *Socialist Review* 19 (1): 57–74.

990. Burg, S. L. October 1990. The European Republics of the Soviet Union. *Current History* 89 (549): 321–324, 340–342.

991. Burg, S. L. 1991. Nationalism and Democratization in Yugoslavia. *Washington Quarterly* 14 (4): 5–19.

992. Burg, S. L. April 1993. Nationalism Redux: Through the Glass of the Post-Communist States Darkly. *Current History* 92: 162–168.

993. Burke, C. G. 1983. The Control of Professionals in a Democracy. *International Journal of Public Administration* 5 (3): 291–320.

994. Burke, J. P. April 1983. *See* Black, C. E. (April 1983).

995. Burke, J. P. March 1989. Reconciling Public Administration and Democracy: The Role of the Responsible Administrator. *Public Administration Review* 49 (2): 180–185.

996. Burkhart, R. E., and M. S. Lewis-Beck. December 1994. Comparative Democracy: The Economic Development Thesis. *American Political Science Review* 88 (4): 903–910.

997. Burlatskii, F. December 1992. *See* Alekseev, S. (December 1992).

998. Burley, A. M. S. 1992. Democracy and Judicial Review in the European Community. *University of Chicago Legal Forum* 81–91.

999. Burley, A. M. S. March 1992. Toward an Age of Liberal Nations. *Harvard International Law Journal* 33: 393–405.

1000. Burnell, P. June 1994. Zambia at the Crossroads. *World Affairs* 157 (1): 19–28.

1001. Burnham, W. D. September 1984. *See* Eckstein, H. (September 1984).

1002. Burnham, W. D. September 1986. Periodization Schemes and "Party Systems": The "System of 1896" as a Case in Point. *Social Science History* 10 (3): 263–314.

1003. Burns, N. November 1994. *See* Schlozman, K. L. (November 1994).

1004. Burns, N. E. August 1990. *See* King, G. (August 1990).

1005. Burstein, P. 1981. The Sociology of Democratic Politics and Government. *Annual Review of Sociology* 7: 291–319.

1006. Burton, A. R. March 1981. Political Parties: Effects on the Presidency. *Presidential Studies Quarterly* 11 (2): 289–298.

1007. Burton, B. January 1984. Brunei: Newest and Richest in Asia; Now Independent but Democracy Lags. *International Perspectives* 27–29.

1008. Burton, M. G. February 1989. *See* Higley, J. (February 1989).

1009. Burton, M. G., and J. Higley. June 1987. Elite Settlements. *American Sociological Review* 552 (3): 295–307.

1010. Busch, E. 1983. *See* Bohr, C. E. (1983).

1011. Buse, D. K. September 1990. Party Leadership and Mechanisms of Unity: The Crisis of German Social Democracy Reconsidered. *Journal of Modern History* 62 (3): 477–502.

1012. Buss, T. F., and F. S. Redburn. June 1983. Deepening Citizen Participation. *American Review of Public Administration* 17 (2–3): 121–130.

1013. Bustamante, F. December 1990. The Military in Latin America: Is the Retreat for Good? *Bulletin of Peace Proposals* 21: 371–384.

1014. Bustamante, F. January 1992. Fuerzas Armadas en Ecuador: ¿Peude Institucionalizarse la Subordinacion al Poder Civil? *Sintesis* 17: 179–202.

1015. Bustelo, P. April 1992. Economic Development and Political Transition in Taiwan and Spain: A Comparative Analysis. *Issues and Studies* 28 (4): 67–82.

1016. Butenko, A. P. 1989. Political Power and the Struggle for It under Socialism.* *Sovetskoe Gosudarstvo Pravo* (3): 121–133.

1017. Butenko, A. P., and L. Golden. August 1988. USSR: Perestroika and Democracy: Who Is to Blame? What's to Be Done? Two Views on Present-Day Priorities. *New Times (Moscow)* 33: 24–29.

1018. Butler, C. E. 1977. *See* Hill, L. E. (1977).

1019. Butler, D., and A. Ranney (eds.). May 1994. Over Their Head: The Growing Use of Referendums and Initiatives around the World. *American Enterprise* 5 (3): 58–65. 4 articles.

1020. Butler, W. E. September 1988. Legal Reform in the Soviet Union. *Harriman Institute Forum* 1: 1–8.

1021. Butora, M. March 1992. Foreword: The Delayed Return of Prodigal Sons: Reflections on Emerging Democracies in Central and Eastern Europe. *American University Journal of International Law and Policy* 7: 435–447.

1022. Butora, M., Z. Butorova, and T. Rosova. December 1991. The Hard Birth of Democracy in Slovakia: The Eighteen Months Following the "Tender" Revolution. *Journal of Communist Studies* 7 (4): 435–459.

1023. Butorova, Z. December 1991. *See* Butora, M. (December 1991).

1024. Butter, L. E. December 1980. Northern Ireland and Theories of Ethic Politics. *Journal of Conflict Resolution* 24 (4): 613–640.

1025. Buultjes, R. 1992. The Destiny of Freedom: Political Cycles in the Twentieth Century. *Ethics and International Affairs* 6: 57–67.

ᘓ

1026. Cabrija, D. D. 1986. Democratic Centralism: Certain Issues of Theory and Practice.* *Sovetskoe Gosudarstvo Pravo* 1: 31–37.

1027. Caceras, J. 1988. Introduction: The Modalities of a Problematic Democratization. *Estudios Sociales Centroamericanos* 47: 33–36.

1028. Caciagli, M. April 1984. Spain: Parties and the Party System in the Transition. *West European Politics* 7 (2): 84–98.

1029. Cadart, C. March 1981. For a Complete Modernization of China.* *Politique Internationale* 11: 127–142.

1030. Cadoux, C. May 1984. The Republic of the Philippines: Towards the End of the Marcos Era.* *Revue du Droit Public et de la Science Politique* 3: 607–656.

1031. Cafferta, G. L. June 1982. The Building of Democratic Organizations: An Embryological Metaphor. *Administrative Science Quarterly* 27 (2): 280–303.

1032. Cahen, M. October 1991. Island Breezes: The Victory of the Opposition in the Cape Verde and São Tome and Principe Islands.* *Politique Africaine* 43: 63–78.

1033. Caine, B. 1983. Judicial Review: Democracy vs. Constitutionality. *Temple Law Quarterly* 56 (2): 297–350.

1034. Caldeira, G. A. 1987. *See* Brunk, G. G. (1987).

1035. Calderon, E., E. Martinez, and D. Cazes. 1992. Informatics and Democracy. *IFIP Transactions* 13: 281–287.

1036. Calderon, R. A. March 1982. The Christian Democrats in Latin America: The Fight for Democracy. *Caribbean Review* 11 (2): 34–37.

1037. Calderon, R. A. December 1986. Political Systems as Export Commodity: Democracy and the Role of the U.S. in Central America. *Caribbean Review* 15 (1): 21–23,37.

1038. Calderon, R. A. December 1987. Panama: Disaster or Democracy. *Foreign Affairs* 66: 328–347.

1039. Calderon, R. A. June 1990. Popular Sovereignty and the Liberation of Pana-

ma. *Caribbean Review* 16 (3–4): 10–11, 76–77.

1040. Caldwell, L. K. 1985. Biocracy and Democracy: Science, Ethics, and the Law. *Politics and the Life Sciences* 3 (2): 137–149.

1041. Calhoun, C. December 1992. Some Thoughts on a Revolution: Intellectual Sphere, Sphere of Power and Democracy in China.* *Actes de la Recherche en Sciences Sociales* (95): 26–36.

1042. Calhoun, C. December 1993. Nationalism and Civil Society: Democracy, Diversity and Self-Determination. *International Sociology* 8 (4): 387–412.

1043. Calhoun, C. J. 1980. Democracy, Autocracy, and Intermediate Associations in Organizations: Flexibility or Unrestrained Change. *Sociology* 14 (3): 345–361.

1044. Calinescu, M., and V. Tismaneanu. January 1991. The 1989 Revolution and Romania's Future. *Problems of Communism* 40 (1–2): 42–59.

1045. Calise, M. 1994. The Italian Particracy: Beyond President and Parliament. *Political Science Quarterly* 109 (3): 441–460. Discussion 461–482.

1046. Callaghy, T. October 1994. Africa: Back to the Future? *Journal of Democracy* 5 (4): 133–145.

1047. Callaway, H. G. January 1993. Democracy, Value Inquiry, and Dewey Metaphysics. *Journal of Value Inquiry* 27 (1): 13–27.

1048. Callus, R. 1984. Self-Management Research and Technological Change: Towards Industrial Democracy in an Australian Public Utility. *Economic and Industrial Democracy* 5 (4): 469–493.

1049. Calvert, P. January 1985. Demilitarization in Latin America. *Third World Quarterly* 7 (1): 31–43.

1050. Cameron, D. December 1993. The Beginning of the End Game: Canada's Recent General Election. *Queen's Quarterly* 100 (4): 763–774.

1051. Cammack, P. June 1988. The "Brazilianization" of Mexico? *Government and Opposition* 23 (3): 304–320.

1052. Cammack, P. November 1991. Brazil: The Long March to the New Republic. *New Left Review* 190: 21–58.

1053. Camp, R. A. 1994. The Cross in the Polling Booth: Religion, Politics, and the Laity in Mexico. *Latin American Research Review* 29 (3): 69–100.

1054. Campaninni, G. January 1985. Ethics and Democracy Facing the Totalitarian Challenge.* *Aggiornamenti Sociali* 36 (1): 35–50.

1055. Campbell, A., and M. Warner. March 1985. Changes in the Balance of Power in the British Mineworkers' Union: An Analysis of National Top-Office Elections, 1974–1984. *British Journal of Industrial Relations* 23: 1–24.

1056. Campbell, B. December 1982. Poliatrics: Physicians and the Physician Analogy within Fourth Century Athens. *American Political Science Review* 76 (4): 810–824.

1057. Campbell, B. June 1989. Paradigms Lost: Classical Athenian Politics in Modern Myth. *History of Political Thought* 10 (2): 189–213.

1058. Campbell, B. C. 1977. Did Democracy Work- Prohibition in Late Nineteenth-Century Iowa: A Test Case. *Journal of Interdisciplinary History* 8 (1): 87.

1059. Campbell, C. April 1988. The Political Roles of Senior Government Officials in Advanced Democracies. *British Journal of Political Science* 18 (2): 243–272.

1060. Campbell, D. E. June 1975. Income Distribution under Majority Rule and Alternative Taxation Criteria. *Public Choice* 22: 23–35.

1061. Campbell, D. T. June 1992. *See* Rosenwein, R. E. (June 1992).

1062. Campbell, F. G. June 1977. Central Europe's Bastion of Democracy. *East European Quarterly* 11 (2): 155–176.

1063. Campbell, F. G., G. Stokes, and R. Szporluk. March 1985. Empty Pedestals? *Slavic Review* 44 (1): 1–29.

1064. Campbell, I. C. March 1992. The Emergence of Parliamentary Politics in Tonga. *Pacific Studies* 15: 77–97.

1065. Campbell, J. C., A. King, J. D. Aberbach, B. A. Rockman, D. E. Ashford, T. J. Anton, and G. Esping-Anderson. March 1985. Governmental Response to Budget Scarcity. *Policy Studies Journal* 13 (3): 471–546.

1066. Campbell, R. M. December 1984. Post-Keynesian Politics and the Post-Schumpeterian World. *Canadian Journal of Political Science* 8 (1–2): 72–91.

1067. Campbell, S. H. June 1991. *See* Morgan, T. C. (June 1991).

1068. Campbell, T. D. June 1994. Democracy, Human Rights, and Positive Law. *Sydney Law Review* 16: 195–212.

1069. Campeanu, P., and S. Steriade. December 1993. The Revolution: The Beginning of the Transition [in East Europe]. *Social Research* 60 (4): 916–932.

1070. Campero, G. 1989. The Chilean Managers and the Democratization Process.* *Problemes d'Amerique Latine* 94: 102–112.

1071. Campero, G., and R. Cortazar. December 1988. Actores Sociales y La Transicion a La Democracia en Chile. *Coleccion Estudios* 15: 115–158.

1072. Campodonico, H. September 1992. Las Relaciones Peru-Estados Unidos: Dos Audiencias Polemicas. *QueHacer* 79: 24–29.

1073. Camps, V. January 1986. Beyond Ends and Means: The Pragmatism of Politics.* *Sistema* 70: 63–76.

1074. Canham Clyne, J. March 1994. U. S. Policy on Haiti: Selling Out Democracy. *Covert Action* 4–9+.

1075. Cannon, G. E. January 1982. Consociational vs. Control: Canada as a Case Study. *Western Political Quarterly* 35 (1): 50–64.

1076. Canon, J. J. 1990. Political Pacts and Democratization in Colombia.* *Politeia* (*Caracas*) 14: 445–472.

1077. Cansino, C. October 1993. The Consolidation of Democracy in Latin America.* *Foro Internacional* 134: 716–736.

1078. Cantori, L. J. January 1980. Egypt at Peace. *Current History* 78 (453): 26–29,38.

1079. Cantori, L. J. March 1991. Report: Middle East Study Group, American Political Science Association, Overview. *American-Arab Affairs* 36: 1–2.

1080. Caplan, R. L. 1981. The Paradoxes of Judicial Review in a Constitutional Democracy. *Buffalo Law Review* 30 (3): 451–498.

1081. Cappell, C. L. 1979. *See* Halliday, T. C. (1979).

1082. Caputo, D. A. 1975. New Perspectives on Public-Policy Implications of Defense and Welfare Expenditures in Four Modern Democracies. *Policy Sciences* 6 (4): 423–446.

1083. Carapico, S. November 1993. Elections and Mass Politics in Yemen. *Middle East Report* 23: 2–6.

1084. Carballal, T., and R. Russell. May 1987. Democracy and Authoritarianism in Argentina: Obstacles to Re-Democratization. *Sintesis* 2: 181–207.

1085. Carballo de Cilley, M. May 1993. *See* Turner, F. C. (May 1993).

1086. Carcassone, G. 1993. On Parliamentary Democracy [in France].* *Pouvoirs* 64: 35–41.

1087. Cardoso, F. H. 1981. State Expansion and Democracy.* *Revue de l'Institut de Sociologie* 1–2: 231–238.

1088. Cardoso, F. H. 1986. Democracy in Latin America. *Politics and Society* 15 (1): 23–41.

1089. Cardoso, F. H. May 1987. Democracy in Latin America.* *Sintesis* 2: 11–30.

1090. Care, N. S. July 1978. Participation and Policy. *Ethics* 88 (4): 316–337.

1091. Carew, G. M. 1993. Development Theory and the Promise of Democracy: The Future of Postcolonial African States. *Africa Today* 40 (4): 31–54.

1092. Carey, A. 1979. The Norwegian Experiments in Democracy at Work: A Critique and a Contribution to Reflexive Sociology. *Australian and New Zealand Journal of Sociology* 15 (1): 13–23.

1093. Carey, G. W., and J. McClellan. August 1976. Towards the Restoration of the American Political Tradition. *Journal of Politics* 38 (3): 110–127.

1094. Carino, L. V. July 1989. Bureaucracy for a Democracy: The Struggle of the Philippines Political Leadership and the Civil Service in the Post-Marcos Period. *Philippine Journal of Public Administration* 33: 207–252.

1095. Carlisle, M. December 1979. Changing the Rules of the Game in the U.S. Senate. *Policy Review* 7: 79–92.

1096. Carlsnaes, W. 1981. Foreign Policy and the Democratic Process. *Scandinavian Political Studies* 4 (2): 81–108.

1097. Carmine, E. G., and M. Berkman. June 1994. Ethos, Ideology, and Partisanship: Exploring the Paradox of Conservative Democrats. *Political Behavior* 16 (2): 203–218.

1098. Carmona, J. D. D. December 1983. Transicion a la Democracia: Problemas y Perspectivas. *Politica (Santiago, Chile)* 4: 217–231.

1099. Carniol, B. 1983. Democracy and Community Development in Canada. *Community Development Journal* 18 (3): 247–250.

1100. Carnoy, M. 1980. The Challenge of Democracy. *Social Policy* 11 (2): 3–5.

1101. Carnoy, M. 1981. Education, Industrial Democracy and the State. *Economic and Industrial Democracy* 2 (2): 243–260.

1102. Carnoy, M. 1983. Education, Democracy, and Social Conflict. *Harvard Educational Review* 53 (4): 398–402.

1103. Carothers, T. July 1981. Spain, NATO and Democracy. *World Today* 37 (7–8): 298–303.

1104. Carothers, T. June 1994. Democracy and Human Rights: Policy Allies or Rivals. *Washington Quarterly* 17 (3): 109–120.

1105. Carpenter, T. G. September 1991. The New World Disorder. *Foreign Policy* (84): 24–39.

1106. Carr, M. July 1994. El Salvador: Two Cheers for Democracy. *Race and Class* 36 (1): 1–22.

1107. Carreton, M. A. December 1988. Popular Mobilization, Authoritarian Regime and Transition to Democracy in Chile.* *Mundo* 2 (1): 49–57.

1108. Carrington, P. D. February 1992. Butterfly Effects: The Possibilities of Law Teaching in a Democracy. *Duke Law Journal* 41 (4): 741–805.

1109. Carrino, A. July 1991. Science and Democracy: Hans Kelsen's Critical Decisionism.* *Democrazia e Diritto* 31 (4): 265–284.

1110. Carro Martinez, A. January 1983. Genuine Democracy.* *Revista de Administracion Publica* 100–102: 181–194.

1111. Carter, D. March 1994. Leadership in a Democratic Society. *Public Manager* 23 (1): 25–26.

1112. Carter, G. M. April 1976. South Africa: Paradox for Democracy. *Common Ground* 2 (2): 33–43.

1113. Carter, M. December 1990. The Role of the Paraguayan Catholic Church in the Downfall of the Stroessner Regime. *Journal of Interamerican Studies and World Affairs* 32 (4): 67–121.

1114. Carter, S. L. 1987. The Constitution, the Uniqueness Puzzle, and the Economic Conditions of Democracy. *George Washington Law Review* 56 (1): 136–148.

1115. Carty, A. 1988. Liberal Economic Rhetoric as an Obstacle to the Democratization of the World Economy. *Ethics* 98 (4): 742–756.

1116. Casanova, J. December 1983. Modernization and Democratization: Reflections on Spain's Transition to Democracy. *Social Research* 50 (4): 929–973.

1117. Casanova, P. G. March 1989. Liberation Struggles in Latin America. *Social Justice* 16 (1): 109–118.

1118. Casanova, P. G. December 1992. Thinking about Cuba. *Social Justice* 19 (4): 153–158.

1119. Casas-Alvarez, P. January 1994. The 1993 [Spanish] Legislative Elections: A Perspective.* *Revista de Estudios Politicos* 83: 313–338.

1120. Case, W. June 1993. Semi-Democracy in Malaysia: Withstanding the Pressures for Regime Change. *Pacific Affairs* 66 (2): 183–205.

1121. Case, W. October 1994. The UMNO Party Election in Malaysia: One for the Money. *Asian Survey* 34 (10): 916+.

1122. Casper, B. M. 1976. Technology Policy and Democracy. *Science* 194 (4260): 29–35.

1123. Caspi, D., and M. A. Seligson. January 1983. Toward an Empirical Theory of Tolerance: Radical Groups in Israel and

Costa Rica. *Comparative Political Studies* 15 (4): 385–404.

1124. Cassidy, K. J. June 1990. Economic Conversion: Industrial Policy and Democratic Values. *Policy Studies Review* 9 (4): 775–786.

1125. Castaneda, J. G. June 1990. Latin America and the End of the Cold War. *World Policy Journal* 7 (3): 469–492.

1126. Castaneda, J. G. September 1993. Can NAFTA Change Mexico? *Foreign Affairs* 72: 66–80.

1127. Castelfranci, C., R. Conte, and M. Diani. October 1994. Cognitive Paradoxes of Democracy and the Limits of the Citizen's Action.* *Parolechiave* 5: 31–63.

1128. Castillo, M. I. September 1990. *See* Becker, D. (September 1990).

1129. Castillo, P. 1990. La Financiacion de los Partidos Politicos ante la Opnion Publica. *Revista de Derecho Politico* 31: 123–141.

1130. Castles, F. G. 1975. Swedish Social Democracy: Conditions of Success. *Political Quarterly* 46 (2): 171–185.

1131. Castles, F. G. June 1981. How Does Politics Matter? Structure or Agency in the Determination of Public Policy Outcomes. *European Journal of Political Research* 9 (2): 119–132.

1132. Castor, S. December 1992. Democracy and Society in Haiti: Structures of Domination and Resistance to Change. *Social Justice* 19 (4): 126–137.

1133. Castoriadis, C. January 1986. The Greek Polis and the Creation of Democracy.* *Le Debat* 38: 126–144.

1134. Castro Escudero, T. July 1986. Popular Movement and Democracy in Chile.* *Revista Mexicana de Sociologia* 48 (3): 51–73.

1135. Castro Moran, M. April 1989. Relaciones entre el ejercito y la Democracia en El Salvador. *Presencia* (*El Salvador*) 2: 26–50.

1136. Catrain, P. June 1984. Democratic Transition, Social Democracy and the Working Class in the Dominican Republic.* *Archipelago* 5: 84–107.

1137. Catudal, H. M. 1976. University Reform in Federal Republic: Experiment in Democratization at Free University of Berlin. *Comparative Education* 12 (3): 231–241.

1138. Cavanagh, T. E. January 1982. The Calculus of Representation: A Congressional Perspective. *Western Political Quarterly* 35 (1): 120–129.

1139. Cavarero, A. March 1990. The Democratic Model: The Horizon of Gender Differences.* *Democrazia e Diritto* 30 (2): 221–241.

1140. Cavarozzi, M. 1982. Developmentism and the Relations between Democracy and Capitalism Dependent on Dependence and Development in Latin America.* *Latin American Research Review* 17 (1): 152–165.

1141. Cavarozzi, M. October 1991. Mas alla de las Transiciones a la Democracia en America Latina. *Revista de Estudios Politicos* 74: 85–112.

1142. Cavarozzi, M. October 1992. Beyond Transitions to Democracy in Latin America. *Journal of Latin American Studies* 24: 665–684.

1143. Cavazza, F. L. March 1992. The Italian Paradox: An Exit from Communism. *Daedalus* 121 (2): 217–249.

1144. Cavendish, J. C. June 1994. Christian Base Communities and the Building of Democracy: Brazil and Chile. *Sociology of Religion* 55 (2): 179–195.

1145. Cayrol, R. June 1983. The Crisis of the French Socialist Party. *New Political Science* 12: 7–18.

1146. Cazes, D. 1992. *See* Calderon, E. (1992).

1147. Cazzola, F. 1985. Notes for an Analysis of Italian Democracy.* *Teoria Politica* 1 (2): 23–42.

1148. Cea, J. L. June 1987. Chile's Difficult Return to Constitutional Democracy. *PS: Political Science & Politics* 20 (3): 665–673.

1149. Ceaser, J. September 1985. Alexis de Tocqueville on Political Science, Political Culture, and the Role of the Intellectual. *American Political Science Review* 79 (3): 656–672.

1150. Cefai, D. April 1993. The Metamorphoses of the Judicial-Legal System during the Democratic Transition [in Brazil].* *Problemes d'Amerique Latine* 9: 109–123.

1151. Celedon, C. June 1993. *See* Munoz-Goma, O. (June 1993).

1152. Centeno, M. A. 1994. Between Rocky Democracies and Hard Markets: Dilemmas of the Double Transition. *Annual Review of Sociology* 20: 125–147.

1153. Center, J. A. 1974. Democratic Convention Reforms and Party Democracy. *Political Science Quarterly* 89 (2): 325–350.

1154. Cerroni, U. 1978. Democracy and Socialism. *Economy and Society* 7 (3): 241–283.

1155. Cerroni, U. April 1983. Democracy as a Problem of Mass Society.* *Estudios Politicos* 2 (2): 54–64.

1156. Cerroni, U. July 1983. Democracy as a Problem of Mass Society.* *Estudios Politicos* 2 (3): 70–83.

1157. Cerroni, U. April 1986. Democracy as a Problem of Mass Society.* *Estudios Politicos* 5 (2): 9–34.

1158. Cessou, S. July 1994. Prisons d'Afrique: Plus Ça Change, Moins Ca Change. *Jeune Afrique Economie* 74–75.

1159. Ch'en, C. November 1987. Fang Li-Chich: Theorist of the Mainland Chinese Democratic Movement. *Issues and Studies* 23 (11): 50–68.

1160. Cha, V. D. September 1993. Politics and Democracy [in South Korea] under the Kim Young Sam Government: Something Old, Something New. *Asian Survey* 33 (9): 849–863.

1161. Cha, Y. K. June 1992. *See* Kim, T. (June 1992).

1162. Chabal, P. January 1994. Democracy and Daily Life in Black Africa. *International Affairs (London)* 70 (1): 83–91.

1163. Chacaltana, J., R. Guzman, and M. Tanaka. September 1993. Crisis of Political Representation and the Popular Classes [in Peru].* *Socialismo y Participacion* 62: 37–45.

1164. Chacon, V. July 1984. Revolution through Votes.* *Revista Brasileira de Estudos Politicos* 50: 71–121.

1165. Chadjipadelis, T., and C. Zafiropoulos. November 1994. Electoral Changes in Greece 1981–1990: Geographical Patterns and the Uniformity of the Vote. *Political Geography* 13 (6): 492–514.

1166. Chaffee, W. A. October 1984. The Political Economy of Revolution and Democracy. *American Journal of Economics and Sociology* 43 (4): 385–398.

1167. Chakravorti, R. July 1992. Capitalist Democracy and Status of Blacks. *Economic and Political Weekly* 27 (30): 1599–1600.

1168. Chalfont, L. December 1977. Freedom in Danger: The External and Internal Threats. *International Lawyer* 11: 193–206.

1169. Chalker, L. January 1994. Development and Democracy: What Should the Commonwealth be Doing? *Round Table* 329: 23–26.

1170. Chalmers, D. A., and C. H. Robinson. March 1982. Why Power Contenders

Choose Liberalization: Perspectives from South America. *International Studies Quarterly* 26 (1): 3–36.

1171. Chamarik, S. March 1985. *See* Neuhaus, R. J. (March 1985).

1172. Chamberlin, C., and D. Sawada. 1987. Democracy, Community, Responsibility and Influence in Teacher Education. *Journal of Education for Teaching* 13 (1): 61–76.

1173. Chambers, R. L. December 1977. The Executive Power: A Preliminary Study of the Concept and of the Efficacy of Presidential Powers. *Presidential Studies Quarterly* 7 (1): 21–37.

1174. Chambers, R. L. March 1980. Guidelines for Choosing a President. *Presidential Studies Quarterly* 10 (2): 156–162.

1175. Champaud, J. (ed.). October 1992. Le Mali: La Transition. *Politique Africaine* 2–107. 9 articles; English summaries 177–180.

1176. Champin, C. August 1993. Malawi: Premiere Victoire Electorale. *Jeune Afrique Economie* 74–5.

1177. Chan, S. (Stephen). April 1992. Democracy in Southern Africa: The 1990 Elections in Zimbabwe and 1991 Elections in Zambia. *Round Table* 322: 183–201.

1178. Chan, S. (Steve). December 1984. Mirror, Mirror on the Wall . . . Are the Freer Countries More Pacific? *Journal of Conflict Resolution* 28 (4): 617–648.

1179. Chan, S. (Steve). June 1992. National Security in the Asia-Pacific: Linkages among Growth, Democracy and Peace. *Contemporary Southeast Asia* 14: 13–32.

1180. Chan, S. (Steve). 1993. Democracy and War: Some Thoughts on Future Research Agenda. *International Interactions* 18 (3): 205–213.

1181. Chan, S. (Steve), and C. Clark. December 1992. The Price of Economic Success: South Korea and Taiwan Sacrifice Political Development. *Harvard International Review* 15 (2): 24–26.

1182. Chandhoke, N. January 1983. The Prospects for Liberal Democracy in Zimbabwe. *Indian Political Science Review* 17 (1): 52–64.

1183. Chandhoke, N. October 8, 1994. Why Should People Have Rights? *Economic and Political Weekly* 29 (41): 2697–2699.

1184. Chaney, D. 1986. *See* Pickering, M. (1986).

1185. Chang, C. 1979. Democracy and Human Rights: The Fifth Modernization. *Issues and Studies* 15 (5): 1–3.

1186. Chang, C. P. 1989. The Rise of the Democracy Movement among Overseas Chinese. *Issues and Studies* 25 (9): 4–6.

1187. Chang, D. W. May 1989. Political Development in Taiwan: The Sun Yat-Sen Model for National Reconstruction. *Issues and Studies* 25 (5): 11–32.

1188. Chang, D. W. 1990. Confucianism, Democracy, and Communism: The Chinese Example in Search of a New Political Typology for Systemic Integration. *Issues and Studies* 26 (11): 53–74.

1189. Chang, P. January 1983. Taiwan in 1982: Diplomatic Setback Abroad and Demands for Reforms at Home. *Asian Survey* 23 (1): 38–46.

1190. Chang, P. January 1992. China's Relations with Hong Kong and Taiwan. *Annals of the American Academy of Political and Social Science* (519): 127–139.

1191. Chang, T. July 1994. Democratization and Constitutional Reform in Taiwan [Republic of China].* *Etudes et Documents (Taipei)* 27–33.

1192. Chao, C. November 1990. Transition from Authoritarian Rule: Is Eastern Europe's Today Mainland China's Tomorrow? *Issues and Studies* 26 (11): 33–52.

1193. Chao, H. Y. 1979. Chinese Communist Socialist Democracy and the Socialist Legal System: Analysis. *Issues and Studies* 15 (10): 58–74.

1194. Chao, L., and R. H. Myers. March 1994. The First Chinese Democracy: Political Development of the Republic of China on Taiwan, 1986–1994. *Asian Survey* 34 (3): 213–230.

1195. Chaoul, M. 1981. Kuwait and Bahrein, or the Ambiguity of the Democratic Experience in the Present Arab Societies.* *L'Afrique et l'Asie Modernes* 128: 20–42.

1196. Chapin, C. 1994. Malawi: The End of a Reign.* *L'Afrique* 259–269.

1197. Chapman, D. August 10, 1990. Can Democracy Survive in the Philippines? *Editorial Research Reports* 2 (6): 446–459.

1198. Charles, D. 1989. Keeping Semiconductors Safe for Democracy. *Bulletin of the Atomic Scientists* 45 (9): 8–10.

1199. Charlick, R. B. 1992. Corruption in [Africa's] Political Transition: A Governance Perspective. *Corruption and Reform* 7 (3): 177–187.

1200. Charnock, D. March 1994. Explaining Why the Pendulum Can Be Improved: A Comment on the Adjusted Electoral Pendulum. *Electoral Studies* 13 (1): 77–79.

1201. Charoenmuang, T. December 1988. General Prem's Eight-Year Premiership and Its Implications for the Thai Democracy. *Asian Survey* 16 (6): 501–514.

1202. Chatterji, R. April 23, 1988. Democracy and the Opposition in India. *Economic and Political Weekly* 23 (17): 843–847.

1203. Chaudhry, K. A., and P. McDonough. October 1983. State, Society, and Sin: The Political Beliefs of University Students in Pakistan. *Economic Development and Cultural Change* 32 (1): 11–44.

1204. Chaudhuri, M. D. 1985. On the Political Structure of a Liberal Democracy. *Economic and Political Weekly* 20 (22): 958–959.

1205. Chauvin, M. P. March 1993. Towards the Establishment of Constitutionalism in Russia. *Indiana International & Comparative Law Review* 3: 271–290.

1206. Chavkin, S. 1986. Uruguay under Civilian Rule: The Rough Road Back to Democracy. *Nation* 242 (7): 199–202.

1207. Chazan, N. November 1989. Planning Democracy in Africa: A Comparative Perspective on Nigeria and Ghana. *Policy Sciences* 22 (3–4): 325–357.

1208. Chazan, N. March 1992. Africa's Democratic Challenge. *World Policy Journal* 9 (2): 279–307.

1209. Chebali, H. E. December 1980. The Absence of Consociationalism in Sri Lanka. *Plural Societies* 11 (4): 55–65.

1210. Chee, C. H. January 1994. Democracy, Human Rights, and Social Justice as Key Factors in Balanced Development. *Round Table* 329: 27–32.

1211. Cheek, H. L. , Jr. March 1991. A Note on the Platonic and Aristotelian Critique of Democratic Man. *International Social Science Review* 66 (2): 59–63.

1212. Cheibub, Z. B. 1993. *See* Reis, E. P. (1993).

1213. Chemerinsky, E. 1988. Protecting the Democratic Process: Voter Standing to Challenge Abuses of Incumbency. *Ohio State Law Journal* 49: 773–798.

1214. Chen, Y. F. 1980. Rural Elections in Wartime Central China: Democratization of Sub-Bureaucracy. *Modern China* 6 (3): 267–310.

1215. Cheng, J. Y. S. June 1989. The Democracy Movement in Hong Kong. *International Affairs (London)* 65 (3): 443–462.

1216. Cheng, J. Y. S. November 1989. Political Modernization in Hong Kong. *Journal of Commonwealth and Comparative Politics* 27 (3): 294–320.

1217. Cheng, J. Y. S. January 1990. Prospects for Democracy in Hong Kong after the Beijing Massacre. *Australian Journal of Chinese Affairs* 23: 161–185.

1218. Cheng, T. July 1989. Democratizing the Quasi-Leninist Regime in Taiwan. *World Politics* 41 (4): 471–499.

1219. Cheng, T. March 1993. Democracy and Taiwan–Mainland China Ties: A Critique of Three Dominant Views. *Journal of Northeast Asian Studies* 12 (1): 72–89.

1220. Cheng, T., and S. Haggard. March 1990. Taiwan in Transition. *Journal of Democracy* 1 (2): 62–74.

1221. Cheng, T., and L. B. Krause. June 1991. Democracy and Development: With Special Attention to Korea. *Journal of Northeast Asian Studies* 10 (2): 3–25.

1222. Chenoweth, E. November 1988. Poland Today: Democracy Aborning. *Freedom at Issue* 105: 10–13.

1223. Chenu, G. January 1991. Democracy in Africa.* *Revue Juridique et Politique, Independance et Cooperation* 45 (1): 6–9.

1224. Cheresky, I. July 1980. Democracy and Authoritarianism in Dependent Capitalisms: The Argentina and Brazil Cases.* *Revista Mexicana de Sociologia* 42 (3): 1071–1103.

1225. Cheresky, I. June 1988. Argentina: A Blackmailed Democracy. *Telos* 75: 148–160.

1226. Cherne, L. March 1979. Ideology and the Balance of Power. *Annals of the American Academy of Political and Social Science* 442: 46–56.

1227. Cheru, F. March 1988. The Garden of Eden Revisited: Why Has African Development Gone Wrong? *Food Monitor* 10–12.

1228. Chervonnaya, S. A. September 1992. Critical Choices of Russia's Democracy. *William and Mary Bill of Rights Journal* 1 (2): 227–244.

1229. Cheung, A. B. L. January 1992. Democracy and the Democratic Movement in Hong Kong: Origin and Prospects. *Politics, Administration, and Change* 18: 19–38.

1230. Chevalier, J. September 1984. Public Service from Myth to Reality. *Projet* 188: 879–896.

1231. Chew, M. November 1994. Human Rights in Singapore: Perceptions and Problems. *Asian Survey* 34 (11): 933–948.

1232. Chey, M. July 1989. *See* Shin, D. C. (July 1989).

1233. Chhabra, H. S. 1992. Democratic South Africa: Prospects. *Africa Quarterly* 32 (1–4): 91–106.

1234. Chhachhi, A., R. A. Palat, and P. Kurian. 1982. Movement towards Workers' Democracy: Solidarity in Poland. *Economic and Political Weekly* 17 (26): 1073–1079.

1235. Chicoine, D. L. January 1993. *See* Deller, S. C. (January 1993).

1236. Chicoine, D. L., M. Walzer, and S. C. Deller. 1989. Representative vs. Direct Democracy and Government Spending in a Median Voter Model. *Public Finance* 44 (2): 225–236.

1237. Chikulo, B. C. June 1993. End of an Era: An Analysis of the 1991 Zambian Presidential and Parliamentary Elections. *Politikon* 20 (1): 87–104.

1238. Chilcote, R. H. February 1984. Toward the Democratic Opening in Latin America: The Case of Brazil. *Monthly Review* 35: 15–24.

1239. Chilton, P. March 1994. Mechanics of Change: Social Movements, Transnational Coalitions, and the Transformation

Processes in Eastern Europe. *Democratization* 1 (1): 151–181.

1240. Chin, J. October 1994. The Sabah Elections in 1994: End of Kadazan Unity. *Asian Survey* 34 (10): 904–915.

1241. Chinchilla, N. S. 1991. Marxism, Feminism, and the Struggle for Democracy in Latin America. *Gender & Society* 5 (3): 291–310.

1242. Ching, F. September 1989. Red Star over Hong Kong. *World Policy Journal* 6 (5): 657–665.

1243. Chinje, E. December 1993. The Media in Emerging African Democracies: Power, Politics, and the Role of the Press. *Fletcher Forum of World Affairs* 17: 49–65.

1244. Chinweizu. July 1976. Education and Democracy in Industrial America: Bicentennial Perspective. *Black Scholar* 7 (10): 7–22.

1245. Chiou, C. L. January 1993. The 1990 National Affairs Conference and the Future of Democracy in Taiwan. *Bulletin of Concerned Asian Scholars* 25 (1): 17–32.

1246. Chiriboga, M. January 1992. Movimiento Campesino e Indigena y Participacion Politica en Ecuador: La Construccion de Identidades en una Sociedad Heterogenea. *Sintesis* 17: 227–253.

1247. Chiriyankandath, J. March 1992. Democracy under the Raj: Elections and Separate Representation in British India. *Journal of Commonwealth and Comparative Politics* 30 (1): 39–63.

1248. Chitrit, A. 1994. *See* Lajoie, A. (1994).

1249. Chiu, H. December 1990. The National Affairs Conference and Constitutional Reform in the Republic of China on Taiwan. *Issues and Studies* 26 (12): 12–22.

1250. Chiu, H. 1993. Hong Kong's Transition to 1997: Background, Problems and Prospects. *Occasional Papers: Reprints Series in Contemporary Asia* 5: 1–24.

1251. Chiu, H. January 1993. Constitutional Development and Reform in the Republic of China on Taiwan. *Issues and Studies* 29 (1): 1–38.

1252. Chladek, T. October 25, 1987. The Western Democracies and Their Struggle against International Terrorism.* *Europa Archiv: Zeitschrift für Internationale Politik* 42 (20): 577–586.

1253. Choi, Y. H. March 1978. Failure of Democracy in Legislative Processes: The Case of South Korea. *World Affairs* 140 (4): 331–340.

1254. Chong, D., H. McClosky, and J. Zaller. October 1983. Patterns of Support for Democratic and Capitalist Values in the United States. *British Journal of Political Science* 13 (4): 401–440.

1255. Choper, J. H. April 1974. Supreme Court and the Political Branches: Democratic Theory and Practice. *University of Pennsylvania Law Review* 122: 810–858.

1256. Choper, J. H. December 1993. Thoughts on the Federalist Vision of Representative Democracy as Viewed at the End of the 20th Century: How Have We Used the Legacy of the Federalist Papers. *Harvard Journal of Law and Public Policy* 16 (1): 35–41.

1257. Chorney, H., and P. Hansen. 1985. Neo-Conservatism, Social Democracy and Province Building: The Experience of Manitoba. *Canadian Review of Sociology and Anthropology* 22 (1): 1–29.

1258. Chou, Y., and A. J. Nathan. March 1987. Democratizing Transition in Taiwan. *Asian Survey* 27 (3): 277–299.

1259. Choudhury, D. 1987. Challenges to Democracy in Bangladesh. *Regional Studies* 5 (4): 23–32.

1260. Choza, J. January 1994. El Problema de la Aceptacion del Extranjero.* *Revista de Estudios Politicos* 83: 191–200.

1261. Chretien, J. P. March 1993. Rwanda and France: Democracy and Ethnicity in Africa. *Esprit* 3–4: 190–195.

1262. Christensen, S. R. February 1990. Thailand in 1989: Consensus at Bay. *Asian Survey* 30 (2): 178–186.

1263. Christensen, T. 1979. Organizational Leadership: External Effectiveness and Internal Democracy in a Particular Case.* *Tidsskrift für Samfunnsforskning* 20 (4): 335–358.

1264. Christiano, T. October 1993. *See* Fishkin, J. (October 1993).

1265. Christie, D. 1984. Recent Calls for Economic Democracy. *Ethics* 95 (1): 112–128.

1266. Christison, K. September 1985. Israel and the Double Standard. *American-Arab Affairs* 7: 18–25.

1267. Chua, B. H. 1979. Democracy as Textual Accomplishment. *Sociological Quarterly* 20 (4): 541–549.

1268. Chua, B. H. July 1993. Singapore: Democracy, Ethnicity, and Development. *Ethnic Studies Report* 11 (2): 143–161.

1269. Chua, B. H. September 1993. Looking for Democratization in Post-Soeharto Indonesia. *Contemporary Southeast Asia* 15 (2): 131–160.

1270. Chuang, R. Y. October 1989. The Sino-British Joint Declaration on Hong Kong and the Direct Election Controversy. *Revue de Droit International de Sciences Diplomatiques et Politiques* 67 (4): 239–253.

1271. Chubin, D. E. 1985. Open Science and Closed Science: Trade-Offs in a Democracy. *Science Technology and Human Values* (51): 73–81.

1272. Chung, E. S. February 1989. Transition to Democracy in South Korea. *Asian Profile* 17 (1): 25–38.

1273. Chung, J. December 1976. *See* Pae, S. M. (December 1976).

1274. Chung, S. W. 1994. Local and Regional Council Elections in 1991: Features and Political Implications. *Korean Studies* 18: 123–138.

1275. Churchill, M. March 1988. Parliaments, Congresses, and the Nurturing of Democracy. *Washington Quarterly* 11 (2): 15–26.

1276. Cifford, W. June 1983. Policing a Democracy. *Police Studies* 6: 3–21.

1277. Cima, R. J. January 1990. Vietnam in 1989: Initiating the Post-Cambodian Period. *Asian Survey* 30 (1): 88–95.

1278. Cintra, A. O., and L. A. Gama de Andrade. September 1985. Development, Equality and Democracy: The Prospects for Political Transition in Brazil.* *Cadernos de Departamento de Ciencia Politica* 7: 37–56.

1279. Cirtautas, A. M., and E. Mokrzycki. December 1993. The Articulation and Institutionalization of Democracy in Poland. *Social Research* 60 (4): 787–820.

1280. Cisneros, H. G. January 1988. Our Economic Engines Are Threatened. *National Civic Review* 77 (1): 8–21.

1281. Cisneros, H. G. December 1991. Revitalizing Citizen Activism and Participatory Democracy. *National Civic Review* 80 (1): 5–15.

1282. Cisneros, H. G., and J. Parr. September 1990. Reinvigorating Democratic Values: Challenge and Necessity. *National Civic Review* 79 (5): 408–413.

1283. Claeys, G. 1982. Paternalism and Democracy in the Politics of Robert Owen. *International Review of Social History* 27 (2): 161–207.

1284. Claeys, G. April 1985. "The Lion and the Unicorn," Patriotism, and Orwell's Politics. *Review of Politics* 47 (2): 186–211.

1285. Claeys, G. February 1987. Justice, Independence and Industrial Democracy: The Development of John Stuart Mills'

Views on Socialism. *Journal of Politics* 49 (1): 122–147.

1286. Clapham, C. 1993. Democratization in Africa: Obstacles and Prospects. *Third World Quarterly* 14 (3): 423–438.

1287. Clapham, C. 1993. *See* Qadir, S. (1993).

1288. Clark, B. S. 1992. Political Economy, Democracy and Eastern Europe. *International Journal of Social Economics* 19 (7–9): 259–272.

1289. Clark, C. December 1992. *See* Chan, S. (Steve). (December 1992).

1290. Clark, D. February 1979. Invention and Contention in the Quaker City. *Journal of Urban History* 5 (2): 265–271.

1291. Clark, R. C. December 1990. Presidential Emergency Powers: The Contribution of Lindsay Rogers. *Presidential Studies Quarterly* 20 (1): 13–30.

1292. Clark, T. D. 1989. State Society Relations in the Soviet Union: A Model of "Demokratizatsiia." *Crossroads* 28: 63–74.

1293. Clark, T. N. May 1993. Local Democracy and Innovation in Eastern Europe. *Environment and Planning C: Government and Planning* 11 (2): 171–198.

1294. Clark, W. D., and H. F. Houser. September 1988. Codetermination: Is There a Better Way? *Tennessee Business and Economic Review* 15: 13–16.

1295. Clarke, C. J., and V. L. Pavlov. September 1985. The Degree of Bureaucratization at the Societal Level and Political Democracy: Cross National Evidence. *Journal of Political and Military Sociology* 13 (2): 265–282.

1296. Clarke, E. H. March 1977. Some Aspects of the Demand-Revealing Process. *Public Choice* 29 (2): 37–50.

1297. Clarke, H. D. June 1984. *See* Le Duc, L. (June 1984).

1298. Clarke, H. D. September 1994. *See* Kornberg, A. (September 1994).

1299. Clarke, H. D., N. Dutt, and A. Kornberg. November 1993. The Political Economy of Attitudes toward Polity and Society in Western European Democracies. *Journal of Politics* 55 (4): 998–1021.

1300. Clarke, H. D., and A. Kornberg. November 1994. The Politics and Economics of Constitutional Choice: Voting in Canada's 1992 National Referendum. *Journal of Politics* 56 (4): 940–962.

1301. Clarke, L. 1989. Capitalism Is Richer, Democracy Is Safer. *Society* 27 (1): 17–18.

1302. Claus, J. F. November 1981. *See* Hamilton, S. F. (November 1981).

1303. Clausen, A. R., S. Holmberg, and L. De Haven-Smith. May 1983. Contextual Factors in the Accuracy of Leader Perceptions of Constituents' Views. *Journal of Politics* 45 (2): 449–472.

1304. Cleary, R. E. 1989. Dialog, Negotiation, and the Advancement of Democracy: Reflections on Minnowbrook. *Public Administration Review* 49 (2): 226–227.

1305. Cleary, R. E. 1989. Reconciling Public Administration and Democracy: The Role of the Responsible Administrator: Response. *Public Administration Review* 49 (2): 186.

1306. Cleary, R. E. March 1989. *See* Mayer, R. T. (March 1989).

1307. Cleghorn, J. S. 1987. Can Workplace Democracy Transform Capitalist Society: Durkheim and Burawoy Compared. *Sociological Inquiry* 57 (3): 304–315.

1308. Clem, A. L., and W. O. Faber. May 1979. Manipulated Democracy: The Multi-Member District. *National Civic Review* 68 (5): 235–243.

1309. Clemmen, R. O. June 1980. *See* Jorgenson, J. G. (June 1980).

1310. Cline, M., and S. Fisher. July 8, 1994. Czech Republic and Slovakia: Views on Politics and the Economy. *RFE/RL Research Report* 3: 33–39.

1311. Clingermayer, J. C. December 1994. Electoral Representation, Zoning Politics, and the Exclusion of Group Homes. *Political Research Quarterly* 47 (4): 969–983.

1312. Clinton, D. December 1988. Tocqueville's Challenge. *Washington Quarterly* 11 (1): 173–189.

1313. Clinton, D. June 1993. Tocqueville on Democracy, Obligation, and the International System. *Review of International Studies* 19 (3): 227–243.

1314. Clinton, R. L. May 1994. Game Theory, Legal History, and the Origins of Judicial Review: A Revisionist Analysis of *Marbury vs. Madison*. *American Journal of Political Science* 38 (2): 285–302.

1315. Clinton, R. L. December 1994. Judicial Review, Nationalism, and the Commerce Clause: Contrasting Antebellum and Postbellum Supreme Court Decision Making. *Political Research Quarterly* 47 (4): 857–876.

1316. Clinton, W. D., and D. G. Lang. December 1993. What Makes a Successful Presidential Transition? The Case of Foreign Affairs. *Presidential Studies Quarterly* 23 (1): 41–56.

1317. Clive, N. 1990. The Dilemma of Democracy in Greece. *Government and Opposition* 25 (1): 115–122.

1318. Clor, H. M. March 1994. Chief Justice Rehnquist and the Balances of Constitutional Democracy. *Rutgers Law Journal* 25: 557–576.

1319. Close, D. March 1991. Central American Elections 1989–1990: Costa Rica, El Salvador, Honduras, Nicaragua, Panama. *Electoral Studies* 10: 60–76.

1320. Close, D. H. 1977. Collapse of Resistance to Democracy: Conservatives, Adult Suffrage, and Second Chamber Reform, 1911–1928. *Historical Journal* 20 (4): 893–918.

1321. Cloward, R. A. June 1990. *See* Bennett, S. E. (June 1990).

1322. Clubb, O. E. September 1980. China and the "Industrial Democracies." *Current History* 79 (458): 5–8, 42–43.

1323. Clune, W. H. 1985. Unreasonableness and Alienation in the Continuing Relationships of Welfare State Bureaucracy: From Regulatory Complexity to Economic Democracy. *Wisconsin Law Review* (3): 707–740.

1324. Cmiel, K. December 1992. A Broad, Fluid Language of Democracy: Discovering the American Idiom. *Journal of American History* 79 (3): 913–936.

1325. Coates, J. F. 1990. Democracy in America: A Darkening Future. *Technological Forecasting and Social Change* 38 (1): 101–106.

1326. Coates, K. November 1976. Industrial Democracy: New Perspectives on the British Labor Movement.* *Argument* 18: 989–995.

1327. Coats, A. W. June 1988. Economists in Government: A Historical and Comparative Perspective. *Economic Papers (Australia)* 7: 89–102.

1328. Cochran, A. B., and C. V. Scott. March 1992. Class, State, and Popular Organizations in Mozambique and Nicaragua. *Latin American Perspectives* 19 (2): 105–124.

1329. Cockcroft, J. D. June 1990. In Latin America: The New Politics Challenge. *New Politics* 3 (1): 16–31.

1330. Cogniot, G. 1976. Democracy and Education.* *Pensée* (186): 104–111.

1331. Cohen, D. K. May 1984. The American Common School: A Divided Vision. *Education and Urban Society* 16 (3): 253–261.

1332. Cohen, E., and N. Ben Yehuda. September 1987. Countercultural Movements and Totalitarian Democracy. *Sociological Inquiry* 57 (4): 372–393.

1333. Cohen, H. J. June 1991. Africa: Democracy and U.S. Policy. *Mediterranean Quarterly* 2 (3): 51–55.

1334. Cohen, J. June 1986. Reflections on Rousseau: Autonomy and Democracy. *Philosophy and Public Affairs* 15 (3): 275–297.

1335. Cohen, J. October 1986. An Epistemic Conception of Democracy. *Ethics* 97 (1): 26–38.

1336. Cohen, J. 1989. The Economic Basis of Deliberative Democracy. *Social Philosophy and Policy* 6 (2): 25–50.

1337. Cohen, J. 1994. Critical Viewing and Participatory Democracy. *Journal of Communication* 44 (4): 98–113.

1338. Cohen, J., and J. Rogers. December 1992. Secondary Associations and Democratic Governance. *Politics & Society* 20 (4): 393–472. Introduction pp. 391–392.

1339. Cohen, J., and J. Rogers. June 1993. Associations and Democracy. *Social Philosophy and Policy* 10 (2): 282–312.

1340. Cohen, J. L. December 1985. Strategy or Identity: New Theoretical Paradigms and Contemporary Social Movements. *Social Research* 52 (4): 663–716.

1341. Cohen, L. J. May 1980. Politics as an Avocation: Legislative Professionalization and Participation in Yugoslavia. *Legislative Studies Quarterly* 5 (2): 175–209.

1342. Cohen, M. J. September 1987. One China or Two: Facing Up to the Taiwan Question. *World Policy Journal* 4 (4): 621–649.

1343. Cohen, P. July 1994. Sweden: The Model That Never Was. *Monthly Review* 46: 41–59.

1344. Cohen, S. 1979. Does Public Employee Unionism Diminish Democracy? *Industrial and Labor Relations Review* 32 (2): 189–195.

1345. Cohen, S. December 1992. *See* Allison, G. T. (December 1992).

1346. Cohen, S. R. January 1983. From Industrial Democracy to Professional Adjustment: The Development of Industrial Sociology in the United States, 1900–1955. *Theory and Society* 12 (1): 47–67.

1347. Cohen, Y. October 1987. Democracy from Above: The Political Origins of Military Dictatorship in Brazil. *World Politics* 40 (1): 30–54.

1348. Cohen-Almagor, R. February 1994. Disqualification of Lists in Israel (1948–1984): Retrospect and Appraisal. *Law and Philosophy* 13: 43–95.

1349. Colaco Antunes, L. F. March 1985. Federalism and Municipalism in the Portuguese Political Thought during the 19th Century. *Il Politico* 50 (1): 83–100.

1350. Colbjornsen, T. 1980. Union Activities and Participatory Democracy.* *Tidsskrift for Samfunnsforskning* 21 (1): 25–50.

1351. Cole, J. R. I. February 1992. Iranian Millenarianism and Democratic Thought in the 19th Century. *International Journal of Middle East Studies* 24 (1): 1–26.

1352. Coleman, J. March 1992. Democracy in Permanently Divided Systems. *American Behavioral Scientist* 35 (4–5): 363–374.

1353. Coleman, J., and J. Ferejohn. October 1986. Democracy and Social Choice. *Ethics* 97 (1): 6–25.

1354. Coleman, W. D. April 1985. *See* Atkinson, M. M. (April 1985).

1355. Collier, D., and D. L. Norden. January 1992. Strategic Choice Models of Political Change in Latin America.* *Comparative Politics* 24 (2): 229–243.

1356. Collins, W. P. 1986. Does Democracy Inevitably Imply Hierarchy? *Quality & Quantity* 20 (4): 405–417.

1357. Colman, W. March 1982. Painful Adjustments: Long Overdue. *National Civic Review* 71 (3): 126–135.

1358. Colombo, A. March 1985. Nitti and the Concept of Democracy.* *Il Politico* 50 (1): 23–39.

1359. Colomer, J. M. July 1987. The Theory of Democracy and Utilitarianism.* *Revista de Estudios Politicos* 57: 7–30.

1360. Colomer, J. M. December 1991. Transitions by Agreement: Modeling the Spanish Way. *American Political Science Review* 85 (4): 1283–1302.

1361. Colomer, J. M., and M. Pascual. September 1994. The Polish Games of Transition. *Communist and Post-Communist Studies* 27 (3): 275–294.

1362. Colton, T. December 1992. *See* Allison, G. T. (December 1992).

1363. Colton, T. J. October 1990. The Politics of Democratization: The Moscow Election of 1990. *Soviet Economy* 6 (4): 285–344.

1364. Combellas, R. 1990. The Democracy in Venezuela.* *Politica (Caracas)* 14: 197–217.

1365. Comiskey, M. October 1993. Electoral Competition and the Growth of Public Spending in 13 Industrial Democracies, 1950–1983. *Comparative Political Studies* 26 (3): 350–374.

1366. Commeau-Rufin, I. 1990. USSR: What Kind of Democracy?* *Pouvoirs* 52: 87–99.

1367. Committee for the Study of the American Electorate. March 1990. Creating the Opportunity: Voting and the Crisis of Democracy. *Policy Studies Review* 9 (3): 583–601.

1368. Conaghan, C. M. March 1989. Ecuador Swings toward Social Democracy. *Current History* 88 (536): 137–141, 154.

1369. Conaghan, C. M. 1990. Business and the "Boys": The Politics of Neoliberalism in the Central Andes. *Latin American Research Review* 25 (2): 3–30.

1370. Conaghan, C. M., and R. Espinal. October 1990. Unlikely Transitions to Uncertain Regimes? Democracy without Compromise in the Dominican Republic and Ecuador. *Journal of Latin American Studies* 22: 553–574.

1371. Conca, K. March 1992. Technology, the Military and Democracy in Brazil. *Journal of Interamerican Studies and World Affairs* 34 (1): 141–177.

1372. Condit, C. M. 1987. Democracy and Civil Rights: The Universalizing Influence of Public Argumentation. *Communication Monographs* 54 (1): 1–18.

1373. Confalonieri, M. A. April 1989. Political Generations in the New Democracies of Southern Europe.* *Biblioteca della Liberta* 105: 111–149.

1374. Congdon, L. June 1980. Hungary in Crisis: Communism and the Intellectuals, 1918. *East European Quarterly* 14 (2): 155–169.

1375. Congdon, T. 1975. Economics of Industrial Democracy. *New Society* 34 (682): 255–257.

1376. Conk, M. A. December 1981. Immigrant Workers in the City, 1870–1930: Agents of Growth or Threats to Democracy. *Social Science Quarterly* 62 (4): 704–720.

1377. Conlon, D. E. June 1991. *See* Murnighan, J. K. (June 1991).

1378. Connolly, J. 1987. Purging the Teamsters: Why Not Try Union Democracy. *Nation* 245 (6): 192.

1379. Connolly, W. E. December 1991. Democracy and Territoriality. *Millennium* 20 (3).

1380. Connors, D. L., and M. E. High. June 1986. Public Trust Doctrine and Private Rights: The Democratization of Trust Resources by the Judicial System Leads to Uncertainty about Owners' Settled Expectations. *Real Estate Review* 16: 51–58.

1381. Conradt, D. P. December 1982. The End of an Era in West Germany. *Current History* 81 (479): 405–408, 438.

1382. Constable, P. March 1989. *See* Valenzuela, A. (March 1989).

1383. Constable, P. March 1994. Haiti: A Nation in Despair, Λ Policy Adrift. *Current History* 93: 108–114+.

1384. Constable, P., and A. Valenzuela. December 1989. Chile's Return to Democracy. *Foreign Affairs* 68 (5): 169–186.

1385. Constable, P., and A. Valenzuela. March 1990 [Chile after Pinochet]: Democracy Restored. *Journal of Democracy* 1 (2): 3–12.

1386. Conte, R. October 1994. *See* Castelfranci, C. (October 1994).

1387. Contee, C. E. June 1987. *See* Sewell, J. W. (June 1987).

1388. Conway, M. M. June 1977. Participatory Democracy and the Democratic Party in the House of Representatives: Implications for Policy Making. *Policy Studies Journal* 5 (4): 459–464.

1389. Cook, R. C. October 1994. Four Years of the Ghana District Assemblies in Operation: Decentralization, Democratization, and Administrative Performance. *Public Administration and Development* 14 (4): 339–364.

1390. Cook, S. D. August 1976. Democracy and Tyranny in America: The Radical Paradox of the Bicentennial and Blacks in the American Political System. *Journal of Politics* 38 (3): 276–294.

·1391. Cook, T. E. February 1975. Rousseau: Education and Politics. *Journal of Politics* 37 (1): 108–128.

1392. Cooke, P., and G. Rees. December 1981. The Industrial Restructuring of South Wales: The Career of a State-Managed Region. *Policy Studies Journal* 10 (2): 284–296.

1393. Cooly, M. 1986. Socially Useful Design: A Form of Anticipatory Democracy. *Economic and Industrial Democracy* 7 (4): 553–559.

1394. Coombe, R. J. August 1993. Tactics of Appropriation and the Politics of Recognition in Late Modern Democracies. *Political Theory* 21 (3): 411–433.

1395. Cooper, J. F. June 1988. Ending Martial Law in Taiwan: Implications and Prospects. *Journal of Northeast Asian Studies* 7 (2): 3–19.

1396. Cooper, J. W. September 1982. The Outlines of Political Theology in the Protestant Reformation. *Teaching Political Science* 10 (1): 43–51.

1397. Cooper, M. April 1993. Information in the Age of Democracy. *Bulletin of the American Society for Information Science* 19 (4): 7.

1398. Cooper, M. H. June 17, 1983. Employee Ownership. *Editorial Research Reports* 455–472.

1399. Cooper, P. J. March 1994. *United States vs. Alvarez-Machain* [112 S. Ct. 2188 (1992)]: Douglas Was Right—The Bill of Rights Is Not Enough. *Chicano-Latino Law Review* 15: 38–73.

1400. Cooper, R. M. 1985. Saccharin: Of Risk and Democracy. *Food and Drug Cosmetic Law Journal* 40 (1): 34–65.

1401. Cooper, T. L., and T. L. Lui. May 1990. Democracy and the Administrative State: The Case of Hong Kong. *Public Administration Review* 50 (3): 332–344.

1402. Coppedge, M. October 1992. Venezuela's Democracy. *Journal of Democracy* 3 (4): 32–44.

1403. Coppedge, M. April 1993. Parties and Society in Mexico and Venezuela: Why Competition Matters. *Comparative Politics* 25 (3): 253–274.

1404. Coppedge, M. June 1994. Prospects for Democratic Governability in Venezuela. *Journal of Interamerican Studies and World Affairs* 36 (2): 39–63.

1405. Coppedge, M., and W. H. Reinicke. March 1990. Measuring Polyarchy. *Studies in Comparative International Development* 25 (1): 51–72.

1406. Copper, J. F. October 1981. Taiwan's Recent Election: Progress toward a Democratic System. *Asian Survey* 21 (10): 1029–1039.

1407. Copper, J. F. April 1986. Taiwan: New Challenges to Development. *Current History* 85 (510): 168–171, 183–184.

1408. Copper, J. F. January 1987. Taiwan in 1986: Back on Top Again. *Asian Survey* 27 (1): 81–91.

1409. Copper, J. F. April 1989. Taiwan: A Nation in Transition. *Current History* 88 (537): 172–176, 198–199.

1410. Copper, J. F. March 1992. Totalitarianism, Authoritarianism, and the Pursuit of Democracy: Lessons from Taiwan and China. *Midsouth Political Science Journal* 13: 51–64.

1411. Coquery-Vidrovitch, C. June 1992. History and Historiography of Politics in Africa: The Need for a Critical Re-reading Regarding Democracy.* *Politique Africaine* 46: 31–40.

1412. Coraggio, J. L. 1984. Revolution and Democracy in Nicaragua.* *Estudios Sociales Centroamericanos* 13 (38): 83–113.

1413. Coraggio, J. L., and G. Irvin. March 1985. Revolution and Democracy in Nicaragua. *Latin American Perspectives* 12 (2): 23–37.

1414. Cordes, H., and H. H. Hartwich. 1987. State Neutrality and Labor Struggle in Welfare State Democracy. *Gegenwartskunde: Gesellschaft, Staat, Erziehung* 36 (1): 107–141.

1415. Cordova, A. March 1991. Modernization and Democracy.* *Revista Mexicana de Sociologia* 53 (1): 261–281.

1416. Corkill, D. October 1993. The Political System and the Consolidation of Democracy in Portugal. *Parliamentary Affairs* 46 (4): 517–533.

1417. Corn, D. 1989. David vs. Goliath: Struggling for Union Democracy. *Nation* 248 (2): 48+.

1418. Cornelius, W. A. June 1994. Mexico Delayed Democratization. *Foreign Policy* (95): 53–71.

1419. Cornell, A., and K. Roberts. November 1990. Democracy, Counterinsurgency, and Human Rights: The Case of Peru. *Human Rights Quarterly* 12 (4): 529–553.

1420. Cornell, D. L. 1991. Gender Hierarchy, Equality, and the Possibility of Democracy. *American Imago* 48 (2): 247–263.

1421. Coronel, S. S. September 1991. Dateline Philippines: The Lost Revolution. *Foreign Policy* (84): 166–185.

1422. Coronil, F., and J. Skurski. April 1991. Dismembering and Remembering the Nation: The Semantics of Political Violence in Venezuela. *Comparative Studies in Society and History* 33 (2): 288–337.

1423. Corradi, J. 1984. Two Cheers (and a Prayer) for Argentine Democracy. *Dissent* 31 (2): 203–206.

1424. Corradi, J. June 1988. A Difficult Transition to Democracy [in Argentina]. *Telos* 75: 141–147.

1425. Correa, J. S. 1992. Dealing with Past Human Rights Violations: The Chilean Case after Dictatorship. *Notre Dame Law Review* 67: 1455–1485.

1426. Corso, G. 1979. Partecipazione e Democrazia: Un Rapporto Problematico. *Rivista di Servizio Sociale* 19 (2): 3–13.

1427. Cortazar, R. January 1986. *See* Arellano, J. P. (January 1986).

1428. Cortazar, R. December 1987. La No Transicion a la Democracia en Chile y el Plebiscito de 1988. *Coleccion Estudios* 14: 111–128.

1429. Cortazar, R. December 1988. *See* Campero, G. (December 1988).

1430. Cortazar, R., and R. Downey. 1977. Effectos Redistributivos de la Reforma Agraria. *Trimestre Economico* 44 (3): 685–713.

1431. Cortright, D. 1976. Can Democracy Stand It. *Nation* 223 (12): 357–361.

1432. Cortright, D. August 1977. Unions in the Military? Pro and Con: Unions and Democracy. *Military Review* 57 (8): 35–44.

1433. Cotterrell, R. 1988. Feasible Regulation for Democracy and Social Justice. *Journal of Law and Society* 15 (1): 5–24.

1434. Cotton, J. June 1989. From Authoritarianism to Democracy in South Korea. *Political Studies* 37 (2): 244–259.

1435. Cotton, J. December 1989. Redefining Taiwan: "One Country, Two Governments." *World Today* 45 (12): 213–216.

1436. Cotton, J. September 1991. The Limits of Liberalization in Industrializing Asia: Three Views of the State. *Pacific Affairs* 64 (3): 311–327.

1437. Cotton, T. Y. C. December 1986. War and American Democracy: Electoral Costs of the Last Five Wars. *Journal of Conflict Resolution* 30 (4): 616–635.

1438. Cotturi, G. December 1975. Alle Origini di Magistratura Democratica. *Politica del Diritto* 6: 685–720.

1439. Couch, C. J. June 1981. *See* Katovich, M. (June 1981).

1440. Coulson, D. C. March 1980. Antitrust Law and the Media: Making the Newspapers Safe for Democracy. *Journalism Quarterly* 57 (1): 79–85.

1441. Court, R. 1981. *See* Turner, R. (1981).

1442. Courtney, J. C. March 1984. Has the Canadian Prime Minister Become "Presidentialized"? *Presidential Studies Quarterly* 14 (2): 238–241.

1443. Coury, C. A. June 1994. Direct Democracy through Initiative and Referendum: Checking the Balance. *Notre Dame Journal of Law, Ethics and Public Policy* 8: 573–597.

1444. Coverdale, J. F. 1977. Spain from Dictatorship to Democracy. *International Affairs (London)* 53 (4): 615–630.

1445. Cox, G. W., and F. Rosenbluth. March 1994. Reducing Nomination Errors: Factional Competition and Party Strategy in Japan. *Electoral Studies* 13 (1): 4–16.

1446. Coyle, D. J. March 1988. The Balkans by the Bay. *Public Interest* (91): 67–78.

1447. Craig, P. P. 1989. Bentham, Public Law and Democracy. *Public Law* 1989: 407–427.

1448. Craig, P. P. January 1990. Dicey: Unitary, Self-Correcting Democracy and Public Law. *Law Quarterly Review* 106: 105–143.

1449. Crain, W. M., and R. B. Ekelund, Jr. April 1978. Deficits and Democracy. *Southern Economic Journal* 44 (4): 813–828.

1450. Crainc, S. June 16, 1986. Pakistan: Millions Demand End of Zia Dictatorship. *Intercontinental Press* 24: 364–366.

1451. Craven, D. June 1990. The State of Cultural Democracy in Cuba and Nicaragua during the 1980s. *Latin American Perspectives* 17 (3): 100–119.

1452. Crawford, J. 1993. Democracy and International Law. *British Year Book of International Law* 64: 113–133.

1453. Crawford, K. L. 1990. Due Obedience and the Rights of Victims: Argentina's Transition to Democracy. *Human Rights Quarterly* 12 (1): 17–52.

1454. Crawford, N. C. June 1994. A Security Regime among Democracies: Cooperation among Iroquois Nations. *International Organization* 48 (3): 345–385.

1455. Creed, G. W. 1993. Rural-Urban Oppositions in the Bulgarian Transition. *Suedosteuropa* 42 (6): 369–382.

1456. Crenshaw, E. M. December 1992. Cross-National Determinants of Income Inequality: A Replication and Extension Using Ecological-Evolutionary Theory. *Social Forces* 71 (2): 339–363.

1457. Crepaz, M. M. L. 1990. The Impact of Party Polarization and Postmaterialism on Voter Turnout: A Comparative Study of 16 Industrial Democracies. *European Journal of Political Research* 18 (2): 183–205.

1458. Crepaz, M. M. L. April 1991. *See* Lijphart, A. (April 1991).

1459. Crepaz, M. M. L. July 1992. Corporatism in Decline: An Empirical Analysis of the Impact of Corporatism on Macroeconomic Performance and Industrial Disputes in 18 Industrialized Democracies. *Comparative Political Studies* 25 (2): 139–168.

1460. Creppell, I. 1989. Democracy and Literacy: The Role of Culture in Political Life. *Archives Europeennes de Sociologie* 30 (1): 22–47.

1461. Crespo, I., P. Mieres, and R. Perez. October 1991. Uruguay: De la Quiebra Institucional a la Presidencia de Lacalle (1971–1991). *Revista de Estudios Politicos* 74: 297–322.

1462. Crisp, B. October 1994. Limitations to Democracy in Developing Capitalist Societies: The Case of Venezuela. *World Development* 22 (10): 1491–1510.

1463. Cristi, R. June 1993. Carl Schmitt on Liberalism, Democracy, and Catholicism. *History of Political Thought* 14 (2): 281–300.

1464. Crittenden, B. 1994. Conflicting Traditions and Education in a Democracy: Can Liberalism Provide Defensible Common Values. *Curriculum Inquiry* 24 (3): 293–326.

1465. Cronin, J. E. March 1983. Politics, Class Structure, and the Enduring Weakness of British Social Democracy. *Journal of Social History* 16 (3): 123–142.

1466. Cronin, J. E. July 1988. The British State and the Structure of Political Opportunity. *Journal of British Studies* 27 (3): 199–231.

1467. Cronin, T. E. 1987. Leadership and Democracy. *Liberal Education* 73 (2): 35–38.

1468. Cronin, T. E. 1988. Public Opinion and Direct Democracy. *PS: Political Science & Politics* 21 (3): 612–619.

1469. Cropsey, J. 1986. On the Mutual Compatibility of Democracy and Marxian Socialism. *Social Philosophy and Policy* 3 (2): 3–18.

1470. Crotty, W. December 1993. Notes on the Study of Political Parties in the Third World. *American Review of Politics* 14: 659–694.

1471. Crouch, H. July 1979. Patrimonialism and Military Rule in Indonesia. *World Politics* 31 (4): 571–587.

1472. Crouch, H. December 1993. Democratic Prospects in Indonesia. *Asian Journal of Political Science* 1 (2): 77–92.

1473. Crowe, W. J. , Jr. June 1986. The Role of Military Strength in the World We Face. *Presidential Studies Quarterly* 16 (3): 428–434.

1474. Crowther, W. April 1991. The Politics of Ethno-National Mobilization: Nationalism and Reform in Soviet Moldavia. *Russian Review* 50 (2): 183–202.

1475. Cruikshank, B. August 1993. Revolutions Within: Self-Government and Self-Esteem.* *Economy and Society* 22 (3): 327–344.

1476. Crystall, J. March 1991. The Human Rights Movement in the Arab World. *American-Arab Affairs* 36: 14–15.

1477. Cubertafond, B. January 1988. Islam and Democracy. *Revue Juridique et Politique, Independance et Cooperation* 42 (1): 74–87.

1478. Cubertafond, B. 1990. Algeria's Search for Democracy.* *Pouvoirs* 52: 117–125.

1479. Cuervo, R. E. June 1986. The Continuing Relevance of Classic Postwar Theories of Executive Legislative Relations. *Presidential Studies Quarterly* 16 (3): 481–490.

1480. Cullen, R. November 1992. Hong Kong: Where Is It Going? *Law Institute Journal* 66: 1004–1007.

1481. Cullis, J. G. 1986. *See* Jones, P. R. (1986).

1482. Cummings, B. January 1989. The Abortive Abertura: South Korea in the Light of Latin American Experience. *New Left Review* 173: 5–32.

1483. Cummings, W. K., and V. N. Kobayashi. December 1985. Education in Japan. *Current History* 84 (506): 422–425, 432–433.

1484. Cumplido, F., J. Guzman, and G. Dietze. June 1984. Pluralism and Outlawing of Anti-Democratic Parties.* *Estudios Publicos* 13: 5–22.

1485. Cunningham, F. November 1989. Democracy and Socialism: Problems of Method.* *Critica Marxistas* 27 (6): 19–35.

1486. Cunningham, F. January 1990. The Socialist Retrieval of Liberal Democracy. *International Political Science Review* 11 (1): 87–97.

1487. Cunningham, F. 1992. University Autonomy and Contexts of Democracy. *Interchange* 23 (1–2): 43–50.

1488. Cunningham, R. M. October 1980. Labor-Management Relations in the Federal Sector: Democracy or Paternalism. *Labor Law Journal* 31 (10): 636–644.

1489. Curbelo, J. L. October 1993. *See* Ortiz, I. (October 1993).

1490. Curran, W. J. December 1988. On Democracy and Economics. *Antitrust Bulletin* 33: 753–777.

1491. Curry, R. L. July 1986. Adaptation of Botswana's Development Strategy to Meet Its People's Needs for Land, Jobs. *American Journal of Economics and Sociology* 45 (3): 297–312.

1492. Curtis, M. September 1982. The Evolution of Israeli Politics. *Middle East Review* 15 (1–2): 59–63.

1493. Curtis, M. E. 1994. *See* Horowitz, I. L. (1994).

1494. Curzan, M. P., and M. L. Pelesh. 1980. Revitalizing Corporate Democracy: Control of Investment Managers Voting on Social-Responsibility Proxy Issues. *Harvard Law Review* 93 (4): 670–700.

1495. Cusicanqui, S. R. June 1990. Liberal Democracy and Ayllu Democracy: The Case of Northern Potosi, Bolivia. *Journal of Development Studies* 26 (4): 97–121.

1496. Cutcomb, S. W. March 1987. *See* Robertson, J. D. (March 1987).

1497. Cuthbert, N. H., and R. Dobbins. 1980. Industrial Democracy, Economic Democracy, and the Ownership of British Industry: Scenarios for the 1980s. *International Journal of Social Economics* 7 (5): 286–295.

1498. Cutler, N. September 1976. Watergate, International Style. *Foreign Policy* (24): 160–171.

1499. Cuzan, A. G. October 1981. Political Profit: Taxing and Spending in Democracies and Dictatorships. *American Journal of Economics and Sociology* 40 (4): 329–340.

૨૾

1500. D'Alimonte, R. August 1989. Democracy and Competition.* *Rivista Italiana di Scienza Politica* 19 (2): 301–319.

1501. D'Angelo, A. November 1992. Democracy in Spain: An Open Problem.* *Critica Marxistas* 6: 32–42.

1502. D'Araujo, M. C. October 1991. *See* Soares, G. A. D. (October 1991).

1503. Da Cruz, J. D. A. September 1993. Democratic Consolidation and the Socio-Economic Crisis of Latin America. *Journal of Interamerican Studies and World Affairs* 35 (1): 145–152.

1504. Da Lage, O. June 1990. The Wind of Democracy Blows Also upon Kuwait.* *Defense Nationale* 119–126.

1505. Da Silva, C. E. L. March 1993. Brazil Struggles with Democracy. *Current History* 92 (572): 126–129.

1506. Daalder, H. 1974. Dutch Universities between New Democracy and New Management. *Minerva* 12 (2): 221–357.

1507. Daalder, H. January 1984. On the Origins of the Consociational Democracy Model. *Acta Politica* 19 (1): 97–116.

1508. Daalder, H. November 1986. Changing Procedures and Changing Strategies in Dutch Coalition Building. *Legislative Studies Quarterly* 11 (4): 507–531.

1509. Dabezies, P. May 1992. Towards African Democratization.* *Defense Nationale* 21–33.

1510. Dachler, P. H., and B. Wilperd. March 1978. Conceptual Dimensions and Boundaries of Participation in Organizations: A Critical Evaluation. *Administrative Science Quarterly* 23 (1): 1–39.

1511. Dacosta, F. F. 1981. Cooperative Democracy among Consumers and Workers. *Annals of Public and Co-operative Economy* 52 (1–2): 101–115.

1512. Dahl, R. A. March 1977. On Removing Certain Impediments to Democracy in the United States. *Political Science Quarterly* 92 (1): 1–20.

1513. Dahl, R. A. 1978. Removing Certain Impediments to Democracy in the United States. *Dissent* 25 (3): 310–324.

1514. Dahl, R. A. January 1978. Pluralism Revisited. *Comparative Politics* 10 (2): 191–203.

1515. Dahl, R. A. 1979. Procedural Democracy.* *Rivista Italiana di Scienza Politica* 9 (1): 3–36.

1516. Dahl, R. A. December 1980. The Moscow Discourse: Fundamental Rights in a Democratic Order. *Government and Opposition* 15 (1): 3–30.

1517. Dahl, R. A. 1983. Federalism and the Democratic Process. *Nomos* 25: 95–108.

1518. Dahl, R. A. December 1984. Democracy in the Workplace: Is It a Right or a Privilege? *Dissent* 31 (1): 54–60.

1519. Dahl, R. A. 1987. Sketches for a Democratic Utopia. *Scandinavian Political Studies* 10 (3): 195–206.

1520. Dahl, R. A. September 1990. Myth of the Presidential Mandate. *Political Science Quarterly* 105 (3): 355–372.

1521. Dahl, R. A. September 1991. Democracy, Majority Rule, and Gorbachev's Referendum. *Dissent* 38 (4): 491–496.

1522. Dahl, R. A. October 1992. The Problem of Civic Competence. *Journal of Democracy* 3 (4): 45–59.

1523. Dahlstrom, E. 1977. Efficiency, Satisfaction and Democracy in Work: Conceptions of Industrial-Relations in Post-War Sweden. *Acta Sociologica* 20 (1): 25–53.

1524. Dahrendorf, R. October 1980. Effectiveness and Legitimacy on the "Governability" of Democracy. *Political Quarterly* 51 (4): 393–410.

1525. Dahrendorf, R. January 1990. The Road to Freedom: Problems of Transition from Dictatorship to Democracy.* *Biblioteca della Liberta* 108: 3–15.

1526. Dahrendorf, R. June 1990. Transitions: Politics, Economics and Liberty. *Washington Quarterly* 13 (3): 133–142.

1527. Dalimonte, R. 1977. Towards a Theory of Competitive Democracy.* *Rivista Italiana di Sciencza Politica* 7 (1): 3–25.

1528. Dallas, R. April 1984. Democracy and Debt in Latin America. *World Today* 40 (4): 160–165.

1529. Dallas, R. April 1987. Will Latin American Democracy Last? *World Today* 43 (4): 70–72.

1530. Dallmayr, F. 1987. *See* Kateb, G. (1987).

1531. Dallmayr, F. February 1993. Post-metaphysics and Democracy. *Political Theory* 21 (1): 101–127.

1532. Dallmayr, F. R. 1987. Democracy and Post-Modernism. *Human Studies* 10 (1): 143–170.

1533. Daloz, J. 1992. New Republic—New Replica? Transforming Inclinations and Perpetuations of Political Behavior in Nigeria.* *Année Africaine* 59–88.

1534. Daloz, J. 1994. Zambia: Analysis of a Foreseeable Drift.* *L'Afrique Politique* 231–244.

1535. Dalton, R. J. October 1994. Communists and Democrats: Democratic Attitudes in the Two Germanies. *British Journal of Political Science* 24 (4): 469–493.

1536. Damgaard, E. September 1994. Termination of Danish Government Coalitions: Theoretical and Empirical Aspects. *Scandinavian Political Studies* 17 (3): 193–212.

1537. Damico, A. J. 1975. Democracy and the Case for Amnesty. *University of Florida Social Sciences Monograph* 55: 1–78.

1538. Damico, A. J. February 1986. Impractical America: Reconsideration of the Pragmatic Lesson. *Political Theory* 14 (1): 83–104.

1539. Damore, L. J. 1977. Saint-John 1986: Anticipatory Democracy in Action. *Business Quarterly* 42 (3): 20–31.

1540. Dandeker, C. March 1994. National Security and Democracy: The United Kingdom Experience. *Armed Forces and Society* 20 (3): 353–374.

1541. Daniels, B. C. 1975. Democracy and Oligarchy in Connecticut Towns: General-Assembly Office Holding, 1701–1790. *Social Science Quarterly* 56 (3): 460–475.

1542. Daniels, M. September 1993. *See* Brooks, A. (September 1993).

1543. Daniels, O. C. B. 1976. Bicentennial: Contradictions in American Democracy. *Black Scholar* 7 (10): 2–6.

1544. Daniels, R. 1988. Finishing the Unfinished Democracy. *Black Scholar* 19 (2): 29–30.

1545. Danilenko, V. N. December 1984. The Legal Mechanism of Public Finance of Political Parties in the Bourgeois Countries. *Sovetskoe Gosudarstvo Pravo* 12: 96–101.

1546. Danis, R. 1984. Policy Changes in Local Schools: The Dissatisfaction Theory of Democracy. *Urban Education* 19 (2): 125–144.

1547. Dannhauser, W. J. 1984. Some Thoughts on Liberty, Equality, and Tocqueville's *Democracy in America. Social Philosophy and Policy* 2 (1): 141–160.

1548. Danopoulos, C. P. March 1985. From Balconies to Tanks: Post-Junta Civil Military Relations in Greece. *Journal of Political and Military Sociology* 13 (1): 83–98.

1549. Danopoulos, C. P. October 1991. Democratising the Military: Lessons from Mediterranean Europe. *West European Politics* 14 (4): 25–41.

1550. Dantonia, W. V. December 1994. Autonomy and Democracy in an Autocratic Organization: The Case of the Roman Catholic Church. *Sociology of Religion* 55 (4): 379–396.

1551. Darcy, R., and M. Marsh. March 1994. Decision Heuristics: Ticket-Splitting and the Irish Vote. *Electoral Studies* 13 (1): 38–49.

1552. Darling, F. C. December 1976. Thailand: Return to Military Rule. *Current History* 71 (422): 197–200, 223, 229–230.

1553. Darling, F. C. February 1977. Thailand in 1977: Another Defeat for Constitutional Democracy. *Asian Survey* 17 (2): 116–132.

1554. Darling, F. C. December 1978. Thailand: Transitional Military Rule? *Current History* 75 (442): 208–211.

1555. Darling, F. C. December 1980. Thailand in the 1980s. *Current History* 79 (462): 185–188, 195.

1556. Darmau, M. July 1994. A New but Ambiguous Malawi.* *Afrique Contemporaine* 171: 34–38.

1557. Darnton, R. June 1991. Adventures of a Germanophobe. *Wilson Quarterly* 15 (3): 113–119.

1558. Darwall, S. L. 1983. Equal Representation. *Nomos* 25: 51–68.

1559. Das, S. July 1994. Democratization and World Petroleum Trade in the Year 2000. *Energy* 19 (7): 783–793.

1560. Dash, S., and R. G. Niemi. March 1992. Democratic Attitudes in Multicultural Settings: A Cross-National Assessment of Political Socialization. *Youth and Society* 23 (3): 313–334.

1561. Dassin, J. R. August 1984. The Brazilian Press and the Politics of "Abertura." *Journal of Interamerican Studies and World Affairs* 26 (3): 385–414.

1562. Dau, R., R. Fricke, and U. Pfefferling. 1988. The Growing Role of the Work Collective in the Perfecting of Socialist Democracy.* *Deutsche Zeitschrift für Philosophie* 36 (7): 610–618.

1563. Dauer, M. J., and M. Sievers. July 1985. The Constitutional Initiatives: Problems in Florida. *National Civic Review* 74 (7): 316–319.

1564. Davallon, J. 1981. Public Opinion in the Democratic Model: On the Making of Consensus.* *Proces* 8: 31–61.

1565. Davalos, J. January 1993. La Democracia Sindical. *Boletin Mexicano de Derecho Comparado* 26 (76): 439–460.

1566. David, D. 1978. Political Campaigning and Democracy. *Revue Française du Marketing* 72: 71–80.

1567. Davies, I. 1994. Whatever Happened To Political Education. *Educational Review* 46 (1): 29–37.

1568. Davies, P. J., and A. V. Ozolins. December 1994. Moving towards Western Democracy: The Latvian Election of 1993 and the UK Connection. *Talking Politics* 6 (2): 110+.

1569. Davis, C. R. March 1990. Public Organizational Existence: A Critique of Individualism in Democratic Administration. *Polity* 22 (3): 397–418.

1570. Davis, D. 1993. *See* Brachet-Marquez, V. (1993).

1571. Davis, D. E. September 1989. Divided over Democracy: The Embeddedness of State and Class Conflicts in Contemporary Mexico. *Politics and Society* 17 (3): 247–280.

1572. Davis, D. E. May 1994. Failed Democratic Reform in Contemporary Mexico: From Social Movement to the State and Back Again. *Journal of Latin American Studies* 26 (2): 375–408.

1573. Davis, D. M. March 1991. Remaking the South African Legal Order. *Social Justice* 18 (1–2): 65–82.

1574. Davis, M. March 1983. Liberalism and/or Democracy? *Social Theory and Practice* 9 (1): 51–72.

1575. Davis, M. January 1986. The Lesser Evil? The Left and the Democratic Party. *New Left Review* 155: 5–36.

1576. Davis, S. September 1981. Jamaican Politics, Economics and Culture: An Interview with Edward Seaga. *Caribbean Review* 10 (4): 14–17.

1577. Davis, S. September 1984. Justice Rehnquist's Judicial Philosophy: Democracy Versus Equality. *Polity* 17 (1): 88–117.

1578. Davis, T. R., and S. M. Lynn Jones. March 1987. "City Upon a Hill." *Foreign Policy* 66: 20–38.

1579. Davison, J. 1992. *See* Abraham, H. J. (1992).

1580. Dawisha, A. June 1986. Power, Participation, and Legitimacy in the Arab World. *World Policy Journal* 3: 517–534.

1581. Day, F. A., and A. L. Jones. 1994. A Portrait of Modern Texas Politics: The Regional Geography of the 1990 Government Race. *Social Science Journal* 31 (2): 99–110.

1582. De Andrada, A. July 1983. A Justica Social Como "Principio-Limite" da Liberdada na Reestructuracao das Democracias: A Proposito de uma Reconstituicao Historica da Ideologia Politica do Governo Vargas. *Revista de Informacao Legislativa* 20: 5–108.

1583. De Caires, D. January 1988. Guyana after Burnham: A New Era? Or Is President Hoyte Trapped in the Skin of the Old PNC? *Caribbean Affairs* 1 (1): 183–198.

1584. De Figueiredo, P. N. A. January 1987. Contribuicao ao Estudo de um Modelo Politico Brasileiro. *Revista de Informacao Legislativa* 15: 11–44.

1585. De Haven-Smith, L. May 1983. *See* Clausen, A. R. (May 1983).

1586. De Hoog, R. H. September 1992. *See* Lowery, D. (September 1992).

1587. De Jonge, H. November 1993. Democracy and Economic Development in the Asia-Pacific Region: The Role of Parliamentary Institutions. *Human Rights Law Journal* 14 (30): 301–307.

1588. De La Madrid, M. September 1984. Mexico: The New Challenges. *Foreign Affairs* 63 (1): 62–76.

1589. De La Torre, E. March 1987. On the Post-Marcos Transition and Popular Democracy. *World Policy Journal* 4: 333–351. Interview.

1590. De Leon, R. 1978. Die Rolle Der Christlichen Demokratie Im Kampt Um Eine Neue Demokratie In Lateinamerika. *Oesterreichische Monatshefte* 34 (7/8): 14–19.

1591. De Marneffe, P. July 1994. Contractualism, Liberty, and Democracy. *Ethics* 104: 764–783.

1592. De Meur, G. April 1994. *See* Berg-Schlosser, D. (April 1994).

1593. De Nevers, R. June 1993. Democratization and Ethnic Conflict. *Survival* 35 (2): 31–48.

1594. De Oliveira, F. March 1985. Heterodox Reflections on the Transition in

Brazil.* *Cahiers des Ameriques Latines* 1: 5–28.

1595. De Onis, J. 1982. Puerto Rico Showcase of Democracy Versus Caribbean Basin Initiative. *Journal of the Institute for Socioeconomic Studies* 7: 569–599.

1596. De Onis, J. September 1989. Brazil on the Tightrope toward Democracy. *Foreign Affairs* 68 (4): 127–143.

1597. De Ridder, M., R. L. Peterson, and R. Wirth. February 1978. Images of Belgium Politics: The Effects of Cleavages on the Political System. *Legislative Studies Quarterly* 3 (1): 83–108.

1598. De Ritter, M. November 1986. *See* Peterson, R. L. (November 1986).

1599. De Romilly, J. 1979. Ideology and Athenian Democracy or On the Use of the Word.* *Revue Europeenne des Sciences Sociales* 46: 27–33.

1600. De Sierra, G. 1991. Dictadura y Restauracion Democratica en El Uruguay Contemporaneo, Limites y Desafios. *Revista de Ciencias Sociales* (6): 66–81.

1601. De Siqueira, G. P. June 1985. The Socialist International: Focus on Brazil. *World Marxist Review* 28: 100–105.

1602. De Soto, H. December 1989. The Informals Pose an Answer to Marx. *Washington Quarterly* 12 (1): 165–172.

1603. De Souza, A. February 1981. A Abertura Politica. *Carta Mensal* 26: 3–14.

1604. De Souza, A., M. Arruda, and P. Flores. December 1984. Economic Dictatorship Versus Democracy in Brazil. *Latin American Perspectives* 11 (1): 13–25.

1605. De Villiers, B. 1993. Federalism in South Africa: Implications for Individual and Minority Protection. *South African Journal of Human Rights* 9 (3): 373–387.

1606. Deacon, A. 1974. Local Democracy and Central Policy: Issues of Pauper Votes in the 1920s. *Policy and Politics* 2 (4): 347–364.

1607. Dealy, G. C. 1974. Tradition of Monistic Democracy in Latin America. *Journal of the History of Ideas* 35 (4): 625–646.

1608. Dealy, G. C. December 1984. The Pluralistic Latins. *Foreign Policy* 57: 108–127.

1609. Dealy, G. C. 1987. Is the United States a School for Central America? *Virginia Quarterly Review* 63: 587–599.

1610. Deane, S. E. March 1990. After the Bloc Party. *Wilson Quarterly* 14 (2): 48–58.

1611. Debbasch, C. et al. February 3, 1994. Une Certaine Idee du Togo. *Jeune Afrique* 34: 40–76.

1612. Debeus, J., and T. Koelble. 1994. Debating the Quality of Life: Social Democracy during the 1980s. *Government and Opposition* 29 (4): 515–535.

1613. Debow, M. E. 1991. The Social Costs of Populist Antitrust: A Public Choice Perspective. *Harvard Journal of Law and Public Policy* 14 (1): 204–223.

1614. Debrito, A. B. October 1993. Truth and Justice in the Consolidation of Democracy in Chile and Uruguay. *Parliamentary Affairs* 46 (4): 579–593.

1615. Debrizzi, J. A. 1982. Marx and Lenin: Class, Party and Democracy. *Studies in Soviet Thought* 24 (2): 95–116.

1616. Debuyst, F. 1982. State, Democracy, and Development in Latin America.* *Culture et Developpement* 14 (4): 563–588.

1617. Decalo, S. January 1992. The Process, Prospects and Constraints of Democratization in Africa. *African Affairs* 91 (362): 7–35.

1618. Decalo, S. November 1994. The Future of Participatory Democracy in Africa. *Futures* 26 (9): 987–992.

1619. Decoudras, P. 1994. Niger: Democratization a Success; Future in Suspense.* *L'Afrique Politique* 45–58.

1620. Decrespigny, A. 1981. Democracy, South Africa and Partition. *Politics* 16 (1): 7–17.

1621. Decter, M. June 1980. Benign Victimization. *Policy Review* 13: 65–72.

1622. Dedeken, J. J. 1992. Social Policy and the Politics of Solidarity: Are There Any Prospects for Social Democracy in East-Central Europe.* *Sociologicky Casopis* 28 (3): 351–368.

1623. Deethardt, J. F. 1983. Inventing Democracy: Future Alternatives for Social Action. *Communication Education* 32 (2): 153–166.

1624. Degen, G. R. 1976. Trade Unions in Great Britain: Social Contracts and Democratization Concept as Cornerstones of Trade Union Programs.* *Gewerkschaftliche Monatshefte* 27 (9): 528–541.

1625. Degenhart, C. 1992. Direct Democracy in the (FDR) Lander: Impulses for the Basic Law.* *Der Staat* 31 (1): 77–97.

1626. Degregori, C. I. 1992. Militarisierung als Politikersatz: Peru: Die Neudefinition der Rolle des Militaers in einer Situation Subversiver Gewalt und der Kollaps des Demokratischen Regimes. *Lateinamerika (Hamburg)* 21: 79–90.

1627. Dehan, N., and A. Percheron. 1980. Democracy at School.* *Revue Française de Sociologie* 21 (3): 379–407.

1628. Dekker, H. 1994. World In Transition—Can Democracies Thrive—Democratic Transitions—International and Cross National Perspectives on Democratization in the 1990s. *Politics and the Individual* 4 (1): 105–108.

1629. Dekmejian, R. H. January 1978. Consociational Democracy in Crisis: The Case of Lebanon. *Comparative Politics* 10 (2): 251–265.

1630. Del Aguila, J. M. August 1982. The Limits of Reform Development in Contemporary Costa Rica. *Journal of Interamer-ican Studies and World Affairs* 24 (3): 355–374.

1631. Del Aguila, J. M. June 1985. Central American Vulnerability to Soviet-Cuban Penetration. *Journal of Interamerican Studies and World Affairs* 27 (2): 77–97.

1632. Del Aguila, J. M. December 1987. Cuba's Declining Fortunes. *Current History* 86 (524): 425–428, 434.

1633. Delamotte, Y. May 1977. The "Reform of the Enterprise" in France. *Annals of the American Academy of Political and Social Science* 431: 54–62.

1634. Deleon, P. March 1992. The Democratization of the Policy Sciences. *Public Administration Review* 52 (2): 125–129.

1635. Deleon, P. June 1994. Democracy and the Policy Sciences: Aspirations and Operations. *Policy Studies Journal* 22 (2): 200–212.

1636. Delgado, M. March 1985. *See* Neuhaus, R. J. (March 1985).

1637. Delgado, R. September 1994. Rodrigo's Seventh Chronicle: Race, Democracy, and the State. *UCLA Law Review* 41: 721–757.

1638. Delich, F. July 1985. From Democracy as Necessity to Democracy as Precondition.* *Estudios Internacionales* 71: 370–381.

1639. Delima, O. B. 1993. The Reform of Political Institutions: The Brazilian Experience and the Perfecting of Democracy.* *Dados: Revista de Ciencias Sociais* 36 (1): 89–117.

1640. Della Cava, R. September 1990. The Church and the "Opening" in Brazil 1974–1985. *Sintesis* 12: 51–77.

1641. Delladora, D. 1976. Democracy and Education: Who Owns the Curriculum. *Educational Leadership* 34 (1): 51+.

1642. Dellenbrandt, J. A., and V. Pestoff. 1980. Elites as Gatekeepers: Democratic and Oligarchic Tendencies in Swedish Co-operative Organizations. *Statsvetenskaplig Tidskrift* 4: 235–243.

1643. Deller, S. C. 1989. *See* Chicoine, D. L. (1989).

1644. Deller, S. C., and D. L. Chicoine. January 1993. Representative Versus Direct Democracy: A Test of Allocative Efficiency in Local Government Expenditures. *Public Finance Quarterly* 21 (1): 100–114.

1645. Delley, J. 1987. Direct Democracy [in Switzerland]: An "Open Doors" Political System.* *Pouvoirs* 43: 101–114.

1646. Delors, J. May 1981. Social Democracy and the Evolution of Capitalism: The Double Compromise.* *Socialisme* 28 (165): 247–261.

1647. Delors, J. September 1990. Europe's Ambitions. *Foreign Policy* (80): 14–27.

1648. Demaio, G. June 1987. *See* Bolce, L. (June 1987).

1649. Demarneffe, P. July 1994. Contractualism, Liberty, and Democracy. *Ethics* 104 (4): 764–783.

1650. Demarquez, V. B. 1981. Politics, Bureaucracy, and Industrial Democracy: A Comparative Framework for the Analysis of Worker Control in Latin America. *Sociology of Work and Occupations* 8 (2): 165–179.

1651. Demetrius, F. J., E. J. Tregurtha, and S. B. MacDonald. 1986. A Brave New World: Debt, Default and Democracy in Latin America. *Journal of Interamerican Studies and World Affairs* 28 (2): 17–38.

1652. Demirovic, A. 1991. Civil Society, Public Sphere, Democracy.* *Argument* 33 (1): 41–55.

1653. Denbaum, L. H. 1985. *See* Lansing, P. (1985).

1654. Dencik, P. 1976. Planning National Business Enterprise and Democracy: In-

troductory Considerations.* *Sociologisk Forskning* 13 (1): 3–9.

1655. Denmark, D. July 1994. Programmic Intransigence and the Limits of the Modern Campaign: New Zealand Labour in 1990. *Political Science* 46 (1): 22–39.

1656. Denisov, A. I., and A. A. Kenenov. August 1982. V. I. Lenin on the Class Character of Democracy.* *Sovetskoe Gosudarstvo Pravo* 8: 117–125.

1657. Denninger, E. 1978. Verfassung und Gesetz: Aktuelle Randbemerkungen zu einer Theory der Freiheitlichen. *Frankfurter Hefte* 33 (3): 27–40.

1658. Depenheuer, O. 1994. Democracy before Wealth?* *Der Staat* 33 (3): 329–350.

1659. Derber, M. May 1977. Collective Bargaining: The American Approach to Industrial Democracy. *Annals of the American Academy of Political and Social Science* 431: 83–94.

1660. Derian, J. C. 1975. Nuclear-Emergency and Exercise of Democracy.* *Futuribles* 3: 205–212.

1661. Derlien, H., and G. J. Szablowski (eds.). July 1993. Special Issue on Regime Transitions, Elites, and Bureaucracies in Eastern Europe. *Governance* 6: 304–453. 10 articles.

1662. Derrick, P. 1981. Prospects for Industrial Cooperatives: An Alternative to Industrial Democracy. *Long Range Planning* 14 (4): 106–114.

1663. Derryck, V. L. January 1991. The Velvet Revolution. *Africa Report* 36: 24–26.

1664. Derthick, M. January 1987. American Federalism: Madison's Middle Ground in the 1980s. *Public Administration Review* 47 (1): 66–74.

1665. Dervin, B. July 1994. Information—Democracy: An Examination of Underlying Assumptions. *Journal of the American Society for Information Science* 45 (6): 369–385.

1666. Desario, J., and S. Langton. February 1984. Citizen Participation and Technocracy. *Policy Studies* 3 (2): 223–233.

1667. Desbrousses-Pe Loille, H. December 1984. Representations of "Republic" and "Democracy." *Revue Française de Science Politique* 34 (6): 1211–1235.

1668. Desert, M. December 1992. Democratization and the Labor Movement.* *Politique Etrangere* 57 (1): 101–110.

1669. Desouza, A. 1991. *See* Lamounier, B. (1991).

1670. Desouza, P. R. January 1990. Pluralisation of World Views and Charismatic Domination. *Indian Journal of Social Science* 3 (1): 31–51.

1671. Desouza-Martins, M. 1990. Market and Democracy: The Perverse Relation.* *Tempo Relation* 2 (1): 7–22.

1672. Destexhe, A. 1988. Haiti (1986–1988): From Duvalier's Fall to Leslie Manigat's Oathtaking.* *Problemes d'Amerique Latine* 87: 25–45.

1673. Detjen, J. August 9, 1991. Natural Law in Pluralist Democracy?* *Aus Politik und Zeitgeschichte* 33: 19–30.

1674. Deussner, R. 1985. *See* Kolland, F. (1985).

1675. Deutsch, S. 1981. Work-Environment Reform and Industrial Democracy. *Sociology of Work and Occupations* 8 (2): 180–194.

1676. Deutsch, S. 1983. *See* Albrecht, S. L. (1983).

1677. Deutsch, S. 1988. Workplace Democracy and Worker Health: Strategies for Implementation. *International Journal of Health Services* 18 (4): 647–658.

1678. Deutscher, E. 1989. The Function and Role of the Political Parties in the Process of Democratization of Central America.* *Estudios Sociales Centroamericanos* 50: 25–32.

1679. Deutscher, E. July 1989. La Funcion y el Papel de los Partidos Politicos en el Proceso de Democratizacion. *Presencia* (*El Salvador*) 2: 67–74.

1680. Devall, W. B., and J. Harry. 1975. Associational Politics and Internal Democracy. *Journal of Voluntary Action and Internal Democracy* 4 (1–2): 90–97.

1681. Devaranjan, S. January 1993. *See* Lindenberg, M. (January 1993).

1682. Devi, K. D. 1978. Trade Union Democracy in India: Review of Theory and Practice. *Indian Journal of Social Work* 39 (1): 69–77.

1683. Devine, D. 1981. An Aborted Democracy. *Worldview* 24 (5): 19–20.

1684. Devine, F. E. August 1975. Democracy of Indefeasible Right: Hobbes Versus Locke. *Journal of Politics* 37 (3): 736–768.

1685. Devine, I. September 1983. *See* Gaertner, G. H. (September 1983).

1686. Deviney, S. June 1992. *See* Abbott, A. (June 1992).

1687. Devlin, K. March 1979. Eurocommunism: Between East and West. *International Security* 3 (4): 81–107.

1688. Devoluy, P. March 22, 1991. Algerie: La Verite en Face. *L'Express* 22–25.

1689. Di Lellio, A. September 1981. The Democratic Management of the Crisis.* *Democrazia e Diritto* 21 (5): 115–128.

1690. Di Palma, G. March 1980. Founding Coalitions in Southern Europe: Legitimacy and Hegemony. *Government and Opposition* 15 (2): 162–189.

1691. Di Palma, G. May 1982. Successor Democracies: The Italian Case.* *Revista de Estudios Politicos* 27: 137–170.

1692. Di Palma, G. 1983. Government by Parties and Democratic Reproducibility: The Dilemma of the New Democracies. *Rivista Italiana di Scienza Politica* 13 (1): 3–36.

1693. Di Palma, G. April 1984. Government Performance: An Issue and Three Cases in Search of Theory. *West European Politics* 7 (2): 172–187.

1694. Di Palma, G. April 1988. The Democratic Consolidation: A Minimalist Vision.* *Revista Espanola de Investigaciones Sociologicas* 42: 67–92.

1695. Di Palma, G. August 1990. Democratic Transitions in Eastern Europe: A Comparative Perspective. *Rivista Italiana di Scienza Politica* 20 (2): 203–242.

1696. Di Palma, G. October 1991. Legitimation from the Top to Civil Society: Politico-Cultural Change in Eastern Europe. *World Politics* 44 (1): 49–79.

1697. Di Palma, G. December 1991. Why Democracy Can Work in Eastern Europe. *Journal of Democracy* 2 (1): 21–31.

1698. Di Quattro, A. May 1980. The Market and Liberal Values. *Political Theory* 8 (2): 183–202.

1699. Di Tella, T. S. March 1984. The October 1983 Elections in Argentina. *Government and Opposition* 19 (2): 188–192.

1700. Di Tella, T. S. March 1984. The Popular Parties: Brazil and Argentina in a Latin American Perspective. *Government and Opposition* 19 (2): 250–268.

1701. Di Zerega, A. September 1988. Equality, Self-Government, and Democracy: A Critique of Dahl's Political Equality. *Western Political Quarterly* 41 (3): 447–468.

1702. Diagna, P. June 1976. De la Democratie Traditionnelle: Probleme de Definition. *Presence Africaine* 18–42.

1703. Diallo, S. March 6, 1991. *See* Girard, P. (March 6, 1991).

1704. Diamandour, P. N. January 1988. *See* Lijphart, A. (January 1988).

1705. Diamandouros, P. N. April 1974. Transition to, and Consolidation of Democratic Politics in Greece, 1974–1984: A

Tentative Assessment. *West European Politics* 7 (2): 50–71.

1706. Diamanti, I. May 1994. Politics as Marketing [in Italy].* *MicroMega* 2: 60–77.

1707. Diamond, L. March 1983. Nigeria in Search of Democracy. *Foreign Affairs* 62 (4): 905–927.

1708. Diamond, L. July 1983. Class, Ethnicity, and the Democratic State: Nigeria, 1950–1966. *Comparative Studies in Society and History* 25 (3): 457–489.

1709. Diamond, L. May 1987. Nigeria Between Dictatorship and Democracy. *Current History* 86 (520): 201–204, 222–224.

1710. Diamond, L. December 1989. Beyond Authoritarianism and Totalitarianism: Strategies for Democratization. *Washington Quarterly* 12 (1): 141–163.

1711. Diamond, L. June 1990. Three Paradoxes of Democracy. *Journal of Democracy* 1 (3): 48–60.

1712. Diamond, L. 1991. Nigeria Third Quest for Democracy. *Current History* 90 (556): 201+.

1713. Diamond, L. March 1991. Nigeria's Search for a New Political Order. *Journal of Democracy* 2 (2): 54–69.

1714. Diamond, L. March 1992. Economic Development and Democracy Reconsidered. *American Behavioral Scientist* 35 (4–5): 450–499.

1715. Diamond, L. March 1992. *See* Marks, G. (March 1992).

1716. Diamond, L. June 1992. Promoting Democracy. *Foreign Policy* (87): 25–46.

1717. Diamond, L. July 1992. A Constitution That Works: Some Options. *South Africa International* 22: 45–48.

1718. Diamond, L. July 1994. Toward Democratic Consolidation. *Journal of Democracy* 5 (3): 4–17.

1719. Diamond, L., S. M. Lipset, and J. Linz. March 1987. Building and Sustaining Democratic Government in Developing Countries: Some Tentative Findings. *World Affairs* 150 (1): 5–19.

1720. Diamond, L., and G. Marks (eds.). March 1992. Comparative Perspectives on Democracy: Essays in Honor of Seymour Martin Lipset. *American Behavioral Scientist* 35: 352–629. 13 articles.

1721. Diamond, M. September 1975. The Declaration and the Constitution: Liberty, Democracy and the Founders. *Public Interest* 41: 39–55.

1722. Diamond, M. June 1978. The Separation of Powers and the Mixed Regime. *Publius* 8 (3): 33–44.

1723. Diamond, M. December 1978. The Electoral College and the Idea of Federal Democracy. *Publius* 8 (1): 63–77.

1724. Diana, M. October 1994. *See* Castelfranci, C. (October 1994).

1725. Dias David, M., and B. Vicro Schmidt. 1994. Democratization and Social Policy: Notes on the Present Brazilian Conjuncture.* *Lusotopie* 1–2: 367–379.

1726. Diaz, E. May 1985. Justifying Democracy.* *Sistema* 66: 3–23.

1727. Diaz, E. October 1988. Democratic Socialism: Political Institutions and Social Movements.* *Revista de Estudios Politicos* 62: 41–67.

1728. Dickey, C. 1984. The Elections Promise Further Carnage, Not Democracy: El Salvador Lost Hope. *New Republic* 190 (12): 180+.

1729. Dickman, H. 1984. Exclusive Representation and American Industrial Democracy: An Historical Reappraisal. *Journal of Labor Research* 5 (4): 325–350.

1730. Dickson, J. W. 1977. Adoption of Industrial Democracy. *Personnel Review* 6 (4): 15–19.

1731. Dicortona, P. G. 1991. From Communism to Democracy: Rethinking Regime Change in Hungary and Czecho-

slovakia. *International Social Science Journal* 43 (2): 315–330.

1732. Diderichsen, F. 1982. Ideologies in the Swedish Health Sector Today: The Crisis of the Social Democracy. *International Journal of Health Services* 12 (2): 191–200.

1733. Diederich, B. June 1982. *See* Bohning, D. (June 1982).

1734. Diedericx, G. 1977. *See* Obler, J. (1977).

1735. Diehl, O. June 1991. *See* Broer, M. (June 1991).

1736. Diericky, G. February 1978. Ideological Opposition and Consociational Attitudes in the Belgian Parliament. *Legislative Studies Quarterly* 3 (1): 133–160.

1737. Dietz, M. G. September 1987. Context Is All: Feminism and Theories of Citizenship. *Daedalus* 116 (4): 1–24.

1738. Dietze, G. June 1984. *See* Cumplido, F. (June 1984).

1739. Dietzel, H. 1984. International Social Democracy for Securing Peace and Overcoming Crises. *IPW Berichte* 13 (10): 21+.

1740. Difilippo, A. 1983. Market and Democracy. *Trimestre Economico* 50 (197): 245–267.

1741. Dijmarescu, E. December 1978. Democratization and Liberalization in the International Trade in Manufactures: Building Factors of a New International Economic Order. *Revue Roumaine des Sciences Sociales (Serie des Sciences Economiques)* 22: 183–196.

1742. Dilla Alfonso, H. July 1986. Democracy and Revolutionary Power in Cuba.* *Revista de Ciencias Sociales* 25 (3–4): 359–380.

1743. Dilla Alfonso, H. January 1988. Democracy and Revolutionary Power in Cuba.* *El Caribe Contemporaneo* 16: 89–105.

1744. Diller, J. M. April 1993. Constitutional Reform in a Repressive State: The Case of Burma (Myanmar). *Asian Survey* 33 (4): 393–407.

1745. Dillon-Soares, G. A. 1984. The Future of Democracy in Latin America.* *Dados* 27 (3): 269–292.

1746. Dillon-Soares, G. A. April 1984. The Future of Democracy in Latin America.* *Estudios Internacionales* 66: 101–134.

1747. DiLorenzo, T. J. September 1986. *See* Bennett, J. T. (September 1986).

1748. DiLorenzo, T. J. 1987. *See* Bennett, J. T. (1987).

1749. DiLorenzo, T. J. 1987. *See* Bennett, J. T. (1987).

1750. DiMaggio, P., and M. Useem. December 1978. Cultural Democracy in a Period of Cultural Expansion: The Social Composition of Art Audiences in the United States. *Social Problems* 26 (2): 179–197.

1751. Dimitrov, R. 1994. Building a Democratic Public in Eastern Europe. *Berliner Journal für Soziologie* 4 (4): 543–580.

1752. Dimock, M. January 1990. The Restorative Qualities of Citizenship. *Public Administration Review* 50 (1): 21–25.

1753. Dimock, M. A. August 1994. *See* Jacobson, G. C. (August 1994).

1754. Dinges, J. 1983. Stirrings of Democracy in Chile: Winter of Discontent. *New Republic* 189 (3): 13–15.

1755. Diniz, E. June 1986. The Political Transition in Brazil: A Reappraisal of the Dynamics of the Political Opening. *Studies in Comparative International Development* 21 (2): 63–73.

1756. Diniz, E. 1994. Economic Reforms and Democracy in Brazil in the 1990s: Sectoral Chambers as Negotiating Forums. *Dados: Revista de Ciencias Sociais* 37 (2): 277–316.

1757. Dinkel, R. September 1976. Collusion in Spatial Models of Party Competition. *Public Choice* 27: 97–99.

1758. Diokno, J., and R. Falk. December 1984. On the Struggle for Democracy. *World Policy Journal* 1 (2): 433–445.

1759. Dion, S. 1984. Negotiation in Local Politics: Neo-Corporatism and Democracy.* *Sociologie du Travail* 2: 121–140.

1760. Dion, S. December 1986. Liberalism and Democracy: A Plea for the Ruling Ideology.* *Politique* 9: 5–38.

1761. Dion, S. February 1993. *See* Blais, A. (February 1993).

1762. Diouf, M. October 1993. African Intellectuals and the Democratic Enterprise: Between Citizens and Expertise.* *Politique Africaine* 51: 36–47.

1763. Diouf, M. 1994. The Failure of Senegal's Democratic System, 1981–1993.* *Africa Spectrum* 29 (1): 47–64.

1764. Dippie, B. W. June 1990. The Winning of the West Reconsidered. *Wilson Quarterly* 14 (3): 70–85.

1765. Diskin, M. March 1984. *See* Sharpe (March 1984).

1766. Dittmar, M. L., and G. Stiehler. 1985. Aspects of Socialist Democracy in Material Production.* *Deutsche Zeitschrift für Philosophie* 33 (10): 893–902.

1767. Dittmer, L. January 1981. China in 1980: Modernization and Its Discontents. *Asian Survey* 21 (1): 31–50.

1768. Dittmer, L. September 1986. Hong Kong and China's Modernization. *Orbis* 30 (3): 525–542.

1769. Dittmer, L., A. J. Nathan, A. G. Walder, and J. T. Dreyer. September 1989. Tiananmen Square 1989: A Symposium. *Problems of Communism* 38 (5): 2–48.

1770. Diuk, N., and A. Karatnycky. September 1990. Nationalism: Part of the Solution. *Orbis* 34 (4): 531–546.

1771. Divine, D. R. May 1979. Political Legitimacy in Israel: How Important is the State? *International Journal of Middle East Studies* 10 (2): 205–224.

1772. Divine, D. R. June 1979. A Political Theory of Bureaucracy. *Public Administration* 57 (2): 143–158.

1773. Dix, R. H. April 1980. Consociational Democracy: The Case of Colombia. *Comparative Politics* 12 (3): 303–321.

1774. Dix, R. H. December 1982. The Breakdown of Authoritarian Regimes. *Western Political Quarterly* 35 (4): 554–573.

1775. Dix, R. H. 1985. Populism: Authoritarian and Democratic. *Latin American Research Review* 20 (2): 29–52.

1776. Dix, R. H. January 1992. Democratization and Institutionalization of Latin American Political Parties. *Comparative Political Studies* 24 (4): 488–511.

1777. Dix, R. H. October 1994. History and Democracy Revisited. *Comparative Politics* 27 (1): 91–105.

1778. Dixon, D. F. June 1992. Consumer Sovereignty, Democracy, and the Marketing Concept: A Macromarketing Perspective. *Canadian Journal of Administrative Sciences* 9 (2): 116–125.

1779. Dixon, W. J. March 1993. Democracy and the Management of International Conflict. *Journal of Conflict Resolution* 37 (1): 42–68.

1780. Dixon, W. J. March 1994. Democracy and the Peaceful Settlement of International Conflict. *American Political Science Review* 88 (1): 14–32.

1781. Dizerega, G. March 1989. Democracy as a Spontaneous Order. *Critical Review* 3 (2): 206–240.

1782. Dizerega, G. March 1991. Elites and Democratic Theory: Insights from the Self-Organizing Model. *Review of Politics* 53 (2): 340–372.

1783. Djian, J. M. July 1991. L'Afrique Culturelle. *Apres-Demain* 3–16.

1784. Djilas, M. March 1980. Yugoslavia and the Expansionism of the Soviet State. *Foreign Affairs* 58 (4): 852–866.

1785. Djiwandodo, J. S. 1989. Progress in Democratic Experiment in Indonesia? *Southeast Asian Affairs* 155–167.

1786. Dobbins, R. 1980. *See* Cuthbert, N. H. (1980).

1787. Dobbs, D. November 1984. Public Choice and Political Rhetoric. *American Behavioral Scientist* 28 (2): 203–210.

1788. Dobratz, B. A. January 1988. Foreign Policy and Economic Orientations Influencing Party Preference in the Socialist Nation of Greece. *East European Quarterly* 21 (4): 413–430.

1789. Dobriansky, P. J. March 1989. Human Rights and U.S. Foreign Policy. *Washington Quarterly* 12 (2): 153–169.

1790. Dobson, J. December 1991. Ethics of Shareholder Referendums: Corporate Democracy or Hypocrisy? *Review of Business (St. John's University)* 13: 22–26.

1791. Dobson, M. March 1986. Democratic Ideals and Contemporary Central American Politics. *Scandinavian Journal of Development Alternatives* 5 (1): 95–114.

1792. Doctor, A. H. February 1994. Resistance Politics: Its Implications for Democracy. *Human Rights Quarterly* 16 (1): 273–290.

1793. Dodd, C. October 1992. The Revival of Turkish Democracy. *Asian Affairs (London)* 79 (3): 305–314.

1794. Dodd, L. C. July 1984. The Study of Cabinet Durability: Introduction and Commentary. *Comparative Political Studies* 17 (2): 155–162.

1795. Dodero, P. May 1990. The Nepalese Road to Pluralism.* *Politica Internazionale* 18 (5–7): 39–52.

1796. Doherty, W. C. September 1989. Debt in Latin America: Toward Democracy or Dictatorship? *Freedom at Issue* 110: 31–35.

1797. Dolan, J. P. 1981. A Catholic Romance with Modernity. *Wilson Quarterly* 5 (5): 120–133.

1798. Dolbeare, K. September 1990. The Decay of Liberal Democracy. *Policy Studies Review* 10 (1): 141–150.

1799. Dole, R. J. March 1985. *See* Lugar, R. G. (March 1985).

1800. Domenach, J. 1990. China: The Long March to Democracy.* *Pouvoirs* 52: 55–64.

1801. Domes, J. October 1981. Political Differentiation in Taiwan: Group Formation within the Ruling Party and the Opposition Circles, 1979–1980. *Asian Survey* 21 (10): 1011–1028.

1802. Domes, J. January 1993. Taiwan in 1992: On the Verge of Democracy. *Asian Survey* 33 (1): 54–60.

1803. Dominick, R. 1977. Democracy or Socialism: A Case Study of Vorwarts in the 1890s. *Central European History* 10 (4): 186–311.

1804. Domke, W. K., R. C. Eichenberg, and C. M. Kelleher. March 1983. The Illusion of Choice: Defense and Welfare in Advanced Industrial Democracies, 1948–1978. *American Political Science Review* 77 (1): 19–35.

1805. Dommen, A. J. September 1993. Sowing Peace in the Killing Fields. *Freedom Review* 24: 32–34.

1806. Domrin, A. N. March 1993. Issues and Options in the Soviet Transition to the Rule of Law. *Coexistence* 30 (1): 57–68.

1807. Donath, F. 1981. Istvan Bibo and the Fundamental Issue of Hungarian Democracy. *Socialist Register:* 221–246.

1808. Donnelly, J. March 1992. Human Rights in the New World Order. *World Policy Journal* 9 (2): 249–277.

1809. Donnorummo, R. June 1994. Poland's Political and Economic Transition. *East European Quarterly* 28 (2): 259–280.

1810. Donovan, T. June 1992. *See* Bowler, S. (June 1992).

1811. Doran, C. F. June 1978. U.S. Foreign Aid and the Unstable Polity: A Regional Case Study. *Orbis* 22 (2): 435–452.

1812. Doran, G. August 1979. Is the Hare Voting Scheme Representative? *Journal of Politics* 41 (3): 918–922.

1813. Dorce, F. August 4, 1991. Les Seychelles Aspirent au Changement: La Contagion Democratique. *Jeune Afrique* 31: 28–29.

1814. Dorff, R. H. March 1985. *See* Steiner, J. (March 1985).

1815. Dorff, R. H., and J. Steiner. July 1987. Decision Cases in Western Democracies: A Data Bank. *Comparative Political Studies* 20 (2): 160–173.

1816. Dorling, H. June 1986. *See* Barton, T. (June 1986).

1817. Dorn, J. A. September 1993. Economic Liberty and Democracy in East Asia. *Orbis* 37 (4): 599–619.

1818. Dornbusch, R. November 1988. Peru on the Brink. *Challenge* 31: 31–37.

1819. Doronila, A. 1992. The Role of Media in Strengthening [Philippine] Democracy. *Democratic Institutions* 1: 39–47.

1820. Dossantos, M. R. January 1991. Governability during the Transition to Democracy in Argentina.* *Revista Mexicana de Sociologia* 53 (1): 293–304.

1821. Dost, A., and E. Lieberam. 1990. Change Processes and Prospects of Bourgeois Democracy. *Staat und Recht* 39 (4): 296–303.

1822. Dougherty, A. F. 1979. Concentration, Conglomeration, and Economic Democracy: A "Concurrent Divestiture" Proposal. *Antitrust Law and Economic Review* 11 (1): 29–54.

1823. Doughtie, J. C., M. McCulloch, and B. G. Peters. April 1977. Types of Democratic Systems and Types of Public Policy: An Empirical Examination. *Comparative Politics* 9 (3): 327–355.

1824. Douglas, R. B. June 1994. The Renewal of Democracy and the Communitarian Prospect. *Responsive Community* 4 (3): 55–62.

1825. Douglas, W. A. June 1981. *See* Samuels, M. A. (June 1981).

1826. Douglas, W. A. September 1982. Helping Democracy Abroad: A U.S. Program. *Freedom at Issue* 68: 15–19.

1827. Doukas, G. October 1993. Party Elites and Democratization in Greece. *Parliamentary Affairs* 46 (4): 506–516.

1828. Dow, G. 1991. The Swedish Model and the Anglo-Saxon Model: Reflections on the Fate of Social Democracy in Australia. *Economic and Industrial Democracy* 12 (4): 515–526.

1829. Dow, G. February 1993. What Do We Know about Social Democracy. *Economic and Industrial Democracy* 14 (1): 11–48.

1830. Downey, R. 1977. *See* Cortazar, R. (1977).

1831. Downing, B. M. 1988. Constitutionalism, Warfare, and Political Change in Early Modern Europe. *Theory and Society* 17 (1): 7–56.

1832. Downing, L. June 1991. *See* Thigpen, R. B. (June 1991).

1833. Downing, L., and R. B. Thigpen. February 1982. A Liberal Dilemma: The Application of Unger's Critique of Formalism to Lowi's Concept of Juridical Democracy.* *Journal of Politics* 44 (1): 230–246.

1834. Downs, A. June 1987. The Evolution of Democracy: How Its Axioms and Institutional Forms Have Been Adapted to Changing Social Forces. *Daedalus* 116 (3): 119–148.

1835. Downs, C. October 1987. Regionalization, Administrative Reforms and Democratization: Nicaragua, 1979–1984. *Public Administration and Development* 7 (4): 363–381.

1836. Doyle, M. W. December 1986. Liberalism and World Politics. *American Political Science Review* 80 (4): 1151–1169.

1837. Drake, P. W. December 1985. The Rebirth of Democracy in Chile: Historical and Comparative Approaches.* *Revista de Ciencia Politica* 7 (2): 117–128.

1838. Draper, T. 1978. Capitalism, Socialism, and Democracy. *Commentary* 65 (4): 36–37.

1839. Dreyer, J. T. September 1989. The Role of the Military. *World Policy Journal* 6 (4): 647–655.

1840. Dreyer, J. T. September 1989. *See* Dittmer, L. (September 1989).

1841. Dreyer, J. T. January 1990. Taiwan in 1989: Democratization and Economic Growth. *Asian Survey* 30 (1): 52–58.

1842. Dreyer, R. 1990. Independent Namibia: Testing National Reconciliation.* *Année Africaine* 261–283.

1843. Dreyfus, F. G. December 1990. The Weight and Place of the Christian Democracy.* *Revue Française de Science Politique* 40 (6): 845–863.

1844. Droz, J. 1976. Historiography of a Century of German Social Democracy.* *Mouvement Social* (95): 3–23.

1845. Drucker, H. 1984. Intra-Party Democracy in Action: The Election of Leader and Deputy Leader by the Labor

Party in 1983. *Parliamentary Affairs* 37 (3): 283–300.

1846. Dryzek, J. S. August 1988. The Mismeasure of Political Man. *Journal of Politics* 50 (3): 705–725.

1847. Dryzek, J. S. September 1989. Policy Sciences of Democracy. *Polity* 22 (1): 97–118.

1848. Dryzek, J. S. July 1994. Australian Discourses of Democracy. *Australian Journal of Political Science* 29 (2): 221–239.

1849. Dryzek, J. S., and J. Berejikian. March 1993. Reconstructive Democratic Theory. *American Political Science Review* 87 (1): 48–60.

1850. Dryzek, J. S., and D. Torgerson (eds.). August 1993. Democracy and the Policy Sciences. *Policy Sciences* 26: 127–270. 6 articles.

1851. Drzemczewski, A. September 30, 1993. The Council of Europe's Co-operation and Assistance Programmes with Central and Eastern European Countries in the Human Rights Field, 1990 to September 1993. *Human Rights Law Journal* 14: 229–248.

1852. Du Toit, P. July 1987. Consociational Democracy and Bargaining Power. *Comparative Politics* 19 (4): 419–430.

1853. Duarte, J. N. October 1988. The CBI Is an Important Plan to Help Change Economic Structures in the Region. *Caribbean Affairs* 1 (4): 123–131.

1854. Dubiel, H. 1990. Civic Religion in Mass Democracy? Critique of a Classic Theory of Post-Traditional Legitimation.* *Soziale Welt* 41 (2): 125–143.

1855. Dubiel, H. April 1990. The Democratic Question. *Blaetter für Deutsche und Internationale Politik* 35 (4): 409–418.

1856. Dubois De Qaudusson, J. October 1992. Thirty Years of Constitutional and Political Institutions in Africa: Landmarks and Questions. *Afrique Contemporaine* 164: 50–58.

1857. Ducanson, I. November 1988. Law, Democracy and the Individual. *Legal Studies* 8: 303–316.

1858. Ducatenzeiler, G. 1987. Political Opening, Democratic Transition and Working Class in Argentina.* *Politique* 12: 63–91.

1859. Ducatenzeiler, G. et al. 1993. Amerique Latine: Les Echecs du Liberal-Populisme. *Canadian Journal of Development Studies* 14 (2): 173–195.

1860. Ducatenzeiler, G., and P. Oxhorn. April 1994. Democracy, Authoritarianism, and the Problem of Governability in Latin America.* *Desarrollo Economico: Revista de Ciencias Sociales* 34 (133): 31–52.

1861. Duch, R. M. September 1991. *See* Gibson, J. L. (September 1991).

1862. Duch, R. M. May 1992. *See* Gibson, J. L. (May 1992).

1863. Duch, R. M. September 1993. Tolerating Economic Reform: Popular Support for Transition to a Free Market in the Former Soviet Union. *American Political Science Review* 87 (3): 590–608.

1864. Duch, R. M. March 1994. *See* Gibson, J. L. (March 1994).

1865. Duchacek, I. D. March 1985. Consociational Cradle of Federalism. *Publius* 15 (2): 35–48.

1866. Duckles, M. M., R. Duckles, and M. MacCoby. July 1977. The Process of Change at Bolivar. *Journal of Applied Behavioral Science* 13 (3): 387–399.

1867. Duckles, R. July 1977. *See* Duckles, M. M. (July 1977).

1868. Duffey, J. D. June 1977. The Perspective of a New Administration. *International Educational and Cultural Exchange* 13 (1): 7–9.

1869. Duffy, T. December 1994. UNTAC's Mission in Cambodia: Prospects for

Democracy and Human Rights. *Asian Affairs* (*New York*) 20: 218–240.

1870. Dugard, J. March 1991. The Role of International Law in the Struggle for Liberation in South Africa. *Social Justice* 18 (1–2): 83–94.

1871. Duguid, S. 1981. Moral Development, Justice and Democracy in the Prison. *Canadian Journal of Criminology* 23 (2): 147–162.

1872. Duguid, S. September 1987. Democratic Praxis and Prison Education. *Howard Journal of Criminal Justice* 26: 57–65.

1873. Duignan, P. J. March 1987. The Case against Divestment. *Orbis* 31 (1): 6–14.

1874. Duignan, P. J. 1991. Towards South African Democracy: De Klerk Can Handle the Transition. *Orbis* 35 (4): 483–498.

1875. Duncan, G. June 1985. A Crisis of Social Democracy? *Parliamentary Affairs* 38 (3): 267–281.

1876. Duncan, T. 1990. Community Councils in Glasgow: The Development of an Urban Grass-Roots Democracy. *Local Government Studies* 16 (2): 8–16.

1877. Dunlop, J. B. March 1991. Crackdown. *National Interest* (23): 24–32.

1878. Dunlop, J. B. June 1991. Russia's Surprising Reactionary Alliance. *Orbis* (35): 3.

1879. Dunmoye, R. A. March 1984. Ethnic Ideology, Bourgeois Democracy, and Nigerian Politics. *Journal of Ethnic Studies* 12 (1): 123–137.

1880. Dunn, J. October 1974. Democracy Unretrieved, or Political Theory of Professor MacPherson. *British Journal of Political Science* 4: 489–499. Review article.

1881. Dunn, M. C. 1993. Islamism Parties in Democratizing States: A Look at Jordan and Yemen. *Middle East Policy* 2 (2): 16–27.

1882. Dupret, B. February 1992. Waiting for Democracy for Thirty Years [in Algeria].* *La Revue Nouvelle* 2–3: 9–17.

1883. Duran, K. June 1989. The Second Battle of Algiers. *Orbis* 33 (3): 403–421.

1884. Duran, K. November 1990. The Predictable Failure of Benazir Bhutto. *World and I* 5: 110–116.

1885. Durao Barroso, J. 1987. Democratization in Portugal: A Tentative Systemic Interpretation.* *Analise Social* 95: 15–36.

1886. Durham, W. L. October 1984. The Proposed Vredeling Directive: A Modest Proposal or the Exportation of Industrial Democracy? *Virginia Law Review* 70 (7): 1469–1503.

1887. Durr, W. 1975. Ahrensberg Model: Example of Cooperative Entrepreneurial Democracy. *Politische Vierteljahresschrift* 16 (6): 401–410.

1888. Durrance, J. C. 1992. The White House Conference and Democracy: A Missed Opportunity. *Government Information Quarterly* 9 (3): 341–346.

1889. Dutt, N. November 1993. *See* Clarke, H. D. (November 1993).

1890. Dutt, V. P. December 1976. The Emergency in India: Background and Rationale. *Asian Survey* 16 (12): 1124–1138.

1891. Dutter, L. E. January 1978. The Netherlands as a Plural Society. *Comparative Political Studies* 10 (4): 555–588.

1892. Duus, P. June 1978. Yoshino Sazuko: The Christian as Political Critic. *Journal of Japanese Studies* 4 (2): 301–326.

1893. Dworkin, R. September 1987. What Is Equality? Part 4: Political Equality. *University of San Francisco Law Review* 22: 1–30.

1894. Dworkin, R. October 1987. What Is Equality? Part 3: The Place of Liberty. *Iowa Law Review* 73: 1–133.

1895. Dworkin, R. 1990. Equality, Democracy, and Constitution: We the People in Court. *Alberta Law Review* 28 (2): 324–346.

1896. Dybbroe, O. 1979. Why Property Owning Democracy? Some Notes on the Defeat of Social Housing and on the Role of the Architect Planner in a Capitalist Society. *Habitat International* 4 (3): 253–263.

1897. Dymski, G. A., and J. E. Elliott. 1988. Capitalism and the Democratic Economy. *Social Philosophy and Policy* 6 (1): 140–164.

1898. Dyson, S. October 1994. Polls Apart? The 1990 Nicaraguan and 1992 British General Elections. *Political Quarterly* 65 (4): 425–431.

1899. Dziewiecka-Bokun, L. 1991. From Communism to Democracy: The Polish Revolution of 1989 and Its Aftermath. *Polish Political Science Yearbook* 21: 37–43.

1900. Dzouza, F. November 1994. Democracy as a Cure for Famine. *Journal of Peace Research* 31 (4): 369–374.

1901. Eakin, J. M. 1984. Hospital Power-Structure and the Democratization of Hospital Administration in Quebec. *Social Science & Medicine* 18 (3): 221–228.

1902. Eakin, J. M. 1984. Survival of the Fittest: The Democratization of Hospital Administration in Quebec. *International Journal of Health Services* 14 (3): 397–412.

1903. Eastman, T. March 1984. The Burger Court and the Founding Fathers. *Policy Review* 28: 14–19.

1904. Easton, S. T. February 1992. *See* Warwick, P. (February 1992).

1905. Ebeling, T., and P. Staber. 1985. Education, Libraries, and Democracy after the Boom: A Comment on Some Consequences of the Increasing Crisis of Social Policy in the FRG.* *Zentralblatt für Bibliothekswesen* 99 (1): 17–22.

1906. Eberstadt, N. September 1989. Democracy and Development in East Asia. *Global Affairs* 4 (4): 74–86.

1907. Ebert, F. 1974. Staat und Demokratie unserer Sozialistischen Gesellschaft. *Einheit* 29 (4): 396–403.

1908. Ebisch, G. A. 1977. Democracy and General Will. *Journal of Thought* 12 (1): 14–20.

1909. Eccles, A. J. 1977. Industrial Democracy and Organizational Change. *Personnel Review* 6 (1): 43–49.

1910. Echenique, L. J. 1989. Les Deux Faces du Boom Agricole. *Notes et Etudes Documentaires* (4): 66–84.

1911. Echeverria, J. 1987. Modernisation Politique, Systeme Institutionnel et Mouvements Sociaux. *Mondes en Developpement* 15 (60): 35–51.

1912. Ecklein, J. L., and J. Z. Giele. June 1981. Women's Lives and Social Policy in East Germany and the United States. *Studies in Comparative Communism* 14 (2–3): 191–207.

1913. Eckstein, G. G. 1979. Ist Demokratischer Sozialismus Moeglich? Skeptische Betrachtungen Aus Amerikanischer Sicht. *Frankfurter Hefte* 34 (6): 20–29.

1914. Eckstein, H., and W. D. Burnham. September 1984. Civic Inclusion and Its Discontents. *Daedalus* 113 (4): 107–160.

1915. Edelstein, J. D., and M. Warner. 1977. Research Areas in National Union Democracy. *Industrial Relations* 16 (2): 186–198.

1916. Eden, R. August 1982. Doing without Liberalism: Weber's Regime Politics. *Political Theory* 10 (3): 379–407.

1917. Eden, R. July 1983. Bad Conscience for a Nietzschean Age: Weber's Calling for Science. *Review of Politics* 45 (3): 366–392.

1918. Eden, R. June 1986. Tocqueville on Political Realignment and Constitutional Forms. *Review of Politics* 48 (3): 349–373.

1919. Edersheim, J. G. June 1985. Free Speech and Union Newspapers: Internal Democracy and Title I Rights. *Harvard Civil Rights-Civil Liberties Law Review* 20 (2): 485–523.

1920. Edinger, L. J. 1985. Politics of the Aged: Orientations and Behavior in Major Liberal Democracies. *Zeitschrift für Gerontologie* 18 (2): 58–64.

1921. Edles, L. D. September 1993. The Sacred and the Spanish Transition to Democracy. *Social Compass* 40 (3): 399–414.

1922. Eduards, M. L. September 1991. Toward a Third Way: Women's Politics and Welfare Policies in Sweden. *Social Research* 58 (3): 677–705.

1923. Edwards, A. C., and S. Edwards. March 1992. Markets and Democracy: Lessons from Chile. *World Economy* 15 (2): 203–219.

1924. Edwards, M. June 1981. Foreign Policy: The Case for a Third Option. *World Affairs* 144 (1): 3–13.

1925. Edwards, S. March 1992. *See* Edwards, A. (March 1992).

1926. Eggers, W. D. July 1991. The New Opposition: The Official, Illustrated Soviet Democracy Movement Guide. *Reason* 23: 40–43.

1927. Eich, D. 1981. Spanien: Von der Diktatur zur Behinderten Demokratiserung. *Gewerkschaftliche Monatshefte* 32 (1): 22–34.

1928. Eichenberg, R. C. March 1983. *See* Domke, W. K. (March 1983).

1929. Eichenberger, J. Y. 1974. Industrial Democracy and the French Board of Directors. *Journal of General Management* 1 (4): 48–58.

1930. Eichner, A. S. March 1982. Reflections on Social Democracy: A "Good Society" in the Coming Era Would Require a New International Economic Order. *Challenge* 25: 33–42.

1931. Eide, I. 1982. Thoughts on the Democratization of Education in Europe. *Prospects* 12 (1): 79–88.

1932. Eidelberg, P. September 1991. The End of Ideology and the Decay of Politics. *Perspectives on Political Science* 20 (4): 203–210.

1933. Eilts, H. F. September 1990. Islamic Fundamentalism: A Quest for a New Order. *Mediterranean Quarterly* 1 (4): 27–45.

1934. Einhorn, E. S. 1988. *See* Logue, J. E. (1988).

1935. Eisel, S. March 1986. Consensus in Conflict: The Survival of Liberal Democracy between Totalitarianism and Anarchy. *Aus Politik und Zeitgeschichte* 10 (8): 3–15.

1936. Eisenstein, Z. 1991. Privatizing the State: Reproductive Rights, Affirmative Action, and the Problem of Democracy. *Frontiers: A Journal of Women Studies* 12 (1): 98–125.

1937. Ekelund, R. B., Jr. April 1978. *See* Crain, W. M. (April 1978).

1938. Ekert Jaffe, O. 1985. School Attendance between the Ages of Seven and Twenty: Democratization or Exacerbation of Inequalities.* *Population* 40 (3): 491–505.

1939. Ekiert, G. July 1991. Democratization Processes in East Central Europe: A Theoretical Reconsideration. *British Journal of Political Science* 21 (3): 285–313.

1940. Ekiert, G. December 1992. Peculiarities of Post-Communism Politics: The Case of Poland. *Studies in Comparative Communism* 25 (4): 341–361.

1941. El Mikawy, N. March 1991. The Egyptian Parliament and Transition to Democracy. *American-Arab Affairs* 36: 18–20.

1942. Elaigwu, J. I. September 1991. Federalism and the National Leadership in Nigeria. *Publius* 21 (4): 125–144.

1943. Elazar, D. J. June 1978. The Constitution, the Union, and the Liberties of the People: Abraham Lincoln's Teaching about the American Political System as Articulated on His Tour from Springfield to Washington in February, 1861. *Publius* 8 (3): 141–176.

1944. Elazar, D. J. September 1980. The Political Theory of Covenant: Origins and Modern Development. *Publius* 10 (4): 3–30.

1945. Elazar, D. J. March 1985. Federalism and Consociational Regimes. *Publius* 15 (2): 17–34.

1946. Elazar, D. J. March 1990. "To Secure the Blessings of Liberty": Liberty and American Federal Democracy. *Publius* 20 (2): 1–13.

1947. Elazar, D. J. March 1993. Communal Democracy and Liberal Democracy in the Jewish Political Tradition. *Jewish Political Studies Review* 5 (1–2): 5–31.

1948. Elazar, D. J. March 1993. Communal Democracy and Liberal Democracy: An Outside Friend's Look at the Swiss Political Tradition. *Publius* 23 (2): 3–18.

1949. Elcock, H. June 1992. Making Bricks without Straw: The Polish Ombudsman and the Transition to Democracy. *International Journal of the Sociology of Law* 20 (2): 173–182.

1950. Elden, J. M. March 1981. Political Efficacy at Work: The Connection between More Autonomous Forms of Workplace Organization and a More Participatory Politics. *American Political Science Review* 75 (1): 43–58.

1951. Elden, M. 1983. Democratization and Participative Research in Developing Local Theory. *Journal of Occupational Behavior* 4 (1): 21–33.

1952. Elgin, D. March 1993. Revitalizing Democracy through Electronic Town Meetings. *Spectrum* 66 (2): 6–13.

1953. Eling, L. 1980. Democracy in Asia: The Political Situation in the ASEAN States.* *Politische Meinung* 191: 61–71.

1954. El-Khazen, F. 1994. Lebanon's First Postwar Parliamentary Elections, 1993. *Middle East Policy* 3 (1): 120–136.

1955. Elkin, S. L. June 1990. Citizenship and Constitutionalism in Post Communist Regimes. *PS: Political Science & Politics* 23 (2): 163–166.

1956. Elklit, J. 1994. Denmark's Electoral System.* *Statsvetenskaplig Tidskrift* 97 (1): 3–9.

1957. Ellenman, D. P. September 1984. Theory of Legal Structure: Worker Cooperatives. *Journal of Economic Issues* 18 (3): 861–891.

1958. Ellingsen, M. 1992. The American Republic: A Paradigm for Democratization in the Communist World? *Journal of Interdisciplinary Studies* 4 (1–2): 81–101.

1959. Elliott, J. April 1978. Conflict or Co-operation? The Growth of Industrial Democracy. *Employment Gazette* 86: 404–406.

1960. Elliott, J. August 1981. In Search of a Alternative Power Basis. *Education and Urban Society* 13 (4): 507–529.

1961. Elliott, J. 1984. Towards Parliamentary Democracy in the Third World: The Case of Thailand. *Parliamentary Affairs* 37 (2): 216–228.

1962. Elliott, J. E., and J. V. Scott. 1987. Theories of Liberal Capitalist Democracy: Alternative Perspectives. *International Journal of Social Economics* 14 (7–9): 52–87.

1963. Elliott, J. E. 1988. *See* Dymski, G. A. (1988).

1964. Ellis, M. S. March 1992. The Democratization of Central and Eastern Europe: An Afterword. *American University Journal of International Law and Policy* 7: 743–748.

1965. Ellison, J. 1981. Anticipatory Democracy in Action: Colorado Front Range Project. *Futurist* 15 (6): 10–14.

1966. Ellner, S. July 12, 1993. Venezuela Takes the Next Step. *New Leader* 76: 5–7.

1967. Ellner, S. December 1993. The Deepening of Democracy in a Crisis Setting: Political Reform and the Electoral Process in Venezuela. *Journal of Interamerican Studies and World Affairs* 35 (4): 1–42.

1968. El-Shagi, E. 1986. Demokratie und Wirtschaftliche Entwicklung. *Zeitschrift für Wirtschafts Politik* 35 (2): 131–144.

1969. Ely, J. 1977. That No Office Whatever Be Held during Life or Good Behavior: Judicial Impeachment and the Struggle for Democracy in South Carolina. *Vanderbilt Law Review* 30 (2): 167–209.

1970. Ely, J. 1981. Democracy and the Right to Be Different. *New York University Law Review* 56 (2–3): 397–405.

1971. Ember, C. R., M. Ember, and B. M. Russett. July 1992. Peace Between Participatory Politics: A Cross-Cultural Test of the "Democracies Rarely Fight Each Other" Hypothesis. *World Politics* 44 (4): 573–599.

1972. Ember, C. R., B. Russett, and M. Ember. February 1993. Political Participation and Peace: Cross-Cultural Codes. *Cross-Cultural Research* 27 (1–2): 97–145.

1973. Ember, M. July 1992. *See* Ember, C. R. (July 1992).

1974. Ember, M. February 1993. *See* Ember, C. R. (February 1993).

1975. Emberley, P. 1989. Places and Stories: The Challenges of Technology. *Social Research* 56 (3): 741–785.

1976. Emery, F. 1976. Implications of Democratization of Work. *Ekistics* 42 (250): 169–172.

1977. Emmanual, A. July 1977. The "Transitional" State.* *L'Homme et la Societe* 45–46: 169–190.

1978. Emmanual, P. March 1981. Elections and Parties in the Eastern Caribbean: A Historical Survey. *Caribbean Review* 10 (2): 14–17.

1979. Emmons, J. June 1991. *See* Siverson, R. M. (June 1991).

1980. Enders, T. O. March 1982. A Comprehensive Strategy for the Caribbean Basin: The U.S. and Her Neighbors. *Caribbean Review* 11 (2): 10–13.

1981. Enelow, J. M., and M. J. Hinich. February 1982. Nonspatial Candidate Characteristics and Electoral Competition. *Journal of Politics* 44 (1): 115–130.

1982. Engberg, J., and J. Gidlund. 1982. Organizations and Pluralist Democracy. *Scandinavian Political Studies* 5 (4): 315–335.

1983. Engedayehu, W. 1993. Ethiopia: Democracy and the Politics of Ethnicity. *Africa Today* 40 (2): 29–52.

1984. Engelmann, H. O. December 1991. A Sociohistorical Perspective for East European Developments. *Journal of Political and Military Sociology* 19 (2): 217–231.

1985. Engels, J. 1992. The Development of Attic Democracy in the Era of Eubulus and Lycurgus (355–322 BC) and Consequences of the Internal Migration of Citizens in Attica. *Hermes: Zeitschrift für Klassische Philologie* 120 (4): 425–453.

1986. Engelstein, S. 1982. Supreme Court Sets Back Union Democracy. *Dissent* 29 (4): 394–399.

1987. Engeman, T. S. September 1991. William Dean Howells' "Poor Real Life": The Royal Road to the American Character. *Interpretation* 19 (1): 29–42.

1988. England, R. E. November 1988. *See* Morgan, D. R. (November 1988).

1989. England, R. W. June 1976. Criminal Justice in the American Democracy. *Current History* 70 (417): 241–244, 277.

1990. Engle, H. E. March 1986. *See* Roberts, W. R. (March 1986).

1991. Englund, T. July 1994. Education as a Citizenship Right: A Concept in Transition—Sweden Related to Other Western Democracies and Political Philosophy. *Journal of Curriculum Studies* 26 (4): 383–399.

1992. Engstrom, R. L. December 1994. The Voting Rights Act: Disfranchisement, Dilution, and Alternative Election Systems. *PS: Political Science & Politics* 27 (4): 685–688.

1993. Engstrom, R. L., and M. D. McDonald. December 1993. "Enhancing" Factors in At-Large Plurality and Majority Systems: A Reconsideration. *Electoral Studies* 12 (4): 385–401.

1994. Enloe, C. H. September 1977. Internal Colonialism, Federalism and Alternative State Development. *Publius* 7 (4): 145–160.

1995. Ensalaco, M. May 1994. In With the New, Out With the Old? The Democratising Impact of Constitutional Reform in Chile. *Journal of Latin American Studies* 26 (2): 409–429.

1996. Entelis, J. P. September 1988. Algeria Under Chadli: Liberalization without Democratization or, Perestroika, Yes; Glasnost, No! *Middle East Insight* 6: 47–64.

1997. Entelis, J. P. May 1992. The Crisis of Authoritarianism in North Africa: The Case of Algeria. *Problems of Communism* 41: 71–81.

1998. Entelis, J. P., and L. J. Arone. 1992. Algeria in Turmoil: Islam Democracy and the State. *Middle East Policy* 1 (2): 23–35.

1999. Entman, R. M. 1993. Putting the First Amendment in Its Place: Enhancing American Democracy through the Press. *University of Chicago Legal Forum:* 61–82.

2000. Epee, M. January 1991. Evolution a Pas Mesures au Cameroun: Le "Our Mai" a La Democratie. *Jeune Afrique* 31: 26–28.

2001. Epstein, B. 1989. The Reagan Doctrine and Right-Wing Democracy. *Socialist Review* 19 (1): 9–38.

2002. Epstein, E. C. October 1984. Legitimacy, Institutionalization, and Opposition in Exclusionary Bureaucratic-Authoritarian Regimes: The Situation of the 1980s. *Comparative Politics* 17 (1): 37–64.

2003. Epstein, L. D. 1994. Changing Perceptions of the British System. *Political Science Quarterly* 109 (3): 483–497. Discussion, 498–514.

2004. Erdmann, G. January 1991. Democratization in Africa: Prospects and Conditions.* *Blatter für Deutsche und Internationale Politik* 36 (1): 51–69.

2005. Erh-Soon Tay, A. June 1990. Communist Visions, Communist Realities, and the Role of Law. *Journal of Law and Society* 17 (2): 155–169.

2006. Ericson, E. L. 1976. CIA and Crisis of Democracy. *Humanist* 36 (1): 26–27.

2007. Erkins, R. 1983. The Recent Discussion on Consociational Democracy and Its Importance for South Africa. *Politeia (UNISA)* 2 (2): 27–45.

2008. Erlich, H. S. 1974. *See* Klein, H. (1974).

2009. Ermann, M. D. December 1981. *See* Waegel, W. B. (December 1981).

2010. Ernst, P. 1990. Democratization of Economic Management. *Politicka Ekonomie* 38 (4): 399–412.

2011. Ersan, T. 1982. Turkey's Battered Democracy: After Violence, Bloodshed and a Military Coup, What Are the Prospects for the Future? *Index on Censorship* 11: 11–14.

2012. Erskov, S. August 1993. Industrial Democracy in the System of Market Relations. *Problems of Economic Transition* 36 (4): 81–96.

2013. Ersson, S. April 1989. *See* Lane, J. E. (April 1989).

2014. Ersson, S., K. Janda, and J. Lane. July 1985. Ecology of Party Strength in Western Europe: A Regional Analysis. *Comparative Political Studies* 18 (2): 170–205.

2015. Ersson, S., and J. Lane. January 1981. The Socio-Economic Structure of European Democracies. *West European Politics* 4 (1): 120–133.

2016. Ersson, S., and J. Lane. 1983. Political Stability in European Democracies. *European Journal of Political Research* 11 (3): 245–264.

2017. Ertukel, A. D. September 1985. Debating Initiative Reform: A Summary of the Second Annual Symposium on Elections at the Center for the Study of Law and Politics. *Journal of Law and Politics* 2: 313–334.

2018. Eschetschwarz, A. 1989. Quasi-Representative Democracy in Switzerland: Between Theory and Reality, 1879–1987. *Canadian Journal of Political Science* 22 (4): 739–764.

2019. Eschetschwarz, A. December 1989. The Role of Semi-Direct Democracy in Shaping Swiss Federalism: The Behavior of Cantons Regarding Revision of the Constitution, 1866–1981. *Publius* 19 (1): 79–106.

2020. Eschetschwarz, A. March 1990. The Swiss Labor Party between the Yoke of Federalism and the Institutions of Semi-Direct Democracy. *Studies in Comparative Communism* 23 (1): 73–87.

2021. Escudero, J. C. 1981. Democracy, Authoritarianism, and Health in Argentina. *International Journal of Health Services* 11 (4): 559–572.

2022. Esherick, J. W., and J. N. Wasserstrom. November 1990. Acting Out Democracy: Political Theater in Modern China. *Journal of Asian Studies* 49 (4): 835–865.

2023. Espinal, R. October 1990. *See* Conaghan, C. M. (October 1990).

2024. Espinal, R. October 1992. Development, Neoliberalism and Electoral Politics in Latin America. *Development and Change* 23 (4): 27–48.

2025. Esping-Anderson, G. October 1978. Social Class, Social Democracy, and the State: Party Policy and Party Decomposition in Denmark and Sweden. *Comparative Politics* 11 (1): 42–58.

2026. Esping-Anderson, G. March 1985. *See* Campbell, J. C. (March 1985).

2027. Esposito, J. L., and J. P. Piscatori. June 1991. Democratization and Islam. *Middle East Journal* 45 (3): 427–440.

2028. Esquith, S. L. May 1988. The Original Position as Social Practice. *Political Theory* 16 (2): 300–334.

2029. Esquith, S. L. March 1991. Liberal Education and Citizenship. *Perspectives on Political Science* 20 (2): 69–72.

2030. Estavam-Martins, C. 1981. Three Concepts of Democracy and Contemporary Marxism.* *Dados* 24 (3): 305–329.

2031. Esterhuyse, W. June 1992. Scenarios for South Africa: Instability and Violence or Negotiated Transition? *Long Range Planning* 25: 21–26.

2032. Esteves Cardosa, M. 1986. Democratic Authority and the System of Political Authorization: A Concept and a Model.* *Analise Social* 91: 231–257.

2033. Estlund, D. M. June 1993. Who's Afraid of Deliberate Democracy? On the Strategic Deliberative Dichotomy in Recent Constitutional Jurisprudence. *Texas Law Review* 71 (7): 1437–1477.

2034. Estlund, D. M. March 1994. Opinion Leaders, Independence, and Condorcet Jury Theorem. *Theory and Decision* 36 (2): 131–162.

2035. Ethier, D. July 1991. Democratic Consolidation in Southern Europe, Latin America, and Southeast Asia: Comparative Perspectives. *Journal of Developing Societies* 7 (2): 195–217.

2036. Ettema, J. S., and T. L. Glasser. March 1994. The Irony in and of Journalism: A Case Study in the Moral Language of Liberal Democracy. *Journal of Communication* 44 (2): 5–28.

2037. Etzioni, A. March 1992. On the Place of Virtues in a Pluralistic Democracy. *American Behavioral Scientist* 35 (4–5): 530–540.

2038. Etzioni-Halevy, E. September 1975. Protest Politics in the Israeli Democracy. *Political Science Quarterly* 90 (3): 497–520.

2039. Etzioni-Halevy, E. April 1988. Inherent Contradictions of Democracy: Illustrations from National Broadcasting Corporations. *Comparative Politics* 20 (3): 325–340.

2040. Etzioni-Halevy, E. 1989. The Contradiction of Power, Conflict and Change in a Democracy: A Demo-Elite Perspective. *Current Perspectives in Social Theory* 9: 177–197.

2041. Etzioni-Halevy, E. March 1989. Elite Power, Manipulation and Corruption: A Demo-Elite Perspective. *Government and Opposition* 24 (2): 215–231.

2042. Etzioni-Halevy, E. 1990. Democratic-Elite Theory: Stabilization vs. Breakdown of Democracy. *Archives Europeennes de Sociologie* 31 (2): 317–350.

2043. Etzioni-Halevy, E. 1994. The Religious Elite Connection and Some Problems of Israeli Democracy. *Government and Opposition* 29 (4): 477–493.

2044. Euben, J. P. August 1986. The Battle of Salamis and the Origins of Political Theory. *Political Theory* 14 (3): 359–390.

2045. Euben, J. P. September 1993. Democracy Ancient and Modern. *PS: Political Science & Politics* 26 (3): 478–480.

2046. Eule, J. N. 1990. Judicial Review of Direct Democracy. *Yale Law Journal* 99 (7): 1503–1590.

2047. Evan, W. M. January 1977. Hierarchy, Alienation, Commitment, and Organizational Effectiveness. *Human Relations* 30 (1): 77–94.

2048. Evans, G. October 1994. *See* Heath, A. (October 1994).

2049. Evans, G. January 1994. *See* Whitefield, S. (January 1994).

2050. Evans, G., and S. Whitefield. October 1993. Identifying the Bases of Party Competition in Eastern Europe. *British Journal of Political Science* 23: 521–548.

2051. Evans, J. W. 1979. Liberal Democracy. *Search* 10 (7–8): 260–262.

2052. Evriviades, M. L. November 1979. Greece after Dictatorship. *Current History* 77 (451): 162–166.

2053. Evriviades, M. L. May 1981. A New Era in Greece. *Current History* 80 (466): 218–219, 229–232.

2054. Ewell, J. January 1986. Venezuela: Interim Report on a Social Pact. *Current History* 85 (507): 25–28, 39–40.

2055. Ewing, K. February 1983. The Politics of Sufism: Redefining the Saints of Pakistan. *Journal of Asian Studies* 42 (2): 251–268.

2056. Ezrahi, Y. September 1992. Technology and Civil Epistemology of Democracy. *Inquiry* 35 (3–4): 363–376.

2057. Fabbrini, S. 1988. The New Characteristics of Political Change and the Problem of Its Institutionalization.* *Teoria Politica* 4 (2): 107–134.

2058. Faber, W. O. May 1979. *See* Clem, A. L. (May 1979).

2059. Faes, G. August 1991. Le Role Des Avocats. *Jeune Afrique Economie* 74–76.

2060. Faes, G. April 7, 1994. Centrafrique: Les Infortunes de l'Amitie. *Juene Afrique* 34: 14–17.

2061. Fagerberg, J. May 1990. The Decline of Social Democratic State Capitalism in Norway. *New Left Review* 181: 60–94.

2062. Fairbanks, J. D. March 1981. The Priestly Functions of the Presidency: A Discussion of the Literature on Civil Religion and Its Implications for the Study of Presidential Leadership. *Presidential Studies Quarterly* 11 (2):

2063. Fajnzylber, F. 1986. Reflexoes Sobre os Limites e Potencialidades Economicas da Democratizacao. *Revista de Economia Politica* 6 (1): 5–34.

2064. Faksh, M. A., and R. F. Faris. 1993. The Saudi Conundrum: Squaring the Security-Stability Circle. *Third World Quarterly* 14 (2): 277–293.

2065. Falcoff, M. July 1982. Eduardo Frei Montalva (1911–1982). *Review of Politics* 44 (3): 323–327.

2066. Falcoff, M. March 1986. Chile: The Dilemma for U.S. Policy. *Foreign Affairs* 64 (4): 833–848.

2067. Falcoff, M. March 1990. The Democratic Prospect in Latin America. *Washington Quarterly* 13 (2): 183–192.

2068. Falk, R. December 1976. Human Rights in South Korea: The Desperate Prospect. *International and Comparative Public Policy* 1 (1): 21–28.

2069. Falk, R. September 1982. The Global Setting and Transition to Democracy: Preliminary Conjectures. *Alternatives* 8 (2): 193–208.

2070. Falk, R. December 1984. *See* Diokno, J. (December 1984).

2071. Falk, R. January 1986. Solving the Puzzles of Global Reform. *Alternatives* 11 (1): 45–81.

2072. Falk, R. June 1986. Nuclear Weapons and the Renewal of Democracy. *Scandinavian Journal of Development Alternatives* 5 (2–3): 25–47.

2073. Falk, R. 1987. The Surge to Democracy. *Center Magazine* 20 (3): 44–46.

2074. Falk, R. March 1991. Reflections on Democracy and the Gulf War. *Alternatives* 16 (2): 263–274.

2075. Falkenheim, V. C. September 1980. Liberalization and Reform in Chinese Politics. *Current History* 79 (458): 33–36, 45.

2076. Fallend, F. 1990. 100 Years of Austrian Social Democracy: Retrospective and Perspectives for the Future.* *Zeitgeschichte* 17 (7–8): 330–346.

2077. Fan, L. M. 1990. On Mainland China and Democratization. *Issues and Studies* 26 (8): 67–80.

2078. Fandy, M. 1994. Tribe vs. Islam: The Post-Colonial Arab State and the Democratic Imperative. *Middle East Policy* 3 (2): 40–51.

2079. Farago, B. September 1993. Democracy and the Problem of National Minorities.* *Le Debat* 76: 5–24.

2080. Farber, S. March 1982. Economism and Social Democracy in the Russian Revolutionary Movement. *Journal of Social Political and Economic Studies* 7 (1–2): 95–114.

2081. Farer, T. J. September 1980. Searching for Defeat. *Foreign Policy* 40: 155–174.

2082. Farer, T. J. September 1983. Manage the Revolution? *Foreign Policy* 52: 96–117.

2083. Farer, T. J. March 1984. Breaking the Deadlock in Central America. *Washington Quarterly* 7 (2): 100–113.

2084. Farer, T. J. June 1985. Contadora: The Hidden Agenda. *Foreign Policy* 59: 59–72.

2085. Farer, T. J. May 1988. The United States as Guarantor of Democracy in the Caribbean Basin: Is There a Legal Way? *Human Rights Quarterly* 10 (2): 157–176.

2086. Farer, T. J. 1989. Elections, Democracy, and Human Rights: Toward Union. *Human Rights Quarterly* 11 (4): 504–521.

2087. Farer, T. J. August 1989. Reinforcing Democracy in Latin America: Notes toward an Appropriate Legal Framework. *Human Rights Quarterly* 11 (3): 434–451.

2088. Farer, T. J. November 1993. Collective Defending Democracy in a World of Sovereign States: The Western Hemisphere's Prospect. *Human Rights Quarterly* 15 (4): 716–750.

2089. Farhang, M. January 1993. The United States and the Question of Democracy in the Middle East. *Current History* 92 (570): 1–5.

2090. Faria, J. E. July 1982. *See* Lamounier, B. (July 1982).

2091. Faris, R. F. 1993. *See* Faksh, M. A. (1993).

2092. Farnham, P. G. March 1990. The Impact of Citizen Influence on Local Government Expenditure. *Public Choice* 64 (3): 201–212.

2093. Farrell, M. J. 1985. The Judiciary and Popular Democracy: Should Courts Review Ballot Measures Prior to Democracy. *Fordham Law Review* 53 (4): 919–935.

2094. Farren, G. C. October 1989. Procesos de Transicion a la Democratie: Una Vi-sion Personel. *Politica (Santiago, Chile)* 20: 47–56.

2095. Farren, G. C. June 1990. Las Fuerzas Armadas y Transicion a la Democracia en America Latina. *Politica* (22–23): 83–99.

2096. Fassbinder, H. 1981. Self-Determination in Housing: Approaches to the Democratization of the Housing Administration in the Netherlands. *Oesterreichische Zeitschrift für Politikwissenschaft* 10 (3): 347–360.

2097. Fastnow, C. September 1994. *See* Squire, P. (September 1994).

2098. Fatton, R. , Jr. June 1985. The Political Ideology of Julius Nyerere: The Structural Limitations of "African Socialism." *Studies in Comparative International Development* 20 (2): 3–24.

2099. Fatton, R. , Jr. September 1986. The Democratization of Senegal (1976–1983): "Passive Revolution" and the Democratic Limits of Liberal Democracy. *Review (F. Braudel Center)* 10 (2): 279–312.

2100. Fatton, R. , Jr. September 1990. Liberal Democracy in Africa. *Political Science Quarterly* 105 (3): 455–473.

2101. Fatton, R. , Jr. September 1991. Democracy and Civil Society in Africa. *Mediterranean Quarterly* 2 (4): 83–95.

2102. Faulhaber, R. W. 1985. Of Power and Authority, People and Democracy. *Review of Social Economy* 2: 193–211.

2103. Faure, M. 1994. South Africa's New Proportional Electoral System: How Does it Work?* *Politeia (UNISA)* 13 (1): 31–50.

2104. Faure, Y. A. 1990. On Democratization in the Ivory Coast: Past and Present.* *Année Africaine* 115–160.

2105. Faure, Y. A. October 1991. The Political Economy of One Democratization: A Tentative Analysis of a Recent Experiment in the Ivory Coast.* *Politique Africaine* 43: 31–49.

2106. Fauriol, G. A. February 1990. The Shadow of Latin American Affairs. *Foreign Affairs* 69 (1): 116–134.

2107. Faus Belau, A. April 1985. *See* Lopez-Escobar, E. (April 1985).

2108. Faux, J. November 1982. Who Plans? Current Economic Planning Procedures and Some Proposals for Democratizing Them. *Working Papers for a New Society* 99: 12–16.

2109. Feagans, T. L. 1984. SEC Rule 14A-8: New Restrictions on Corporate Democracy? *Buffalo Law Review* 33 (1): 225–267.

2110. Feenberg, A. September 1992. Subversive Rationalization: Technology, Power and Democracy. *Inquiry* 35 (3–4): 301–322.

2111. Feher, F. 1994. *See* Heller, A. (1994).

2112. Feher, F., and A. Heller. March 1983. Class, Democracy, Modernity. *Theory and Society* 12 (2): 211–244.

2113. Feinerman, J. V. September 1989. Human Rights in China. *Current History* 88 (539): 273–276, 293–295.

2114. Feinerman, J. V. September 1990. Deteriorating Human Rights in China. *Current History* 89 (548): 265–269, 279–280.

2115. Feis, W. J. 1976. Is Shareholder Democracy Attainable? *Business Lawyer* 31 (2): 621–643.

2116. Feiwel, G. R. 1987. Arrow and His Thoughts on Equality, Efficiency and Democracy.* *Trimestre Economico* 54 (215): 457–485.

2117. Fejto, F. 1990. Democracy in Hungary. *Pouvoirs* 52: 77–86.

2118. Feldberg, R. L., and E. N. Glenn. 1983. Incipient Workplace Democracy among United States Clerical Workers. *Economic and Industrial Democracy* 4 (1): 47–67.

2119. Feldman, H. J. September 1987. Taiwan: The Great Step Forward. *National Interest* 9: 85–91.

2120. Feldman, R. L., S. Kafatou, R. Taylor, and R. Wood. 1981. Self-Management, Democracy, Socialism. *Socialist Review* 56: 137–140.

2121. Fellman, D. July 1975. The Separation of Powers and the Judiciary. *Review of Politics* 37 (3): 357–376.

2122. Fellner, G. 1980. Hartman, Ludo, Moritz: Between Bourgeoise and Social Democracy 1848–1918.* *Zeitgeschichte* 8 (3): 83–108.

2123. Femenia, N. A. 1987. Argentine Mothers of Plaza De Mayo: The Mourning Process from Junta to Democracy. *Feminist Studies* 13 (1): 9–18.

2124. Femia, J. V. September 1985. Marxism and Radical Democracy. *Inquiry* 28 (3): 293–319.

2125. Fenmore, B., and T. J. Volgy. December 1978. Short-Term Economic Change and Political Instability in Latin America. *Western Political Quarterly* 31 (4): 548–564.

2126. Ferdo, M. 1985. Is There Too Much Democracy in the USSR.* *Annales Economies Societes Civilisations* 40 (4): 811–827.

2127. Ferejohn, J. October 1986. *See* Coleman, J. (October 1986).

2128. Ferge, Z. 1993. Social Change in Eastern-Europe: Social Citizenship in the New Democracies.* *Sociologicky Casopis* 29 (2): 149–166.

2129. Ferguson, T. December 1984. From Normalcy to New Deal: Industrial Structure, Party Competition, and American Public Policy in the Great Depression. *International Organization* 38 (1): 41–94.

2130. Ferleger, L., and J. R. Mandle. December 1987. Democracy and Productivity in the Future American Economy. *Review of Radical Political Economics* 19 (4): 1–15.

2131. Fernandez, G., and L. Narvaez. June 1987. Refugees and Human Rights in Costa Rica: The Mariel Cubans. *International Migration Review* 21 (2): 406–415.

2132. Fernandez-Balboa, J. M., and J. P. Marshall. May 1994. Dialogical Pedagogy in Teacher Education: Toward an Education for Democracy. *Journal of Teacher Education* 45 (3): 172–182.

2133. Fernandez-Jilberto, A. E. 1989. *See* Holman, O. (1989).

2134. Fernandez-Jilberto, A. E. March 1993. Transition to Democracy in a Neoliberal Economy: Rethinking State-Society Relations in Chile. *International Journal of Political Economy* 23 (1): 13–34.

2135. Fernos, A. September 1992. Trading Winds in Puerto Rico: The Dawn of Self-Determination Shines on a Legal System. *William and Mary Bill of Rights Journal* 1 (2): 285–298.

2136. Ferreira Nunes, B., and E. Nascimento. June 1987. Towards a New [Brazilian] Constitution: The Long Transition.* *Les Temps Modernes* 491: 44–61.

2137. Ferrer, A. 1984. Deuda, Soberania y Democracia en America Latina. *Comer Exterior (Mexico)* 34 (10): 988–993.

2138. Ferrera, M. December 1984. Schumpeter and the Debate on the "Competitive" Theory of Democracy.* *Rivista Italiana di Scienza Politica* 14 (3): 413–432.

2139. Fesmire, J. M., and E. C. Beauvals. 1978. Budget Size in a Democracy Revisited: Public Supply of Private, Public, and Semi-Public Goods. *Southern Economic Journal* 45 (2): 477–493.

2140. Fessele, B. H. September 1991. *See* Richardson, W. D. (September 1991).

2141. Fetscher, I. March 1983. Some Problems of Democracy (Can It Remain Vital in Advanced Countries?). *Dissent* 30 (2): 199–208.

2142. Feuer, B. February 1991. Mining Unionism, Political Democracy and Revealed Preferences: The Quid Pro Quo of Labour Relations in Bolivia, Chile and Peru, 1950–1980. *Economic and Industrial Democracy* 12 (1): 97–118.

2143. Feuilherade, P. August 1992. *See* Shahin, M. (August 1992).

2144. Feyerabend, P. 1980. Democracy, Elitism, and the Scientific Method. *Inquiry* 23 (1): 3–18.

2145. Field, M. December 1992. Egypt at the Threshold of Democracy? *Vierteljahresberichte* 130: 329–341.

2146. Fieldman, N. 1981. Ideology, Democracy and the National Front. *Ethnic and Racial Studies* 4 (1): 56–74.

2147. Fierbeck, K. 1994. Economic Liberalization as a Prologue to Democracy: The Case of Indonesia. *Canadian Journal of Development Studies* 15 (2): 151–169.

2148. Fierot, D. 1984. The Theme of Democracy in Mosco and Pareto.* *Pensiero Politico* 17 (3): 335–351.

2149. Figal, G. 1993. Philosophy and Democracy. *Filosoficky Casopis* 41 (2): 203–216.

2150. Filgueira, C. 1987. Uruguay: De la Transition Politique à la Consolidation de la Democratie. *Notes et Etudes Documentaires* 86 (4): 23–41.

2151. Filippov, F. 1990. Continuous Education, Democracy, and Society. *Soviet Education* 32 (3): 44–56.

2152. Filton, T. A. June 1979. A Swedish Road to Socialism: Ernst Wigforss and the Ideological Foundations of Swedish Social Democracy. *American Political Science Review* 73 (2): 505–520.

2153. Fincham, R., and G. Zulu. April 1980. Work Councils in Zambia: The Implementation of Industrial Participatory Democracy. *Labour and Society* 5: 171–190.

2154. Fincher, J. September 1989. Zhao's Fall, China's Loss. *Foreign Policy* 76: 3–25.

2155. Fine, D. March 1991. The Changing Role of Paralegals in Building a Post-Apartheid South Africa. *Social Justice* 18 (1–2): 154–169.

2156. Finer, S. E. 1976. Kinds of Democracy. *New Society* 37 (729): 664–665.

2157. Finer, S. E. January 1985. The Retreat to the Barracks: Notes on the Practice and the Theory of Military Withdrawal from the Seats of Power. *Third World Quarterly* 7 (1): 16–30.

2158. Finer, S. E. June 1990. Problems of the Liberal-Democratic State: An Historical Overview. *Government and Opposition* 25 (3): 334–358.

2159. Finkelstein, B. 1984. Education and the Retreat from Democracy in the United States. *Teachers College Record* 86 (2): 275–282.

2160. Fiorina, M. P., and R. G. Noll. November 1978. Majority Rule Models and Legislative Elections. *Journal of Politics* 41 (4): 1081–1104.

2161. Fiotito, J., and W. E. Hendricks. July 1987. Union Characteristics and Bargaining Outcomes. *Industrial and Labor Relations Review* 40: 569–584.

2162. Fischer, F. 1993. Citizen Participation and the Democratization of Policy Expertise: From Theoretical Inquiry to Practical Cases. *Policy Sciences* 26 (3): 165–187.

2163. Fischer, H. 1993. European Democracy on Trail.* *Europaeische Rundschau* 21 (4): 81–87.

2164. Fisher, S. July 8, 1994. *See* Cline, M. (July 8, 1994).

2165. Fishkin, J., and T. Christiano. October 1993. Democracy and Deliberation: New Directions for Democratic Reform. *Ethics* 104 (1): 179–180.

2166. Fishman, E. January 1985. What Makes Rabbit Run? Updike's Hero as Tocqueville's American Democrat. *American Politics Quarterly* 13 (1): 79–100.

2167. Fishman, N. 1989. Extending the Scope of Representative Democracy. *Political Quarterly* 60 (4): 442–455.

2168. Fishman, R. M. April 1982. The Labor Movement in Spain: From Authoritarianism to Democracy. *Comparative Politics* 14 (3): 281–305.

2169. Fishman, R. M. April 1990. Rethinking State and Regime: Southern Europe's Transition to Democracy. *World Politics* 42 (3): 422–440.

2170. Fishman, W. K. March 1981. Right-Wing Reaction and Violence: A Response to Capitalism's Crises. *Social Research* 48 (1): 157–182.

2171. Fisichella, D. 1980. Interest Groups and Pressure Groups in a Modern Democracy: Outline for Interpretation.* *Rivista Italiana di Scienza Politica* 10 (1): 53–71.

2172. Fisichella, D. 1984. The Second Ballot Majority System and Difficult Democracies.* *Rivista Italiana di Scienza Politica* 14 (2): 309–329.

2173. Fiss, O. M. June 1992. Capitalism and Democracy. *Michigan Journal of International Law* 13: 908–920.

2174. Fistie, P. December 1986. What Is the State of Democracy in Thailand.* *Defense Nationale* 117–132.

2175. Fitzgerald, F. T. 1988. *See* Petras, J. (1988).

2176. Fitzgerald, M. S. June 1980. Computing Democracy: An Analysis of California's New Love Affair with the Initiation Process. *California Journal* 11: 229–243.

2177. Fitzgerald, R. March 1985. Human Needs and Politics: The Ideas of Christian Bay and Herbert Marcuse. *Political Psychology* 6 (1): 87–108.

2178. Fitzmaurice, J. December 1990. Eastern Germany. *Electoral Studies* 9 (4): 327–336.

2179. Flaherty, P. June 1989. Perestroika and the Soviet Working Class. *Studies in Political Economy: A Socialist Review* 39–61.

2180. Flam, H. 1985. Democracy in Debt: Credit and Politics in Paterson, NJ, 1890–1930. *Journal of Social History* 18 (3): 439–462.

2181. Flechtheim, O. K. 1982. The Democratic Dilemma.* *Wirtschaft und Gesellschaft* 8 (2): 429–445.

2182. Fleischer, D. V. November 1983. Political Engineering in South America: Brazil under Comparative Analysis.* *Revista de Estudios Politicos* 36: 61–105.

2183. Flemingmathur, M. E. 1975. Body Polity: Iroquois Village Democracy. *Indian Historian* 8 (1): 31–47.

2184. Fletcher, F. J. August 1987. Mass Media and Parliamentary Elections in Canada. *Legislative Studies Quarterly* 12 (3): 341–372.

2185. Fletcher, J. F. October 1990. Participation and Attitudes toward Civil Liberties: Is There an "Educative" Effect? *International Political Science Review* 11 (4): 439–459.

2186. Fletcher, R. A. June 1983. Cobden as Educator: The Free Trade Internationalism of Eduard Berstein, 1899–1914. *American Historical Review* 88 (3): 561–578.

2187. Fleurbaey, M. June 1993. An Egalitarian Democratic Private Ownership Economy. *Politics and Society* 21 (2): 215–233.

2188. Flint, J. T. October 1976. Conceptual Translations in Comparative Study. *Comparative Studies in Society and History* 18 (4): 502–516.

2189. Flood, M. M. November 1978. Let's Redesign Democracy. *Behavioral Science* 23 (6): 429–440.

2190. Flores, P. 1984. *See* Aguiar, M. A. D. (1984).

2191. Flores, P. December 1984. *See* Desouza, A. (December 1984).

2192. Flores-Olea, V. April 1993. Political Systems and Their Crisis. Part I: Dissolution with the Systems.* *Revista Mexicana de Ciencias Politicas y Sociales* 152: 129–142.

2193. Flynn, P. July 1989. Brazil and Inflation: A Threat to Democracy. *Third World Quarterly* 11 (3): 50–70.

2194. Fogarty, M. P. 1976. The Place of Managers in Industrial Democracy. *British Journal of Industrial Relations* 14 (2): 119–127.

2195. Foglesong, R. E. March 1990. *See* Beauregard, R. A. (March 1990).

2196. Fogt, H. 1984. Basisdemokratie oder Herrschaft der Aktivisten? Zum Politikverstaendnis der Greunen. *Politische Vierteljahresschrift* 25 (1): 97–120.

2197. Fomerand, J. October 1975. Policy Formulation and Change in Gaullist France: The 1968 Orientation Act of Higher Education. *Comparative Politics* 8 (1): 59–89.

2198. Fond, J., and R. Goma. 1991. The Democratization Process in Nicaragua: Players, Strategies, and Conflict.* *Afers Internacionals* 20: 49–75.

2199. Fontaine, J. A. September 1993. Transicion Economica Y Politica En Chile: 1970–1990. *Estudios Publicos* 50: 229–279.

2200. Forbath, W. E. December 1994. The Present of the Past: Voluntarism, Producerism, and the Fate of Economic Democracy. *Law and Social Inquiry* 19 (1): 201–215.

2201. Ford, G. W. 1984. The Democratization of Work in Australia. *Economic Analysis (Belgrade)* 18 (1): 77–102.

2202. Ford, M. 1992. *See* Holmquist, F. (1992).

2203. Forde, H. October 1990. Human Rights and the Evolution of International Norms. *Round Table* 316: 350–366.

2204. Forde, S. June 1986. Thucydides on the Causes of Athenian Imperialism. *American Political Science Review* 80 (2): 433–448.

2205. Forester, T. 1980. Whatever Happened to Industrial Democracy? *New Society* 53 (922): 120–122.

2206. Forkosch, M. D. July 1985. On Perennial Re-Examination of the U.S. Constitution. *American Journal of Economics and Sociology* 44 (3): 348–350.

2207. Formanek, M. 1977. Socialist Democracy.* *Sociologicky Casopis* 13 (5): 467–480.

2208. Formanek, M. 1980. The Development of Personality as Product and Presumption of the Deepening of Socialist Democracy.* *Filosoficky Casopis* 28 (4): 457–481.

2209. Formisano, R. P. June 1976. Toward a Reorientation of Jacksonian Politics: A Review of the Literature, 1959–1975. *Journal of American History* 63 (1): 42–65.

2210. Forndran, E. 1993. Democracy in a Crisis.* *Gegenwartskunde: Gesellschaft, Staat, Erziehung* 42 (4): 495–525.

2211. Forrest, J. B. September 1992. A Promising Start: The Inauguration and Consolidation of Democracy in Namibia. *World Policy Journal* 9 (4): 739–753.

2212. Forrest, J. B. July 1994. Namibia: The First Post-Apartheid Democracy. *Journal of Democracy* 5 (3): 88–100.

2213. Forsythe, D. P. November 1992. Democracy, War, and [U.S.] Covert Action. *Peace Research* 29 (4): 385–395.

2214. Fortin, W. June 1984. The Democratic Challenge in Latin America.* *Sistema* 60–61: 63–71.

2215. Fossum, T. E. 1994. Nationalism, Federalism, and Constitutionalism: Three Central Metaphors in Canadian Politics.* *Internasjonal Politikk* 52 (3): 363–390.

2216. Foster, F. H. April 1993. Procedure as a Guarantee of Democracy: The Legacy of the Perestroika Parliament. *Vanderbilt Journal of Transnational Law* 26: 1–109.

2217. Foster, F. H. November 1993. Izvestiia as a Mirror of Russia Legal Reform: Press, Law, and Crisis in the Post-Soviet Era. *Vanderbilt Journal of Transnational Law* 26: 675–748.

2218. Foster, G. D. September 1982. Consensus and National Security Policy. *Bureaucrat* 11 (3): 49–53.

2219. Foster, J. F. December 1981. The United States, Russia, and Democracy. *Journal of Economic Issues* 15 (4): 975–980.

2220. Fott, D. 1991. John Dewey and the Philosophical Foundations of Democracy. *Social Science Journal* 28 (1): 29–44.

2221. Foweraker, J. October 1987. Corporatist Strategies and the Transition to Democracy in Spain. *Comparative Politics* 20 (1): 57–72.

2222. Fowler, A. March 1991. The Role of NGOs in Changing State Society Relations: Perspectives from Eastern and Southern Africa. *Development Policy Review* 9: 53–84.

2223. Fowler, A. May 1993. Nongovernmental Organizations as Agents of Democratization: An African Perspective. *Journal of International Development* 5: 325–339.

2224. Fowler, D. 1990. Democracy Next Generation. *Educational Leadership* 48 (3): 10+.

2225. Fowler, M. R. 1992. *See* Abraham, H. J. (1992).

2226. Fowler, R. B. 1979. Founding Principles of American Government: Two Hundred Years of Democracy on Trial. *Polity* 12 (1): 142–148.

2227. Fox, D. T., and A. Stetson. March 1992. The 1991 Constitutional Reform: Prospects for Democracy and the Rule of Law in Colombia. *Case Western Reserve Journal of International Law* 24: 139–163.

2228. Fox, J. January 1994. The Difficult Transition from Clientelism to Citizenship: Lessons from Mexico. *World Politics* 46 (2): 151–184.

2229. Fox, J. April 1994. Latin America's Emerging Local Politics. *Journal of Democracy* 5 (2): 105–116.

2230. Fox, J., and L. Hernandez. March 1992. Mexico's Difficult Democracy: Grassroots Movements, NGOs and Local Government. *Alternatives* 17 (2): 165–208.

2231. Foxley, A. December 1982. Algunas Condiciones Para una Democratizacion Estable: El Caso de Chile. *Coleccion Estudios* 9: 139–169.

2232. Fradkin, H. G. September 1988. The "Separation" of Religion and Politics: The Paradox of Spinoza. *Review of Politics* 50 (4): 603–627.

2233. Frakt, P. M. July 1977. Democracy, Political Activity, Economic Development, and Governmental Responsiveness: The Case of Labor Policy. *Comparative Political Studies* 10 (2): 177–212.

2234. Francis, W. L., L. W. Kenny, R. B. Morton, and A. B. Schmidt. November 1994. Retrospective Voting and Political Mobility. *American Journal of Political Science* 38 (4): 999–1024.

2235. Franck, T. M. January 1992. The Emerging Right to Democratic Governance. *American Journal of International Law* 86 (1): 46–91.

2236. Franco, V. July 1981. USA: Democracy and Participation.* *Critica Marxistas* 19 (4): 143–161.

2237. Franda, M. F. April 1976. India's New Authoritarianism. *Common Ground* 2 (2): 11–21.

2238. Frank, A. G. April 1990. Revolution in Eastern Europe: Lessons for Democratic Social Movements (and Socialists?). *Third World Quarterly* 12: 36–52.

2239. Frank, A. G. December 1990. No End to History! History to No End? *Social Justice* 17 (4): 7–29.

2240. Frank, H. 1976. Future of Corporate Democracy. *Baylor Law Review* 28 (1): 39–58.

2241. Frank, L. January 1981. Khama and Jonathan: Leadership Strategies in Contemporary Southern Africa. *Journal of Developing Areas* 15 (2): 173–198.

2242. Frankel, C. 1978. Capitalism, Socialism, and Democracy. *Commentary* 65 (4): 37–39.

2243. Frankel, F. R. June 1990. India's Democracy in Transition. *World Policy Journal* 7 (3): 521–555.

2244. Frankland, E. G. December 1988. The Role of the Greens in West German Parliamentary Politics, 1980–87. *Review of Politics* 50 (1): 99–122.

2245. Frankland, E. G. June 1989. Parliamentary Politics and the Development of the Green Party in West Germany. *Review of Politics* 51 (3): 386–411.

2246. Franklin, M. N., and T. T. Mackie. July 1983. Familiarity and Inertia in the Formation of Governing Coalitions in Parliamentary Democracies. *British Journal of Political Science* 13 (3): 275–298.

2247. Franklin, M. N., and T. T. Mackie. November 1984. Reassessing the Importance of Size and Ideology for the Formation of Governing Coalitions in Parliamentary Democracies. *American Journal of Political Science* 28 (4): 671–692.

2248. Franklin, M. N., R. Niemi, and G. Whitten. October 1994. The Two Faces of Tactical Voting. *British Journal of Political Science* 24 (4): 549–556.

2249. Franz, G. September 1985. Deficit Spending in Competitive Democracies as Perceived by the Electorate and the Elected: Theoretical and Empirical Analysis.* *Zeitschrift für Soziologie und Sozialpsychologie* 37 (3): 478–502.

2250. Fraser, D. M. 1974. Democracy and Representation in the Presidential Nominating Process. *Forensic Quarterly* 48 (3): 357–370.

2251. Fraser, E. E. January 1994. Reconciling Conceptual and Measurement Problems in the Comparative Study of Human Rights. *International Journal of Comparative Sociology* 35 (1–2): 1–18.

2252. Fraser, P. March 1982. British War Policy and the Crisis of Liberalism in May 1915. *Journal of Modern History* 54 (1): 1–26.

2253. Fraser, S. 1983. Industrial Democracy in the 1980s. *Socialist Review* 72: 98–122.

2254. Frederickson, H. G., and D. K. Hart. September 1985. The Public Service and the Patriotism of Benevolence. *Public Administration Review* 45 (5): 547–553.

2255. Frederiksen, B., L. Johannsen, and A. Pedersen. December 1993. Democratic Consolidation in the Baltic Countries.* *Politica* 25 (4): 381–398.

2256. Fredman, L. E. June 1980. Why Great Men Are, or Are Not, Elected President; Some British Views on the Presidency. *Presidential Studies Quarterly* 10 (3): 296–305.

2257. Freeman, D. M. December 1993. The U.S. Presidential Election of 1992 and Its Impact on Asia. *Asian Journal of Political Science* 1 (2): 144–176.

2258. Freeman, G. M. September 1980. The Process of Covenant. *Publius* 10 (4): 71–81.

2259. Freeman, J. R. April 1980. The Logic of Franchisement: A Decision Theoretic Analysis. *Comparative Political Studies* 13 (1): 61–95.

2260. Freeman, J. R., and D. Snidal. 1982. Diffusion, Development and Democratization: Enfranchisement in Western Europe. *Canadian Journal of Political Science/Revue Canadienne de Science Politique* 15 (2): 299–329.

2261. Freeman, R. B. April 1977. Political Power, Desegregation, and Employment of Black School Teachers. *Journal of Political Economy* 85 (2): 299–322.

2262. Freeman, S. 1990. Constitutional Democracy and the Legitimacy of Judicial Review. *Law and Philosophy* 9 (4): 327–370.

2263. Fregosi, R. July 1993. Paraguayan Society and the Democratic Transition.* *Problemes d'Amerique Latine* 10: 3–29.

2264. Frendreis, J. P. July 1984. *See* Browne, E. C. (July 1984).

2265. Frendreis, J. P. August 1986. *See* Browne, E. C. (August 1986).

2266. Frendreis, J. P., D. W. Gleiber, and E. C. Browne. November 1986. The Study of Cabinet Dissolution in Parliamentary Democracies. *Legislative Studies Quarterly* 11 (4): 619–628.

2267. Frenkel, M. March 1993. The Communal Basis of Swiss Liberty. *Publius* 23 (2): 61–70.

2268. Frenkin, A. 1987. Glasnost, an Expression of Soviet Democracy: Openness Is Not an End in Itself but Rather an Instrument of Reorganization.* *Beitraege zur Konfliktforschung* 17 (2): 27–47.

2269. Frescobaldi, D. October 1974. La Difficile Stada turna alla Democrazia. *Affari Esteri* 6: 51–65.

2270. Freudenstein, R. June 25, 1993. Polen 1993: Licht Am Ende des Tunnels? *Europa Archiv: Zeitschrift für Internationale Politik* 48: 361–368.

2271. Frey, B. S. 1978. *See* Pommerehne, W. W. (1978).

2272. Frey, B. S. 1978. Eine Theorie Demokratischer Wirtschaftspolitik. *Kyklos* 31 (2): 208–234.

2273. Frey, B. S. 1979. Politometrics of Government Behavior in a Democracy. *Scandinavian Journal of Economics* 81 (2): 308–322.

2274. Frey, B. S. May 1994. Direct Democracy: Politico-Economic Lessons from Swiss Experience. *American Economic Review* 84 (2): 338–342.

2275. Frey, B. S., and I. Bohnet. March 1993. Democracy by Competition: Referenda and Federalism in Switzerland. *Publius* 23 (2): 71–82.

2276. Frey, R. 1974. Communal Partitioning and Administrative Reform: For or Against More Democracy.* *Gegenwartskunde: Gesellschaft, Staat, Erziehung* 23 (4): 415–427.

2277. Fricke, R. 1988. *See* Dau, R. (1988).

2278. Friedheim, D. V. September 1993. Bringing Society Back into Democratic Transition Theory after 1989: Pact Making and Regime Collapse. *East European Politics and Societies* 7 (3): 482–512.

2279. Friedman, E. Summer 1989a. Modernization and Democratization in Leninist States: The Case of China. *Studies in Comparative Communism* 22 (2–3): 251–264.

2280. Friedman, E. Summer 1989b. Democratization and Re-Stalinization in China. *Telos* 80: 27–36.

2281. Friedman, J. June 1989. The New Consensus. *Critical Review* 3 (3–4): 373–410.

2282. Friedman, M. 1978. Capitalism, Socialism, and Democracy. *Commentary* 65 (4): 39–41.

2283. Friend, T. September 1988. Marcos and the Philippines. *Orbis* 32 (4): 569–586.

2284. Frisch, A. 1981. Eine Partei im Schwebezustand:Union pour la Democratie Française, die Hausmacht Giscard d'Estaings. *Dokumente* 37 (2): 115–118.

2285. Frisch, H. September 1993. The Druze Minority in the Israeli Military: Traditionalizing an Ethnic Policing Role. *Armed Forces & Society* 20 (1): 51–67.

2286. Frisch, M. J. June 1978. Hamilton's Report on Manufactures and Political Philosophy. *Publius* 8 (3): 129–140.

2287. Frisch, M. J. March 1987. Leo Strauss and the American Regime. *Publius* 17 (2): 1–5.

2288. Fritz, H. W. 1976. Racism and Democracy in Tocqueville's America. *Social Science Journal* 13 (3): 65–75.

2289. Froehle, B. T. June 1994. Religious Competition, Community Building, and Democracy in Latin America: Grass-Roots Religious Organizations in Venezuela. *Sociology of Religion* 55 (2): 145–162.

2290. Frognier, H. P. 1986. Corruption and Consociational Democracy: First Thoughts on the Belgium Case. *Corruption and Reform* 1 (2): 143–148.

2291. Frohlich, N., and J. A. Oppenheim. February 1990. Redistributive Politics: A Theory of Taxation for an Incumbent in a Democracy. *Public Choice* 64 (2): 135–153.

2292. Frohlich, N., and J. A. Oppenheim. June 1990. Choosing Justice in Experimental Democracies with Production. *American Political Science Review* 84 (2): 461–477.

2293. Fromm, E. 1976. Freedom, Democracy, Justice: Imperialist Reality and Bourgeoise Demagogy. *IPW Berichte* 5 (7): 6–13.

2294. Frost, A. June 1994. *See* Macun, I. (June 1994).

2295. Frundt, H. J. September 1990. Guatemala in Search of Democracy. *Journal of International Studies and World Affairs* 32 (3): 25–74.

2296. Frydman, R. July 1988. Political Democracy and Social Democracy.* *Projet* 212: 57–68.

2297. Fuentes, C. 1992. The State of the World and Democracy: The Problem of the New Order.* *Teoria Politica* 8 (1–2): 3–17.

2298. Fuerst, J. S. 1984. Democracy's Precarious Showcase. *Christianity and Crisis* 44 (6): 14–17.

2299. Fukuda, K. 1976. Parliamentary Democracy and Political Corruption. *Japan Interpreter* 11 (2): 159–166.

2300. Fukuyama, F. June 1991. The Next South Africa. *National Interest* 24: 13–28.

2301. Fukuyama, F. December 1991. Liberal Democracy as a Global Phenomenon. *PS: Political Science & Politics* 24 (4): 659–664.

2302. Fulcher, J. 1987. Labor Movement Theory Versus Corporatism: Social Democracy in Sweden. *Sociology* 21 (2): 231–252.

2303. Fullbright, J. W. March 1979. The Legislator as Educator. *Foreign Affairs* 57 (4): 719–732.

2304. Fuller, E. January 1, 1993. Transcaucasia: Ethnic Strife Threatens Democratization. *RFE/RL Research Report* 2: 17–24.

2305. Fuller, E. V. September 1991. *See* Perry, E. (September 1991).

2306. Fuller, G. E. June 1991. Respecting Regional Realities. *Foreign Policy* (83): 39–46.

2307. Fuller, G. E. December 1991. Soviet Nationalities and Democratic Reform. *Global Affairs* 6: 23–39.

2308. Fuller, L. K. April 1991. Tiananmen as Treated by the *Christian Science Monitor.* *Political Communication and Persuasion* 8 (2): 79–91.

2309. Fuller, T. September 1992. The End of Socialism's Historical Theology and its Rebirth in Fukuyama's Thesis. *Perspectives on Political Science* 21 (4): 189–192.

2310. Fuller, W. A. 1979. Conservatism and Mysticism, Democracy and Things. *Arctic* 32 (3): 179–188.

2311. Fulop, M. 1992. *See* Andrassy, G. (1992).

2312. Fung, E. 1991. The Alternative of Loyal Opposition: The Chinese Youth Party and Chinese Democracy, 1937–1949. *Modern China* 17 (2): 260–289.

2313. Funston, R. September 1975. The Supreme Court and Critical Elections. *American Political Science Review* 69 (3): 795–812.

2314. Furlong, W. L. September 1993. Panama: The Difficult Transition towards Democracy. *Journal of Interamerican Studies and World Affairs* 35 (3): 19–64.

2315. Furstenburg, F. May 1977. West German Experience with Industrial Democracy. *Annals of the American Academy of Political and Social Science* 431: 44–53.

2316. Fusaro, A. March 1979. Two Faces of British Nationalism: The Scottish National Party and Plaid Cymru Compared. *Polity* 11 (3): 362–386.

2317. Fusi, J. P. July 1982. Spain: The Fragile Democracy. *West European Politics* 5: 222–235.

2318. Gabanyi, A. U. 1990. Romania from Dictatorship to Democracy.* *Osteuropa* 40 (9): 793–801.

2319. Gabis, S. T. August 1978. Political Secrecy and Cultural Conflict: A Plea for Formalism. *Administration and Society* 10 (2): 139–175.

2320. Gaboury, W. J. 1977. G.W. Murray and the Fight for Political Democracy in South Carolina. *Journal of Negro History* 62 (3): 258–269.

2321. Gabricidze, B. N. 1989. The Culture of Socialist Democratism in the Work of Soviets and Their Organs.* *Sovetskoe Gosudarstvo Pravo* 2: 3–11.

2322. Gabriel, O. W. March 1989. Change of Government and Political Support: Party Competition and Structure of Political Support in a Democracy.* *Politische Vierteljahresschrift* 30 (1): 75–93.

2323. Gabriel, O. W. September 1989. Federalism and Party Democracy in West Germany. *Publius* 19 (4): 65–80.

2324. Gadberry, S. 1976. *See* Graubert, J. (1976).

2325. Gaenszle, M. November 1991. Blood in Exchange for Democracy: The Struggle for a New Constitution in Nepal, 1990.* *Internationales Asienforum* 22 (3–4): 233–258.

2326. Gaertner, G. H., K. N. Gaertner, and I. Devine. September 1983. Federal Agencies in the Context of Transition: A Contrast between Democratic and Organizational Theories. *Public Administration (London)* 43 (5): 421–432.

2327. Gaertner, K. N. September 1983. *See* Gaertner, G. H. (September 1983).

2328. Gafke, R., and D. Leuthold. September 1979. The Effect on Voters of Misleading, Confusing, and Difficult Ballot Titles. *Public Opinion Quarterly* 43 (3): 394–401.

2329. Gagel, W. 1974. Democratization and Freedom as Counterparts: Discussions with H. Schelsky.* *Gegenwartskunde: Gesellschaft, Staat, Erziehung* 23 (2): 199–202.

2330. Gagel, W. (ed.). 1980. Massenkommunikation in der Demokratie. *Politische Bildung* 13 (1): 3–85. 5 articles.

2331. Gaillard, P. March 12, 1992. Cameroun: La Vraie Mort du Parti Unique. *Jeune Afrique* 32: 16–18.

2332. Gaitan Pavia, P. September 1993. Considerations on the Debate Concerning Democracy.* *Analisis Politico* 20: 47–57.

2333. Galante, S. 1975. Sulle "Condizioni" della Democrazia Progressiva Nella Linea Politica del PCI (Italian Communist Party) (1943–1948). *Politico* 40 (3): 455–74.

2334. Galeano, E. 1989. Democracy in Latin America: Best Is That Which Best Creates. *Social Justice* 16 (1): 119–126.

2335. Galenson, W. 1974A. Communists and Trade Union Democracy. *Industrial Relations* 13 (3): 228–236.

2336. Galenson, W. 1974B. Communists and Trade Union Democracy: A Rejoinder. *Industrial Relations* 13 (3): 239–243.

2337. Galeotti, G. April 1990. Consensus and Constitution: The Problems of Democracy in James Buchanan's Economic Analysis.* *Stato e Mercato* 28: 103–116.

2338. Gall, N. January 1975. Oil and Democracy in Venezuela. *Common Ground* 1 (1): 53–61.

2339. Gall, N. July 1977. Peru's Schools: Words and Letters. *Common Ground* 3 (3): 21–38.

2340. Gallagher, C. F. April 1976. The Spanish Succession. *Common Ground* 2 (2): 87–100.

2341. Gallagher, T. March 1981. The Growing Pains of Portuguese Democracy. *World Today* 37 (3): 102–109.

2342. Gallagher, T. March 1985. Democracy in Portugal since the 1974 Revolution. *Parliamentary Affairs* 38 (2): 202–218.

2343. Gallagher, T. April 1986. Portugal's Second Decade of Democracy. *World Today* 42 (4): 67–69.

2344. Galli Della Loggia, E. July 1983. Politics and Mythical-Symbolic Integration. *Il Mulino* 228: 538–558.

2345. Galston, M. March 1994. Taking Aristotle Seriously: Republican-Oriented Legal Theory and the Moral Foundation of Deliberative Democracy. *California Law Review* 82 (2): 329–399.

2346. Galston, W. A. 1987. Tocqueville on Liberalism and Religion. *Social Research* 54 (3): 499–518.

2347. Galston, W. A. September 1988. Socratic Reason and Lockean Rights: The Place of the University in a Liberal Democracy. *Interpretation* 16 (1): 101–109.

2348. Galston, W. A., and G. L. Tibbetts. June 1994. Reinventing Federalism: The Clinton/Gore Program for a New Partnership among the Federal, State, Local, and Tribal Governments. *Publius* 24 (3): 23–48.

2349. Gama de Andrade, L. A. September 1985. *See* Cintra, A. O. (September 1985).

2350. Gamarra, E. 1985. *See* Molloy, J. M. (1985).

2351. Gandasegui, M. A. 1988. Democracy in Panama. *Estudios Sociales Centroamericanos* 47: 113–132.

2352. Gangemi, G. 1987. Logical Conventionalism and Democratic Culture.* *Teoria Politica* 3 (3): 101–125.

2353. Ganley, G. D. March 1991. Power to the People via Personal Electronic Media. *Washington Quarterly* 14 (2): 5–22.

2354. Gans, C. March 1988. Justice-Conditioned and Democracy-Based Obedience. *Oxford Journal of Legal Studies* 8: 92–110.

2355. Gans, C. D. June 1990. *See* Bennett, S. E. (June 1990).

2356. Gans, H. J. 1983. News Media, News Policy, and Democracy: Research for the Future. *Journal of Communication* 33 (3): 174–184.

2357. Gant, M. M., and W. Lyons. April 1993. Democratic Theory, Nonvoting, and Public Policy: The 1972–1988 Presidential Elections. *American Political Quarterly* 21: 185–204.

2358. Gao, X. 1989. Political Structural Reform and the Future of Democratization in China. *Journal of Legislation* 16 (1): 47–57.

2359. Garcia, J. Z. December 1988. Democratic Consolidation in El Salvador. *Current History* 87 (533): 421–424, 437–438.

2360. Garcia-Alvarez, M. B. 1977. Political Clubs in People's Democracies. *East European Quarterly* 11 (4): 477–492.

2361. Garcia-Morales, F. 1977. Crisis of Democracy.* *Estudios Sociales Centroamericanos* 6 (16): 23–43.

2362. Gardbaum, S. A. December 1993. Broadcasting, Democracy, and The Market. *Georgetown Law Journal* 82 (2): 373–396.

2363. Gardell, B. 1982. Worker Participation and Autonomy: A Multilevel Approach to Democracy at the Workplace. *International Journal of Health Services* 12 (4): 527–558.

2364. Gardner, N. 1974. Power Diffusion in the Public Sector: Collaboration for Democracy. *Journal of Applied Behavioral Science* 10 (3): 367–372.

2365. Gardner, R. N. June 1990. The Comeback of Liberal Internationalism. *Washington Quarterly* 13 (3): 23–39.

2366. Gargin, T. 1992. France and Democratization in Africa.* *Le Trimestre du Monde* 17: 135–144.

2367. Garner, L. M. March 1992. Unresolved Issues in Brazil: Challenges to the Political Leadership in the 1990s. *Journal of Third World Studies* 9: 59–79.

2368. Garreton, M. M. A. 1981. The Sociopolitical Forces and the Problem of Democracy in Chile.* *Trimestre Economico* 48 (1): 101–120.

2369. Garreton, M. M. A. 1985. Chile: In Search of the Lost Democracy.* *Desarrollo Economico* 25 (99): 381–397.

2370. Garreton, M. M. A. October 1985. Socio-Political Actors and Democratization (in Chile).* *Revista Mexicana de Sociologia* 47 (4): 5–16.

2371. Garreton, M. M. A. June 1988. Problems of Democracy in Latin America: On the Processes of Transition and Consolidation. *International Journal* 43 (3): 357–377.

2372. Garreton, M. M. A. December 1988. Fear and Military Dictatorships.* *La Revue Nouvelle* 12: 21–31.

2373. Garreton, M. M. A. 1989. Les Partis Politiques Chiliens Face à la Transition Democratique.* *Notes et Etudes Documentaires* 4: 35–51.

2374. Garreton, M. M. A. 1990. Democratic Inauguration in Chile: From Pinochet to Aylwin. *Third World Quarterly* 12 (3–4): 64–80.

2375. Garreton, M. M. A. 1991. Political Redemocratization in Chile: Transition, Inauguration and Evolution.* *Estudios Publicos* 42: 101–133.

2376. Garreton, M. M. A. January 1991. From Authoritarianism to Political Democracy [in Latin America].* *Revista Mexicana de Sociologia* 53 (1): 283–292.

2377. Garreton, M. M. A. July 1991. Democracy between Two Eras: Latin America in 1990.* *Foro Internacional* 125: 47–64.

2378. Garreton, M. M. A. November 1991. The 1990s: A Hinge between Two Eras [in Latin America].* *Politica Internazionale* 19 (6): 7–21.

2379. Garreton, M. M. A. February 1994. Human Rights in Processes of Democratization. *Journal of Latin American Studies* 26 (1): 221–234.

2380. Garrett, G. August 1985. *See* Lange, P. (August 1985).

2381. Garrett, G. June 1991. *See* Alvarez, R. M. (June 1991).

2382. Garrett, G. January 1993. The Politics of Structural Change: Swedish Social Democracy and Thatcherism in Comparative Perspective. *Comparative Political Studies* 25 (4): 521–547.

2383. Garrett, G., and P. Lange. July 1986. Performance in a Hostile World: Economic Growth in Capitalist Democracies. *World Politics* 38 (4): 517–545.

2384. Garrett, G., and P. Lange. August 1989. Government Partisanship and Economic Performance: When and How Does "Who Governs" Matter? *Journal of Politics* 51 (3): 676–693.

2385. Garrison, J. W. 1988. Democracy, Scientific Knowledge, and Teacher Empowerment. *Teachers College Record* 89 (4): 487–504.

2386. Garrison, J. W., and K. S. Lawwill. 1993. Democratic Science Teaching: A Role for the History of Science. *Interchange* 24 (1–2): 29–39.

2387. Garro, A. 1993. Nine Years of Transition to Democracy in Argentina: Partial Failure or Qualified Success? *Columbia Journal of Transnational Law* 31 (1): 1–102.

2388. Garson, R. A. 1977. Political Fundamentalism and Popular Democracy in the 1920s. *South Atlantic Quarterly* 76 (2): 219–233.

2389. Gartner, R. February 1990. The Victims of Homicide: A Temporal and Cross-National Comparison. *American Sociological Review* 55 (1): 92–106.

2390. Gartner, R. 1991. Family Structure, Welfare Spending, and Child Homicide in Developed Democracies. *Journal of Marriage and the Family* 53 (1): 231–240.

2391. Garver, J. W. September 1991. Chinese Foreign Policy: The Diplomacy of Damage Control. *Current History* 90 (557): 241–246.

2392. Gasiorowski, M. J. September 1986. Dependency and Cliency in Latin America. *Journal of Interamerican Studies and World Affairs* 28 (3): 47–65.

2393. Gasiorowski, M. J. January 1988. Economic Dependence and Political Democracy: A Cross-National Study. *Comparative Political Studies* 20 (4): 489–515.

2394. Gaskil, R. D. December 1985. The Past, Present and Future of Democracy. *Journal of International Affairs* 38 (2): 161–179.

2395. Gaskil, R. D. March 1990. The Comparative Survey of Freedom: Experiences and Suggestions. *Studies in Comparative International Development* 25 (1): 25–50.

2396. Gasparovic, I. October 1993. Slovakia's Constitution: The Route away from Communism. *Parliamentarian* 74: 201–202.

2397. Gastil, J. March 1992. Why We Believe in Democracy: Testing Theories of Attitude Functions and Democracy. *Journal of Applied Social Psychology* 22 (6): 423–450.

2398. Gastil, J. August 1992. A Definition of Small-Group Democracy. *Small Group Research* 23 (3): 278–301.

2399. Gastil, J. February 1993. Identifying Obstacles to Small Group Democracy. *Small Group Research* 24 (1): 5–27.

2400. Gastil, R. D. October 1978. Pluralist Democracy and the Third World: Political Options and Conflicting Needs. *Worldview* 21 (10): 37–41.

2401. Gati, C. April 1977. The "Europeanization" of Communism. *Foreign Affairs* 55 (3): 539–553.

2402. Gaubatz, K. T. June 1991. Election Cycles and War. *Journal of Conflict Resolution* 35 (2): 212–244.

2403. Gaud, M., and L. Porges. July 1993. Presidents and Transitions.* *Afrique Contemporaine* 167: 29–39.

2404. Gaulme, F. October 1991. Gabon in Search of a New Political and Social Ethos.* *Politique Africaine* 43: 50–62.

2405. Gaulme, F. December 1991. Uncertain Africa.* *Etudes* 581–590.

2406. Gaus, G. F. September 1991. Public Justification and Democratic Adjudication. *Constitutional Political Economy* 2 (3): 251–281.

2407. Gauthiez-Rieucau, D. January 1985. Democracy in Senegal.* *L'Afrique Contemporaine* 133: 12–32.

2408. Gawthrop, L. C. 1989. Ethics and Democracy: The Moral Dimension. *Journal of State Government* 62 (5): 180–184.

2409. Gay, R. August 1990. Popular Incorporation and Prospects for Democracy: Some Implications of the Brazilian Case. *Theory and Society* 19 (4): 447–463.

2410. Gayle, D. J. December 1983. Democratic Pluralism and Economic Growth Reflections on the Costa Rica Case. *Journal of Social, Political and Economic Studies* 8 (4): 355–371.

2411. Gebert, K. December 1991. Anti-Semitism in the 1990 Polish Presidential Election. *Social Research* 58 (4): 723–755.

2412. Geddes, B. June 1991. A Game Theoretical Model of Reform in Latin American Democracies. *American Political Science Review* 85 (2): 371–392.

2413. Geddes, B. October 1994. Challenging the Conventional Wisdom. *Journal of Democracy* 5 (4): 104–118.

2414. Gedicks, F. M., and R. Hendrix. 1987. Democracy, Autonomy, and Values: Some Thoughts on Religion and Law in Modern America. *Southern California Law Review* 60 (6): 1579–1619.

2415. Gedman, J. March 1990. Reconstructing Germany. *World Affairs* 152 (4): 191–194.

2416. Gehlot, N. S. January 1991. The Appointment of Chief Election Commissioner in India: A Critical Study. *Journal of Constitutional and Parliamentary Studies* 25 (1–4): 56–66.

2417. Geiger, J. O. 1974. Aquinas and Education for a Just Technological Democracy. *Education Theory* 24 (4): 394–409.

2418. Geiger, R. L. 1977. Democracy and Crowd: Social-History of an Idea in France and Italy, 1890–1914. *Societas: A Review of Social History* 7 (1): 47–71.

2419. Geisler, G. December 1993. Fair? What Has Fairness Got to Do With It? Vagaries of Election Observations and Democratic Standards. *Journal of Modern African Studies* 31 (4): 613–637.

2420. Geissler, R. April 1979. Participatory Pluralist Democracy and the Media Content.* *Publizistik* 24 (2): 171–187.

2421. Gelb, A. September 1986. *See* Auty, R. (September 1986).

2422. Gelb, J., and M. L. Palley. July 1977. Women and Interest Group Politics: A Case Study of the Equal Credit Opportunity Act. *American Politics Quarterly* 5 (3): 331–352.

2423. Gellner, E. August 1991. Civil Society in Historical Context. *International Social Science Journal* 43 (3): 495–510.

2424. Gelman, A., and G. King. May 1994. A Unified Method of Evaluating Electoral Systems and Redistricting Plans. *American Journal of Political Science* 38 (2): 514–554.

2425. Gelman, A., and G. King. September 1994. Enhancing Democracy through Legislative Redistricting. *American Political Science Review* 88 (3): 541–559.

2426. Gemayel, A. March 1985. The Price and the Promise. *Foreign Affairs* 63 (4): 759–777.

2427. Gendrot, S. November 1980. New York: Democracy Trapped.* *Etudes* 465–477.

2428. Genov, N. May 1991. The Transition to Democracy in Eastern Europe: Trends and Paradoxes of Social Rationalization. *International Social Science Journal* 43 (2): 331–341.

2429. Genovese, E. 1978. Capitalism, Socialism, and Democracy. *Commentary* 65 (4): 41–43.

2430. Gensen, J. June 1993. Democratic Culture and the Arts: Constructing a Useable Past. *Journal of Arts Management, Law and Society* 23: 110–120.

2431. Gensicke, K. H. 1990. Peace and Democracy in the Mass Consciousness of the Federal Republic of Germany.* *IPW Berichte* 19 (1): 18–23.

2432. Gentili, A. M. July 1991. A New African Revolution.* *Il Mulino* 336: 626–636.

2433. Gentleman, J., and V. Zubek. March 1992. International Integration and Democratic Development: The Cases of Poland and Mexico. *Journal of Interamerican Studies and World Affairs* 34 (1): 59–109.

2434. George, B., and P. Millett. 1984. Papua New Guinea: A South Pacific Democracy. *World Today* 40 (8–9): 377–385.

2435. George, L. N. March 1990. Tocqueville's Caveat: Centralized Executive Foreign Policy and American Democracy. *Polity* 22 (3): 419–441.

2436. Geras, N. January 1994. Democracy and the Ends of Marxism. *New Left Review* 203: 92–106.

2437. Gerber, A. November 1994. *See* Ansolabehere, S. (November 1994).

2438. Gerber, D. A. July 1984. The Pathos of Exile: Old Lutheran Refugees in the United States and South Australia. *Comparative Studies in Society and History* 26 (3): 498–522.

2439. Gerchikov, V. I. 1992. The Democratization of Ruling and the Forms of Property.* *Sotsiologicheskie Issledovaniia* (1): 58–70.

2440. Geremek, B. June 1990. Postcommunism and Democracy in Poland. *Washington Quarterly* 13 (3): 125–131.

2441. Geremek, B. April 1992. Problems of Postcommunism: Civil Society Then and Now. *Journal of Democracy* 3 (2): 3–12.

2442. Gerety, T. 1981. Doing without Privacy. *Ohio State Law Journal* 42 (1): 143–166.

2443. Germann, R. E. 1993. Introducing Instruments of Direct Democracy in the German Constitution: What Can Be Learned from the Swiss Experiences?* *Jahrbuch für Politik* 3 (2): 219–238.

2444. Germann, R. E., and J. Steiner. January 1985. Comparing Decision Modes at the Country Level: Some Methodological Considerations Using Swiss Data. *British Journal of Political Science* 15 (1): 123–126.

2445. Gershman, C. 1978. Capitalism, Socialism, and Democracy. *Commentary* 65 (4): 43–45.

2446. Gershman, C. December 1989. The United States and the World Democratic Revolution. *Washington Quarterly* 12 (1): 127–139.

2447. Gershman, C. March 1990. Freedom Remains the Touchstone. *National Interest* 19 (1): 83–86.

2448. Gerston, L. N. December 1989. Policy Making by Referendum in Palau: Grassroots Democracy or Political Paralysis. *Asian Affairs (New York)* 16: 175–185.

2449. Gersuny, C. September 1990. Citizenship and Industrial Relations. *Employee Responsibilities and Rights Journal* 3 (3): 185–197.

2450. Geva, N. September 1993. *See* Mintz, A. (September 1993).

2451. Ghabra, S. March 1991. Voluntary Associations in Kuwait: The Foundation of a New System? *Middle East Journal* 45 (2): 199–215.

2452. Ghabra, S. 1994. Democratization in a Middle Eastern State: Kuwait, 1993. *Middle East Policy* 3 (1): 102–119.

2453. Ghejan, A. M. March 1990. Mass Communications in the Libyan Jamahiriya. *Journal of Black Studies* 20 (3): 324–334.

2454. Ghosh, A. 1988. Centrism, Decentralization and Democracy. *Economic and Political Weekly* 5: 175–176.

2455. Ghosh, A. November 1992. Federalism, Democracy and Decentralization. *Economic and Political Weekly* 27 (46): 2453–2455.

2456. Ghosh, A. January 2, 1993. Market System, Socialism, and Democracy. *Economic and Political Weekly* 28 (1–2): 13–15.

2457. Ghosh, A. April 3, 1993. Socialism, Modern Capitalism, and Democracy. *Economic and Political Weekly* 28 (14): 551–554.

2458. Ghosh, A. December 11, 1993. Democracy, Human Rights and Management of Technological Change. *Economic and Political Weekly* 28 (50): 2697–2699.

2459. Ghosh, K. K. 1977. Indonesia's Transition to Guided Democracy, 1949–1965. *Indian Journal of Politics* 11 (1): 19–29.

2460. Giakoumis, P. 1990. Die Rolle der Armee im Politischen System Griechenlands. *Suedosteuropa Mitteilungen* 30 (3): 191–199.

2461. Gibbons, J. J. 1976. Governance of Industrial Corporations in an Industrial Democracy. *Business Lawyer* 31 (1): 1393–1400.

2462. Gibney, F. B. December 1992. The Promise of the Pacific. *Wilson Quarterly* 16 (1): 64–75.

2463. Gibson, E. L. September 1990. Democracy and the New Electoral Right in Argentina. *Journal of Interamerican Studies and World Affairs* 32 (3): 177–228.

2464. Gibson, J. L. June 1988. Political Intolerance and Political Repression during the McCarthy Red Scare. *American Political Science Review* 82 (2): 511–529.

2465. Gibson, J. L., and R. D. Bingham. March 1984. Skokie, Nazis, and the Elitist Theory of Democracy. *Western Political Quarterly* 37 (1): 32–47.

2466. Gibson, J. L., and R. M. Duch. September 1991. Elitist Theory and Political Tolerance in Western Europe. *Political Behavior* 13 (3): 191–212.

2467. Gibson, J. L., and R. M. Duch. March 1994. Postmaterialism and the Emerging Soviet Democracy. *Political Research Quarterly* 47 (1): 5–39.

2468. Gibson, J. L., R. M. Duch, and K. L. Tedin. May 1992. Democratic Values and the Transformation of the Soviet Union. *Journal of Politics* 54 (2): 329–371.

2469. Gidengil, E. September 1993. *See* Blais, A. (September 1993).

2470. Gidlund, J. 1982. *See* Engberg, J. (1982).

2471. Giele, J. Z. June 1981. *See* Ecklein, J. L. (June 1981).

2472. Gilberg, T. December 1990. Romania: Will History Repeat Itself? *Current History* 89 (551): 409–412, 431–433.

2473. Gilbert, A. 1986. Democracy and Individuality. *Social Philosophy and Policy* 3 (2): 19–58.

2474. Gilbert, A. February 1992. Must Global Politics Constrain Democracy? Realism, Regimes and Democratic Internationalism. *Political Theory* 20 (1): 8–37.

2475. Gilbert, C. E. July 1976. The Shaping of Public Policy. *Annals of the American Academy of Political and Social Science* 426: 116–151.

2476. Gilbert, R. B. 1986. Press Libertarianism's Toll on Democracy. *Journal of Social, Political, and Economic Studies* 11 (2): 175–188.

2477. Giles, M. W., and T. D. Lancaster. September 1989. Political Transition, Social Development and Legal Mobilization in Spain. *American Political Science Review* 83 (3): 817–833.

2478. Giliomee, H. January 1992. The Last Trek? Afrikaners in the Transition to Democracy. *South Africa International* 22: 111–120.

2479. Giliomee, H. October 1992. *See* Rantete, J. (October 1992).

2480. Gill, C. G. 1984. Swedish Wage-Earner Funds: The Road to Economic Democracy. *Journal of General Management* 9 (3): 37–59.

2481. Gillespie, C. G. April 1989. Democratic Consolidation in the Southern Cone and Brazil: Beyond Political Disarticulation. *Third World Quarterly* 11 (2): 93–113.

2482. Gillespie, C. G. September 1990. Paraguay after Stroessner: Democratizing a One-Party State. *Journal of Democracy* 1 (4): 49–58.

2483. Gillespie, R. January 1993. "Programa 2000": The Appearance and Reality of Socialist Renewal in Spain. *West European Politics* 16: 78–96.

2484. Gillespie, R. October 1993. The Continuing Debate on Democratization in Spain. *Parliamentary Affairs* 46 (4): 534–548.

2485. Gilli, D. C. August 1991. From Communism to Democracy in Central Europe: Hungary and Czechoslovakia.* *Rivista Italiana di Scienza Politica* 21 (2): 282–313.

2486. Gilligan, J. J. June 1993. A Search for Community: The Problem of Governance in a Democratic Society. *University of Cincinnati Law Review* 62 (1): 101–112.

2487. Gills, B. 1993. *See* Qadir, S. (1993).

2488. Gills, B., and J. Rocamora. 1992. Low Intensity Democracy. *Third World Quarterly* 13 (3): 501–523.

2489. Gilmore, D. D. January 1993. The Democratization of Ritual: Andalusian Carnival after Franco. *Anthropological Quarterly* 66 (1): 37–47.

2490. Gilmore, H. L. April 1988. Industrial Democracy in Zambia: Is It Working? *Labor Law Review* 39 (4): 195–207.

2491. Gilmour, I. 1983. Tories, Social Democracy and the Center. *Political Quarterly* 54 (3): 257–267.

2492. Gindin, S. April 1991. *See* Panitch, L. (April 1991).

2493. Giner, S. April 1984. Southern European Socialism in Transition. *West European Politics* 7 (2): 135–157.

2494. Giner, S. January 1986. The Logical Structure of Democracy. *Sistema* 70: 3–25.

2495. Ginsberg, B., and E. Sanders. December 1990. Theodore Lowi and Juridical Democracy. *PS: Political Science & Politics* 23 (4): 563–566.

2496. Ginsburg, V., and P. Michel. 1982. Democracy and Dynamic Welfare Optima. *Economic Letters* 9 (4): 315–318.

2497. Gintis, H. May 1978. *See* Bowles, S. (May 1978).

2498. Gintis, H. 1980. Communication and Politics: Marxism and the Problem of Liberal Democracy. *Socialist Review* (50–5): 189–232.

2499. Gintis, H. October 1989. *See* Bowles, S. (October 1989).

2500. Girard, P. May 22, 1991. Burkina: Chronique d'une Perestroika. *Jeune Afrique* 31: 41+. 3 articles and interviews.

2501. Girard, P., and S. Diallo (eds.). March 6, 1991. Gabon: Une Democratie Reussie? *Jeune Afrique* 37+. 7 articles and interviews.

2502. Giraudineau, L. October 15, 1991. *See* Soudan, F. (October 15, 1991).

2503. Girault, C. A. 1988. Election and Progress toward Democracy in the Dominican Republic 1978–1986.* *Problemes d'Amerique Latine* 89: 29–53.

2504. Girault, C. A. December 1988. The Haitian Diaspora: A Prescription for Decency. *Caribbean Review* 16 (2): 14–15, 37–38.

2505. Girling, J. 1988. Development and Democracy in Southeast Asia. *Pacific Review* 1 (4): 332–340.

2506. Girling, J. August 1990. The New Social Forces and the Demand for Democracy.* *Politica Internazionale* 18 (8–10): 71–81.

2507. Girling, R. K. 1980. Industrial Democracy: Teaching by Symposium. *Exchange Organizational Behavior Teaching Journal* 5 (2): 31–33.

2508. Giroux, H. A. 1991. Democracy and the Discourse of Cultural Difference: Towards a Politics of Border Pedagogy. *British Journal of Sociology of Education* 12 (4): 501–519.

2509. Giroux, H. A., and P. McLaren. 1986. Teacher Education and the Politics of Engagement: The Case for Democratic Schooling. *Harvard Educational Review* 56 (3): 213–238.

2510. Gitlin, T. 1980. Making Democracy Safe for America. *Columbia Journalism Review* 18 (6): 53+.

2511. Gittell, M. 1981. Localizing Democracy Out of Schools. *Social Policy* 12 (2): 4–11.

2512. Glahe, F. September 1989. *See* Vorhies, F. (September 1989).

2513. Glahe, F., and F. Vorhies. September 1989. Religion, Liberty and Economic Development: An Empirical Investigation. *Public Choice* 62 (3): 201–215.

2514. Glasser, T. L. March 1994. *See* Ettema, J. S. (March 1994).

2515. Glaudio, D. September 1979. *See* Soares, G. A. D. (September 1979).

2516. Glazer, A., and M. Robbins. May 1985. Congressional Responsiveness to Constituency Change. *American Journal of Political Science* 29 (2): 259–273.

2517. Glazer, N. 1978. Capitalism, Socialism, and Democracy. *Commentary* 65 (4): 45–46.

2518. Gleason, P. March 1987. Pluralism, Democracy, and Catholicism in the Era of World War II. *Review of Politics* 49 (2): 208–230.

2519. Gleditsch, K. S. 1994. Towards Democracy in Mexico.* *Internasjonal Politikk* 52 (1): 89–104.

2520. Gleditsch, N. P. November 1992. Democracy and Peace. *Journal of Peace Research* 29 (4): 369–376.

2521. Gleiber, D. W. August 1986. *See* Browne, E. C. (August 1986).

2522. Gleiber, D. W. July 1984. *See* Browne, E. C. (July 1984).

2523. Gleiber, D. W. November 1986. *See* Frendreis, J. P. (November 1986).

2524. Gleijeses, P. January 1988. The Decay of Democracy in Argentina. *Current History* 87 (525): 5–8, 43.

2525. Glenn, E. N. 1983. *See* Feldberg, R. L. (1983).

2526. Gleysteen, W. H., Jr., and A. D. Romberg. June 1987. Korea: Asian Paradox. *Foreign Affairs* 65 (5): 1037–1054.

2527. Glickman, H. July 1988. Frontiers of Liberal and Non-Liberal Democracy in Tropical Africa. *Journal of Asian and African Studies* 23 (3–4): 234–254.

2528. Glinkin, A. December 1985. New Trends in Latin America. *International Affairs (Moscow)* 12: 49–57.

2529. Glosemeyer, I. September 1993. The First Yemeni Parliamentary Elections in 1993: Practicing Democracy. *Orient* 34 (3): 439–451.

2530. Gluhova, A. V. 1993. Political Conflicts and Crises: Consensus and Political Methods for Attaining It.* *Gosudarstvo i Pravo* 6: 3–14.

2531. Goati, V. 1992. Majoritarian Democracy in (the Yugoslav) Postcommunist Multi-National States.* *Teorija in Praksa* 29 (3–4): 238–245.

2532. Godeau, R. February 25, 1993. Cap Vert de Bonne Experance. *Jeune Afrique* 33: 37–39+.

2533. Godeau, R., and Z. Limam. July 8, 1993. Democratisation et Crise Economique: Double Defi pour le Gabon. *Jeune Afrique* 33: 27+.

2534. Godoy Arcaya, O. 1984. Aristotle and Democratic Theory.* *Revista de Ciencia Politica* 6 (2): 7–46.

2535. Goerl, G. F. March 1992. *See* Bellone, C. J. (March 1992).

2536. Goertzel, T. G. 1984. Costa Rica: Democracy and Antimilitarism. *Dissent* 31 (3): 333–337.

2537. Goetschy, J. 1983. A New Future for Industrial Democracy in France. *Economic and Industrial Democracy* 4 (1): 85–101.

2538. Goetschy, J. May 1985. La Democratie Industrielle a l'Epreuve de la Crise: Grande-Bretagne, Suede, Allemagne. *Economie et Humanisme* 62–71.

2539. Goetting, D. January 1993. Die Mongolei: Die Zentralasiatische Republik Ist Vom Zusammenbruch des Sozialismus Besonders Betroffen. *Indo Asia: Für Politik, Kultur, und Wirtschaft in Indiens und Suedost Asiens* 35: 36–41.

2540. Goggin, M. L. 1987. How Democratic Is Science Policy? *Scientist* 1 (10): 18.

2541. Gohan, B. April 1988. South Korea: Road to Democracy. *Pakistan Horizon* 41 (2): 50–68.

2542. Goidel, R. K., and D. A. Gross. April 1994. A Systems Approach to Campaign Finance in the U.S. House Elections. *American Politics Quarterly* 22 (2): 125–153.

2543. Gold, L. E. 1982. *See* Bernstein, J. (1982).

2544. Goldbard, A. 1981. *See* Adams, D. (1981).

2545. Goldberg, J. September 1982. *See* Huffschmid, J. (September 1982).

2546. Goldberg, M. A., and M. D. Levi. December 1994. Growing Together or Apart: The Risks and Returns of Alternative Constitutions of Canada. *Canadian Public Policy* 20 (4): 341–352.

2547. Goldburg, C. B. November 1994. The Accuracy of Game Theory Predictions to Political Behavior: Cumulative Voting in Illinois. *Journal of Politics* 56 (4): 885–900.

2548. Golden, L. August 1988. *See* Butenko, A. (August 1988).

2549. Goldey, D. B. 1983. Elections and the Consolidation of Portuguese Democracy, 1974–1983. *Electoral Studies* 2 (3): 229–240.

2550. Goldey, D. B. December 1993. The French General Elections of 21–28 March 1993. *Electoral Studies* 12 (4): 291–314.

2551. Goldfarb, J. December 1983. *See* Arato, A. (December 1983).

2552. Goldfarb, J. C. September 1990. Post-Totalitarian Politics: Ideology Ends Again. *Social Research* 57 (3): 533–554.

2553. Goldman, J. R. June 1985. Consociational Authoritarian Politics and the 1974 Yugoslav Constitution: A Preliminary Note. *East European Quarterly* 19 (2): 241–249.

2554. Goldman, K. 1981. Democracy Does Not Work in Foreign and Defense Policy: Specification of a Hypothesis.* *Statsvetenskaplig Tidskrift* 3: 123–134.

2555. Goldman, M. September 1983. Human Rights in the People's Republic of China. *Daedalus* 112 (4): 111–138.

2556. Goldman, M. 1990. China's Sprouts of Democracy. *Ethics and International Affairs* 4: 71–90.

2557. Goldman, P. March 1985. Combating the Opposition: English and United States Restrictions on the Public Right to Access to Government Information. *Hastings International and Comparative Law Review* 8: 249–303.

2558. Goldman, P. June 1994. The Democratization of the Development of United States Trade Policy. *Cornell International Law Journal* 27: 631–697.

2559. Goldman, R. M., and H. Pascual. March 1988. NAMFREL: Spotlight for Democracy. *World Affairs* 150 (4): 223–231.

2560. Goldschmidt, D. 1976. Participatory Democracy in Schools and Higher Education: Emerging Problems in the Federal Republic of Germany and Sweden. *Higher Education* 5 (2): 113–133.

2561. Goldsmith, A. A. January 1986. Democracy, Political Stability, and Economic Growth in Developing Countries: Some Evidence on Olson's Theory of Distributional Coalitions. *Comparative Political Studies* 18 (4): 517–531.

2562. Goldsmith, A. A. March 1994. Political Freedom and the Business Climate: Outlook for Development in Newly Democratizing States. *Social Science Quarterly* 75 (1): 115–124.

2563. Goldsmith, M. 1979. *See* Boaden, N. (1979).

2564. Goldstein, L. F. 1987. Judicial Review and Democratic Theory: Guardian Democracy vs. Representative Democracy. *Western Political Quarterly* 40 (3): 391–412.

2565. Goldstein, L. F. 1987. Europe Looks at American Women, 1820–1840. *Social Research* 54 (3): 519–542.

2566. Golembiewski, R. T. 1981a. The Ideational Poverty of Two Modes of Coupling Democracy and Administration: Democracy Versus Administration. *International Journal of Public Administration* 3 (1): 1–65.

2567. Golembiewski, R. T. 1981b. A Third Mode of Coupling Democracy and Administration: Another Way of Making a Crucial Point. *International Journal of Public Administration* 3 (4): 423–453.

2568. Golembiewski, R. T., and L. Tanner. 1984. One Perspective on Democracy Versus Efficiency: Testing Mutuality via the Laboratory Approach. *International Journal of Public Administration* 6 (1): 125–149.

2569. Golomb, N. February 1975. *See* Katz, D. (February 1975).

2570. Golub, S. March 1993. Assessing and Enhancing the Impact of Democratic Development Projects: A Practitioner's Perspective Studies in Comparative International Development. *Comparative International Development* 28 (1): 54–70.

2571. Goma, R. 1991. *See* Fond, J. (1991).

2572. Gomes, C. November 1993. Education, Democracy, and Development in Latin America. *International Review of Education* 39 (6): 531–540.

2573. Gomez, E. September 1990. *See* Becker, D. (September 1990).

2574. Gomulka, S. 1977. Economic Factors in the Democratization of Socialism and the Socialization of Capitalism. *Journal of Comparative Economics* 1 (4): 189–406.

2575. Gomulka, S. 1994. Economic and Political Constraints during Transition. *Europe-Asia Studies* 46 (1): 89–106.

2576. Goncalves Ferreira Filho, M. July 1984. The Revision of Democratic Theory.* *Revista Brasileira de Estudos Politicos* 59: 7–39.

2577. Gong, G. W. March 1990. Afterimage: Tiananmen a Year Later. *Mediterranean Quarterly* 1 (2): 58–71.

2578. Gonidec, P. F. 1986. Democratic Concepts in Third World States. *Revue Juridique et Politique, Independance et Cooperation* 40 (1–2): 1–15.

2579. Gontcharoff, G. March 1985. Local Democracy Questioned. *Revue Internationale d'Action Communautaire* 53: 119–124.

2580. Gonzales, S. December 1992. The Strengthening of Democracy in Nicaragua: The Armed Forces and Political Parties in a Frail Democracy.* *America Latina* 5: 64–70.

2581. Gonzalez, E. July 1976. The Party Congress and Poder Popular: Orthodoxy, Democratization, and the Leaders Dominance. *Cuban Studies* 6 (2): 1–14.

2582. Gonzalez, E. October 1992. The Transition to Democracy in Eastern Europe: A Comparative Analysis.* *Revista de Estudios Politicos* 78: 195–217.

2583. Gonzalez, M. 1975. Psychodynamics of Ideological Democracy.* *Acta Psiquiatrica y Psicologica de America Latina* 21 (2): 137–142.

2584. Gonzalez, S. S. September 1992. Emergent New Democracies: The Case of Spain. *William and Mary Bill of Rights Journal* 1 (2): 267–283.

2585. Gonzalez-Casanova, P. September 1986. Foreign Debt, the Threat of Foreign Intervention, and Democracy in Latin America. *Contemporary Marxism* 14: 34–48.

2586. Good, I. J. March 1977. Justice in Voting by Demand Evaluation. *Public Choice* 29 (2): 65–70.

2587. Goodin, R. E. 1993. Democracy, Preferences, and Paternalism. *Policy Sciences* 26 (3): 229–247.

2588. Gooding, J. April 1990. Gorbachev and Democracy. *Soviet Studies* 42 (2): 195–231.

2589. Goodman, D. S. G. 1980. Opposition und Widerspruch in der Volksrepublik China: Die Demokratiebewegung und das Potential Fuer Ablehnung. *Europa Archiv: Zeitschrift für Internationale Politik* 35 (13): 425–434.

2590. Goodman, D. S. G. June 1985. The Chinese Political Order after Mao: Socialist Democracy and the Exercise of State Power. *Political Studies* 33 (2): 218–235.

2591. Goodman, L. W. September 1993. Democracy, Sovereignty, and Intervention. *American University Journal of International Law and Policy* 9: 27–32.

2592. Goodsell, C. T. January 1975. That Confounding Revolution in Peru. *Current History* 68 (401): 20–23.

2593. Goodsell, C. T. March 1989. Does Bureaucracy Hurt Democracy? *Bureaucrat* 18 (1): 45–48.

2594. Goodstadt, L. 1977. Democracy Versus Dynasties: 11th Congress of the Chinese Communist Party. *Round Table* 268: 337–344.

2595. Goodstadt, L. 1979. Democracy and Development: Chinese Debate in the Wake of the Disgrace of the Gang of Four. *Round Table* (273): 12–19.

2596. Goodstein, J. T. 1978. *See* Goodstein, L. D. (1978).

2597. Goodstein, L. D., and J. T. Goodstein. 1978. Democratization of Research. *Society* 16 (1): 12–13.

2598. Goralczyk, B. 1992. Central and Eastern Europe in Transition: Democracy Half Done. *Bulletin of Peace Proposals* 23 (2): 197–203.

2599. Gorbachev, M. March 10, 1986. Political Report of the CPSU Central Committee to the 27th Congress of the Communist Party of the Soviet Union. *New Times (Moscow)* 13–48.

2600. Gorden, W. I. December 1988. Range of Employee Voices. *Employee Responsibilities and Rights Journal* 1 (4): 283–299.

2601. Gorden, W. I., K. Holmberg, and D. R. Heisey. June 1994. Equality and the Swedish Work Environment. *Employee Responsibilities and Rights Journal* 7: 141–160.

2602. Gordon, D. December 1993. They're Over Here from Over There! More and More Legislatures Are Finding Their Capitols and Sessions Drawing International Scrutiny. *State Legislatures* 19: 19–22.

2603. Gordon, J. February 1990. Political Opposition in Egypt. *Current History* 89 (544): 65–68, 79–80.

2604. Gordon, L. A. December 1993. Russian Workers and Democracy: A Study of Mineworker Activists in the Kuzbass. *International Journal of Sociology* 23: 3–99.

2605. Gordon, S. October 1991. Political Transition Processes in Central America. *Foro Internacional* 126: 273–284.

2606. Goriely, G. 1979. Un Paradoxe Historique: La Social Democratie Allemande Inspiratrice du Bolchevisme. *Revue des Pays de l'Est* 20 (1): 1–20.

2607. Goriely, G. July 1983. A Historical Paradox: German Social Democracy Inspiring Bolshevism.* *Cahiers Internationaux de Sociologie* 75: 197–214.

2608. Gotham, K. December 1994. Domestic Security in the American State: The FBI, Covert Repression, and Democratic Legitimacy. *Journal of Political and Military Sociology* 22 (2): 203–222.

2609. Gott, M., and G. Warren. 1991. Neighbourhood Health Forums: Local Democracy at Work. *World Health Forum* 12 (4): 413–418.

2610. Gottdiener, M. January 1985. *See* Neiman, M. (January 1985).

2611. Gottschling, E. 1975. Militant Democracy as an Instrument against Social Progress.* *IPW Berichte* 4 (9): 46–54.

2612. Gouaud, C. January 1991. Research on Democratic Transition.* *Revue du Droit Public et de la Science Politique* 1: 81–120.

2613. Gould, F., and F. Zarkesh. 1986. Local Government Expenditures and Revenues in Western Democracies: 1960–1982. *Local Government Studies* 12 (1): 33–42.

2614. Gourdon, H. 1977. Citizen, Worker, Brother: The Second Constitutionalization of the Algerian Political System. *Annuaire de l'Afrique du Nord* 16: 99–121.

2615. Gourevitch, P. A. August 1993. Democracy and Economic Policy: Elective Affinities and Circumstantial Conjunctions. *World Development* 21 (8): 1271–1280.

2616. Gouws, A. June 1993. Political Tolerance and Civil Society: The Case of South Africa. *Politikon* 20 (1): 15–31.

2617. Goyard-Fabre, S. 1990. Democracy and Authority.* *Archiv für Rechts- und Sozialphilosophie* 76 (1): 1–11.

2618. Grabb, E. G. June 1981. The Ranking of Self-Actualization Values: The Effects of Class, Stratification, and Occupational Experiences. *Sociological Quarterly* 22 (3): 373–383.

2619. Grabendorff, W. 1984. Argentina's New Foreign Policy: Democratization and Indebtedness.* *Europa Archiv: Zeitschrift für Internationale Politik* 39 (19): 595–604.

2620. Grabovsek, B. April 20, 1982. Myth and Reality of the European Left: Social Democracy and the Communist Parties of West Europa. *Review of International Affairs* 33: 26–29.

2621. Grady, R. C. April 1978. Interest Group Liberalism and Juridical Democracy: Two Theses in Search of Legitimacy. *American Politics Quarterly* 6 (2): 213–236.

2622. Grady, R. C. March 1984. Juridical Democracy and Democratic Values: An Evaluation of Lowi's Alternative to Interest Group Liberalism. *Polity* 16 (3): 404–422.

2623. Grady, R. C. 1986. Reindustrialization, Liberal Democracy, and Corporatist Representation. *Political Science Quarterly* 101 (3): 415–423.

2624. Grady, R. C. February 1990. Workplace Democracy and Possessive Individualism. *Journal of Politics* 52 (1): 146–166.

2625. Graebner, N. A. 1976. Christianity and Democracy: Tocqueville's Views of Religion in America. *Journal of Religion* 56 (3): 263–273.

2626. Graf, W. January 1989. Issues and Substance in the Prescription of Liberal-Democratic Forms for Nigeria's Third Republic. *African Affairs* 350: 91–100.

2627. Graham, C. L. March 1989. The Latin American Quagmire: Beyond Debt and Democracy. *Brookings Review* 7: 42–47.

2628. Graham, J. Q., Jr. February 1982. Legislative Careers in the French Chamber and U.S. House, 1871–1940. *Legislative Studies Quarterly* 7 (1): 37–56.

2629. Graham, R. A. December 1989. Soviet New Thinking: History Versus Human Development Research. *Political Psychology* 10 (4): 767–777.

2630. Graham-Yooll, A. July 1985. Argentina: The State of Transition, 1983–1985. *Third World Quarterly* 7 (3): 573–593.

2631. Gramm, W. S. June 1980. Oligarchic Capitalism: Arguable Reality, Thinkable Future? *Journal of Economic Issues* 14 (2): 411–432.

2632. Gramm, W. S. June 1981. Property Rights in Work: Capitalism, Industrialism, and Democracy. *Journal of Economic Issues* 15 (2): 363–375.

2633. Granahan, C. M. March 1992. The Prospects of a Successful Reunification of Hong Kong and China in Light of the Events at Tiananmen Square. *Boston University International Law Journal* 10: 83–117.

2634. Granat, M. December 1992. The Essence of Political and Constitutional Change in the Countries of Central and Eastern Europe.* *Revue d'Etudes Comparatives Est-Ouest* 23 (4): 5–21.

2635. Grandjean, B. D. October 1981. *See* Bollen, K. A. (October 1981).

2636. Grano, J. D. 1981. Ely's Theory of Judicial Review: Preserving the Significance of the Political Process. *Ohio State Law Review* 42 (1): 167–186.

2637. Grant, F., and J. Kipper. 1978. Press Martyrs for Democracy and Peace: Chamorro, Pedro, Joaquin, Sebai, Yousef. *Worldview* 21 (5): 24–26.

2638. Graubard, A. 1984. Ideas of Economic Democracy: Workers' Control and Public Rights. *Dissent* 31 (4): 415–423.

2639. Graubert, J., S. Gadberry, and B. Ross. 1976. Classroom Adventure in Participatory Democracy. *High School Behavioral Science* 3 (2): 75–79.

2640. Graves, D. R. July 1978. Elections and National Mobilization in India. *Comparative Political Studies* 11 (2): 255–278.

2641. Gravil, R. April 1991. *See* Merrett, C. (April 1991).

2642. Gray, B. March 19, 1993. Shoot-Out in Dodge City. *Investors Chronicle* 103: 22–23.

2643. Gray, J. 1993. Hayek: Spontaneous Order in Transitional Post-Communist Societies.* *Estudios Publicos* 50: 131–149.

2644. Grayson, G. W. November 1977. Portugal's Crisis. *Current History* 73 (431): 169–173, 179–180.

2645. Grayson, G. W. December 1984. Venezuela and the Puerto Ordaz Agreement. *Inter-American Economic Affairs* 38 (3): 49–73.

2646. Graziano, L. May 1985. The Pluralist Foundations of Democracy.* *Democrazia e Diritto* 25 (3–4): 243–260.

2647. Graziano, L. July 1988. Sartori and the "Double Soul" of Democracy.* *Biblioteca della Liberta* 102: 75–83.

2648. Grebenik, E. 1989. Demography, Democracy, and Demonology. *Population and Development Review* 15 (1): 1–22.

2649. Grebing, H. 1976. Conditions for Realizing Union Goals in a Parliamentary Democracy.* *Gewerkschaftliche Monatshefte* 27 (5): 257–267.

2650. Greco, E. 1979. Testimonial to Greek Democracy.* *Recherche* 10 (103): 904–905.

2651. Green, F. January 1981. The United States and Asia in 1980. *Asian Survey* 21 (1): 1–13.

2652. Green, J. D. 1991. USAID's Democratic Pluralism Initiative: Pragmatism or

Altruism? *Ethics and International Affairs* 5: 215–231.

2653. Green, J. D. July 1992. Islam and Democratization in the Middle East.* *Relaciones Internacionales (Mexico)* 55: 7–13.

2654. Green, J. N. December 1994. The Emergence of the Brazilian Gay Liberation Movement, 1977–1981. *Latin American Perspectives* 21 (1): 38–55.

2655. Green, P. 1978. Social Democracy and Its Critics: The Case of England. *Dissent* 25 (3): 334–340.

2656. Greenawalt, K. June 1993. The Role of Religion in a Liberal Democracy: Dilemmas and Possible Resolutions. *Journal of Church and State* 35: 503–519.

2657. Greenberg, E. S. March 1980. Participation in Industrial Decision-Making and Work Satisfaction: The Case of Producer Cooperatives. *Social Science Quarterly* 60 (4): 551–569.

2658. Greenberg, E. S. November 1981. Industrial Democracy and the Democratic Citizen. *Journal of Politics* 43 (4): 964–981.

2659. Greenberg, E. S. 1983. Context and Cooperation: Systematic Variation in the Political Effects on Workplace Democracy. *Economic and Industrial Democracy* 4 (2): 191–223.

2660. Greenberg, J. April 1974. Litigation for Social Change: Methods, Limits, and Role in Democracy. *Record* 29: 320–375.

2661. Greene, J. P. July 1976. Values and Society in Revolutionary America. *Annals of the American Academy of Political and Social Science* 426: 53–69.

2662. Greene, J. P. March 1978. Paine, America, and the "Modernization" of Political Consciousness. *Political Science Quarterly* 93 (1): 73–92.

2663. Greene, J. P. January 1994. *See* Peterson, P. E. (January 1994).

2664. Greene, K. V. December 1990. *See* Balkan, E. M. (December 1990).

2665. Greenhouse, C. J. September 1994. Democracy and Demography. *Indiana Journal of Global Legal Studies* 2: 21–29.

2666. Greenstein, F. I. 1975. Benevolent Leader Revisited: Children's Images of Political Leaders in Three Democracies. *American Political Science Review* 69 (4): 1371–1398.

2667. Greer, D. L. September 1985. *See* Manaster, G. J. (September 1985).

2668. Gregor, A. J. March 1987. After the Fall: The Prospects for Democracy after Marcos. *World Affairs* 149 (4): 195–208.

2669. Gregory, B. A. September 1993. Envisioning Futures: The Battle over Democracy in Hong Kong. *North Carolina Journal of International Law and Commercial Regulation* 19: 175–207.

2670. Gregory, F. December 1986. Policing the Democratic State: How Much Force? *Conflict Studies* 194: 1–25.

2671. Greider, W. September 1988. The Money Question. *World Policy Journal* 5 (4): 567–613.

2672. Greilsammer, I. 1979. Democratization of a Community: French Jewry and the Fonds Social Juif Unifie. *Jewish Journal of Sociology* 21 (2): 109–124.

2673. Greven, M. T. September 1993. Democracy and Modernity? The Crisis of Rationality in Political Societies.* *Politische Vierteljahresschrift* 34 (3): 399–413.

2674. Grey, R. D., L. A. Jennisch, and A. S. Tyler. June 1990. Soviet Public Opinion and the Gorbachev Reforms. *Slavic Review* 49 (2): 261–271.

2675. Grieve, M. J. December 1992. International Assistance and Democracy: Assessing Efforts to Assist Post-Communist Development. *Studies in Comparative International Development* 27 (4): 80–101.

2676. Griffin, C. July 1993. Election Watch: Lesotho Returns to Democracy

Freely, Fairly and with Quiet Enthusiasm. *Parliamentarian* 74 (3): 133–136.

2677. Griffin, C. E. 1992. Haiti's Democratic Challenge. *Third World Quarterly* 13 (4): 663–673.

2678. Griffin, C. E. April 1993. Democracy in the Commonwealth Caribbean. *Journal of Democracy* 4 (2): 84–94.

2679. Griffin, C. E. July 1994. The Opposition and Policy Making in the Caribbean: The Emergence of High Consensus Politics in St. Kitts and Nevis. *Journal of Commonwealth and Comparative Politics* 32 (2): 230–243.

2680. Griffin, L. J., P. J. O'Connell, and H. J. McCammon. 1989. National Variation in the Context of Struggle: Postwar Class Conflict and Market Distribution in the Capitalist Democracies. *Canadian Review of Sociology and Anthropology* 26 (1): 37–68.

2681. Griffin, R. D. July 19, 1991. Mexico's Emergence: Will Economic Reform Work? Can Democracy Wait? *CQ Researcher* 1: 491–511.

2682. Griffin, R. D. March 12, 1993. Aid to Russia: Can Its Democracy Survive without Western Aid? *CQ Researcher* 3: 219–239.

2683. Griffith, R. June 1978. The Chilling Effect. *Wilson Quarterly* 2 (3): 135–136.

2684. Grilli Di Cortona, P. May 1991. From Communism to Democracy: Rethinking Regime Change in Hungary and Czechoslovakia. *International Social Science Journal* 43 (2): 315–330.

2685. Gripp, R. G. April 1989. Political Reform in Three Asian Polities. *Asian Profile* 17 (2): 189–197.

2686. Grittnet, F. M. 1977. Democratization of the Foreign-Language Program through Individualized Instruction. *System* 5 (2): 84–99.

2687. Grobovsek, B. July 1982. West European Social Democracy and the "Third World." *Review of International Affairs* 33: 32–35.

2688. Grofman, B. September 1993. Lessons of Athenian Democracy: Editor's Introduction. *PS: Political Science & Politics* 26 (3): 471–474.

2689. Grondona, M. June 1978. Reconciling Internal Security and Human Rights. *International Security* 3 (1): 3–16.

2690. Grondona, M. C. 1974. Socialism and Democracy.* *Revista Usem* 25: 1–2.

2691. Grondsmat, T. November 1979. *See* Van Den Poel, H. (November 1979).

2692. Groseclose, T., and K. Krebiel. February 1994. Golden Parachutes, Rubber Checks, and Strategic Retirement from the 102d House. *American Journal of Political Science* 38 (1): 75–99.

2693. Gross, D. A. April 1994. *See* Goidel, R. K. (April 1994).

2694. Gross, J. 1980. Church and Democracy in Poland. *Dissent* 27 (3): 321–322.

2695. Gross, P. June 1991. Restricting the Free Press in Romania. *Orbis* 35 (3): 365–375.

2696. Grosscup, B. March 1982. The Neoconservative State and the Politics of Terrorism. *New Political Science* 8: 39–62.

2697. Groth, A. J. et al. December 1993. Welfare-Military Trade-Offs among Oligarchies and Polyarchies: Some Cross-Sectional Aspects. *Coexistence* 30 (4): 289–302.

2698. Grotzky, J. May 1991. The Hard Road towards Democracy: Observations in Albania.* *Osteuropa* 41 (5): 431–437.

2699. Grundy, K. W. March 1983. South Africa's Domestic Strategy. *Current History* 82 (482): 110–114, 132–133.

2700. Grundy, K. W. May 1993. South Africa's Tortuous Transition. *Current History* 92: 229–233.

2701. Gruner, E. 1987. Direct Democracy [in Switzerland] on Trial.* *Annuaire Suisse de Science Politique* 27: 283–313.

2702. Gryski, G. S., G. Zuk, and D. J. Barrow. November 1994. A Bench That Looks like America: Representation of African Americans and Latinos on the Federal Courts. *Journal of Politics* 56 (4): 1076–1086.

2703. Grzybowski, C. July 1990. Rural Workers' Movements and Democratization in Brazil. *Journal of Development Studies* 26 (4): 19–43.

2704. Guacang, H. September 1989. The Events of Tiananmen Square. *Orbis* 33 (4): 487–500.

2705. Gueguen, J. A. September 1982. Reflections on Statesmanship and the Presidency. *Presidential Studies Quarterly* 12 (4): 470–484.

2706. Guervara, P. 1992. The Constitution of Elites in Representative Democracy.* *Politeia (Caracas)* 15: 305–330.

2707. Guess, G. 1978. The Narrowing Base of Costa Rican Democracy. *Development and Change* 9 (4): 599–611.

2708. Guha, R. 1976. India's Democracy: Long Dead, Now Buried. *Journal of Contemporary Asia* 6 (1): 39–53.

2709. Guidi, M. E. L. 1985. An Unpublished Text of Francesco S. Nitti on Democracy.* *Pensiero Politico* 18 (1): 55–64.

2710. Guilherme Dos Santos, W. 1985. Michel's Century: Oligopolistic Competition, Authoritarian Logic and Transition in Latin America.* *Dados* 28 (3): 283–310.

2711. Guilhon Alburquerque, J. A. October 1992. Plebiscitarian Presidentialism and the Instability of Democracies.* *Cuestiones Politica* 9: 5–15.

2712. Guillebaud, J. September 1991. Crisis of the Media or Crisis of Democracy?* *Le Debat* 66: 63–74.

2713. Guillebaud, J. March 1993. Are the News Media for or against Democracy in the World?* *Esprit* (3–4): 86–101.

2714. Guimaraes, R. March 1986. New Social and Political Actors in the Democratic Transition.* *Politica Internazionale* 14 (3–4): 88–95.

2715. Guinier, L. November 1993. [E]Racing Democracy: The Voting Rights Cases. *Harvard Law Review* 108: 109–137.

2716. Guinot, C. N. October 1993. Transicion y Consolidacion Democratica en America Latina. *Revista de Estudios Politicos* (82): 107–136.

2717. Gulick, L. 1977. Democracy and Administration Face the Future. *Public Administration Review* 37 (6): 706–711.

2718. Gulowsen, J. 1985. Hearocracy: The Deterioration of Democracy in a Norwegian Trade Union. *Organization Studies* 6 (4): 439–365.

2719. Gunlicks, A. B. September 1989. Federalism and Intergovernmental Relations in West Germany: A 40th Year Appraisal—Introduction. *Publius* 19 (4): 1–15.

2720. Gunn, G. June 1990. Will Castro Fall? *Foreign Policy* 79: 132–150.

2721. Gunn, G. C. August 1979. Ideology and the Concept of Government in the Indonesian New Order. *Asian Survey* 19 (8): 751–769.

2722. Gunn, P. F. 1981. Initiatives and Referendums: Direct Democracy and Minority Interests. *Urban Law Annual* 22: 135–159.

2723. Gunnell, J. G. March 1978. The Myth of the Tradition. *American Political Science Review* 72 (1): 122–134.

2724. Gunnell, J. G. August 1985. Political Theory and Politics: The Case of Leo Strauss. *Political Theory* 13 (3): 339–361.

2725. Gunter, M. M. June 1988. The Kurdish Problem in Turkey. *Middle East Journal* 42 (3): 389–406.

2726. Gunther, R. January 1988. *See* Lijphart, A. (January 1988).

2727. Gupta, A. July 5, 1992. Bangladesh: Democracy Dhaka-Style. *Economic and Political Weekly* 27 (30): 1601–1602.

2728. Gupta, A. September 5, 1992. Neighbors and Borders: Democracy in the Himalayas. *Economic and Political Weekly* 27 (36): 1897+.

2729. Gupta, A. October 24, 1992. Neighbors and Borders: Four South Asian Democracies—Old and New. *Economic and Political Weekly* 27 (43–44): 2354–2356.

2730. Gupta, A. April 1994. *See* Austin, D. (April 1994).

2731. Gupta, A. October 22, 1994. Nepali Congress and Post-Panchayat Politics. *Economic and Political Weekly* 29 (43): 2798–2801.

2732. Gupta, N. S. 1975. Nuevas Experimentos con la Democracia en el Tercer Mundo. *Revista Interamericana de Sociologia* 5 (15–16): 67–85.

2733. Gupta, S. D. 1986. Soviet Socialism and the Question of Democracy in Recent Times. *Calcutta Journal of Political Studies* 6 (1–2): 70–85.

2734. Gupta, V. 1992. Violence and Regionalism Delay Democratization. *Africa Quarterly* 32 (1–4): 107–114.

2735. Gupta, V. S. January 1978. Illiteracy: A Challenge to Democracy. *Journal of Constitutional and Parliamentary Studies* 12 (1): 85–91.

2736. Gurian, P., and J. A. Wolfe. 1994. Regional Primaries and [U.S.] Presidential Campaign Coverage. *Social Science Journal* 31 (1): 17–28.

2737. Gurian, W. October 1978. The Totalitarian State. *Review of Politics* 40 (4): 514–527.

2738. Gurr, T. R. 1988. *See* King, D. S. (1988).

2739. Gurr, T. R. December 1991. America as a Model for the World? A Skeptical View. *Political Science and Politics* 24 (4): 664–667.

2740. Gurr, T. R., K. Jaggers, and W. H. Moore. March 1990. The Transformation of the Western State: The Growth of Democracy, Autocracy and State Power since 1800. *Studies in Comparative International Development* 25 (1): 73–108.

2741. Gustaffs, B. 1974. Social Democracy in New Zealand: New Directions in a Welfare State. *Round Table* 255: 331–345.

2742. Gustafson, W. E., and W. L. Richter. February 1981. Pakistan in 1980: Weathering the Storm. *Asian Survey* 21 (2): 162–171.

2743. Gusy, C. July 1980. The "Liberal Democratic Order" in the Jurisprudence of the Federal Constitutional Court.* *Archiv des Offentlichen Rechts* 105 (2): 279–310.

2744. Gusy, C. September 1981. The Majority Principle in the Democratic State.* *Archiv des Offentlichen Rechts* 106 (3): 329–354.

2745. Gusy, C. June 1985. The Principle of Consensus or Democracy: The Debate on the Majority Principle.* *Zeitschrift für Politik* 32 (2): 133–152.

2746. Gusy, C. September 1989. Democratic Representation.* *Zeitschrift für Politik* 36 (3): 264–285.

2747. Gutmann, G. December 1975. Market Economics and Constitutional Order with Respect to Freedom and Democracy.* *Zeitschrift für Politik* 22 (4): 338–354.

2748. Guy, M. E. March 1989. *See* Mayer, R. T. (March 1989).

2749. Guyer, J. I. April 1992. Representation without Taxation: An Essay on Democracy in Rural Nigeria 1952–1990. *African Studies Review* 35 (1): 41–79.

2750. Guyon, R. March 1992. Violent Repression in Burma: Human Rights and the Global Response. *UCLA Pacific Basin Law Journal* 10: 409–459.

2751. Guyot, J. F., and J. Badgley. February 1990. Myanmar in 1989. *Asian Survey* 30 (2): 187–195.

2752. Guzda, H. P. May 1984. Industrial Democracy—Made in the U.S.A.: Labor Management Cooperation to Improve the Quality of Products, Worklife, and the Effectiveness of Companies Can Be Traced to the Early 19th Century. *Monthly Labor Review* 107 (5): 26–33.

2753. Guzel, M. July 1992. Le Reveil du Mouvement Ouvrier. *Peuples Mediterraneens* 59–78.

2754. Guzman, J. June 1984. *See* Cumplido, F. (June 1984).

2755. Guzman, R. September 1993. *See* Chacaltana, J.(September 1993).

2756. Gwin, C., and L. A. Veit. March 1985. The Indian Miracle. *Foreign Policy* (58): 79–98.

2757. Gyimah-Boadi, E. April 1994. Ghana's Uncertain Political Opening. *Journal of Democracy* 5 (2): 75–86.

2758. Haarh, J. H. 1994. Democracy and Interdependence in Modern Society.* *Politica* 26 (3): 328–347.

2759. Haas, A. 1986. Social Bases of Support for Workplace Democracy: Trends among Swedish Workers in Gothenburg 1977–1980. *Work and Occupations* 13 (2): 241–263.

2760. Habermas, J. March 1979. *See* Marcuse, H. (March 1979).

2761. Habermas, J. April 1994. Three Normative Models of Democracy. *Constellations* 1 (1): 1–10.

2762. Habiby, R. June 1978. Qadhafi's Thoughts on True Democracy. *Middle East Review* 10 (4): 29–35.

2763. Haddad, L. 1994. The World Bank and the Process of Transition in Eastern Europe: Lessons from China and Vietnam. *Journal of Contemporary Asia* 24 (4): 441–458.

2764. Hadenius, A. 1988. Democracy and Capitalism: Collective Action Theory and Structural Analysis. *Scandinavian Political Studies* 11 (1): 21–43.

2765. Haemmerli, A. B. June 1976. International Norm-Creating for a Divided Society: A Reappraisal of Some Perennial Problems. *Orbis* 20 (2): 315–341.

2766. Haerpfer, C. 1994. *See* Rose, R. (1994).

2767. Hafemann, H. 1993. On the Problem of Practicing Democracy and Self-Organization: Experience with the Organization of the Thuringia State Jugendring.* *Zeitschrift für Paedagogik* S30: 283–297.

2768. Hafen, B. C. 1993. Schools As Intellectual and Moral Associations. *Brigham Young University Law Review* 1993: 605–621.

2769. Hafner, D. F. December 1992. Political Modernization in Slovenia in the 1980s and the Early 1990s. *Journal of Communist Studies* 8 (4): 210–226.

2770. Hage, J., and Z. J. Shi. October 1993. Alternative Strategies for the Reconstruction of the State during Economic Reform. *Governance* 6 (4): 463–491.

2771. Haggard, S. March 1990. *See* Cheng, T. (March 1990).

2772. Haggard, S. 1992. Democracy and Economic Development: A Comparative Perspective. *Democratic Institutions* 1: 49–62.

2773. Haggard, S., and R. R. Kaufman. October 1994. The Challenges of Consolidation. *Journal of Democracy* 5 (4): 5–16.

2774. Haghayeghi, M. March 1994. Islam and Democratic Politics in Central Asia. *World Affairs* 156 (4): 186–198.

2775. Hagopian, F. July 1990. "Democracy by Undemocratic Means"? Elites, Political Pacts, and Regime Transition in Brazil. *Comparative Political Studies* 23 (2): 147–170.

2776. Hagopian, F. April 1993. After Regime Change: Authoritarian Legacies, Political Representation and the Democratic Future of South America. *World Politics* 45 (3): 464–500.

2777. Hagopian, F., and S. Mainwaring. June 1987. Democracy in Brazil: Problems and Prospects. *World Policy Journal* 4 (3): 485–514.

2778. Hahn, E. 1976. Democracy, Society and Ideology.* *Deutsche Zeitschrift für Philosophie* 24 (8): 901–914.

2779. Hahn, E. 1977. Democracy and Society: A World-View.* *Filosoficky Casopis* 25 (6): 825–837.

2780. Hahn, J. W. January 1989. Power to the Soviets? *Problems of Communism* 38 (1): 34–46.

2781. Hahn, J. W. March 1990. Boss Gorbachev Confronts His New Congress. *Orbis* 34 (2): 163–178.

2782. Hahn, W. March 1987. Electoral Choice in the Soviet Bloc. *Problems of Communism* 36: 29–39.

2783. Haig, A. M. December 1980. Reflections on Energy and Western Security. *Orbis* 23 (4): 755–760.

2784. Haiman, F. S. 1991. The First Amendment in Its Third Century: The Majoritarian Challenge. *Free Speech Yearbook* 29: 1–8.

2785. Hainsworth, G. B. April 1983. The Political Economy of Pancasila in Indonesia. *Current History* 82 (483): 167–171, 178–179.

2786. Hairong, L. October 1990. *See* Jianhua, Z. (October 1990).

2787. Hajjar, S. G. June 1980. The Jamahiriya Experiment in Libya: Qadhafi and Rousseau. *Journal of Modern African Studies* 18 (2): 181–200.

2788. Hakansson, A., and T. Niklasson. 1990. The Democratization Process in Eastern Europe: Trade, Development and Electoral Result.* *Statsvetenskaplig Tidskrift* 93 (4): 335–361.

2789. Hakim, M. A. August 1994. The Mirpur Parliamentary By-Election in Bangladesh. *Asian Survey* 34 (8): 738–747.

2790. Hakim, P. July 1993. The OAS: Putting Principle into Practice. *Journal of Democracy* 4 (3): 39–49.

2791. Hakim, P., and A. F. Lowenthal. June 1991. Latin America's Fragile Democracies. *Journal of Democracy* 2 (3): 16–29.

2792. Halberstam, M. December 1993. The Copenhagen Document: Intervention in Support of Democracy. *Harvard International Law Journal* 34 (1): 163–175.

2793. Hale, W. 1977. Turkish Democracy in Travail: The Case of State Security Courts. *World Today* 33 (5): 186–194.

2794. Halevi, J. June 1979. Comments on Professor Lerner's Paper: A Marxist View. *Social Research* 46 (2): 240–254.

2795. Hall, A. 1992. Constructing Democracy: Progress and Prospects in Nepal. *Journal of Commonwealth and Comparative Politics* 30 (1): 85–95.

2796. Hall, G. January 1987. The White House Conspiracy against Democracy. *Political Affairs* 66: 3–11.

2797. Hall, J. S., and P. K. Piele. September 1976. Selected Determinants of Precinct Voting in School Budget Elections. *Western Political Quarterly* 29 (3): 441–456.

2798. Halliday, T. C. 1975. Politics of Universal Participatory Democracy: A Canadian Case Study. *Minerva* 13 (3): 404–427.

2799. Halliday, T. C., and C. L. Cappell. 1979. Indicators of Democracy in Professional Associations: Elite Recruitment, Turnover, and Decision-Making in a Metropolitan Bar Association. *American Bar Foundation Research Journal* (4): 697–767.

2800. Hallin, D. C. March 1992. Sound Bite Democracy. *Wilson Quarterly* 16 (2): 34–37.

2801. Halperin, M. December 1992. Limited Constitutional Democracy: Lessons from the American Experience. *American University Journal of International Law and Policy* 8: 523–529.

2802. Halperin, M. H. September 1988. Lawful Wars. *Foreign Policy* 72: 173–195.

2803. Halperin, M. H. June 1993. Guaranteeing Democracy. *Foreign Policy* (91): 105–122.

2804. Halperin, M. H., and K. Lomasney. July 1993. Toward a Global "Guarantee Clause." *Journal of Democracy* 4 (3): 60–69.

2805. Halpern, M. January 1987. Choosing between Ways of Life and Death and between Forms of Democracy: An Archetypal Analysis. *Alternatives* 12 (1): 5–35.

2806. Halpern, N. P. June 1989. Economic Reform and Democratization in Communist Systems: The Case of China. *Studies in Comparative Communism* 22 (2–3): 139–152.

2807. Halpern, S. C. July 1981. The Hidden Agenda of Environmental Reform. *Society* 18 (5): 27–33.

2808. Halpern, S. M. April 1986. The Disorderly Universe of Consociational Democracy. *West European Politics* 9 (2): 181–197.

2809. Halsey, A. H. 1981. Democracy and Education. *New Society* 56 (967): 346–348.

2810. Hamalainen, P. K. 1986. The Finnish Solution. *Wilson Quarterly* 10 (4): 59–75.

2811. Hambleton, R. 1988. Consumerism, Decentralization and Local Democracy. *Public Administration* 66 (2): 125–147.

2812. Hambleton, R. July 1992. Decentralization and Democracy in UK Local Government. *Public Money and Management* 12: 9–20.

2813. Hambleton, R. October 1993. Reflections on Urban Government in the USA. *Policy and Politics* 21 (4): 245–257.

2814. Hamilton, N., and E. M. Kim. 1993. Economic and Political Liberalisation in South Korea and Mexico. *Third World Quarterly* 14 (1): 109–136.

2815. Hamilton, S. F., and J. F. Claus. November 1981. Inequality and Youth Unemployment: Can Work Programs Work? *Education and Urban Society* 14 (1): 103–126.

2816. Hammock, D. C. August 1978. Elite Perceptions of Power in the Cities of the United States, 1880–1900: The Evidence of James Bryce, Moisei Ostrogorski, and Their American Informants. *Journal of Urban History* 4 (4): 363–397.

2817. Hammond, J. L. March 1982. The Armed Forces Movement and the Portuguese Revolution: Two Steps Forward, One Step Back. *Journal of Political and Military Sociology* 10 (1): 71–101.

2818. Hammond, T. H., and G. J. Miller. December 1987. The Core of the Constitution. *American Political Science Review* 81 (4): 1155–1174.

2819. Hampsher-Monk, I. April 1980. Classical and Empirical Theories of Democracy: The Missing Historical Dimension? *British Journal of Political Science* 10 (2): 241–252.

2820. Hampton, W. 1979. *See* Boaden, N. (1979).

2821. Han, S. J. 1975. South Korea in 1974: Korean Democracy on Trial. *Asian Survey* 15 (1): 35–42.

2822. Han, S. J. January 1988. South Korea in 1987: The Politics of Democratization. *Asian Survey* 28 (1): 52–61.

2823. Han, S. J. January 1989. South Korea in 1988: A Revolution in the Making. *Asian Survey* 29 (1): 29–38.

2824. Han, S. J. March 1991. The [South] Korean Experiment. *Journal of Democracy* 2 (2): 92–104.

2825. Han, S. J. 1992. Korea's Democratic Experiment 1987–1991. *Democratic Institutions* 1: 63–78.

2826. Hanak, P. June 1994. A National Compensation for Backwardness. *Studies in East European Thought* 46 (1–2): 33–45.

2827. Hancock, M. D. October 1978. Productivity, Welfare, and Participation in Sweden and West Germany: A Comparison of Social Democratic Reform Prospects. *Comparative Politics* 11 (1): 4–23.

2828. Hancock, M. D., and J. Logue. December 1984. Sweden: The Quest for Economic Democracy. *Polity* 17 (2): 248–270.

2829. Handelman, H. 1977. Oligarchy and Democracy in Two Mexican Labor Unions: A Test of Representation Theory. *Industrial and Labor Relations Review* 30 (2): 205–218.

2830. Handelman, H. November 1981. Labor-Industrial Conflict and the Collapse of Uruguayan Democracy. *Journal of Interamerican Studies and World Affairs* 23 (4): 371–394.

2831. Handle, W. 1989. China Is Different: Economic Reform, Democratic Opening. *Aussenpolitik* 40 (2): 129–138.

2832. Handy, J. November 1986. Resurgent Democracy and the Guatemalan Military. *Journal of Latin American Studies* 18: 383–408.

2833. Hanf, T., and H. Weiland. 1978. Concord Democracy for South Africa: The Significance of New Debate on Constitutionality.* *Europa Archiv: Zeitschrift für Internationale Politik* 33 (23): 755–770.

2834. Hankiss, E. December 1990. In Search of a Paradigm. *Daedalus* 119 (1): 183–214.

2835. Hankiss, E. 1994. Our Recent Pasts: Recent Developments in East Central Europe in the Light of Various Social Philosophies. *East European Politics and Societies* 8 (3): 531–542.

2836. Hanninen, S. 1986. On the Democratic Language of Comparison.* *Politiika* 28 (1): 11–20.

2837. Hanrahan, P. M. December 1994. No Home? No Vote: Homeless Are Often Denied That Most Basic Element of Democracy. *Human Rights* 21: 8–9+.

2838. Hansch, K. 1986. European Integration and Parliamentary Democracy.* *Europa Archiv: Zeitschrift für Internationale Politik* 41 (7): 191–200.

2839. Hansen, E. 1977. Workers and Socialists: Relations between the Dutch Trade Union Movement and Social Democracy, 1894–1914. *European Studies Review* 7 (2): 199–226.

2840. Hansen, G. E. February 1976. Indonesia 1975: National Resilience and Continuity of the New Order Struggle. *Asian Survey* 16 (2): 146–158.

2841. Hansen, P. 1985. *See* Chorney, H. (1985).

2842. Hansen, S. B. September 1984. On the Making of Unpopular Decisions: A Typology and Some Evidence. *Policy Studies Journal* 13 (1): 23–43.

2843. Hansmann, H. June 1990. When Does Worker Ownership Work? ESOPs, Law Firms, Codetermination, and Economic Democracy. *Yale Law Review* 99 (8): 1749–1816.

2844. Hanson, C., and P. Rathkey. July 1984. Industrial Democracy: A Post-Bullock Shopfloor View. *British Journal of Industrial Relations* 22 (2): 154–168.

2845. Hansot, E. June 1981. *See* Tyack, D. (June 1981).

2846. Hanzel, J. March 1981. Palacky and Czech Culture in the First Half of the Nineteenth Century. *East European Quarterly* 15 (1): 57–64.

2847. Hao Wang. June 1990. *See* Waterman, H. (June 1990).

2848. Hao, W. September 1992. Mainland Chinese Political Opposition in 1989: Causes and Characteristics. *Issues and Studies* 28 (9):

2849. Happ, T. June 1992. *See* Bowler, S. (June 1992).

2850. Haque, A. February 1980. Bangladesh 1979: Cry For Sovereign Parliament. *Asian Survey* 20 (2): 217–230.

2851. Harber, C. July 1994. Ethnicity and Education for Democracy in Sub-Saharan Africa. *International Journal of Educational Development* 14 (3): 255–264.

2852. Hardin, R. January 1982. *See* Allen, G. O. (January 1982).

2853. Harding, T., and J. Petras. June 1988. Democratization and Class Struggle [in Latin America]. *Latin American Perspectives* 15 (3): 3–17.

2854. Hare, F. K. 1990. *See* Oriordan, T. (1990).

2855. Harel, A. September 1994. Free Speech Revisionism: Doctrinal and Philosophical Challenges. *Boston University Law Review* 74: 687–714.

2856. Harik, J. P., and H. Khashan. December 1993. Lebanon's Divisive Democracy: The Parliamentary Elections of 1992. *Arab Studies Quarterly* 15: 41–59.

2857. Harisalo, R. March 1993. Powers Shifts in Democracy, Public Services, and Local Government. *Local Government Studies* 19 (1): 16–27.

2858. Harlow, K. S. June 1984. *See* Warren, R. (June 1984).

2859. Harlow, L. F. 1992. Democracy Efficiently at Work Better Government for All: A How-To Book. *International Journal of Public Administration* 15 (1–4): 1–1049.

2860. Harman, M. M. 1974. Social Equity and Organizational Man: Motivation and Organizational Democracy. *Public Administration Review* 34 (1): 11–18.

2861. Harmel, R. April 1981. Environment and Party Decentralization: A Cross-National Analysis. *Comparative Political Studies* 14 (1): 75–99.

2862. Harmel, R. October 1985. On the Study of New Parties. *International Political Science Review* 6 (4): 403–418.

2863. Harmel, R., and J. D. Robertson. October 1985. Formation and Success of New Parties: A Cross-National Analysis. *International Political Science Review* 6 (4): 501–523.

2864. Harnecker, M. December 1992. Democracy and Revolutionary Movement. *Social Justice* 19 (4): 60–73.

2865. Harre, E. 1985. The Development of Individuality in the Process of Perfecting Socialist Democracy.* *Deutsche Zeitschrift für Philosophie* 33 (10): 903–908.

2866. Harries, O. September 1988. "Exporting Democracy" and Getting It Wrong. *National Interest* 13: 3–12.

2867. Harrigan, N., and P. I. Varlack. June 1977. The U.S. Virgin Islands and the Black Experience. *Journal of Black Studies* 7 (4): 387–410.

2868. Harrington, M. 1978. Democracy and Social Decay: A Comment. *Socialist Review* (40–4): 49–52.

2869. Harrington, M. 1981. The Virtues and Limitation of Liberal Democracy. *Center Magazine* 14 (2): 50–53.

2870. Harrington, M. J. 1976. The United States in Italian Democracy. *Nation* 223 (1): 16–18.

2871. Harris, E., M. Lopez, J. Arevalo, J. Bellatin, A. Belli, J. Moran, and C. Orrego. January 1993. Short Courses on DNA Detection and Amplification for Public Health in Central and South America: The Democratization of Molecular Biology. *Biochemical Education* 21 (1): 16–22.

2872. Harris, F. P. 1975. Tangential Thoughts on Democracy and the Individual in Japan. *Pacific Community* 7 (1): 132–141.

2873. Harris, J. H. 1979. Enduring Chinese Dimensions in Peking's Military Policy and Doctrine: Return of the Western Democracies. *Issues and Studies* 15 (7): 77–88.

2874. Harris, K. 1992. Schooling, Democracy, and Teachers as Intellectual Vanguard. *New Zealand Journal of Educational Studies* 27 (1): 21–33.

2875. Harris, R. (ed). March 1985. Nicaragua: Democracy and Revolution. *Latin American Perspectives* 12: 3–111. 5 articles.

2876. Harrison, P. 1979. Pretense of Democracy. *New Society* 47 (849): 67–69.

2877. Harrison, S. S. June 1987. Dateline South Korea: A Divided Seoul. *Foreign Policy* (67): 154–175.

2878. Harrison, S. S. March 1988. Taiwan after Chaing Ching-kua. *Foreign Affairs* 66 (4): 790–808.

2879. Harrop, J. 1978. Industrial Democracy: Can Britain Leap Ahead of European Experience. *Annals of Public and Cooperative Economy* 49 (1): 103–119.

2880. Harry, J. 1975. *See* Devall, W. B. (1975).

2881. Harsanyi, D., and N. Harsanyi. June 1993. Romania: Democracy and the Intellectuals. *East European Quarterly* 27 (2): 243–260.

2882. Harsanyi, N. June 1993. *See* Harsanyi, D. (June 1993).

2883. Harsch, E. May 27, 1985. Senegal: Cracks in a Bastion of Neocolonialism— IMF Austerity Plan Provokes Strikes, Political Ferment. *Intercontinental Press* 23: 302–305.

2884. Harsch, E. 1993. Structural Adjustment and Africa's Democracy Movements. *Africa Today* 40 (4): 7–29.

2885. Hart, D. K. September 1985. *See* Frederickson, H. G. (September 1985).

2886. Hart, D. K. March 1989. A Partnership in Virtue among All Citizens: The Public Service and Civic Humanism. *Public Administration Review* 49 (2): 101–105.

2887. Hartfiel, G. 1974. Co-determination of Parity: More Democracy, Little Efficiency.* *Gegenwartskunde: Gesellschaft, Staat, Erziehung* 23 (2): 129–140.

2888. Hartlandsberg, M. 1981. *See* Lembcke, J. (1981).

2889. Hartley, D. 1991. Democracy, Capitalism and the Reform of Teacher Education. *Journal of Education for Teaching* 17 (1): 81–95.

2890. Hartley, R. C. 1982. The Framework of Democracy in Union Government. *Catholic University Law Review* 32 (1): 13–128.

2891. Hartlyn, J. May 1984. Military Government and the Transition to Civilian Rule: The Colombian Experience of 1957–1958. *Journal of Interamerican Studies and World Affairs* 26 (2): 245–281.

2892. Hartweg, F. 1980. Union pour la Democratie Française: Oder die Partei des Praesidenten. *Dokumente* 36 (4): 309–318.

2893. Hartwich, H. 1981. The Change in Significance of the Concept of Democracy in the Federal Republic of Germany. *Gegenwartskunde: Gesellschaft, Staat, Erziehung* 30 (1): 5–22.

2894. Hartwich, H. 1987. *See* Cordes, H. (1987).

2895. Hartwich, H. 1990. Western Democracy as a Constitutional Form and East Germany.* *Gegenwartskunde: Gesellschaft, Staat, Erziehung* 39 (2): 149–164.

2896. Harvey, R. January 1979. Portugal: Democracy's Balance Sheet. *World Today* 35 (1): 24–30.

2897. Harvey, R. March 1980. Spain's Democracy: A Remarkable First Year. *World Today* 36 (3): 102–107.

2898. Hasan, F. R. October 29, 1994. Limits and Possibilities of Law and Legal Literacy: Experience of Bangladesh Women. *Economic and Political Weekly* 29 (44): WS69-WS76.

2899. Haseler, S. March 1978. Europe after the French Elections: A Counter-Strategy for the West. *Policy Review* 4: 7–20.

2900. Haseman, J. B. March 1993. Destruction of Democracy: The Tragic Case of Burma. *Asian Affairs (New York)* 20: 17–26.

2901. Hasenritter, K. H. April 1982. Party Organisation and Intra-Party Democracy.* *Aus Politik und Zeitgeschichte* 14–15: 19–28.

2902. Haskell, J. December 1992. The Paradox of Plebiscitary Democracy in Presidential Nomination Campaigns. *Western Political Quarterly* 45 (4): 1001–1019.

2903. Hastings, M. June 1989. The Media and Modern Warfare. *Conflict Quarterly* 9: 5–20.

2904. Hatchard, J. December 1993. Re-Establishing a Multi-Party State: Some Constitutional Lessons from the Seychelles. *Journal of Modern African Studies* 31 (4): 601–612.

2905. Hattenhauer, H. 1979. Dreissig Jahre Grundgesetz: Was Ist die "Freiheitliche Demokratrische Grundordnung"? *Neue Ordnung* 33 (3): 161–175.

2906. Hattich, M. May 1985. Act: Back to Origins?* *Politische Studien* 281: 246–253.

2907. Hauofa, E. September 1994. Thy Kingdom Come: The Democratization of Aristocratic Tonga. *Contemporary Pacific* 6 (2): 414–428.

2908. Hauser, W., and W. Singer. September 1986. The Democratic Rite: Celebration and Participation in the Indian Elections. *Asian Survey* 26 (9): 941–958.

2909. Hauss, C., and D. Rayside. 1978. The Development of New Parties in Western Democracies since 1945. *Sage Electoral Studies Yearbook* 4: 31–57.

2910. Havens, A. E. November 1983. *See* Petras, J. (November 1983).

2911. Havlovic, S. J. June 1990. German Works' Councils: A Highly Evolved Institution of Industrial Democracy. *Labor Studies Journal* 15 (2): 62–73.

2912. Hawes, G. March 1989. Acquino and Her Administration: A View from the Countryside. *Pacific Affairs* 62 (1): 9–28.

2913. Hawkins, R. B. , Jr. March 1978. Federal Principles for Government Reorganization. *Publius* 8 (2): 133–140.

2914. Hawthorn, G. 1987. Practical Reason and Social Democracy: Reflections on Unger's Passion and Politics. *Northwestern University Law Review* 81 (4): 766–790.

2915. Hawthorn, G. August 1993. Liberalization and "Modern Liberty": Four Southern States. *World Development* 21 (8): 1299–1312.

2916. Hayat, S. March 1984. American Democratic Theory: An Appraisal of

Robert Dahl's Contribution. *Pakistan Journal of American Studies* 2 (1): 36–53.

2917. Hayden, F. G., and L. D. Swanson. June 1980. Planning through the Socialization of Property Rights: The Community Reinvestment Act. *Journal of Economic Issues* 14 (2): 351–369.

2918. Hayek, F. A. March 1978. The Miscarriage of the Democratic Ideal. *Encounter* 50 (3): 14–17.

2919. Hayes, E. December 1983. Presidential Participation: Decentralization from Lyndon Johnson to Ronald Reagan: On Programs and Presidential Control. *Urbanism Past and Present* 8 (1): 1–11.

2920. Hayhoe, R. June 1990. China's Returned Scholars and the Democratic Movement. *China Quarterly* 122: 293–302.

2921. Hayhoe, R. 1992. Universities, Cultural Identity, and Democracy: Some Canada-China Comparisons. *Interchange* 23 (1–2): 165–180.

2922. Haynes, F. 1986. Curriculum, Democracy, and Evaluation. *Teachers College Record* 88 (1): 81–94.

2923. Haynes, J. 1991. Human Rights and Democracy in Ghana: The Record of the Rawlings Regime. *African Affairs* 90 (360): 407–425.

2924. Haynes, J. 1993. Sustainable Democracy in Ghana? Problems and Prospects. *Third World Quarterly* 14 (3): 451–468.

2925. Haysom, N. March 1991. Democracy, Constitutionalism, and the ANC's Bill of Rights for a New South Africa. *Social Justice* 18 (1–2): 40–48.

2926. Hayward, B. July 1993. Participating Democracy: Questions Raised by Feminist Involvement with Practice and Theory. *Political Science* 45 (1): 27–39.

2927. He, B. G. 1990. A Critique of the Chinese Paternalistic Model of Democracy. *Issues and Studies* 26 (10): 24–42.

2928. He, B. G. 1991. Democracy as Viewed by Three Chinese Liberals: Wei Jingsheng, Hu Ping and Yan Jiagi. *China Information* 6 (2): 23–43.

2929. He, B. G. March 1992. Democratization: Antidemocratic and Democratic Elements in the Political Culture of China. *Australian Journal of Political Science* 27 (1): 120–136.

2930. He, B. G. September 1993. Challenge of Exception to Procedural Democracy: Constitutional Emergency Power. *Journal of Contemporary China* 4: 35–57.

2931. He, B. G. December 1993. Infusing Morality into [Chinese] Political Institutions. *Journal of Contemporary China* 2: 35–52.

2932. He, B. G. March 1994. Dual Roles of Semi-Civil Society in Chinese Democratization. *Australian Journal of Political Science* 29 (1): 154–171.

2933. Healey, J., R. Ketley, and M. Robinson. January 1993. Will Political Reform Bring About Improved Economic Management in Sub-Saharan Africa. *IDS Bulletin (Institute of Development Studies)* 24 (1): 31–38.

2934. Hearn, F. March 1985. Durkheim's Political Sociology: Corporatism, State Autonomy, and Democracy. *Social Research* 52 (1): 151–177.

2935. Heath, A., and G. Evans. October 1994. Tactical Voting: Concepts, Measurement, and Findings. *British Journal of Political Science* 24 (4): 557+.

2936. Heath, A. F. April 1994. *See* Weakliem, D. L. (April 1994).

2937. Heck, D. February 1981. Nepal in 1980: The Year of the Referendum. *Asian Survey* 21 (2): 181–187.

2938. Heidar, K. March 1984. Party Power: Approaches in a Field of Unfilled Classics. *Scandinavian Political Studies* 7 (1): 1–16.

2939. Heilbroner, R. L. 1978. Capitalism, Socialism, and Democracy. *Commentary* 65 (4): 46–48.

2940. Heilbroner, R. L. 1981. Was Schumpeter Right? *Social Research* 48 (3): 456–471.

2941. Hein, G. R. February 1990. Indonesia in 1989: A Question of Openness. *Asian Survey* 30 (2): 221–230.

2942. Hein, L. E. August 1994. In Search of Peace and Democracy: Japanese Economic Debate in Political Context. *Journal of Asian Studies* 53 (3): 752–778.

2943. Heineman, R. September 1983. "E Pluribus Unum"? Recent Critique of Liberal Democracy. *Political Science Review* 13: 69–98.

2944. Heini, J. December 1988. Transition to Nowhere: How Haiti's Democratic Transition Might Have Worked. *Caribbean Review* 16 (2): 4–6, 26.

2945. Heinin, J. 1992. Polish Democracy Is a Masculine Democracy. *Women's Studies International Forum* 15 (1): 129–138.

2946. Heisey, D. R. June 1994. *See* Gorden, W. I. (June 1994).

2947. Heisler, M. O. September 1977. Managing Ethnic Conflict in Belgium. *Annals of the American Academy of Political and Social Science* 433: 32–46.

2948. Heisler, M. O. May 1986. Transnational Migration as a Small Window on the Diminished Autonomy of the Modern Democratic State. *Annals of the American Academy of Political and Social Science* 485: 153–166.

2949. Held, D. 1990. Democracy, Nation-State and the Global System.* *Teoria Politica* 6 (3): 3–44.

2950. Held, D. March 1991. Democracy and Globalization. *Alternatives* 16 (2): 201–208.

2951. Held, D. May 1991. Democracy, the Nation-State and the Global System. *Economy and Society* 20 (2): 138–172.

2952. Held, D. 1992a. Democracy: From City-State to a Cosmopolitan Order.* *Teoria Politica* 8 (1–2): 19–63.

2953. Held, D. 1992b. Democracy: From City-State to a Cosmopolitan Order. *Political Studies* 40: 10–39. Special issue.

2954. Held, D. April 1993. Liberalism, Marxism, and Democracy. *Theory and Society* 22 (2): 249–281.

2955. Held, D. June 1993. Democracy: Past, Present, and Possible Futures. *Alternatives* 18 (3): 259–271.

2956. Held, D., and A. McGrew. March 1993. Globalization and the Liberal Democratic State. *Government and Opposition* 28 (2): 261–288.

2957. Heller, A. December 1978. The Past, Present, and Future of Democracy. *Social Research* 45 (4): 866–886.

2958. Heller, A. 1981. Rationality and Democracy. *Philosophy & Social Criticism* 8 (3): 243+.

2959. Heller, A. March 1983. *See* Feher, F. (March 1983).

2960. Heller, A. 1988. Political Principles. *Teoria Politica* 4 (2): 3–17.

2961. Heller, A., and F. Feher. 1994. Democracy in Absolute Present Tense.* *Internationale Politik und Gesellschaft* 1: 7–14.

2962. Heller, M. A. February 1990. The Middle East: Out of Step with History. *Foreign Affairs* 69 (1): 152–171.

2963. Helliwell, J. F. April 1994. Empirical Linkages between Democracy and Economic Growth. *British Journal of Political Science* 24 (2): 225–248.

2964. Hellman, J. A. March 1994. Mexican Popular Movements, Clientelism, and the Process of Democratization. *Latin American Perspectives* 21 (2): 124–142.

2965. Helms, A. R. C. December 1982. Procedural Democracy and the Terrorist Threat. *Police Studies* 4: 23–32.

2966. Henberg, M. December 1994. *See* Zirker, D. (December 1994).

2967. Henderson, A. 1982. Finnegan vs. Leu: Promoting Union Democracy by Suppressing Internal Dissent. *Catholic University Law Review* 32 (1): 287–315.

2968. Henderson, C. W. November 1981. Comment: Consociational Democracy and the Case of Switzerland. *Journal of Politics* 43 (3): 1232–1235.

2969. Henderson, C. W. 1991. Conditions Affecting the Use of Political Repression. *Journal of Conflict Resolution* 35 (1): 120–142.

2970. Henderson, J. S. December 1976. *See* Reid, W. M. (December 1976).

2971. Henderson, M. October 1979. Setting India's Democratic House in Order: Constitutional Amendments. *Asian Survey* 19 (10): 946–956.

2972. Hendricks, W. E. July 1987. *See* Fiotito, J. (July 1987).

2973. Hendrickson, D. C. December 1994. The Democratic Crusade: Intervention, Economic Sanctions, and Engagement. *World Policy Journal* 11 (4): 18–30.

2974. Hendrix, R. 1987. *See* Gedicks, F. M. (1987).

2975. Henke, W. 1986. Democracy as a Legal Concept.* *Der Staat* 25 (2): 157–171.

2976. Henkin, L. March 1989. Treaties in a Constitutional Democracy. *Michigan Journal of International Law* 10: 406–429.

2977. Henkin, L. September 1992. Constitutionalism, Democracy and Foreign Affairs. *Indian Law Journal* 67 (4): 879–886.

2978. Henkin, S. M. April 1983. The Liquidation of the Franco Dictatorship in Spain. *Voprosy Istorii* 4: 48–61.

2979. Hennesy, T. M., and B. G. Peters. March 1975. Political Paradoxes in Post-Industrialism: A Political Economy Perspective. *Policy Studies Journal* 3 (3): 233–240.

2980. Henningsen, M. July 1989. Democracy: The Future of a Western Political Formulation. *Alternatives* 14 (3): 327–342.

2981. Hennis, W. September 1988. Tocqueville's Perspective: *Democracy in America* —In Search of the "New Science of Politics." *Interpretation* 16 (1): 61–86.

2982. Henry, N. August 1984. Scattered Thoughts on a Democratic Dilemma. *Policy Studies Review* 4 (1): 28–34.

2983. Henson, G. M. May 1982. Education Levels, Participation Rates, and Policy Output Efforts in the Fifty States. *State and Local Government Review* 14 (2): 75–79.

2984. Henze, P. B. 1982. On thc Rebound. *Wilson Quarterly* 6 (5): 109–125.

2985. Heper, M. October 1976. Political Modernization as Reflected in Bureaucratic Change: The Turkish Bureaucracy and a "Historical Bureaucratic Empire" Tradition. *International Journal of Middle East Studies* 7 (4): 507–521.

2986. Heper, M. April 1992. Consolidating Democracy. *Journal of Democracy* 3 (2): 105–117.

2987. Heper, M. July 1992. The Strong State as a Problem for the Consolidation of Democracy: Turkey and Germany Compared. *Comparative Political Studies* 25 (2): 169–194.

2988. Herbeson, E. 1992. *See* Winchester, I. (1992).

2989. Herbst, J. May 1992. The American People's College: The Lost Promise of Democracy in Education. *American Journal of Education* 100 (3): 275–297.

2990. Herd, J. P. March 1994. The Cuban Democracy Act: Another Extraterritorial

Act That Won't Work. *Brooklyn Journal of International Law* 20: 397–442.

2991. Herf, J. 1990. Asymmetric Strategic Interaction: Democracy, Dictatorship and the Euromissile Dispute in West Germany. *Journal of Strategic Studies* 13 (2): 54–81.

2992. Herman, E. S., and J. Petras. 1985. Resurgent Democracy: Rhetoric and Reality. *New Left Review* (154): 83–98.

2993. Herman, E. S., and J. Petras. July 6, 1985. Resurgent Democracy in Latin America: Rhetoric and Reality. *Economic and Political Weekly* 20 (27): 1147–1152.

2994. Hermann, J. 1992. Sudeafrika: Der Weg Aus der Apartheid. *Weltgeschehen* 1: 8–154.

2995. Hermanson, T., S. Aro, and C. L. Bennett. June 22, 1994. Finland Health Care System: Universal Access to Health Care in a Capitalistic Democracy. *Journal of the American Medical Association* 271 (24): 1957–1962.

2996. Hermansson, J. 1986. Democracy in the Western Sense.* *Statsvetenskaplig Tidskrift* 89 (4): 253–264.

2997. Hermansson, J. 1992. Democratization of Eastern Europe: A Game Theoretic Perspective. *Scandinavian Political Studies* 15 (3): 217–233.

2998. Hermele, K. October 1993. The Past and Future of Swedish Social Democracy: A Response. *Monthly Review* 45 (5): 32–37.

2999. Hermens, F. A. 1978. Return to Democratic Government. *Year Book of World Affairs* 32: 191–207.

3000. Hermens, F. A. September 1978. The New Dilemma of Democracy. *Freedom at Issue* 47: 13–18.

3001. Hermet, G. 1977. Spain: Change of Society, Authoritarian Modernization and Democracy Conceded.* *Revue Française de Science Politique* 27 (4–5): 582–600.

3002. Hermet, G. June 1984. Predestination or Strategy?* *Esprit* 6: 131–141.

3003. Hermet, G. 1986. Reflections for a Study of "Granted" Democracy. *Teoria Politica* 2 (1): 49–71.

3004. Hermet, G. March 1986. The European Left and Central America. *Washington Quarterly* 9 (2): 37–43.

3005. Hermet, G. December 1986. On Democracy in Latin America.* *Politique Internationale* 34: 271–279.

3006. Hermet, G. June 1990. Amicable Democratization: From Spain to Poland.* *Commentaire* 50: 279–286.

3007. Hermet, G. August 1991. The Disenchantment of the Old Democracies.* *International Social Science Journal* 43 (3): 451–461.

3008. Hermosa Andujar, A. March 1986. From Direct to Representative Democracy.* *Revista de Estudios Politicos* 50: 101–141.

3009. Hernandez, C. G. December 1985. Constitutional Authoritarianism and the Prospects of Democracy in the Philippines. *Journal of International Affairs* 38 (2): 243–258.

3010. Hernandez, C. G. February 1988. The Philippines in 1987: Challenges of Redemocratization. *Asian Survey* 28 (2): 229–241.

3011. Hernandez, C. G. February 1989. The Philippines in 1988: Reaching Out to Peace and Economic Recovery. *Asian Survey* 29 (2): 154–164.

3012. Hernandez, H. H. 1978. On Dimensions in Kelsen's Writing.* *Boletin de Ciencias Politicas y Sociales* 23: 145–173.

3013. Hernandez, L. March 1992. See Fox, J. (March 1992).

3014. Hernes, G. 1991. The Dilemmas of Social Democracies: The Case of Norway and Sweden. *Acta Sociologica* 34 (4): 239–260.

3015. Hernes, H. M. 1988. Scandinavian Citizenship. *Acta Sociologica* 31 (3): 199–215.

3016. Hero, R. E. June 1986. The Urban Service Delivery Literature: Some Questions and Considerations. *Polity* 18 (4): 659–677.

3017. Herrera, R., and M. K. Taylor. December 1994. The Structure of Opinion in American Political Parties. *Political Studies* 42 (4): 676–689.

3018. Herrick, N. Q. 1985. Is the Time Finally Ripe for Educational Democracy. *Social Policy* 16 (2): 53–56.

3019. Herrick, R. December 1994. *See* Nixon, D. L. (December 1994).

3020. Herring, R. J. December 1978. Radical Politics and Revolution in South Asia. *Peasant Studies* 7 (1): 1–10.

3021. Hershey, M. R. December 1994. The Meaning of a Mandate: Interpretation of Mandate in 1984 Presidential Election Coverage. *Polity* 27 (2): 225–254.

3022. Herskovits, J. December 1979. Democracy in Nigeria. *Foreign Affairs* 58 (2): 314–335.

3023. Herskovits, J. March 1984. Dateline Nigeria: Democracy Down but Not Out. *Foreign Policy* 54: 171–190.

3024. Hersom, N. January 1994. Democracy and University Governance: One President's Perspective. *Interchange* 25 (1): 19–23.

3025. Herzberg, R. June 1986. *McCloskey vs. McIntyre:* Implications of Contested Elections in a Federal Democracy. *Publius* 16 (3): 93–109.

3026. Herzog, D. April 1994. Democratic Credentials. *Ethics* 104: 467–479.

3027. Hesli, V. L. April 1994. *See* Reisinger, W. M. (April 1994).

3028. Hetzner, C. May 1985. Social Democracy and Bureaucracy: The Labour Party and Higher Civil Service Recruit-ment. *Administration and Society* 17 (1): 97–128.

3029. Heuer, U. 1990. Marxist Theory and Democracy.* *Kritische Justiz* 23 (2): 198–208.

3030. Heumos, P. 1987. The Working Classes and Social Democracy in Eastern Central-Europe, 1944–1948. *Geschichte und Gesellschaft* 13 (1): 22–38.

3031. Hewitt, C. June 1977. The Effect of Political Democracy and Social Democracy on Equality in Industrial Societies: A Cross-National Comparison. *American Sociological Review* 42 (3): 450–464.

3032. Hewitt, W. E. October 1989. *See* Bruneau, T. C. (October 1989).

3033. Hewitt, W. E. June 1990. Religion and the Consolidation of Democracy in Brazil: The Role of the Comunidades Eclesias de Base (CEBs). *Sociological Analysis* 51 (2): 139–152.

3034. Heydemann, S. March 1991. Can We Get There from Here? The Syrian Case. *American-Arab Affairs* 36: 27–30.

3035. Heywood, P. April 1987. Mirror-Images: The PCE and PSOE in the Transition to Democracy in Spain. *West European Politics* 10: 193–210.

3036. Hibbing, J. R., and S. C. Patterson. December 1994. Public Trust in the New Parliaments of Central and Eastern Europe. *Political Studies* 42 (4): 570–592.

3037. Hibbs, D. A. , Jr. 1985. Macroeconomic Performance, Policy and Electoral Politics in Industrial Democracies. *International Social Science Journal* 37 (1): 63–74.

3038. Hibbs, D. A. , Jr., and H. J. Madsen. April 1981. Public Reactions to the Growth of Taxation and Government Expenditure. *World Politics* 33 (3): 413–435.

3039. Hibert, T. 1975. Comprehensive Schools and Democratization of Education.* *Orientation Scolaire et Professionnelle* 4 (4): 407–420.

3040. Hibri, A. Y. December 1992. Islamic Constitutionalism and the Concept of Democracy. *Case Western Reserve Journal of International Law* 24: 1–27.

3041. Hic, M. June 1992. Market Economy and Democracy: Turkey as a Case Study for Developing Countries and Eastern Europe. *Orient* 33: 205–226.

3042. Hickey, D. V. V. 1991. Tiananmen Tremors: The Economic, Political, and Strategic Impact of the Democracy Movement on Taiwan. *Issues and Studies* 27 (2): 36–57.

3043. Hickey, D. V. V. March 1992. Perceptions, Misperceptions, and Policy: Taiwan's Assessment of the Democracy Movement in the People's Republic of China. *Asian Affairs: An American Review* 19 (1): 35–47.

3044. Hicks, A. August 1988. Social Democratic Corporatism and Economic Growth. *Journal of Politics* 50 (3): 677–704.

3045. Hicks, A. April 1994. *See* Misra, J. (April 1994).

3046. Hicks, A., and J. Misra. November 1993. Political Resources and the Growth of Welfare in Affluent Capitalist Democracies, 1960–1982. *American Journal of Sociology* 99 (3): 668–710.

3047. Hicks, A., and W. D. Patterson. August 1989. On the Robustness of the Left Corporatist Model of Economic Growth. *Journal of Politics* 51 (3): 662–675.

3048. Hicks, A., and D. H. Swank. April 1984. On the Political Economy of Welfare Expansion: A Comparative Analysis of 18 Advanced Capitalist Democracies, 1960–1971. *Comparative Political Studies* 17 (1): 81–119.

3049. Hicks, A., and D. H. Swank. December 1984. Government Redistribution in Rich Capitalist Democracies. *Policy Studies Journal* 13 (2): 265–286.

3050. Hicks, A., and D. H. Swank. March 1992. Politics, Institutions, and Welfare Spending in Industrial Democracies 1960–1982. *American Political Science Review* 86 (3): 658–674.

3051. High, M. E. June 1986. *See* Connors, D. L. (June 1986).

3052. Higham, J. December 1984. Herbert Baxter Adams and the Study of Local History. *American Historical Review* 89 (5): 1225–1239.

3053. Higley, J. June 1987. *See* Burton, M. G. (June 1987).

3054. Higley, J., and M. G. Burton. February 1989. The Elite Variable in Democratic Transitions and Breakdowns. *American Sociological Review* 54 (1): 17–32.

3055. Hilb, C. January 1984. Reflections on the Democratization of Authoritarian Regimes. *L'Homme et la Societe* 71–72: 55–64.

3056. Hildreth, A. May 1994. The Importance of Purposes in "Purposive" Groups: Incentives and Participation in the Sanctuary Movement. *American Journal of Political Science* 38 (2): 447–463.

3057. Hill, L. E., C. E. Butler, and S. A. Lorenzen. 1977. Inflation and Destruction of Democracy: The Case of the Weimar Republic. *Journal of Economic Issues* 11 (2): 299–313.

3058. Hill, R. C. September 1983. Market, State, and Community: National Urban Policy in the 1989s. *Urban Affairs Quarterly* 19 (1): 5–20.

3059. Hillal Dessouki, A. E. January 1990. Egypt's Political Evolution: Democratic Pluralism or Neo-Authoritarianism?* *Maghreb-Machrek* 127: 7–16.

3060. Hillebrand, E. 1993. Democratization as Recycling of Elites: The Case of Gabon.* *Afrika Spectrum* 28 (1): 73–92.

3061. Hillebrand, E. 1994. Afterthoughts on Civil Society and Democracy in Africa. *Internationale Politik und Gesellschaft* 1: 57–71.

3062. Hilliard, A. G. III. May 1984. The School's Response to Youth Unemployment. *Education and Urban Society* 16 (3): 354–359.

3063. Hills, J. January 1993. Telecommunications and Democracy: The International Experience. *Telecommunication Journal* 60 (1): 21–29.

3064. Hillyard, P., and J. Percy Smith. October 1989. The Coercive State Revisited. *Parliamentary Affairs* 42 (4): 533–547.

3065. Hilt, E. April 1993. *See* Pastor, M., Jr. (April 1993).

3066. Hilton, R. C. 1978. Public Support for Library Service: Revolutionary Democracy in Action. *Library Journal* 103 (12): 1223–1228.

3067. Himmelstrand, U. 1983. Sweden Toward Economic Democracy: A Social Democratic Government Contemplates New Policies. *Dissent* 30 (3): 329–336.

3068. Hinckley, C. J. September 1990. Tocqueville on Religious Truth and Political Necessity. *Polity* 23 (1): 39–52.

3069. Hindess, B. May 1991. Imaginary Presuppositions of Democracy. *Economy and Society* 20 (2): 173–195.

3070. Hindess, B. August 1993. Liberalism, Socialism, and Democracy: Variations on a Governmental Theme. *Economy and Society* 22 (3): 300–313.

3071. Hinich, M. J. February 1982. *See* Enelow, J. M. (February 1982).

3072. Hinnebusch, R. A. March 1984. The Reemergence of the Wafd Party: Glimpses of the Liberal Opposition in Egypt. *International Journal of Middle East Studies* 16 (1): 99–121.

3073. Hintze, W. 1975. The International Monopoly Capital's Part in the Struggle against Democracy in Portugal.* *IPW Berichte* 4 (5): 66–72.

3074. Hirschkop, K. 1986. Bakhtin, Discourse and Democracy. *New Left Review* (160): 92–112.

3075. Hirschman, A. O. 1989. Opinionated Opinions and Democracy. *Dissent* 36 (3): 393–395.

3076. Hirschman, A. O. May 1994. Social Conflict as Pillars of Democratic Market Society. *Political Theory* 22 (2): 203–218.

3077. Hirst, M., and R. Russell. October 1987. Democracy and Foreign Policy: The Case of Argentina and Brazil.* *Estudios Internacionales* 80: 442–490.

3078. Hirst, P. April 1988. Representative Democracy and Its Limits. *Political Quarterly* 59 (2): 190–205.

3079. Hirst, P. December 1992. Comments on "Secondary Associations and Democratic Governance." *Politics and Society* 20 (4): 473–481.

3080. Hirst, P. March 1994. Associative Democracy. *Dissent* 41 (2): 241–248.

3081. Hirst, P., and J. Zeitlin. 1991. State, Democracy, Socialism: Introduction. *Economy and Society* 20 (2): 133–137.

3082. Hirttio, K., J. Husa, and T. Saarelainen. 1994. Democracy from the Viewpoint of Publicity and Values: The Model of Competing Values.* *Hallinnon Tutimus* 13 (1): 22–37.

3083. Hiskes, R. P. September 1988. Emergent Risks and Convergent Interest: Democratic Policy Making for Biotechnology. *Policy Studies Journal* 17 (1): 73–82.

3084. Ho, S. March 1992. Walking the Tightrope: The ROCs Democratization, Diplomacy, and Mainland Policy. *Issues and Studies* 28 (3): 1–20.

3085. Hodge, R. W. June 1979. *See* Tyree, A. (June 1979).

3086. Hodgson, G., I. Kristal, and G. Tullock. March 1988. The Virtues and Vices of Democracy in Conducting Foreign Affairs. *University of Miami Law Review* 43: 211–222.

3087. Hoepken, W. 1980. Das Yugoslawische Delegietensystem als Modell Unmittelbaren Demokratie: Aspekte der Praxis der Nuen Vertretungssystem in Yugoslawien. *Politische Vierteljahresschrift* 21 (1): 62–87.

3088. Hoffman, E., and E. W. Packel. January 1982. A Stochastic Model of Committee Voting with Exogenous Cost: Theory and Experiments. *Behavioral Science* 27 (1): 43–56.

3089. Hoffmann, G. R. March 1994. Philosophy and Democracy from an Intercultural Perspective: International Conference at Erasmus University in Rotterdam, October 29–30, 1993.* *Argument* 36 (2): 277–279.

3090. Hoffmann, R. June 1984. Democracy between Representation and Anarchy.* *Zeitschrift für Politik* 31 (2): 123–134.

3091. Hoffmann, S. December 1979. Fragments Floating in the Here and Now. *Daedalus* 108 (1): 1–26.

3092. Hoffmann, S. 1980. Some Notes on Democratic Theory and Practice. *Tocqueville Review* 2 (1): 59–75.

3093. Hoffmann, S. June 1984. Less Ambition, Far More Result.* *Politique Internationale* 24: 23–36.

3094. Hofmeister, W. October 19, 1990. The Chilean Road towards Democracy.* *Aus Politik und Zeitgeschichte* 43: 44–54.

3095. Hohm, K. 1983. Parteidemokratie und Volkentscheid: Stabilisierung der Parteiendemokratie durch die Einfuehrung Direkt-Demokratischer. *Demokratie und Recht* 11 (4): 406–411.

3096. Hojman, D. E. June 1993. Nongovernmental Organisations (NGOs) and the Chilean Transition to Democracy. *Revista Europea Estudios Latinoamericanos y del Caribe:* 7–24.

3097. Holbrook, D. 1990. The Health Service: A Triumph of Democracy. *Political Quarterly* 61 (1): 93–97.

3098. Holbrok, T. M. November 1994. Campaigns, National Conditions, and United States Presidential Elections. *American Journal of Political Science* 38 (4): 973–998.

3099. Holbrooke, R. June 1976. A Sense of Drift, a Time for Calm. *Foreign Policy* 23: 97–112.

3100. Holbrooke, R. March 1986. East Asia: The Next Challenge. *Foreign Affairs* 64 (4): 732–751.

3101. Holden, B. June 1988. New Directions in Democratic Theory. *Political Studies* 36 (2): 324–333.

3102. Holdren, J. P. March 1976. The Nuclear Controversy and the Limitations of Decision-Making by Experts. *Bulletin of the Atomic Scientists* 32 (3): 20–22.

3103. Holesovsky, V. June 1981. Ideas of Industrial Democracy in Eastern Europe: Dilemmas and Blind Alleys. *Association of Comparative Economic Studies Bulletin* 23: 71–79.

3104. Hollerman, L. August 1979. International Economic Controls in Occupied Japan. *Journal of Asian Studies* 38 (4): 707–720.

3105. Holm, H. December 1990. The Democratic Victory: What Will Happen to Foreign Policy? *Cooperation and Conflict* 25 (4): 195–206.

3106. Holm, J. D. June 1987. Botswana: A Paternalistic Democracy. *World Affairs* 150 (1): 21–30.

3107. Holm, J. D. 1990. *See* Molutsi, P. P. (1990).

3108. Holm, J. D., and P. P. Molutsi. 1990. Monitoring the Development of Democracy: Our Botswana Experience. *Journal of Modern African Studies* 28 (3): 535–543.

3109. Holm, J. D., and G. Somolekae. 1989. Democracy in Botswana.* *Année Africaine* 129–149.

3110. Holman, O., and A. E. Fernandez-Jilberto. 1989. Social Classes, Crisis of the Authoritarian Regime and Democratic Transition: The Case of Brazil and Spain in a Comparative Light.* *Afers Internacionals* 16: 5–22.

3111. Holmberg, K. June 1994. *See* Gorden, W. I. (June 1994).

3112. Holmberg, S. May 1983. *See* Clausen, A. R. (May 1983).

3113. Holmberg, S. December 1990. *See* Branberg, D. (December 1990).

3114. Holmes, M. 1983. Freedom and Control in Education: How Can We Escape Public Opinion in a Democracy: Response. *Interchange* 14 (3): 64–71.

3115. Holmquist, F., and M. Ford. 1992. Kenya: Slouching toward Democracy. *Africa Today* 39 (3): 97–111.

3116. Holtz Bacha, C. et al. January 1994. Political Television Advertising in Western Democracies: A Comparison of Campaign Broadcasts in the United States, Germany, and France. *Political Communication* 11: 67–80.

3117. Holway, R. November 1994. Achilles, Socrates, and Democracy. *Political Theory* 22 (4): 561–590.

3118. Holzer, M. March 1989. *See* Mayer, R. T. (March 1989).

3119. Homann, B. 1982. Das Konkordanzsystem der Schweiz: Kritik und Alternative Konkordanztheoretischer Ansaetze. *Politische Vierteljahresschrift* 23 (4): 418–438.

3120. Homer, F. D., and G. Massey. March 1979. On Being Canned: Personnel Decisions in Democratic Bureaucracies. *Bureaucrat* 8 (1): 33–39.

3121. Homerin, E. June 1986. The Arabi in the People's Assembly: Religion, Press, and Politics in Sadat's Egypt. *Middle East Journal* 40 (3): 462–477.

3122. Homig, H. 1978. Absolutism and Democracy: The Dargenson Reform Program.* *Historische Zeitschrift* 226 (2): 349–380.

3123. Honderich, T. 1974. Difficulty with Democracy. *Philosophy and Public Affairs* 3 (2): 221–226.

3124. Honderich, T. March 1994. Hierarchical Democracy. *New Left Review* (204): 48–66.

3125. Hooghe, I. 1989. Democracy and Modernization: Constraints or Choice.* *Res Publica* 31 (4): 565–591.

3126. Hook, S. 1978. Capitalism, Socialism, and Democracy. *Commentary* 65 (4): 48–50.

3127. Hopkins, S. September 1993. The French Communist Party in the Legislative Elections [21 and 28 March 1993]. *Communist Studies* 9 (3): 278–288.

3128. Hoppe, H. September 1991. Bulgaria's Difficult Road towards Democracy.* *Osteuropa* 41 (9): 887–904.

3129. Hoppe, H. July 1992. Demokratischer Machtwechsel in Albanien. *Osteuropa* 42: 609–620.

3130. Hoppe, T. June 1992. Die Chinesische Position in Ost-Turkestan, Xinjiang. *China Aktuell* 21: 358–365.

3131. Hormats, R. D. December 1978. Managing Economic Problems in the Industrialized Democracies. *Department of State Bulletin* 78: 32–36.

3132. Horn, G., and R. Schifter. December 1990. A Hungarian Looks at Human Rights. *Mediterranean Quarterly* 1 (1): 26–36.

3133. Horner, S. July 1991. Democracy in the English-Speaking Caribbean. *Courier* 44: 73–76.

3134. Hornung, K. 1985. Welfare State Democracy and Safety Political Self-Assertion: The Federal Republic of Germany.* *Beitraege zur Konfliktforschung* 15 (1): 5–30.

3135. Horowitz, A. M. December 1981. *See* Waegel, W. B. (December 1981).

3136. Horowitz, D. L. October 1993. Democracy in Divided Societies. *Journal of Democracy* 4 (4): 18–38.

3137. Horowitz, F. D. 1982. Educating for Human Development, for Democracy: An Essay. *Peabody Journal of Education* 59 (2): 79–88.

3138. Horowitz, I. L. May 1977. Can Democracy Cope with Terrorism? *Civil Liberties Review* 4 (1): 29–37.

3139. Horowitz, I. L. 1979. Beyond Democracy: Interest Groups and the Patriotic Core. *Humanist* 39 (5): 4–10.

3140. Horowitz, I. L. January 1981. Military Origins of Third World Dictatorship and Democracy. *Third World Quarterly* 3 (1): 36–47.

3141. Horowitz, I. L. 1983. Printed Words, Computers, and Democratic Societies (Political and Social Impact of Computer and Information Technologies). *Virginia Quarterly Review* 59: 620–636.

3142. Horowitz, I. L., and M. E. Curtis. 1994. Politics and Publishing in a Democratic Society: Technical Breakthroughs and Research Agendas. *Publishing Research Quarterly* 10 (3): 22–30.

3143. Horowitz, R. B. July 1994. The Uneasy Relationship between Political and Economic Reform in South Africa: The Case of Telecommunications. *African Affairs* 93 (372): 361–386.

3144. Horvath, L. 1976. Participation and Factory Democracy. *Eastern European Economics* 14 (3): 59–83.

3145. Horwitt, S. D. September 1990. America's Number-One Problem: Democracy. *National Civic Review* 79 (5): 414–416.

3146. Hossain, G. 1985. "Civilianizing" Ziaur Rahman's Army Regime: Bangladesh Model. *Regional Studies* 3 (4): 42–57.

3147. Hottinger, A. 1976. Portuguese Democracy under Verification: Results of a Revolution Two and a Half Years Later.* *Europa Archiv: Zeitschrift für Internationale Politik* 31 (15): 487–496.

3148. Hottinger, A. 1977. Spain Headed for a Democracy.* *Europa Archiv: Zeitschrift für Internationale Politik* 32 (16): 515–524.

3149. Hottinger, A. 1977. Spain on the Road to Democracy. *World Today* 33 (9): 353–362.

3150. Hottinger, A. 1979. Spain's Transition to Democracy: Successes and Difficulties.* *Beitraege zur Konfliktforschung* 9 (1): 21–40.

3151. Hottinger, A. 1981. Spanish Democracy in Crisis. *Europa Archiv: Zeitschrift für Internationale Politic* 36 (12): 353–362.

3152. Hottinger, A. April 1987. The Return of the Political Pendulum in Turkey: Democracy Comes Back after the Third Military Intervention.* *Schweizer Monatshefte* 67 (4): 277–284.

3153. Hough, J. F. September 1990. Gorbachev's Endgame. *World Policy Journal* 7 (4): 639–672.

3154. Hough, J. F. January 1994. The Russian Election of 1993: Public Attitudes toward Economic Reform and Democratization. *Post-Soviet Affairs* 10 (1): 1–37.

3155. Houppert, E. March 1993. *See* Padilla, D. (March 1993).

3156. Houser, H. F. September 1988. *See* Clark, W. D. (September 1988).

3157. Houska, J. 1984. Theoretical Aspects of the Present Struggle for Democracy in Capitalist Countries.* *Sociologicky Casopis* 20 (5): 472–486.

3158. Housman, R. F. June 1994. Democratizing International Trade Decision-

Making. *Cornell International Law Journal* 27: 699–747.

3159. Howard, A. E. D. June 1986. "Garcia" of Federalism and Constitutional Values. *Publius* 16 (3): 17–31.

3160. Howard, A. E. D. January 1992. Drafting Constitutions for New Democracies. *Problems of Communism* 41 (1–2): 63–65.

3161. Howard, M. February 1990. The Springtime of Nations. *Foreign Affairs* 69 (1): 17–32.

3162. Howe, J. September 1978. Toward a Broader Democracy. *Africa:* 58–60.

3163. Howe, K. R. September 1992. Liberal Democracy, Equal Educational Opportunity, and the Challenge of Multiculturalism. *American Educational Research Journal* 29 (3): 455–470.

3164. Howell, S. E. April 1994. Racism, Cynicism, Economics, and David Duke [in Louisiana Elections]. *American Political Quarterly* 22 (2): 190–207.

3165. Hoxie, R. G. September 1988. Alexander Hamilton and the Electoral System Revisited. *Presidential Studies Quarterly* 18 (4): 717–720.

3166. Hoxie, R. G. December 1993. Democracy in Transition. *Presidential Studies Quarterly* 23 (1): 27–36.

3167. Hoyos Vasquez, G. September 1993. Discussive Ethics, Law, and Democracy.* *Analisis Politico* 20: 5–19.

3168. Hrabovska, A. 1993. *See* Plichtova, J. (1993).

3169. Hsiao, D. H. April 1992. Invisible Cities: The Constitutional Status of Direct Democracy in a Democratic Republic. *Duke Law Journal* 41 (5): 1267–1310.

3170. Hsiao, H. M. July 1990. Emerging Social Movements and the Rise of a Demanding Civil Society in Taiwan. *Australian Journal of Chinese Affairs* 24: 163–180.

3171. Hsuan, C. W. 1976. Criticizing Concerning Socialist Democracy and Legal System. *Issues and Studies* 12 (2): 109–135.

3172. Hsuan, C. W. 1977. Criticism of Socialist Democracy and the Legal System. *Chinese Law and Government* 10 (3): 76–112.

3173. Hua, S. P. January 1992. All Roads Lead to Democracy: A Critical Analysis of the Writings of Three Chinese Reformist Intellectuals. *Bulletin of Concerned Asian Scholars* 24 (1): 43–56.

3174. Hua, S. P. June 1992. *See* So, A. Y. (June 1992).

3175. Huan, G. September 1989. The Roots of the Political Crisis. *World Policy Journal* 6 (4): 609–620.

3176. Huang, P. H. 1990. The Overseas Ramifications of Mainland China Democracy Movement. *Issues and Studies* 26 (4): 12–22.

3177. Huang, Y. December 1990. The Origins of China's Pro-Democracy Movement and the Government's Response: A Tale of Two Reforms. *Fletcher Forum of World Affairs* 14 (1): 30–39.

3178. Hubell, S. November 9, 1992. Elections in Kuwait: Democracy Is Still a Mirage. *Nation* 255 (15): 539+.

3179. Hubener, K. L. March 1982. The Socialist International and Latin America: Problems and Possibilities. *Caribbean Review* 11 (2): 38–41.

3180. Huber, E., C. Ragin, and J. D. Stephens. November 1993. Social Democracy, Christian Democracy, Constitutional Structure, and the Welfare State. *American Journal of Sociology* 99 (3): 711–749.

3181. Huber, E., D. Rueschemeyer, and J. D. Stephens. June 1993. The Impact of Economic Development on Democracy. *Journal of Economic Perspectives* 7 (3): 71–86.

3182. Huber, E., and J. D. Stephens. 1993. Political Parties and Public Pensions: A Quantitative Analysis. *Acta Sociologica* 36 (4): 309–325.

3183. Huber, J. January 1983. Basic Democracy and Parliamentarism: The "Greens" Conception of Politics.* *Aus Politik und Zeitgeschichte* 15 (2): 33–45.

3184. Huber, J. D., and G. B. Powell. April 1994. Congruence between Citizens and Policy Makers in Two Visions of Liberal Democracy. *World Politics* 46 (3): 291–326.

3185. Hudec, R. E. December 1993. "Circumventing" Democracy: The Political Morality of Trade Negotiations. *New York University Journal of International Law and Politics* 25: 311–322.

3186. Hudson, M. C. March 1976. The Lebanese Crisis: The Limits of Consociational Democracy. *Journal of Palestine Studies* 5 (3–4): 104–122.

3187. Hudson, M. C. December 1985. The Breakdown of Democracy in Lebanon. *Journal of International Affairs* 38 (2): 277–292.

3188. Hudson, M. C. December 1988. Democratization and the Problem of Legitimacy in Middle East Politics. *Middle East Studies Association Bulletin* 22 (2): 157–171.

3189. Hudson, M. C. June 1991. After the Gulf War: Prospects for Democratization in the Arab World. *Middle East Journal* 45 (3): 407–426.

3190. Hueglin, T. O. March 1985. Yet the Age of Anarchism? *Publius* 15 (2): 101–112.

3191. Huerta, M. M. October 1991. *See* Rodriguez, A. M. (October 1991).

3192. Hufford, L. 1985. Promoting Democracy in Central America: The U.S. Policy of Deceit. *Current Research on Peace and Violence* 8 (2): 75–85.

3193. Huffschmid, J., and J. Goldberg. September 1982. A Right Turn under Social Democracy in Germany. *Political Affairs* 61: 18–27.

3194. Hugeux, V. June 1994. L'An Prochain à Port-au-Prince. *Politique Internationale* 66: 225–239.

3195. Hughes, A. 1982. The Limits of "Consociational Democracy" in the Gambia. *Civilisations* 31 (2): 65–96.

3196. Hull, R. W. May 1990. United States Policy in Southern Africa. *Current History* 89 (547): 193–196, 228–231.

3197. Huneeus, M. C. October 1982. The Transition to Democracy in South America: Approaching Its Study.* *Revista Espanola de Investigaciones Sociologicas* 20: 59–80.

3198. Huneeus, M. C. December 1984. Political Parties and the Transition to Democracy in Present Chile. *Estudios Publicos* 15: 57–88.

3199. Huneeus, M. C. 1986. Inaugurating Democracy in Chile. Procedural Reform and Break in Democratic Content?* *Revista de Ciencia Politica* 8 (1–2): 22–87.

3200. Hunley, J. D. 1974. Working Classes, Religion and Social Democracy in the Düsseldorf Area, 1867–1878. *Societas: A Review of Social History* 4 (2): 131–149.

3201. Hunt, F. 1979. Lawyers' War against Democracy. *Commentary* 68 (4): 45–51.

3202. Hunt, G. C. February 1992. Division of Labor, Life-Cycle and Democracy in Worker Cooperatives. *Economic and Industrial Democracy* 13 (1): 9–43.

3203. Hunt, R. J. December 1980. The Crisis of Liberal Democracy. *Polity* 13 (1): 312–326.

3204. Hunter, G. July 1987. *See* Pollack, B. (July 1987).

3205. Huntington, S. P. September 1975. The Democratic Distemper. *Public Interest* 41: 9–38.

3206. Huntington, S. P. March 1982. Reform and Stability in South Africa. *International Security* 6 (4): 3–25.

3207. Huntington, S. P. June 1984. Will More Countries Become Democratic? *Political Science Quarterly* 99 (2): 193–218.

3208. Huntington, S. P. March 1988. One Soul at a Time: Political Science and Political Reform. *American Political Science Review* 82 (1): 3–10.

3209. Huntington, S. P. June 1989. The Essential Meaning of Democracy.* *Estudios Publicos* 33: 5–30.

3210. Huntington, S. P. March 1991. Democracy's Third Wave. *Journal of Democracy* 2 (2): 12–34.

3211. Huntington, S. P. June 1991. Religion and the Third Wave. *National Interest* 24: 29–42.

3212. Huntington, S. P. December 1991. How Countries Democratize. *Political Science Quarterly* 106 (4): 579–616.

3213. Huntington, S. P. December 1992. What Cost Freedom? Democracy and/or Economic Reform. *Harvard International Review* 15 (2): 8–13.

3214. Huntley, J. R. 1983. The Alliance of Democracies: A New Strategy. *Washington Quarterly* 6 (4): 53–61.

3215. Hurd, H. M. 1991. Challenging Authority. *Yale Law Journal* 100 (6): 1611–1677.

3216. Hurwitz, L. 1976. Watergate and Détente: A Content Analysis of Five Communist Newspapers. *Studies in Comparative Communism* 9 (3): 244–256.

3217. Husa, J. 1994. *See* Hirttio, K. (1994).

3218. Husen, T. 1992. The Applicability of Democratic Principles and the Mission of the University. *Interchange* 23 (1–2): 11–18.

3219. Huterer, M. June 1992. *See* Weidefeld, W. (June 1992).

3220. Hutter, J. L., and S. E. Sciuer. October 1984. Representativeness: From Caucus to Convention in Iowa. *American Political Quarterly* 12 (4): 431–448.

3221. Hyde, A. April 1984. Democracy in Collective Bargaining. *Yale Law Journal* 93 (5): 793–856.

3222. Hyden, G., and S. Reutlinger. September 1992. Foreign Aid in a Period of Democratization: The Case of Politically Autonomous Food Funds. *World Development* 20: 1253–1260.

3223. Hyer, E. July 1991. United States' Response to the Tiananmen Massacre: Congressional Values and Executives Interests. *Conflict* 11 (3): 169–183.

3224. Hyland, W. G. March 1990. America's New Course. *Foreign Affairs* 69 (2): 1–12.

3225. Hyman, R. 1991. European Unions: Towards 2000. *Work Employment and Society* 5 (4): 621–639.

&

3226. Iakovlev, A. 1990. Constitutional Socialist Democracy: Dream or Reality. *Columbia Journal of Transnational Law* 28 (1): 117–132.

3227. Ibrahim, J. December 1988. (Nigerian) Society against a Two-Party System.* *Politique Africaine* 32: 7–20.

3228. Ibrahim, S. E. March 1993. Crises, Elites, and Democratization in the Arab World. *Middle East Journal* 47 (2): 292–305.

3229. Ichilov, O., D. Bar-Tal, and A. Mazawi. December 1989. Israeli Adolescents' Comprehension and Evaluation of Democracy. *Youth and Society* 21 (2): 153–169.

3230. Iguiniz, J. June 1986. Peru Requires Deep Changes in Democracy.* *Socialismo y Participacion* 34: 1–17.

3231. Ihonvbere, J. O. 1990. Structural Adjustment, the April 1990 Coup and Democratization in Nigeria. *Africa Quarterly* 29 (3–4): 17–39.

3232. Ihonvbere, J. O. June 1992. The Military and Political Engineering under Structural Adjustment: The Nigerian Experience since 1985. *Journal of Political and Military Sociology* 20: 107–131.

3233. Ihonvbere, J. O. January 1994. The "Irrelevant" State, Ethnicity, and the Quest for Nationhood in Africa. *Ethnic and Racial Studies* 17 (1): 42–60.

3234. Ihonvbere, M. C. 1991. State Power and Political Change in Fiji. *Journal of Contemporary Asia* 21 (1): 78–106.

3235. Ikeda, D. March 1991. The Triumph of Democracy: Toward a Century of Hope. *Bulletin of Peace Proposals* 22 (1): 31–39.

3236. Ikonitskii, I. V. 1978. Crisis of Bourgeois Democracy and Violation of Human Rights in the Capitalist World. *Soviet Studies in Philosophy* 16 (3): 69–77.

3237. Iliescu, D. 1976. *See* Anghene, M. (1976).

3238. Immergut, E. M. December 1992. An Institutional Critique of Associative Democracy: Commentary on "Secondary Associations and Democratic Governance." *Politics and Society* 20 (4): 481–486.

3239. Inbar, D. E. 1986. Educational Policy Making and Planning in a Small Centralized Democracy. *Comparative Education* 22 (3): 271–281.

3240. Indorf, H. H. December 1978. Malaysia at the Polls. *Current History* 75 (442): 217–220/229.

3241. Ingavata, C. February 1990. Community Development and Local-Level Democracy in Thailand: The Role of Tambol Councils. *Sojourn* 5: 113–143.

3242. Ingberman, D. E. 1985. Running against the Status Quo: Institutions for Direct Democracy Referenda and Allocations over Time. *Public Choice* 46 (1): 19–43.

3243. Ingberman, D. E., and J. Villani. May 1993. An Institutional Theory of Divided Government and Party Polarization. *American Journal of Political Science* 37 (2): 429–471.

3244. Ingberman, D. E., and D. A. Yao. 1991. Circumventing Formal Structure through Commitment: Presidential Influence and Agenda Control. *Public Choice* 70 (2): 151–179.

3245. Inglehart, R. 1988. Political Culture and Stable Democracy. *Politische Vierteljahresschrift* 29 (3): 369–387.

3246. Inglehart, R. December 1988. The Renaissance of Political Culture. *American Political Science Review* 82 (4): 1203–1230.

3247. Ingram, D. May 1993. The Limits and Possibilities of Communicative Ethics for Democratic Theory. *Political Theory* 21 (2): 294–321.

3248. Ingrao, P. November 1992. Democracy and the Crisis of Political Representation.* *Critica Marxistas* 6: 10–16.

3249. Inkeles, A. 1990. On Measuring Democracy: An Introduction. *Studies in Comparative International Development* 25 (1): 3–6.

3250. Inkeles, A. March 1990. *See* Sirowy, L. (March 1990).

3251. Inkeles, A. May 1991. Transitions to Democracy. *Society* 28 (4): 67–72.

3252. Inoguchi, T. March 1991. The Nature and Functioning of Japanese Politics. *Government and Opposition* 26: 185–198.

3253. Inoue, K. 1987. Democracy in the Ambiguities of Two Languages and Cultures: The Birth of a Japanese Constitution. *Linguistics* 25 (3): 595–606.

3254. Iokibe, M. June 1990. Japan Meets the United States for the Second Time. *Daedalus* 119 (3): 91–106.

3255. Ionescu, D. August 27, 1993. Has Romania's Ruling Party Become Stronger or Weaker? *RFE/RL Research Report* 2: 15–20.

3256. Ionescu, G. December 1994. Peace, Commerce, and Democracy. *Government and Opposition* 29 (1): 42–47.

3257. Ip, H. Y. October 1991. Liang Shuming and the Idea of Democracy in Modern China. *Modern China* 17 (4): 469–508.

3258. Irele, A. June 1992. The Crisis of Legitimacy in Africa: A Time of Change and Despair. *Dissent* 39 (3): 296–302.

3259. Irvin, G. March 1985. *See* Coraggio, J. L. (March 1985).

3260. Irvine, W. January 1988. Corporate Democracy and the Rights of Shareholders. *Journal of Business Ethics* 7 (1–2): 99–108.

3261. Irwin, T. H. March 1989. Socrates and Athenian Democracy. *Philosophy and Public Affairs* 18 (2): 184–205.

3262. Isaac, J. C. March 1994. Oasis in the Desert: Hannah Arendt on Democratic Politics. *American Political Science Review* 88 (1): 156–168.

3263. Isenberg, M. T. 1976. Mirror of Democracy: Reflections of War Films of World War I, 1917–1919. *Journal of Popular Culture* 9 (4): 878–885.

3264. Isensee, J. 1981. Human Rights and Democracy: "Polar" Legitimation in the Basic Law.* *Der Staat* 20 (2): 161–176.

3265. Ishibashi, M., and S. R. Reed. April 1992. Second-Generation Diet Members and Democracy in Japan: Hereditary Seats. *Asian Survey* 32 (4): 366–379.

3266. Islam, N. February 1981. Islam and National Identity: The Case of Pakistan and Bangladesh. *International Journal of Middle East Studies* 13 (1): 55–72.

3267. Islam, S. S. February 1987. Bangladesh in 1986: Entering a New Phase. *Asian Survey* 27 (2): 163–172.

3268. Ispahani, M. 1989. Varieties of Muslim Experience. *Wilson Quarterly* 13 (4): 63–72.

3269. Issouf, A. September 1993. Benin: Deux Ans àpres la Democratisation. *Information Economique Africaine* 26–27.

3270. Ito, N. August 1992. National Question, Nationalism and Democracy in Asia. *History of European Ideas* 15 (4–6): 773–777.

3271. Itscherenska, I. 1980. Sozialdemokratische Auffassunger zu Problemen einer Internationalen Wirtschaftsordnung. *Asien, Afrika, Lateinamerika* 8 (5): 809–824.

3272. Ivancenko, A. V. 1987. The Great October [1917] and the Revolutionary Confirmation of Political Rights and Freedom of Citizens. *Sovetskoe Gosudarstvo Pravo* 11: 17–26.

3273. Ivancenko, A. V. 1989. Democratic Institutions in the History of the Soviet State. *Sovetskoe Gosudarstvo Pravo* (1): 118–126.

3274. Iverson, T. February 1994. Political Leadership and Representation in West European Democracies: A Test of Three Models of Voting. *American Journal of Political Science* 38 (1): 45–74.

3275. Iyengar, S. December 1994. *See* Ansolabehere, S. (December 1994).

3276. Jackman, R. W. 1974. Political Democracy and Equality: Comparative Analysis. *American Sociological Review* 39 (1): 29–45.

3277. Jackman, R. W. February 1980. Socialist Parties and Income Inequality in Western Industrial Societies. *Journal of Politics* 42 (1): 135–149.

3278. Jackman, R. W. August 1985. *See* Bollen, K. A. (August 1985).

3279. Jackman, R. W. October 1986. Elections and the Democratic Class Struggle. *World Politics* 39 (1): 123–146.

3280. Jackman, R. W. February 1987. The Politics of Economic Growth in the Industrial Democracies, 1974–1980: Leftish Strength or North Sea Oil. *Journal of Politics* 49 (1): 242–256.

3281. Jackman, R. W. June 1987. Political Institutions and Voter Turnout in the Industrial Democracies. *American Political Science Review* 81 (2): 405–423.

3282. Jackman, R. W. August 1989. The Politics of Economic Growth, Once Again. *Journal of Politics* 51 (3): 646–661.

3283. Jackman, R. W. August 1989. *See* Bollen, K. A. (August 1989).

3284. Jackman, S. June 1994. *See* Western, B. (June 1994).

3285. Jackman, S. July 1994. Measuring Electoral Bias: Australia 1949–1993. *British Journal of Political Science* 24 (3): 319–367.

3286. Jackman, S., and G. N. Marks. July 1994. Forecasting Australian Elections 1993, and All That. *Australian Journal of Political Science* 29 (2): 277–291.

3287. Jackson, D. 1979. Disappearance of Strikes in Tanzania: Income Policy and Industrial Democracy. *Journal of Modern African Studies* 17 (2): 219–251.

3288. Jackson, D. W. September 1990. A Conceptual Framework for the Comparative Analysis of Judicial Review. *Policy Studies Journal* 19 (1): 161–171.

3289. Jackson, K. October 1993. Problems of Democracy in a Majoritarian System: New Zealand and Emancipation from the Westminster Model. *Round Table* 328: 401–417.

3290. Jackson, M. 1978. Industrial Democracy: Review of the Bullock Report. *Scottish Journal of Sociology* 2 (2): 241–246.

3291. Jackson, M. September 1986. Statehood for D. C.: A Struggle for Democracy Too Long Denied. *Political Affairs* 65: 17–24.

3292. Jackson, M. W. September 1988. The Public Interest, Public Service and Democracy. *Australian Journal of Public Administration* 47 (3): 241–251.

3293. Jackson, R. H., and C. G. Rosberg. July 1984. Personal Rule: Theory and Practice in Africa. *Comparative Politics* 16 (4): 421–442.

3294. Jackson, R. H., and C. G. Rosberg. December 1985. Democracy in Tropical Africa: Democracy vs. Autocracy in African Politics.* *Journal of International Affairs* 38 (2): 293–305.

3295. Jackson, R. W. August 1989. *See* Bollen, K. A. (August 1989).

3296. Jacob, M. C. June 1991. The Enlightenment Redefined: The Formation of Modern Civil Society. *Social Research* 58 (2): 475–495.

3297. Jacob, P. September 1975. Autonomy and Political Responsibility: The Enigmatic Verdict of a Cross-National Comparative Study of Community Dynamics. *Urban Affairs Quarterly* 11 (1): 36–57.

3298. Jacobs, J. B. 1991. Democracy and China. *Economic and Political Weekly* 26 (33): 1905–1906.

3299. Jacobs, L. R., and R. Y. Shapiro. March 1994. Studying Substantive Democracy. *PS: Political Science & Politics* 27 (1): 9–16.

3300. Jacobson, A. J. December 1983. Democratic Participation and the Legal Structure of the Economy of Firms. *Social Research* 50 (4): 803–849.

3301. Jacobson, G. C., and M. A. Dimock. August 1994. Checking Out: The Effects of Bank Overdrafts on the 1992 House Elections. *American Journal of Political Science* 38 (3): 681–624.

3302. Jacobson, J. June 1986. Socialism and the Third Camp. *New Politics* 1 (1): 5–37.

3303. Jacoby, T. June 1986. The Reagan Turnaround on Human Rights. *Foreign Affairs* 64 (5): 1066–1086.

3304. Jaeggi, U. 1976. Tactics: Incessant Social Democratization Process or New Communism.* *Argument* 18: 580–594.

3305. Jafrey, N. A. April 1991. Concept of State and Political System in Islam. *Journal of Islamic Banking and Finance* 8: 31–41.

3306. Jaggers, K. March 1990. *See* Gurr, T. R. (March 1990).

3307. Jaguaribe, H. 1983. Democracy and Society. *Trimestre Economico* 50 (197): 349–358.

3308. Jahn, D. 1988. Logics of Collective Action and Trade Union Democracy: Organizational Democracy and New Politics in German and Swedish Unions. *Economic and Industrial Democracy* 9 (3): 319–343.

3309. Jain, P. C. November 1993. A New Political Era in Japan: The 1993 Election. *Asian Survey* 33 (11): 1071–1082.

3310. Jakobsen, U. 1994. *See* Bang, H. P. (1994).

3311. Jakovlev, A. 1990. Constitutional Socialist Democracy: Dream or Reality? *Columbia Journal of Transnational Law* 28 (1): 117–132.

3312. Jakubowicz, K. 1985. Mass (?) Communication (?): As Contemporary Broadcasting Evolves Both Terms Are Acquiring Quite New Meanings. *Gazette* 36 (1): 39–53.

3313. James, E. N. March 1978. Union Democracy and the Labor Management Reporting and Disclosure Act: Autocracy and Insurgency in National Union Elections. *Civil Rights-Civil Liberties Law Review* 13 (2): 247–356.

3314. James, I. December 1990. *See* Vivekananda, F. (December 1990).

3315. James, K. E. June 1994. Tonga's Pro-Democracy Movement. *Public Affairs* 67 (2): 242–263.

3316. James, M. February 1981. Public Interest and Majority Rule in Bentham's Democratic Theory. *Political Theory* 9 (1): 49–64.

3317. James, P. July 1991. Germany United: The 1990 All-Germany Election. *West European Politics* 14 (3): 215–220.

3318. James, T. 1982. Tuition Tax Credits and the Pains of Democracy. *Phi Delta Kappan* 63 (9): 606–609.

3319. Jamison, M. S. December 1985. The Joys of Gardening: Collectivist and Bureaucratic Cultures in Conflict. *Sociological Quarterly* 26 (4): 473–490.

3320. Jancar, B. June 1990. Democracy and the Environment in Eastern Europe and the Soviet Union. *Harvard International Review* 12: 13–14+.

3321. Janda, K. July 1985. *See* Ersson, S. (July 1985).

3322. Jannazzo, A. 1987. Representative Government and Democracy in Sonnino's Thought.* *Il Pensiero Politico* 20 (1): 79–91.

3323. Janos, A. C. October 1981. Social Science, Communism, and the Dynamics of Political Change. *World Politics* 44 (1): 81–111.

3324. Janowski, K. B. 1983. Issues of Socialist Democracy in Poland. *Polish Political Science* 13: 123–138.

3325. Jaquitte, J. S. 1994. Women's Movements and the Challenge of Democratic Politics in Latin America. *Social Politics* 1 (3): 335–340.

3326. Jaraquemada Roblero, J. December 1989. *See* Benavente Urbinā, A. (December 1989).

3327. Jarnagin, L. February 1984. *See* Pang, E. S. (February 1984).

3328. Jarnagin, L. February 1985. *See* Pang, E. S. (February 1985).

3329. Jarre, D. 1986. Why NGOs? The Role of Non-Governmental Organizations in Parliamentary Democracy. *Annuaire Europeen* 34: 33–34.

3330. Jasanoff, S. September 1990. American Exceptionalism and the Political Acknowledgment of Risk. *Daedalus* 119 (4): 61–81.

3331. Jasiewitz, K. April 1992. From Solidarity to Fragmentation. *Journal of Democracy* 3 (2): 55–69.

3332. Jayasekera, P. V. J. February 1977. Sri Lanka in 1976: Changing Strategies and Confrontation. *Asian Survey* 17 (2): 208–217.

3333. Jefferies, T. R. September 1993. The Cuban Democracy Act of 1992: A Rotten Carrot and a Broken Stick? *Houston Journal of International Law* 16: 75–100.

3334. Jefferson, T., E. McLaughlin, and L. Robertson. 1988. Monitoring the Monitors: Accountability, Democracy and Police Watching in Britain. *Contemporary Crises* 12 (2): 91–106.

3335. Jelin, E. March 1994. The Politics of Memory: The Human Rights Movement and the Construction of Democracy in Argentina. *Latin American Perspectives* 21 (2): 38–58.

3336. Jencks, H. W. September 1989. The Military in China. *Current History* 88 (539): 265–268, 291–293.

3337. Jenkins, H. W. 1988. Gorbachev's Economic Reforms: A Structural or a Technical Alternation? *International Journal of Social Economics* 15 (1): 3–32.

3338. Jennings, B. 1983. Liberal Democracy and the Problem of Scarcity. *International Political Science Review* 4 (3): 375–383.

3339. Jennings, B. 1984. Science and Democracy: A Commentary. *Politics and the Life Sciences* 3 (1): 47–48.

3340. Jennings, B. 1990. Democracy and Justice in Health Policy. *Hastings Center Report* 20 (5): 22–23.

3341. Jennings, B. 1991. Possibilities of Consensus: Toward Democratic Moral Discourse. *Journal of Medicine and Philosophy* 16 (4): 447–463.

3342. Jennisch, L. A. June 1990. *See* Grey, R. D. (June 1990).

3343. Jensen, R. March 1983. How Democracy Works: The Linkage between Micro and Macro Political History. *Journal of Social History* 16 (3): 27–34.

3344. Jenson, J. June 1984. *See* Le Duc, L. (June 1984).

3345. Jenson, J., and R. Mahon. September 1993. Representing Solidarity: Class, Gender, and the Crisis in Social Democratic Sweden. *New Left Review* 201: 76–100.

3346. Jerez, C. 1988. *See* Marchetti, P. (1988).

3347. Jesse, E. March 1986. Democracy and Its Opponents.* *Politische Studien* 286: 150–163.

3348. Jesse, E. March 1992. The Changing Concept of Conflict Democracy (in the FRG).* *Recht und Politik* 28 (1): 20–28.

3349. Jewell, M. E. November 1978. Legislative Studies in Western Democracies: A

Comparative Perspective. *Legislative Studies Quarterly* 3 (4): 537–554.

3350. Jewell, M. E. October 1994. State Legislative Elections: What We Know and Don't Know. *American Politics Quarterly* 22 (4): 483–501.

3351. Jezer, M., and E. Miller. June 1994. Money Politics: Campaign Finance and the Subversion of American Democracy. *Notre Dame Journal of Law, Ethics and Public Policy* 8: 467–498.

3352. Ji, G. June 1987. ASEAN Countries in Political and Economic Perspectives. *Asian Affairs* 74 (2): 157–166.

3353. Jianhua, Z., Z. Xinshu, and L. Hairong. October 1990. Public Political Consciousness in China: An Empirical Profile. *Asian Survey* 30 (10): 992–1006.

3354. Jilberto, A. E. F. December 1991. Military Bureaucracy, Political Opposition, and Democratic Transition. *Latin American Perspectives* 18 (1): 33–65.

3355. Jinadu, L. A. March 1985. Federalism, the Consociational State, and Ethnic Conflict in Nigeria. *Publius* 15 (2): 71–100.

3356. Joffe, G. July 1993. Political Institutions and Political Culture in the Southern Mediterranean. *International Spectator* 28 (3): 33–51.

3357. Joffe, J. December 1988. Tocqueville Revisited: Are Good Democracies Bad Players in the Game of Nations. *Washington Quarterly* 11 (1): 161–172.

3358. Johannesson, C. 1985. Political Science and the Theory of Labor Union Democracy.* *Statsvetenskaplig Tidskrift* 88 (3): 231–245.

3359. Johansen, B. E. 1990. Native-American Societies and the Evolution of Democracy in America, 1600–1800. *Ethnohistory* 37 (3): 279–290.

3360. Johansen, R. C. March 1991. Real Security Is Democratic Security. *Alternatives* 16 (2): 209–241.

3361. Johansen, R. C. 1992. Military Policies and the State System as Impediments to Democracy. *Political Studies* 40: 99–115. Special issue.

3362. Johanson, J. E., and M. Mattla. December 1994. The Vicious Circle of Cutback Policies: Citizens' Attitudes toward Cutbacks in Finnish Welfare Services. *Scandinavian Political Studies* 17 (4): 289–304.

3363. Johnakin, S. G. 1984. Self-Governance in Timeshare Projects: Mail-Order Democracy. *Real Property Probate and Trust Journal* 19 (3): 705–720.

3364. Johnannsen, L. December 1993. *See* Frederiksen, B. (December 1993).

3365. Johnson, A. T. December 1979. Potential Groups and Agenda Responsiveness. *Polity* 12 (2): 349–358.

3366. Johnson, C. December 1986. Tanaka Kakuei, Structural Corruption, and the Advent of Machine Politics in Japan. *Journal of Japanese Studies* 12 (1): 1–28.

3367. Johnson, C., and K. Um. January 1987. The United States and Asia in 1986: Demands for Democracy. *Asian Survey* 27 (1): 10–22.

3368. Johnson, D. R., J. A. Williams, Jr., and L. St. Peter. February 1977. Comments on Jackman's "Political Elites, Mass Publics, and Support For Democratic Principles." *Journal of Politics* 39 (1): 176–184.

3369. Johnson, J. May 1994. *See* Knight, J. (May 1994).

3370. Johnson, J. T. 1990. Is Democracy an Ethical Standard? *Ethics and International Affairs* 4: 1–17.

3371. Johnson, J. T. 1992. Does Democracy "Travel"? Some Thoughts on Democracy and Its Cultural Context. *Ethics and International Affairs* 6: 41–55.

3372. Johnson, K. F. 1982. The 1980 Image: Index Survey of Latin American Political Democracy. *Latin American Research Review* 17 (3): 193–201.

3373. Johnson, L. K. March 1985. Legislative Reform of Intelligence Policy. *Polity* 17 (3): 549–573.

3374. Johnson, P. December 1985. The Almost-Chosen People. *Wilson Quarterly* 9 (5): 78–89.

3375. Johnston, A. October 1994. South Africa: The Election and the Emerging Party System. *International Affairs (London)* 70 (4): 721–736.

3376. Johnston, R. May 1992. Party Identification Measures in the Anglo-American Democracies: A National Survey Experiment. *American Journal of Political Science* 36 (2): 542–549.

3377. Johnston, R. J. September 1987. Dealignment, Viability, and Electoral Geography. *Studies in Comparative International Development* 22 (3): 3–25.

3378. Johnston, R. J., S. Openshaw, D. W. Rhind, and D. J. Rossiter. 1984. Spatial Scientists and Representational Democracy: The Role of Information-Processing Technology in the Design of Parliamentary and Other Constituencies. *Environment and Planning C: Government and Policy* 2 (1): 57–66.

3379. Johnston, R. J., D. J. Rossiter, C. J. Pattie, and A. T. Russell. October 1994. The Definition of Parliamentary Constituencies in England: Searching for Principles in the Work of the Boundary Commission for England. *Policy and Politics* 22 (4): 267–286.

3380. Johnstone, D. B. 1992. The University, Democracy, and the Challenge to Meritocracy. *Interchange* 23 (1–2): 19–23.

3381. Jonas, S. June 1988. Contradictions of Guatemala's "Political Opening." *Latin American Perspectives* 15 (3): 26–46.

3382. Jonas, S., and N. Stein. June 1990. The Construction of Democracy in Nicaragua. *Latin American Perspectives* 17 (3): 10–37.

3383. Jones, A. L. 1994. *See* Day, F. A. (1994).

3384. Jones, B. June 1994. British Democracy Today. *Talking Politics* 6 (3): 143–146.

3385. Jones, D. C. 1977. The Bullock Report Commenting on the Report of the Committee of Inquiry on Industrial Democracy: Great Britain. *Economic Analysis (Belgrade)* 11 (3–4): 245–279.

3386. Jones, G. 1992. *See* Winchester, I. (1992).

3387. Jones, G., and S. Ranson. 1989. Is There a Need for Participative Democracy: An Exchange. *Local Government Studies* 15 (3): 1–10.

3388. Jones, K. B. 1994. Identity, Action, and Locale: Thinking about Citizenship, Civil Action, and Feminism. *Social Politics* 1 (2): 256–270.

3389. Jones, P. March 1988. Intense Preferences, Strong Beliefs and Democratic Decision-Making. *Political Studies* 36 (1): 7–29.

3390. Jones, P. R., and J. G. Cullis. 1986. Is Democracy Regressive: A Comment on Political Participation. *Public Choice* 51 (1): 101–107.

3391. Jones, R. S. December 1980. Democratic Values and Pre-Adult Virtues: Tolerance, Knowledge, and Participation. *Youth and Society* 12 (2): 189–220.

3392. Jones, R. V. 1976. Knowledge and Power: Thoughts on Intelligence in a Democracy. *Minerva* 14 (2): 241–250.

3393. Jorge Lazarte, R. October 1991. Partidos, Democracia, Problemas de Representacion e Informalizacion de la Politica (El Caso de Bolivia). *Revista de Estudios Politicos* 74: 579–614.

3394. Jorgenson, J. G., and R. O. Clemmen. June 1980. On Washburn's "On the Trail of the Activist Anthropologist": A Rejoiner to a Reply. *Journal of Ethnic Studies* 82: 85–94.

3395. Jose, L. July 1991. *See* Simon, G. (July 1991).

3396. Jose, P. January 1989. Il Cile e La Sua Lotta per Ristabilire la Democrazia. *Affari Esteri* 21: 72–86.

3397. Joseph, A. June 1994. Pathways to Capitalist Democracy: What Prevents Social Democracy. *British Journal of Sociology* 45 (2): 211–246.

3398. Joseph, L. B. February 1981. Democratic Revisionism Revisited. *American Journal of Political Science* 25 (1): 160–187.

3399. Joseph, L. B. November 1982. Neoconservatism in Contemporary Political Science: Democratic Theory and the Party System. *Journal of Politics* 44 (4): 955–982.

3400. Joseph, L. B. December 1982. Corporate Political Power and Liberal Democratic Theory. *Polity* 15 (2): 246–267.

3401. Joseph, R. A. 1978. Dominican Republic: Democracy Has a Prayer. *Nation* 227 (4): 106–108.

3402. Joseph, R. A. October 1981. Democratization under Military Tutelage: Crisis and Consensus in the Nigerian 1979 Election. *Comparative Politics* 14 (1): 75–100.

3403. Joseph, R. A. March 1984. The Overthrow of Nigeria's Second Republic. *Current History* 83 (491): 122–124, 138.

3404. Joseph, S. February 20, 1993. Social Movements, State, and Democracy. *Economic and Political Weekly* 28 (8–9): 330–332.

3405. Joseph, W. A. September 1985. The Dilemmas of Political Reform in China. *Current History* 84 (503): 252–255, 279–280.

3406. Josephs, H. K. March 1992. The Chinese Democracy Movement in U.S. Perspective. *UCLA Pacific Basin Law Journal* 10: 285–328.

3407. Joset, J. 1977. Spain in 1977: The Nature of Democracy.* *Socialisme* 139: 3–14.

3408. Joslyn, R. December 1988. *See* Ross, M. H. (December 1988).

3409. Jost, K. August 17, 1990. Initiatives: True Democracy or Bad Lawmaking? *Editorial Research Reports* 2 (7): 462–475.

3410. Jost, K. January 14, 1994. South Africa's Future: Can South Africa Make the Transition to a Non-Racial Democracy? *CQ Researcher* 4: 27–47.

3411. Jost, K. April 29, 1994. Talk Show Democracy: Are Call-In Programs Good for the Political System? *CQ Researcher* 4: 363–383.

3412. Joyaux, F. March 1988. South Korea: Time for Democracy?* *Politique Internationale* 39: 313–320.

3413. Juchler, J. February 1994. Difficult Democratization Processes: Political Development in the Reforming Countries of Eastern Europe. *Osteuropa* 44 (2): 125–141.

3414. Judd, D. R. September 1980. *See* Kerstein, R. (September 1980).

3415. Judin, J. A. 1992. New Trends of Constitutional Development in the African Countries.* *Gosudarstvo I Pravo* 12: 117–126.

3416. Jukam, T. 1980. *See* Muller, E. N. (1980).

3417. Jung, D. J., and D. L. Kirp. September 1984. Law as an Instrument of Educational Policy-Making. *American Journal of Comparative Law* 32 (4): 625–678.

3418. Jung, K. D. December 1985. Democracy and Dissidence in South Korea. *Journal of International Affairs* 38 (2): 181–191. Interview.

3419. Jung, K. D. et al. December 1986. South Korea: Voices for Democracy. *World Policy Journal* 4: 16–178. Interviews.

3420. Jung, O. 1987. People's Legislation in Germany. *Leviathan* 15 (2): 242–265.

3421. Jung, O. October 1990. Direct Democracy (in the FRG): State and Aims of Research. *Zeitschrift für Parlamentsfragen* 21 (3): 491–504.

3422. Junghanns, R. 1987. *See* Baltodano, M. P. (1987).

3423. Junior, D. P. March 1990. Guns or Butter? Arms Industry, Technology and Democracy in Brazil. *Bulletin of Peace Proposals* 21: 49–57.

3424. Justel, M. April 1990. Panorama de la Abstencion Electoral en Espana. *Revista de Estudios Politicos* (*Neuva Epoca*) 343–396.

3425. Kaarsholm, P. 1990. Mental Colonization or Catharsis: Theater, Democracy and Cultural Struggle from Rhodesia to Zimbabwe. *Journal of Southern African Studies* 16 (2): 246–275.

3426. Kaase, M. 1990. Political Violence and the Democratic State. *Scandinavian Political Studies* 13 (1): 1–19.

3427. Kaase, M., and H. D. Klingeman. 1982. Social Structure, Value Orientations, and the Party System: The Problem of Interest Accommodation in Western Democracy. *European Journal of Political Research* 10 (4): 367–386.

3428. Kabaya Katambwa, J. J. June 1986. The Concept of Power and Democracy in Black Africa after Independence.* *Le Mois en Afrique* 245–246: 23–38.

3429. Kafatou, S. 1981. *See* Feldman, R. L. (1981).

3430. Kahane, R. March 1986. Informal Agencies of Socialization and the Integration of Immigrant Youth into Society: An Example from Israel. *International Migration Review* 20 (1): 21–39.

3431. Kahlenberg, F. P. December 1992. Democracy and Federalism: Changes in the National Archival System. *American Archivist* 55 (1): 72–85.

3432. Kahler, M. April 1981. Political Regime and Economic Actors: The Response of Firms to the End of Colonial Rule. *World Politics* 33 (3): 383–412.

3433. Kahn, G. March 1981. In Perpetual Tension: Executive-Legislative Relations and the Case of the Legislative Veto. *Presidential Studies Quarterly* 11 (2): 271–279.

3434. Kahn, K. F. February 1994. Does Gender Make a Difference? An Experimental Examination of Sex Stereotypes and Press Patterns in Statewide Campaigns. *American Journal of Political Science* 38 (1): 162–195.

3435. Kahn, P. R. 1974. Philippines without Democracy. *Foreign Affairs* 52 (3): 612–632.

3436. Kaidi, H. April 1992. Le Togo à Son Destin. *Jeune Afrique* 32: 123+.

3437. Kaidi, H. February 11, 1993. Rwanda: Au Dessous du Volcan. *Jeune Afrique* 33: 24–25.

3438. Kalaycioglu, E. October 1994. Elections and Party Preferences in Turkey: Changes and Continuities in the 1990s. *Comparative Political Studies* 27 (3): 402–424.

3439. Kalipeni, E. March 1992. Political Development and Prospects for Democracy in Malawi. *Transafrica Forum* 9 (1): 27–40.

3440. Kallgren, J. K. January 1980. China 1979. *Asian Survey* 20 (1): 1–18.

3441. Kalluza, H. W. November 1982. Austria: Direct Democracy under the Test of Socialism.* *Politische Studien* 33: 679–682.

3442. Kaltoft, G. September 1993. *See* Brooks, A. (September 1993).

3443. Kamanga, K. 1993. The Malawi Republic Constitution and Multi-Partyism: Main Concerns.* *Verfassung und Recht in Ubersee* 26 (3): 245–257.

3444. Kamata, T. 1990. Contemporary Democracy in a Parliamentary System: Authority of the National and Local Governments under the Constitution. *Law and Contemporary Problems* 53 (1–2): 163–164.

3445. Kamath, P. M. October 1985. Politics of Defection in India in the 1980s. *Asian Survey* 25 (10): 1039–1054.

3446. Kamenskaya, G. V. 1994. The Genesis of Ideas about Democracy.* *Sotsiologicheskie Issledovaniia* (4): 29–40.

3447. Kamers, D. H. 1988. Education and Democracy: A Comparative Institutional Analysis. *Sociology of Education* 61 (2): 114–127.

3448. Kaminski, A. Z. 1977. State Bureaucracy and Parliamentary Democracy in the Development of a Liberal Democratic State. *Polish Sociological Bulletin* (2): 37–48.

3449. Kaminski, B. June 1991. Systemic Underpinnings of the Transition in Poland: The Shadow of the Round-Table Agreement. *Studies in Comparative Communism* 24 (2): 173–190.

3450. Kaminsky, L. 1994. Refuge Refused: Haitians, Borders, and Democracy. *Public Culture* 7 (1): 102–106.

3451. Kamlet, M. S. February 1993. *See* Su, T. T. (February 1993).

3452. Kammler, H. September 1985. Security-Related Efforts in Western Democracies: Toward a Comparative Political Economy of Defense. *European Journal of Political Research* 13 (3): 311–325.

3453. Kammler, H. September 1986. Promises of Democracies? Security and Other Public Goods.* *Zeitschrift für Politik* 33 (3): 235–253.

3454. Kammler, H. 1989. The Efficiency of Security Policy: An Achilles Heel for the Western World? *Beitraege zur Konfliktforschung* 19 (3): 65–81.

3455. Kampelman, M. M. September 1978. The Power of the Press: A Problem for Our Democracy. *Policy Review* 6: 7–39.

3456. Kampelman, M. M. June 1990. Speeches by Max Kampelman. *World Affairs* 153 (1): 9–22.

3457. Kamrava, M. June 1989. Intellectuals and Democracy in the Third World. *Journal of Social, Political, and Economic Studies* 14 (2): 227–234.

3458. Kanapa, J. January 1977. "A New Policy" of the French Communists? *Foreign Affairs* 55 (2): 280–294.

3459. Kanev, Y. December 1991. Freedom, Environment Linked in Bulgaria. *Forum for Applied Research and Public Policy* 6 (4): 56–60.

3460. Kang, S. October 1979. Graham Wallas and Liberal Democracy. *Review of Politics* 41 (1): 536–560.

3461. Kann, M. E. December 1979. A Standard for Democratic Leadership. *Polity* 12 (2): 202–224.

3462. Kann, M. E. July 1981. Political Education and Equality: Gramsci against "False Consciousness." *Teaching Political Science* 8 (4): 417–446.

3463. Kann, R. 1977. Demokratie des Politischen Alltags: Europaische Rundschau. *Vierteljahreszeitschrift für Politik, Wirtschaft und Zeitgeschichte* 5 (1): 59–66.

3464. Kannabiran, K. G. August 15, 1992. Creeping Decay in Institutions of Democracy. *Economic and Political Weekly* 27 (33): 1718–1720.

3465. Kannappan, S. June 1988. India at Forty: Democracy, Economy, and International Relations. *Atlantic Community Quarterly* 26: 199–213.

3466. Kannappan, S., and V. N. Krishnan. May 1977. Participative Management in India: Utopia or Snare? *Annals of the American Academy of Political and Social Science* 431: 95–102.

3467. Kante, B. January 1994. Senegal's Empty Elections. *Journal of Democracy* 5 (1): 96–108.

3468. Kantor, P. June 1987. The Dependent City: The Changing Political Economy of Urban Economic Development in the United States. *Urban Affairs Quarterly* 22 (4): 493–520.

3469. Kaplan, F. L. September 1977. Czechoslovakia's Experiment in Humanizing Socialism: An Examination of Ideological and Tactical Implications. *East European Quarterly* 11 (3): 303–316.

3470. Kaplan, M. July 1985. Argentina from Dictatorship to Democracy.* *Nuestro Tiempo* 44 (4): 28–49.

3471. Kaplan, M. A. July 1989. Steps toward a Democratic World Order. *International Journal on World Peace* 6 (3): 23–44.

3472. Karasimeonov, G. March 1992. From Communism to Democracy in Bulgaria.* *Aus Politik und Zeitgeschichte* 27 (14): 13–22.

3473. Karasyov, K. October 1977. Further Extension of Soviet Democracy: On the Draft of the New Constitution of the USSR. *World Marxist Review* 20: 96–104.

3474. Karatnycky, A. September 1990. *See* Diuk, N. (September 1990).

3475. Karatnycky, A. April 1992. The Battle for the Trade Unions. *Journal of Democracy* 3 (2): 43–54.

3476. Karelis, C. H. 1986. A Note on Democracy and Liberal Education. *Liberal Education* 72 (4): 319–322.

3477. Karier, C. 1977. Making the World Safe for Democracy: Historical Critique of J. Dewey's Pragmatic Liberal Philosophy in the Warfare State. *Educational Theory* 27 (1): 12–47.

3478. Karikari, K. January 1993. Africa: The Press and Democracy. *Race and Class* 34 (3): 55–66.

3479. Karklins, R. June 1986. Soviet Elections Revisited: Voter Abstention in Noncompetitive Balloting. *American Political Science Review* 80 (2): 449–469.

3480. Karl, B. D. January 1987. The American Bureaucrat: A History of a Sheep in Wolves' Clothing. *Public Administration Review* 47 (1): 26–34.

3481. Karl, T. L. March 1985. After La Palma: The Prospects for Democratization in El Salvador. *World Policy Journal* 2 (2): 305–330.

3482. Karl, T. L. 1987. Petroleum and Political Pacts: The Transition to Democracy in Venezuela. *Latin American Research Review* 22 (1): 63–94.

3483. Karl, T. L. October 1990. Dilemmas of Democratization in Latin America. *Comparative Politics* 23 (1): 1–21.

3484. Karl, T. L. June 1991. *See* Schmitter, P. C. (June 1991).

3485. Karl, T. L. March 1994. *See* Schmitter, P. C. (March 1994).

3486. Karl, T. L., and P. C. Schmitter. May 1991. Modes of Transition in Latin America, Southern and Eastern Europe. *International Social Science Journal* 43 (2): 269–284.

3487. Karnig, A. K. April 1976. *See* Sigelman, L. (April 1976).

3488. Karumanchi, R. L. October 1990. Political Liberalization and the Democratization Process in Brazil in the 1980s: A Reassessment. *International Studies* 27 (4): 325–349.

3489. Karumanchi, R. L. July 1991. *See* Narayanan, R. (July 1991).

3490. Kasfir, N. 1992. Popular Sovereignty and Popular Participation: Mixed Constitutional Democracy in the Third World. *Third World Quarterly* 13 (4): 587–605.

3491. Kasl, E. September 1993. *See* Brooks, A. (September 1993).

3492. Kassalov, E. M. July 1982. Industrial Democracy and Collective Bargaining: A Comparative View. *Labour and Society* 7: 209–229.

3493. Kassebaum, N. L. March 1988. To Form a More Perfect Union. *Presidential Studies Quarterly* 18 (2): 241–249.

3494. Kasza, G. J. August 1986. Democracy and the Founding of Japanese Public Radio. *Journal of Asian Studies* 45 (4): 745–767.

3495. Kateb, G. December 1979. On the "Legitimation Crisis." *Social Research* 46 (4): 695–727.

3496. Kateb, G. April 1981. The Moral Distinctiveness of Representative Democracy. *Ethics* 91 (3): 357–374.

3497. Kateb, G. 1983. Remarks on Robert B. McKay's "Judicial Review in a Liberal Democracy." *Nomos* 25: 145–152.

3498. Kateb, G. August 1984. Democratic Individuality and the Claims of Politics. *Political Theory* 12 (3): 331–360.

3499. Kateb, G. November 1990. Walt Whitman and the Culture of Democracy. *Political Theory* 18 (4): 545–600.

3500. Kateb, G., and F. Dallmayr. 1987. Death and Politics: Hannah Arendt's Reflections on the American Constitution. *Social Research* 54 (3): 605–628.

3501. Kates, G. October 1989. From Liberalism to Radicalism: Tom Paine's "Rights of Man." *Journal of the History of Ideas* 50 (4): 569–587.

3502. Katovich, M., M. W. Weiland, and C. J. Couch. June 1981. Access to Information and Internal Structures of Partisan Groups: Some Notes on the Iron Law Oligarchy. *Sociological Quarterly* 22 (3): 431–445.

3503. Katz, C. J. 1988. *See* Mahler, V. A. (1988).

3504. Katz, D., and N. Golomb. February 1975. Integration, Effectiveness, and Adaptation in Social Systems: A Comparative Analysis of Kibbutzim Communities (Part 2). *Administration and Society* 6 (4): 389–421.

3505. Katz, R. S. January 1984. Dimensions of Partisan Conflict in Swiss Cantons. *Comparative Political Studies* 16 (4): 505–527.

3506. Katz, R. S. July 1985. Preference Voting in Italy: Votes of Opinion, Belonging, or Exchange. *Comparative Political Studies* 18 (2): 229–249.

3507. Katz, R. S. et al. October 1992. The Membership of Political Parties in European Democracies, 1960–1990. *European Journal of Political Research* 22 (3): 329–345.

3508. Katz, S. September 1985. The Succession of Power and the Power of Succession: Nyayoism in Kenya. *Journal of African Studies* 12 (3): 155–161.

3509. Katznelson, I. October 1978. Consideration on Social Democracy in the United States. *Comparative Politics* 11 (1): 77–99.

3510. Kauffman, K. G., and A. Shorett. September 1977. A Perspective on Public Involvement in Water Management Decision Making. *Public Administration Review* 37 (5): 467–472.

3511. Kauffman, L. A. 1990. Democracy in a Postmodern World. *Social Policy* 21 (2): 6–15.

3512. Kaufman, M. 1988. Democracy and Social Transformation in Jamaica. *Social and Economic Studies* 37 (3): 45–73.

3513. Kaufman, R. R. May 1981. Liberalization and Democratization in the Bureaucratic-Authoritarian States.* *Il Mulino* 275: 385–418.

3514. Kaufman, R. R. June 1985. Democratic and Authoritarian Responses to the Debt Issue: Argentina, Brazil, Mexico. *International Organization* 39 (3): 472–503.

3515. Kaufman, R. R. October 1994. *See* Haggard, S. (October 1994).

3516. Kaufmann, E. 1974. Basic Facts and Basic Concepts of Democracy.* *Politische Studien* 25 (218): 567–582.

3517. Kauzyo, J. July 1994. *See* Bertrand, J. (July 1994).

3518. Kawar, A. June 1989. Issue Definition, Democratic Participation, and Genetic Engineering. *Policy Studies Journal* 17 (4): 719–744.

3519. Kay, C. October 1991. La Politica Agraria del Gobierno de Aylwin: Continuidad o Cambio? *Comer Exterior (Mexico)* 41: 934–941.

3520. Kay, R. S. 1981. Preconstitutional Rules. *Ohio State Law Journal* 42 (1): 187–208.

3521. Kay, W. D. March 1994. Democracy and Super Technologies: The Politics of the Space Shuttle and Space Station Freedom. *Science, Technology, and Human Values* 19: 131–151.

3522. Kazancigil, A. May 1991. Democracy in Muslim Hands: Turkey in Comparative Perspective. *International Social Science Journal* 43 (2): 343–360.

3523. Kazarinov, S. April 1978. *See* Markovitz, A. S. (April 1978).

3524. Kazin, A. 1976. Democracy According to Whitman. *Commentary* 61 (6): 52–58.

3525. Keane, J. December 1983. Democracy and the Theory of Ideology. *Canadian Journal of Political and Social Theory* 7 (1–2): 5–17.

3526. Keane, J. August 1991. Democracy and the Media. *International Social Science Journal* 43 (3): 523–540.

3527. Keane, J. 1992. Democracy and the Media: Without Foundations. *Political Studies* 40: 116–129. Special issue.

3528. Kearny, E. N. June 1984. Presidential Nominations and Representative Democracy: Proposals for Change. *Presidential Studies Quarterly* 14 (3): 348–356.

3529. Keck, M. E. 1986. Democratization and Dissention: The Formation of the Workers Party. *Politics and Society* 15 (1): 67–95.

3530. Kedourie, E. 1976. Is Democracy Doomed? *Commentary* 62 (5): 39–43.

3531. Kedourie, E. 1984. Why Growth and Democracy Stall in the Third-World: The Development Delusion. *New Republic* 191 (25): 13–18.

3532. Keehn, N. H. September 1976. A World of Becoming: From Pluralism to Corporatism. *Polity* 9 (1): 19–39.

3533. Keehn, N. H. December 1980. Liberal Democracy: Impediment to Anti-Inflation Policy. *Polity* 13 (1): 207–229.

3534. Keeling, D. T. March 1994. *See* Mancini, G. F. (March 1994).

3535. Keiber, D. A. September 1985. *See* Manaster, G. J. (September 1985).

3536. Keiichi, M. 1984. Half Democracy. *Japan Quarterly* 31 (1): 6–10.

3537. Keim, G. D., B. D. Baysinger, and R. E. Meiners. May 1981. Corporate Democracy Act: Would The Majority Rule? *Business Horizons* 24 (2): 30–35.

3538. Keita, M. K. October 1992. Reflexion sur la Presse Ecrite. *Politique Africaine* 79–90.

3539. Keith, K. J. December 1985. A Bill of Rights for New Zealand? Judicial Review Versus Democracy. *New Zealand University Law Review* 11: 307–322.

3540. Keith, R. C. September 1980. Socialist Legality and Democracy in the People's Republic of China. *Canadian Journal of Political Science* 13 (3): 565–582.

3541. Keithlucas, B. 1976. What Price Local Democracy? *New Society* 37 (723): 340–341.

3542. Kelleher, C. M. March 1983. *See* Domke, W. K. (March 1983).

3543. Kelleher, C. M., W. Domke, and R. Eichenberg. 1980. Guns, Butter, and Growth: Expenditure Patterns in Four Advanced Democracies. *Zeitschrift für Soziologie* 9 (2): 149–158.

3544. Keller, E. F. March 1983. Feminism, Science, and Democracy. *Democracy* 3 (2): 50–58.

3545. Keller, E. J. September 1993. Towards a New African Order? *African Studies Review* 36 (2): 1–10.

3546. Keller, E. J. September 1994. *See* Thomas Woolley, B. (September 1994).

3547. Keller, J. 1992. Nationalism as an Unintended Consequence of the Democratization of Society.* *Sociologicky Casopis* 28 (1): 38–48.

3548. Keller, J. F. 1974. Democracy in the Hearing-Impaired Classroom. *American Annals of the Deaf* 119 (3): 307–313.

3549. Keller, M. September 1978. Reflections on Politics and Generations in America. *Daedalus* 107 (4): 123–135.

3550. Kelliher, D. July 1993. Keeping Democracy Safe from the Masses: Intellectuals and Elitism in the Chinese Protest Movement. *Comparative Politics* 25 (4): 379–396.

3551. Kellner, D. March 1979. Critical Theory, Democracy, and Human Rights. *New Political Science* 1 (1): 12–18.

3552. Kellner, D. September 1992. *See* Antonio, R. J. (September 1992).

3553. Kellner, M. M. November 1975. Democracy and Civil Disobedience. *Journal of Politics* 37 (4): 899–911.

3554. Kelly, A. H., and R. D. Miles. July 1976. Maintenance of Revolutionary Values. *Annals of the American Academy of Political and Social Science* 426: 25–52.

3555. Kelly, E. P., and J. Zoric. September 1988. Employee Ownership and Industrial Democracy: The Pursuit of Free Enterprise. *Proteus* 5: 18–22.

3556. Kelly, G. A. December 1982. Faith, Freedom, and Disenchantment: Politics and the American Religious Consciousness. *Daedalus* 111 (1): 127–148.

3557. Kelman, M. 1988. On Democracy Bashing: A Skeptical Look at the Theoretical and Empirical Practice of the Public Choice Movement. *Virginia Law Review* 74 (2): 199–273.

3558. Kemal, A. March 1984. Military Rule and the Future of Democracy in Turkey. *Middle East Research & Information Project Reports* 14: 12–15.

3559. Keman, H. 1984. Politics, Policies and Consequences: A Cross-National Analysis of Public-Policy Formation in Advanced Capitalist Democracies. *European Journal of Political Research* 12 (2): 147–170.

3560. Keman, H. 1985. Economic Decline, Cold War Structure and the Trade-Off Between Welfare in Seventeen Capitalist Democracies. *Current Research on Peace and Violence* 8 (1): 24–36.

3561. Keman, H. April 1990. Social Democracy and the Politics of Welfare Statism. *Netherlands Journal of Social Sciences* 26 (1): 17–34.

3562. Keman, H. April 1990. *See* Budge, I. (April 1990).

3563. Keman, H. July 1993. Theoretical Approaches to Social Democracy. *Journal of Theoretical Politics* 5 (3): 291–316.

3564. Keman, H. July 1993. *See* Wolden-dorp, J. (July 1993).

3565. Keman, H., and D. Braun. 1984. The Limits of Political Control: A Cross-National Comparison of Economic Policy Responses in 18 Capitalist Democracies. *European Journal of Political Research* 12 (1): 101–108.

3566. Kemble, P. 1978. Capitalism, Social-ism, and Democracy. *Commentary* 65 (4): 50–53.

3567. Kemmis, D. September 1991. Com-munity and the Quest for Excellence. *National Civic Review* 80 (4): 358–361.

3568. Kemp, J. F. March 1985. *See* Lugar, R. G. (March 1985).

3569. Kendal, W. December 1984. Bipar-tisanship and Majority-Rule Democracy. *World Affairs* 147 (3): 201–210.

3570. Kende, P. August 1976. Commu-nism and Democracy.* *Paysans* 20: 11–28.

3571. Kenenov, A. A. August 1982. *See* Denisov, A. I. (August 1982).

3572. Kenis, P. 1989. Public Ownership: Economizing Democracy or Democratiz-ing Economy. *Economic and Industrial Democracy* 10 (1): 81–97.

3573. Kennedy, D. 1991. Turning to Mar-ket Democracy: A Tale of Two Architec-tures. *Harvard International Law Journal* 32 (2): 373–396.

3574. Kennedy, E. M. March 1985. *See* Lugar, R. G. (March 1985).

3575. Kennedy, K. C. September 1987. Voluntary Restraint Agreements: A Threat to Representative Democracy. *Hastings In-ternational and Comparative Law Review* 11: 1–40.

3576. Kennedy, M. D. December 1990. The Constitution of Critical Intellectuals: Polish Physicians, Peace Activists and De-mocratic Civil Society. *Studies in Compara-tive Communism* 23 (3–4): 281–303.

3577. Kenny, L. W. 1978. The Collective Allocation of Commodities in a Democra-tic Society: A Generalization. *Public Choice* 33 (2): 117–120.

3578. Kenny, L. W. November 1994. *See* Francis, W. L. (November 1994).

3579. Kenworthy, E. December 1983. Dilemmas of Participation in Latin Amer-ica. *Democracy* 3 (1): 72–83.

3580. Kenworthy, E. 1985. Cuba's Experi-ment with Local Democracy. *Journal of Community Psychology* 13 (2): 194–203.

3581. Kerimov, D. A. 1984. The Democra-tic Character of Soviet State Construction: Problem of Theory and Practice.* *Voprosy Filosofii* 84 (4): 3–21.

3582. Kerimov, D. A., and N. G. Kobec. 1986. The 27th CPSU Congress and the Development of Socialist Democracy. *Sovetskoe Gosudarstvo Pravo* 4: 3–10.

3583. Kerimov, D. A., and G. W. Malzef. 1977. Democracy and the Political System in a Socialist Society. *Sowjetwissenschaft: Gesellschaft Wissenschaftliche Beitrage* 30 (12): 1239–1253.

3584. Kerr, H. H. February 1978. The Structure of Opposition in the Swiss Par-liament. *Legislative Studies Quarterly* 3 (1): 51–62.

3585. Kerrine, T. M., and R. J. Neuhaus. November 1979. Mediating Structures: A Paradigm for Democratic Pluralism. *An-nals of the American Academy of Political and Social Science* 446: 10–18.

3586. Kersberger, K., and U. Becker. Oc-tober 1988. The Netherlands: A Passive Social Democratic Welfare State in a Christian Democratic Ruled Society. *Jour-nal of Social Policy* 17: 477–499.

3587. Kershaw, R. October 1979. Thai-land's Return to Limited Democracy. *Asian Affairs (London)* 66: 304–313.

3588. Kerstein, R. December 1987. Un-locking the Doors to Democracy: Election

Process Reform. *Florida State University Law Review* 15: 687–730.

3589. Kerstein, R., and D. R. Judd. September 1980. Achieving Less Influence with More Democracy: The Permanent Legacy of the War on Poverty. *Social Science Quarterly* 61 (2): 208–220.

3590. Kesselman, M. March 1980. Continuity and Change on the French Left: Revolutionary Transformation or Immobilism? *Social Research* 47 (1): 93–113.

3591. Kessler, S. February 1977. Tocqueville on Civil Religion and Liberal Democracy. *Journal of Politics* 39 (1): 119–146.

3592. Kessler, S. March 1989. Tocqueville on Sexual Morality. *Interpretation* 16 (3): 465–480.

3593. Ketley, R. January 1993. *See* Healey, J. (January 1993).

3594. Keyder, C. May 1979. The Political Economy of Turkish Democracy. *New Left Review* 115: 3–36.

3595. Keyfitz, N. November 1988. The Asian Road to Democracy. *Society* 26 (1): 71–76.

3596. Keynes, E. January 1981. Democracy, Judicial Review, and the War Powers. *Ohio Northern University Law Review* 8: 69–101.

3597. Khadka, N. 1986. Crisis in Nepal Partyless Panchayat System: The Case for More Democracy. *Pacific Affairs* 59 (3): 429–454.

3598. Khadka, N. March 1993. Democracy and Development in Nepal: Prospects and Challenges. *Pacific Affairs* 66 (1): 44–71.

3599. Khagram, S. 1993. Democracy and Democratization in Africa: A Plea for Pragmatic Possibilism. *Africa Today* 40 (4): 55–72.

3600. Khan, A. 1985. Zia Islamic Democracy: Leading Pakistan into the Past. *Nation* 25: 791–794.

3601. Khan, B. Z. 1990. *See* Sokoloff, K. L. (1990).

3602. Khan, Z. R. February 1993. Bangladesh in 1992: Dilemmas of Democratization. *Asian Survey* 33 (2): 150–156.

3603. Khare, B. B. April 1991. Caste and Religion: Conflicts Dividing the Indian Society. *Conflict (New York)* 11: 99–111.

3604. Khashan, H. March 1991. The Limits of Arab Democracy. *World Affairs* 153 (4): 127–135.

3605. Khashan, H. December 1992. The Quagmire of Arab Democracy. *Arab Studies Quarterly* 14 (1): 17–33.

3606. Khashan, H. December 1993. *See* Harik, J. P. (December 1993).

3607. Khilnani, S. May 1991. Democracy and Modern Political Community: Limits and Possibilities. *Economy and Society* 20 (2): 196–204.

3608. Khoryama, G. October 1984. Liberia: Rough Road to Democracy. *Africa* 23–25.

3609. Khu, J. M. T. 1990. Student Organization in the 1989 Chinese Democracy Movement. *Bulletin of Concerned Asian Scholars* 22 (3): 3–12.

3610. Kieh, G. K. 1992. *See* Agbese, P. O. (1992).

3611. Kieh, G. K., and P. O. Agbese. November 1993. From Politics Back to the Barracks in Nigeria: A Theoretical Explanation. *Journal of Peace Research* 30 (4): 409–426.

3612. Kielmansegg, P. September 1981. Freedom and Political Participation.* *Merkur* 35 (9–10): 941–953.

3613. Kielmansegg, P. December 1982. The Democratic Revolution and the Scope of Political Action.* *Merkur* 36 (12): 1150–1163.

3614. Kielmansegg, P. October 1989. West Germany's Constitution: Response to the Past or Design for the Future? *World Today* 45: 175–179.

3615. Kielmansegg, P. March 1994. Can There Be a Democratic Constitution of the European Community?* *Europaeische Rundschau* 22 (2): 23–33.

3616. Kiely, R. October 1993. *See* Berry, S. (October 1993).

3617. Kieve, R. A. April 1981. Pillars of Sand: A Marxist Critique of Consociational Democracy in the Netherlands. *Comparative Politics* 13 (3): 313–337.

3618. Kievenhéim, C. March 1977. Scientific Socialism Requires Internal Party and Social Democracy.* *Argument* 19: 192–204.

3619. Kiewiet, D. R. September 1979. Approval Voting: The Case of the 1968 Election. *Polity* 12 (1): 170–161.

3620. Kihl, Y. W. April 1989. South Korea's Rise to Prominence. *Current History* 88 (537): 165–168, 192–193.

3621. Kihl, Y. W. 1990. South Korea in 1989: Slow Progress toward Democracy. *Asian Survey* 30 (1): 67–73.

3622. Kihl, Y. W. January 1990. South Korea in 1990: Diplomatic Activism and a Partisan Quagmire. *Asian Survey* 31 (1): 64–70.

3623. Kil, S. September 1993. Political Reform of the Kim Young Sam Government. *Korea and World Affairs* 17 (3): 419–431.

3624. Kilgour, D. M. June 1991. Domestic Political Structure and War Behavior: A Game-Theoretical Approach. *Journal of Conflict Resolution* 35 (2): 266–284.

3625. Kilker, E. June 1989. Max Weber and Plebiscitarian Democracy: A Critique of the Mommsen Thesis. *International Journal of Politics, Culture, and Society* 2 (4): 429–465.

3626. Kim, B. 1993. The Democratization of Public Administration in (South) Korea. *Korean Social Science Journal* 17: 97–108.

3627. Kim, C. 1976. Détente and the Future of South Korean Democracy. *Pacific Community* 7 (2): 283–295.

3628. Kim, C. I. E. April 1978. Emergency, Development, and Human Rights: South Korea. *Asian Survey* 18 (4): 363–378.

3629. Kim, C. I. E. August 1978. The Value Congruence between ROK Civilian and Former Military Party Elites. *Asian Survey* 18 (8): 838–846.

3630. Kim, C. I. E. January 1987. South Korea in 1986: Preparing for a Power Transition. *Asian Survey* 27 (1): 64–74.

3631. Kim, C. L. February 1978. *See* Lowenberg, G. (February 1978).

3632. Kim, C. L., and S. C. Patterson. July 1988. Parliamentary Elite Integration in Six Nations. *Comparative Politics* 20 (4): 379–399.

3633. Kim, D. R. September 1993. Reform and National Development. *Korea and World Affairs* 17 (3): 405–418.

3634. Kim, E. M. 1993. *See* Hamilton, N. (1993).

3635. Kim, H. December 1994. A Theory of Government-Driven Democratization: The Case of Korea. *World Affairs* 156 (3): 130–140.

3636. Kim, H. N. December 1987. Political Changes in South Korea and Their Implications for U.S.-Korean Security Relations. *Korea and World Affairs* 11 (4): 649–665.

3637. Kim, H. N. May 1989. The 1988 Parliamentary Election in South Korea. *Asian Survey* 29 (5): 480–495.

3638. Kim, K. D. 1984. Socio-Economic Changes and Political Selectivity in the Development of Industrial Democracy in the Republic of Korea. *Economic and Industrial Democracy* 5 (4): 445–467.

3639. Kim, K. W. July 1989. *See* Shin, D. C. (July 1989).

3640. Kim, P. S. September 1994. A Theoretical Overview of Representative Bureaucracy: Synthesis. *International Review of Administrative Sciences* 60 (3): 385–398.

3641. Kim, S. S. September 1990. Chinese Foreign Policy after Tiananmen. *Current History* 89 (548): 245–248, 280–282.

3642. Kim, T., and Y. K. Cha. June 1992. Prospects for Political Change and Liberalization in North Korea. *Washington Quarterly* 15 (3): 155–169.

3643. Kim, Y. C. November 1977. Korea's Future: Pyongyang's Perspective. *Asian Survey* 17 (11): 1077–1087.

3644. Kimenyi, M. S. 1989. Interest Groups, Transfer Seeking and Democratization: Competition for the Benefits of Governmental Power May Explain African Political Instability. *American Journal of Economics and Sociology* 48 (3): 339–349.

3645. Kinciad, D. D. December 1978. The Arkansas Plan: Coon Dogs or Community Services. *Publius* 8 (1): 117–133.

3646. King, A. March 1985. *See* Campbell, J. C. (March 1985).

3647. King, D. E. December 1992. The Thai Parliamentary Elections of 1992: Return to Democracy in an Atypical Year. *Asian Survey* 32 (12): 1109–1123.

3648. King, D. S. November 1987. The State and the Social Structure of Welfare in Advanced Industrial Democracy. *Theory and Society* 16 (6): 841–868.

3649. King, D. S., and T. R. Gurr. 1988. The State and Fiscal Crisis in Advanced Industrial Democracies. *International Journal of Urban and Regional Research* 12 (1): 87–106.

3650. King, D. S., and M. Wickham Jones. July 1990. Social Democracy and Rational Workers. *British Journal of Political Science* 20: 387–413.

3651. King, E. G. 1990. Reconciling Democracy and the Crowd in Turn-of-the-Century American Social-Psychological Thought. *Journal of the History of the Behavioral Sciences* 26 (4): 334–344.

3652. King, G. May 1990. Electoral Responsiveness and Partisan Bias in Multiparty Democracies. *Legislative Studies Quarterly* 15 (2): 159–181.

3653. King, G. May 1994. *See* Gelman, A. (May 1994).

3654. King, G. July 1994. *See* Alt, J. E. (July 1994).

3655. King, G. September 1994. *See* Gelman, A. (September 1994).

3656. King, G., J. E. Alt, N. E. Burns, and M. Laver. August 1990. A Unified Model of Cabinet Dissolution in Parliamentary Democracies. *American Journal of Political Science* 34 (3): 846–871.

3657. King, R. F. 1991. On Watersheds, Reforms, and Public Goods: Comment. *American Politics Quarterly* 19 (4): 494–504.

3658. King, R. R. 1976. Essays on So-Called Socialist Democracy in Romania: Multiple Candidates in the 1975 Elections.* *Osteuropa* 26 (5): 382–388.

3659. Kinnvall, C., and A. Uhlin. 1993. Global Democratization: Transitions from Authoritarian Rule during 1989–1991. *Statsvetenskaplig Tidskrift* 96 (1): 7–38.

3660. Kintner, W. R. March 1977. A Program for America: Freedom and Foreign Policy. *Orbis* 21 (1): 139–156.

3661. Kintner, W. R. March 1986. The Elements of Peace. *World Affairs* 148 (4): 187–198.

3662. Kinzer, D. M. May 1980. A Provider Perspective on PL 93–641. *State and Local Government Review* 12 (2): 57–61.

3663. Kinzo, M. D. G. October 1991. La Eleccion Presidencial de 1989: El Comportamiento Electoral en Uno Ciudad Brasilena. *Revista de Estudios Politicos* 74: 257–276.

3664. Kipper, J. 1978. *See* Grant, F. (1978).

3665. Kirby, D. 1974. Stockholm, Petrograd, Berlin: International Social Democracy and Finnish Independence, 1917. *Slavonic and East European Review* 52 (126): 63–84.

3666. Kirchner, E. March 1984. *See* Broughton, D. (March 1984).

3667. Kirk, D. June 1981. Democracy in the Philippines. *New Leader* 64: 5–8.

3668. Kirk, D. March 8, 1982. Democracy without Dissent in Korea: The Plight of Kim Dae Jung. *New Leader* 65: 5–7.

3669. Kirkby, R. G. September 1989. Whose Company Is It Anyway? *Journal of Portfolio Management* 16: 13–18.

3670. Kirkland, L. 1978. Free Trade Unions: Force for Democracy. *AFL-CIO American Federationist* 85 (4): 1–5.

3671. Kirkpatrick, J. J. June 1978. Martin Diamond and the American Idea of Democracy. *Publius* 8 (3): 7–32.

3672. Kirkpatrick, J. J. 1982. Human Rights and the Foundations of Democracy. *World Politics* 144 (3): 196–203.

3673. Kirkpatrick, J. J. September 1984. Democratic Elections and Democratic Government. *World Affairs* 147 (2): 61–69.

3674. Kirkpatrick, J. J. February 1990. Beyond the Cold War. *Foreign Affairs* 69 (1): 1–16.

3675. Kirlin, J. J. February 1975. Electoral Conflict and Democracy in Cities. *Journal of Politics* 37 (1): 262–269.

3676. Kirp, D. L. September 1984. *See* Jung, D. J. (September 1984).

3677. Kirschner, B. H. September 1991. Electronic Democracy in the 21st Century. *National Civic Review* 80 (4): 406–412.

3678. Kirwan, K. A. September 1981. Historicism and Statemanship: In the Reform Argument of Woodrow Wilson. *Interpretation* 9 (2–3): 339–351.

3679. Kiser, E., and Y. Barzel. October 1991. The Origins of Democracy in England. *Rationality and Society* 3 (4): 396–422.

3680. Kiser, L. L. June 1984. Toward an Institutional Theory of Citizen Coproduction. *Urban Affairs Quarterly* 19 (4): 485–510.

3681. Kisiel, W., and D. Taebel. 1994. Poland's Quest for Local Democracy: The Role of Polish Mayors in an Uncertain Environment. *Journal of Urban Affairs* 16 (1): 51–66.

3682. Kiss, E. March 1992. Democracy without Parties: Civil Society in East-Central Europe. *Dissent* 39 (2): 226–231.

3683. Kissler, L., and U. Sattel. 1980. Economic Democracy: Theories, Strategies, Programs.* *Gegenwartskunde: Gesellschaft, Staat, Erziehung* 29 (1): 35–46.

3684. Kitschelt, H. March 1992. The Formation of Party Systems in East-Central Europe. *Politics and Society* 20 (1): 7–50.

3685. Kitschelt, H. July 1993. Social Movement, Political Parties, and Democratic Theory. *Annals of the American Academy of Political and Social Science* 528: 13–29.

3686. Kitschelt, H. April 1994. Austrian and Swedish Social Democrats in Crisis: Party Strategy and Organization in Corporatist Regimes. *Comparative Political Studies* 27: 3–39.

3687. Kitschelt, H. P. January 1986. Political Opportunity Structures and Political Protest: Anti-Nuclear Movements in Four

Democracies. *British Journal of Political Science* 16: 57–85.

3688. Kitschelt, H. P. January 1988. Left-Libertarian Parties: Explaining Innovation in Competitive Party Systems. *World Politics* 40 (2): 194–234.

3689. Kittrie, N. N. December 1992. Democracy: An Institution Whose Time Has Come—From Classical Greece to the Modern Pluralistic Society. *American University Journal of International Law and Policy* 8: 375–388.

3690. Kizuk, R. June 1984. Democratization and Consumption (Some Theoretical Aspects).* *Revue d'Etudes Comparatives Est-Ouest* 15 (2): 111–125.

3691. Klapp, O. E. July 1975. Opening and Closing in Open Systems. *Behavioral Science* 20 (4): 251–257.

3692. Klare, H. J. 1975. Barbican Center: Experiment in Voluntarism and Democracy. *Human Context* 7 (3): 602–604.

3693. Klare, K. E. 1988a. The Labor-Management Cooperation Debate: A Workplace Democracy Perspective. *Harvard Civil Rights-Civil Liberties Law Review* 23 (1): 40–83.

3694. Klare, K. E. 1988b. Workplace Democracy and Market Reconstruction: An Agenda for Legal Reform. *Catholic University Law Review* 38 (1): 1–68.

3695. Klein, H., and H. S. Erlich. 1974. Is Hospital Democracy Possible. *Mental Health and Society* 1 (1): 34–48.

3696. Klein, R. October 1977. Democracy: The Welfare State and Social Policy. *Political Quarterly* 48 (4): 448–458.

3697. Kleinewefers, H. 1992. Outline of a Dynamic Model of Free Elections and Stable Parliamentary Democracy.* *Jahrbuch für Sozialwissenschaft* 43 (1): 108–129.

3698. Klen, M. November 1992. La Detresse de Madagascar. *Defense Nationale* 48: 143–153.

3699. Klepak, H. P. November 1983. Trying Democracy in Spain: One Year of Socialist Government; Democracy Fit but Struggling. *International Perspectives* 17–19.

3700. Klieman, A. S. 1978. Emergency Powers and Liberal Democracy in Britain. *Journal of Commonwealth and Comparative Politics* 16 (2): 190–211.

3701. Klieman, A. S. June 1981. Indira's India: Democracy and Crisis Government. *Political Science Quarterly* 96 (2): 241–259.

3702. Kline, J. M. August 1992. The Role of Transnational Corporations in Chile's Transition: Beyond Dependency and Bargaining. *Transnational Corporations* 1 (2): 81–95.

3703. Klingeman, H. D. 1982. *See* Kaase, M. (1982).

3704. Kljamkin, I. 1990. Transition from Totalitarianism to Democracy in the Soviet Union: Trends, Problems, Possible Steps. *Osteuropa* 40 (6): 479–494.

3705. Klock, J. J. 1974. Democracy in the UMW. *Labor Law Journal* 25 (10): 625–631.

3706. Klosko, G. June 1993. Rawls's Political Philosophy and American Democracy. *American Political Science Review* 87 (2): 348–359.

3707. Klosterman, R. E. January 1985. Arguments for and against Planning Formal Governmental Efforts at the Local and Regional Level; Western Democracy. *Town Planning Review* 56: 5–20.

3708. Kly, Y. N. September 1993. African-Americans and the Right of Self-Determination. *Hamline Law Review* 17: 4–45.

3709. Knabe, H. 1991. Democratization and Political Reform: On the Critical Discussion of Legitimacy and Legitimization in the GDR. *Studies in GDR Culture and Society* 10: 31–51.

3710. Knapp, T. June 1988. *See* Antonio, R. (June 1988).

3711. Knella, P. 1977. Renunciation of Democracy in India: Interpretation from the Viewpoint of Traditional Indian Sociology.* *Indo Asia: für Politik, Kultur, und Wirtschaft Indiens und Suedost Asiens* 19 (1): 30–37.

3712. Knight, J., and J. Johnson. May 1994. Aggregation and Deliberation: On the Possibility of Democratic Legitimacy. *Political Theory* 22 (2): 277–296.

3713. Knight, N. 1990. On Contradiction and On New Democracy: Contrasting Perspectives on Causation and Social Change in the Thought of Mao Zedong. *Bulletin of Concerned Asian Scholars* 22 (2): 18–34.

3714. Knight, V. C. May 1991. Mozambique's Search for Stability. *Current History* 90 (556): 217–220, 226.

3715. Knopff, R. December 1978. Democracy Versus Liberal Democracy: The Nationalist Conundrum (Quebec). *Dalhousie Review* 58: 638–646.

3716. Knopff, R. December 1980. Pierre Trudeau and the Problem of Liberal Democratic Statesmanship. *Dalhousie Review* 60: 712–726.

3717. Knopff, R. March 1982. Liberal Democracy and the Challenge of Nationalism in Canadian Politics. *Canadian Review of Studies in Nationalism* 9: 23–42.

3718. Knopfle, F. 1978. Crisis of Representative Democracy.* *Politische Studien* 29 (240): 341–357.

3719. Knutsen, O. January 1985. *See* Lafferty, W. M. (January 1985).

3720. Knutsen, O. July 1988. The Impact of Structural and Ideological Party Cleavages in West European Democracies: A Comparative Empirical Analysis. *British Journal of Political Science* 18: 323–352.

3721. Knutsen, O. October 1990. Materialist and Postmaterialist Values and Social Structures in the Nordic Countries. *Comparative Politics* 23 (1): 85–104.

3722. Kobach, K. W. December 1993. Recent Developments in Swiss Direct Democracy. *Electoral Studies* 12 (4): 342–365.

3723. Kobayashi, V. N. December 1985. *See* Cummings, W. K. (December 1985).

3724. Kobec, N. G. 1986. *See* Kerimov, D. A. (1986).

3725. Koblik, S. 1977. Symbolism and Reality. *Wilson Quarterly* 1 (5): 103–110.

3726. Koelble, T. 1994. *See* Debeus, J. (1994).

3727. Koelble, T. A. July 1989. Party Structures and Democracy: Michels, McKenzie, and Duverger Revisited via the Examples of the West German Green Party and the British Social Democratic Party. *Comparative Political Studies* 22 (2): 199–216.

3728. Koelble, T. A. March 1992. Recasting Social Democracy in Europe: A Nested Games Explanation of Strategic Adjustment in Political Parties. *Politics and Society* 20 (1): 51–70.

3729. Koh, B. C. March 1985. The Recruitment of Higher Civil Servants in Japan: A Comparative Perspective. *Asian Survey* 25 (3): 292–309.

3730. Koh, B. C. September 1985. The 1985 Parliamentary Election in South Korea. *Asian Survey* 25 (9): 883–897.

3731. Koh, H. H. September 1994. Democracy and Human Rights in the United States Foreign Policy? Lessons from the Haitian Crisis. *SMU Law Review* 48: 189–202.

3732. Kohl, H. 1981. *See* Nathan, J. (1981).

3733. Kohler, J. M. 1987. Colony or Democracy: The New Caledonian Dilemma. *Australian Journal of Politics and History* 33 (2): 47–59.

3734. Kohli, A. July 1980. Democracy, Economic Growth, and Inequality in

India's Development. *World Politics* 32 (4): 623–638.

3735. Kohli, A. October 1988. The NTR Phenomenon in Andhra Pradesh: Political Change in a South Indian State. *Asian Survey* 28 (10): 991–1017.

3736. Kohli, A. January 1992. Indian Democracy: Stress and Resilience. *Journal of Democracy* 3 (1): 52–64.

3737. Kohli, A. April 1993. Democratic Transitions in the Developing Countries.* *Politica Internazionale* 21 (2): 19–34.

3738. Kohli, A. November 1993. Democracy Amid Economic Orthodoxy: Trends in Developing Countries. *Third World Quarterly* 14 (4): 671–690.

3739. Kohlmeier, L. M. March 1980. Economic Policy Disarray Threatens Political Freedom. *Financier* 4: 7–11.

3740. Kohn, W. S. G. March 1983. Democratic Government in the Twentieth Century: The New Model Takes Shape. *Midwest Quarterly* 24: 248–260.

3741. Kohno, M. January 1994. The Politics of Coalition Building in Japan: The Case of the Katayama Government Formation in 1947. *British Journal of Political Science* 24 (1): 148–157.

3742. Koizumi, T. 1988. Knowledge, Power and Democracy. *Cybernetica* 31 (3): 215–224.

3743. Koja, F. 1993. Instruments of Direct Democracy in the Austrian Federal State and Its Lander. *Austrian Journal of Public and International Law* 45 (1): 33–45.

3744. Kolakowski, L. January 1979. The Meaning of Social Democracy: The Possibilities and the Limits of Humane Political Action. *New Leader* 62: 9–13.

3745. Kolakowski, L. September 1983. Marxism and Human Rights. *Daedalus* 112 (4): 81–92.

3746. Kolakowski, L. 1990. Dangers to Democracy. *Society* 27 (4): 77–79.

3747. Kolakowski, L. December 1990. Uncertainties of a Democratic Age. *Journal of Democracy* 1 (1): 47–50.

3748. Kolane, J. T., and M. D. Thulo. July 1993. Constituent Assembly: Lesotho's Return to Parliamentary Democracy. *Parliamentarian* 74: 130–132.

3749. Kolikova, G. B. May 1985. Improving Soviet Democracy at the Stage of Developed Socialism.* *Voprosy Istorii* 5: 3–21.

3750. Kolland, F. 1984. The Contribution of the Third World Movement to the Political Culture of Austria.* *Oesterreichische Zeitschrift für Politikwissenschaft* 13 (2): 165–181.

3751. Kolland, F., and R. Deussner. 1985. Democracy and Regional Inequality: Two Aspects of Cuban Development. *Oesterreichische Zeitschrift für Politikwissenschaft* 14 (1): 39–56.

3752. Kolson, K. April 1978. Party, Opposition and Political Development. *Review of Politics* 40 (2): 163–182.

3753. Koltay, J. 1986. Economic Reform and Industrial Democracy in Hungary. *Revue d'Etudes Comparatives Est-Quest* 17 (2): 41–52.

3754. Komila-A-Iboanga, F. January 1991. The Resistance of Power to the Establishment of Pluralist Democracy in Africa: The Case of Gabon.* *Revue Juridique et Politique Independence et Cooperation* 45 (1): 10–33.

3755. Komisar, L. 1981. The Old Order Endureth: Spain's Fragile Democracy. *Nation* 223 (14): 437.

3756. Komisar, L. 1984. Spain's Socialists: Democracy First, Then Revolution. *Nation* 238 (5): 158–160.

3757. Kommers, D. P. November 1976. Judicial Review: Its Influence Abroad. *Annals of the American Academy of Political and Social Science* 428: 52–64.

3758. Kommers, D. P. March 1977. Abortion and the Constitution: United States and West Germany. *American Journal of Comparative Law* 25 (2): 255–285.

3759. Kondracke, M. 1986. Reagan's Fragile Legacy: How to Save Democracies. *New Republic* 195 (25): 23–25.

3760. Koniusz, M. 1984. Democracy in Karl Renner's Political Doctrine.* *Nauk Politycznych* 69: 27–47.

3761. Koo, H. August 1991. Middle Classes, Democratization, and Class Formation: The Case of South Korea. *Theory and Society* 20 (4): 485–509.

3762. Kopf, E. 1975. Reactionary Criticism of Marx after Gotha Program of German Social Democracy.* *Deutsche Zeitschrift für Philosophie* 23 (5): 706–713.

3763. Kopp, E. December 1992. *See* Bieber, R. (December 1992).

3764. Kopp, M. S. 1990. Anxiety, Freedom and Democracy. *Behavioral Psychotherapy* 18 (3): 189–192.

3765. Korab, W. April 1980. Responsibility in Democracy.* *Oesterreichische Zeitschrifte für Offentliches Recht und Volkerrecht* 31 (1–2): 75–91.

3766. Koritansky, J. C. 1974. Two Forms of Love of Equality in Tocqueville's Practical Teaching for Democracy. *Polity* 6 (4): 488–499.

3767. Koritansky, J. C. 1976. Democracy and Nobility: Comments on Tocqueville's *Democracy in America*. *Intercollegiate Review* 12 (1): 13–27.

3768. Koritansky, J. C. March 1990. Civil Religion in Tocqueville's "Democracy in America." *Interpretation* 17 (3): 389–400.

3769. Kornberg, A. November 1993. *See* Clarke, H. D. (November 1993).

3770. Kornberg, A. November 1994. *See* Clarke, H. D. (November 1994).

3771. Kornberg, A. August 1990. Political Support in Democratic Societies: The Case of Canada. *Journal of Politics* 52 (3): 709–716.

3772. Kornberg, A., and H. D. Clarke. September 1994. Beliefs about Democracy and Satisfaction with Democratic Government: The Canadian Case. *Political Science Quarterly* 47 (3): 537–564.

3773. Kornblith, M. September 1991. The Politics of Constitution-Making: Constitutions and Democracy in Venezuela. *Journal of Latin American Studies* 23: 61–89.

3774. Kornbluh, H. May 1984. Work-Place Democracy and Quality of Work Life: Problems and Prospects. *Annals of the American Academy of Political and Social Science* 473: 88–95.

3775. Kornhauser, L. A. March 1994. *See* Benoit, J. P. (March 1994).

3776. Korosenyi, A. December 1990. Hungary. *Electoral Studies* 9 (4): 337–345.

3777. Korosenyi, A. December 1993. Stable or Fragile Democracy: Political Cleavages and Party System. *Government and Opposition* 28 (1): 87–104.

3778. Korosenyi, A. October 1994. Intellectuals and Democracy in Eastern Europe. *Political Quarterly* 65 (4): 415–424.

3779. Korpi, W. 1979. Variations of the Welfare State: Research Problems Concerning Social-Political Strategies in the Capitalist Democracies.* *Sociologisk Forskning* 16 (1): 3–18.

3780. Korpi, W. October 1980. Social Policy and Distributional Conflict in the Capitalist Democracies: A Preliminary Comparative Framework.* *West European Politics* 3 (3): 296–316.

3781. Korpi, W. 1991. Political and Economic Explanations for Unemployment: A Cross-National and Long Term Analysis. *Statsvetenskaplig Tidskrift* 94 (2): 101–124.

3782. Korson, J. H., and M. Maskiell. June 1985. Islamization and Social Policy in Pakistan: The Constitutional Crisis and the Status of Women. *Asian Survey* 25 (6): 589–612.

3783. Korzeniewicz, R. P., and K. Awbrey. December 1992. Democratic Transitions and the Semiperiphery of the World Economy. *Sociological Forum* 7 (4): 609–640.

3784. Koschwitz, H. 1977. Streitkraefte und Politisches System: Zur Rolle und Entwicklung des Militaers in Den Demokratien des Westens. *Deutsche Studien* 15 (59): 249–264.

3785. Koscr, M. I. 1974. *See* Beljajewa, S. (1974).

3786. Koslowski, P. June 1983. Are Market and Democracy Powerless? The Limits of Individualist Social Decision with Special Reference to the Questions of Environmental and Nuclear Energy.* *Politische Vierteljahresschrift* 24 (2): 166–187.

3787. Kosminski, J. September 1991. Arsenals of Democracy: Defense Strategies for a Revolutionary Decade. *Policy Review* 58: 66–71.

3788. Koszinowski, T. September 1984. The Process of Democratization in Egypt: Mubarak's Policy in the Light of the Parliamentary Elections of May 1984.* *Orient* 25 (3): 335–360.

3789. Kothari, R. January 1989. The Democratic Challenge (in India).* *Projet* 215: 19–28.

3790. Kothari, R. July 1989. The New Détente: Some Reflections from the South. *Alternatives* 14 (3): 289–299.

3791. Kothari, R. September 1989. The Indian Enterprise Today. *Daedalus* 118 (4): 51–67.

3792. Kourliandsky, J. (ed.). 1994. Les Democraties de Basse Intensite. *Relations Internationales et Strategiques* (2): 43–149. 13 articles.

3793. Kouvetaris, G. A. June 1989. Political Elites and Party Organization in Greece: An Entrepreneurial Model. *Journal of Social, Political, and Economic Studies* 14 (2): 189–214.

3794. Kouzmine, E. August 1985. The Worsening of the Crisis of Traditional Bourgeois Political Institutions. *La Vie Internationale* 8: 66–75.

3795. Kovalskys, J. September 1990. *See* Becker, D. (September 1990).

3796. Kovecses, Z. 1994. Tocqueville's Passionate Beast: A Linguistic Analysis of the Concept of American Democracy. *Metaphor and Symbolic Activity* 9 (2): 113–133.

3797. Kowalski, R. 1977. Social Democracy and Social Market Economics.* *IPW Berichte* 6 (11): 47–50.

3798. Kowalski, S. December 1990. *See* Pelczynski, Z. (December 1990).

3799. Kowarich, L., and N. Bonduki. 1987. Urban and Political Space in São Paulo from Brazilian Populism to the Return of Democracy.* *Estudios Sociales Centroamericanos* 44: 45–61.

3800. Kozinski, A. January 1991. Death, Lies and Videotape: The Ceausescu Show Trial and the Future of Romania. *American Bar Association Journal* 77: 70–73.

3801. Kpatinde, F. February 20, 1991. Mali: Le Front du Refus. *Jeune Afrique* 31: 10–13.

3802. Kpatinde, F. March 19, 1992. Democratisation: Bilan des Années Folles. *Jeune Afrique* 32: 20–24.

3803. Kpundeh, S., and S. P. Riley. July 1992. Political Choice and the New Democratic Politics in Africa. *Round Table* 323: 263–271.

3804. Kramer, K. W. February 1985. *See* Plumtree, J. P. (February 1985).

3805. Kramer, M. January 1993. Islam Versus Democracy. *Commentary* 95 (1): 35–42.

3806. Krancberg, S. July 1982. Karl Marx and Democracy. *Studies in Soviet Thought* 24 (1): 23–35.

3807. Krannich, R. L. May 1979. Politics of Intergovernmental Relations in Thailand. *Asian Survey* 19 (5): 506–522.

3808. Krasner, S. D. February 1992. Realism, Imperialism, and Democracy: A Response to Gilbert. *Political Theory* 20 (1): 38–52.

3809. Krasnov, V. N. July 1985. Political Regimes of the Bourgeois Countries. *Sovetskoe Gosudarstvo Pravo* 7: 105–111.

3810. Kraus, J. May 1989. Economic Adjustment and Regime Creation in Nigeria. *Current History* 88 (538): 233–237, 249–250.

3811. Kraus, J. 1991. Building Democracy in Africa. *Current History* 90 (556): 209–212.

3812. Kraus, P. A. June 1990. Elements of a Theory of Democratic Transition in the Southern European Context.* *Politische Vierteljahresschrift* 31 (2): 191–213.

3813. Kraus, W. June 1985. Democracy: A Lack of Ideals?* *Europaeische Rundschau* 13 (3): 131–139.

3814. Krause, E. March 1989. England, the United States, and the Export of Democracy. *Washington Quarterly* 12 (2): 189–197.

3815. Krause, L. B. June 1991. *See* Cheng, T. (June 1991).

3816. Krause, R., and G. Liebscher. 1979. Die Haltung der Internationales Sozialdemokratie zum Kampf der Voelker Afrikas und Lateinamerikas um Nationale Unabhaengigkeit und Sozialen Fortschritt. *Asien, Afrika, Lateinamerika* 7 (5): 813–824.

3817. Kraynak, R. P. December 1987. Tocqueville's Constitutionalism. *American Political Science Review* 81 (4): 1175–1195.

3818. Krebiel, K. February 1994. *See* Groseclose, T. (February 1994).

3819. Krebs, H. P. 1990. Authoritarian State, Democracy and Social Movements. *Argument* 32 (3): 429–431.

3820. Kremendahl, H. August 1980. Upon the Problem of a Systems Comparison.* *Aus Politik und Zeitgeschichte* 31: 42–46.

3821. Kremsmayer, U. 1989. Instrumentalized Intelligence: Social Democracy and Intellectuals. *Oesterreichische Zeitschrift für Politikwissenschaft* 18 (4): 361–372.

3822. Kress, P. F. June 1978. Of Action and Virtue: Notes on the Presidency, Watergate, and Liberal Society. *Polity* 10 (4): 510–523.

3823. Kressley, K. March 1990. The Red and the Green: Antecedents to the Political Consciousness of Germany's Green Party. *Southeastern Political Review* 18 (1): 3–25.

3824. Krieger, W. April 1979. Worrying about West German Democracy. *Political Quarterly* 50 (2): 192–204.

3825. Kriek, D. J. 1987. The Institutionalization of Democracy in a Plural Society: Prospects of Acceptance of Democracy and of Its Protection.* *Politeia (UNISA)* 6 (1): 62–71.

3826. Kriek, D. J. 1988. Decision-Making in Democracies: Introductory Remarks.* *Politeia (UNISA)* 7 (2): 2–11.

3827. Krimerman, L., and F. Lindenfeld. March 1990. Contemporary Workplace Democracy in the United States: Taking Stock of an Emerging Movement. *Socialism and Democracy* 109–139.

3828. Krischke, P. 1990. Social Movements and Political Participation: Contributions of Grassroots Democracy in Brazil. *Canadian Journal of Development Studies* 11 (1): 173–184.

3829. Krischke, P. J. July 1991. Church Base Communities and Democratic Change in Brazilian Society. *Comparative Political Studies* 24 (2): 186–210.

3830. Krishnan, V. N. May 1977. *See* Kannappan, S. (May 1977).

3831. Kristal, I. March 1988. *See* Hodgson, G. (March 1988).

3832. Kristol, I. 1978. Capitalism, Socialism, and Democracy. *Commentary* 65 (4): 53–54.

3833. Kristol, I. December 1987. "The Spirit of '87." *Public Interest* 86: 3–9.

3834. Krivoguz, I. M. June 1976. Historical Experience and Current Problems of Participation by Communists in the Governments of Noncommunist Countries. *Soviet Law and Government* 15: 3–33.

3835. Krjazkov, V. A. 1988. The Development of Direct Democracy Institutions in the Present Period [in the USSR].* *Sovetskoe Gosudarstvo Pravo* 9: 21–30.

3836. Kroeber, A. R. 1988. India's Democracy: Strained but Stable. *Dissent* 35 (3): 275–278.

3837. Kroes, B. June 1986. Cruise Missiles and the Western Party System: Some Dutch Lessons. *Armed Forces and Society* 12 (4): 581–590.

3838. Krosnick, J. A. August 1994. *See* Rahn, W. M. (August 1994).

3839. Krouse, R. March 1982. Polyarchy and Participation: The Changing Democratic Theory of Robert Dahl. *Polity* 14 (3): 441–463.

3840. Krouse, R. May 1982. Two Concepts of Democratic Representation: James and John Stuart Mill. *Journal of Politics* 44 (2): 509–537.

3841. Krouse, R., and G. Marcus. 1984. Electoral Studies and Democratization Theory Reconsidered. *Political Behavior* 6 (1): 23–39.

3842. Krouse, R., and M. McPherson. October 1986. A "Mixed"-Property Regime: Equality and Liberty in a Market Economy. *Ethics* 97 (1): 119–138.

3843. Kruis, K. 1979. Professional Officialdom: Nuisance or Challenge to Free Democracy in Constitutional and Welfare State.* *Politische Studien* 30 (244): 189–201.

3844. Krumwiede, H. W. March 1986. Military Leadership and (Re)Democratization in Central America.* *Aus Politik und Zeitgeschichte* 9 (1): 17–29.

3845. Kruze, U. April 1991. Sino-Japanese Relations. *Current History* 90 (555): 156–159, 179.

3846. Kryzanek, M. J. May 1977. Political Party Decline and the Failure of Liberal Democracy: The PRD in Dominican Politics. *Journal of Latin American Studies* 9: 115–143.

3847. Kuan, H. December 1991. Power Dependence and Democratic Transition: The Case of Hong Kong. *China Quarterly* 128: 774–793.

3848. Kubicek, P. December 1994. Delegative Democracy in Russia and Ukraine. *Communist and Post-Communist Studies* 27 (4): 423–442.

3849. Kubik, J. December 1994. The Role of Decentralization and Cultural Revival in Post-Communist Transformations: The Case of Cieszyn Silesia, Poland. *Communist and Post-Communist Studies* 27 (4): 331–356.

3850. Kucinskas, L. September 1991. Lithuania's Independence: The Litmus Test for Democracy in the USSR. *Lituanus* 37: 5–50.

3851. Kuhn, D., and C. E. Zech. 1986. Labor Law and the Political Process in Labor Unions: Leviathan vs. Voter Responsive Democracy. *Labor Law Journal* 37 (5): 259–272.

3852. Kuhnau, K. 1988. The Achievement of Socialist Democracy [in the GDR].* *Staat und Recht* 37 (5): 370–377.

3853. Kuhnel, K., and G. Moller. 1989. On the Development of Democracy and the Challenge of Comprehensive Intensification in the German Democratic Republic. *Deutsche Zeitschrift für Philosophie* 37 (6): 557–560.

3854. Kukla, C. G. 1994. *See* Monshipouri, M. (1994).

3855. Kuklinski, J. H. March 1977. Constituency Opinion: A Test of the Surrogate Model. *Public Opinion Quarterly* 41 (1): 34–40.

3856. Kulenovic, M. June 1993. Predefence of Democracy: Leaders, Followers, Masses. *Collegium Antropologicum* 17 (1): 159–170.

3857. Kulikov, V. V. 1989. Societal Ownership and the Democratization of Economic Life. *Politicka Ekonomie* 37 (3): 249–262.

3858. Kumar, A. 1987. Accountability and Autonomy in Higher Education: Needed Internal Democracy. *Economic and Political Weekly* 22 (44): 1858–1861.

3859. Kumar, D. D. 1990. Science for Democracy: Communicating Science for Knowledge Equity. *Bulletin of Science, Technology and Society* 10 (5–6): 290–292.

3860. Kumar, K. June 1992. The Revolutions of 1989: Socialism, Capitalism, and Democracy. *Theory and Society* 21 (3): 309–356.

3861. Kummer, J. 1985. *See* Weede, E. (1985).

3862. Kuo, T., and R. H. Myers. September 1988. The Great Transition: Political Change and the Prospects for Democracy in the Republic of China on Taiwan. *Asian Affairs: An American Review* 15 (3): 115–133.

3863. Kuran, T. October 1991. Now Out of Never: The Element of Surprise in the East European Revolution of 1989. *World Politics* 44 (1): 7–47.

3864. Kurian, P. 1982. *See* Chhachhi, A. (1982).

3865. Kurth, J. R. December 1979. The Political Consequences of the Product Cycle: Industrial History and Political Outcomes. *International Organization* 33 (1): 1–34.

3866. Kurtz, P. 1976. Journey to India: End of Indian Democracy. *Humanist* 36 (2): 12–14.

3867. Kuruvilla, S. July 1992. *See* Pontussen, J. (July 1992).

3868. Kusin, V. V. November 1987. Reform and Dissidence in Czechoslovakia. *Current History* 86 (523): 361–364, 383–384.

3869. Kuzmin, E. May 1993. Russian Libraries during the Transition from a Authoritarian System to a Democracy. *Zeitschrift für Bibliothekswesen und Bibliographie* 40 (3): 245–253.

3870. Kuzmin, E. L. 1978. Critique of Bourgeois and Revisionist Views of Democracy and the State. *Soviet Studies in Philosophy* 16 (3): 52–68.

3871. Kuzmin, E. L. 1986. Bourgeois Democracy: Its Limits and Possibilities.* *Sovetskoe Gosudarstvo Pravo* (5): 109–117.

3872. Kuzmin, E. L. 1987. Democracy for the People and Democracy for the Elite.* *Mirovaia Ekonomika i Mezdunarodyne Otnoshenia Nauk* 6: 3–13.

3873. Kvaternik, E. 1978. Political Parties and Democracy in Argentina between 1955–1966. *Desarrollo Economico* 18 (71): 409–431.

3874. Kweit, M. G., and R. W. Kweit. May 1987. Citizen Participation: Enduring Issues for the Next Century. *National Civic Review* 76 (3): 191–198.

3875. Kweit, R. W. May 1987. *See* Kweit, M. G. (May 1987).

3876. Kwitko, L. 1990. *See* So, A. Y. (1990).

3877. Kwon, W. H. February 1978. *See* Boynton, G. R. (February 1978).

3878. Kwong, J. September 1988. The 1986 Student Demonstrations in China: A Democratic Movement? *Asian Survey* 28 (9): 970–985.

3879. Kyle, K. 1976. Bringing Democracy to Brussels: Towards a Directly Elected European Parliament. *Round Table* (264): 323–330.

3880. Kyu, H. Y. 1989. Press Freedom in "Democratic" South Korea: Moving from Authoritarianism to Libertarian? *Gazette* 1: 53–71.

3881. Kyungmo, C. 1974. The Second Liberation of South Korea and Democratization of Japan. *Japan Interpreter* 9 (2): 177–197.

3882. Laakkonen, V. 1976. Democracy and Efficiency in Co-operative. *Annals of Public and Co-operative Economy* 47 (1): 37–45.

3883. Laakso, M. 1980. Representative Democracy and Political Science.* *Politiika* 22 (4): 337–357.

3884. Laaksonen, O. 1984. Participation Down and Up the Line: Comparative Industrial Democracy Trends in China and Europe. *International Social Science Journal* 36 (2): 299–318.

3885. Laband, D. N. 1984. Is There a Relationship between Economic Conditions and Political Structure. *Public Choice* 42 (1): 25–37.

3886. Labastida, J. April 1991. Mexico: Democratic Transition and Economic Reform.* *Revista Mexicana de Sociologia* 53 (2): 127–139.

3887. Labaune, P. 1981. Tribal Democracy and the Political System in the Yemen Arab Republic.* *Revue Française de Science Politique* 31 (4): 745–768.

3888. Laber, J. January 14, 1993. Slouching toward Democracy and the Future of Albania. *New York Review of Books* 40 (1–2): 24–27.

3889. Laclau, E., and C. Mouffee. November 1987. Post-Marxism without Apologies. *New Left Review* 166: 79–106.

3890. Ladd, E. C. March 1981. The Brittle Mandate: Electoral Dealignment and the 1980 Presidential Election. *Political Science Quarterly* 96 (1): 1–25.

3891. Lafer, C. 1978. Growth Equality and Democracy.* *Dados Revista de Ciencias Sociais* (18): 123–133.

3892. Lafer, C. March 1984. The Brazilian Political System: Trends and Perspectives. *Government and Opposition* 19 (2): 178–187.

3893. Lafferty, W. M. 1984. Workplace Democratization in Norway: Current Status and Future Prospects with Special Emphasis on the Role of the Public Sector. *Acta Sociologica* 27 (2): 123–138.

3894. Lafferty, W. M. January 1990. The Political Transformation of a Social Democratic State: As the World Moves In, Norway Moves Right. *West European Politics* 13: 79–100.

3895. Lafferty, W. M., and O. Knutsen. January 1985. Postmaterialism in a Social Democratic State: An Analysis of the Distinctness of the Inglehart Value Syndrome in Norway. *Comparative Political Studies* 17 (4): 411–430.

3896. Lahav, P. 1977. World Jewry and the Ballot: Defense of Democracy at the World Zionist Federation and Its Potential Impact on Israel's Constitutional Law. *Israel Law Review* 12 (3): 318–329.

3897. Laird, F. N. June 1993. Participatory Analysis, Democracy, and Technological Decision-Making. *Science, Technology, and Human Values* 18 (3): 341–361.

3898. Laitin, D. D. October 1991. The National Uprisings in the Soviet Union. *World Politics* 44 (1): 139–177.

3899. Lajoie, A., S. Perrault, H. Quillinan, and A. Chitrit. 1994. Jean Beetz: Sur la Societe Libre et Democratique. *La Revue Juridique Themis* 28: 557–611.

3900. Lajoie, A., and L. Rolland. October 1993. Gerald LeDain: Sur la Societe Libre et Democratique. *McGill Law Journal* 38: 899–938.

3901. Lake, A. January 1994. A Strategy of Enlargement and the Developing World. *Foreign Policy Bulletin* 4: 91–94.

3902. Lake, D. A. March 1992. Powerful Pacifists: Democratic States and War. *American Political Science Review* 86 (1): 24–37.

3903. Lakoff, S. June 1990. Autonomy and Liberal Democracy. *Review of Politics* 52 (3): 378–396.

3904. Laloupo, F. 1992. The Benin National Conference: A New Concept of Political Regime Change.* *Année Africaine* 89–114.

3905. Lam, J. T. M. July 1993. Chris Patten's Constitutional Reform Package: Implications for Hong Kong's Political Transition. *Issues and Studies* 29 (7): 55–72.

3906. Lam, J. T. M. December 1993. Democracy or Convergence: The Dilemma of Political Reform in Hong Kong. *Asian Journal of Public Administration* 15 (2): 225–253.

3907. Lam Kabore, G. June 12, 1991. Tchad: Trente Mois pour Oublier le Passe. *Jeune Afrique* 31: 33–49.

3908. Lamberti, M. March 1992. Elementary School Teachers and the Struggle against Social Democracy in Wilhelmine Germany. *History of Education Quarterly* 32 (1): 73–97.

3909. Lambright, W. H., and D. Rahm. June 1987. Science, Technology, and Democracy. *Teaching Political Science* 14 (4): 179–183.

3910. Lameyer, J. 1981. Democracy at Issue.* *Jahrbuch des Oeffenlichen Rechts der Gegenwalt* 30: 147–196.

3911. Lamounier, B. March 1984. Opening through Elections: Will the Brazilian Case Become a Paradigm? *Government and Opposition* 19 (2): 167–177.

3912. Lamounier, B. 1986. Authoritarian Brazil Revisited: The Impact of Election on the Brazilian Political Liberalization, 1974–1982. *Dados* 29 (3): 283–317.

3913. Lamounier, B. March 1990. Brazil's New Beginning. *Journal of Democracy* 1 (2): 87–98.

3914. Lamounier, B., and A. Desouza. 1991. Changing Attitudes towards Democracy and Institutional Reform in Brazil.* *Dados: Revista de Ciencias Sociais* 34 (3): 311–347.

3915. Lamounier, B., and J. E. Faria. July 1982. A Debate on the Future of the Political Opening of Democracy.* *Revista Mexicana de Sociologia* 44 (3): 999–1071.

3916. Lancaster, C. December 1991. Democracy in Africa. *Foreign Policy* 85: 148–165.

3917. Lancaster, C. 1993. Democratization in Sub-Saharan Africa. *Survival* 35 (3): 38–50.

3918. Lancaster, T. D. September 1989. *See* Giles, M. W. (September 1989).

3919. Lancaster, T. D. January 1994. A New Phase For Spanish Democracy? The General Election Of June 1993. *West European Politics* 17 (1): 183–190.

3920. Landau, D. 1980. *See* Bordo, M. (1980).

3921. Landerman, R. October 1984. *See* Zipp, J. F. (October 1984).

3922. Landers, R. K. February 19, 1988. Why America Doesn't Vote. *Editorial Research Reports* 82–95.

3923. Landi, B. 1984. *See* Lanuti, J. (1984).

3924. Landor, J. February 1993. Democracy by Minority and the Limited Mandate of the Kuwaiti Parliament. *Index on Censorship* 22 (2): 24.

3925. Lane, J. January 1981. *See* Ersson, S. (January 1981).

3926. Lane, J. July 1985. *See* Ersson, S. (July 1985).

3927. Lane, J. July 1991. Interpretations of the Swedish Model. *European Politics* 14 (3): 1–7.

3928. Lane, J. 1993. Democracy: Institutions and Interests. *Politeia (UNISA)* 12 (2): 56–67.

3929. Lane, J., and S. Ersson. April 1989. Unpacking the Political Development Concept. *Political Geography Quarterly* 8: 123–144.

3930. Lane, R. E. 1981. Cognition, Consciousness, and Depression: Effect on the Market and the Democratic State. *Micropolitics* 1 (1): 1–43.

3931. Lane, R. E. June 1985. From Political to Industrial Democracy? *Polity* 17 (4): 623–648.

3932. Lane, R. E. May 1994. Democracies, Institutions, and Persons' Quality of Life and Quality of Persons: A New Role for Government. *Political Theory* 22 (2): 219–252.

3933. Lang, D. G. December 1993. *See* Clinton, W. D. (December 1993).

3934. Lang, G. J. 1993. Hungary: Building Democracy through Law. *Legal Reference Services Quarterly* 13: 31–90.

3935. Lange, P. July 1986. *See* Garrett, G. (July 1986).

3936. Lange, P. June 1991. *See* Alvarez, R. M. (June 1991).

3937. Lange, P., and G. Garrett. August 1985. The Politics of Growth: Strategic Interaction and Economic Performance in the Advanced Industrial Democracies, 1974–1980. *Journal of Politics* 47 (3): 792–827.

3938. Langton, S. February 1984. *See* Desario, J. (February 1984).

3939. Lanoue, D. J. November 1994. *See* Bowles, S. (November 1994).

3940. Lansbury, R. D., and G. J. Prideaux. 1981. Industrial Democracy: Toward an Analytical Framework. *Journal of Economic Issues* 15 (2): 325–338.

3941. Lansing, P.., and L. H. Denbaum. 1985. A Setback for Democracy in Union Elections: *Sadlowski vs. United Steelworkers of America. Denver University Law Review* 62 (2): 653–656.

3942. Lansley, S. 1980. Is This the End of Local Democracy? *New Society* 54 (943): 510–511.

3943. Lanuti, J., and B. Landi. 1984. La Socialdemocracia en America Latina. *Realidad Economica* 2: 77–88.

3944. Lanzalaco, L. 1988. The Institutionalization of Democratic Competition and the Theory of Rational Choice.* *Teoria Politica* 4 (3): 91–113.

3945. LaPalombara, J. March 1988. Partitocrazia. *Wilson Quarterly* 12 (2): 99–117.

3946. Lapidus, G. W. March 1987. Gorbachev and the Reform of the Soviet System. *Daedalus* 116 (2): 1–30.

3947. Lapitan, A. E. June 1989. The Re-Democratization of the Philippines: Old Wine in a New Bottle. *Asian Profile* 17 (3): 235–242.

3948. Lappe, F. M. December 26, 1983. Nicaragua: Revolution and/or Democracy? *Christianity and Crisis* 43: 502–508.

3949. Lappe, F. M. July 1989. Politics for a Troubled Planet. *National Civic Review* 78 (4): 255–258.

3950. Lappe, F. M. September 1990. *See* Boyte, H. C. (September 1990).

3951. Laptef, O. 1974. Rigorously Enforced Laws on Collective Farm Democracy. *Soviet Law and Government* 13 (3): 79–85.

3952. Lara, F., Jr., and H. Morales, Jr. July 1990. The Peasant Movement and the Challenge of Democratization in the Philippines. *Journal of Development Studies* 26 (4): 143–162.

3953. Large, S. S. November 1976. Nishio Suehiro and the Japanese Social Democratic Movement, 1920–1940. *Journal of Asian Studies* 36 (1): 37–56.

3954. Larmore, C. 1993. Symposium on Jurgen Habermas: Factitiousness and Validity: Roots of Radical Democracy.* *Deutsche Zeitschrift für Philosophie* 41 (2): 321–327.

3955. Larmour, P. March 1994. "A Foreign Flower"? Democracy in the South Pacific. *Pacific Studies* 17 (1): 45–77.

3956. Larrain, F. April 1991. Os Desafios Economicos Desenvolvimento Democratico no Chile. *Pesquisa e Planejamento Economico* 21: 25–53.

3957. Larrain Fernandez, H. December 1984. Democracy, Political Parties and Transition: The Chilean Case.* *Estudios Publicos* 15: 89–121.

3958. LaRue, L. H. December 1988. Antitrust and Politics. *Antitrust Bulletin* 33: 745–752.

3959. Lasch, C. June 1975. The Democratization of Culture: A Reappraisal. *Change* 7 (6): 14–24.

3960. Lateef, N. September 1981. Allocating Justice: The Danger of Judicial Triage. *Judicature* 64: 312–319.

3961. Latey, M. 1990. Germany 1: Two Cheers for Democracy. *World Today* 46 (5): 77–78.

3962. Latham, R. June 1993. Democracy and War-Making: Locating the International Liberal Context. *Millennium* 22 (2): 139–164.

3963. Lauber, V. 1978. Ecology Politics and Liberal Democracy. *Government and Opposition* 13 (2): 199–217.

3964. Lauder, H. 1991. Education, Democracy and the Economy. *British Journal of Sociology of Education* 12 (4): 417–431.

3965. Laughton, J. June 1993. Cultural Democracy, Issues of Multiculturalism, and the Arts. *Journal of Arts Management, Law and Society* 23: 121–126.

3966. Laurell, A. C. 1989. The Role of Union Democracy in the Struggle for Workers' Health in Mexico. *International Journal of Health Services* 19 (2): 279–293.

3967. Laurell, A. C. July 1992. Democracy in Mexico: Will the First Be the Last? *New Left Review* 194: 33–53.

3968. Laurell, A. C. December 1992. For an Alternative Social Policy: The Production of Public Services. *Social Justice* 19 (4): 92–109.

3969. Laurent, P. H. April 1976. Old Dilemmas and New Problems in Belgium. *Current History* 70 (415): 168–172, 184.

3970. Lavados, I. 1992. La Educacion Superior en Chile. *Estudios Sociales* (2): 137–153.

3971. Lavau, G. 1990. Brief Remarks on the Risk of Democracy. *Pouvoirs* 52: 35–42.

3972. Laver, M. November 1986. *See* Budge, I. (November 1986).

3973. Laver, M. August 1990. *See* King, G. (August 1990).

3974. Laver, M. J. May 1994. *See* Strom, K. (May 1994).

3975. Lavoie, D. June 1992. Democracy, Markets, and the Legal Order: Notes on the Nature of Politics in a Radical Liberal Society. *Social Philosophy and Policy* 10 (2): 103–120.

3976. Lavoie, D. December 1992. Glasnost and the Knowledge Problem: Rethinking Economic Democracy. *Cato Journal* 11 (3): 435–455.

3977. Lawler, P. A. 1983. Tocqueville on the Place of Liberal Education in a Democracy. *Liberal Education* 69 (4): 301–306.

3978. Lawler, P. A. September 1988. Thoughts on America's "Catholic Movement." *Political Science Reviewer* 18: 197–220.

3979. Lawless, P. August 1988. Urban Development Corporations and Their Alternatives. *Cities* 5: 277–289.

3980. Lawrence, S. E. March 1991. Participation through Mobilization of the Law: Institutions Providing Indigents with Access to the Civil Courts. *Polity* 23 (3): 423–442.

3981. Lawrence, S. E. September 1991. Justice, Democracy, Litigation, and Political Participation. *Social Science Quarterly* 72 (3): 464–477.

3982. Lawson, N. August 1977. How Bullock Got the Sums Wrong: The Bullock Report on Industrial Democracy. *Banker (London)* 127: 31–33.

3983. Lawson, S. January 1993. Conceptual Issues in the Comparative Study of Regime Change and Democratization. *Comparative Politics* 25 (2): 183–205.

3984. Lawson, S. May 1993. Institutionalising Peaceful Conflict: Political Opposition and the Challenge of Democratization in Asia. *Australian Journal of International Affairs* 47 (1): 15–30.

3985. Lawwill, K. S. 1993. *See* Garrison, J. W. (1993).

3986. Laxman, R. K. September 1989. Freedom to Cartoon, Freedom to Speak. *Daedalus* 118 (4): 69–91.

3987. Laycock, D. 1989. Representative Economic Democracy and the Problem of Policy Influence: The Case of Canadian Co-operatives. *Canadian Journal of Political Science* 22 (4): 765–792.

3988. Layne, C. 1994. Kant or Cant. *International Security* 19 (2): 5–49.

3989. Layton-Henry, Z. 1978. Democracy and Reform in the Conservative Party. *Journal of Contemporary History* 13 (4): 653–670.

3990. Lazer, H. June 1976. British Populism: The Labour Party and the Common Market Parliamentary Debate. *Political Science Quarterly* 91 (2): 259–277.

3991. Le Duc, L., J. Jenson, J. H. Pammett, and H. D. Clarke. June 1984. Partisan Instability in Canada: Evidence from a New Panel Study. *American Political Science Review* 78 (2): 470–484.

3992. Le Roux, P. March 1991. The South African Economy and the Democratic Imperative. *Social Justice* 18 (1–2): 230–242.

3993. Le Roy, E. 1992. Peasant Movement and Democratic Transition in Southern Mali.* *Année Africaine* 145–159.

3994. Le Troquer, Y. 1993. The Islamists, Democracy and the Palestinian Issue in Jordan after 1988.* *Revue du Monde Musulman et de la Mediterranee* 68–69: 133–150.

3995. Leane, G. W. G. 1991. Environmental Contacts: A Lesson in Democracy from the Japanese. *University of British Columbia Law Review* 25 (2): 361–385.

3996. Leathers, C. G. July 1989. Thorstein Vebler's Theories of Governmental Failure: The Critic of Capitalism and Democracy Neglected Some Useful

Insights, Hindsight Shows. *American Journal of Economics and Sociology* 48 (3): 293–306.

3997. Leburton, E. 1978. Parliamentary Form of Democracy.* *Socialisme* (146): 183–193.

3998. Lechner, N. 1985. From Revolution to Democracy: The Intellectual Debate in South America.* *Cuestiones Politica* 1: 49–66.

3999. Lechner, N. August 1991. The Search for Lost Community: Challenges to Democracy in Latin America. *International Social Science Journal* 43 (3): 541–553.

4000. Lecomte, P. July 1994. Strategies of Media Power: Drift toward Telecracy?* *Regards sur l'Actualite* 203: 15–35.

4001. Lederer, A. L. December 1985. The Democratization of the Computer. *Business Forum* 10: 22–25.

4002. Lee, H. May 1981. The Prosperity for Democracy in [South] Korea. *Asian Affairs (New York)* 8 (5): 281–286.

4003. Lee, H. Y. January 1993. South Korea in 1992: A Turning Point in Democratization. *Asian Survey* 33 (1): 32–42.

4004. Lee, J. July 1991. Transition to Communist Rule: The Limits of the Democratic Movement in Hong Kong, 1984–1990. *Politics, Administration, and Change* 17: 1–23.

4005. Lee, J. July 1993. The Politics of Consent in Hong Kong's Transition Politics. *Administration and Change* 21: 1–16.

4006. Lee, J. H. 1990. Reunification, Democratization and Education. *International Review of Education* 36 (2): 159–169.

4007. Lee, K. December 1991. The Road to Democracy: Taiwan's Experience. *Asian Profile* 19 (6): 489–504.

4008. Lee, K. C. March 1993. The Socialization through Curricula Control in Korea: An Analysis of Primary School Moral Textbooks. *Korea Observer* 24: 71–90.

4009. Lee, M. C. M., and T. Boasberg. April 1994. Broken Promises: Hong Kong Faces 1997. *Journal of Democracy* 5 (2): 42–57.

4010. Lee, M. M. June 1976. Why Few Women Hold Public Office: Democracy and Sexual Roles. *Political Science Quarterly* 91 (2): 297–314.

4011. Lee, R. 1986. The New Populist Campaign for Economic Democracy: A Rhetorical Exploration. *Quarterly Journal of Speech* 72 (3): 274–289.

4012. Lee, R. D., Jr. August 1991. Legal Parameters of Administration in a Democratic Society: The Case of Australia. *Administration and Society* 23 (2): 201–226.

4013. Lee, S. March 1986. Democratic Propensity in the Soviet Bloc States. *Korea and World Affairs* 10 (1): 72–90.

4014. Lee, S. September 1993. Transitional Politics of [South] Korea: 1987–1992: Activation of Civil Society. *Pacific Affairs* 66 (3): 351–367.

4015. Lee, T. Y. 1979. Striking a Balance between Democracy and Centralism. *International Development Review* 21 (2): 39–40.

4016. Lee, W. November 1993. *See* Bray, M. (November 1993).

4017. Leeson, S. M. March 1979. Philosophic Implications of the Ecological Crisis: The Authoritarian Challenge to Liberalism. *Polity* 11 (3): 303–318.

4018. Lefort, C. November 1985. Human Rights and the Welfare State.* *Esprit* 11: 65–79.

4019. Lefort, C. 1990. Rebirth of Democracy?* *Pouvoirs* 52: 5–22.

4020. Leftwich, A. 1993. Governance, Democracy and Development in the Third World. *Third World Quarterly* 14 (3): 605–624.

4021. Legassick, M. 1985. South Africa in Crisis: What Route to Democracy? *African Affairs* 84 (337): 587–603.

4022. Legault, A. July 1989. Democracy and Chinese Acupuncture circa 2000 BC.* *Cahiers Internationaux de Sociologie* 87: 337–351.

4023. Legum, C. December 1990. The Coming of Africa's Second Independence. *Washington Quarterly* 13 (1): 129–140.

4024. Lehman, J. 1985. Dictatorship and Development in Pacific Asia: Wider Implications. *International Affairs (London)* 64 (4): 591–606.

4025. Lehmbruch, G. March 1993. Consociational Democracy and Corporatism in Switzerland. *Publius* 23 (2): 43–60.

4026. Lehner, F. 1984. Consociational Democracy in Switzerland: A Political-Economic Explanation and Some Empirical Evidence. *European Journal of Political Research* 12 (1): 25–42.

4027. Lehner, O. 1983. The Development of Austrian Social Democracy as Illustrated by Its Understanding of Property.* *Zeitgeschichte* 11 (1): 1–18.

4028. Lehner, P. U. 1984. Striving for the Democratization of Business.* *Oesterreichische Zeitschrift für Politikwissenschaft* 13 (3): 353–362.

4029. Leibfried, S. October 1978. Public Assistance in the United States and the Federal Republic of Germany: Does Social Democracy Make a Difference? *Comparative Politics* 11 (1): 59–76.

4030. Leibovici, M. February 1991. Rosa Luxemburg (Revolution and Democracy).* *Revue Française de Science Politique* 41 (1): 59–80.

4031. Leiva, F. I. June 1988. *See* Petras, J. (June 1988).

4032. Leiva, F. I., and J. Petras. September 1986. Chile's Poor in the Struggle for Democracy. *Latin American Perspectives* 13 (4): 5–25.

4033. Leiva, F. I., and J. Petras. July 1987. Chile: New Urban Movements and the Transition to Democracy. *Monthly Review* 39 (3): 109–124.

4034. Lejeune, A. December 1981. Chile's Mild Authoritarianism. *Policy Review* 15: 160–165.

4035. Lekachman, R. 1978. Capitalism, Socialism, and Democracy. *Commentary* 65 (4): 54–56.

4036. Lelart, M. 1992. The International Monetary Fund and Democracy.* *Le Trimestre du Monde* 17: 91–107.

4037. Leliaert, R. M. January 1976. The Religious Significance of Democracy in the Thoughts of Orestos A. Brownson. *Review of Politics* 38 (1): 3–27.

4038. Lemarchand, R. October 1992. Africa's Troubled Transitions. *Journal of Democracy* 3 (4): 98–109.

4039. Lembcke, J., and M. Hartlandsberg. 1981. Economic Democracy: Dealing Capital In or Out in the 80s. *Contemporary Crises* 5 (1): 1–13.

4040. Lembruch, G. 1975. Consociational Democracy in the International System. *European Journal of Political Research* 3 (4): 377–391.

4041. LeMoyne, J. June 1989. El Salvador's Forgotten War. *Foreign Affairs* 68 (3): 105–125.

4042. Lendvai, P. July 1990. Eastern Europe: Liberalism vs. Nationalism. *World Today* 46 (7): 131–133.

4043. Leng, S. C., and C. Y. Lin. December 1993. Political Change on Taiwan: Transition to Democracy? *China Quarterly* (136): 805–838.

4044. Lengnick-Hall, C. June 1992. *See* Lengnick-Hall, M. L. (June 1992).

4045. Lengnick-Hall, M. L., and C. Leng-nick-Hall. June 1992. Effective Participative Decision Making: A Joint Responsibility for Success. *Employee Responsibilities and Rights Journal* 5 (2): 101–116.

4046. Lennertz, J. E. September 1986. Human Rights and Institutional Process: Abortion Policy in Six Nations. *Policy Studies Journal* 15 (1): 147–157.

4047. Lennox-Boyd, M. April 1994. Turks and Caicos Islands: A New Constitutional Plan from the British Government. *Parliamentarian* 75: 99–104.

4048. Lentini, P. March 1994. Women and 1989 Elections to the USSR Congress of People's Deputies. *Coexistence* 31 (1): 1–28.

4049. Leo Grande, W. M. March 1979. The Theory and Practice of Socialist Democracy in Cuba: Mechanisms of Elite Accountability. *Studies in Comparative Communism* 12 (1): 39–62.

4050. Leo Grande, W. M. January 1986. The United States and Latin America. *Current History* 85 (507): 1–4, 40–42.

4051. Leo Grande, W. M. March 1990. After the Battle of San Salvador. *World Policy Journal* 7 (2): 331–356.

4052. Leon, F. July 1992. Cuba: Procesos y Dilemas. *Estudios Internacionales* 25: 365–377.

4053. Leonard, J. December 1987. *See* Leveillee, J. (December 1987).

4054. Leonard, Y. (ed.). 1994. Le Portugal: Vingt Ans àpres la Revolution des Oeillets. *Notes et Etudes Documentaires* (6): 1–238. Selection of articles.

4055. Leonardi, R. April 1984. The Italian Parliamentary Elections of 1983: The Making and Unmaking of Myths. *West European Politics* 7 (2): 188–191.

4056. Leonardson, G., and D. Mircev. January 1979. A Structure for Participatory Democracy in the Local Community: The Yugoslav Constitution of 1974. *Comparative Politics* 11 (2): 189–203.

4057. Leonidov, E. November 1982. Genuine and Illusory Democracy.* *La Vie Internationale* 11: 3–11.

4058. Leorardi, L. July 1994. Open Society and Democracy. Reflections Inspired by Ralf Dahrendorf's Political Sociology.* *Rassegna Italiana di Sociologia* 35 (3): 309–333.

4059. Lepsius, M. R. March 1985. The Nation and Nationalism in Germany. *Social Research* 52 (1): 43–64.

4060. Lerner, B. 1981. Representative Democracy, Men of Zeal, and Testing Legislation. *American Psychologist* 36 (3): 270–275.

4061. Lerner, B. April 1985. The Revival of Political Democracy in Latin America. *Revista Mexicana de Ciencias Politicas y Sociales* 120: 135–148.

4062. Lesage, M. December 1992. The Role of the (East European) Head of State During the Period of Transition.* *Revue d'Etudes Comparatives Est-Ouest* 23 (4): 41–48.

4063. Lesch, A. M. September 1989. Democracy in Doses: Mubarak Launches His Second Term as President. *Arab Studies Quarterly* 11 (4): 87–107.

4064. Lesemann, F. 1978. Local Community Service Centers and Democratization of Health. *Canada's Mental Health* 26 (1): 14–17.

4065. Lesquins, J. L. February 1993. Uneasiness in Regard to Modern Concepts of Democracy.* *Temps Modernes* 49 (559): 97–112.

4066. Lessnoff, M. 1979. Capitalism, Socialism and Democracy. *Political Studies* 27 (4): 594–602.

4067. Letamendia, P. December 1989. Back to Democracy in Chile.* *Etudes:* 497–607.

4068. Letterie, J. W., and R. A. G. Van Puyenbroek. July 1985. Welfare Policies: The Interaction Effects of Collective Demands and Liberal Democracy in a Cross-Sectional Analysis of 115 Countries. *Acta Politica* 20 (3): 331–352.

4069. Letwin, S. R. March 1979. Politics and Language: Why There Are No "Authoritarianism." *Policy Review* 8: 97–102.

4070. Leung, J. January 1986. Community Development in Hong Kong: Contributions towards Democratization. *Community Development Journal* 21 (1): 3–10.

4071. Leuthold, D. September 1979. *See* Gafke, R. (September 1979).

4072. Levada, I. December 1992. The Strains and Stresses of Democracy: Russian Public Opinion in 1991.* *Politique Etrangere* 57 (1): 89–100.

4073. Levantrosser, W. F. March 1981. Financing Presidential Campaigns: The Impact of Reform Finance Laws on the Democratic Presidential Nomination of 1976. *Presidential Studies Quarterly* 11 (2): 280–288.

4074. Leveillee, J., and J. Leonard. December 1987. The Montreal Citizens' Movement Comes to Power. *International Journal of Urban and Regional Research* 11: 567–580.

4075. Leven, P. 1978. Labor Democracy in Difficulties: Case Study.* *Revista Usem* (48): 26–28.

4076. Levi, M. D. December 1994. *See* Goldberg, M. A. (December 1994).

4077. Levine, A. 1978. Conceptual Problem for Liberal Democracy. *Journal of Philosophy* 75 (6): 302–308.

4078. Levine, A. December 1992. Soft on Capitalism: Prospects for Secondary Associations and Democratic Governance. *Politics and Society* 20 (4): 487–492.

4079. Levine, B. B. December 1988. The Shifting Sands of Haitian Legitimacy. *Caribbean Review* 16 (2): 3, 47.

4080. Levine, D. H. February 1976. Democracy and the Church in Venezuela. *Journal of Interamerican Studies and World Affairs* 18 (1): 3–24.

4081. Levine, D. H. April 1988. Paradigm Lost: Dependence to Democracy. *World Politics* 40 (3): 377–384.

4082. Levine, G. D. June 1977. Should Civil Disobedience Be Legalized? Reflections on Coercive Protest and the Democratic Regime of Law. *Southwestern Law Journal* 31: 617–648.

4083. Levine, M. A. March 1988. Is a Presidential System for Everyone? Some Reflections on the Dutch Rejection of an American-Style Presidency. *Presidential Studies Quarterly* 18 (2): 277–281.

4084. Levine, R. M. February 1979. Brazil's Definition of Democracy. *Current History* 76 (444): 70–73, 83.

4085. Levine, R. M. February 1980. Brazil: Democracy without Adjectives. *Current History* 78 (454): 49–52, 82–83.

4086. Levine, R. M. February 1982. Brazil: The Dimensions of Democratization. *Current History* 81 (472): 60–63, 86–87.

4087. Levine, S., and N. S. Roberts. July 1994. The New Zealand General Elections and Electoral Referendum of 1993. *Political Science* 46 (1): 40–69.

4088. Levine, V. T. 1992. Administrative Corruption and Democratization in Africa: Aspects of the Theoretical Agenda. *Corruption and Reform* 7 (3): 271–278.

4089. Levinson, M. June 1985. Brazil's Fragile Democracy. *Worldview* 28: 4–6.

4090. Levitt, S. D. March 1994. An Empirical Test of Competing Explanations for the Midterm Gap in the U.S. House. *Economics and Politics* 6 (1): 25–37.

4091. Levy, E. March 20, 1991. Brazzaville s'Enivre de Mots. *Jeune Afrique* 31: 20–22.

4092. Levy, F. June 1979. On Understanding Proposition 13. *Public Interest* 56: 66–89.

4093. Levy, J., and N. D. Mills. December 1984. The Challenge to Democratic Reformism in Ecuador. *Studies in Comparative International Development* 18 (4): 3–33.

4094. Levy, L. April 1989. Vers le Pluralisme en Yougoslavie: La specificite Slovene. *Cosmopolitiques* 106–111.

4095. Levy-Garboua, L. February 1991. General Interest and Redistribution with Self-Interested Voters: Social Contract Revisited. *Public Choice* 69 (2): 175–196.

4096. Lew, R. June 1989. La Chine en Transes. *Monde Diplomatique* 36: 1+.

4097. Lewandowski, M. J. June 1993. Democracy in the Workplace: Working Women in Midwestern Unions, 1943–1945. *Prologue: Quarterly of the National Archives* 25 (2): 157–169.

4098. Lewin, M. 1987. Kurt Lewin and the Invisible Bird on the Flagpole: A Reply to Graebner. *Journal of Social Issues* 43 (3): 23–139.

4099. Lewis, B. March 1994. Why Turkey Is the Only Muslim Democracy. *Middle East Quarterly* 1 (1): 41–49.

4100. Lewis, G. K. December 1980. On the Limits of the New Cuban Presence in the Caribbean. *Caribbean Studies* 9 (1): 33–35.

4101. Lewis, J. R., and A. M. Williams. April 1984. Social Cleavages and Electoral Performance: The Social Basis of Portuguese Political Parties. *West European Politics* 7 (2): 119–137.

4102. Lewis, K. A. December 1993. *See* Abrams, B. A. (December 1993).

4103. Lewis, P. G. December 1990. Democratization in Eastern Europe. *Coexistence* 27 (4): 245–267.

4104. Lewis, P. M. July 1994. Endgame in Nigeria: The Politics of Failed Democratic Transition. *African Affairs* 93 (372): 323–340.

4105. Lewis, W. June 1990. Algeria and the Magreb at the Turning Point. *Mediterranean Quarterly* 1 (3): 62–74.

4106. Lewis-Beck, M. S. 1987. *See* Brunk, G. G. (1987).

4107. Lewis-Beck, M. S. December 1994. *See* Burkhart, R. E. (December 1994).

4108. Lewy, G. September 1983. Can Democracy Keep Secrets? Do We Need an Official Secrets Act? *Policy Review* 26: 17–29.

4109. Lewy, G. September 1987. Does America Need a Verfassungsschutzbericht? *Orbis* 31 (3): 275–292.

4110. Leymarie, P. October 1992. Les Voices Incertaines de la Cooperation Franco-Africaine: Deux Ans de Malentendus et de Deceptions. *Monde Diplomatique* 39: 22–23.

4111. Leys, C., and J. S. Saul. March 1994. Liberation without Democracy: The SWAPO Crisis of 1976. *Journal of Southern African Studies* 20 (1): 123–147.

4112. Li, H. 1989. The Democratic Management of Enterprises and Workers Awareness of Democracy. *Chinese Economic Studies* 22 (4): 69–80.

4113. Li, H. L. 1987. How to Implement a High-Level Democracy. *Chinese Law and Government* 20 (1): 57–60.

4114. Li, I. 1976. Concerning Socialist Democracy and Legal System: Dedicated to Chairman Mao and the Fourth National People's Congress. *Issues and Studies* 12 (1): 110–148.

4115. Li, I. C. 1977. Socialist Democracy and the Legal System. *Chinese Law and Government* 10 (3): 15–75.

4116. Li, J. March 1994. *See* Mayer, W. (March 1994).

4117. Li, S. 1988. The Road to Freedom: Can Communist Societies Evolve into Democracy. *World Affairs* 150 (3): 183–189.

4118. Li, S. June 1988. The Road to Freedom: Can Communist Societies Evolve into Democracy.* *Issues and Studies* 24 (6): 92–104.

4119. Liang, Y. Y. March 1994. The Political Reforms Adopted by the Hong Kong Legislative Council. *Issues and Studies* 30 (3): 129–133.

4120. Liao, H. S. June 1991. Recent Political Reform in Mongolia. *Issues and Studies* 27 (6): 86–101.

4121. Licht, R. A. March 1993. Communal Democracy, Modernity, and the Jewish Political Tradition. *Jewish Political Studies Review* 5 (1–2): 95–127.

4122. Licht, S. June 1989. The Yugoslav Experience: The Failure of Reform without Democracy. *New Politics* 2: 152–165.

4123. Lichtenstein, N. 1982. Industrial Democracy, Contract Unionism, and the National War Labor Board. *Labor Law Journal* 33 (8): 524–531.

4124. Lichtenstein, P. M. 1984. Economic Democracy: The Rawls-Vanek-Sraffa Connection. *Review of Social History* 42 (2): 170–181.

4125. Lichtenstein, P. M. July 1984. Some Theoretical Coordinates of Radical Liberalism. *American Journal of Economics and Sociology* 43 (3): 333–339.

4126. Lichtenstein, P. M. January 1985. Radical Liberalism and Radical Education: A Synthesis and Critical Evaluation of Illich, Freire, and Dewcy. *American Journal of Economics and Sociology* 44 (1): 39–53.

4127. Liddle, R. W. July 1992. Indonesia's Democratic Past and Future. *Comparative Politics* 24 (4): 443–462.

4128. Lie, J. 1991. Democratization and Its Discontents: Origins of the Present Crisis in South Korea. *Monthly Review* 42 (9): 38–52.

4129. Lie, J. 1991. The Prospects for Economic Democracy in South Korea. *Economic and Industrial Democracy* 12 (4): 501–513.

4130. Lieberam, E. 1990. *See* Dost, A. (1990).

4131. Liebman, L. 1974. Social Intervention in a Democracy. *Public Interest* 34: 14–29.

4132. Liebscher, G. 1979. *See* Krause, R. (1979).

4133. Lienesch, M. January 1983. Historical Theory and Political Reform: Two Perspectives on Confederation Politics. *Review of Politics* 45 (1): 94–115.

4134. Lienesch, M. November 1992. Wo(e)begon(e) Democracy. *American Journal of Political Science* 36 (4): 1004–1014.

4135. Lienesch, M. November 1992. *See* Mueller, J. (November 1992).

4136. Lieten, G. K. 1978. Scope for People's Democracy in Indian Studies: Case for Kerala. *Journal of Contemporary Asia* 8 (4): 513–530.

4137. Lievrouw, L. A. July 1994. Information Resources and Democracy: Understanding the Paradox. *Journal of the American Society for Information Science* 45 (6): 350–357.

4138. Light, M. December 1993. Democracy Russian-Style. *World Today* 49 (12): 228–231.

4139. Lijphart, A. September 1979. Consociation and Federation: Conceptual and Empirical Links. *Canadian Journal of Political Science* 12 (3): 499–516.

4140. Lijphart, A. 1981. Power Sharing vs. Majority Rule: Patterns of Cabinet Formation in Twenty Democracies. *Government and Opposition* 16 (4): 395–413.

4141. Lijphart, A. 1982. The Relative Salience of the Socioeconomic and Religious Issue Dimensions: Coalition Formations in Ten Western Democracies, 1919–1979. *European Journal of Political Research* 10 (3): 201–211.

4142. Lijphart, A. January 1984. The Politics of Accommodation: Reflections Fifteen Years Later. *Acta Politica* 19: 9–18.

4143. Lijphart, A. July 1984. A Note on the Meaning of Cabinet Durability. *Comparative Political Studies* 17 (2): 163–166.

4144. Lijphart, A. March 1985. Non-Majoritarian Democracy: A Comparison of Federal and Consociational Theories. *Publius* 15 (2): 3–15.

4145. Lijphart, A. December 1985. The Pattern of Electoral Rules in the United States: A Deviant Case among the Industrialized Democracies. *Government and Opposition* 20 (1): 18–28.

4146. Lijphart, A. 1988. Citation Classic: The Politics of Accommodation—Pluralism and Democracy in the Netherlands. *Current Contents: Social and Behavioral Sciences* 39 (14): 14.

4147. Lijphart, A. January 1989. Democratic Political Systems: Types, Cases, Causes and Consequences. *Journal of Theoretical Politics* 1 (1): 33–48.

4148. Lijphart, A. June 1990. The Political Consequences of Electoral Laws, 1945–1985. *American Political Science Review* 84 (2): 481–496.

4149. Lijphart, A. December 1990. The Southern European Examples of Democratization: Six Lessons for Latin America. *Government and Opposition* 25 (1): 68–84.

4150. Lijphart, A. August 1991. Majority Rule in Theory and Practice: The Tenacity of a Flawed Paradigm. *International Social Science Journal* 43 (3): 483–493.

4151. Lijphart, A. April 1992. Democratization and Constitutional Choices in Czecho-Slovakia, Hungary and Poland, 1989–1991. *Journal of Theoretical Politics* 4 (2): 207–223.

4152. Lijphart, A. 1994. On S. E. Finer's Electoral Theory. *Government and Opposition* 29 (5): 623–635.

4153. Lijphart, A. January 1994. Democracies: Forms, Performance, and Constitutional Engineering. *European Journal of Political Research* 25 (1): 1–17.

4154. Lijphart, A., T. C. Bruneau, P. N. Diamandour, and R. Gunther. January 1988. A Mediterranean Model of Democracy: The Southern European Democracies in Comparative Perspective. *West European Politics* 11 (1): 7–25.

4155. Lijphart, A., and M. M. L. Crepaz. April 1991. Corporatism and Consensus Democracy in Eighteen Countries: Conceptual and Empirical Linkages. *British Journal of Political Science* 21 (2): 235–246.

4156. Limam, Z. July 8, 1993. *See* Godeau, R. (July 8, 1993).

4157. Limberes, N. M. January 1986. The Greek Election of June 1985: A Socialist Entrenchment. *West European Politics* 9: 142–147.

4158. Limongi, F. June 1993. *See* Przeworski, A. (June 1993).

4159. Limongi, F. July 1994. *See* Przeworski, A. (July 1994).

4160. Limonov, E. September 1992. A Sham Democracy and a Sham Revolution. *Russian Politics and Law* 31 (2): 40–44.

4161. Lin, C. Y. December 1993. *See* Leng, S. C. (December 1993).

4162. Lin, T. T. 1991. The Role of the Mass Media in the ROC's Political Democratization. *Issues and Studies* 27 (10): 158–172.

4163. Lin, Z. 1990. What Kind of Democracy Do We Need? *World Affairs* 152 (3): 167–172.

4164. Lind, G., J. Sandberger, and T. Bargel. September 1981. Moral Judgment, Ego Strength, and Democratic Orientation: Some Theoretical Contiguities and Empirical Findings. *Political Psychology* 3 (3–4): 70–110.

4165. Lind, J. E. September 1994. Dominance and Democracy: The Legacy of Woman Suffrage for Voting Rights. *UCLA Women's Law Journal* 5 (1): 103–216.

4166. Lindbeck, A., and J. W. Weibull. June 1993. A Model of Political Equilibrium in a Representative Democracy. *Journal of Public Economics* 51 (2): 195–209.

4167. Lindblad, S., and E. Wallin. January 1993. On Transitions of Power, Democracy and Education in Sweden. *Journal of Curriculum Studies* 25 (1): 77–88.

4168. Lindblom, C. 1978. Capitalism, Socialism, and Democracy: A Symposium. *Commentary* 65 (4): 57–58.

4169. Lindblom, C. E. March 1982. Another State of Mind. *American Political Science Review* 76 (1): 9–21.

4170. Linde, J. E. December 1984. Title III of the Labor Management Relations and Disclosure Act: For Greater Judicial Protection of Union Democracy and Local Autonomy. *Journal of Corporation Law* 9 (2): 271–320.

4171. Lindenberg, M., and S. Devaranjan. January 1993. Prescribing Strong Economic Medicine: Revisiting the Myths about Structural Adjustment, Democracy, and Economic Performance in Developing Countries. *Comparative Politics* 25 (2): 169–182.

4172. Lindenfeld, F. March 1990. *See* Krimerman, L. (March 1990).

4173. Lindholm, L. M. April 1988. Judicial Supremacy, Right-To-Life and the Abortion Decision. *Public Affairs Quarterly* 2: 1–20.

4174. Lindner, R. 1985. Nicaragua Way in National Democracy.* *Osteuropa* 35 (7–8): 593–603.

4175. Lindsay, T. K. February 1992. Aristotle's Qualified Defense of Democracy Through "Political Mixing." *Journal of Politics* 54 (1): 101–119.

4176. Lindsay, T. K. August 1992. Liberty, Equality, Power: Aristotle's Critique of the Democratic "Presupposition." *American Journal of Political Science* 36 (3): 743–761.

4177. Lindsey, B. December 1991. System Overload: The Size of Our Government Is Unsafe for Democracy. *Policy Review* 55: 52–56.

4178. Ling, D. L. June 1977. Education in the Western World: Looking toward the Year 2000. *International Educational and Cultural Exchange* 13 (1): 25–32.

4179. Ling, T., and R. H. Myers. April 1990. Winds of Democracy: The 1989 Taiwan Elections. *Asian Survey* 30 (4): 360–379.

4180. Ling, T., and R. H. Myers. March 1992. Surviving the Rough-and-Tumble of Presidential Politics in an Emerging Democracy: The 1990 Elections in the Republic of China on Taiwan. *China Quarterly* (129): 123–148.

4181. Lingle, C. December 1989. Populism and Rent-Seeking in Post-Apartheid South Africa. *Politikon* 16 (2): 5–21.

4182. Lingle, C. 1991. An Austrian Public Choice Analysis of Representative Democracy.* *Hallinnon Tutimus* 10 (4): 252–258.

4183. Lingle, C. January 1991. The EC Social Charter, Social Democracy and Post-1992 Europe. *West European Politics* 14: 129–138.

4184. Link, R. 1977. Open Government: Democracy? You Don't Know the Meaning of the Word until You've Seen the

Swedish Government in Action. *Sweden Now* 11 (5): 34–37+.

4185. Linstone, H. A. 1989. Mediacracy, Mediocracy, or New Democracy: Where Are the Information-Age Jeffersons and Madisons When We Need Them? *Technological Forecasting and Social Change* 36 (1–2): 153–169.

4186. Linz, J. J. December 1979. Europe's Southern Frontier: Evolving Trends. *Daedalus* 108 (1): 175–209.

4187. Linz, J. J. December 1986. From Authoritarianism to Democracy.* *Estudios Publicos* 23: 5–58.

4188. Linz, J. J. March 1987. *See* Diamond, L. (March 1987).

4189. Linz, J. J. June 1990. Transitions to Democracy. *Washington Quarterly* 13 (3): 143–164.

4190. Linz, J. J. September 1990. Presidents vs. Parliaments: The Virtues of Parliamentarism. *Journal of Democracy* 1 (4): 84–91.

4191. Linz, J. J. 1991. Church and State from the Civil War to the Return of Democracy. *Daedalus* 120 (3): 159–178.

4192. Linz, J. J. January 1992. *See* Shain, Y. (January 1992).

4193. Linz, J. J., and A. Stepan. March 1992. Political Identities and Electoral Sequences: Spain, the Soviet Union, and Yugoslavia. *Daedalus* 121 (2): 123–139.

4194. Lipietz, A. March 1990. Post-Fordism and Democracy.* *Les Temps Modernes* 524: 97–121.

4195. Lipietz, A. 1991. Democracy after Fordism. *Argument* 33 (5): 677–694.

4196. Lipkin, R. J. March 1994. The Quest for the Common Good: Neutrality and Deliberative Democracy in Sunstein's Conception of America Constitutionalism. *Connecticut Law Review* 26: 1039.

4197. Lippmann, W. March 1985. The Public Policy. *World Affairs* 147 (4): 315–339.

4198. Lipschitz, G. 1990. Hungary from Socialist Legality to Constitutional State. *Rivista Trimestrale di Diritto Publico* 2: 563–586.

4199. Lipset, S. M. 1978. Capitalism, Socialism, and Democracy. *Commentary* 65 (4): 58–59.

4200. Lipset, S. M. December 1978. Marx, Engels, and American Political Parties. *Wilson Quarterly* 2 (1): 90–104.

4201. Lipset, S. M. March 1987. *See* Diamond, L. (March 1987).

4202. Lipset, S. M. April 1987. Notes on Democratic Systems and the Social Sciences.* *Biblioteca della Liberta* 97: 73–89.

4203. Lipset, S. M. 1988. Citation Classic: Union Democracy—The Internal Politics of the International Typographical Union. *Current Contents: Social & Behavioral Sciences* 20 (16): 16.

4204. Lipset, S. M. January 1994. The Requisites of Democracy Revisited. *Biblioteca della Liberta* 124: 3–40.

4205. Lipset, S. M. February 1994. The Social Requisites of Democracy Revisited: 1993 Presidential Address. *American Sociological Review* 59 (1): 1–22.

4206. Lipset, S. M., K. Seong, and J. C. Torres. May 1993. A Comparative Analysis of the Social Requisites of Democracy. *International Social Science Journal* 45 (2): 155–175.

4207. Lipson, L. November 1976. European Responses to the American Revolution. *Annals of the American Academy of Political and Social Science* 428: 22–32.

4208. Lipson, L. 1989. Power, Principles, and Democracy. *Political Science* 41 (2): 1–17.

4209. Lipton, D. June 1990. *See* Sachs, J. (June 1990).

4210. Lipton, L. M. December 1985. The Philosophy of Democracy: Can Its Contradiction Be Reconciled. *Journal of International Affairs* 38 (2): 151–160.

4211. Lira, E. September 1990. *See* Becker, D. (September 1990).

4212. Lissner, W. January 1979. On the Centenary of Progress and Poverty. *American Journal of Economics and Sociology* 38 (1): 1–16.

4213. Listhaug, O., S. E. MacDonald, and G. Rabinowitz. December 1994. Issue Perception of Parties and Candidates: A Comparison of Norway and the United States. *Scandinavian Political Studies* 17 (4): 273–288.

4214. Little, D. R. May 1980. Regional Legislatures in the Soviet Political System. *Legislative Studies Quarterly* 5 (2): 233–246.

4215. Little, R. October 1977. *See* McKinlay, R. D. (October 1977).

4216. Little, W. June 1994. Democracy in Latin America: Problems and Prospects. *Democratization* 1 (2): 193–208.

4217. Liu, L. Y. April 1982. Taiwan's Role in the Western Pacific. *Current History* 81 (474): 164–167, 176–177.

4218. Liu, L. Y. June 1991. Self-Determination, Independence and the Process of Democratization in Taiwan. *Asian Profile* 19 (3): 197–205.

4219. Liu, S. C. 1989. The 1989 Peking Student Pro-Democracy Movement in Retrospect. *Issues and Studies* 25 (12): 31–46.

4220. Liu, W. November 1992. Politics on Taiwan: Democratization and Relations with the Mainland. *China Newsletter* 2–7+.

4221. Liu, W. H. December 1991. *See* Richdale, K. G. (December 1991).

4222. Liviga, A. J. July 1990. *See* Van Donge, J. K. (July 1990).

4223. Livingston, W. S. November 1976. Britain and America: The Institutionalization of Accountability. *Journal of Politics* 38 (4): 879–894.

4224. Livingstone, J. June 1983. The Presidency and the People. *Democracy* 3 (3): 50–57.

4225. Livingstone, K. March 1992. Can Democracy Survive in Russia. *New Left Review* (192): 98–104.

4226. Lloyd, A. 1983. Europe Examines Electronic Democracy. *New Scientist* 98 (1360): 634–635.

4227. Lloyd, J. April 1993. Democracy in Russia. *Political Quarterly* 64 (2): 147–155.

4228. Lo, C. W. H. December 1992. Trials on Dissidents of the 1989 Democracy Movement: The Limits of Criminal Justice under Teng Hsiao-Ping. *Issues and Studies* 28 (12): 23–45.

4229. Lo, S. December 1989. Aspects of Political Development in Macao. *China Quarterly* 120: 837–851.

4230. Lo, S. May 1990. Democratization in Hong Kong: Reasons, Phases, and Limits. *Issues and Studies* 26 (5): 100–117.

4231. Loaeza, S. October 1991. Los Partidos y el Cambio Politico en Mexico. *Revista de Estudios Politicos* 74: 389–404.

4232. Lobel, J. December 1987. The New Nicaraguan Constitution: Uniting Participatory and Representative Democracy. *Monthly Review* 39 (7): 1–17.

4233. Lobel, J. 1988. The Meaning of Democracy: Representative and Participatory Democracy in the New Nicaraguan Constitution. *University of Pittsburgh Law Review* 49 (3): 823–889.

4234. Lobkowicz, N. 1977. From Democratization to Bureaucratization: Sins of Secondary School Policies.* *Zeitschrift für Politik* 24 (3): 291–303.

4235. Locander, R. March 1978. The President, the Press, and the Public: Friends and Enemies of Democracy. *Presidential Studies Quarterly* 8 (2): 140–150.

4236. Lockerbie, B. February 1994. *See* Wielhouwer, P. W. (February 1994).

4237. Lodge, J. January 1994. The European Parliament and the Authority Democracy Crises. *Annals of the American Academy of Political and Social Science* 531: 69–83.

4238. Loebl, E. 1978. Capitalism, Socialism, and Democracy. *Commentary* 65 (4): 59–63.

4239. Loew, K. January 1974. Das Selbstverstaendis des Grundgesetzes und Wirklich Allgemeine Wahlen. *Politische Studien* 25: 19–29.

4240. Loewy, A. H. March 1993. Freedom of Speech as a Product of Democracy. *University of Richmond Law Review* 27: 427–439.

4241. Loffredo, S. April 1993. Poverty, Democracy and Constitutional Law. *University of Pennsylvania Law Review* 141 (4): 1277–1389.

4242. Loftager, J. 1990. Public Opinion between State and Civil Society.* *Politica* 22 (2): 208–223.

4243. Logue, J. 1977. Industrial Democracy, Yesterday and Today. *Scandinavian Review* 2: 4–11.

4244. Logue, J. December 1984. *See* Hancock, M. D. (December 1984).

4245. Logue, J. 1985. Stable Democracy without Majorities? Scandinavian Parliamentary Government Today. *Policy Studies Review* 73: 39–45.

4246. Logue, J., and E. S. Einhorn. 1988. Restraining the Governors: Limiting the Strong State. *Scandinavian Political Studies* 11 (1): 45–67.

4247. Lomasney, K. July 1993. *See* Halperin, M. H. (July 1993).

4248. Lombardi, G. March 1982. Democracy and Constitution in Italy. *Revista de Estudios Politicos* 26: 119–125.

4249. Lombardi, G. May 1982. Currents and Internal Democracy in Political Parties.* *Revista de Estudios Politicos* 27: 7–28.

4250. Lombardo, P. A. 1981. Historic Echoes: Romantic Emphasis in Tocqueville's *Democracy in America*. *Journal of Thought* 16 (2): 67–80.

4251. Lomme, R. June 1988. L'URSS et la Social-Democratie Europeenne: Enjeux Strategiques et Ideologiques d'un Dialogue. *Cosmopolitiques* 47–53.

4252. London, B., and B. A. Williams. December 1990. National Politics, International Dependency, and Basic Needs Provision: A Cross-National Analysis. *Social Forces* 69 (2): 565–584.

4253. Lonergan, E. August 1986. *See* Tidmarch, C. M. (August 1986).

4254. Long, J. 1979. Organization and Management: Industrial Democracy. *Local Government Studies* 5 (2): 54–56.

4255. Long, N. E. September 1987. The Citizenships: Local, State, and National. *Urban Affairs Quarterly* 23 (1): 4–14.

4256. Lonky, E., J. M. Reihman, and R. C. Serlin. June 1981. Political Values and Moral Judgement in Adolescence. *Youth and Society* 12 (4): 423–441.

4257. Lonowski, D. December 1993. Capitalism and Democracy: A Play. *PS: Political Science & Politics* 26 (4): 760–763.

4258. Loomis, B. A. June 1979. The Congressional Office as a Small Business: New Members Set Up Shop. *Publius* 9 (3): 35–55.

4259. Lopez, M. January 1993. *See* Harris, E. (January 1993).

4260. Lopez-Escobar, E., and A. Faus Belau. April 1985. Broadcasting in Spain: A History of Heavy-Handed State Control. *West European Politics* 8: 122–136.

4261. Lopez-Nieto, L. July 1993. *See* Alda Fernandez, M. (July 1993).

4262. Lopez-Pintor, R. July 1981. The Socio-Economic Determinants of Political Action in the Democratic Transition.* *Revista Espanola de Investigaciones Sociologicas* 15: 9–31.

4263. Lorenzen, S. A. 1977. *See* Hill, L. E. (1977).

4264. Lorig, W. 1984. Protest Behavior and New Social Movements: Comments on the Present Challenges of the Parliamentary Democracy. *Gegenwartskunde: Gesellschaft, Staat, Erziehung* 33 (2): 163–174.

4265. Lorincz, L. December 1992. Constitutional and Administrative Reform in Hungary.* *Revue d'Etudes Comparatives Est-Ouest* 23 (4): 49–61.

4266. Los, M. 1991. Legitimation, State and Law in the Central-European Return to Democracy. *Polish Sociological Bulletin* 96: 231–249.

4267. Loughlin, K. September 1993. *See* Brooks, A. (September 1993).

4268. Loulis, J. C. September 1981. *See* Alexander, G. M. (September 1981).

4269. Love, N. S. 1987. Class or Mass: Marx, Nietzsche, and Liberal Democracy. *Studies in Soviet Thought* 33 (1): 43–64.

4270. Love, N. S. December 1989. Foucault and Habermas on Discourse and Democracy. *Polity* 22 (2): 269–293.

4271. Loveman, B. June 1994. Protected Democracies and Military Guardianship: Political Transitions in Latin America, 1978–1993. *Journal of Interamerican Studies and World Affairs* 36 (2): 105–189.

4272. Low, K. 1975. Civil and Socialist Democracy Viewed by Marxist-Leninist Party.* *Zeitschrift für Politik* 22 (2): 95–110.

4273. Lowe, M. 1986. The BMA and Trade Union Democracy: New Style Council Elections. *British Medical Journal* 292 (6512): 70–72.

4274. Lowenberg, G., and C. L. Kim. February 1978. Comparing the Representativeness of Parliaments. *Legislative Studies Quarterly* 3 (1): 27–49.

4275. Lowenthal, A. F. January 1988. The United States and South America. *Current History* 87 (525): 1–4, 42–43.

4276. Lowenthal, A. F. June 1991. *See* Hakim, P. (June 1991).

4277. Lowenthal, A. F. 1993. Latin America: Ready for Partnership? *Foreign Affairs* 72 (1): 74–92.

4278. Lowenthal, A. F. October 1994. *See* Armijo, L. E. (October 1994).

4279. Lowenthal, R. June 1976. Social Transformation and Democratic Legitimacy. *Social Research* 43 (2): 246–275.

4280. Lowenthal, R. 1977. Post-War Transformation of European Social Democracy. *Dissent* 24 (3): 248–260.

4281. Lowenthal, R. 1979. Political Legitimacy and Cultural Change in West and East. *Social Research* 46 (3): 401–435.

4282. Lowenthal, R. March 1980. Democratic Socialism as an International Force. *Social Research* 47 (1): 63–92.

4283. Lowenthal, R. February 1981. The "Missing" Revolution of Our Time: Reflections on New Post-Marxist Fundamentals of Social Change. *Encounter* 56 (2–3): 10–18.

4284. Lowenthal, R. September 1981. Party Competition and Inner-Party Democracy: Motives and Remedies for Conflict of Functions.* *Merkur* 35 (9–10): 953–959.

4285. Lowery, D., R. H. De Hoog, and W. E. Lyons. September 1992. Citizenship in the Empowered Locality: An Elaboration, a Critique, and a Partial Test. *Urban Affairs Quarterly* 28 (1): 69–102.

4286. Lowi, T. J. February 1988. *See* Schaefer, D. L. (February 1988).

4287. Lowi, T. J. September 1990. Risks and Rights in the History of American Governments. *Daedalus* 119 (4): 17–40.

4288. Lowi, T. J. 1994. Presidential Democracy in America: Toward the Homogenized Regime. *Political Science Quarterly* 109 (3): 401–414. Discussion, 415–440.

4289. Lozano, L. November 1991. Adjustment and Democracy in Latin America.* *Cuadernos Americanos* 30: 87–103.

4290. Lozano, L. December 1992. Adjustment and Democracy in Latin America. *Social Justice* 19 (4): 48–59.

4291. Lu, A. Y. November 1985. Future Domestic Development in the Republic of China on Taiwan. *Asian Survey* 25 (11): 1075–1095.

4292. Lu, Z. C. 1982. Stability, Unity and Socialist Democracy. *Chinese Law and Government* 15 (3–4): 116–123.

4293. Lubar, R. September 1980. Making Democracy Less Inflation Prone: Can Our Political System Tame the Monster It Helped to Create. *Fortune* 102 (6): 78–86.

4294. Lubbe, H. March 1985. The Advantages of Formal Democracy over Moral Rigorism.* *Politische Meinung* 219: 33–43.

4295. Luciak, I. A. October 1987. Popular Democracy in the New Nicaragua: The Case of a Rural Mass Organization. *Comparative Politics* 20 (1): 35–55.

4296. Luciak, I. A. June 1990. Democracy in the Nicaraguan Country: A Comparative Analysis of Sandinista Grassroots Movements. *Latin American Perspectives* 17 (3): 55–75.

4297. Luciani, G. September 1988. Economic Foundations of Democracy and Authoritarianism: The Arab World in Comparative Perspective. *Arab Studies Quarterly* 10 (4): 457–475.

4298. Ludington, N. S., and J. W. Spain. March 1983. Dateline Turkey: The Case for Patience. *Foreign Policy* 50: 150–168.

4299. Ludlow, H. T. June 1975. The Role of Trade Unions in Poland. *Political Science Quarterly* 90 (2): 315–324.

4300. Luebbe, P. November 1988. Wandelt Sich das "Sozialreformistische" Feindbild in der DDR? *Deutschland Archiv* 21: 1178–1188.

4301. Luebbert, G. M. July 1984. A Theory of Government Formation. *Comparative Political Studies* 17 (2): 229–264.

4302. Luebbert, G. M. July 1987. Social Foundations of Political Order in Interwar Europe. *World Politics* 39 (4): 449–478.

4303. Luebke, P. October 1984. *See* Zipp, J. F. (October 1984).

4304. Lugar, R. G., J. F. Kemp, E. M. Kennedy, and R. J. Dole. March 1985. Foreign Policy Agenda. *Washington Quarterly* 8 (2): 3–23.

4305. Luhmann, N. July 1987. *See* Zolo, D. (July 1987).

4306. Lui, T. L. May 1990. *See* Cooper, T. L. (May 1990).

4307. Luik, J. C. 1991. Democracy, Elitism, and the Academy: Some Thoughts After Bloom. *Interchange* 22 (1–2): 5–14.

4308. Lujan, C. January 1991. Redemocratizacion y Politica Exterior en el Uruguay. *Sintesis* 16: 359–377.

4309. Lukacs, G. 1977. Bolshevism as a Moral Problem. *Social Research* 44 (3): 416–424.

4310. Lummis, C. D. December 1991. Development against Democracy. *Alternatives* 16 (1): 31–66.

4311. Lundahl, M. March 1989. History as a Obstacle to Change: The Case of Haiti. *Journal of Interamerican Studies and World Affairs* 31 (1–2): 1–21.

4312. Lundmark, C. 1990. The Perfect Politician: From a Liberal to a Feminist Perspective on Democracy. *Statsvetenskaplig Tidskrift* 93 (3): 235–245.

4313. Lundquist, L. 1980. Lenin's Concept of Democracy.* *Statsvetenskaplig Tidskrift* 83: 1–21.

4314. Lundquist, L. 1992. Administrative Leadership and Democracy.* *Statsvetenskaplig Tidskrift* 95 (3): 234–256.

4315. Lundstedt, S. B. September 1989. Democracy, Technology, and Privacy. *Forum for Applied Research and Public Policy* 4 (3): 68–74.

4316. Lunn, E. 1986. Cultural Populism and Egalitarian Democracy: Herder and Michelet in the 19th Century. *Theory and Society* 15 (4): 479–517.

4317. Lunsgaard, D. C. 1993. *See* Utter, R. F. (1993).

4318. Lusinchi, J. April 1988. Thirty Years Ago: The First Dawn of Democracy in Venezuela's Troubled History. *Caribbean Affairs* 1 (2): 142–149.

4319. Lustick, I. April 1979. Stability in Deeply Divided Societies: Consociationalism Versus Control. *World Politics* 31 (3): 325–344.

4320. Lustick, I. S. September 1987. Israel's Dangerous Fundamentalists. *Foreign Policy* 68: 118–139.

4321. Luterbacher, U. March 1985. The Frustrated Commentator: An Evaluation of the Work of Raymond Aron. *International Studies Quarterly* 29 (1): 39–49.

4322. Lutrin, C. E., and A. K. Settle. June 1975. The Public and Ecology: The Role of Initiatives in California's Environmental Politics. *Western Political Quarterly* 28 (2): 352–371.

4323. Lutz, D. S. March 1979. The Theory of Consent in Early State Constitutions. *Publius* 9 (2): 11–42.

4324. Lynn-Jones, S. M. March 1987. *See* Davis, T. R. (March 1987).

4325. Lyons, W. 1993. *See* Gant, M. M. (1993).

4326. Lyons, W. E. September 1992. *See* Lowery, D. (September 1992).

4327. Lyrintzis, C. April 1984. Political Parties in Post-Junta Greece: A Case of "Bureaucratic Clientelism." *West European Politics* 7 (2): 99–118.

4328. Lyttkens, C. H. January 1994. A Predatory Democracy: An Essay on Taxation in Classical Athens. *Explorations in Economic History* 31 (1): 62–90.

4329. Ma, A. 1990. *See* Tong, J. (1990).

4330. MacCoby, M. July 1977. *See* Duckles, M. M. (July 1977).

4331. MacDonald, A. M. December 1994. Rethinking Restatement: Challenging Our Nation's Malapportioned, Undemocratic Presidential Election System. *Marquette Law Review* 77: 201–264.

4332. MacDonald, S. B. 1986. *See* Demetrius, F. J. (1986).

4333. MacDonald, S. B. March 1988. Insurrection and Redemocratization in Suriname? The Ascendance of the "Third Path." *Journal of Interamerican Studies and World Affairs* 30 (1): 105–132.

4334. MacDonald, S. B. January 1992. Turkey's Elections: Democracy Renewed or the Past Revisited? *Middle East Insight* 8: 25–30.

4335. MacDonald, S. E. December 1994. *See* Listhaug, O. (December 1994).

4336. MacDougall, T. E. January 1988. Yoshida Shigeru and the Japanese Transition to Liberal Democracy. *International Political Science Review* 9 (1): 55–69.

4337. Mace, G. December 1987. *See* Melone, A. P. (December 1987).

4338. Macey, J. R. December 1993. Representative Democracy. *Harvard Journal of Law and Public Policy* 16 (1): 49–54.

4339. Macey, J. R., and G. P. Miller. March 1992. The End of History and the New World Order: The Triumph of Capitalism and the Competition between Liberalism and Democracy. *Cornell International Law Journal* 25: 277–303.

4340. Machado, K. G. February 1979. The Philippines 1978: Authoritarian Consolidation Continues. *Asian Survey* 19 (2): 131–140.

4341. Machetzki, R. May 1989. "55 Tage in Peking": Zur Uberrechenbarkeit der Volksrepublik China. *China Aktuell* 18: 352–356.

4342. Machncke, D. 1982. The Participation of Public Opinion to Foreign Policy from an International Comparative Point of View: Forces and Weakness of Democratic States.* *Oesterreichische Zeitschrift für Aussenpolitik* 22 (2): 94–103.

4343. Macho, T. H. September 1993. From Elite to Prominence: The Structural Change of Political Leadership.* *Merkur* 47 (9–10): 762–769.

4344. Maciag, Z. 1988. Bureaucracy, Parties, Society in Poland.* *Der Staat* 27 (1): 127–138.

4345. MacIntosh, M. L. 1982. The South Australian Public Service Board Industrial Democracy Policies 1973–1979. *Australian Journal of Public Administration* 41 (4): 355–371.

4346. MacIsaacs, D., and S. F. Wells, Jr. March 1979. A "Minuteman" Tradition. *Wilson Quarterly* 3 (2): 109–123.

4347. MacKenzie, K. 1981. Nigeria's New Democracy. *Round Table* (283): 258–263.

4348. MacKey, E. M. 1991. Industrialization and Two-Party Democracy. *Midsouth Political Science Journal* 12: 100–112.

4349. Mackie, T. T. July 1983. *See* Franklin, M. N. (July 1983).

4350. Mackie, T. T. November 1984. *See* Franklin, M. N. (November 1984).

4351. Mackintosh, J. P. July 1978. Has Social Democracy Failed in Britain? *Political Quarterly* 49: 259–270.

4352. MacKuen, M. September 1979. *See* Miller, A. H. (September 1979).

4353. MacLean, J. 1978. Democracy and Social Decay: Response. *Socialist Review* (40–44): 42–48.

4354. Macmillan, G. March 1992. The Referendum, the Courts and Representative Democracy in Ireland. *Political Studies* 40 (1): 67–78.

4355. MacPherson, C. B. 1976. Humanist Democracy and Elusive Marxism: Response to Minogue and Svacek. *Canadian Journal of Political Science* 9 (3): 423–430.

4356. Macrae, N. March 1980. The New Entrepreneurial Revolution. *Policy Review* 12: 79–88.

4357. Macridis, R. C. Greece in Flux. *Current History* 85 (514): 369–372, 389.

4358. Macun, I., and A. Frost. June 1994. Living Like There's No Tomorrow: Trade Union Growth in South Africa, 1979–1991. *Social Dynamics* 20 (2): 67–90.

4359. Maddox, G. 1986. The Christian Democracy of A. D. Lindsay. *Political Studies* 34 (3): 441–455.

4360. Maddox, G. November 1986. Contours of a Democratic Polity. *Politics* 21 (1): 1–11.

4361. Maddox, G. 1993. Republic or Democracy? *Australian Journal of Political Science* 28: 9–26. Special issue.

4362. Madec, A., and C. Mouton. June 1978. Democratie Economique et Agriculture. *Revue des Etudes Cooperatives* 35–57.

4363. Madeley, J. T. S. 1977. Scandinavian Christian Democracy: Throwback or Portent. *European Journal of Political Research* 5 (3): 267–286.

4364. Maderthaner, W. 1989. Becoming of a Disciplined Mass Party: Development of the Organizational Structure of the German Social Democracy in Austria, 1889–1913.* *Oesterreichische Zeitschrift für Politikwissenschaft* 18 (4): 347–358.

4365. Madison, G. B. December 1991. The Politics of Postmodernity. *Critical Review* 5 (1): 53–79.

4366. Madsen, H. J. 1980. Class Power and Participatory Equality: Attitudes towards Economic Democracy in Denmark and Sweden. *Scandinavian Political Studies* 3 (4): 277–298.

4367. Madsen, H. J. April 1981. *See* Hibbs, D. A., Jr. (April 1981).

4368. Maechling, C. , Jr. September 1983. Human Rights Dehumanized. *Foreign Policy* 52: 118–135.

4369. Maga, T. P. December 1990. The New Frontier Versus Guided Democracy: JFK, Sukarno, and Indonesia, 1961–1963. *Presidential Studies Quarterly* 20 (1): 91–102.

4370. Magagna, V. V. June 1988. Representing Efficiency: Corporatism and Democratic Theory. *Review of Politics* 50 (3): 420–444.

4371. Magalhaes, R. D. A. December 1985. La Transition Bresilienne: Un Cas Particular.* *Notes et Etudes Documentaires* 61–77.

4372. Maghraoui, A. July 1992. *See* Shahin, E. E. (July 1992).

4373. Magleby, D. B. 1985. Is Direct Democracy a Failed Democracy. *Center Magazine* 18 (4): 51–55.

4374. Magleby, D. B. March 1986. Legislatures and the Initiative: The Politics of Direct Democracy. *State Government* 59 (1): 31–39.

4375. Magleby, D. B. 1988. Taking the Initiative: Direct Legislation and Direct Democracy in the 1980s. *PS: Political Science & Politics* 21 (3): 600–611.

4376. Magnusson, J. 1992. The Process of Democratization in Eastern Europe 1989 as a "Garbage Can."* *Statsvetenskaplig Tidskrift* 95 (1): 1–30.

4377. Magri, L. 1977. Italy, Social Democracy, and Revolution in the West. *Socialist Revolution* 36: 105–142.

4378. Maguire, R. 1986. Standing Tall: Balanced Development in Brazil. *Grassroots Development* 10 (2): 8–11.

4379. Maguire, R. December 1987. The U.S. and a New Haiti. *Caribbean Review* 15 (3): 3.

4380. Mahant, E. E. 1977. Strange Fate of a Liberal Democracy: Political Opposition and Civil Liberties in Guyana. *Round Table* 267 (77–89):

4381. Maher, K. H. April 1994. *See* Reisinger, W. M. (April 1994).

4382. Maheshwari, S. August 1976. Constituency Linkage of National Legislators in India. *Legislative Studies Quarterly* 1 (3): 331–354.

4383. Mahler, J. G. July 1987. Structural Decision Making in Public Organizations. *Public Administration Review* 47 (4): 336–342.

4384. Mahler, V. A., and C. J. Katz. October 1988. Social Benefits in Advanced Capitalist Countries: A Cross-National Assessment. *Comparative Politics* 21 (1): 37–51.

4385. Mahmud, S. 1993. The Failed Transition to Civilian Rule in Nigeria: Its Implications for Democracy and Human Rights. *Africa Today* 40 (4): 87–95.

4386. Mahon, R. September 1993. *See* Jenson, J. (September 1993).

4387. Mahon, R., and R. Meidner. 1993. System Shift: Or, What is the Future of Swedish Social Democracy. *Socialist Review* 23 (4): 57–77.

4388. Mahoney, K. December 1993. Hungary: Sudden Democracy or Incomplete Transition? *State Legislatures* 19: 29–33.

4389. Mahrad, A. 1983. Zur Person des Gruenders der Iranischer Sozialistischen Partei: Khalil Maleki. *Orient* 24 (4): 645–655.

4390. Maier, C. S. July 1994. Democracy and Its Discontents. *Foreign Affairs* 73 (4): 48–64.

4391. Maier, C. S. October 1994. Moral Crisis of Democracy.* *Parolechiave* 5: 93–110.

4392. Maier, H., and H. Oberreuter (eds.). 1977. Pluralismus.* *Politische Bildung* 10 (1): 3–100.

4393. Maihold, G. October 1990. Democracy by a Show of Hands? The Army and Democratic Change in Latin America. *Aus Politik und Zeitgeschichte* 43: 17–29.

4394. Maina, K. W. 1992. The Future of Democracy in Kenya. *Africa Today* 39 (1–2): 122–127.

4395. Maingot, A. P. September 1983. Options for Grenada: The Need to Be Cautious. *Caribbean Review* 12 (4): 24–28.

4396. Maingot, A. P. March 1985. Politics Caribbean Style: Lessons from Grenada. *Caribbean Review* 14 (2): 4–6, 36–37.

4397. Maingot, A. P. December 1986. Haiti: Problems of a Transition to Democracy in an Authoritarian Soft State. *Journal of Interamerican Studies and World Affairs* 28 (4): 75–102.

4398. Mainwaring, S. December 1985. *See* Viola, E. (December 1985).

4399. Mainwaring, S. 1986. *See* Share, D. (1986).

4400. Mainwaring, S. January 1986. *See* Share, D. (January 1986).

4401. Mainwaring, S. March 1986. The Transition to Democracy in Brazil. *Journal of Interamerican Studies and World Affairs* 28 (1): 149–179.

4402. Mainwaring, S. June 1987. *See* Hagopian, F. (June 1987).

4403. Mainwaring, S. July 1987. Urban Popular Movements, Identity, and Democratization in Brazil. *Comparative Political Studies* 20 (2): 131–159.

4404. Mainwaring, S. July 1993. Presidentialism, Multipartism, and Democracy: The Difficult Combination. *Political Studies* 26 (2): 198–228.

4405. Mainwaring, S., and E. Viola. October 1985. The New Social Movements, Political Cultures and Democracy: Brazil and Argentina in the 1980s.* *Revista Mexicana de Sociologia* 47 (4): 35–85.

4406. Mair, P. July 1979. The Autonomy of the Political: The Development of the Irish Party System. *Comparative Politics* 11 (4): 445–466.

4407. Mair, S. April 25, 1994. Clientelism as Obstacle to Democracy in Africa.* *Europa Archiv: Zeitschrift für Internationale Politik* 49 (8): 231–238.

4408. Maira, L. May 1987. Predictions and Realities of Democracy and Social Change in Latin America.* *Sintesis* 2: 31–38.

4409. Major, L. 1990. *See* Znoj, M. (1990).

4410. Makinda, S. M. October 1992. Kenya: Out of the Strait-Jacket Slowly. *World Today* 48 (10): 188–192.

4411. Makorovic, J. 1994. Where Is Democracy Today in the Countries of the Habsburg Crown?* *Teorija in Praksa* 31 (5–6): 519–534.

4412. Makram-Ebeid, M. June 1989. Political Opposition in Egypt: Democratic

Myth or Reality? *Middle East Journal* 43 (3): 423–436.

4413. Malamud-Goti, J. February 1990. Transitional Governments in the Breach: Why Punish State Criminals? *Human Rights Quarterly* 12 (1): 1–16.

4414. Maletz, D. J. November 1991. The Place of Constitutionalism in the Education of Public Administrators. *Administration and Society* 23 (3): 374–394.

4415. Maley, M., and R. Medew. March 1991. Some Approaches to Election Night Forecasting in Australia. *Australian Journal of Political Science* 26 (1): 51–62.

4416. Malfa, U. L. 1978. Communism and Democracy in Italy. *Foreign Affairs* 56 (3): 476–488.

4417. Malik, Y. K. October 1979. Trust, Efficacy, and Attitude toward Democracy: A Case Study from India. *Comparative Education Review* 23 (3): 433–442.

4418. Malik, Y. K., and J. F. Marquette. February 1975. Democracy and Alienation in North India. *Journal of Politics* 37 (1): 35–55.

4419. Malik, Y. K., and D. K. Vajpeyi. March 1989. The Rise of Hindu Militancy: India's Secular Democracy at Risk. *Asian Survey* 29 (3): 308–325.

4420. Malitza, M. 1994. Culture and Democracy in Southeastern Europe. *Suedosteuropa Mitteilungen* 34 (1): 1–8.

4421. Maller, J. May 1994. Worker Participation and Trade Unionism: Case Studies of Workplace Democracy in South Africa. *Economic and Industrial Democracy* 15 (2): 241–257.

4422. Mallmann, C. A. 1985. *See* Arienza, M. (1985).

4423. Mallo, S., and M. Serna. November 1993. Razon y Tradicion: Los Partidos en Argentina y Uruguay. *Revista de Ciencias Sociales* 8: 29–44.

4424. Malloy, J. M. January 1987. Bolivia's Economic Crisis. *Current History* 86 (516): 9–12, 37–38.

4425. Malloy, J. M. June 1991. Democracy, Economic Crisis and the Problems of Governance: The Case of Bolivia. *Studies in Comparative International Development* 26 (2): 37–57.

4426. Malone, C. R. March 1991. High-Level Nuclear Waste Disposal: A Perspective on Technocracy and Democracy. *Growth and Change* 22 (2): 69–74.

4427. Maltz, E. M. 1981. Federalism and the Fourteenth Amendment: A Comment on "Democracy and Distrust." *Ohio State Law Journal* 42 (1): 209–222.

4428. Malvoz, L. January 1989. La Democratie Locale en Suede. *Credit Communal de Belgique* 43: 21–49.

4429. Malzef, G. W. 1977. *See* Kerimov, D. A. (1977).

4430. Mamdini, M. March 1986. Peasants and Democracy in Africa. *New Left Review* 156: 37–49.

4431. Mamdini, M. June 1992. Africa: Democratic Theory and Democratic Struggles. *Dissent* 39 (3): 312–318.

4432. Manaev, O. 1990. Discordant Audience (Alteration of Mass Media Effectiveness Criteria in Accordance with Democratization of Society).* *Sotsiologichicheskie Issledovaniia* 6: 26–37.

4433. Manaev, O. 1991. The Influence of Western Radio on the Democratization of Soviet Youth. *Journal of Communication* 41 (2): 72–91.

4434. Manaev, O. 1991. The Disagreeing Audience: Change in Criteria for Evaluating Mass Media Effectiveness with the Democratization of Soviet Society. *Communication Research* 18 (1): 25–52.

4435. Manaster, G. J., D. L. Greer, and D. A. Keiber. September 1985. Youth's Outlook on the Future III: A Second Past-

Present Comparison. *Youth and Society* 17 (1): 97–112.

4436. Manatt, C. T. March 1984. Campaign '84: The Contest of National Leadership. *Presidential Studies Quarterly* 14 (2): 179–182.

4437. Mancini, G. F., and D. T. Keeling. March 1994. Democracy and the European Court of Justice. *Modern Law Review* 57 (2): 175–190.

4438. Mandel, D. 1988. Economic Reform and Democracy in the Soviet Union. *Socialist Register* 132–153.

4439. Mandel, M. 1984. Democracy, Class, and Canadian Sentencing Law. *Crime and Social Justice* 21–22: 163–182.

4440. Mandini, M., T. Mkandawire, and W. Wanbadia. 1988. Social Movements, Social Transformation and Struggle for Democracy in Africa. *Economic and Political Weekly* 23 (19): 973+.

4441. Mandle, J. R. December 1987. *See* Ferleger, L. (December 1987).

4442. Mandt, H. June 1985. The Critique of Formal Democracy and Loss of Formality of the Political Debate.* *Zeitschrift für Politik* 32 (2): 115–132.

4443. Manes, S. W. May 1994. *See* Wertheimen, F. (May 1994).

4444. Manfredi, C. P. September 1994. Appropriate and Just in the Circumstances: Public Policy and the Enforcement of Rights under the Canadian Charter of Rights and Freedoms. *Canadian Journal of Political Science* 27 (3): 435–464.

4445. Mangin, M. September 1993. Philippines: La Fin du Feodalisme? *Politique Internationale* 61: 369–379.

4446. Mango, A. November 1983. Turkey: Democracy under Military Tutelage. *World Today* 39 (11): 429–435.

4447. Manheim, J. B. March 1976. Can Democracy Survive Television? *Journal of Communication* 26 (2): 84–90.

4448. Manicas, P. T. March 1988. The Foreclosure of Democracy in America. *History of Political Thought* 9 (7): 137–160.

4449. Maniruzzaman, T. August 1975. Bangladesh: An Unfinished Revolution. *Journal of Asian Studies* 34 (4): 891–911.

4450. Manley, J. F. September 1990. American Liberalism and the Democratic Dream: Transcending the American Dream. *Policy Studies Review* 10 (1): 89–102.

4451. Manley, M. September 1983. Grenada in the Context of History: Between Neocolonialism and Independence. *Caribbean Review* 12 (4): 7–9, 45–47.

4452. Mann, E. 1988. Cooperation or Democracy: New Directions for the UAW. *Nation* 246 (23): 816–818.

4453. Mannathoko, C. 1994. Democracy in the Management of Teacher Education in Botswana. *British Journal of Sociology of Education* 15 (4): 481–496.

4454. Manning, F. E. March 1981. Race and Democracy in Bermuda. *Caribbean Review* 10 (2): 20–23.

4455. Manning, R. E. 1985. Diversity in a Democracy: Expanding the Recreation Opportunity Spectrum. *Leisure Sciences* 7 (4): 377–399.

4456. Manoff, R. K. 1984. The Media: Nuclear Secrecy Versus Democracy. *Bulletin of the Atomic Scientists* 40 (1): 26–29.

4457. Manor, J. March 1986. India: Awakening and Decay. *Current History* 85 (509): 101–104, 136–137.

4458. Mansbridge, J. April 1981. Living with Conflict: Representation in the Theory of Adversary Democracy. *Ethics* 91 (3): 466–476.

4459. Mansbridge, J. February 1990. Self-Interest in Political Life. *Political Theory* 18 (1): 132–153.

4460. Mansbridge, J. December 1992. A Deliberate Perspective on Neocorporatism. *Politics and Society* 20 (4): 493–506.

4461. Mansbridge, J. April 1994. Using Power/Fighting Power. *Constellations* 1 (1): 53–73.

4462. Mansfield, H. C. June 1979. The Media World and Democratic Representation. *Government and Opposition* 14: 318–334.

4463. Mansfield, H. C. December 1981. The American Election (1980): Towards Constitutional Democracy? *Government and Opposition* 16 (1): 3–18.

4464. Mansfield, H. C. December 1983. The Forms and Formalities of Liberty. *Public Interest* 70: 121–131.

4465. Mansfield, H. C. December 1987. Constitutional Government: The Soul of Modern Democracy. *Public Interest* (86): 53–64.

4466. Mansilla, H. C. F. 1981. The New Absolutism: Industrialization without Democracy in the Third World. *Folia Humanistica* 19 (225): 629–634.

4467. Mansilla, H. C. F. 1982. Conflict, Pluralism and Free Market as Elements of Modern Democracy. *Folia Humanistica* 20 (237): 617–636.

4468. Mansilla, H. C. F. May 1984. Conflict, Pluralism and Market as Elements of Modern Democracy.* *Revista de Estudios Politicos* 39: 29–48.

4469. Mansilla, H. C. F. October 1991. Aspectos Antidemocraticos y Antipluralistas en la Cultura Politica Latinoamericana. *Revista de Estudios Politicos* 74: 17–42.

4470. Mantovani, G. January 1994. Is Computer-Mediated Communication Intrinsically Apt to Enhance Democracy in Organizations. *Human Relations* 47 (1): 45–62.

4471. Manuat, R. B. September 1993. Identity Crisis: The Military in Changing Times. *Report on the Americas* 27: 15–19.

4472. Manza, J. December 1992. Postindustrial Capitalism, the State, and the Prospects for Economic Democracy. *Journal of Political and Military Sociology* 20 (2): 209–241.

4473. Maor, M. July 1991. The 1990 Danish Election: An Unnecessary Contest? *West European Politics* 14 (3): 209–214.

4474. Maoz, Z., and N. Abdolani. March 1989. Regime Types and International Conflict, 1816–1976. *Journal of Conflict Resolution* 33 (1): 3–35.

4475. Maoz, Z., and B. M. Russett. September 1993. Normative and Structural Causes of Democratic Peace, 1946–1986. *American Political Science Review* 87 (3): 624–638.

4476. Maphai, V. April 1993. Prospects for a Democratic South Africa. *International Affairs (London)* 69 (2): 223–237.

4477. Mara, G. M. September 1989. Virtue and Pluralism: The Problem of the One and the Many. *Polity* 22 (1): 25–48.

4478. Mara, G. M. December 1993. Cries, Eloquence, and Judgment: Interpreting Political Voice in Democratic Regimes. *Polity* 26 (2): 155–187.

4479. Marable, M. May 1984. Race and Democracy in Cuba. *Black Scholar* 15 (3): 22–37.

4480. Marable, M. July 1993. Beyond Racial Identity Politics: Towards a Liberation Theory for Multicultural Democracy. *Race and Class* 35 (1): 113–130.

4481. Marando, V. L. December 1981. *See* Thomas, R. D. (December 1981).

4482. Marantis, D. J. March 1994. Human Rights, Democracy, And Development: The European Community Model. *Harvard Human Rights Journal* 7: 1–32.

4483. Maravall, J. M. 1993. *See* Pereira, L. C. B. (1993).

4484. Maravall, J. M. December 1981. The Transition to Democracy: Political Alignments and Elections in Spain.* *Rivista Italiana di Scienza Politica* 11 (3): 377–421.

4485. Maravall, J. M. January 1991. Democracia y Socialdemocracia: Quince Anos de Politica en España. *Sistema* 41–67.

4486. Maravall, J. M. October 1994. The Myth of the Authoritarian Advantage. *Journal of Democracy* 5 (4): 17–31.

4487. Marcella, G. 1979. The Chilean Military Government and the Prospects for Transition to Democracy. *Inter-American Economic Affairs* 33 (2): 3–19.

4488. Marcella, G. July 1986. Security, Democracy, and Development: The United States and Latin America in the Next Decade. *Air University Review* 37: 2–14.

4489. Marcella, G. March 1990. The Latin American Military, Low Intensity Conflict, and Democracy.* *Journal of Interamerican Studies and World Affairs* 32 (1): 45–82.

4490. March, J. G., and J. P. Olsen. October 1986. Popular Sovereignty and the Search for Appropriate Institutions. *Journal of Public Policy* 6 (4): 341–370.

4491. Marchetti, P., and C. Jerez. 1988. Democracy and Militarization: War and Development. *IDS Bulletin (Institute of Development Studies)* 19 (3): 3–11.

4492. Marciszewski, W. 1979. Epistemological Foundations of Democratism in Cartesian Philosophy. *Poznan Studies* 5 (1–4): 77–86.

4493. Marcus, G. 1984. *See* Krouse, R. (1984).

4494. Marcus, G. E. September 1988. Democratic Theories and the Study of Public Opinion. *Polity* 21 (1): 25–44.

4495. Marcuse, H., and J. Habermas. March 1979. A Discussion on Democracy and Critical Theory. *New Political Science* 1 (1): 19–29.

4496. Marcy, C. 1975. Foreign Policy Debate in a Democracy. *Bulletin of the Atomic Scientists* 31 (9): 36–37.

4497. Maren, M. P. May 1987. Kenya: The Dissolution of Democracy. *Current History* 86 (520): 209–212, 228–229.

4498. Margolin, J. December 1990. Singapore: Possibilities and Difficulties of Opening of an Authoritarian Regime.* *Politique* 17: 91–111.

4499. Margolin, J. 1992. Development and Democracy in Southeast Asia. *Politique Etrangere* 57 (3): 571–583.

4500. Margolis, M. March 1984. Public Opinion, Polling, and Political Behavior. *Annals of the American Academy of Political and Social Science* 472: 61–71.

4501. Mariam, Y. H. October 29, 1994. Ethiopian Women in the Period of Socialist Transformation. *Economic and Political Weekly* 29 (44): 57–62.

4502. Marican, Y. M. July–September and October–November 1977. Democracy and National Integration. *Political Science Review* 16 (3 and 4): 45–52.

4503. Marinelli, J. September 1983. Making the Stock Market Safe for Democracy. *Environmental Action* 1: 23–26.

4504. Marini, R. M. December 1994. Latin America at the Crossroads. *Latin American Perspectives* 21 (1): 99–114.

4505. Marion, D. E. July 1980. Alexander Hamilton and Woodrow Wilson on the Spirit and Form of a Responsible Republican Government. *Review of Politics* 42 (3): 309–328.

4506. Maritain, J. March 1991. A Christian Philosophy of Democracy. *Civitas (Roma)* 42 (2): 3–103.

4507. Marko, K. 1975. Social Democracy of the Polish Realm and Lithuania.* *Oesterreichische Osthefte* 17 (1): 96–100.

4508. Markoff, J. 1993. *See* Montecinos, V. (1993).

4509. Markoff, J., and S. R. D. Baretta. July 1990. Economic Crisis and Regime Change in Brazil: The 1960s and the 1980s. *Comparative Politics* 22 (4): 421–444.

4510. Markovic, B. 1981. International Conceptions of Social-Democratic and Socialist Parties in Western Europe. *Review of International Affairs* 32 (5): 11–14.

4511. Markovitz, A. S. March 1986. The Vicissitudes of West German Social Democracy in the Crisis of the 1980s. *Studies in Political Economy* 83–112.

4512. Markovitz, A. S., and S. Kazarinov. April 1978. Class Conflict, Capitalism and Social Democracy: The Case of Migrant Workers in the Federal Republic of Germany. *Comparative Politics* 10 (3): 373–391.

4513. Marks, G. March 1992. Rational Sources of Chaos in Democratic Transition. *American Behavioral Scientist* 35 (4–5): 397–421.

4514. Marks, G. March 1992. *See* Diamond, L. (March 1992).

4515. Marks, G., and L. Diamond. March 1992. Seymour Martin Lipset and the Study of Democracy. *American Behavioral Scientist* 35 (4–5): 352–362.

4516. Marks, G. N. July 1994. *See* Jackman, S. (July 1994).

4517. Marks, S. P. September 1994. The New Cambodian Constitution: From Civil War to a Fragile Democracy. *Columbia Human Rights Law Review* 26: 45–110.

4518. Marody, M. June 1990. Perception of Politics in Polish Society. *Social Research* 57 (2): 257–274.

4519. Marot, J. E. September 1993. Marxism, Science, Materialism: Toward a Deeper Appreciation of the 1908–1909 Philo-

sophical Debate in Russian Social Democracy. *Studies in East European Thought* 45 (3): 147–167.

4520. Marquand, D. 1987. Beyond Social Democracy. *Political Quarterly* 58 (3): 243–253.

4521. Marquand, D. June 1988. Preceptoral Politics, Yeoman Democracy and the Enabling State. *Government and Opposition* 23 (3): 261–275.

4522. Marquardt, P. D. March 1994. Deficit Reduction: Democracy, Technocracy, and Constitutionalism in the European Union. *Duke Journal of Comparative and International Law* 4: 265–290.

4523. Marquette, J. F. February 1975. *See* Malik, Y. K. (February 1975).

4524. Marquis, A. 1976. Democracy Startles Holtville. *Nation* 222 (3): 79–83.

4525. Marrengane, N. 1994. Voting in Exile: South Africans in the United States Discuss the May Elections. *Black Scholar* 24 (3): 28–32.

4526. Marrero, S. G. October 1991. La Transicion a la Democracia en Nicaragua. *Revista de Estudios Politicos* 74: 449–470.

4527. Marsh, M. March 1994. *See* Darcy, R. (March 1994).

4528. Marsh, R. M. September 1991. Authoritarian and Democratic Transitions in National Political Systems. *International Journal of Comparative Sociology* 32 (3–4): 219–232.

4529. Marshall, J. June 1988. *See* O'Tolle, D. E. (June 1988).

4530. Marshall, J. P. May 1994. *See* Fernandez-Balboa, J. M. (May 1994).

4531. Marshall, S. January 1986. The Trade Unions and Peace: New Development. *Political Affairs* 65: 23–17.

4532. Marshall, W. P. September 1994. Free Speech and the "Problem" of Democracy. *Northwestern University Law Review* 89: 191–211.

4533. Marston, B. 1991. Libraries and Democracies: Information for All. *Wilson Library Bulletin* 65 (7): 47+.

4534. Martell, E. P. December 1993. *See* Vasconi, T. A. (December 1993).

4535. Martin, D. July 1993. Tanzania and the Multiparty System.* *Afrique Contemporaine* 167: 3–13.

4536. Martin, J. A. 1983. Science and Democracy in a Age of Technology: Separating Fact from Value. *American Statistician* 37 (4): 367–371.

4537. Martin, M. L. March 1994. National Security and Democracy: The Dilemma from a French Perspective. *Armed Forces and Society* 20 (3): 395–421.

4538. Martin, P. Y. 1989. *See* Whiddon, B. (1989).

4539. Martineau, J. C. March 1991. Mali: L'Ouverture ou l'Emeute. *Jeune Afrique Economie* 46–48.

4540. Martinez, A. April 15, 1991. En Chile la Violencia Extremista Pone en Jaque la Democracia. *Cambio* 16: 76–77.

4541. Martinez, E. 1992. *See* Calderon, E. (1992).

4542. Martinez, I. C. October 1991. La Problematica Transicional y el Desafio de la Consolidacion (Argentina, Uruguay y Chile). *Revista de Estudios Politicos* 74: 661–670.

4543. Martinez, M. S. 1980. The Role of Christian Democracy at the Present Juncture in Central America.* *Estudios Sociales Centroamericanos* 9 (27): 277–289.

4544. Martinez, P. A. July 1987. Democracy and National Sovereignty in the Caribbean: The Case of the Dominican Republic.* *Caribe Contemporaneo* 14: 53–66.

4545. Martinez, R. E. November 1988. Spain: Pragmatism and Continuity. *Current History* 87 (532): 373–376, 389–390.

4546. Martinez Valenzuela, C. I. January 1988. Movimientos Sociales, Sistema Electoral y Perspectivas Democraticas en Haiti. *Estudios Latinoamericanos* 3: 68–72.

4547. Martini, G. May 1993. Culture and Democratic Development in Central-Eastern Europe.* *Aggiornamenti Sociali* 44 (5): 385–400.

4548. Martins, C. E. 1981. Concepts of Democracy and Contemporary Marxism. *Dados: Revista de Ciencias Sociais* 24 (3): 305–329.

4549. Martins, J. D. S. 1990. Mercado e Democracia: A Relacao Perversa. *Tempo Social: Revista de Sociologia de Universidade de Sao Paulo* 2: 7–22.

4550. Martins, L. 1985. Easy Transition, Difficult Democracy.* *Problemes d'Amerique Latine* 78: 53–60.

4551. Marty, M. E. 1979. "In Every Way Religious." *Social Research* 46 (3): 580–599.

4552. Martz, J. D. February 1980. Quest for Popular Democracy in Ecuador. *Current History* 79 (454): 66–70, 84.

4553. Martz, J. D. February 1984. The Crisis of Venezuelan Democracy. *Current History* 83 (490): 73–77, 89.

4554. Martz, J. D. February 1985. Ecuador: The Right Takes Command. *Current History* 84 (499): 69–72, 84–85.

4555. Martz, J. D. January 1988. Instability in Ecuador. *Current History* 87 (525): 17–20, 37–38.

4556. Martz, J. D. March 1990. Electoral Campaigning and Latin American Democratization: The Grancolombian Experience. *Journal of Interamerican Studies and World Affairs* 32 (1): 17–43.

4557. Martz, J. D. September 1992. Party Elites and Leadership in Colombia and Venezuela. *Journal of Latin American Studies* 24: 87–121.

4558. Martz, J. D. March 1994. Colombia: Democracy, Development, and Drugs. *Current History* (581): 134–137.

4559. Maryniak, I. March 1993. Democracy Playground: Byelarus. *Index on Censorship* 22 (3): 4.

4560. Maskiell, M. June 1985. *See* Korson, J. H. (June 1985).

4561. Maskova, E. 1991. Realization of Economic Democracy by Collective Forms.* *Ekonomicky Casopis* 39 (8): 592–602.

4562. Mason, A. T. June 1976. America's Political Heritage: Revolution and Free Government, A Bicentennial Tribute. *Political Science Quarterly* 91 (2): 193–217.

4563. Mason, D. S. November 1985. Stalemate and Apathy in Poland. *Current History* 84: 377–380.

4564. Mason, D. S. March 1989. Solidarity as a New Social Movement. *Political Science Quarterly* 104 (1): 41–58.

4565. Mason, D. S., D. N. Nelson, and B. M. Szklarski. 1991. Apathy and the Birth of Democracy: The Polish Struggle. *East European Politics and Societies* 5 (2): 205–233.

4566. Mass, P. F. April 1986. Coalition Negotiations in the Dutch Multi-Party System. *Parliamentary Affairs* 39: 214–220.

4567. Massey, G. March 1979. *See* Homer, F. D. (March 1979).

4568. Masson, G. March 1975. Crise de l'Etat: Autoritarisme ou Democratisation? *Cahiers du Communisme* 51: 42–54.

4569. Massoud, H. January 1986. Egypt under Mubarak: Progress since Sadat, Even Some Democracy. *International Perspectives:* 22–25.

4570. Masters, M. F., R. S. Atkin, and G. Schoenfeld. September 1990. A Survey of USWA Local Officers' Commitment-Support Attitudes. *Labor Studies Journal* 15 (3): 51–80.

4571. Masters, M. F., and J. D. Robertson. December 1988. Class Compromises in Industrial Democracies. *American Political Science Review* 82 (4): 1183–1201.

4572. Masters, R. D. 1984. Ostracism, Voice, and Exit: The Biology of Social Participation. *Social Science Information* 23 (6): 877–893.

4573. Mastnak, T. December 1990. Civil Society in Slovenia: From Opposition to Power. *Studies in Comparative Communism* 23 (3–4): 305–317.

4574. Mateju, P. 1986. Democratization of Education and Reproduction of the Educational Structure in Czechoslovakia in the Light of Mobility Data.* *Sociologicky Casopis* 22 (2): 131–152.

4575. Matel, P. March 5, 1993. The Czech Constitution. *RFE/RL Research Report* 2: 53–57.

4576. Matheny, A. R., and B. A. Williams. July 1988. Strong Democracy and the Challenge of Siting Hazardous Waste Disposal Facilities in Florida. *National Civic Review* 77 (4): 323–341.

4577. Mather, M. E. F. March 1975. The Body Politic: Iroquois Village Democracy. *Indian Historian* 8 (1): 31–48.

4578. Mathews, D. November 1984. In the Beginning . . . Was the Public Not the Government. *National Civic Review* 73 (10): 491–496.

4579. Mathews, D. July 1989. The Politics of Community. *National Civic Review* 78 (4): 271–278.

4580. Mathews, J. 1989. The Democratization of Capital. *Economic and Industrial Democracy* 10 (2): 165–193.

4581. Mathews, J. D. H. 1975. Arts and People: The New Deal Quest for a Cultural Democracy. *Journal of American History* 62 (2): 316–339.

4582. Mathijsen, P. September 1993. The Power of Co-Decision of the European

Parliament Introduced by the Maastricht Treaty. *Tulane European and Civil Law Forum* 8: 81–93.

4583. Mathur, A. B. July 1981. Democracy on the Defensive. *Administrative Change* 9 (1): 19–33.

4584. Matland, R. E. March 1994. *See* Studlar, D. T. (March 1994).

4585. Matlosa, K. 1992. Multi-Partyism Versus Democracy in Southern Africa: "Whither Lesotho." *Verfassung und Recht in Ubersee* 25 (3): 327–340.

4586. Matta, E. July 1982. Brazil's Institutional Problematics.* *Revista Brasileira de Estudos Politicos* 55: 139–161.

4587. Mattel, F., and H. F. Weisberg. October 1994. Presidential Succession Effect in Voting. *British Journal of Political Science* 24 (4): 495–515.

4588. Mattelard, A. 1986. Communication in Nicaragua between War and Democracy.* *Estudios Sociales Centroamericanos* 41: 17–46.

4589. Matteucci, N. September 1985. Democracy and Autocracy in N. Bobbio's Thoughts.* *Il Mulino* 301: 701–721.

4590. Mattfeldt, H. May 1984. Keynesianism, Monetarism and Democracy. *Argument* 26: 391–408.

4591. Matthews, B. April 1992. Trouble in Sri Kotha: Strains and Perils of Democracy in Sri Lanka. *Round Table* 322: 215–227.

4592. Matthews, B. January 1993. Myanmar's Agony: The Struggle for Democracy. *Round Table* 325: 37–49.

4593. Mattla, M. December 1994. *See* Johanson, J. E. (December 1994).

4594. Matzka, M. 1975. *See* Ohlinger, T. (1975).

4595. Maung, M. June 1990. The Burma Road from the Union of Burma to Myanmar. *Asian Survey* 30 (6): 602–624.

4596. Maura, J. R. 1976. After Franco, Franquismo Armed Forces, Crown and Democracy. *Government and Opposition* 11 (1): 35–64.

4597. Mauzy, D. K. February 1988. Malaysia in 1987: Decline of "The Malay Way." *Asian Survey* 28 (2): 213–222.

4598. Maxwell, K. March 1983. The Emergence of Democracy in Spain and Portugal. *Orbis* 27 (1): 151–184.

4599. Maxwell, K. 1991. Spain's Transition to Democracy: A Model for Eastern Europe? *Proceedings of the Academy of Political Science* 38 (1): 35–49.

4600. May, J. D. 1974a. Democracy and Rural Over-representation. *Australian Quarterly* 46 (2): 52–56.

4601. May, J. D. 1974b. Bigness, Technology and Democracy. *Search* 5 (6): 249–255.

4602. May, J. D. 1976. Locating Democracy: C. B. MacPherson's Deviant Estimate. *Politics* 11 (2): 165–169.

4603. May, J. D. 1978. Defining Democracy: A Bid for Coherence and Consensus. *Political Studies* 26 (1): 1–14.

4604. May, J. D. December 1980. Popular Conceptions of Democracy. *International Journal of Political Education* 3 (4): 323–350.

4605. May, S. H. June 1993. *See* So, A. Y. (June 1993).

4606. Mayall, J. 1978. Threats to Democracy: Reflections on the First Indo-British Exchange. *Round Table* (270): 112–119.

4607. Mayall, J. December 1993. The Commonwealth in Cyprus. *World Today* 49: 239–241.

4608. Mayer, L. C. June 1988. Teaching Industrial Democracies: Balancing Theory and Information for Undergraduates. *Teaching Political Science* 15 (4): 140–146.

4609. Mayer, R. T., M. E. Guy, M. Holzer, D. O. Porter, M. T. Bailey, and R. E.

Cleary. March 1989. Meadowbrook II: Conclusions and Reflections. *Public Administration Review* 49 (2): 218–227.

4610. Mayer, T. June 1982. Markets and Democracy: A Critique of Charles E. Lindblom. *New Political Science* 3 (1–2): 71–92.

4611. Mayer, W., and J. Li. March 1994. Interest Groups, Electoral Competition, and Probabilistic Voting for Trade Policies. *Economics and Politics* 6 (1): 59–77.

4612. Mayer-Tasch, P. C. December 1992. How Many Shepherds Destroy the Vineyard? Democracy and the Middle Ages.* *Zeitschrift für Politik* 39 (4): 421–435.

4613. Mayhem, R. J. 1977. Industrial Democracy and Universities. *New Universities Quarterly* 31 (4): 496–502.

4614. Maynes, C. W. September 1990. The New Decade. *Foreign Policy* 80: 3–13.

4615. Maynes, C. W. December 1993. A Workable Clinton Doctrine. *Foreign Policy* 93: 3–21.

4616. Maza, H. June 1984. Foreign Service Mandarins and Democracy. *World Affairs* 147 (1): 43–49.

4617. Mazawi, A. December 1989. *See* Ichilov, O. (December 1989).

4618. Maziarski, J. November 1979. Democracy and Efficiency.* *Perspectives Polonaises* 22 (11): 15–24.

4619. Mazrui, A. A. 1992. Planned Governance and the Liberal Revival in Africa: The Paradox of Anticipation. *Cornell International Law Journal* 25: 541–553.

4620. Mbachu, O. September 1990. Capitalism, Socialism and Democracy: A Nigerian Perspective. *Coexistence* 27 (3): 187–197.

4621. Mbachu, O. March 1991. Democratization and the Economy. *Africa (Roma)* 46 (1): 40–53.

4622. Mbachu, O. September 1992. The Impact of Perestroika and Glasnost on African Politics. *Coexistence* 29 (3): 297–304.

4623. Mbachu, O. June 1994. Democracy in Africa: A Theoretical Overview. *Coexistence* 31 (2): 147–157.

4624. Mbaku, J. M. August 1991. Military Expenditures and Bureaucratic Competition for Rents. *Public Choice* 71: 19–31.

4625. Mbaku, J. M. September 1992. Political Democracy and the Prospects of Development in Post–Cold War Africa. *Journal of Social, Political, and Economic Studies* 17 (3–4): 345–371.

4626. Mbaku, J. M. March 1993. Political Democracy, Military Expenditure, and Economic Growth in Africa. *Scandinavian Journal of Development Alternatives* 12 (1): 49–64.

4627. Mbogua, J. P. July 1977. The Current Political Problems of Southern Africa. *Journal of Southern African Affairs* 2 (3): 371–378.

4628. McAllister, S. W. December 1994. Political Participation in Postcommunist Russia: Voting, Activism, and the Potential for Mass Protest. *Political Studies* 42 (4): 593–615.

4629. McArdle, A. L. September 1989. In Defense of State and Local Government Anti-Apartheid Measures: Infusing Democratic Values into Foreign Policy Making. *Temple Law Review* 62: 813–847.

4630. McBrien, J. P. April 14, 1989. Conscience and the Law: A Step Too Far? *Solicitors' Journal* 133 (15): 472–473.

4631. McCaffery, J., and J. H. Bowman. 1978. Participatory Democracy and Budgeting: Effects of Proposition 13. *Public Administration Review* 38 (6): 530–538.

4632. McCammon, H. J. 1989. *See* Griffin, L. J. (1989).

4633. McCargo, D. October 1992. Thailand's Democracy: The Long Vacation. *Politics* 12 (2): 3–8.

4634. McCarthy, C. August 1992. The Southern African Customs Union in a Changing Economic and Political Environment. *Journal of World Trade* 26: 5–24.

4635. McCaughan, E. March 1989. Human Rights and Peoples' Rights: An Introduction. *Social Justice* 16 (1): 1–7.

4636. McCaughey, E. P. December 1993. Democracy at Risk: The Dangerous Flaws in the Electoral College. *Policy Review* 63: 79–81.

4637. McChesney, R. W. 1991. Free Speech and Democracy: Louis G. Caldwell. *American Journal of Legal History* 35 (4): 351–392.

4638. McClellan, J. August 1976. *See* Carey, G. W. (August 1976).

4639. McClendon, B. March 1991. Customer Service: A New Philosophy towards Effective City Planning. *Journal of the American Planning Association* 57 (2): 205–211.

4640. McClesky, C. May 1984. Parties at the Bar: Equal Protection, Freedom of Association, and the Rights of Political Organizations. *Journal of Politics* 46 (2): 346–368.

4641. McClintock, C. January 1989. The Prospects for Democratic Consolidation in a "Least Likely" Case: Peru. *Comparative Politics* 21 (2): 127–148.

4642. McClintock, C. March 1993. Peru-Fujimori: A Caudillo Derails Democracy. *Current History* 92 (572): 112.

4643. McClosky, H. October 1983. *See* Chong, D. (October 1983).

4644. McColm, R. B. May 1986. Democracy and Peace in Central America. *Freedom at Issue* 90: 5–11.

4645. McCord, W. February 10 1986. Venezuela's Determined Democracy. *New Leader* 69: 4–6.

4646. McCormick, B. L. January 1994. Democracy or Dictatorship?: A Response to Gordon White. *Australian Journal of Chinese Affairs* 31: 95–110.

4647. McCormick, B. L., S. Su, and X. Xiao. June 1992. The 1989 Democratic Movement: A Review of the Prospects for Civil Society in China. *Pacific Affairs* 65 (2): 183–202.

4648. McCormick, J. M. July 1988. *See* Mitchell, N. J. (July 1988).

4649. McCoy, J. L. 1989. Labor and the State in a Party-Mediated Democracy: Institutional Change in Venezuela. *Latin American Research* 24 (2): 35–67.

4650. McCoy, J. L. December 1992. Trouble Ahead, Trouble Behind: Can Latin America Stay on the Democratic Road? *Harvard International Review* 15 (2): 28–30.

4651. McCulloch, A. M. September 1983. Voting Paradoxes and Primary Politics: A Dilemma for Democracy. *Presidential Studies Quarterly* 13 (4): 575–588.

4652. McCulloch, M. April 1977. *See* Doughtie, J. C. (April 1977).

4653. McDonagh, E. L. December 1992. Representative Democracy and State Building in the Progressive Era. *American Political Science Review* 86 (4): 938–950.

4654. McDonald, M. D. December 1993. *See* Enstrom, R. L. (December 1993).

4655. McDonald, R. H. February 1985. Confrontation and Transition in Uruguay. *Current History* 84 (499): 57–60, 87–88.

4656. McDonald, R. H. January 1988. The Dilemma of Normalcy in Uruguay. *Current History* 87: 25–28.

4657. McDonough, P. October 1982. Repression and Representation in Brazil. *Comparative Politics* 15 (1): 73–99.

4658. McDonough, P. October 1983. *See* Chaudhry, K. A. (October 1983).

4659. McDonough, P. 1985. *See* Barnes, S. H. (1985).

4660. McDonough, P., S. H. Barnes, and A. L. Pina. August 1984. Authority and Associations: Spanish Democracy in Comparative Perspective. *Journal of Politics* 46 (3): 652–688.

4661. McDowell, B. 1983. *See* Peck, R. S. (1983).

4662. McEachern, W. A. 1987. Federal Advisory Commissions in an Economic Model of Representative Democracy. *Public Choice* 54 (1): 41–62.

4663. McFaul, M. et al. April 1994. Is Russian Democracy Doomed? *Journal of Democracy* 5 (2): 4–41.

4664. McFerson, H. M. August 1992. Democracy and Development in Africa. *Journal of Peace Research* 29 (3): 241–248.

4665. McGary, J., and S. J. R. Noel. March 1989. The Prospects for Consociational Democracy in South Africa. *Journal of Commonwealth and Comparative Politics* 27 (1): 3–22.

4666. McGee, R. W. March 1992. The Theory of Secession and Emerging Democracies: A Constitutional Solution. *Stanford Journal of International Law* 28 (2): 451–476.

4667. McGregor, J. January 22, 1993. How Electoral Laws Shape Eastern Europe's Parliaments. *RFE/RL Research Report* 2: 11–18.

4668. McGrew, A. March 1993. *See* Held, D. (March 1993).

4669. McInerney, T. J. March 1981. Eisenhower's Governance and the Power of Command: A Perspective on Presidential Leadership. *Presidential Studies Quarterly* 11 (2): 262–270.

4670. McIntosh, C. A. June 1981. Low Fertility and Liberal Democracy in Western Europe. *Population and Development* 7 (2): 181–207.

4671. McKay, R. B. 1983. Judicial Review in a Liberal Democracy. *Nomos* 25: 121–144.

4672. McKibben, C. R. September 1976. *See* Bogue, A. G. (September 1976).

4673. McKinlay, R. D., and R. Little. October 1977. A Foreign Policy Model of U.S. Bilateral Aid Allocation. *World Politics* 30 (1): 58–86.

4674. McLachlan, H. V. 1976. Universities, Schools and Democracy. *Oxford Review of Education* 2 (2): 171–178.

4675. McLaren, P. 1986. *See* Giroux, H. A. (1986).

4676. McLaughlin, E. 1988. *See* Jefferson, T. (1988).

4677. McLaverty, P. May 1991. Democratizing Local Government: The Sheffield and Doncaster Experience. *Economic and Industrial Democracy* 12 (2): 203–230.

4678. McLean, I. March 1994. Democratization and Economic Liberalization: Which Is the Chicken and Which Is the Egg? *Democratization* 1 (1): 27–40.

4679. McMillion, C. W. April 1981. International Integration and Intra-National Disintegration: The Case of Spain. *Comparative Politics* 13 (3): 291–313.

4680. McNeill, P. 1988. Party Politics in Democracy. *New Society* 83 (1310): 39.

4681. McNelly, T. June 1977. American Political Traditions and Japan's Postwar Constitution. *World Affairs* 140 (1): 58–68.

4682. McPherson, M. October 1986. *See* Krouse, R. (October 1986).

4683. McQuaid, K. January 1976. An American Owenite: Edward A. Filene and the Parameters of Industrial Reform, 1890–1937. *American Journal of Economics and Sociology* 35 (1): 77–94.

4684. McQuillan, W. June 1979. *See* Metcalfe, L. (June 1979).

4685. McSherry, J. P. September 1992a. Military Power, Impunity, and State Society Change in Latin America. *Canadian Journal of Political Science* 25 (3): 463–488.

4686. McSherry, J. P. Fall 1992b. Confronting the Question of Justice in Guatemala. *Social Justice* 19 (3): 1–28.

4687. McSweeney, D., and C. Tempest. September 1993. The Political Science of Democratic Transition in Eastern Europe. *Political Studies* 41 (3): 408–419.

4688. McWilliams, W. C. December 1992. *See* Schneck, S. (December 1992).

4689. Meacham, C. E. March 1994. The Role of the Chilean Catholic Church in the New Chilean Democracy. *Journal of Church and State* 36: 277–299.

4690. Meadows, M. January 1977. Constitutional Crisis in the United Kingdom: Scotland and the Devolution Controversy. *Review of Politics* 39 (1): 41–59.

4691. Meaglia, P. 1985. Tocqueville and the Problem of Democracy.* *Teoria Politica* 1 (3): 41–70.

4692. Meaglia, P. April 1987. Democracy and Interest in Kelsen.* *Revista Mexicana de Sociologia* 49 (2): 3–20.

4693. Mease, E. III. September 1987. Bicentennial Considerations on Establishing Justice and Securing Liberty. *Presidential Studies Quarterly* 17 (4): 661–671.

4694. Medard, J. October 1991. Authoritarianism and Democracy in Sub-Saharan Africa.* *Politique Africaine* 43: 92–104.

4695. Medew, R. March 1991. *See* Maley, M. (March 1991).

4696. Medhurst, K. April 1984. Spain's Evolutionary Pathway from Dictatorship to Democracy. *West European Politics* 7 (2): 30–49.

4697. Medvedenko, A. December 1985. Uruguay: Democratization an Uphill Struggle. *New Times (Moscow)* (52): 26–27.

4698. Meehan, E. April 1993. Citizenship and the European Community. *Political Quarterly* 64 (2): 172–186.

4699. Meehl, P. E. March 1977. The Selfish Voter Paradox and the Thrown-Away Vote Argument. *American Political Science Review* 71 (1): 11–30.

4700. Meeks, B. 1989. C. Y. Thomas, the Authoritarian State and Revolutionary Democracy. *Social and Economic Studies* 38 (1): 161–185.

4701. Meeks, J. E. 1981. Symposium: Judicial Review Versus Democracy: Foreword. *Ohio State Law Journal* 42 (1): 1–3.

4702. Megged, M. 1982. Censorship in the West Bank: How Democracy Can Be Distorted. *Nation* 235 (11): 333–336.

4703. Meicheong, N. January 1990. O Fim da Era de Deng Xiaoping? *Politica Internacional (Lisbon)* 1: 37–62.

4704. Meidner, R. 1993. *See* Mahon, R. (1993).

4705. Meier, C. 1978. Entstehung und Besonderheit der Griechischen Demokratie. *Zeitschrift für Politik* 25 (1): 1–31.

4706. Meier, K. J., and K. B. Smith. December 1994. Representative Democracy and Representative Bureaucracy: Examining the Top-Down and Bottom-Up Linkage. *Social Science Quarterly* 75 (4): 790–803.

4707. Meighan, R. 1987. Concepts of Democracy: Comment. *Journal of Education for Teaching* 13 (1): 77–78.

4708. Meili, S. March 1987. Cleaning House: Democracy and Environmentalism in Brazil. *Amicus Journal* 9: 11–13.

4709. Meiners, R. E. May 1981. *See* Keim, G. D. (May 1981).

4710. Meisler, S. October 1977. Spain's New Democracy. *Foreign Affairs* 56 (1): 190–208.

4711. Melamed, A. March 1993. The Attitude towards Democracy in Medieval Jewish Philosophy. *Jewish Political Studies Review* 5 (1–2): 33–56.

4712. Mellucci, A. July 1992. Liberation or Meaning: Social Movements, Culture, and Democracy. *Development and Change* 23 (3): 43–77.

4713. Melocchi, L. 1979. Democracy and Bureaucracy: Participation and Opposition in an Industrial Venture.* *Quaderni di Sociologia* 28 (4): 445–478.

4714. Melone, A. P., and G. Mace. December 1987. Judicial Review: The Usurpation and Democracy Question. *Judicature* 71: 202–210.

4715. Meltzer, A. A., and S. F. Richard. June 1978. Why Government Grows (and Grows) in a Democracy. *Public Interest* 52: 111–118.

4716. Melville, L. J., and D. K. Osborne. September 1990. Constitutional Democracy and the Theory of Agency. *Constitutional Political Economy* 1 (3): 21–47.

4717. Menacker, J. 1979. Democracy and College Admission Policy: German Perspectives. *College and University* 55 (1): 27–40.

4718. Menchu, R. June 1992. The Quincentennial, a Gift of Life: A Message from the Indigenous People of Guatemala. *Social Justice* 19 (2): 63–72.

4719. Mendelsohn, M. March 1994. The Media's Persuasive Effects: The Priming of Leadership in the 1988 Canadian Election. *Canadian Journal of Political Science* 27 (1): 81–97.

4720. Mendes, C. 1980. The Post-1964 Brazilian Regime: Outward Re-democratization and Inner Institutionalization. *Government and Opposition* 15 (1): 48–74.

4721. Mendes, C. March 1984. The 1982 Elections in Brazil. *Government and Opposition* 19 (2): 152–156.

4722. Mendes-Fernandes, R. 1994. Guinea-Bissau: A Democratic Transition?* *L'Afrique Politique* 81–91.

4723. Mendez, A. May 1994. *See* Roman, A. (May 1994).

4724. Mendras, M. April 1994. Russia Votes and Parts.* *Pouvoirs* 69: 173–181.

4725. Menendez Carrion, A. May 1991. Pendant Democracy and Political Representation in Latin America: Dilemmas and Possibilities, A Few Loud Ideas.* *Sintesis* 14: 43–67.

4726. Menendez Carrion, A. January 1992. La Democracia en El Ecuador: Desafios, Dilemas y Perspectivas. *Sintesis* 15: 101–123.

4727. Menezes, D. et al. October 1979. Is Democracy an Ideology?* *Revista de Ciencia Politica* 22 (4): 3–22.

4728. Mengel, H. J. June 1984. Basic Preconditions of Democratic Legislation.* *Zeitschrift für Rechtspolitik* 17 (6): 153–162.

4729. Menges, C. C. 1978. Spain: Struggle for Democracy Today. *Washington Papers* 6 (58): 7–80.

4730. Menges, C. C. April 1978. Deepening Shadows over a Fragile Democracy: Right and Left vs. Center in Spain. *Worldview* 21: 14–18.

4731. Menges, C. C. January 1988. How Democracies Keep Secrets. *Public Opinion (American Enterprise Institute)* 10: 10–13.

4732. Meredith, C. W. 1986. Democracy in the Family. *Individual Psychology* 42 (4): 602–610.

4733. Merelman, R. M. June 1980. Democratic Politics and the Culture of American Education. *American Political Science Review* 74 (2): 319–332.

4734. Merelman, R. M. September 1985. Role and Personality among Adolescent Political Activists. *Youth and Society* 17 (1): 37–68.

4735. Merkel, W. March 1993. Power Resources, Constraints and Strategic Choice: The Logic of Social Democracy in the Field of Economic Policy.* *Politische Vierteljahresschrift* 34 (1): 3–28.

4736. Merkel, W. 1994. Restrictions and Opportunities of Democratic Consolidation in Postcommunist Societies: A Comparison of Countries in East-Central Europe.* *Berliner Journal für Soziologie* 4 (4): 463–484.

4737. Merkel, W. May 1994. System Change: Problems of Democratic Strengthening in East Central Europe. *Aus Politik und Zeitgeschichte* 6 (18–19): 3–11.

4738. Merkl, P. H. October 1981. Democratic Development Breakdowns and Fascism. *World Politics* 34 (1): 114–135.

4739. Merkl, P. H. October 1985. Mapping the Temporal Universe of Party Governments. *Review of Politics* 47 (4): 483–515.

4740. Merkl, P. H. May 1993. Which Are Today's Democracies? *International Social Science Journal* 45 (2): 257–270.

4741. Meron, G. March 1990. Democracy, Dependency, and Destabilization: The Shaking of Allende's Regime. *Political Science Quarterly* 105 (1): 75–95.

4742. Meron, T. June 1990. Democracy and the Rule of Law. *World Affairs* 153 (1): 23–27.

4743. Merrett, C., and R. Gravil. April 1991. Comparing Human Rights: South Africa and Argentina, 1976–1989. *Comparative Studies in Society and History* 33 (2): 255–287.

4744. Merritt, R. L. November 1976. American Influences in the Occupation of Germany. *Annals of the American Academy of Political and Social Science* 428: 91–103.

4745. Mershon, C. A. January 1989. Between Workers and Union: Factory Councils in Italy. *Comparative Politics* 21 (2): 215–235.

4746. Merz, J. 1993. Mongolia on the Road to Pluralist Democracy and Market Economy: The New Mongolian Constitution of 1992.* *Verfassung und Recht in Ubersee* 26 (1): 82–100.

4747. Mes, G. M. 1977. Requiem for Democracy. *Mankind Quarterly* 17 (3): 208–214.

4748. Messas, K. December 1992. Democratization of Military Regimes: Contending Explanation. *Journal of Political and Military Sociology* 20 (2): 243–255.

4749. Mestak, P. 1986. A Social Reformist Understanding of the State and Democracy. *Filosoficky Casopis* 34 (2): 281–289.

4750. Metcalfe, L., and W. McQuillan. June 1979. Corporation or Industrial Democracy? *Political Studies* 27 (2): 266–282.

4751. Meuschel, S. 1989. The SED: From Stalinism to Democracy or Nationhood. *Revue d'Etudes Comparatives Est-Ouest* 20 (4): 47–67.

4752. Mewes, H. September 1991. German Unification, Nationalism and Democracy. *Telos* 89: 65–84.

4753. Meyer, D. S. September 1993. Protest Cycles and Political Process: American Peace Movements in the Nuclear Age. *Political Research Quarterly* 46 (3): 451–479.

4754. Meyer, L. October 1991. La Prolongada Transicion Mexicana: Del Autoritarismo Hacia Dondo. *Revista de Estudios Politicos* 74: 363–388.

4755. Meyer, W. J. 1974. Democracy: Needs over Wants. *Political Theory* 2 (2): 197–214.

4756. Meyerberg Leycegui, Y. April 1985. Mexico and Spain: A Comparative Analysis of Political Reform. *Revista Mexicana de Ciencias Politicas y Sociales* 120: 103–131.

4757. Meyerson, A. June 1984. Better Off Than Four Years Ago? *Policy Review* (29): 41–43.

4758. Meyerson, A. December 1984. Elliot Abrams for Human Rights. *Policy Review* (27): 78–79.

4759. Meyerson, A. March 1985. Brave New Hemisphere: Latin America's Democratic Renaissance. *Policy Review* (32): 24–27.

4760. Miara, L. October 1991. Notas Sobre le Transicion Chilena. *Revista de Estudios Politicos* 74: 323–362.

4761. Michaels, A. L. February 1976. The Alliance for Progress and Chile's Revolution in Liberty, 1964–1970. *Journal of Interamerican Studies and World Affairs* 18 (1): 74–99.

4762. Michel, P. 1982. *See* Ginsburg, V. (1982).

4763. Michelman, F. June 1992. Universities, Racist Speech, and Democracy in America: An Essay for the ACLU. *Harvard Civil Rights-Civil Liberties Law Review* 27 (2): 339–369.

4764. Michels, J. 1994. National Vision and the Negotiation of Narratives: The Oslo Agreement. *Journal of Palestine Studies* 24 (1): 28–38.

4765. Michnik, A. December 1991. Nationalism. *Social Research* 58 (4): 757–763.

4766. Middlebrook, K. J. 1989. Union Democratization in the Mexican Automobile Industry: A Reappraisal. *Latin American Research Review* 24 (2): 69–93.

4767. Midgley, G. April 1993. Empowerment, Participation, and Democracy. *Systems Practice* 6 (2): 211.

4768. Midlarsky, M. I. September 1992. The Origins of Democracy in Agrarian Society: Land Inequality and Political Rights. *Journal of Conflict Resolution* 36 (3): 454–477.

4769. Mieli, R. 1978. Eurocommunism and Western Democracy. *Atlantic Community Quarterly* 16 (3): 282–289.

4770. Mieres, P. October 1991. *See* Crespo, I. (October 1991).

4771. Migranjan, A. M. 1986. The Crisis of the Liberal Theory of Democracy.* *Sovetskoe Gosudarstvo Pravo* 3: 86–92.

4772. Migranjan, A. M. 1986. Crisis of the Theories of Democracy in the West.* *Voprosy Filosofii* 9: 122–132.

4773. Migranjan, A. M. 1989. Interrelations of the Individual, Society, and the State in the Political Theory of Marxism: The Problem of the Democratization of Socialist Society. *Soviet Studies in Philosophy* 27 (3): 6–34.

4774. Migue, J. 1976. Le Marche Politique et les Choix Collectives. *Revue d'Economie Politique* 27 (6): 984–1007.

4775. Mihajlov, M. 1979. After Tito: Prospects for Democracy. *New Leader* 62 (8): 12–13.

4776. Mihut, L. December 1994. The Emergence of Political Pluralism in Romania. *Communist and Post-Communist Studies* 27 (4): 411–422.

4777. Mikuriya, T. December 1993. A Blast from the Past. *Look Japan* 39: 10–12.

4778. Milacic, S. December 1992. Legal Order and Democracy in Eastern Europe: Some Views Regarding the Highly Institutional Times of Democratic Transition.* *Revue d'Etudes Comparatives Est-Ouest* 23 (4): 23–40.

4779. Miles, R. D. July 1976. *See* Kelly, A. H. (July 1976).

4780. Milette, J. December 1990. Parliamentary Democracy in the Caribbean. *Transafrica Forum* 7 (4): 21–34.

4781. Milgate, M. December 1993. *See* Stimson, S. C. (December 1993).

4782. Milimo, J. T. March 1993. Multiparty Democracy in Africa: Lessons from

Zambia. *International Journal on World Peace* 10 (1): 35–42.

4783. Milisavljevic, M. August 1983. Business Planning and Employee Democracy in Yugoslavia, 1940–1976. *Long Range Planning* 16 (4): 84–89.

4784. Millan, V., and M. A. Morris. April 1990. Conflicts in Latin America: Democratic Alternatives in the 1990s. *Conflict Studies* 230: 1–47.

4785. Millard, F. 1994. The Shaping of the Polish Party System, 1989–1993. *East European Politics and Societies* 8 (3): 467–494.

4786. Millard, F. September 1994. The Polish Parliamentary Elections of September 1993. *Communist and Post-Communist Studies* 27 (3): 295–314.

4787. Miller, A. H. April 1994. *See* Reisinger, W. M. (April 1994).

4788. Miller, A. H., and M. MacKuen. September 1979. Learning about the Candidates: The 1976 Presidential Debates. *Public Opinion Quarterly* 43 (3): 326–346.

4789. Miller, D. January 1978. Democracy and Social Justice. *British Journal of Political Science* 8: 1–19.

4790. Miller, D. December 1980. Jerusalem Not Yet Built: A Reply to Lessnoff on Capitalism, Socialism and Democracy. *Political Studies* 28 (4): 584–589.

4791. Miller, D. September 1984. The Use and Abuse of Political Violence. *Political Studies* 32 (3): 401–419.

4792. Miller, D. 1992. Deliberative Democracy and Social Choice. *Political Studies* 40: 54–67. Special issue.

4793. Miller, E. June 1994. *See* Jezer, M. (June 1994).

4794. Miller, G. J. December 1987. *See* Hammond, T. H. (December 1987).

4795. Miller, G. P. March 1992. *See* Macey, J. R. (March 1992).

4796. Miller, J. March 1983. Scientific Literacy: A Conceptual and Empirical Review. *Daedalus* 112 (2): 29–48.

4797. Miller, J. February 1988. The Ghostly Body Politic: *The Federalist Papers* and Popular Sovereignty. *Political Theory* 16 (1): 99–119.

4798. Miller, J. 1991. Direct Democracy and the Puritan Theory of Membership. *Journal of Politics* 53 (1): 57–74.

4799. Miller, J. March 1993. The Challenge of Radical Islam. *Foreign Affairs* 72: 43–56.

4800. Miller, M. J. December 1989. Dual Citizenship: A European Norm? *International Migration Review* 23 (4): 945–950.

4801. Miller, M. J., and W. W. Boyer. December 1982. Foreign Workers in the USVI: History of a Dilemma. *Caribbean Review* 11 (1): 48–51.

4802. Miller, R. W. 1986. Democracy and Class Dictatorship. *Social Philosophy and Policy* 3 (2): 59–76.

4803. Miller, T. C. November 1989. The Operation of Democratic Institutions. *Public Administration Review* 49 (6): 511–521.

4804. Millett, P. 1984. *See* George, B. (1984).

4805. Millett, R. March 1985. Guatemala: Progress and Paralysis. *Current History* 84 (500): 109–113, 136.

4806. Millett, R. December 1986. Guatemala's Painful Progress. *Current History* 85 (515): 413–416, 430–431.

4807. Millett, R. June 1988. Looking Beyond Noriega. *Foreign Policy* (71): 46–63.

4808. Millett, R. L. 1994. Beyond Sovereignty: International Efforts to Support Latin American Democracy. *Journal of Interamerican Studies and World Affairs* 36 (3): 1–24.

4809. Millette, J. December 1990. Parliamentary Democracy in the Caribbean. *TransAfrica Forum* 7: 21–34.

4810. Millon, D. April 1992. Objectivity and Democracy. *New York University Law Review* 67 (1): 1–66.

4811. Mills, C. W. 1990. Getting out of the Cave: Tension between Democracy and Elitism in Marx Theory of Cognitive Liberation. *Social and Economic Studies* 39 (1): 1–50.

4812. Mills, G. January 1992. Zambia and the Winds of Change. *World Today* 48 (1): 16–18.

4813. Mills, N. D. December 1984. *See* Levy, J. (December 1984).

4814. Mills, T. November 1978. Europe's Industrial Democracy: An American Response. *Harvard Business Review* 56 (6): 143–152.

4815. Minehart, T. G. August 1984. *See* Brunk, G. G. (August 1984).

4816. Minford, P. 1988. Interest Rates and Bond Financed Deficits in a Ricardian Two Party Democracy. *Weltwirtschaftliches Archiv* 124 (3): 387–402.

4817. Minogue, K. R. 1976. Humanist Democracy: Political Thought of C. B. MacPherson. *Canadian Journal of Political Science* 9 (3): 377–394.

4818. Minty, A. S. March 1993. South Africa: From Apartheid to Democracy. *Security Dialogue* 24 (1): 69–84.

4819. Mintz, A., and N. Geva. September 1993. Why Don't Democracies Fight Each Other: An Experimental Study. *Journal of Conflict Resolution* 37 (3): 484–503.

4820. Minzberg, H. 1983. Why America Needs, but Cannot Have, Corporate Democracy. *Organizational Dynamics* 11 (4): 5–20.

4821. Mioni, F. April 1990. Tocqueville and the American Democratic Culture of the Eighteenth Century. *Il Politico* 55 (2): 251–273.

4822. Miranda, F. B. June 1993. Democratization in the Philippines: Recent Developments, Trends, and Prospects. *Asian Journal of Political Science* 1 (1): 85–112.

4823. Mircev, D. January 1979. *See* Leonardson, G. (January 1979).

4824. Miric, J. 1989. Speaking about Democracy.* *Politicka Misao* 26 (2): 3–11.

4825. Miric, J. 1990. Speech and Democracy.* *Politicka Misao* 27 (2): 133–137.

4826. Mirkovic, D. September 1987. Sociological Reflections on Yugoslav Participatory Democracy and Social Ownership. *East European Quarterly* 21 (3): 319–332.

4827. Mirsky, Y. September 1993. Democratic Politics, Democratic Culture. *Orbis* 37 (4): 567–580.

4828. Mishler, W. April 1994. *See* Rose, R. (April 1994).

4829. Mishler, W., and R. Rose. February 1994. Support for Parliaments and Regimes in the Transition toward Democracy in Eastern Europe. *Legislative Studies Quarterly* 19 (1): 5–32.

4830. Misra, J. November 1993. *See* Hicks, A. (November 1993).

4831. Misra, J., and A. Hicks. April 1994. Catholicism and Unionization in Affluent Postwar Democracies: Catholicism, Culture, Party, and Unionization. *American Sociological Review* 59 (2): 304–326.

4832. Misra, R. N. July 1982. Some Observations on Democracy. *Indian Political Science Review* 16 (2): 166–175.

4833. Miszlivetz, F. September 1989. Europa: Redefining the Possible. *Peace Review* 1 (4): 4–7.

4834. Miszlivetz, F. December 1991. The Unfinished Revolutions of 1989: The Decline of the Nation-State? *Social Research* 58 (4): 781–804.

4835. Misztal, B. March 1984. *See* Misztal, B. A. (March 1984).

4836. Misztal, B. A. 1989. Political Transformations of Authoritarian Regimes. *Polish Sociological Bulletin* 86: 17–33.

4837. Misztal, B. A. 1992. Must Eastern Europe Follow the Latin American Way? *Archives Europeennes de Sociologie* 33 (1): 151–179.

4838. Misztal, B. A. August 1993. Understanding Political Change in Eastern Europe: A Sociological Perspective. *Sociology* 27 (3): 451–470.

4839. Misztal, B. A., and B. Misztal. March 1984. Urban Social Problems in Poland: The Macrosocial Determinants. *Urban Affairs Quarterly* 19 (3): 315–328.

4840. Mitchell, M. J. April 1989. *See* Rochon, T. R. (April 1989).

4841. Mitchell, N. J., and J. M. McCormick. July 1988. Economic and Political Explanations of Human Rights Violations. *World Politics* 40 (4): 476–498.

4842. Mitchell, W. C. 1984. Schumpeter and Public Choice, Part II: Democracy and the Demise of Capitalism: The Missing Chapter in Schumpeter. *Public Choice* 42 (2): 161–174.

4843. Mitman, G. 1990. Evolution as Gospel: William Patten, the Language of Democracy. *ISIS* 81 (308): 446–463.

4844. Mitra, S. K. 1979. Political Democracy and Modernization: Some Implications of the Existing Paradigm. *Teaching Politics* 5 (1–2): 32–39.

4845. Mitra, S. K. 1988. India: Dynastic Rule or the Democratization of Power. *Third World Quarterly* 10 (1): 129–159.

4846. Mitra, S. K. August 1991. Crisis and Resilience in Indian Democracy.* *International Social Science Journal* 43 (3): 555–570.

4847. Mitra, S. K. March 1992. Democracy and Political Change in India. *Journal of Commonwealth and Comparative Politics* 30 (1): 9–38.

4848. Mitran, I. 1981. The Functionality of Socialist Democratic Structures. *Revue Roumaine des Sciences Sociales (Serie de Sociologie)* 25: 9–16.

4849. Mitter, W. November 1993. Education, Democracy, and Development in a Period of Revolutionary Change. *International Review of Education* 39 (6): 463–471.

4850. Mitterer, J., and K. Oneill. 1992. The End of Information: Computers, Democracy, and the University. *Interchange* 23 (1–2): 123–139.

4851. Mitterlehner, G. 1990. Authoritarian State, Democracy and Social Movements. *Argument* 32 (3): 431–432.

4852. Mitzman, A. July 1987. Danton Michelet and the Corruption of Revolutionary Virtue. *Journal of the History of Ideas* 48 (3): 453–466.

4853. Mizrahi, Y. February 1994. Rebels without a Cause? The Politics of Entrepreneurs in Chihuahua [Mexico]. *Journal of Latin American Studies* 26 (1): 137–158.

4854. Mkandawire, T. 1988. *See* Mandini, M. (1988).

4855. Mladenka, K. R. 1977. Citizen Demand and Bureaucratic Response: Direct Dialing Democracy in a Major American City. *Urban Affairs Quarterly* 12 (3): 273–290.

4856. Mo, J. January 1992. *See* Brady, D. (January 1992).

4857. Modelski, G., and G. Perry. 1991. Democratization in Long Perspective. *Technological Forecasting and Social Change* 39 (1–2): 23–34.

4858. Moeller, J. February 1985. Alexander M. Bickel: Toward a Theory of Politics. *Journal of Politics* 47 (1): 113–139.

4859. Mohr, L. B. October 1977. Authority and Democracy in Organizations. *Human Relations* 30 (10): 919–947.

4860. Mohr, L. B. January 1994. Authority in Organizations: On the Reconciliation of Democracy and Expertise. *Journal of Public Administration Research and Theory* 4 (1): 49–65.

4861. Mohs, R. M. January 1992. *See* Repnik, H. P. (January 1992).

4862. Moises, J. A. March 1990. Dilemmas of Democratic Consolidation in Brazil.* *Sintesis* 11: 213–243.

4863. Moises, J. A. March 1991. Democracy Threatened: The Latin American Paradox. *Alternatives* 16 (2): 141–159.

4864. Mokrzycki, E. 1991. Inheritance of the Real Socialism and the Western Democracy: The Sociological Sketch.* *Sociologicky Casopis* 27 (6): 751–757.

4865. Mokrzycki, E. June 1991. The Legacy of Real Socialism and Western Democracy. *Studies in Comparative Communism* 24 (2): 211–217.

4866. Mokrzycki, E. December 1993. *See* Cirtautas, A. M. (December 1993).

4867. Molin, K. March 1983. Social Democracy after the Second World War. *Scandinavian Review* 71: 58–62.

4868. Molitor, M. December 1988. The Revival of Chilean Democracy.* *La Revue Nouvelle* 12: 3–20.

4869. Moller, G. 1989. *See* Kuhnel, K. (1989).

4870. Molloy, J. M., and E. Gamarra. January 1985. La Transicion a la Democracia en Bolivia. *Apuntes* 87–108.

4871. Mols, M. 1978. Bundestag Electoral Fight 1976: Indication of the Direction for the Future of Our Democracy.* *Politische Studien* 29 (237): 33–42.

4872. Mols, M. 1985. Possibilities for Europe to Aid the Consolidation of Latin American Democracies.* *Europa Archiv: Zeitschrift für Internationale Politik* 40 (19): 581–590.

4873. Mols, M., and U. Wolf. 1987. Risks to Democracy in Latin America.* *Aussenpolitik* 38 (2): 194–208.

4874. Molt, P. March 1993. Chances and Preconditions.* *Aus Politik und Zeitgeschichte* 19 (12): 12–21.

4875. Molutsi, P. P. 1990. *See* Holm, J. D. (1990).

4876. Molutsi, P. P., and J. D. Holm. 1990. Developing Democracy When Civil Society Is Weak: The Case of Botswana. *African Affairs* 89 (356): 323–340.

4877. Molyneux, M. June 1994. Women's Rights and the International Context: Some Reflections on the Post-Communist States. *Millennium* 23 (2): 287–314.

4878. Mommsen, M. 1974. Contradictions in Proporz Democracy. *Politische Vierteljahresschrift* 15 (2): 175–212.

4879. Mommsen, M. February 1986. Women's Political Role: East and West.* *Aus Politik und Zeitgeschichte* 8 (6–7): 3–13.

4880. Monaco, F. May 1994. Italy Turns to the Right. The 27–28 March [1994] Elections. *Aggiornamenti Sociali* 45 (5): 325–332.

4881. Monberg, J. 1993. Intangible Consequences of Target Marketing: Hidden Threats to a Democratic Social Order. *Bulletin of Science, Technology and Society* 13 (5): 264–267.

4882. Monclaire, S. September 1994. Le Quasi-Impeachment du President Collor: Questions sur la "Consolidation de la Democratie" Bresilienne. *Revue Française de Science Politique* 44: 23–48.

4883. Monconduit, F. March 1986. State and Democracy.* *Revue du Droit Public et de la Science Politique* 2: 327–344.

4884. Moncrieff, A. March 1993. Thailand's Slow March To Democracy. *World Today* 49 (3): 56–59.

4885. Monereo Perez, M. November 1994. The Crisis of Politics and European Institutions.* *Sistema* 123: 81–93.

4886. Monette, R. A. June 1994. A New Federalism for Indian Tribes: The Relationship between the United States and Tribes in Light of Our Federalism and Republican Democracy. *University of Toledo Law Review* 25: 617–672.

4887. Mong, Xiong. November 1990. *See* Petracca, M. P. (November 1990).

4888. Monga, C. January 1991. Cameroun: L'Enjeu des Libertes. *Jeune Afrique Economie:* 74–77.

4889. Mongardini, C. June 1981. Vilfredo Pareto and Democracy.* *Storia e Politica* 20 (2): 296–322.

4890. Monks, R. A. July 1987. Shareholder Democracy Isn't Working: How Can Shareholders Act as a Group When They Don't Know Who the Others Are? *Pension World* 23: 24–26.

4891. Monroe, B. L. December 1994. Understanding Electoral Systems: Beyond Plurality Versus PR. *PS: Political Science & Politics* 27 (4): 677–682.

4892. Monroe, L. January 1992. Un Pays en Psychanalyse. *Croissance* 34–36.

4893. Monshipouri, M., and C. G. Kukla. 1994. Islam, Democracy and Human Rights: The Continuing Debate in the West. *Middle East Policy* 3 (2): 22–39.

4894. Montecinos, V. March 1993. Economic Policy Elites and Democratization. *Studies in Comparative International Development* 28 (1): 25–53.

4895. Montecinos, V., and J. Markoff. 1993. Democrats and Technocrats: Professional Economists and Regime Transitions in Latin America. *Canadian Journal of Development Studies* 14 (1): 7–22.

4896. Montefiore, A. 1992. The Role of Democracy in the University: The University and Its Old Members. *Interchange* 23 (1–2): 51–62.

4897. Montero, C., and O. Munoz (eds.). December 1993. Hacia Donde va la Sociedad Chilena? *Coleccion Estudios* 10: 95–154. Round-table discussion.

4898. Montero, J. R. January 1994. Religiosity, Ideology, and Vote in Spain.* *Revista de Estudios Politicos* 83: 77–111.

4899. Moody, P. R. April 1983. The Erosion of the Function of Political Parties in the Post-Liberal State. *Review of Politics* 45 (2): 254–279.

4900. Moody, P. R. December 1991. The Democratization of Taiwan and the Reunification of China. *Journal of East Asian Affairs* 5: 144–184.

4901. Moon, J. D. 1983. Can Liberal Democracy Cope with Scarcity. *International Political Science Review* 5 (3): 385–400.

4902. Moore, A. March 1984. From Council to Legislature: Democracy, Parliamentarianism, and the San Blas Cuna. *American Anthropologist* 86 (1): 28–42.

4903. Moore, C. H. March 1987. Prisoners' Financial Dilemmas: A Consociational Future for Lebanon? *American Political Science Review* 81 (1): 201–218.

4904. Moore, C. H. March 1991. Democratic Passions and Economic Interest. *American-Arab Affairs* 36: 7–9.

4905. Moore, D. T. 1981. Will Robots Save Democracy. *Futurist* 15 (4): 14–19.

4906. Moore, D. W. June 1975. Repredicting Voting Patterns in the General Assembly. *International Studies Quarterly* 19 (2): 199–211.

4907. Moore, J. N. June 1988. An Overview Democratic Strategy of Strength and Principle. *Global Affairs* 3 (3): 76–79.

4908. Moore, M. May 1990. Economic Liberalization Versus Political Pluralism in

Sri Lanka. *Modern Asian Studies* 24 (2): 341–383.

4909. Moore, M. March 1992. Retreat from Democracy in Sri Lanka? *Journal of Commonwealth and Comparative Politics* 30 (1): 64–84.

4910. Moore, M. March 1994. "Guided Democracy" in Sri Lanka: The Electoral Dimension. *Journal of Commonwealth and Comparative Politics* 32 (1): 1–30.

4911. Moore, R. A. August 1979. Reflections on the Occupation of Japan. *Journal of Asian Studies* 38 (4): 721–734.

4912. Moore, T. G. June 1991. Privatization Now or Else: The Impending Failure of Democracy and Freedom in Central Europe.* *Revue d'Etudes Comparatives Est-Ouest* 22 (2): 85–103.

4913. Moore, W. H. March 1990. *See* Gurr, T. R. (March 1990).

4914. Moore, W. J. September 17, 1988. Election-Day Lawmaking: Skipping the Legislative Process. *National Journal* 20: 2296–2301.

4915. Morales, C. January 1986. Individual Autonomy Politics.* *Cuadernos Americanos* 45 (1): 141–155.

4916. Morales, H., Jr. July 1990. *See* Lara, F. (July 1990).

4917. Morales, W. Q. February 1980. Bolivia Moves toward Democracy. *Current History* 79 (454): 76–79, 86–88.

4918. Moran, J. January 1993. *See* Harris, E. (January 1993).

4919. Moran, J. P. March 1994. The Communist Torturers of Eastern Europe: Prosecute and Punish or Forgive and Forget? *Communist and Post-Communist Studies* 27: 95–109.

4920. Moravcsik, M. J. 1987. Some Thoughts for the Discussion on Decision Making within Science and Technology: Is Democracy Possible. *Bulletin of Science, Technology and Society* 7 (5–6): 697–699.

4921. Morawski, W. March 1990. Town-Country Economic Relations Versus Stability of the System of Parliamentary Democracy in Poland of the 1920s. *East European Quarterly* 24 (1): 47–56.

4922. Moreau Defarges, P. March 1993. The Crisis of Politics and the Maastricht Turmoil.* *Politique Etrangere* 58 (1): 93–104.

4923. Moreira-Alves, M. H. December 1984. Grassroots Organizations, Trade Unions, and the Church: A Challenge to the Controlled Abertura in Brazil. *Latin American Perspectives* 11 (1): 73–102.

4924. Moreira-Alves, M. H. June 1988. Dilemmas of the Consolidation of Democracy from the Top in Brazil: A Political Analysis. *Latin American Perspectives* 15 (3): 47–63.

4925. Moreira, M. M. March 1984. Political Liberalization and Economic Crisis. *Government and Opposition* 19 (2): 157–166.

4926. Morel, Y. June 1992. Democratization in Africa: The "National Conferences."* *Etudes* 733–743.

4927. Morena-Valencia, F. 1987. Church and Democracy.* *Revista de Ciencia Politica* 9–10 (2–1): 29–50.

4928. Moreno, F. J. 1975. Breakdown of Chilean Democracy. *World Affairs* 138 (1): 19–25.

4929. Morera, E. March 1990. Gramsci and Democracy. *Canadian Journal of Political Science* 23 (1): 23–38.

4930. Morgan, C. 1976. Lies, Secrecy, Bribery: Democracy Can't Stand It. *Nation* 222 (22): 690–692.

4931. Morgan, D. R., and R. E. England. November 1988. The Two Faces of Privatization. *Public Administration Review* 48 (6): 979–987.

4932. Morgan, R. December 1982. Social Democracy in Europe: A Comparative Examination. *Government and Opposition* 17 (1): 22–34.

4933. Morgan, T. C. 1993. Democracy and War: Reflections on the Literature. *International Interactions* 18 (3): 197–203.

4934. Morgan, T. C., and S. H. Campbell. June 1991. Domestic Structure, Decision Constraints, and War: So Why Kant Democracies Fight? *Journal of Conflict Resolution* 35 (2): 187–211.

4935. Morgandini, C. 1977. Democracy or Plutocracy. *Sociological Analysis and Theory* 7 (2): 83–97.

4936. Morgenthau, H. March 1977. Hannah Arendt on Totalitarianism and Democracy. *Social Research* 44 (1): 127–131.

4937. Morigiwa, Y. September 1992. The Laws of a Nation: The Essential Formula for a Liberal and Democratic State. *William and Mary Bill of Rights Journal* 1 (2): 187–204.

4938. Morlan, R. L. December 1980. Consolidation vs. Confederation in European Municipal Reform. *National Civic Review* 69 (11): 601–607.

4939. Morlan, R. L. September 1982. Sub-Municipal Governance in Practice: The Rotterdam Experience. *Western Political Quarterly* 35 (3): 425–441.

4940. Morlan, R. L. October 1984. Communication with Citizens: The Movement in European Cities. *National Civic Review* 73 (9): 441–445.

4941. Morley, J. W. December 1986. The North's Dilemma Is the South's Opportunity. *Korea and World Affairs* 10 (4): 695–727.

4942. Morley, M. November 1983. *See* Petras, J. (November 1983).

4943. Morley, M. 1991. *See* Petras, J. (1991).

4944. Morlino, L. 1975. Measures of Democracy and Freedom: Some Empiri-

cal Analyses Discussed.* *Rivista Italiana di Scienza Politica* 5 (1): 131–166.

4945. Morlino, L. July 1979. Political Regimes and Freedom.* *Biblioteca della Liberta* 74–75: 5–26.

4946. Morlino, L. December 1985. ¿Cual Es la Crisis Democratica de Italia? *Critica y Utopia* (13): 65–106.

4947. Morlino, L. July 1986. Democratic Consolidation: Definition, Models, Hypotheses.* *Revista Espanola de Investigaciones Sociologicas* 35: 7–61.

4948. Morlino, L. August 1986. Democratic Consolidation: Definition and Models.* *Rivista Italiana di Scienza Politica* 16 (2): 197–238.

4949. Morlino, L. December 1986. Democratic Consolidation: A Few Explanatory Hypotheses.* *Rivista Italiana di Scienza Politica* 16 (3): 439–459.

4950. Morlino, L. January 1991. Democratic Consolidation: Definition, Models, Hypothesis. *Sintesis* 13: 37–86.

4951. Morocco, M. 1990. Rediscovering the Roots of American Democracy. *Human Rights* 17 (3): 38–39.

4952. Morrice, D. December 1994. C. B. MacPherson's Critique of Liberal Democracy and Capitalism. *Political Studies* 42 (4): 646–661.

4953. Morris, M. A. April 1990. *See* Millan, V. (April 1990).

4954. Morris, R. B. February 1977. "We the People of the United States": The Bicentennial of a People's Revolution. *American Historical Review* 92 (1): 1–20.

4955. Morris, S. D. March 1992. Political Reformism in Mexico: Salinas at the Brink. *Journal of Interamerican Studies and World Affairs* 34 (1): 27–57.

4956. Morris-Jones, W. H. 1979. The West and the Third World: Whose Democracy, Whose Development? *Third World Quarterly* 1 (3): 31–42.

4957. Mortati, C. February 1975. La Repubblica e Fondata sul Lavoro. *Politica del Diritto* 6: 19–71.

4958. Mortimer, R. A. January 1993. Algeria: The Clash between Islam, Democracy, and the Military. *Current History* 92 (570): 37–41.

4959. Morton, B. March 1993. A Question of Time: The Real Message from the Tongan Elections Is That Support for Change Is Real. *Pacific Islands Monthly* 63: 11–13.

4960. Morton, F. L. 1984. Sexual Equality and the Family in Tocqueville's *Democracy in America*. *Canadian Journal of Political Science* 17 (2): 309–324.

4961. Morton, F. W. O. July 1985. Brazil's New Democracy. *International Perspectives:* 21–24.

4962. Morton, R. B. November 1994. *See* Francis, W. L. (November 1994).

4963. Morton, S. I. 1991. The Bicentennial of Democracy: A WHCLIS Theme. *Special Libraries* 82 (2): 109–112.

4964. Moschutz, H. D. 1985. Popular Sovereignty and Democratic Centralism. *Staat und Recht* 34 (1): 4–8.

4965. Mosher, S. W. September 1987. Three Steps toward Opening Mainland China. *Orbis* 31 (3): 331–337.

4966. Moss, B. H. October 1985. Marx and Engels on French Social Democracy: Historians or Revolutionaries. *Journal of the History of Ideas* 46 (4): 539–557.

4967. Moss, D. 1991. Psychoanalysis and Democracy: Introduction. *American Imago* 48 (2): 177–180.

4968. Moss, M., and R. Warren. December 1984. Public Policy and Community-Oriented Uses of Cable Television. *Urban Affairs Quarterly* 20 (2): 233–254.

4969. Mosse, C. 1979. Democracy of Athens.* *Histoire* (9): 24–31.

4970. Mosse, C. 1979. Creation of a Political Myth: Solon, Founding Father of the Athenian Democracy.* *Annales: Economies Societes Civilisations* 34 (3): 425–437.

4971. Mostov, J. December 1989. Karl Marx as Democratic Theorist. *Polity* 22 (2): 195–212.

4972. Mostov, J. June 1994. Democracy and the Politics of National Identity. *Studies in East European Thought* 46 (1–2): 9–32.

4973. Motley, L. A. April 1984. Central America: Democracy, Peace, and Development Initiative. *Department of State Bulletin* 84: 72–74.

4974. Motley, L. A. October 1984. Democracy in Latin America and the Caribbean. *Department of State Bulletin* 84: 1–15.

4975. Motofumi, A. January 1990. Democracy, an Unintended Victim. *Japan Quarterly* 37 (1): 4–13.

4976. Mouffe, C. 1990. Radical Democracy or Liberal Democracy. *Socialist Review* 20 (2): 57–66.

4977. Mouffe, C. November 1987. *See* Laclau, E. (November 1987).

4978. Moussalli, A. S. January 1994. Hasan al-Turabi's Islamist Discourse on Democracy and Shura. *Middle Eastern Studies* 30 (1): 52–63.

4979. Mouton, C. 1978. *See* Madec, A. (1978).

4980. Mouzeus, N. February 1983. On the Demise of Oligarchic Parliamentarianism in the Semi-Periphery: A Balkan-Latin American Comparison. *Sociology* 17 (1): 28–43.

4981. Mowery, D. C. February 1993. *See* Su, T. T. (February 1993).

4982. Mowlam, M. March 1979. Popular Access to the Decision-Making Process in Switzerland: The Role of Direct Democracy. *Government and Opposition* 14 (2): 180–197.

4983. Moynihan, D. P. March 1979. Further Thoughts on Words and Foreign Policy. *Policy Review* 8: 53–60.

4984. Moynihan, D. P. May 1985. Indira Gandhi and Democracy. *Freedom at Issue* 84: 17–18.

4985. Msonganzila, M. R. October 29, 1994. Women and Co-operatives in Tanzania: Separatism or Integration. *Economic and Political Weekly* 29 (44): WS86.

4986. Mucha, J. L. December 1991. Democratization and Cultural Minorities: The Polish Case of the 1980s-1990s. *East European Quarterly* 25 (4): 463–482.

4987. Mueller, J. November 1992. Theory and Democracy. *American Journal of Political Science* 36 (4): 1015–1022.

4988. Mueller, J., and M. Lienesch. November 1992. Democracy and Ralph's Pretty Good Grocery: Elections, Equality, and the Minimal Human Being. *American Journal of Political Science* 36 (4): 983–1003. 3 articles.

4989. Mughan, A. September 1986. Toward a Political Explanation of Government: Vote Losses in Midterm. *American Political Science Review* 80 (3): 761–755.

4990. Mujal-Leon, E. March 1982. The Crisis of Spanish Democracy. *Washington Quarterly* 5 (2): 101–107.

4991. Mujal-Leon, E. June 1983. Rei(g)ning in Spain. *Foreign Policy* 51: 101–117.

4992. Mujal-Leon, E. March 1986. Decline and Fall of Spanish Communism. *Problems of Communism* 35 (2): 1–27.

4993. Mukandala, R. S. December 1992. To Be or Not to Be: The Paradoxes of African Bureaucracies in the 1990s. *International Review of Administrative Sciences* 58: 555–576.

4994. Mulgan, G. 1994. Democratic Dismissal, Competition and Contestability among the Quangos. *Oxford Review of Economic Policy* 10 (3): 51–60.

4995. Mulgan, R. G. December 1984. Who Should Have How Much Say About What?: Some Problems in Pluralist Democracy. *Political Science* 36 (2): 12–124.

4996. Mulhlpfordt, G. 1981. Bahrdt's Road to Revolutionary Democratism: The Becoming of His Doctrine of Welfare.* *Zeitschrift für Geschichtswissenschaft* 29 (11): 996–1017.

4997. Muller, E. N. December 1985. Dependent Breakdown in the Third World. *International Studies Quarterly* 29 (4): 445–469.

4998. Muller, E. N. September 1987. *See* Seligson, M. A. (September 1987).

4999. Muller, E. N. February 1988. Democracy, Economic Development, and Income Inequality. *American Sociological Review* 53 (1): 50–68.

5000. Muller, E. N. 1990. *See* Seligson, M. A. (1990).

5001. Muller, E. N., P. Pesonen, and T. Jukam. 1980. Support for the Freedom of Assembly in Western Democracies. *European Journal of Political Research* 8 (3): 265–288.

5002. Muller, E. N., and M. A. Seligson. September 1994. Civic Culture and Democracy: The Question of Causal Relationships. *American Political Science Review* 88 (3): 635–652.

5003. Muller, E. N., M. A. Seligson, and I. Turan. October 1987. Education, Participation, and Support for Democratic Norms. *Comparative Politics* 20 (1): 19–33.

5004. Muller, E. P. 1976. Democratic Socialism and German Social Democracy. *Politische Studien* 27 (228): 355–362.

5005. Muller, K. February 1992. Environmental Policy and Reform of Political System in New Democracies. *IGW* (*Report uber Wissenschaft und Technologie*) 6: 55–70.

5006. Muller, L. March 1991. Building Stones and Ethics of a Market Economy in Accordance with the Requirements of Democracy.* *Politische Studien* 316: 147–160.

5007. Muller, P. 1989. Democracy or Technology.* *Archiv für Rechts und Sozialphilosophie* 75 (1): 61–71.

5008. Muller, S. December 1994. Democracy in Germany. *Daedalus* 123 (1): 33–56.

5009. Munck, G. L. 1993. Beyond Electoralism in El Salvador: Conflict Resolution through Negotiated Compromise. *Third World Quarterly* 14 (1): 75–93.

5010. Munck, G. L. April 1994. Democratic Transition in Comparative Perspective. *Comparative Politics* 26 (3): 355–375.

5011. Munck, G. L. June 1994. Democratic Stability and Its Limits: An Analysis of Chile's 1993 Elections. *Journal of Interamerican Studies and World Affairs* 36 (2): 1–37.

5012. Munck, R. March 1990. Farewell to Socialism? A Comment on Recent Debates. *Latin American Perspectives* 17 (2): 113–121.

5013. Munck, R. May 1992. The Democratic Decade: Argentina since Malvinas. *Bulletin of Latin American Research* 11: 205–216.

5014. Muni, S. D. May 1991. Patterns of Democracy in South Asia. *International Social Science Journal* 43 (2): 361–372.

5015. Munoz, H. July 1993. The OAS and Democratic Governance. *Journal of Democracy* 4 (3): 29–38.

5016. Munoz, O. 1983. A New Industrialization: Strategy Elements of Development by Democracy.* *Trimestre Economico* 50 (200): 2287–2319.

5017. Munoz, O. December 1993. *See* Montero, C. (ed.) (December 1993).

5018. Munoz-Goma, O., and C. Celedon. June 1993. Chile en Transicion: Estrategia Economica y Politica. *Coleccion Estudios* 20: 101–129.

5019. Munoz-Patraca, V. M. July 1994. The Transition Democracy in Mexico.* *Revista Mexicana de Ciencias Politicas y Sociales* 157: 9–23.

5020. Munro, R. September 1991. The Beijing Trails: Secret Judicial Procedures and the Exclusion of Foreign Observers. *UCLA Pacific Basin Law Journal* 10: 136–150.

5021. Munro, R. H. September 1984. Dateline Manila: Moscow's Next Win? *Foreign Policy* 56: 173–190.

5022. Munslow, B. March 1983. Why Has the Westminster Model Failed in Africa. *Parliamentary Affairs* 36 (2): 218–228.

5023. Munslow, B. October 1993. Democratization in Africa. *Parliamentary Affairs* 46 (4): 478–490.

5024. Munz, T. 1977. Spinoza's Theory of State, Tolerance and Democracy. *Filosoficky Casopis* 25 (5): 772–783.

5025. Mura, V. 1985. Pluralism and Democracy: A Difficult Encounter.* *Teoria Politica* 1 (2): 3–21.

5026. Mura, V. 1990. Ideal Democracy and Real Democracy.* *Teoria Politica* 6 (1): 57–80.

5027. Murauskas, G. T. 1987. *See* Soloman, B. D. (1987).

5028. Muravchik, J. June 1989. U.S. Political Parties Overseas. *Washington Quarterly* 12 (3): 91–100.

5029. Murillo Castano, G., and J. C. Ruiz Vasquez. March 1992. Elections, Political Parties and Democracy in the Andean Countries.* *America Latina* 3: 7–24.

5030. Murnighan, J. K., and D. E. Conlon. June 1991. The Dynamics of Intense

Work Groups: A Study of British String Quartets. *Administrative Science Quarterly* 36 (2): 165–186.

5031. Murphy, B. C. October 1993. A Progress Report on the Democracy Development Initiative. *Federal Bar News and Journal* 40: 579–580.

5032. Murphy, F. X. 1982. City of God. *Wilson Quarterly* 6 (4): 98–112.

5033. Murphy, J. W. March 1986. Yugoslav Self-Management and Social Ontology. *East European Quarterly* 20 (1): 75–89.

5034. Murphy, P. December 1983. Moralities, Rule Choice, and the Universal Legislator. *Social Research* 50 (4): 757–801.

5035. Murphy, R. D. September 1986. The Mayoralty and the Democratic Creed: The Evolution of an Ideology and Institution. *Urban Affairs* 22 (1): 3–23.

5036. Murray, B. April 1990. Tiananmen: The View from Taipei. *Asian Survey* 30 (4): 348–359.

5037. Murray, P. V. 1986. Educating for Participatory Democracy in the Effective School. *Education* 106 (4): 409–412.

5038. Murshid, T. M. 1993. Bangladesh: The Challenge of Democracy: Language, Culture and Political Identity. *Contemporary South Asia* 2 (1): 67–73.

5039. Murteira, M. 1986. From Obsolete State to Democratic Nation: Portugal in Europe's Periphery in the Second Half of the 20th Century. *Analise Social* 91: 259–277.

5040. Musgrave, R. A. March 1979. The Tax Revolt: Causes and Cure. *Social Science Quarterly* 59 (4): 697–703.

5041. Mushkat, M. December 1990. The Political Economy of Constitutional Change in Hong Kong. *Asian Economies* 19: 33–53.

5042. Musil, J. March 1992. Czechoslovakia in the Middle of Transition. *Daedalus* 121 (2): 175–196.

5043. Muslih, M. March 1993. Palestinian Civil Society. *Middle East Journal* 47: 258–274.

5044. Muslih, M., and A. R. Norton. June 1991. The Need for Arab Democracy. *Foreign Policy* 83: 3–19.

5045. Musolf, L. D., and J. F. Springer. May 1977. Legislatures and Divided Societies: The Malaysian Parliament and Multi-Ethnicity. *Legislative Studies Quarterly* 2 (2): 113–136.

5046. Musso, R. 1976. Gli Interrogativi sul Futuro Capitalismo e della Democrazia. *Civitas (Roma)* 27 (5): 3–22.

5047. Musso, R. 1991. Science and Democracy: Scientific Institutions in Advanced Societies. *Mondes en Developpement* 74: 33–39.

5048. Muthayya, B., and S. Rangacharyulu. 1980. Relationship between Faith in People and Opinion on Democracy. *Behavioural Sciences and Rural Development* 3 (2): 140–144.

5049. Muzzio, D. June 1987. *See* Bolce, L. (June 1987).

5050. Muzzopappa, H. 1989. El Retorno del Ciudadano: Democracia y Politica Bajo el Gobierno Radical. *Nuevo Proyecto* 5–6: 7–25.

5051. Myers, M. S. September 1979. Towards Organisational Democracy: "Win-Lose Adversary," "Collaborative Adversary," and "Organizational Democracy": Models of the Union Company Relationship. *ASCI Journal of Management* 9 (1): 33–49.

5052. Myers, R. September 1991. Democracy According to Heredotus: A Study of the Debate on the Regimes. *Canadian Journal of Political Science* 24 (3): 541–555.

5053. Myers, R. H. September 1988. *See* Kuo, T. (September 1988).

5054. Myers, R. H. April 1990. *See* Ling, T. (April 1990).

5055. Myers, R. H. March 1994. *See* Chao, L. (March 1994).

5056. Myers, R. J. 1988. The End of the Hermit Kingdom. *Ethics and International Affairs* 2: 99–114.

5057. Mygind, N., and C. P. Rock. May 1993. Financial Participation and the Democratization of Work. *Economic and Industrial Democracy* 14 (2): 163–183.

5058. Myrdal, G. June 1987. Inequalities of Justice. *Review of Black Political Economy* 16 (1–2): 81–98.

૨૰

5059. Nabi, S. A. 1991. *See* Pruthi, S. (1991).

5060. Naby, E. March 1993. Tajik Political Legitimacy and Political Parties. *Iranian Journal of International Affairs* 5: 195–201.

5061. Nadeau, R., R. G. Niemi, and T. Amato. June 1994. Expectations and Preferences in British General Elections. *American Political Science Review* 88 (2): 371–383.

5062. Nagel, J. H. April 1993. Populism, Heresthetics and Political Stability: Richard Seddon and the Art of Majority-Rule. *British Journal of Political Science* 23: 139–174.

5063. Nagel, R. F. 1983. Interpretation and Importance in Constitutional Law: A Re-Assessment of Judicial Restraint. *Nomos* 25: 181–207.

5064. Nagel, S. S. January 1986. Using Microcomputers to Choose among Government Structures. *International Political Science Review* 7 (1): 27–37.

5065. Nahrstedt, W. 1981. Joblessness as a Goal of Learning: Organized Boredom or Democratization of Total Time.* *Zeitschrift für Paedagogik* 17: 107–110.

5066. Najjar, F. June 1989. Elections and Democracy in Egypt. *American-Arab Affairs* 29: 96–113.

5067. Nakamura, H. March 1978. Japan, Incorporated and Postwar Democracy. *Japanese Economic Studies* 6 (3–4): 68–109.

5068. Nakarada, R. March 1990. The Constitutional Promotion of Human Rights in Eastern Europe. *Alternatives* 15 (2): 227–240.

5069. Nakarada, R. March 1991. Democratic Alternatives: A Perspective from Eastern Europe. *Alternatives* 16 (2): 129–140.

5070. Nalbandian, J. November 1990. Tenets of Contemporary Professionalism in Local Government. *Public Administration Review* 50 (4): 654–662.

5071. Nandy, A. July 1975. The Economic and Psychoeconomic Contexts of Political Commitment and Dissent. *Economic Development and Cultural Change* 23 (4): 653–660.

5072. Nandy, A. September 1989. The Political Culture of the Indian State. *Daedalus* 118 (4): 1–26.

5073. Nankin, K. S. October 1993. The Future of the Democracy Development Initiative. *Federal Bar News and Journal* 40: 581–583.

5074. Nannan, S. S. January 1992. Africa: The Move towards Democracy. *Strategic Analysis* 14 (10): 1221–1232.

5075. Narain, I. October 1976. Cultural Pluralism, National Integration and Democracy. *Asian Survey* 16 (10): 903–917.

5076. Narain, I. February 1986. India in 1985: Triumph of Democracy. *Asian Survey* 26 (2): 253–269.

5077. Narain, I. June 1992. Future of Democracy in India: Some Reflections in the Context of Tenth Lok Sabha Poll Verdict. *Indian Journal of Social Science* 5 (2): 227–239.

5078. Narain, S. September 1992. *See* Agarwal, A. (September 1992).

5079. Narayanan, R., and R. L. Karumanchi. July 1991. Democracy at the Polls: A Comparative Analysis of Elections in Latin America, 1989–1990. *International Studies* 28 (3): 229–248.

5080. Narr, W. February 1991. The Liberalism of the Exhausted.* *Blaetter für Deutsche und Internationale Politik* 36 (2): 216–227.

5081. Narvaez, L. June 1987. *See* Fernandez, G. (June 1987).

5082. Narveson, J. December 1992. Democracy and Economic Rights. *Social Philosophy and Policy* 9 (1): 29–61.

5083. Nascimento, E. June 1987. *See* Ferreira Nunes, B. (June 1987).

5084. Nash, J. W. September 1985. What Hath Intervention Wrought: Reflections on the Dominican Republic. *Caribbean Review* 14 (4): 6–11.

5085. Nasr, S. V. R. June 1992. Democracy and the Crisis of Governability in Pakistan. *Asian Survey* 32 (6): 521–537.

5086. Nass, K. O. May 25, 1993. Limitations and Risks of Humanitarian Interventions: Making Way for Peace, Human Rights, Democracy and Development.* *Europa Archiv: Zeitschrift für Internationale Politik* 48 (10): 279–288.

5087. Nassmacher, H. December 1992. Governance and Minorities: Experiences in Western Democracies. *Politische Vierteljahresschrift* 33 (4): 643–660.

5088. Nathan, A. J. March 1987. *See* Chou, Y. (March 1987).

5089. Nathan, A. J. 1989. Chinese Democracy in 1989: Continuity and Change. *Problems of Communism* 38 (5): 16–29.

5090. Nathan, A. J. September 1989. *See* Dittmer, L. (September 1989).

5091. Nathan, A. J. March 1990. Is China Ready for Democracy? *Journal of Democracy* 1 (2): 50–61.

5092. Nathan, A. J. September 1993. Chinese Democracy: The Lessons of Failure. *Journal of Contemporary China* 4: 3–13.

5093. Nathan, A. J., and T. J. Shi. March 1993. Cultural Requisites for Democracy in China: Findings from a Survey. *Daedalus* 122 (2): 95–123.

5094. Nathan, J., and H. Kohl. 1981. Public Alternative Schools and the Future of Democracy. *Phi Delta Kappan* 62 (10): 733–734.

5095. Nathan, L. March 1991. *See* Phillips, M. (March 1991).

5096. Nathan, N. 1981. Poetry Criticism and Democracy. *English Journal* 70 (3): 56–59.

5097. Naumann, J. 1982. *See* Schneider, F. (1982).

5098. Navarro, F. March 1991. *See* Bareiro-Saguier, R. (March 1991).

5099. Navarro, J. C. et al. 1988. Alexis de Tocqueville: 150 Years of *Democracy In America*. The United States Today. *Politeia (Caracas)* 12: 13–55. 5 articles.

5100. Navarro, R. N. January 1991. The Growing Political Crisis in the Philippines: An Analysis of the Internal Military Threat of a Coup d'Etat. *Conflict* 11 (1): 53–68.

5101. Nazimora, A. December 1992. The Russian Parliament: Session One to Five.* *Politique Etrangere* 57 (1): 75–88.

5102. Nazzaro, P. March 1975. Italy in Trouble. *Current History* 68 (403): 101–104, 134.

5103. Nda, P. November 1993. Teacher Struggles, Student Rebellions and Democratization in Black Africa. *International Review of Education* 39 (6): 519–530.

5104. Ndege, W. June 1979. Sadat Gambles with Democracy. *Africa:* 58–60.

5105. Ndiaye, B. December 1992. International Cooperation to Promote Democracy and Human Rights: Principles and Programs. *International Commission of Jurists Review* 49: 23–36.

5106. Ndue, P. N. January 1994. Africa's Turn toward Pluralism. *Journal of Democracy* 5 (1): 45–54.

5107. Neal, F. W. September 1984. Yugoslav Approaches to the Nationalities Problem: The Politics of Circumvention. *East European Quarterly* 18 (3): 327–334.

5108. Neal, P. February 1990. Justice as Fairness: Political or Metaphysical? *Political Theory* 18 (1): 24–50.

5109. Neale, W. C. November 1983. Community Development in India: Progress or Rip-Off? *Asian Survey* 23 (11): 1209–1219.

5110. Nedergaard, P. 1993. The EC and Its Democratic Deficit.* *Politica* 25 (3): 303–322.

5111. Nedzi, L. N. June 1993. Institutionalization of New Democracies: A Fresh Approach to Security. *Mediterranean Quarterly* 4 (3): 1–9.

5112. Nef, J. 1986. Redemocratization in Latin America, or the Modernization of the Status Quo. *Canadian Journal of Latin American and Caribbean Studies* 21 (11): 43–55.

5113. Negt, O. July 1976. No Democracy without Socialism, No Socialism without Democracy.* *Argument* 18: 595–618.

5114. Neher, C. D. December 1975. Stability and Instability in Contemporary Thailand. *Asian Survey* 25 (12): 1097–1113.

5115. Neher, C. D. February 1981. The Philippines in 1980: The Gathering Storm. *Asian Survey* 21 (2): 261–273.

5116. Neher, C. D. February 1988. Thailand in 1987: Semi-Successful Semi-Democracy. *Asian Survey* 28 (2): 192–201.

5117. Neher, C. D. March 1990. Change in Thailand. *Current History* 89 (545): 101–104, 127–130.

5118. Neher, C. D. September 1991. Democratization in Southeast Asia. *Asian Affairs: An American Review* 18 (3): 139–152.

5119. Neher, C. D. November 1994. Asian Style Democracy. *Asian Survey* 34 (11): 949–961.

5120. Nehru, B. K. 1979. Western Democracy and the Third World. *Third World Quarterly* 1 (2): 53–70.

5121. Neier, A. November 1989. Human Rights in the Reagan Era: Acceptance in Principle. *Annals of the American Academy of Political and Social Science* 506: 30–41.

5122. Neiman, M., and M. Gottdiener. January 1985. Qualifying Initiatives: A Heuristic Use of Data to Commend an Unexplored Stage of Direct Democracy. *Social Science Journal* 22 (1): 99–109.

5123. Nejelski, P. October 1977. Judging in a Democracy: The Tension of Popular Participation. *Judicature* 61 (4): 166–175.

5124. Nelson, A., and C. Arnson. 1984. Death Squads, Daubuisson and Democracy. *Nation* 238 (3): 88–90.

5125. Nelson, C. M. December 1993. An Opportunity for Constitutional Reform in Argentina: Reelection 1995. *University of Miami Inter-America Law Review* 25: 283–317.

5126. Nelson, D. N. 1991. *See* Mason, D. S. (1991).

5127. Nelson, D. N. September 1981. Worker-Party Conflict in Romania. *Problems of Communism* 30 (5): 40–49.

5128. Nelson, D. N. April 1982. Leninists and Political Inequalities: The Nonrevolutionary Politics of Communist States. *Comparative Politics* 14 (3): 307–328.

5129. Nelson, D. N. December 1990. Romania. *Electoral Studies* 9 (4): 355–366.

5130. Nelson, D. N. June 1993. Democracy, Markets and Security in Eastern Europe. *Survival* 35 (2): 156–171.

5131. Nelson, J. M. October 1994. Linkage between Politics and Economics. *Journal of Democracy* 5 (4): 49–62.

5132. Nemec, B. 1978. Actual Problems Involved in Theory of Socialist Revolution and in Development of Socialist Democracy in Czechoslovakia.* *Sociologicky Casopis* 14 (4): 337–352.

5133. Neocosmos, M. 1994. Lesotho: Political Liberalization. Recent Developments. *L'Afrique Politique* 269–280.

5134. Neuberger, B. September 1990. Israel Has a Liberal-Democratic Tradition? *Jewish Political Studies Review* 2 (3–4): 85–98.

5135. Neuchterlein, J. A. April 1980. The Dream of Scientific Liberalism: The New Republic and American Progressive Thought, 1914–1920. *Review of Politics* 42 (2): 167–190.

5136. Neuhaus, R. J. November 1979. *See* Kerrine, T. M. (November 1979).

5137. Neuhaus, R. J., A. Wahid, N. Smith, S. Chamarik, J. Bernas, and M. Delgado. March 1985. Religious Freedom in the Third World. *World Affairs* 147 (4): 253–267.

5138. Neuman, R. P. 1974. Sexual Question and Social Democracy in Imperial Germany. *Journal of Social History* 7 (3): 271–286.

5139. Neumann, F. 1994. More Democracy in the Bonn Republic: Cautious or Zero Steps of the Common Constitution Commission of the Bundestag and the Bundesrat.* *Gegenwartskunde: Gesellschaft, Staat, Erziehung* 43 (2): 155–171.

5140. Nevill, C. J. 1981. Democracy and Technology. *Search* 12 (7): 210–213.

5141. Newberg, P. R. June 1989. Pakistan at the Edge of Democracy. *World Policy Journal* 6 (3): 563–587.

5142. Newfield, C. December 1993. What Was Political Correctness, Race, the Right, and Managerial Democracy in the Humanities. *Critical Inquiry* 19 (2): 308–336.

5143. Newland, C. A. June 1979. Present Discontents and Futures of Federal Executives. *Bureaucrat* 8 (2): 49–55.

5144. Newman, F. M. July 1987. Citizenship Education in the United States: A Statement of Needs. *National Civic Review* 76 (4): 280–287.

5145. Newman, K. J. 1980. Hat Die Demokratie Eine Zukunft in Asien? *Indo Asia: für Politik, Kultur, und Wirtschaft Indiens und Suedost Asiens* 22 (1–2): 64–81.

5146. Newson, J. A. March 1994. Subordinating Democracy: The Effects of Fiscal Retrenchment and University Business Partnerships on Knowledge Creation and Knowledge Dissemination in Universities. *Higher Education* 27 (2): 141–161.

5147. Newton, K. June 1982. Is Small Really So Beautiful? Is Big Really So Ugly? Size, Effectiveness, and Democracy in Local Government. *Political Studies* 30 (2): 190–206.

5148. Nguema, I. April 1992. Democracy, Africa and Development.* *Revue Juridique et Politique, Independance et Cooperation* 46 (2): 129–162.

5149. Niam, M. October 1994. Latin America: The Second Stage of Reform. *Journal of Democracy* 5 (4): 32–48.

5150. Nicgorski, W. May 1985. Leo Strauss and Liberal Education. *Interpretation* 13 (2): 233–250.

5151. Nichols, D. K. March 1987. Herbert Croly and the Progressive Rejection of Individual Rights. *Publius* 17 (2): 27–39.

5152. Nickel, J. W. June 1982. Are Human Rights Utopian? *Philosophy and Public Affairs* 11 (3): 246–264.

5153. Nickens, J. M. 1980. *See* Sawyer, J. A. (1980).

5154. Nickson, R. A. November 1992. Democratization and the Growth of Communism in Nepal: A Peruvian Scenario in the Making. *Journal of Commonwealth and Comparative Politics* 30 (3): 358–386.

5155. Niclauss, K. January 1974. Die Entstehung der Bundesrepublik als Demokratiegruendung. *Vierteljahreshefte für Zeitgeschichte* 22: 46–75.

5156. Nicro, S. June 1993. Thailand's NIC Democracy: Studying from General Elections. *Pacific Affairs* 66 (2): 167–182.

5157. Nieh, Y. December 1989. Die Wiederbelebung der Sino-Britischen Kontroverse ueber Hong Kong. *China Aktuell* 18: 931–934.

5158. Nielebock, T. 1993. Peace between Democracies: An Empirical Law of International Relations in Search for Its Own Explanation. *Oesterreichische Zeitschrift für Politikwissenschaft* 22 (2): 179–193.

5159. Nielson, K. June 1989. A Moral Case for Socialism. *Critical Review* 3 (3–4): 542–553.

5160. Niemi, R. October 1994. *See* Franklin, M. (October 1994).

5161. Niemi, R. G. March 1992. *See* Dash, S. (March 1992).

5162. Niemi, R. G. June 1994. *See* Nadeau, R. (June 1994).

5163. Niemi, R. G., and J. D. Barkan. June 1987. Age and Turnout in New Electorates and Peasant Societies. *American Political Science Review* 81 (2): 583–388.

5164. Niethammer, L. July 1975. Aktivitaet und Grenzen der Antifa-Ausschuesse, 1945: da Beispiel Stuttgart. *Vierteljahrshefte für Zeitgeschichte* 23: 297–331.

5165. Nightingale, D. 1976. Industrial Democracy: Strategy for Improving Productivity and Labor-Management. *Business Quarterly* 41 (3): 36–42.

5166. Nigro, L. G., and W. D. Richardson. August 1987. Self-Interest Properly Understood: The American Character and Public Administration. *Administration and Society* 19 (2): 157–177.

5167. Niklasson, T. 1990. *See* Hakansson, A. (1990).

5168. Niklasson, T., and A. Spannerstedt. 1993. Europe Safe for Democracy? The Council of Europe and Democratization in Central and Eastern Europe. *Statsvetenskaplig Tidskrift* 96 (1): 69–81.

5169. Niksch, L. A. February 1989. Thailand in 1988: The Economic Surge. *Asian Survey* 29 (2): 165–173.

5170. Nilsson, A. September 1991. Swedish Social Democracy in Central America: The Politics of Small State Solidarity. *Journal of Interamerican Studies and World Affairs* 33 (3): 169–199.

5171. Nimmo, D. D. September 1976. *See* Yarwood, D. L. (September 1976).

5172. Ninalowo, B. December 1990. On the Structures and Praxis of Domination, Democratic Culture and Social Change: With Inferences from Africa. *Scandinavian Journal of Development Alternatives* 9 (4): 107–123.

5173. Nino, C. S. September 1989. Transition to Democracy, Corporatism and Constitutional Reform in Latin America. *University of Miami Law Review* 44: 129–164.

5174. Nino, C. S. March 1991. The Epistemological Moral Relevance of Democracy. *Ratio Juris* 4: 36–51.

5175. Nino, C. S. March 1994. Positivism and Communitarianism: Between Human Rights and Democracy. *Ratio Juris* 7: 14–40.

5176. Ninou Guinot, C. October 1993. Transition and Democratic Consolidation in Latin America.* *Revista de Estudios Politicos* 82: 107–135.

5177. Nisbet, R. September 1975. Public Opinion Versus Popular Opinion. *Public Interest* 41: 166–192.

5178. Nisbet, R. 1978. Capitalism, Socialism, and Democracy. *Commentary* 65 (4): 62–63.

5179. Nishibe, S. December 1982. Japan as a Highly Developed Mass Society: An Appraisal. *Journal of Japanese Studies* 8 (1): 73–96.

5180. Niskanen, W. A. June 1994. Why Our Democracy Doesn't Work. *Public Interest* (116): 88–95.

5181. Nixon, D. L., and R. Herrick. December 1994. Four Generations and Defense Voting. *Journal of Political and Military Sociology* 22 (2): 223–240.

5182. Njaim, H. 1989. Factors Which Facilitate or Hinder Democracy in Venezuela.* *Revista de la Facultad de Ciencias Juridicas y Politicas* 72: 81–98.

5183. Noam, E. M. August 1980. The Efficiency of Direct Democracy. *Journal of Political Economy* 88 (4): 803–810.

5184. Nodia, G. October 1992. Nationalism and Democracy. *Journal of Democracy* 3 (4): 3–22.

5185. Noel, S. J. R. March 1989. *See* McGary, J. (March 1989).

5186. Noelle-Neumann, E. June 1979. Public Opinion and the Classical Tradition: A Re-evaluation. *Public Opinion Quarterly* 43 (2): 143–156.

5187. Nogeira, M. A. 1986. From the Politics of the Possible to the Possibilities of Politics: Notes on the Democratic Transition in Brazil.* *Perspectives* 9–10: 1–19.

5188. Noguera, P. A. March 1994. More Democracy, Not Less: Confronting the Challenge of Privatization in Public Education. *Journal of Negro Education* 63 (2): 237–250.

5189. Nohlen, D. October 1984. Political Regime Change in Latin America.* *Estudios Internacionales* 68: 548–575.

5190. Nohlen, D. March 1986. Military Regimes and Redemocratization in Latin America.* *Aus Politik und Zeitgeschichte* 9 (1): 3–16.

5191. Nohlen, D. June 1988. More Democracy in the Third World.* *Aus Politik und Zeitgeschichte* 17: 3–18.

5192. Nohlen, D. September 1988. More Democracy in Latin America? Democratization and Consolidation of Democracy in Comparative Perspective.* *Sintesis* 6: 37–63.

5193. Nohlen, D. August 1989. ¿Mas Democracia en America Latina? Democratizacion y Consolidacion de la Democracia en una Perspectiva Comparada. *Cuadernos del CLAEH: Revista Uruguaya de Ciencias Sociales* 14: 135–161.

5194. Nohlen, D. October 1991. Presidencialismo vs. Parlamentarismo en America Latina. *Revista de Estudios Politicos* 74: 43–54.

5195. Nolan, P. March 1994. Democratization, Human Rights and Economic Reform: The Case of China. *Democratization* 1 (1): 73–99.

5196. Noll, R. G. November 1978. *See* Fiorina, M. P. (November 1978).

5197. Nolte, S. H. April 1984. Industrial Democracy for Japan: Tanako Odo and John Dewey. *Journal of the History of Ideas* 45 (2): 277–294.

5198. Nolutshungu, S. C. January 1990. Fragments of a Democracy: Reflections on Class and Politics in Nigeria. *Third World Quarterly* 12 (1): 86–115.

5199. Nolutshungu, S. C. November 1992. Africa in a World of Democracies: Interpretation and Retrieval. *Journal of*

Commonwealth and Comparative Politics 30 (3): 316–334.

5200. Norden, A. 1975. Sozialismus und Demokratie-Eine Untrennbare Einheit. *Einheit* 30 (1): 35–42.

5201. Norden, D. L. January 1992. *See* Collier, D. (January 1992).

5202. Norgaard, O. 1985. The Debate on Democracy and Political Development in the USSR.* *Politica* 17 (1): 56–74.

5203. Norgaard, O. 1991. Post-Stalinism and Democracy.* *Politica* 23 (3): 241–258.

5204. Norgaard, O. March 1992. The Political Economy of Transition in Post-Socialist Systems: The Case of the Baltic States. *Scandinavian Political Studies* 15 (1): 41–60.

5205. Norman, W. J. June 1993. A Democratic Theory for a Democratizing World? A Reassessment of Popper's Political Realism. *Political Studies* 41 (2): 252–268.

5206. Norris, P. October 1985. Women's Legislative Participation in Western Europe. *West European Politics* 8: 90–101.

5207. Norton, A. R. June 1991. *See* Muslih, M. (June 1991).

5208. Norton, A. R. March 1993. The Future of Civil Society in the Middle East. *Middle East Journal* 47 (2): 205–215.

5209. Norton, B. T. April 1986. E.D. Kuskova, S.N. Prokopovich, and the Challenge to Russian Social Democracy. *Russian Review* 45 (2): 183–207.

5210. Norwood, J. L. June 1994. Data Policy and Politics in a Democracy. *Journal of Economic Education* 25 (3): 213–217.

5211. Nossiter, B. D. 1990. Money and Democracy: The Myth of an Independent Fed. *Nation* 251 (23): 837–838.

5212. Nougmanov, A. March 1993. Kazakhstan's Challenges: The Case of a Central Asian Nation in Transition. *Harvard International Review* 15 (3): 10–12, 58–59.

5213. Nourzhanov, A. S. December 1994. The New Kazakhstan: Has Something Gone Wrong? *World Today* 50 (12): 225–228.

5214. Novak, M. July 1977. An Underpraised and Underdeveloped System: In Defense of Democratic Capitalism. *Worldview* 20: 9–12.

5215. Novak, M. 1978. Capitalism, Socialism, and Democracy. *Commentary* 65 (4): 63–64.

5216. Novak, M. July 1981. The Economic System: The Evangelistic Basis of a Social Market Economy. *Review of Politics* 43 (3): 355–380.

5217. Novak, M. September 1986. What Do They Mean by Socialism? *Orbis* 30 (3): 405–425.

5218. Novicki, M. A. March 1994. Interview: President Jerry Rawlings: Ghana's Fourth Republic. *Africa Report* 39 (2): 23–25.

5219. Nozawa, M. April 1982. The Alternative Economic Strategy in Japan Democratization of the Economy. *Kyoto University Economic Review* 52: 38–63.

5220. Nuechterlein, D. E. December 1990. The Reagan Doctrine in Perspective. *Perspectives on Political Science* 19 (1): 43–49.

5221. Nuechterlein, J. A. January 1977. Arthur M. Schlesinger, Jr., and the Discontent of Postwar American Liberalism. *Review of Politics* 39 (1): 3–40.

5222. Nullmeier, F. 1980. Democracy in the Environmental Crisis.* *Gegenwartskunde: Gesellschaft, Staat, Erziehung* 29 (2): 253–271.

5223. Nun, J. April 1987. Elements for a Theory of Democracy: Gramsci and Common Sense. *Revista Mexicana de Sociologia* 49 (2): 21–54.

5224. Nun, J. October 1991. Democracy and Modernization 30 Years Later.* *Desarrollo Economico* 31 (123): 375–393.

5225. Nun, J. September 1993. Democracy and Modernization (in Latin America): Thirty Years Later. *Latin American Perspectives* 20 (4): 7–27.

5226. Nun, J. January 1994. Democracy and Modernization Thirty Years Later.* *America Latina Loy* 7: 7–16.

5227. Nun, J., and J. C. Protantiero. May 1987. Strengthening Democracy in Argentina.* *Sintesis* 2: 226–256.

5228. Nunez de Escorcia, V. September 1984. On Political Democracy in Nicaragua. *World Policy Journal* 2: 169–177. Interview.

5229. Nurmi, H. 1984. Social Choice Theory and Democracy: A Comparison of Two Recent Views. *European Journal of Political Research* 12 (3): 325–333.

5230. Nwajiaku, K. September 1994. The National Conferences in Benin and Togo Revisited. *Journal of Modern African Studies* 32 (3): 429–418.

5231. Nwokedi, E. March 25, 1994. Democracy and Security in Black Africa. *Europa Archiv: Zeitschrift für Internationale Politik* 49 (6): 169–178.

5232. Nwokedi, E. April 1994. Nigeria's Democratic Transition: Explaining the Annulled 1993 Presidential Election. *Round Table* 330: 189–204.

5233. Nyang'oro, J. E. September 1990. The Quest for Pluratist Democracy in Kenya. *Transafrica Forum* 7 (3): 73–82.

5234. Nyang'oro, J. E. July 1993. Development, Democracy and NGOs in Africa. *Scandinavian Journal of Development Alternatives* 12: 277–291.

5235. Nyang'oro, J. E. April 1994. Reform Politics and the Democratization Process in Africa. *African Studies Review* 37 (1): 133–150.

5236. Nyden, P. W. May 1985. Democratizing Organizations: A Case Study of Union Reform Movement. *American Journal of Sociology* 90 (6): 1179–1203.

5237. Nyers, R. 1986. Efficiency and Socialist Democracy. *Acta Oeconomica* 37 (1–2): 1–13.

5238. Nzomo, M. December 1993. The Gender Dimension of Democratization in Kenya: Some International Linkages. *Alternatives* 18 (1): 61–73.

5239. Nzouankeu, J. May 1991. The African Attitude to Democracy. *International Social Science Journal* 43 (2): 373–385.

5240. O'Brien, C. C. March 1992. Nationalism and Democracy. *Queen's Quarterly* 99 (1): 72–83.

5241. O'Brien, D. J. December 1977. The Sociological Perspective and the Liberal Democratic Model. *Social Science Quarterly* 58 (3): 436–448.

5242. O'Brien, D. M. March 1991. The Framers' Muse on Republicanism, the Supreme Court, and Pragmatic Constitutional Interpretivism. *Review of Politics* 53 (2): 251–288.

5243. O'Connell, B. July 1987. Strengthening Philanthropy and Voluntary Action. *National Civic Review* 76 (4): 308–314.

5244. O'Connell, P. J. 1989. *See* Griffin, L. J. (1989).

5245. O'Donnell, G. 1979. What Democracy: Response to a Commentary of E. Kvaternik.* *Desarrollo Economico* 18 (72): 607–612.

5246. O'Donnell, G. 1981. Tensions of the Bureaucratic Authoritarian State and the Question of Democracy. *Revue de l'Institut de Sociologie* 1–2: 9–39.

5247. O'Donnell, G. 1982. Notes for the Study of Political Democratization Processes Beginning with the Bureaucratic Authoritarian State. *Desarrollo Economico* 22 (86): 231–248.

5248. O'Donnell, G. May 1987. Latin America, USA and Democracy: Variation on a Very Old Theme.* *Sintesis* 2: 115–136.

5249. O'Donnell, G. March 1988. Challenges to Democratization in Brazil. *World Policy Journal* 5 (2): 281–300.

5250. O'Donnell, G. July 1993. The State, Democracy and Some Conceptual Problems: Latin American Perspectives with Respect to Postcommunist Countries. *Desarrollo Economico: Revista de Ciencias Sociales* 33 (130): 163–184.

5251. O'Donnell, G. August 1993. On the State, Democratization and Some Conceptual Problems: A Latin American View with Glances at Some Postcommunist Countries. *World Development* 27 (8): 1355–1369.

5252. O'Donnell, G. January 1994. Delegative Democracy [in Latin America]. *Journal of Democracy* 5 (1): 55–69.

5253. O'Flaherty, B. July 1990. Why Are There Democracies? A Principle Agent Answer. *Economics and Politics* 2 (2): 133–155.

5254. O'Flaherty, D. J. June 1978. Finding Jamaica's Way. *Foreign Policy* (31): 137–158.

5255. O'Keefe, M. F. 1979. End of Ideology: Trend Analysis of Communist Party Strength in Ten Advanced Industrial Democracies. *Mid-American Review of Sociology* 4 (2): 55–67.

5256. O'Leary, K. C. June 1994. Herbert Croly and Progressive Democracy. *Polity* 26 (4): 533–552.

5257. O'Lessker, K. April 1985. Democracy in the Third World: Egypt's High-Risk Experiment. *American Spectator* 18: 22–24.

5258. O'Neil, M. J. December 1982. Public Hearing and Public Preferences: The Case of the White House Conference on Families. *Public Opinion Quarterly* 46 (4): 488–502.

5259. O'Neill, J. September 1986. Scientific Socialism and Democracy: A Response to Femia. *Inquiry* 29 (3): 345–353.

5260. O'Tolle, D. E., and J. Marshall. June 1988. Citizen Participation through Budgeting. *Bureaucrat* 17 (2): 51–55.

5261. O'Toole, L. J., Jr. June 1977. Schumpeter's *Democracy:* A Critical View. *Polity* 9 (4): 446–462.

5262. Oberreuter, H. 1977. *See* Maier, H. (1977).

5263. Oberreuter, H. January 1983. Renouncing a Certain Type of Constitution? Current Challenges and Misunderstandings in Parliamentary Democracy.* *Aus Politik und Zeitgeschichte* 15 (2): 19–31.

5264. Oberreuter, H. September 1987. Power Preservation and Power Change: Majority and Minority in Parliamentary Democracy.* *Politische Studien* 295: 521–530.

5265. Oberst, R. C. 1985. Legislative Behavior and Ethnicity in a Third-World Democracy: Sri Lanka. *Pacific Affairs* 58 (2): 265–286.

5266. Oberst, R. C. July 1985. Democracy and the Persistence of Westernized Elite Dominance in Sri Lanka. *Asian Survey* 25 (7): 760–772.

5267. Obler, J. April 1974. Intraparty Democracy and Selection of Parliamentary Candidates: Belgian Case. *British Journal of Political Science* 4: 163–185.

5268. Obler, J., J. Steiner, and G. Diedericx. 1977. Decision-Making in Smaller Democracies: The Consociational Burden. *Sage Professional Paper in Comparative Politics* 6 (106): 5–58.

5269. Oeuvrard, F. 1979. Towards Greater Democracy or Increased Paths of Relegation. *Actes de la Recherche en Sciences Sociales* (30): 87–97.

5270. Offe, C. 1983. Competitive Party Democracy and the Keynesian Welfare State: Sources of Stability and Change. *Dados: Revista de Ciencias Sociais* 26 (1): 29–51.

5271. Offe, C. April 1983. Competitive Party Democracy and the Keynesian Welfare State: Factors of Stability and Disorganization. *Policy Sciences* 15 (3): 225–246.

5272. Offe, C. December 1983. Political Legitimation through Majority Rule? *Social Research* 50 (4): 709–756.

5273. Offe, C. November 1987. Democracy against the Welfare State? Structural Foundations of Neoconservative Political Opportunities. *Political Theory* 15 (4): 501–537.

5274. Offe, C. April 1991. The Dilemma of Simultaneity: Democratization and Market Economy in Eastern Europe.* *Merkur* 45 (4): 279–292.

5275. Offe, C. December 1992. Capitalism by Democratic Design? Democratic Theory and the Triple Transition in East Central Europe. *Revue Francaise de Science Politique* 42 (6): 923–942.

5276. Offe, C., and U. K. Preuss. 1989. Can Democratic Institutions Make Moral Resources.* *Politicka Misao* 26 (4): 85–106.

5277. Offe, C., and E. Richter. December 1991. Capitalism by Democratic Design? Democratic Theory Facing the Triple Transition in East Central Europe. *Social Research* 58 (4): 865–902.

5278. Ogbondah, C. W. April 1991. The Pen Is Mightier than the "Koboko": A Critical Analysis of the Amakiri Case in Nigeria. *Political Communication and Persuasion* 8 (2): 109–124.

5279. Ogden, S. June 1993. The Chinese Communist Party: Key to Pluralism and a Market Economy. *SAIS Review* 13 (2): 107–125.

5280. Ogmundson, R. August 1975. Party Class Images and the Class Vote in Canada. *American Sociological Review* 40 (4): 506–512.

5281. Ohlinger, T., and M. Matzka. 1975. Democracy and Administration: Problem of Constitutional Law.* *Oesterreichische Zeitschrift für Politikwissenschaft* 4 (4): 445–462.

5282. Ohman, B. 1981. Labor Theory of Value and Democracy.* *Sociologisk Forskning* 18 (1): 29–46.

5283. Okan, A. M. March 1979. Our Blend of Democracy and Capitalism: It Works, but Is in Danger. *Across the Board* 16: 69–76.

5284. Okpahu, J. November 1994. Creating a Desirable 21st-Century Africa: The Role of Leadership and Governance. *Futures* 26 (9): 999–1010.

5285. Okun, A. M. 1978. Capitalism and Democracy: Some Unifying Principles. *Columbia Journal of World Business* 13 (4): 22–30.

5286. Olejnik, P. A. 1980. The Individual, Democracy, and Legality.* *Voprosy Filosofii* 7: 34–43.

5287. Oliver, J. D. 1993. What Is Democracy? Some Elucidation and Lessons from the Works of R. A. Dahl and C. B. MacPherson. *Politeia (UNISA)* 12 (2): 2–17.

5288. Olokaonyango, J. 1989. Law, Grass-Roots Democracy and the National Resistance Movement in Uganda. *International Journal of the Sociology of Law* 17 (4): 465–489.

5289. Oloughlin, J. 1980. District Size and Party Electoral Strength: A Comparison of 16 Democracies. *Environment and Planning A* 12 (3): 247–262.

5290. Olsen, E. A. 1979. Movement toward Democracy in South Korea. *Worldview* 22 (10): 24–26.

5291. Olsen, E. A. March 1987. South Korean Political Uncertainty and U.S. Policy. *Washington Quarterly* 10 (2): 165–181.

5292. Olsen, J. P. October 1986. *See* March, J. G. (October 1986).

5293. Olshausen, K. 1976. Participation and Democracy: The Relationship between Political Participation and the Theory of Democracy.* *Beitraege zur Konfliktforschung* 6 (4): 95–117.

5294. Olson, D. M. May 1980. *See* Simon, M. D. (May 1980).

5295. Olson, D. M. May 1993. Compartmentalized Competition: The Managed Transitional Election System of Poland. *Journal of Politics* 55 (2): 415–441.

5296. Olson, J. M. 1977. Radical Social Democracy and School Reform in Wilhelmian Germany. *History of Education Quarterly* 17 (1): 3–16.

5297. Olson, J. P. 1991. Individual Autonomy, Political Authority and Democratic Institutions.* *Nordish Administrativt Tidsskrift* 72 (1): 8–25.

5298. Olson, K. W. 1986. Between East and West. *Wilson Quarterly* 10 (4): 44–58.

5299. Olson, M. September 1993. Dictatorship, Democracy, and Development. *American Political Science Review* 87 (3): 567–576.

5300. Oltay, E. July 16, 1993. Religious Sects at Center of Controversy in Hungary. *RFE/RL Research Report* 2: 37–40.

5301. Olugbade, K. 1989. Sustaining Democratic Virtues in Nigeria: Expectations for the Third Republic. *Corruption and Reform* 4 (3): 245–281.

5302. Omara-Ottunu, A. September 1992. The Struggle for Democracy in Uganda. *Journal of Modern African Studies* 30 (3): 443–463.

5303. Omestad, T. June 1988. Dateline Taiwan: A Dynasty Ends. *Foreign Policy* (71): 176–198.

5304. Omvedt, G. 1989. India's Movements for Democracy: Peasants, Greens, Women and Peoples' Power. *Race and Class* 31 (2): 37–46.

5305. Omvedt, G. 1994. Peasants, Dalits, and Women: Democracy and India's New Social Movements. *Journal of Contemporary Asia* 24 (1): 35–48.

5306. Oneill, K. 1992. *See* Mitterer, J. (1992).

5307. Onis, Z. June 1992. Redemocratization and Economic Liberalization in Turkey: The Limits of State Autonomy. *Studies in Comparative International Development* 27 (2): 3–23.

5308. Oommen, T. K. December 1994. Religion Nationalism and Democratic Polity: The Indian Case. *Sociology of Religion* 55 (4): 455–480.

5309. Opello, W. C. , Jr. April 1981. Local Government and Political Culture in a Portuguese Rural Community. *Comparative Politics* 13 (3): 271–289.

5310. Openshaw, S. 1984. *See* Johnston, R. J. (1984).

5311. Oppenheim, J. A. February 1990. *See* Frohlich, N. (February 1990).

5312. Oppenheim, J. A. June 1990. *See* Forhlich, N. (June 1990).

5313. Oppenheim, L. H. June 1985. Democracy and Social Transformation in Chile: The Debate within the Left. *Latin American Perspectives* 12 (3): 59–76.

5314. Oppenheim, L. H. 1991. Military-rule and the Struggle for Democracy in Chile: Introduction. *Latin American Perspectives* 19 (1): 3–14.

5315. Orbell, J. M., and L. A. Wilson II. June 1978. Institutional Solutions to the N Prisoners' Dilemma. *American Political Science Review* 72 (2): 411–421.

5316. Ordeshook, P. C., and O. V. Shuetsova. February 1994. Ethnic Heterogeneity, District Magnitude, and the Number of Parties. *American Journal of Political Science* 38 (1): 100–123.

5317. Oriordan, T., and F. K. Hare. 1990. Seventh Parliamentary and Scientific Conference of the Committee on Science and Technology of the Parliamentary Assembly of the Council of Europe, Entitled Coping with Global Change: The Role of Science and Democracy. *Environmental Conservation* 17 (2): 186+.

5318. Orkin, M. September 1992. Democracy Knows No Color: Rationales for Guerrilla Involvement among Black South Africans. *Journal of Southern African Studies* 18 (3): 642–669.

5319. Orloff, A. S., and T. Skocpol. December 1984. Why Not Equal Protection: Explaining the Politics of Public Social Spending in Britain, 1900–1911, and the United States, 1880s–1920. *American Sociological Review* 49 (6): 726–750.

5320. Orlow, B. S. 1991. Social Democracy in the Soviet-Union. *Osteuropa* 41 (9): 976–886.

5321. Orme, J. June 1988. Dismounting the Tiger: Lessons from Four Liberations. *Political Science Quarterly* 103 (2): 245–265.

5322. Orme, W. 1985. Mexico's One-Party Democracy Feels the Heat: Fire in the Pan. *New Republic* 192 (18): 19–21.

5323. Ornstein, N. J., and M. Schmitt. June 1990. Dateline Campaign '92: Post-Cold War Politics. *Foreign Policy* (79): 169–186.

5324. Orpen, C. 1980. Management Attitudes to Industrial Democracy: International Assessment. *Management International Review* 20 (1): 111–125.

5325. Orr, D. W. November 1979. U.S. Energy Policy and the Political Economy of Participation. *Journal of Politics* 41 (4): 1027–1056.

5326. Orr, D. W. 1982. Abundance and American Democracy: A Comment. *Journal of Politics* 44 (2): 388–393.

5327. Orr, D. W. May 1982. *See* Ostheimer, J. M. (May 1982).

5328. Orrego, C. January 1993. *See* Harris, E. (January 1993).

5329. Orrego Vicuna, F. January 1992. Las Relaciones entre los Paises de America Latina y los Estados Unidos: Limites Regionales y Entendimientos Globales. *Estudios Internacionales* 25: 23–40.

5330. Ortiz, I., and J. L. Curbelo. October 1993. 15 Anos de Politica Economica en Espana: 1977–1993. *Revista Interamericana de Planificacion* 26: 47–89.

5331. Osborne, D. K. September 1990. *See* Melville, L. J. (September 1990).

5332. Osculati, F., and C. Perugini. 1985. Democracies in Deficit. *Il Politico* 50 (3): 383–417.

5333. Osia, K. September 1992. Leadership and Followship: Nigeria's Problems of Governance. *Scandinavian Journal of Development Alternatives* 11 (3–4): 175–194.

5334. Osiel, M. J. March 1983. The Agonies of Abertura: Brazil Moves a Little Toward Democracy. *Dissent* 30 (2): 217–223.

5335. Osler, A. 1993. Education for Development and Democracy in Kenya: A Case Study. *Educational Review* 45 (2): 165–173.

5336. Osorio, J. December 1992. Liberalism, Democracy, and Socialism. *Social Justice* 19 (4): 25–33.

5337. Ostengard, U. 1985. From Modern to Postmodern Society: Participation or Paternalism, Belief in Progress or Skeptical Relativism. *Politica* 17 (3): 330–358.

5338. Ostensson, B. September 1976. Industrial Democracy in Sweden. *Free Labour World* 20–22.

5339. Ostheimer, J. M., L. G. Ritt, and D. W. Orr. May 1982. Abundance and

American Democracy: A Test of Dire Predictions. *Journal of Politics* 44 (2): 365–393.

5340. Ostrom, E. February 1985. An Alternative Perspective on Democratic Dilemmas. *Policy Studies Review* 4 (3): 412–416.

5341. Ostrom, V. August 1976. The American Contribution to a Theory of Constitutional Choice. *Journal of Politics* 38 (3): 56–78.

5342. Ostrom, V. September 1980. Hobbes, Covenant, and the Constitution. *Publius* 10 (4): 83–100.

5343. Ostrovska, I. March 1993. Women and Politics in Latvia: The Transition to Democracy. *Women's Studies International Forum* 17 (2–3): 301–303.

5344. Otakpor, N. March 1981. Pluralism and Consociational Democracy in Nigeria. *Il Politico* 46 (1–2): 107–125.

5345. Otayek, R. June 1992. The Democratic "Rectification" in Burkina Faso. *Journal of Communist Studies* 8 (2): 82–104.

5346. Ottaway, M. 1991. Liberation Movements and Transition to Democracy: The Case of the ANC. *Journal of Modern African Studies* 29 (1): 61–82.

5347. Otten, W. September 1979. Chile's Far Horizons: The Hard Way Back To Democracy.* *Politische Meinung* 186: 58–64.

5348. Otto, D. September 1993. Challenging the "New World Order": International Law, Global Democracy, and the Possibilities for Women. *Transnational Law & Contemporary Problems* 3: 371–415.

5349. Otunbayeva, R. March 1993. Leap of Faith: Central Asia's Plunge into Democracy. *Harvard International Review* 15 (3): 16–17,60.

5350. Ouellette, R. 1993. Democracia y Reformas Administrativas: Los Casos de Argentina y Uruguay. *Cuadernos del CLAEH: Revista Uruguaya de Ciencias Sociales* 18 (1–2): 75–85.

5351. Overholt, W. H. September 1985. Hong Kong and China: A New Relationship. *Current History* 84 (503): 256–259, 274–275.

5352. Owen, D. 1978. Communism, Socialism and Democracy. *Atlantic Community Quarterly* 16 (2): 154–166.

5353. Owen, J. M. 1994. How Liberalism Produces Democratic Peace. *International Security* 19 (2): 87–125.

5354. Owens, M. T., Jr. May 1986. Alexander Hamilton on Natural Rights and Prudence. *Interpretation* 14 (2–3): 331–351.

5355. Owusa, M. September 1992. Democracy and Africa: A View from the Village. *Journal of Modern African Studies* 30 (3): 369–396.

5356. Oxhorn, P. April 1994. *See* Ducatenzeiler, G. (April 1994).

5357. Oxhorn, P. June 1994. Where Did All the Protesters Go: Popular Mobilization and the Transition to Democracy in Chile. *Latin American Perspectives* 21 (3): 49–68.

5358. Oxhorn, P. October 1994. Understanding Political Change after Authoritarian Rule: The Popular Sectors and Chile's New Democratic Regime. *Journal of Latin American Studies* 26 (3): 737–759.

5359. Oyediran, O., and A. Agbaje. June 1991. Two-Partyism and Democratic Transition in Nigeria. *Journal of Modern African Studies* 29 (2): 213–235.

5360. Oyowe, A. July 1991. Building Democracy with Tribalism. *Courier* 69–72.

5361. Oyserman, D. August 1992. Conflict and Democracy in Action. *Small Group Research* 23 (3): 259–277.

5362. Ozal, T. 1987. Turkey's Path to Freedom and Prosperity. *Washington Quarterly* 10 (4): 161–165.

5363. Ozolins, A. V. December 1994. *See* Davies, P. J. (December 1994).

ઝ&

5364. Pabon Tarantino, E. E. January 1993. Colombia y su Revolucion Pacifica: La Nueva Constitucion del 5 de Julio de 1991: Inicio de un Macro Institucional Dentro de un Contexto Politico Pluralista. *Revista de Estudios Politicos* 161–208.

5365. Pacek, A. C. 1989. Changing Political Processes in Soviet-Type Systems: Toward an Emergent Pluralism. *Crossroads* 28: 75–91.

5366. Pachter, H. June 1978. Freedom, Authority, Participation. *Dissent* 25 (3): 294–309.

5367. Packel, E. W. January 1982. *See* Hoffman, E. (January 1982).

5368. Paddock, R. C. June 1991. Disaster or Democracy? California's Proposition 140 That Limits Legislative Terms Has Put the State at an Historic Turning Point. *State Legislatures* 17: 22–25+.

5369. Padgett, S. January 1993. Social Democracy in Power. *Parliamentary Affairs* 46 (1): 101–120.

5370. Padilla, D., and E. Houppert. March 1993. International Observing: Enhancing the Principle of Free and Fair Elections. *Emory International Law Review* 7: 73–132.

5371. Padilla, L. A. 1988. Guatemala: A Real Transition to Democracy. *Estudios Sociales Centroamericanos* 47: 37–50.

5372. Pae, S. M. June 1992. Korea: Leading the Third World in Democratization. *Asian Affairs: An American Review* 19 (2): 80–96.

5373. Pae, S. M., and J. Chung. December 1976. Attitudes of the Korean Bureaucrats toward Democracy. *Asian Forum* 9: 16–41.

5374. Paehlke, R. 1988. Democracy, Bureaucracy, and Environmentalism. *Environmental Ethics* 10 (4): 291–308.

5375. Pagano, M. A. June 1994. *See* Bowman, A. O. (June 1994).

5376. Pagano, U. 1983. Profit Maximization, Industrial Democracy and the Allocation of Labor. *Manchester School of Economic and Social Studies* 51 (2): 159–183.

5377. Page, B. I. March 1994. Democratic Responsiveness? Untangling the Links Between Public Opinion and Policy. *PS: Political Science & Politics* 27 (1): 25–28.

5378. Page, D. 1984. Community Housing Groups in Argentina's Democracy: Getting In on the Ground Floor. *Grassroots Development* 8 (1): 38–43.

5379. Paggi, L. April 1986. The Problems of Political Democracy in Western Societies.* *Estudios Politicos* 5 (2): 35–45.

5380. Paige, J. M. January 1990. The Social Origins of Dictatorship, Democracy and Socialist Revolution in Central America. *Journal of Developing Societies* 6 (1): 37–42.

5381. Painter, J. July 1986. Guatemala in Civilian Garb. *Third World Quarterly* 8 (3): 818–844.

5382. Palat, R. A. 1982. *See* Chhachhi, A. (1982).

5383. Palda, F. November 1993. Can Repressive Regimes Be Moderated through Foreign Aid? *Public Choice* 77 (3): 535–550.

5384. Palecek, A. June 1979. The Good Genius of Czechoslovak Democracy: Masaryk and Benes, or Svehla? *East European Quarterly* 13 (2): 213–234.

5385. Palermo, V. October 1991. Argentina: Democracia y Populismo en Tiempos Dificiles. *Revista de Estudios Politicos* 74: 211–240.

5386. Palley, M. L. July 1977. *See* Gelb, J. (July 1977).

5387. Palmer, N. D. 1975. Crisis of Democracy in India. *Orbis* 19 (2): 379–401.

5388. Palmer, N. D. February 1976. India in 1975: Democracy in Eclipse. *Asian Survey* 16 (2): 95–111.

5389. Palmer, N. D. February 1977. India in 1976: The Politics of Depoliticization. *Asian Survey* 17 (2): 160–180.

5390. Palterovitch, D. September 1989. Competition and Democratization. *Problems of Economics* 31 (10): 60–77.

5391. Pammett, J. H. June 1984. *See* Le Duc, L. (June 1984).

5392. Pampel, F. C., and J. B. Williamson. December 1985. Age Structure, Politics, and Cross-National Patterns of Public Pension Expenditure. *American Sociological Review* 50 (6): 782–799.

5393. Pampel, F. C., and J. B. Williamson. May 1988. Welfare Spending in Advanced Industrial Democracies, 1950–1980. *American Journal of Sociology* 93 (6): 1424–1456.

5394. Pampel, F. C., J. B. Williamson, and R. Stryker. 1990. Class Context and Pension Response to Demographic Structure in Advanced Industrial Democracies. *Social Problems* 37 (4): 535–550.

5395. Panebianco, A. July 1983. Charismatic Tendencies in Contemporary Societies.* *Il Mulino* 288: 507–537.

5396. Panebianco, A. December 1990. War and Democracy. *Il Mulino* 332: 908–916.

5397. Panebianco, M. 1978. Italian Democracy and Community Democracy. *Scientia* 113 (9–12): 919–934.

5398. Pang, E. S. February 1983. Brazil's New Democracy. *Current History* 82 (482): 54–57, 87–89.

5399. Pang, E. S. January 1988. The Darker Side of Brazil's Democracy. *Current History* 87 (525): 21–24, 40–41.

5400. Pang, E. S., and L. Jarnagin. February 1984. Brazilian Democracy and the Foreign Debt. *Current History* 83 (490): 36–67, 87–88.

5401. Pang, E. S., and L. Jarnagin. February 1985. A Requiem for Authoritarianism in Brazil. *Current History* 84 (499): 61–64, 88–89.

5402. Panitch, L. 1977. Development of Corporatism in Liberal Democracies. *Comparative Political Studies* 10 (1): 61–90.

5403. Panitch, L. 1981. Liberal Democracy and Socialist Democracy: The Antinomies of C. B. MacPherson. *Socialist Register* 144–168.

5404. Panitch, L., and S. Gindin. April 1991. Soviet Workers: A New Beginning? *Monthly Review* 42: 17–35.

5405. Panizza, F. May 1993. Human Rights: Global Culture and Social Fragmentation. *Bulletin of Latin American Research* 12: 205–214.

5406. Panter-Brick, K. March 1994. Prospects for Democracy in Zambia. *Government and Opposition* 29 (2): 231–247.

5407. Pantham, T. 1976. On the Theory of Democracy: A Critique of "The Schumpeter-Dahl Axis." *Journal of the Maharaja Sayajirao University of Baroda* 25 & 26 (2): 65–86.

5408. Pantham, T. May 1983. Thinking with Mahatma Gandhi: Beyond Liberal Democracy. *Political Theory* 11 (2): 165–188.

5409. Papageorgiou, C. I. March 1990. Four or Five Types of Democracy in Aristotle? *History of Political Thought* 11 (1): 1–8.

5410. Pappalardo, A. 1979. The Conditions of Consociational Democracy: A

Logical and Empirical Critique.* *Rivista Italiana di Scienza Politica* 9 (3): 367–445.

5411. Pappalardo, A. April 1980. Consociational Politics and Italian Democracy.* *Rivista Italiana di Scienza Politica* 10 (1): 63–123.

5412. Pappalardo, A. December 1981. The Conditions for Consociational Democracy: A Logical and Empirical Critique. *European Journal of Political Research* 9 (4): 365–390.

5413. Paramio, L. October 1991. El Final de un Ciclo y la Crisis de Unos Actores: America Latina ante la Decada de los 90. *Revista de Estudios Politicos* 74: 131–144.

5414. Pare, L. July 1990. The Challenges of Rural Democratization in Mexico. *Journal of Development Studies* 26 (4): 79–96.

5415. Pareja, C. 1991. La Academia y la Politica: La Reactualizacion de la Alternativa Parlamentarista y los Procesos de Consolidacion Democratica en el Cono Sur. *Cuadernos del CLAEH: Revista Uruguaya de Ciencias Sociales* 16 (1): 25–46.

5416. Parekh, B. 1992. The Cultural Particularity of Liberal Democracy. *Political Studies* 40: 160–175. Special issue.

5417. Paribatra, S. September 1993. State and Society in Thailand: How Fragile the Democracy? *Asian Survey* 33 (9): 879–893.

5418. Paris, D. C. July 1979. *See* Reynolds, J. F. (July 1979).

5419. Paris, D. C. June 1987. Fact, Theory, and Democratic Theory.* *Western Political Quarterly* 40 (2): 215–236.

5420. Paris, D. C., and J. F. Reynolds. November 1978. Paradox, Rationality, and Politics: Wollheim's Democracy. *Journal of Politics* 40 (4): 956–983.

5421. Paris, J. S. September 1993. When to Worry in the Middle East. *Orbis* 37 (4): 553–565.

5422. Park, A. June 1994. Turning-Points of Post-Communist Transition: Lessons from the Case of Estonia. *Government and Opposition* 29 (3): 403–413.

5423. Park, C. W. September 1993. Korean Voters' Candidate Choice in the 1992 Presidential Election: A Survey Data Analysis. *Korea and World Affairs* 17 (3): 432–458.

5424. Park, J. December 1990. Political Change in South Korea: The Challenge of the Conservative Alliance. *Asian Survey* 30 (12): 1154–1168.

5425. Park, J. 1992. Challenges to Korean Democracy. *Pacific Review* 5 (3): 297–301.

5426. Park, J. C. 1980. The New Right: Threat to Democracy in Education. *Educational Leadership* 38 (2): 146–149.

5427. Park, R. L. (ed.). November 1976. The American Revolution Abroad. *Annals of the American Academy of Political and Social Science* 428: 1–133. Preface and 10 articles.

5428. Parker, B. December 1991. Beyond the Vote: Responses to Centralization among Nepal Marpha Thakari. *Human Organization* 50 (4): 349–357.

5429. Parker, J. October 20, 1990. Now What? A Survey of the Soviet Union. *Economist (London)* 317: 66–88.

5430. Parker, J. March 13, 1993. Rejoined: A Survey of Eastern Europe. *Economist (London)* 326: 62–84.

5431. Parker, R. D. 1981. The Past of Constitutional Theory and Its Future. *Ohio State Law Review* 42 (1): 223–260.

5432. Parker, R. D. June 1993. "Here, The People Rule": A Constitutional Populist Manifesto. *Valparaiso University Law Review* 27: 531–584.

5433. Parks, Y. Y. March 1982. Organizational Development and Culture Contact: A Case Study of the Sokagakki in America. *Journal of Ethnic Studies* 10 (1): 1–16.

5434. Parkyn, B. (ed.). 1979. Democracy, Accountability and Participation in Industry. *Management Decision* 17 (1): 5–152. Collection of articles.

5435. Parming, T. 1975. Collapse of Liberal Democracy and Rise of Authoritarianism in Estonia. *Sage Professional Paper in Contemporary Political Sociology* 1 (601): 5–73.

5436. Parr, J. September 1990. *See* Cisneros, H. G. (September 1990).

5437. Parry, G. 1989. Democracy and Amateurism: The Informed Citizen. *Government and Opposition* 24 (4): 489–502.

5438. Parsons, N. January 1993. Botswana: An End to Exceptionality? *Round Table* 325: 73–82.

5439. Parsons, W. 1982. Politics without Promises: The Crisis of "Overload" and Governability. *Parliamentary Affairs* 35 (4): 421–435.

5440. Pascual, H. March 1988. *See* Goldman, R. M. (March 1988).

5441. Pascual, M. September 1994. *See* Colomer, J. M. (September 1994).

5442. Pasha, M. K. March 1993. *See* Blaney, D. L. (March 1993).

5443. Pask, G. 1990. Correspondence, Consensus, Coherence and the Rape of Democracy. *Communication and Cognition* 23 (2–3): 235–244.

5444. Pasour, E. C. September 1992. Economist and Public Policy: Chicago Political Economy Versus Conventional Views. *Public Choice* 74: 153–167.

5445. Pasqualetti, M. J. 1987. *See* Soloman, B. D. (1987).

5446. Pasquini, G. December 1984. Difficult Democracy in Argentina.* *Politica Internazionale* 12 (12): 45–56.

5447. Pasquino, G. September 1979. Skeptical Suggestions to Electoral Engineers.* *Il Mulino* 265: 749–780.

5448. Pasquino, G. July 1981. The Difficult Democracy in Spain.* *Il Mulino* 276: 595–624.

5449. Pasquino, G. May 1985. Democracy and Reformism, a New Mixture.* *Democrazia e Diritto* 25 (3–4): 211–241.

5450. Pasquino, G. January 1987. The Representation of Complexity and Democratic Governability.* *Democrazia e Diritto* 27 (1–2): 49–70.

5451. Pasquino, G. September 1989. Democracy Today: Challenges and Potentialities.* *Il Mulino* 325: 733–751.

5452. Pasquino, G. March 1993. The Opportunities of Democracy.* *Il Mulino* 346: 217–226.

5453. Pasquino, G. July 1994. The Need for Ethics in Democratic Politics.* *Il Mulino* 354: 572–580.

5454. Pasquino, G. September 1994. The Unexpected Alternation: The Italian Elections of March 1994 and Their Consequences.* *Politische Vierteljahresschrift* 35 (3): 383–401.

5455. Passerini, L. March 1994. The Interpretation of Democracy in the Italian Womens Movement of the 1970s and 1980s. *Women's Studies International Forum* 17 (2–3): 235–239.

5456. Passeron, J. C. 1979. Democratization of Higher Education in Europe: A Retrospective View. *Prospects* 9 (1): 43–53.

5457. Passin, H. June 1990. The Occupation: Some Reflections. *Daedalus* 119 (3): 107–129.

5458. Pastor, M. , Jr., and E. Hilt. April 1993. Private Investment and Democracy in Latin America. *World Development* 21 (4): 489–507.

5459. Pastor, R. July 1985. The Dawn of Caciques: History of the Crisis of the Honduras Political System.* *Foro Internacional* 101: 16–30.

5460. Pastor, R. A. December 1988. Securing a Democratic [Latin America] Hemisphere. *Foreign Policy* 73: 41–59.

5461. Pastuhov, V. B. 1990. On the Historical Evaluation of Certain Views of Marxism on Bourgeois Democracy.* *Sovetskoe Gosudarstvo Pravo* 9: 95–102.

5462. Pateman, C. 1974. Criticising Empirical Theories of Democracy: Comment on Skinner. *Political Theory* 2 (2): 215–218.

5463. Pateman, C. May 1975. A Contribution to the Political Theory of Organizational Democracy. *Administration and Society* 7 (1): 5–26.

5464. Pateman, C. 1986. Social Choice or Democracy: A Comment. *Ethics* 97 (1): 39–46.

5465. Patterson, D. October 1994. Electoral Influence and Economic Policy: Political Origins of Financial Aid to Small Business in Japan. *Comparative Political Studies* 27 (3): 425–447.

5466. Patterson, S. C. July 1988. *See* Kim, C. L. (July 1988).

5467. Patterson, S. C. December 1994. *See* Hibbing, J. R. (December 1994).

5468. Patterson, W. D. August 1989. *See* Hicks, A. (August 1989).

5469. Pattie, C. J. October 1994. *See* Johnston, R. J. (October 1994).

5470. Paul, E. C. 1993. Prospects for Liberalization in Singapore. *Journal of Contemporary Asia* 23 (3): 291–305.

5471. Pavlov, V. L. September 1985. *See* Clarke, C. J. (September 1985).

5472. Payne, A. J. March 1988. Creative Politics: Jamaica's Approach to Independence. *Caribbean Review* 16 (1): 4–8, 30–31.

5473. Payne, D. W. March 1985. The "Mantos" of Sandinista Deception. *Strategic Review* 13: 9–10.

5474. Payne, D. W. May 1987. Between Pinochet and Democracy. *Freedom at Issue* 96: 3–9.

5475. Payne, D. W. January 1989. Latin America: Crisis of Democracy. *Freedom at Issue* 106: 9–12.

5476. Payne, D. W. February 1990. A Latin Last Hurrah (in Paraguay). *Society* 27 (2): 41–52.

5477. Payne, D. W. July 1992. Peru: Fujimoro Breaks the Law. *Freedom Review* 23: 8–11.

5478. Payne, J. H. 1992. Economic Assistance to Support Democratization in Developing Countries: A Canadian Perspective. *Development* (3): 12–16.

5479. Payne, L. A. January 1991. Working-Class Strategies in the Transition to Democracy in Brazil. *Comparative Politics* 23 (2): 221–238.

5480. Payne, S. G. November 1977. The Political Transformation of Spain. *Current History* 73 (431): 165–168, 178–179.

5481. Payne, S. G. December 1982. Spain's Political Future. *Current History* 81 (479): 417–421, 434.

5482. Paz, O. April 1983. Latin America and Democracy.* *Merkur* 37 (3): 243–259.

5483. Paz, O. March 1986. Notes on the United States. *Wilson Quarterly* 10 (2): 80–93.

5484. Pazanin, A. 1984. The State and Democracy.* *Politicka Misao* 21 (1–2): 3–19.

5485. Pe Linka, A. 1980. Conditions and Alternatives of the Political System.* *Oesterreichische Zeitschrift für Politikwissenschaft* 9 (1): 25–32.

5486. Pease Garcia, H. April 1988. Peru: Building Democracy upon Precariousness.* *Revista Mexicana de Sociologia* 50 (2): 51–63.

5487. Pecaut, D. 1980. Coffee Politics and Restricted Civilian Democracy: The Case of Colombia.* *Cultures et Development* 12 (3–4): 477–506.

5488. Peck, R. S., and B. McDowell. 1983. Dollar Democracy: An Analysis of Public Financing of State Politics. *Urban Lawyer* 15 (4): 921–946.

5489. Pedersen, A. December 1993. *See* Frederiksen, B. (December 1993).

5490. Pederzoli, P. August 1990. The Judge in Democratic Regimes.* *Rivista Italiana de Scienza Politica* 20 (2): 293–323.

5491. Pehe, J. 1993. The Waning Popularity of the Czech Parliament. *RFE/RL Research Report* 2 (12): 9–13.

5492. Pei, M. October 1994. The Puzzle of East Asian Exceptionalism. *Journal of Democracy* 5 (4): 90–103.

5493. Pejovich, S. 1994. The Market for Institutions vs. Capitalism by Fiat: The Case of Eastern Europe. *Kyklos* 47 (4): 519–529.

5494. Peju, M. March 19, 1992. Sondage Exclusif: Les Africains et la Democratie. *Jeune Afrique* 32: 56–61.

5495. Pelczynski, Z., and S. Kowalski. December 1990. Poland. *Electoral Studies* 9 (4): 346–354.

5496. Peled, Y. June 1992. Ethnic Democracy and the Legal Construction of Citizenship: Arab Citizens of the Jewish State. *American Political Science Review* 86: 432–443.

5497. Pelesh, M. L. 1980. *See* Curzan, M. P. (1980).

5498. Pellegrini, T. December 1994. Brazil in the 1970s: Literature and Politics. *Latin American Perspectives* 21 (1): 56–71.

5499. Pena, F. 1988. The Latin American Summit Meeting of Acapulco: Economic Change, Democratization and International Cooperation.* *Europa Archiv: Zeitschrift für Internationale Politik* 43 (5): 132–138.

5500. Penner, R. January 1994. Unionization, Democracy, and the University. *Interchange* 25 (1): 49–53.

5501. Penniman, H. R. June 1984. U.S. Elections: Really a Bargain? *Public Opinion* 7: 51–53.

5502. Pennock, J. R. 1983. Introduction: Liberal Democracy. *Nomos* 25: 1–12.

5503. Pepin, L. 1990. The Defence of Teachers' Trade Union Rights. *International Labour Review* 129 (1): 59–71.

5504. Pepper, S. April 1982. China's Universities: New Experiments in Socialist Democracy and Administrative Reform: A Research Report. *Modern China* 8 (2): 147–204.

5505. Percheron, A. 1980. *See* Dehan, N. (1980).

5506. Percy Smith, J. October 1989. *See* Hillyard, P. (October 1989).

5507. Percy, S. L. June 1984. Citizen Participation in the Coproduction of Urban Services. *Urban Affairs Quarterly* 19 (4): 431–446.

5508. Pereira, A. W. 1993. Economic Underdevelopment, Democracy and Civil Society: The North-East Brazilian Case. *Third World Quarterly* 14 (2): 365–380.

5509. Pereira, L. C. B., J. M. Maravall, and A. Przeworski. 1993. Economic Reforms in Recent Democracies: A Social Democratic Approach.* *Dados: Revista de Ciencias Sociais* 36 (2): 171–207.

5510. Perelli, C. June 1992. Settling Accounts with Blood Memory: The Case of Argentina. *Social Research* 59 (2): 415–451.

5511. Peres, S. September 1991. The Middle East in a New Era. *Mediterranean Quarterly* 2 (4): 1–14.

5512. Peretz, D. 1983. A Different Place. *Wilson Quarterly* 7 (1): 62–80.

5513. Perez, A. 1992. The International Center for Human Rights and Democratic Development: A New Approach to Politics and Democracy in Developing Countries. *Canadian Journal of Development Studies* 13 (1): 91–102.

5514. Perez, A. G. 1986. Debt or Democracy, the Alternative of Latin America. *Trimestre Economico* 53 (211): 664–671.

5515. Perez, C. A. September 1990. OAS Opportunities. *Foreign Policy* 80: 52–55.

5516. Perez, M. 1990. *See* Trejos, M. E. (1990).

5517. Perez, R. October 1991. *See* Crespo, I. (October 1991).

5518. Perez-Diaz, V. 1990. Inventing a Democratic Tradition in Spain. *Tocqueville Review* 11: 197–217.

5519. Perina, R. M. April 1993. La Promocion de la Democracia en America Latina. *Estudios Internacionales* 26 (102): 204–215.

5520. Peritore, N. P. October 1988. Brazilian Communist Opinion: A Q Methodology Study of Ten Parties. *Journal of Developing Areas* 23 (1): 105–136.

5521. Peritore, N. P. December 1989. Brazilian Party Left Opinion: A Q Methodology Profile. *Political Psychology* 10 (4): 675–702.

5522. Perkins, E. J. December 1993. The United States as a Global Citizen. *Presidential Studies Quarterly* 23 (1): 17–22.

5523. Perkovitz, G. June 1992. Weapons Complexes Versus Democracy. *Bulletin of the Atomic Scientists* 48 (5): 16–17.

5524. Perrault, S. 1994. *See* Lajoie, A. (1994).

5525. Perry, B. A. 1992. *See* Abraham, H. J. (1992).

5526. Perry, C. S. September 1980. Political Constetation in Nations: 1960, 1963, and 1970. *Journal of Political and Military Sociology* 8: 161–174.

5527. Perry, E. June 1980. Report on the Mayors' Delegation to the People's Republic of China. *Urbanism Past and Present* 5 (2): 21–28.

5528. Perry, E., and E. V. Fuller. September 1991. China's Long March to Democracy. *World Policy Journal* 8 (4): 663–685.

5529. Perry, G. 1991. *See* Modelski, G. (1991).

5530. Perry, M. J. 1981. Interpretivism, Freedom of Expression, and Equal Protection. *Ohio State Law Journal* 42 (1): 261–318.

5531. Perry, W. March 1990. In Search of a Latin America Policy: The Elusive Quest. *Washington Quarterly* 13 (2): 125–134.

5532. Perthes, V. January 1993. Incremental Change in Syria. *Current History* 92 (570): 23–26.

5533. Perugini, C. 1985. *See* Osculati, F. (1985).

5534. Pesek, J. 1990. *See* Znoj, M. (1990).

5535. Pesonen, P. 1980. *See* Muller, E.N. (1980).

5536. Pesonen, P. September 1994. The First Direct Elections of Finland's President. *Scandinavian Political Studies* 17 (3): 259–210.

5537. Pestoff, V. 1980. *See* Dellenbrandt, J. A. (1980).

5538. Peter, B. G. October 1993. Searching for a Role: The Civil Service in American Democracy. *International Political Science Review* 14 (4): 373–386.

5539. Peters, B. G. March 1975. *See* Hennesy, T. M. (March 1975).

5540. Peters, B. G. April 1977. *See* Doughtie, J. C. (April 1977).

5541. Peters, J. D. 1989. Democracy and American Mass Communication Theory: Dewey, Lippmann, Lazarfeld. *Communication* 11 (3): 199–220.

5542. Petersen, J. C. 1976. Ideological Diffuseness and Internal Democracy in

Voluntary Associations. *Journal of Voluntary Action Research* 5 (1): 33–41.

5543. Petersen, M. D. 1976. Adams and Jefferson: A Revolutionary Dialogue. *Wilson Quarterly* 1 (1): 108–125.

5544. Peterson, D. L. June 1994. Debunking Ten Myths about Democracy in Africa. *Washington Quarterly* 17 (3): 129–141.

5545. Peterson, M. J. December 1992. Transnational Activity, International Society and World Politics. *Millennium* 21 (3): 371–388.

5546. Peterson, N. March 1985. The Scandilux Experiment: Toward a Transnational Social Democratic Security Perspective. *Cooperation and Conflict* 20: 1–22.

5547. Peterson, P. E., and J. P. Greene. January 1994. Why Executive-Legislative Conflict in the United States Is Dwindling. *British Journal of Political Science* 24 (1): 33–56.

5548. Peterson, R. D. 1978. Pluralist Democracy, Political Economy, and Modern American Capitalism. *Akron Business and Economic Review* 9 (2): 14–19.

5549. Peterson, R. L. 1978. *See* De Ritter, M. (1978).

5550. Peterson, R. L., and M. M. De Ritter. November 1986. Government Formation as a Policy-Making Arena. *Legislative Studies Quarterly* 11 (4): 565–581.

5551. Petersson, O. 1988. The Study of Power and Democracy in Sweden. *Scandinavian Political Studies* 11 (2): 145–158.

5552. Petersson, O. 1994. The Electoral System of France, Belgium, and Germany.* *Statsvetenskaplig Tidskrift* 97 (1): 33–60.

5553. Petr, J. L. December 1987. The Nature and Necessity of the Mixed Economy. *Journal of Economic Issues* 21 (4): 1445–1468.

5554. Petracca, M. P. March 1991. The Rational-Choice Approach to Politics: A Challenge to Democratic Theory. *Review of Politics* 53 (2): 289–319.

5555. Petracca, M. P., and Mong Xiong. November 1990. The Concept of Chinese Neo-Authoritarianism: An Exploration and Democratic Critique. *Asian Survey* 30 (11): 1099–1117.

5556. Petras, J. 1985. Authoritarianism, Democracy and the Transition to Socialism. *Socialist Register* 268–294.

5557. Petras, J. 1985. *See* Herman, E. S. (1985).

5558. Petras, J. July 6, 1985. *See* Herman, E. S. (July 6, 1985).

5559. Petras, J. September 1985. Authoritarianism, Democracy and the Transition to Socialism. *Socialism and Democracy* 1: 5–27.

5560. Petras, J. September 1986. *See* Leiva, F. I. (September 1986).

5561. Petras, J. July 1987. *See* Leiva, F. I. (July 1987).

5562. Petras, J. June 1988. *See* Harding, T. (June 1988).

5563. Petras, J. 1989. State, Regime and the Democratization Muddle. *Journal of Contemporary Asia* 19 (1): 26–32.

5564. Petras, J. 1991. Eastern Europe: Restoration and Crisis. *Journal of Contemporary Asia* 21 (3): 301–326.

5565. Petras, J. December 3, 1994. The 1994 United States Democratic Debacle: Conservative Elections Mandate. *Economic and Political Weekly* 29 (49): 3079–3081.

5566. Petras, J., and F. T. Fitzgerald. 1988. Authoritarianism and Democracy in the Transition to Socialism. *Latin American Perspectives* 15 (1): 93–111.

5567. Petras, J., and F. I. Leiva. June 1988. Chile: The Authoritarian Transition to Electoral Politics: A Critique. *Latin American Perspectives* 15 (3): 97–114.

5568. Petras, J., and M. Morley. 1991. Latin America: Poverty of Democracy and Democracy of Poverty. *Economic and Political Weekly* 26 (30): 103–111.

5569. Petras, J., M. Morley, and A. E. Havens. November 1983. Peru: Capitalist Democracy in Transition. *New Left Review* 142: 30–53.

5570. Petryszak, N. June 1977. The Frankfurt School's Theory of Manipulation. *Journal of Communication* 27 (3): 32–40.

5571. Pettit, P. 1993. Liberalism and Republicanism. *Australian Journal of Political Science* 28 (1): 162–189.

5572. Peukert, D. 1977. Antifaschistischer Konsens als Voraussetzung einer Demokratischen Nachkriegsentwicklung. *Blaetter für Deutsche und Internationale Politik* 22 (11): 1367–1386.

5573. Pfaff, W. 1978. Capitalism, Socialism, and Democracy. *Commentary* 65 (4): 64–65.

5574. Pfaffenberger, B. February 1987. Sri Lanka in 1986: A Nation at the Crossroads. *Asian Survey* 27 (2): 155–162.

5575. Pfefferling, U. 1988. *See* Dau, R. (1988).

5576. Pfersmann, O. July 1989. Consensus and the Possibility of Democracy [in Austria].* *Austriaca* 28: 59–68.

5577. Pfiffner, J. P. January 1987. Political Appointees and Career Executives: The Democracy Bureaucracy Nexus in the Third Century. *Public Administration Review* 47 (1): 57–65.

5578. Pharo, P. July 1990. The Conditions of Legitimacy of Public Actions.* *Revue Française de Sociologie* 31 (3): 389–420.

5579. Pheifer, C. 1992. State or Market? Society or Individual? Background and Prospects of the Democratization Process in Vietnam.* *Internationales Asienforum* 23 (3–4): 347–358.

5580. Philip, G. March 1984. Democratization in Brazil and Argentina: Some Reflections. *Government and Opposition* 19 (2): 269–276.

5581. Philip, G. 1992. Venezuelan Democracy and the Coup Attempt of February 1992. *Government and Opposition* 27 (4): 455–469.

5582. Philip, G. 1993. The New Economic Liberalism and Democracy in Latin America: Friends or Enemies? *Third World Quarterly* 14 (3): 555–571.

5583. Philip, G. June 1994. New Economic Liberalism and Democracy in Spanish America. *Government and Opposition* 29 (3): 362–377.

5584. Philippe, C. May 1992. Democracy in the Congo: A Difficult Transition.* *Defense Nationale* 43–56.

5585. Phillips, A. 1992. Must Feminists Give Up on Liberal Democracy? *Political Studies* 40: 68–82. Special issue.

5586. Phillips, A. January 1992. Democracy and Difference: Some Problems for Feminist Theory. *Political Quarterly* 63 (1): 79–90.

5587. Phillips, A. April 1994. Dealing with Difference: A Politics of Ideas or a Politics of Presence? *Constellations* 1 (1): 74–91.

5588. Phillips, D. R. 1986. Hong Kong: Edging towards Local Democracy. *Geography* 71 (311): 142–146.

5589. Phillips, M., and L. Nathan. March 1991. The Changing of the Guard: The Security Forces in Transition. *Social Justice* 18 (1–2): 105–123.

5590. Picard, R. G. March 1985. Patterns of State Intervention in Western Press Economies. *Journalism Quarterly* 62 (1): 3–9.

5591. Picciotto, S. 1988. The Control of Trans-National Capital and the Democratization of the International State. *Journal of Law and Society* 15 (1): 58–76.

5592. Pick, O. November 1994. The Czech Republic: A Stable Transition. *World Today* 50 (11): 206–207.

5593. Pickel, A. 1993. Authoritarianism or Democracy: Marketization as a Political Problem. *Policy Sciences* 26 (3): 139–163.

5594. Pickering, M., and D. Chaney. 1986. Democracy and Communication: Mass Observation 1937–1943. *Journal of Communication* 36 (1): 41–56.

5595. Piel, G. December 1975. Public Support for Autonomous Universities. *Daedalus* 104 (1): 148–155.

5596. Piele, P. K. September 1976. *See* Hall, J. S. (September 1976).

5597. Pienkos, A. June 1986. Organizational Contradictions and Policy Inertia in Yugoslav Institutional Evolution. *Journal of Economic Issues* 20 (2): 583–592.

5598. Pierce, J. C. January 1986. Vanguards and Rearguards in Environmental Politics: A Comparison of Activists in Japan and the United States. *Comparative Political Studies* 18: 419–447.

5599. Pierre-Charles, G. June 1986. A Difficult Challenge: Building Democracy in Haiti.* *Revista Mexicana de Sociologia* 48 (3): 75–88.

5600. Pierre-Charles, G. June 1988. The Democratic Revolution in Haiti. *Latin American Perspectives* 15 (3): 64–76.

5601. Pierson, C. 1992. Democracy, Markets and Capital: Are There Necessary Economic Limits to Democracy? *Political Studies* 40: 83–98. Special issue.

5602. Pieterse, J. N. May 1993. Fukuyama and Liberal Democracy: The Ends of History. *Economy and Society* 22 (2): 218–232.

5603. Pii, E. May 1993. Republic Democracy: European Links in Montesquieu's Thought.* *Il Pensiero Politico* 26 (2): 215–226.

5604. Pike, D. 1988. Georg Lukacs on Stalinism and Democracy: Before and after Prague, 1968. *East European Politics and Societies* 2 (2): 241–279.

5605. Pilat, J. F. 1982. Democracy or Discontent: Ecologists in the European Electoral Arena. *Government and Opposition* 17 (2): 222–233.

5606. Pildes, R. H., and E. S. Anderson. December 1990. Slinging Arrows at Democracy: Social Choice Theory, Value Pluralism, and Democratic Politics. *Columbia Law Review* 90 (8): 2121–2214.

5607. Pilon, R. December 1992. Individual Rights, Democracy, and Constitutional Order: On the Foundations of Legitimacy. *Cato Journal* 11 (3): 373–390.

5608. Pilon, R. December 1992. On the First Principles of Constitutionalism: Liberty, Then Democracy. *American University Journal of International Law and Policy* 8: 531–549.

5609. Pina, A. L. August 1984. *See* McDonough, P. (August 1984).

5610. Pina, A. L. 1985. *See* Barnes, S. H. (1985).

5611. Pinder, J. 1994. The European Elections of 1994 and the Future of the European Union. *Government and Opposition* 29 (4): 494–514.

5612. Pionberlin, D. October 1992. Military Autonomy and Emerging Democracies in South America. *Comparative Politics* 25 (1): 83–102.

5613. Pious, R. 1994. Presidential and Parliamentary Democracies Which Work Best: Concluding Reflections. *Political Science Quarterly* 109 (3): 541+.

5614. Pipes, R. 1978. Capitalism, Socialism, and Democracy. *Commentary* 65 (4): 65–66.

5615. Piro, T. July 1992. Parliament, Politics and Pluralism in Jordan: Democratic Trends at a Difficult Time. *Middle East Insight* 8: 39–44.

5616. Pisani, D. J. December 1987. Promotion and Regulation: Constitutionalism and the American Economy. *Journal of American History* 74 (3): 740–768.

5617. Piscatori, J. P. June 1991. *See* Esposito, J. L. (June 1991).

5618. Pisier, E. 1986. Public Service and Public Liberties. *Pouvoirs* 36: 143–154.

5619. Piskotin, M. I. May 1981. Democratic Centralism: Problems of the Combination of Centralization and Decentralization.* *Sovetskoe Gosudarstvo Pravo* 5: 39–49.

5620. Pitroda, S. November 1993. Development, Democracy, and the Village Telephone. *Harvard Business Review* 71 (6): 66–68.

5621. Piven, F. F. June 1990. *See* Bennett, S. E. (June 1990).

5622. Pizarro Leongomez, E. May 1994. Elections, Parties, and the New Institutional Setting [in Colombia].* *Analisis Politico* 22: 81–98.

5623. Pizetti, F. April 1994. Electoral Reforms, Majority System, and Constitutional Guarantees.* *Biblioteca della Liberta* 125: 5–23.

5624. Placca, J. April 1993. Mauritanie: Democratie en Construction. *Jeune Afrique Economie* 117–125.

5625. Plaka, S. 1991. European Democratization and Integration. *Est-Ouest* 22 (2): 11–24.

5626. Plank, D. N., and W. L. Boyd. June 1994. Antipolitics, Education, and Institutional Choice: The Flight from Democracy. *American Educational Research Journal* 31 (2): 263–281.

5627. Plasseraud, Y., and S. Pourchier. 1991. The Baltic States: Independence at Last. *Esprit* 10: 31–39.

5628. Platt, M. March 1993. The Banner of Upright Swiss Liberty. *Publius* 23 (2): 97–109.

5629. Plener, U. 1986. The Evolution of the Interpretation of Democracy in the Workers' Movement.* *Zeitschrift für Geschichtswissenschaft* 34 (1): 5–21.

5630. Pleschberger, W. 1975. Bourgeois Theory of Democracy in Search of Strategies for Capitalistic and Functional Democratization.* *Oesterreichische Zeitschrift für Politikwissenschaft* 4 (2): 195–205.

5631. Plichtova, J., and E. Brozmanova. 1994. Concept of Democracy from the Point of View of Slovak Mayors.* *Sociologia* 26 (3): 245–260.

5632. Plichtova, J., and A. Hrabovska. 1993. Construction of the Meaning of Some Political Terms: Pilot Study.* *Ceskoslovenska Psychologie* 37 (2): 111–128.

5633. Plohn, J. 1993. The Hamburg Ruling: Victory for Democracy or Judicial Despotism. *Gegenwartskunde: Gesellschaft, Staat, Erziehung* 42 (3): 341–352.

5634. Plotke, D. 1984. Democracy, Modernization, Democracy. *Socialist Review* (74): 29–53.

5635. Plotke, D. 1990. Talk Democracy: How to Reframe the Public Debates. *Social Policy* 21 (2): 26–36.

5636. Plumtree, J. P., J. D. Starling, and K. W. Kramer. February 1985. Citizen Participation in Water Quality Planning: A Case Study of Perceived Failure. *Administration and Society* 16 (4): 455–474.

5637. Pocock, J. G. A. June 1976. The Classical Theory of Deference. *American Historical Review* 81 (3): 516–523.

5638. Podhoretz, J. December 1982. A Confederacy of Dunces. *Policy Review* 19: 133–135.

5639. Poe, S. C., and C. N. Tate. December 1994. Repression of Human Rights to Personal Integrity in the 1980s: A Global Analysis. *American Political Science Review* 88 (4): 853–872.

5640. Poettgens, H. February 1974. Funktionsgerechte Gestaltung des Staates: Zur Diskussion um Demokratisierung, Partizipation and Raetesystem. *Neue Ordnung* 28: 34–43.

5641. Pogany, I. April 1993. Constitutional Reform in Central and Eastern Europe: Hungary's Transition to Democracy. *International and Comparative Law Quarterly* 42: 332–355.

5642. Pohoryles, R. J. 1989. Do Democracies Need Corruption? A Pragmatic View on a Widespread Phenomenon. *Innovation* 2 (4): 393–399.

5643. Polhemus, J. H. 1983. Botswana Votes: Parties and Elections in an African Democracy. *Journal of Modern African Studies* 21 (3): 397–430.

5644. Polin, C. 1979. Ideology and Athenian Democracy or the Use of the Word Ideology.* *Cahiers Vilfredo Pareto* 17 (46): 35–44.

5645. Pollack, B. 1978. Spain: From Corporate State to Parliamentary Democracy. *Parliamentary Affairs* 31 (1): 52–66.

5646. Pollack, B. 1990. *See* Angell, A. (1990).

5647. Pollack, B., and G. Hunter. July 1987. Spanish Democracy after Four General Elections. *Parliamentary Affairs (London)* 40 (3): 357–373.

5648. Pollack, B., and M. Pollack. October 1993. Overview: The Vulnerability of Democracy.* *Parliamentary Affairs* 46 (1): 447–457.

5649. Pollack, B., and J. Taylor. April 1983. The Transition to Democracy in Portugal and Spain. *British Journal of Political Science* 13 (2): 209–243.

5650. Pollack, M. October 1993. *See* Pollack, B. (October 1993).

5651. Pollard, R. 1992. Ambiguous Democracy [in Africa].* *Année Africaine* 17–57.

5652. Pollitt, C. June 1988. Consumerism and Beyond. *Public Administration* 66: 125–193.

5653. Polsby, N. W. 1980. Autonomous Power in Democracy: Empirical Criticism of Neo-Elitists.* *Rivista Italiana di Scienza Politica* 10 (1): 149–166.

5654. Polvin, M. September 1994. The Election of Civil Servants and Partisan Behavior among Elected Representatives: A Comparative Study of Parliaments and Governments in Five Liberal Democracies [1965 & 1985]. *International Review of Administrative Sciences* 60 (3): 423–446.

5655. Pomery, C. September 1990. Hong Kong: Which Way Forward? *World Policy Journal* 7 (4): 773–790.

5656. Pommerehne, W. W. 1975. Budgetary Redistribution in a Democracy: An Empirical Test for Alternative Hypothesis. *Zeitschrift für Wirtschaft und Sozialwissenschaften* 4: 327–364.

5657. Pommerehne, W. W., and B. S. Frey. 1978. Bureaucratic Behavior in Democracy: Case Study. *Public Finance* 33 (1–2): 98–112.

5658. Pomper, G. M. March 1977. The Decline of the Party in American Elections. *Political Science Quarterly* 92 (1): 21–42.

5659. Pond, D. March 1992. Direct Democracy: The Wave of the Future? *Canadian Parliamentary Review* 15: 11–14.

5660. Pontussen, J. 1984. Behind and Beyond Social Democracy in Sweden. *New Left Review* (143): 69–96.

5661. Pontussen, J. 1987. Radicalization and Retreat in Swedish Social Democracy. *New Left Review* (165): 5–33.

5662. Pontussen, J. September 1992. At the End of the Third Road: Swedish Social Democracy in Crisis. *Politics and Society* 20 (3): 305–332.

5663. Pontussen, J. January 1993. The Comparative Politics of Labor-Initiated Reforms: Swedish Cases of Success and Failure. *Comparative Political Studies* 25: 548–578.

5664. Pontussen, J., and S. Kuruvilla. July 1992. Swedish Wage-Earner Funds: An Experiment in Economic Democracy. *Industrial and Labor Relations Review* 45 (4): 779–791.

5665. Poole, M. 1979. Industrial Democracy: A Comparative Analysis. *Industrial Relations* 18 (3): 262–272.

5666. Poole, M. 1982. Theories of Industrial Democracy: The Emerging Synthesis. *Sociological Review* 30 (2): 181–207.

5667. Popescu, S. 1976. *See* Anghene, M. (1976).

5668. Popovic, M. V. 1988. Crisis of the Yugoslav Society and Social Conflicts. *Est-Ouest* 19 (5): 95–112.

5669. Porges, L. July 1993. *See* Gaud, M. (July 1993).

5670. Porket, J. L. May 1977. The Soviet Model of Industrial Democracy. *Annals of the American Academy of Political and Social Science* 431: 123–132.

5671. Portales, C. C. July 1989. External Factors and the Authoritarian Regime: Evolution and Impact of Chile's International Relations in the Process of Transition to Democracy.* *Estudios Internacionales* 87: 308–341.

5672. Portelli, H. 1978. Representative Democracy, Basic Democracy and Social Movement.* *Pouvoirs* 7: 95–106.

5673. Porter, B. D. November 1993. Can American Democracy Survive? *Commentary* 96: 37–40.

5674. Porter, D. O. March 1989. *See* Mayer, R. T. (March 1989).

5675. Porter, R. B. March 1977. John Stuart Mill and Federalism. *Publius* 7 (2): 101–124.

5676. Portinaro, P. P. October 1979. Democracy and Dictatorship in Guglielmo Ferrero.* *Comunita* 181: 271–296.

5677. Portis, E. B. March 1987. Charismatic Leadership and Cultural Democracy. *Review of Politics* 49 (2): 231–250.

5678. Posadacarbo, E. October 1994. Elections and Civil War in 19th Century Colombia: The 1875 Presidential Campaign. *Journal of Latin American Studies* 26 (3): 621–650.

5679. Posas, M. 1988. Democratization in Honduras. *Estudios Sociales Centroamericanos* (47): 61–78.

5680. Posavec, Z. 1989. The Democratic Constitutional State and Totalitarian Democracy.* *Politicka Misao* 26 (2): 13–19.

5681. Posderac, H. 1986. Democratic Centralism and Pluralism of Self-Management Interests.* *Questions Actuelles du Socialisme* 36 (2): 3–21.

5682. Posner, M. December 1994. Rally Round Human Rights. *Foreign Affairs* (97): 133–139.

5683. Posner, R. A. 1991. Democracy and Distrust Revisited. *Virginia Law Review* 77 (4): 641–651.

5684. Post, R. C. December 1991. Racist Speech, Democracy, and the First Amendment. *William and Mary Law Review* 32: 267–327.

5685. Potter, A. L. May 1981. The Failure of Democracy in Argentina 1916–1930: An Institutional Perspective. *Journal of Latin American Studies* 13: 83–109.

5686. Poulat, E. 1978. Right, Left and Originality of Christian Democracy.* *Pensee* (197): 3–12.

5687. Poulsen, J. December 1986. Natural Society, Reification, and Socialist Institutions in Marx. *Social Research* 53 (4): 591–613.

5688. Pouncy, H. August 1988. Terms of Agreement: Evaluating the Theory of

Symbolic Politics' Impact on the Pluralist Research Program. *American Journal of Political Science* 32 (3): 781–795.

5689. Pourchier, S. 1991. *See* Plasseraud, Y. (1991).

5690. Pourgerami, A. August 1988. The Political Economy of Development: A Cross-National Causality Test of Development Democracy Growth Hypothesis. *Public Choice* 58 (2): 123–141.

5691. Pourgerami, A. April 1991. The Political Economy of Development: An Empirical Examination of the Wealth Theory of Democracy. *Journal of Theoretical Politics* 3 (2): 189–211.

5692. Pourgerami, A. October 1992. Authoritarian Versus Nonauthoritarian Approaches to Economic Development: Update and Additional Evidence. *Public Choice* 74 (3): 365–377.

5693. Pouthier, J. L. January 1993. Christian Democracy in France: An Unattainable Goal.* *Histoire* (162): 48–54.

5694. Powell, C. T. 1993. The External Dimension of the Spanish Transition.* *Revista (IDOB d'Afers Internacionals)* 26: 37–64.

5695. Powell, D. E. October 1988. Soviet Glasnost: Definitions and Dimensions. *Current History* 87 (531): 321–324, 344–345.

5696. Powell, G. B. , Jr. 1981. Party Systems and Political System Performance: Voting Participation, Government Stability and Mass Violence in Contemporary Democracy. *American Political Science Review* 75 (4): 861–879.

5697. Powell, G. B. , Jr. July 1983. Representative or Responsible Party Systems in Parliamentary Democracies.* *Il Mulino* 11 (288): 633–665.

5698. Powell, G. B., Jr. March 1986. American Voter Turnout in Comparative Perspective. *American Political Science Review* 80 (1): 17–43.

5699. Powell, G. B. , Jr. April 1994. *See* Huber, J. D. (April 1994).

5700. Powell, L. W. September 1993. *See* Wilcox, C. (September 1993).

5701. Power, T. J. September 1991. Politicized Democracy: Competition, Institutions, and "Civic Fatique" in Brazil. *Journal of Interamerican Studies and World Affairs* 33 (3): 75–112.

5702. Prager, J. June 1981. Moral Integration and Political Inclusion: A Comparison of Durkheim's and Weber's Theories of Democracy. *Social Forces* 59 (4): 918–950.

5703. Pratt, C. 1978. Democracy and Socialism in Tanzania. *Journal of African Studies* 12 (3): 407–428.

5704. Preciphs, T. September 1993. *See* Brooks, A. (September 1993).

5705. Preobrazenskaja, A. 1993. The Left Wing Bloc before and after the [1993] French Parliamentary Elections.* *Mirovaia Ekonomika i Mezdunarodnye Otnosenija Nauk* 12: 103–114.

5706. Presser, S. B. September 1992. Thwarting the Killing of the Corporation: Limited Liability, Democracy, and Economics. *Northwestern University Law Review* 87 (1): 148–179.

5707. Prestipino, G. January 1979. Crisis of Democracy: Neoliberalism or Progressive Democracy.* *Critica Indixista* 17 (1): 87–103.

5708. Preston, W. May 1977. American Liberty: A Post-Bicentennial Look at Our Unfinished Agenda. *Civil Liberties Review* 4 (1): 38–51.

5709. Pretzell, K. September 1992. Demokratie in Thailand: Getrachtungen zum Sommer 1992. *Suedostasien Aktuell* 11: 475–478.

5710. Pretzell, K. March 1993. Demokratie in Thailand. *Suedostasien Aktuell* 12: 141–144.

5711. Pretzell, K. September 1993. Thailand im Umbruch? Demokratie 1993. *Suedostasien Aktuell* 12: 355–360.

5712. Preuss, U. K. 1989. *See* Offe, C. (1989).

5713. Preuss, U. K. 1991. Perspectives of Democracy and the Rule of Law. *Journal of Law and Society* 18 (3): 353–363.

5714. Prewitt, K. March 1983. Scientific Illiteracy and Democratic Theory. *Daedalus* 112 (2): 49–64.

5715. Price, C. M. April 1983. Recalls at the Local Level: Dimensions and Implications. *National Civic Review* 72 (4): 199–206.

5716. Price, P. 1992. Democracy and Political Development in India: The Case of Tamil Nadu.* *Internasjonal Politikk* 50 (2): 431–437.

5717. Price, P. May 1993. Democracy and Ethnic Conflict in India: Precolonial Legacies in Tamil Nadu. *Asian Survey* 33 (5): 493–506.

5718. Prickett, J. R. 1974. Communists and Trade-Union Democracy: Reply. *Industrial Relations* 13 (3): 237–239.

5719. Prideaux, G. J. 1981. *See* Lansbury R. D. (1981).

5720. Pridham, G. January 1984. Party Government in the New Iberian Democracies. *World Today* 40 (1): 12–21.

5721. Pridham, G. April 1984. Comparative Perspectives on the New Mediterranean Democracies: A Model of Regime Transition. *West European Politics* 7 (2): 1–29.

5722. Pridham, G. October 1990. Political Actors, Linkages and Interactions: Democratic Consolidation in Southern Europe. *West European Politics* 13 (4): 103–117.

5723. Prigogine, I. 1986. Science, Civilization and Democracy: Values, Systems, Structures and Affinities. *Futures* 18 (4): 493–507.

5724. Prindle, D. F. December 1991. Head of State and Head of Government in Comparative Perspective. *Presidential Studies Quarterly* 21 (1): 55–71.

5725. Prins, G. 1991. Home Is Where the Heart Is: Reflections on Social Democracy and Nationalism in the Common European Home. *Political Quarterly* 62 (1): 5–15.

5726. Proenca, D. 1990. Guns and Butter: Arms Industry, Technology and Democracy in Brazil. *Bulletin of Peace Proposals* 21 (1): 49–57.

5727. Protantiero, J. C. May 1987. *See* Nun, J. (May 1987).

5728. Prothro, J. W. 1985. Citation Classic: Fundamental Principles of Democracy: Bases of Agreement and Disagreement. *Current Contents: Social and Behavioral Sciences* (34): 16.

5729. Pruthi, S., and S. A. Nabi. 1991. Scientific Literacy and Democracy: A Case Study of the Attentive Public. *Journal of Scientific & Industrial Research* 50 (8): 589–595.

5730. Prybyla, J. S. September 1981. The Hundred Flowers of Discontent. *Current History* 80 (467): 254–257, 274.

5731. Prybyla, J. S. 1988. Socialist Economic Reform, Political Freedom, and Democracy. *Comparative Strategy* 7 (4): 351–360.

5732. Przeworski, A. 1992. Choosing Institutions in the Transition to Democracy: A Game-Theory Approach.* *Dados* 35 (1): 5–48.

5733. Przeworski, A. 1993. *See* Pereira, L. C. B. (1993).

5734. Przeworski, A., and F. Limongi. June 1993. Political Regimes and Economic Growth. *Journal of Economic Perspectives* 7 (3): 51–69.

5735. Przeworski, A., and F. Limongi. July 1994. Political Regimes and Economic Growth.* *Desarrollo Economico Revista de Ciencias Sociales* 34 (134): 163–179.

5736. Przeworski, A., and M. Wallerstein. June 1982. The Structure of Class Conflict in Democratic Capitalist Societies. *American Political Science Review* 76 (2): 215–238.

5737. Pullo, A. December 1986. The Concept of Direct Democracy in Socialist States.* *Panstwo i Pravo* 41 (12): 24–32.

5738. Punke, H. H. June 1976. Freedom to Contract, as Basic American Democracy. *Commercial Law Journal* 81: 246–248.

5739. Punyaratabandhu Bhakdi, S. February 1984. Thailand in 1983: Democracy, Thai Style. *Asian Survey* 24 (2): 187–194.

5740. Purcell, S. K. September 1985. Demystifying Contadora. *Foreign Affairs* 64 (1): 74–95.

5741. Purcell, S. K. September 1987. The Choice in Central America. *Foreign Affairs* 66 (1): 109–128.

5742. Purcell, T. W., and K. Sawyers. April 1993. Democracy and Ethnic Conflict: Blacks in Costa Rica. *Ethnic and Racial Studies* 16 (2): 298–322.

5743. Purdy, D. November 1994. Citizenship, Basic Income, and the State. *New Left Review* 208: 30–48.

5744. Purdy, S. S. 1983. The Civic Religion Thesis as It Applies to a Pluralistic Society: Pancasila Democracy in Indonesia (1945–1965). *Journal of International Affairs* 36 (2): 307–316.

5745. Pusic, V. 1986. Economic Democracy and Civil Society. *Economic and Industrial Democracy* 7 (3): 275–295.

5746. Pusic, V. July 1994. Dictatorship with Democratic Legitimacy (in Croatia).* *Cahiers Internationaux de Sociologie* 95: 369–388.

5747. Pusic, V. September 1994. Dictatorship with Democratic Legitimacy: Democ-racy Versus Nation. *East European Politics and Societies* 8 (3): 383–401.

5748. Putnum, H. September 1990. A Reconsideration of Deweyan Democracy. *Southern California Law Review* 63 (6): 1671–1697.

5749. Pycroft, C. June 1994. Angola: The Forgotten Tragedy. *Journal of Southern African Studies* 20 (2): 241–262.

5750. Pym, F. June 1982. Defense in Democracies: The Public Dimension. *International Security* 7 (1): 40–44.

5751. Pym, F. 1983. Defense in Democracies: The Public Dimension. *Atlantic Community Quarterly* 20 (4): 327–330.

5752. Pyo, H. H. December 1993. The Transition in the Political Economy of South Korean Development. *Journal of Northeast Asian Studies* 12 (4): 74–86.

5753. Pyrcz, G. 1981. Obedience, Support, and Authority: The Limits of Political Obligation in a Democracy. *Canadian Journal of Political Science* 14 (2): 337–352.

5754. Qadir, S., C. Clapham, and B. Gills. 1993. Democratization in the Third World: An Introduction. *Third World Quarterly* 14 (3): 415–422.

5755. Quandt, W. B. July 1994. The Palestinian Future: The Urge for Democracy. *Foreign Affairs* 73 (4): 2–7.

5756. Quantin, P. 1994. Congo: The Political Origins of the Decay of a Liberalization Process, August 1992–December 1993.* *L'Afrique Politique* 167–190.

5757. Quantin, P. D. October 1991. *See* Bourmaud, D. (October 1991).

5758. Quaritsch, H. 1980. Zur Entstehung der Theorie des Pluralism. *Der Staat* 19 (1): 29–56.

5759. Questor, G. September 1980. Consensus Lost. *Foreign Policy* 40: 18–32.

5760. Quigley, K. F. F. September 1993. Philanthropy's Role in East Europa. *Orbis* 37 (4): 581–598.

5761. Quilitzch, G. 1985. The Relationship between State and Democracy under Socialism.* *Staat und Recht* 34 (11): 867–874.

5762. Quillinan, H. 1994. *See* Lajoie, A. (1994).

5763. Quinault, R. E. 1979. Randolph Churchill and Tory Democracy, 1880–1885. *Historical Journal* 22 (1): 141–165.

5764. Quinlan, D. August 1977. *See* Rubinson, R. (August 1977).

5765. Quinlan, M. October 1993. The Role and Oversight of Armed Forces within Democratic Societies. *NATO Review* 41 (5): 24–28.

5766. Quinlan, T. August 1990. Haiti: Facing Democracy and Disaster. *World and I* 5: 100–107.

5767. Qvale, T. U. 1976. Norwegian Strategy for Democratization of Industry. *Human Relations* 29 (5): 453–469.

5768. Qvale, T. U. 1979. Industrial Democracy in Norway: Experience from the Boardroom. *Journal of General Management* 5 (1): 37–45.

5769. Raaflaub, K. A. November 1983. Democracy, Oligarchy, and the Concept of the "Free Citizen" in Late Fifth Century Athens. *Political Theory* 11 (4): 517–544.

5770. Rabben, L. 1988. Brazil on the Brink: Land, Debt and Democracy. *Nation* 246 (17): 597–601.

5771. Rabello Duarte, C. 1983. The Press and Redemocratization in Brazil.* *Dados* 16 (2): 181–195.

5772. Rabier, J. April 1981. Opinions et Attitudes des Europeens: Dix Années de Recherches Internationales Comparatives. *Futuribles* 43: 3–20.

5773. Rabinowitch, A. March 1987. The Evolution of Local Soviets in Petrograd, November 1917–June 1918: The Case of the First City District Soviet. *Slavic Review* 46 (1): 20–37.

5774. Rabinowitz, G. December 1994. *See* Listhaug, O. (December 1994).

5775. Rabkin, J. December 1987. Disestablished Religion in America. *Public Interest* 86: 124–139.

5776. Rabkin, R. December 1992. The Aylwin Government [in Chile] and "Tutelary" Democracy: A Concept in Search of a Case? *Journal of Interamerican Studies and World Affairs* 34 (4): 119–194.

5777. Rachel, G. 1985. Civic Democracy Myth and Political Reality. *IPW Berichte* 14 (9): 18.

5778. Rachel, G. 1988. Social Democratic Positions on Democracy in the 1980s. *IPW Berichte* 17 (4): 16–22.

5779. Rachwald, A. R. November 1982. Poland: Quo Vadis. *Current History* 81 (478): 371–375, 389–392.

5780. Racz, B. A. October 1984. Recent Developments in Hungarian Enterprise Democracy. *Soviet Studies* 36 (4): 544–559.

5781. Racz, B. A. January 1989. Political Participation and the Expanding Role of the Hungarian Legislature. *East European Quarterly* 22 (4): 459–493.

5782. Radan, P. November 1994. Secessionist Self-Determination: The Cases of

Slovenia and Croatia. *Australian Journal of International Affairs* 48 (2): 183–196.

5783. Radcliff, B. March 1994. Collective Preferences in [U.S.] Presidential Elections. *Electoral Studies* 13 (1): 50–57.

5784. Radcliff, B. July 1994. Turnout and the Democratic Vote. *American Politics Quarterly* 22 (3): 259–276.

5785. Radcliff, B. September 1994. Reward without Punishment: Economic Conditions and the Vote. *Political Research Quarterly* 47 (3): 721–732.

5786. Radev, Y. 1980. Bourgeois Democracy and Socialist Democracy. *Revolutionary World* 37–39: 182–192.

5787. Radin, M. J. December 1994. A Deweyan Perspective on the Economic Theory of Democracy. *Constitutional Commentary* 11 (3): 539–556.

5788. Radojkovic, M. 1984. Eight Considerations on New Information Technology and the Development of Democracy.* *Gazette* 33 (1): 51–58.

5789. Radu, M. 1991. Toward South African Democracy: ANC-Inspired Violence Poses a Threat. *Orbis* 35 (4): 499–513.

5790. Radunski, P. March 1986. The Electoral Struggle in the 1990s: Repoliticization of the Electoral Campaign and the New Techniques in Electoral Campaigns in Western Democracies.* *Aus Politik und Zeitgeschichte* 15 (11): 34–45.

5791. Raftopoulos, B. July 1992. Beyond the House of Hunger: Democratic Struggle in Zimbabwe. *Review of African Political Economy* 19: 59–74.

5792. Ragin, C. November 1993. *See* Huber, E. (November 1993).

5793. Raginowitz, D. March 1994. The Common Memory of Loss: Political Mobilization among Palestinian Citizens of Israel. *Journal of Anthropological Research* 50 (1): 27–49.

5794. Rahm, D. June 1987. *See* Lambright, W. H. (June 1987).

5795. Rahman, M. A. February 1984. Bangladesh in 1983: A Turning Point for the Military. *Asian Survey* 24 (2): 240–249.

5796. Rahman, S. February 1990. Bangladesh in 1989: Internationalization of Political and Economic Issues. *Asian Survey* 30 (2): 150–157.

5797. Rahn, W. M., J. A. Krosnick, and M. Breuning. August 1994. Rationalization and Derivation Process in Survey Studies of Political Candidates Evaluation. *American Journal of Political Science* 38 (3): 582–600.

5798. Rai, L. November 1985. The Question of Democracy and China. *China Report* 21 (6): 473–488.

5799. Railton, P. 1983. Judicial Review, Elites, and Liberal Democracy. *Nomos* 25: 153–180.

5800. Rainey, R. R. November 1993. Law and Religion: Is Reconciliation Still Possible? *Loyola Los Angeles Law Review* 27: 147–192.

5801. Rainey, R. R. December 1993. The Public's Interest in Public Affairs Discourse, Democratic Governance, and Fairness in Broadcasting: A Critical Review of the Public Interest Duties of the Electronic Media. *Georgetown Law Journal* 82: 269–372.

5802. Rais, R. B. September 1985. Elections in Pakistan: Is Democracy Winning? *Asian Affairs (New York)* 12: 43–61.

5803. Rais, R. B. February 1988. Pakistan in 1987: Transition to Democracy. *Asian Survey* 28 (2): 126–136.

5804. Rais, R. B. February 1989. Pakistan in 1988: From Command to Conciliation Politics. *Asian Survey* 29 (2): 199–206.

5805. Rais, R. B. April 1994. Pakistan: Hope amidst Turmoil. *Journal of Democracy* 5 (2): 132–143.

5806. Raison-Jourde, F. December 1993. Completed or Inceptive Transition (in Madagascar)?* *Politique Africaine* 52: 6–18.

5807. Rake, A. July 1991. Wind of Democracy: Thirty Years after Independence a New Kind of Change Is Rushing through Africa. *New African* 8–9.

5808. Rake, A. April 1992. Who Is in Charge of Uganda? *New African* 14–15.

5809. Rake, A. October 1993. What Hope for Democracy? *New African* 10–14.

5810. Rakhimov, A. R. 1978. *See* Belinkii, V. K. (1978).

5811. Rakitskaia, G. 1990. Socialist Democracy: Politico-Economic Aspects. *Problems of Economics* 32 (10): 54–74.

5812. Rallings, C., and M. Thrasher. December 1993. Exploring Uniformity and Variability in Local Electoral Outcomes: Some Evidence from English Local Elections 1985–1991. *Electoral Studies* 12 (4): 366–384.

5813. Rama, C. M. January 1981. The Fragility of Latin America Democracy: The Case of Uruguay. *Cuandernos Americanos* 40 (1): 19–30.

5814. Rama, G. W. 1985. Democracy in Uruguay: A Draft Interpretation.* *Problemes de Amerique Latine* 78: 3–49.

5815. Ramaswany, E. A. 1977. A Participatory Dimension of Trade-Union Democracy: A Comparative Sociological View. *Sociology: The Journal of the British Sociological Association* 11 (3): 465–480.

5816. Ramer, S. C. 1981. Democracy Versus the Rule of a Civic Elite: Novikov, Alexsadr, Ovanovic and the Fate of Self-Government in Russia. *Cahiers du Monde Russe et Sovietique* 22 (2–3): 167–185.

5817. Ramet, P. June 1980. Yugoslavia's Debate over Democratization. *Survey* 25 (3): 43–48.

5818. Ramet, S. P. September 1992. Balkan Pluralism and Its Enemies. *Orbis* 36: 547–564.

5819. Ramet, S. P. 1993. Slovenia's Road to Democracy. *Europe-Asia Studies* 45 (5): 869–886.

5820. Ramharack, B. January 1992. Consociational Democracy: A Democratic Option for Guyana. *Caribbean Studies* 25 (1–2): 75–101.

5821. Raminez, M. 1990. Reflections on Spain's Transition to Democracy.* *Revista de Derecho Politico* 31: 11–25.

5822. Ramondt, J. J. 1977. Industrial Democratization without Workers. *Netherlands Journal of Sociology* 13 (1): 35–43.

5823. Ramsay, H. 1991. The Community, the Multinational, Its Workers and Their Charter: A Modern Tale of Industrial Democracy. *Work Employment and Society* 5 (4): 541–566.

5824. Ranadive, K. January 29, 1994. Market, Democracy, and Unequal Relation. *Economic and Political Weekly* 29 (5): 2–13.

5825. Randall, S. 1993. People's Education and "Nation Building" for a New South Africa. *Review of African Political Economy* (58): 43–60.

5826. Randall, V. 1993. The Media and Democratization in the Third World. *Third World Quarterly* 14 (3): 625–646.

5827. Rangacharyulu, S. 1980. *See* Muthayya, B. (1980).

5828. Rangel Suarez, A. September 1989. Colombia: Uno Democracia sin Partidos. *Revista Foro* 4: 72–78.

5829. Ranis, P. January 1986. The Dilemmas of Democratization in Argentina. *Current History* 85 (507): 29–33, 42.

5830. Ranis, P. 1989. Redemocratization and the Argentine Working Class. *Canadian Journal of Development Studies* 10 (2): 293–302.

5831. Ranney, A. May 1994. *See* Butler, D. (May 1994).

5832. Ransom, H. H. September 1987. The Intelligence Function and the Constitution. *Armed Forces and Society* 14 (1): 43–63.

5833. Ranson, S. 1988. From 1944 to 1988: Education, Citizenship and Democracy. *Local Government Studies* 14 (1): 1–19.

5834. Ranson, S. 1989. *See* Jones, G. (1989).

5835. Ranson, S. December 1993. Markets or Democracy for Education. *British Journal of Education Studies* 41 (4): 333–352.

5836. Rantete, J., and H. Giliomee. October 1992. Transition to Democracy through Transaction: Bilateral Negotiations between the ANC and NP in South Africa. *African Affairs* 91 (365): 515–542.

5837. Rao, V. 1984. Democracy and Economic Development. *Studies in Comparative International Development* 19 (4): 67–81.

5838. Rapport, R. B. November 1994. *See* Stone, W. J. (November 1994).

5839. Raschke, C. A. 1980. Economic Democracy: From Slogan to Program. *Christianity and Crisis* 40 (4): 4–8.

5840. Raschke, J. September 1980. Politics and Value Change in the Western Democracies.* *Aus Politik und Zeitgeschichte* 36 (6): 23–45.

5841. Rashiduzzaman, M. February 1979. Bangladesh 1978: Search for a Political Party. *Asian Survey* 19 (2): 191–197.

5842. Rashiduzzaman, M. November 1994. The Liberals and the Religious Right in Bangladesh. *Asian Survey* 34 (11): 974–990.

5843. Raskin, J. B. 1990. Domination, Democracy, and the District: The Statehood Position. *Catholic University Law Review* 39 (2): 417–440.

5844. Raskin, M. G. June 1976. Democracy Versus the National Security State. *Law and Contemporary Problems* 10 (3): 189–220.

5845. Rassudovskii, V. A. 1992. Scientific Freedom, Human Rights and Democracy.* *Vestnik Rossiiskoi Akademii Nauk* (2): 15–26.

5846. Rath, K. July 1994. The Process of Democratization in Jordan. *Middle Eastern Studies* 30 (3): 530–557.

5847. Rathkey, P. July 1984. *See* Hanson, C. (July 1984).

5848. Ratkovic, R. March 1991. Human Rights in Yugoslavia. *Review of International Affairs* 42: 12–14+.

5849. Ratz, U. 1980. Zur Ideology und Organisationsgeschichte der Sozialdemokratie: Neue Arbeiter ueber die Deutsche Arbeiterbeweging. *Neue Politische Literatur* 25 (4): 475–484.

5850. Rauch, A. M. 1991. *See* Behrens, M. (1991).

5851. Rauter, A. 1981. Cooperatives and the Democracy of Members. *Annals of Public and Co-operative Economy* 52 (1–2): 117–125.

5852. Rawls, J. June 1985. Justice as Fairness: Political, Not Metaphysical. *Philosophy and Public Affairs* 14 (3): 223–251.

5853. Raworth, P. September 1994. A Timid Step Forwards: Maastricht and the Democratisation of the European Community. *European Law Review* 19: 16–33.

5854. Ray, A. K. 1989. Pakistan Post-Colonial Democracy: Implications for Indo-Pak Relations. *Economic and Political Weekly* 24 (16): 866–868.

5855. Ray, J. L. 1993. Wars between Democracies: Rare, or Nonexistent. *International Interactions* 18 (3): 251–276.

5856. Raymond, G. A. March 1994. Democracies, Disputes, and Third-Party

Intermediaries. *Journal of Conflict Resolution* 38 (1): 24–42.

5857. Raynal, J. October 1991. Democratic Revival in Benin: Model or Mirage?* *Afrique Contemporaine* 160: 3–25.

5858. Rayner, L. April 1992. Hong Kong: Prospects for Democracy. *Round Table* 322: 229–235.

5859. Rayside, D. 1978. *See* Hauss, C. (1978).

5860. Raz, J. 1989. Liberalism, Skepticism, and Democracy. *Iowa Law Review* 74 (4): 761–786.

5861. Raz, J. December 1990. The Politics of the Rule of Law. *Ratio Juris* 3: 331–339.

5862. Reading, A. A. March 1984. Backing Democracy and Development. *World Policy Journal* 1 (3): 653–667.

5863. Reburn, F. S. June 1983. *See* Buss, T. F. (June 1983).

5864. Recchia, G. July 1984. Parliamentary Information and Basic Guarantees.* *Revista de Estudios Politicos* 40: 9–24.

5865. Redburn, F. S. June 1983. *See* Buss, T. F. (June 1983).

5866. Reding, A. June 1985. On Nicaraguan Democracy: Conversations with Clemente Guido, Mauricio Diaz Davila, Sixto Ulloa Dona, and Rafael Solis Cerda. *World Policy Journal* 2 (3): 555–567.

5867. Reding, A. March 1986. Costa Rica: Democratic Model in Jeopardy. *World Policy Journal* 3 (2): 301–315.

5868. Reding, A. March 1987. Nicaragua's New Constitution: A Close Reading. *World Policy Journal* 4: 257–294.

5869. Reding, A. March 1991. Mexico: The Crumbling of the "Prefect Dictatorship." *World Policy Journal* 8 (2): 255–284.

5870. Reding, A. A. June 1992. Bolstering Democracy in the Americas. *World Policy Journal* 9 (3): 401–415.

5871. Redish, M. H. 1982. Self-Realization, Democracy, and Freedom of Expression: A Reply. *University of Pennsylvania Law Review* 130 (3): 678–688.

5872. Redor, D. 1986. Economic Reform and Industrial Democracy in Hungary: Comment.* *Revue d'Etudes Comparatives Est-Ouest* 17 (2): 52–53.

5873. Reed, S. R. April 1992. *See* Ishibashi, M. (April 1992).

5874. Reed, S. R. March 1994. Democracy and the Personal Vote: A Cautionary Tale from Japan. *Electoral Studies* 13 (1): 17–28.

5875. Reed, W. R. March 1994. A Retrospective Voting Model with Heterogeneous Politicians. *Economics and Politics* 6 (1): 39–58.

5876. Rees, G. December 1981. *See* Cooke, P. (December 1981).

5877. Reeseschafer, W. 1993. Community Spirit and Liberal Democracy.* *Gegenwartskunde: Gesellschaft, Staat, Erziehung* 42 (3): 305–317.

5878. Regalia, I. November 1984. Democracy and Labor Unions: Preliminaries to a Critical Reflection.* *Il Mulino* 296: 993–1020.

5879. Regalia, I. 1988. Democracy and Unions: Toward a Critical Appraisal. *Economic and Industrial Democracy* 9 (3): 345–371.

5880. Regis Romero, A. January 1990. Una Aproximacion a Rol y a Las Tareas Pendientes de Las Fuerzas Armadas en la Transicion Paraguaya a la Democracia. *Perspectiva Internacional Paraguaya* 2: 95–116.

5881. Rehn, G. March 1984. The Wages of Success. *Daedalus* 113 (2): 137–168.

5882. Reich, R. B. June 1983. Industrial Evolution. *History and Theory* 3 (3): 10–20.

5883. Reich, R. B. June 1985. Public Administration and Public Deliberations: An

Interpretive Essay. *Yale Law Review* 94: 1617–1641.

5884. Reichley, A. J. 1986. Democracy and Religion. *PS: Political Science & Politics* 19 (4): 801–806.

5885. Reichley, A. J. March 1986. Religion and the Future of American Politics. *Political Science Quarterly* 101 (1): 23–47.

5886. Reid, W. A. 1980. Democracy, Perfectability, and the Battle of the Books: Thoughts on the Conception of Liberal Education in the Writings of Schwab. *Curriculum Inquiry* 10 (3): 249–263.

5887. Reid, W. M., and J. S. Henderson. December 1976. Political Obligation: An Empirical Approach. *Polity* 9 (2): 237–252.

5888. Reihman, J. M. June 1981. *See* Lonky, E. (June 1981).

5889. Reinicke, W. H. March 1990. *See* Coppedge, M. (March 1990).

5890. Reis, E. P., and Z. B. Cheibub. 1993. Poverty, Inequality, and Democratic Consolidation [in Brazil].* *Dados: Revista de Ciencias Sociais* 36 (2): 233–259.

5891. Reis, F. W. 1980. Academy, Democracy and Dependence.* *Dados: Revista de Ciencias Sociais* 23 (1): 59–77.

5892. Reis, F. W. 1986. Authoritarianism, Democracy, and Theory: Notes to a Partially Unsuccessful Symposium.* *Dados: Revista de Ciencias Sociais* 29 (2): 257–269.

5893. Reis, F. W. 1988. La Construction Democratique au Brasil: Diagnostic et Perspectives. *Notes et Etudes Documentaires* 4: 3–22.

5894. Reischauer, E. O. June 1977. The Postwar "Miracle." *Wilson Quarterly* 1 (4): 55–59.

5895. Reisinger, W. M., A. H. Miller, V. L. Hesli, and K. H. Maher. April 1994. Political Values in Russia, Ukraine, and Lithuania: Sources and Implications for Democ-racy. *British Journal of Political Science* 24: 183–223.

5896. Reisman, W. M. 1992. International Election Observation. *Pace Yearbook of International Law* 1992: 1–48.

5897. Remington, R. A. 1991. The Road to Multiparty Democracy in Post-Communist Europe. *Punjab Journal of Politics* 15 (1–2): 1–14.

5898. Remington, R. A. November 1991. Eastern Europe after the Revolution. *Current History* 90 (559): 379–383.

5899. Remington, R. A. March 1992. Contradictions on the Road to Democracy and the Market in East-Central Europe. *Midsouth Political Science Journal* 13: 3–25.

5900. Remington, T. F. April 1990. Regime Transformation in Communist Systems: The Soviet Case. *Soviet Economy* 6 (2): 160–190.

5901. Remmer, K. L. May 1977. The Timing, Pace and Sequence of Political Change in Chile, 1891–1925. *Hispanic American Historical Review* 57 (2): 105–230.

5902. Remmer, K. L. April 1980. Political Demobilization in Chile, 1973–1978. *Comparative Politics* 12 (3): 275–301.

5903. Remmer, K. L. April 1985. Redemocratization and the Impact of Authoritarian Rule in Latin America. *Comparative Politics* 17 (3): 253–275.

5904. Remmer, K. L. December 1985. Exclusionary Democracy. *Studies in Comparative International Development* 20 (4): 64–85.

5905. Remmer, K. L. September 1989. State Change in Chile 1973–1988. *Studies in Comparative International Development* 24 (3): 5–29.

5906. Remmer, K. L. April 1990. Democracy and Economic Crisis: The Latin American Experience. *World Politics* 42 (3): 315–335.

5907. Remmer, K. L. July 1991. New Wine or Old Bottlenecks? The Study of Latin American Democracy. *Comparative Politics* 23 (4): 479–495.

5908. Remmer, K. L. September 1991. The Political Impact of Economic Crisis in Latin America in the 1980s. *American Political Science Review* 85 (3): 777–800.

5909. Remmer, K. L. December 1992. The Process of Democratization in Latin America. *Studies in Comparative International Development* 27 (4): 3–24.

5910. Remmer, K. L. June 1993. The Political Economy of Elections in Latin America, 1980–1991. *American Political Science Review* 87 (2): 393–407.

5911. Renn, O. June 1989. Risk Analysis: A Need to Communicate. *Forum for Applied Research and Public Policy* 4 (2): 86–92.

5912. Rennie, E. January 1979. Democracy and the BPS. *Bulletin of the British Psychological Society* 32: 3–5.

5913. Renzsch, W. September 1989. German Federalism in Historical Perspective: Federalism as a Substitute for a National State. *Publius* 19 (4): 17–33.

5914. Repnik, H. P., and R. M. Mohs. January 1992. Good Governance, Democracy and Development Paradigms. *Intereconomics* 27: 28–33.

5915. Resnick, D. August 1990. *See* Bennett, S. E. (August 1990).

5916. Ress, I. December 1992. The Effects of Democratization on Archival Administration and Use in Eastern Middle Europe. *American Archivist* 55 (1): 86–93.

5917. Reuter, J. 1992. Die Innere Entwicklung Albaniens Im Jahre 1991–1992. *Suedosteuropa* 41 (5): 257–271.

5918. Reuter, N. 1994. Institutionalismus, Neo-Institutionalismus, Neue Institutionelle Okonomie und Andere "Institutionalismen": Eine Differenzierung Konträter Konzepte. *Zeitschrift für Wirtschafts- und Sozialwissenschaften* 114 (1): 5–24.

5919. Reutlinger, S. September 1992. *See* Hyden, G. (September 1992).

5920. Revel, J. F. January 1978. Myths of Eurocommunism. *Foreign Affairs* 56 (2): 295–305.

5921. Revel, J. F. 1984. Can the Democracies Survive? *Commentary* 77 (6): 19–28.

5922. Revel, J. F. 1991. Resurrecting Democracy in Eastern Europe. *Orbis* 35 (3): 323–326.

5923. Rey, J. C. October 1991. La Democracia Venezolana y la Crisis del Sistema Populista de Conciliacion. *Revista de Estudios Politicos* 74: 533–578.

5924. Rey, J. N. 1981. Social Democracy at the Crossroads: Ideas for a Debate. *Cahiers Vilfredo Pareto* 19 (59): 159–174.

5925. Reynolds, D. R., and F. M. Shelley. 1985. Procedural Justice and Local Democracy. *Political Geography Quarterly* 4 (4): 267–288.

5926. Reynolds, J. F. November 1978. *See* Paris, D. C. (November 1978).

5927. Reynolds, J. F., and D. C. Paris. July 1979. Concept of "Choice" and Arrow's Theorem. *Ethics* 89 (4): 354–371.

5928. Reyntjens, F. December 1993. The Proof of the Pudding Is in the Eating: The June 1993 Elections in Burundi. *Journal of Modern African Studies* 31 (4): 563–583.

5929. Rhind, D. W. 1984. *See* Johnston, R. J. (1984).

5930. Rial, J. 1988. Gobernabilidad, Partidos Politicos y Reforma Politica: Uruguay a Tres Anos de la Restauracion Democratica. *Revista de Ciencias Sociales (Uruguay)* (3): 127–139.

5931. Rial, J. May 1991. Transitions in Latin America on the Threshold of the 1990s. *International Social Science Journal* 43 (2): 285–300.

5932. Rial, J. October 1991. Las Fuerzas Armadas de America del Sur y su Relacion con el Estado en el Nuevo Contexto Democratico, en Un Mundo en Cambio Constante. *Revista de Estudios Politicos* 74: 55–84.

5933. Riason-Jourde, F. (ed.). December 1993. Madagascar. *Politique Africaine* 1–88. 9 articles; English summaries, 187–189.

5934. Riccucci, N. M. May 1991. Merit, Equity, and Test Validity: A New Look at an Old Problem. *Administration and Society* 23 (1): 74–93.

5935. Riccucci, N. M. November 1991. *See* Thompson, F. J. (November 1991).

5936. Rice, C. April 1992. The Military under Democracy. *Journal of Democracy* 3 (2): 27–42.

5937. Rich, H. 1992. John Porter, Sociology, and Liberal Democracy. *Canadian Journal of Sociology-Cahiers Canadiens de Sociologie* 17 (2): 193–198.

5938. Richard, P. July 1988. Religion and Democracy: The Church of the Poor in Central America. *Alternatives* 13 (3): 357–378.

5939. Richard, S. F. June 1978. *See* Meltzer, A. A. (June 1978).

5940. Richards, G. January 1986. Stabilization Crises and the Breakdown of Military Authoritarianism in Latin America. *Comparative Political Studies* 18 (4): 449–485.

5941. Richardson, D. A. J. 1981. Moral Philosophy and the Search for Fundamental Values in Constitutional Law. *Ohio State Law Journal* 42 (1): 319–334.

5942. Richardson, E. L. 1984. The Democracy of Facts: Comment. *Milbank Memorial Fund Quarterly: Health and Society* 62 (1): 42–47.

5943. Richardson, R. C. III. September 1987. The Democratic Process: People, Politicians, and the Press. *Journal of Social,* *Political, and Economic Studies* 12 (3): 321–335.

5944. Richardson, W. D. August 1987. *See* Nigro, L. G. (August 1987).

5945. Richardson, W. D., and B. H. Fessele. September 1991. Tocqueville's Observations on Racial and Sexual Inequalities in America. *Southeastern Political Review* 19 (2): 248–277.

5946. Richdale, K. G., and W. H. Liu. December 1991. The Politics of Glasnost in China, 1978–1990. *Journal of East Asian Affairs* 5: 104–143.

5947. Richie, M. June 1994. Democratizing the Trade Policy Process: The Lessons of NAFTA and Their Implications for the GATT. *Cornell International Law Journal* 27: 749–754.

5948. Richter, D. K. April 1993. Whose Indian History? *William and Mary Quarterly* 50 (2): 379–393.

5949. Richter, E. December 1991. *See* Offe, C. (December 1991).

5950. Richter, M. May 1982. Legitimacy and Illegitimacy in Post-Revolutionary France, toward a Concept of Political Illegitimacy: Bonapartist Dictatorship and Democratic Legitimacy (Part II). *Political Theory* 10 (2): 185–214.

5951. Richter, W. L. February 1981. *See* Gustafson, W. E. (February 1981).

5952. Richter, W. L. May 1982. Pakistan: A New "Front-Line" State? *Current History* 81 (475): 202–206, 225.

5953. Richter, W. L. February 1986. Pakistan in 1985: Testing Time for the New Order. *Asian Survey* 26 (2): 207–218.

5954. Richter, W. L. March 1986. Pakistan: Out of the Praetorian Labyrinth. *Current History* 85 (509): 113–116, 137–138.

5955. Riddell, R. C. September 1988. New Sanctions against South Africa. *Development Policy Review* 6: 243–267.

5956. Ridder, H. April 1985. The Federal Republic of Germany: What Kind of Democracy Is It?* *Blaetter für Deutsche und Internationale Politik* 30 (4): 430–441.

5957. Riedinger, J. September 1993. Property Rights and Democracy: Philosophical and Economic Considerations. *Capital University Law Review* 22: 893–915.

5958. Riemer, N. September 1980. Covenant and the Federal Constitution. *Publius* 10 (4): 135–148.

5959. Riesman, D. 1978. Capitalism, Socialism, and Democracy. *Commentary* 65 (4): 66–67.

5960. Riggs, F. W. May 1993. Fragility of the Third World's Regimes. *International Social Science Journal* 45: 199–243.

5961. Rijnierse, E. 1993. Democratisation in Sub-Saharan Africa? Literature Overview. *Third World Quarterly* 14 (3): 647–664.

5962. Riker, W. H. June 1988. The Place of Political Science in Public Choice. *Public Choice* 57 (3): 247–257.

5963. Riley, J. December 1985. On the Possibility of Liberal Democracy. *American Political Science Review* 79 (4): 1135–1151.

5964. Riley, J. January 1990. Utilitarian Ethics and Democratic Government. *Ethics* 100 (2): 335–348.

5965. Riley, S. P. October 1991. The Democratic Transition in Africa: An End to the One-Party State? *Conflict Studies* 245: 1–37.

5966. Riley, S. P. 1992. Political Adjustment or Domestic Pressure: Democratic Politics and Political Choice in Africa. *Third World Quarterly* 13 (3): 539–551.

5967. Riley, S. P. July 1992a. Africa's "New Wind of Change." *World Today* 48 (7): 116–119.

5968. Riley, S. P. July 1992b. *See* Kpundeh, S. (July 1992).

5969. Rimlinger, G. W. September 1983. Capitalism and Human Rights. *Daedalus* 112 (4): 51–77.

5970. Rimmerman, C. A. September 1991. Democracy and Critical Education for Citizenship. *Political Science and Politics* 24 (3): 492–495.

5971. Risse-Kappen, T. July 1991. Public Opinion, Domestic Structure, and Foreign Policy in Liberal Democracies. *World Politics* 43 (4): 479–512.

5972. Ritt, L. G. May 1982. *See* Ostheimer, J. M. (May 1982).

5973. Rittberger, V. October 31, 1987. The Democracies' Capacity for Peace: Considerations on the Political Theory of Peace.* *Aus Politik und Zeitgeschichte* 44: 3–12.

5974. Ritter, A. 1980. Los Organos del Poder Popular and Participatory Democracy in Cuba: A Preliminary Analysis. *Social and Economic Studies* 29 (2–3): 193–219.

5975. Ritter, G. A. 1989. Social Democracy in the German Empire from the Social Historical Perspective.* *Historische Zeitschrift* 249 (2): 295–362.

5976. Rivas, E. T. 1984. The Problems of Counter-Revolution and Democracy in Guatemala.* *Estudios Sociales Centroamericanos* 13 (38): 127–142.

5977. Rivera Cusicanqui, S. July 1990. Liberal Democracy and Aylu Democracy in Bolivia: The Case of Northern Potosi. *Journal of Development Studies* 26 (4): 97–121.

5978. Rivera Urrutia, E., and A. Sojo. October 1985. Popular Movement, Social Conflict and Democracy.* *Revista Mexicana de Sociologia* 47 (4): 17–34.

5979. Riviere d'Arc, H. 1991. Du National au Particulier: Le Debat sur la Decentralisation dans Trois Pays d'Amerique Latine (Bresil, Mexique, Cuba). *Cahiers des Ameriques Latines* (11): 7–22.

5980. Roback, T. H. May 1975. Amateurs and Professionals: Delegates to the 1972 Republican National Convention. *Journal of Politics* 37 (2): 436–468.

5981. Robb, C. S. 1987. Developing Democracy at Home and Abroad. *Washington Quarterly* 10 (4): 147–153.

5982. Robbins, B. June 1991. Othering the Academy: Professionalism and Multiculturalism. *Social Research* 58 (2): 355–372.

5983. Robbins, M. May 1985. *See* Glazer, A. (May 1985).

5984. Robers, J. C. d. V. 1992. Paving the Way to Democracy. *Society & Politics* 31 (1–2): 15–24.

5985. Roberts, B. March 1990. Human Rights and International Security. *Washington Quarterly* 13 (2): 65–75.

5986. Roberts, B. June 1991. Democracy and World Order. *Fletcher Forum of World Affairs* 15 (2): 9–25.

5987. Roberts, B. C. July 1977. Participation by Agreement Commenting on the Majority Report Issued by the Committee on Industrial Democracy under the Chairmanship of Lord Bullock. *Lloyds Bank Review* 125: 12–23.

5988. Roberts, D. 1994. Democratic Kampuchea? *Pacific Review* 7 (1): 105–110.

5989. Roberts, H. 1992. The Algerian State and the Challenge of Democracy. *Government and Opposition* 27: 433–454.

5990. Roberts, J. M. June 1991. Prospects for Democracy in Jordan. *Arab Studies Quarterly* 13 (3–4): 119–138.

5991. Roberts, K. 1985. Democracy and the Dependent Capitalist State in Latin America. *Monthly Review* 37 (5): 12–26.

5992. Roberts, K. November 1990. *See* Cornell, A. (November 1990).

5993. Roberts, N. S. July 1994. *See* Levine, S. (July 1994).

5994. Roberts, W. R., and H. E. Engle. March 1986. The Global Information Revolution and the Communist World. *Washington Quarterly* 9 (2): 141–155.

5995. Robertson, G. 1983. The Mother of Parliaments: The Sweatshop of Democracy. *Parliamentarian* 64 (4): 193–196.

5996. Robertson, J. A. December 1990. The ROCs 1990: National Affairs Conference. *Issues and Studies* 26 (12): 23–35.

5997. Robertson, J. D. January 1983. Inflation, Unemployment, and Government Collapse: A Poisson Application. *Comparative Political Studies* 15 (4): 425–444.

5998. Robertson, J. D. 1984. Toward a Political Economic Accounting of the Endurance of Cabinet Administrations: An Empirical Assessment of Eight European Democracies. *American Journal of Political Science* 28 (4): 693–709.

5999. Robertson, J. D. December 1984. Economic Performance and Transient European Cabinet Administrations: Implications for Consociational Parliamentary Democracies. *International Studies Quarterly* 28 (4): 447–466.

6000. Robertson, J. D. September 1985. Economic Issues and the Probability of Forming Minority Coalition Cabinets. *Social Science Quarterly* 66 (3): 687–694.

6001. Robertson, J. D. October 1985. *See* Harmel, R. (October 1985).

6002. Robertson, J. D. November 1986. Economic Polarization and Cabinet Formation in Western Europe. *Legislative Studies Quarterly* 11 (4): 533–549.

6003. Robertson, J. D. December 1988. *See* Masters, M. F. (December 1988).

6004. Robertson, J. D. February 1990. Transaction-Cost Economics and Cross-National Patterns of Industrial Conflict: A Comparative Institutional Analysis. *American Journal of Political Science* 34 (1): 153–189.

6005. Robertson, J. D., and S. W. Cutcomb. March 1987. Parliamentary Executive-Legislative Relations and the Implications of Cabinet Stability "Ballast" and "Energy" in Macroeconomic Policy. *Western Political Quarterly* 40 (1): 7–27.

6006. Robertson, L. 1988. *See* Jefferson, T. (1988).

6007. Robinson, C. H. March 1982. *See* Chambers, D. A. (March 1982).

6008. Robinson, J. P. January 1978. "Massification" and Democratization of the Leisure Class. *Annals of the American Academy of Political and Social Science* 435: 206–225.

6009. Robinson, L. June 1992. Why Central America Is Still Not Democratic. *SAIS Review* 12 (2): 81–96.

6010. Robinson, M. January 1993. *See* Healey, J. (January 1993).

6011. Robinson, P. T. April 1994. Democratization: Understanding the Relationship between Regime Change and the Culture of Politics. *African Studies Review* 37 (1): 39–68.

6012. Robinson, R. June 1992. U.S. Africa Policy: Building a Democratic Peace. *Transafrica Forum* 9: 39–46.

6013. Robinson, R. D. August 1982. Can the Japanese Keep It Up? *Technology Review* 85: 46–52.

6014. Robinson, W. H. September 1991. Congress and Parliaments: Central Europe and the USSR. *Bureaucrat* 20 (3): 45–47.

6015. Roca, B. September 1977. Specific Features of Socialist Democracy in Cuba. *World Marxist Review* 20: 14–20.

6016. Rocamora, J. September 1991. Discontent in the Philippines. *World Policy Journal* 8: 633–661.

6017. Rocamora, J. 1992. *See* Gills, B. (1992).

6018. Rocha, G. M. December 1994. Redefining the Role of the Bourgeoisie in Dependent Capitalist Development: Privatization and Liberalization in Brazil. *Latin American Perspectives* 21 (1): 72–98.

6019. Rocha, R. M., and H. D. Sanford. 1979. Mainstreaming: Democracy in Action. *Social Education* 43 (1): 59–62.

6020. Rocher, G. 1994. Le Droit et les Juristes dans une "Societe Libre et Democratique," Selon Alex de Tocqueville. *La Revue Juridique Themis* 28: 1011–1034.

6021. Rochon, T. R. April 1982. Direct Democracy or Organized Futility? Action Groups in the Netherlands. *Comparative Political Studies* 15 (1): 3–28.

6022. Rochon, T. R. January 1990. Political Movements and State Authority in Liberal Democracies. *World Politics* 42 (2): 299–313.

6023. Rochon, T. R., and M. J. Mitchell. April 1989. Social Bases of the Transition to Democracy in Brazil. *Comparative Politics* 21 (3): 307–322.

6024. Rock, C. P. June 1987. Recent Reforms Democratizing Swedish Economic Institutions. *Journal of Economic Issues* 21 (2): 837–845.

6025. Rock, C. P. May 1993. *See* Mygind, N. (May 1993).

6026. Rock, M. T. March 1994. Transitional Democracies and the Shift to Export-Led Industrialization: Lessons from Thailand. *Studies in Comparative International Development* 29 (1): 18–37.

6027. Rockman, B. A. December 1978. *See* Aberbach, J. D. (December 1978).

6028. Rockman, B. A. March 1985. *See* Campbell, J. C. (March 1985).

6029. Rodel, W. 1983. The Most Important Claims of the Revolutionary German Social-Democracy Concerning Pharmacy Service at the End of the 19th-Century. *Pharmazie* 38 (11): 772–774.

6030. Rodin, D. 1990. Politicization (in Yugoslavia) and Depoliticization.* *Politicka Misao* 27 (2): 155–159.

6031. Rodota, S. December 1993. Sovereignty in the Technopolitical Age: Electronic Democracy and Representative Democracy.* *Politica del Diritto* 24 (4): 569–600.

6032. Rodriguez, A. M. October 1991. Reforma Economica y Liberacion Politica: Dos Inveles de la Transicion Mexicana. *Revista de Estudios Politicos* 74: 671–676.

6033. Rodriguez, A. M., and M. M. Huerta. October 1991. Mexico: En Busca de la Democracia. *Revista de Estudios Politicos* 74: 405–430.

6034. Rodriguez, C. A. J. April 1980. Elaboration and Control of Foreign Policy in a Democratic System.* *Revista de Estudios Internacionales* 1 (2): 403–417.

6035. Rodriguez, D. A. October 1987. A Framework for the Analysis of Political Representation in Democratic Systems.* *Revista de Estudios Politicos* 58: 137–190.

6036. Rodriguez, G. P. 1986. Restauracion de la Democracia en Chile. *Politica* (9): 127–137.

6037. Rodriquez, V. E., and P. M. Ward. 1991. Opposition Politics, Power and Public Administration in Urban Mexico. *Bulletin of Latin American Research* 10 (1): 23–36.

6038. Rodriquez, V. E., and P. M. Ward. December 1994. Disentangling the PRI from the Government in Mexico. *Mexican Studies* 10 (1): 163–186.

6039. Rocder, P. G. January 1994. Varieties of Post-Soviet Authoritarian Regimes. *Post-Soviet Affairs* 10: 61–101.

6040. Roelofs, H. M. June 1986. The American Polity: A Systematic Ambiguity. *Review of Politics* 48 (3): 323–348.

6041. Roemer, J. 1989. Democracy and Production Series: Visions of Capitalism and Socialism. *Socialist Review* 19 (3): 95–100.

6042. Roemer, J. E. June 1994. The Strategic Role of Party Ideology When Voters Are Uncertain about How the Economy Works. *American Political Science Review* 88 (2): 327–335.

6043. Roemer, P. 1981. Demokratie als Inhaltliches Prinzip der Gesamten Gesellschaft: Wolfgang Abendroths Beitrag zur Verteidigung Demokratischer Positionen in der Bundesrepublik Deutschland. *Demokratie und Recht* 8 (2): 123–136.

6044. Roett, R. June 1983. Staying the Course. *Wilson Quarterly* 7 (3): 46–61.

6045. Roett, R. 1984. Democracy and Debt in South America: A Continent's Dilemma. *Foreign Affairs* 62 (3): 695–720.

6046. Roett, R. January 1986. The Transition to Democratic Government in Brazil. *World Politics* 38 (2): 371–382.

6047. Roett, R. March 1989. Brazil's Transition to Democracy. *Current History* 88 (536): 117–120, 149–151.

6048. Roett, R. March 1989. Paraguay after Stroessner. *Foreign Affairs* 68 (2): 124–142.

6049. Roett, R. January 1991. The Reawakening of Democracy and Market Economy in Latin America.* *Europa Archiv: Zeitschrift für Internationale Politik* 46 (1): 7–16.

6050. Roett, R., and S. D. Tollefson. January 1986. The Transition to Democracy in Brazil. *Current History* 85 (507): 21–24.

6051. Rogachev, S. November 1992. First Steps on the Path of Democratization. *Russian Education and Society* 34 (11): 5–15.

6052. Rogers, J. December 1992. *See* Cohen, J. (December 1992).

6053. Rogers, J. June 1993. *See* Cohen, J. (June 1993).

6054. Rogin, M. February 1977. Nature as Politics and Nature as Romance in America. *Political Theory* 5 (1): 5–30.

6055. Rogowski, R. March 1987. Trade and the Variety of Democratic Institutions. *International Organization* 41 (2): 203–223.

6056. Rohrschneider, R. February 1994. How Iron is the Law of Oligarchy: Robert Michels and National Party Delegates in Eleven West European Democracies. *European Journal of Political Research* 25 (2): 207–238.

6057. Rohrschneider, R. December 1994. Report from the Laboratory: The Influence of Institutions on Political Elites' Democratic Values in Germany. *American Political Science Review* 88 (4): 927–941.

6058. Rohwer, J. December 7, 1991. Drunk, Not Sick: A Survey of Brazil. *Economist (London)* 321: 64+.

6059. Roldan, D. January 1993. Democracy in Latin America.* *Esprit* 1: 103–122.

6060. Roldan-Barbero, J. January 1993. Democracy and European Law. *Revista de Instituciones Europeas* 20 (1): 101–137.

6061. Rolland, L. October 1993. *See* Lajoie, A. (October 1993).

6062. Roman, A., and A. Mendez. May 1994. The Spanish Transition to Democracy Seen through the Spanish Database ISOC. *Scientometrics* 30 (1): 201–212.

6063. Roman, P. December 1993. Representative Government in Socialist Cuba. *Latin American Perspectives* 20 (1): 7–27.

6064. Roman, R. 1977. Political Democracy and Mexican Constitutionalists: A Reexamination. *Americas* 34 (1): 81–89.

6065. Romberg, A. D. June 1987. *See* Gleysteen, W. H. , Jr. (June 1987).

6066. Romer, T., and H. Rosenthal. 1979. Bureaucrats Versus Voters: Political Economy of Resource Allocation by Direct Democracy. *Quarterly Journal of Economics* 93 (4): 563–587.

6067. Romero, C. A. January 1989. Pragmatic Democracy and Foreign Policy in the Caribbean. *Caribbean Affairs* 2 (1): 9–18.

6068. Romero-Barcelo, C. September 1980. Puerto Rico, U.S.A.: The Case for Statehood. *Foreign Affairs* 59 (1): 60–81.

6069. Rommetvedt, H. September 1994. Norwegian Coalition Governments and the Management of Party Relations. *Scandinavian Political Studies* 17 (3): 239–258.

6070. Ronai, I., and M. N. Bryant. April 1992. The Role of Hungary's Parliamentary Library in Fostering Democratic Decision Making. *Libri* 42: 135–143.

6071. Ronchey, A. 1979. Guns and Gray Matter: Terrorism in Italy. *Foreign Affairs* 57 (4): 921–940.

6072. Rondinelli, D. A. January 1986. Extending Urban Services in Developing Countries: Policy Options and Organizational Choices. *Public Administration and Development* 6 (1): 1–21.

6073. Ronfeldt, D. F. December 1985. Rethinking the Monroe Doctrine. *Orbis* 28 (4): 634–696.

6074. Roniger, L. September 1989. Democratic Transitions and Consolidation in Contemporary Southern Europe and Latin America. *Journal of Comparative Sociology* 30 (3–4): 211–230.

6075. Roniger, L. September 1994. Civil Society, Patronage, and Democracy. *International Journal of Comparative Sociology* 35 (3–4): 207–220.

6076. Rootes, C. A. December 1981. On the Future of Protest Politics in Western Democracies: A Critique of Barnes, Kaase et al. *European Journal of Political Research* 9 (4): 421–432.

6077. Roper, S. D. December 1994. The Romanian Revolution from a Theoretical Perspective. *Communist and Post-Communist Studies* 27 (4): 411–422.

6078. Roper, S. D. December 1994. The Romanian Party System and the Catch-All Party Phenomenon. *East European Quarterly* 28 (4): 519–532.

6079. Ropp, S. C. December 1987. Panama's Struggle for Democracy. *Current History* 86 (524): 421–424, 434–435.

6080. Ropp, S. C. December 1988. Panama's Defiant Noriega. *Current History* 87 (533): 417–420, 431.

6081. Ropp, S. C. March 1991. Panama: The United States Invasion and Its Aftermath. *Current History* 90 (554): 113–116, 130.

6082. Rorty, R. 1988. Straussianism, Democracy, and Allan Bloom: That Old-Time Philosophy. *New Republic* 198 (14): 28–33.

6083. Rosaldo, R. August 1994. Cultural Citizenship and Educational Democracy. *Cultural Anthropology* 9 (3): 402–411.

6084. Rosberg, C. G. July 1984. *See* Jackson, R. H. (July 1984).

6085. Rose, D. D. 1975. Citizen Preference and Public Policy in American States: Causal Analysis of Non-Democracy. *Tulane Studies in Political Science* 15: 53–94.

6086. Rose, G. 1990. The Struggle for Political Democracy: Emancipation, Gender, and Geography. *Environment and Planning D: Society and Space* 8 (4): 395–408.

6087. Rose, H. April 1993. From Command to Free Politics. *Political Quarterly* 64 (2): 156–171.

6088. Rose, R. 1978. Authority, Effectiveness and Consent in Western Democracies.* *Rivista Italiana di Scienza Politica* 8 (2): 213–242.

6089. Rose, R. April 1992. Toward a Civil Economy. *Journal of Democracy* 3 (2): 13–26.

6090. Rose, R. October 1992. Escaping from Absolute Dissatisfaction: A Trial-and-Error Model of Change in Eastern Europe. *Journal of Theoretical Politics* 4 (4): 371–393.

6091. Rose, R. February 1994. *See* Mishler, W. (February 1994).

6092. Rose, R., and C. Haerpfer. 1994. Mass Response to Transformation in Post-Communist Societies. *Europa-Asia Studies* 46 (1): 3–28.

6093. Rose, R., and W. T. E. Mishler. April 1994. Mass Reaction to Regime Change in Eastern Europe: Polarization or Leaders and Laggards? *British Journal of Political Science* 24 (2): 159–182.

6094. Rose, S. 1974. Sri Lanka at Turning Point: Future of Parliamentary Democracy. *Round Table* (256): 411–422.

6095. Rose-Ackerman, S. June 1991. Justifying Democracy: A Review Essay. *Political Science Quarterly* 106 (2): 313–315.

6096. Rosen, C. M. 1989. Business, Democracy, and Progressive Reform in the Redevelopment of Baltimore After the Great Fire of 1904. *Business History Review* 63 (2): 283–328.

6097. Rosen, S. March 1985. Guangzhou's Democratic Movement in the Cultural Revolution: Perspective. *China Quarterly* 101: 1–31.

6098. Rosen, S. September 1988. Dissent and Tolerance in Chinese Society. *Current History* 87 (530): 261–264, 278–281.

6099. Rosen, S. June 1989. Public Opinion and Reform in the Peoples Republic of China. *Comparative Communism* 22 (2–3): 153–170.

6100. Rosen, S. September 1993. *See* Zhu, J. H. (September 1993).

6101. Rosenberg, M. B. June 1977. Thinking about Costa Rica's Political Future: A Comment. *Inter-American Economic Affairs* 31 (1): 89–94.

6102. Rosenberg, M. B. December 1986. Honduras: The Reluctant Democracy. *Current History* 85 (515): 417–420, 438/448.

6103. Rosenberg, T. 1989. Will Democracy Come to Chile. *Dissent* 36 (3): 294–300.

6104. Rosenberg, T. September 1991. Beyond Elections (in Latin America). *Foreign Policy* 84: 72–91.

6105. Rosenberg, T. 1992. Latin America's Magical Liberalism. *Wilson Quarterly* 16 (4): 58–74.

6106. Rosenberg, W. G. December 1981. The Democratization of Russia's Railroads in 1917. *American Historical Review* 86 (5): 983–1008.

6107. Rosenbloom, D. H. September 1982. Constitutionalism and Public Bureaucrats. *Bureaucrat* 11 (3): 54–56.

6108. Rosenbloom, D. H. March 1984. Public Administrative Professionalism and Public Service Law. *State and Local Government Review* 16 (2): 52–57.

6109. Rosenbloom, D. H. January 1987. Public Administration and the Judiciary; The "New Partnership." *Public Administration Review* 47 (1): 75–83.

6110. Rosenblum, N. L. March 1994. Democratic Character and Community: The Logic of Congruence? *Journal of Political Philosophy* 2 (1): 67–97.

6111. Rosenblum, S. 1980. Swedish Social Democracy: At the Crossroads. *Contemporary Crises* 4 (3): 267–282.

6112. Rosenbluth, F. March 1994. *See* Cox, G. W. (March 1994).

6113. Rosenfeld, S. June 1990. *See* Bello, W. (June 1990).

6114. Rosenstein, E. 1979. *See* Bass, B. M. (1979).

6115. Rosenthal, E. May 1977. Worker Participation in Israel: Experience and Lessons. *Annals of the American Academy of Political and Social Science* 431: 113–122.

6116. Rosenthal, H. 1979. *See* Romer, T. (1979).

6117. Rosenthal, U. July 1986. The Predicament of Democracy. *Acta Politica* 21 (3): 311–326.

6118. Rosentraub, M. S. June 1984. *See* Warren, R. (June 1984).

6119. Rosenwein, R. E., and D. T. Campbell. June 1992. Mobilization to Achieve Collective Action and Democratic Majority Plurality Amplification. *Journal of Social Issues* 48 (2): 125–138.

6120. Rosett, C. November 1987. Cory's Land Grab; Land Reform Will Not Save Philippine Democracy. *American Spectator* 20: 16–18.

6121. Rosh, R. M. September 1986. The Impact of Third-World Defense Burdens on Basic Human Needs. *Policy Studies Journal* 15 (1): 135–146.

6122. Roskin, M. December 1978. Spain Tries Democracy Again. *Political Science Quarterly* 93 (4): 629–646.

6123. Rosner, M., and A. S. Tannenbaum. 1987. Organizational Efficiency and Egalitarian Democracy in a Intentional Communal Society: The Kibbutz. *British Journal of Sociology* 38 (4): 521–545.

6124. Rosova, T. December 1991. *See* Butora, M. (December 1991).

6125. Rosow, S. J. March 1989. Nuclear Deterrence, State Legitimation, and Liberal Democracy. *Polity* 21 (3): 563–586.

6126. Ross, B. 1976. *See* Graubert, J. (1976).

6127. Ross, M. H., and R. Joslyn. December 1988. Election-Night News Coverage as Political Ritual. *Polity* 21 (2): 301–319.

6128. Rossiter, D. J. 1984. *See* Johnston, R. J. (1984).

6129. Rossiter, D. J. October 1994. *See* Johnston, R. J. (October 1994).

6130. Roszak, T. 1986. Partners for Democracy: Public Libraries and Information Technology. *Wilson Library Bulletin* 60 (6): 14–16.

6131. Roth, K. 1991. Albanian Election Aftermath: Democracy's Race against Fear. *Nation* 252 (17): 588+.

6132. Roth, R. 1975. Young Voters and Democracy: Thoughts and Observations on Young Mature Citizens.* *Politische Studien* 26 (219): 27–46.

6133. Rothblatt, D. N. April 1978. Multiple Advocacy: An Approach to Metropolitan Planning. *Journal of the American Institute of Planners* 44 (2): 193–199.

6134. Rothschild-Whitt, J. August 1979. The Collectivist Organization: An Alternative to Rational-Bureaucratic Models. *American Sociological Review* 44 (4): 509–527.

6135. Rothstein, L. September 1988. Industrial Justice Meets Industrial Democracy: Liberty of Expression at Workplace in the U.S. and France. *Labor Studies Journal* 13 (3): 18–39.

6136. Rothstein, P. July 1994. Learning the Preferences of Governments and Voters from Proposed Spending and Aggregated Votes. *Journal of Public Economics* 54 (3): 361–389.

6137. Rothstein, R. L. March 1991. Democracy, Conflict, and Development in the Third World. *Washington Quarterly* 14 (2): 43–63.

6138. Roubini, N., and J. D. Sachs. 1989. Political and Economic Determinants of Budget Deficits in the Industrial Democracies. *European Economic Review* 33 (5): 903–933.

6139. Rouquie, A. January 1983. Democratic Demand and Revolutionary Desire.* *Project* 176: 603–614.

6140. Rousset, M. January 1985. The Difficult Conciliation of Unanimitarian and Democratic Ideology: The Case of Morocco.* *Maghreb Review* 10 (1): 10–14.

6141. Rowat, D. C. October 1985. Why Democracies Need an Access Law. *Transnational Data Report* 8: 364–366.

6142. Rowat, D. D. 1985. Bureaucracy and Policy-Making in Developing Democracies: The Decline of Bureaucratic Influence. *Revue Internationale des Sciences Administration* 51 (3): 189–198.

6143. Roxborough, I. July 1982. *See* Thompson, M. R. (July 1982).

6144. Roy, A. December 3, 1994. Elections without Issues. *Economic and Political Weekly* 29 (49): 3064.

6145. Roy, B. December 3, 1994. West Bengal: Human Rights Abuse Continues Unchecked. *Economic and Political Weekly* 29 (49): 3071–3072.

6146. Roy, D. March 1994. Singapore, China, and the "Soft Authoritarian" Challenge. *Asian Survey* 34 (3): 231–242.

6147. Rozman, F. 1981. The Policy of Slovenian Social Democracy: The Southern Slavic Social Democratic Party during World War I.* *Oesterreichische Osthefte* 23 (2): 196–203.

6148. Rubens, J. 1983. Retooling American Democracy. *Futurist* 17 (1): 59–64.

6149. Rubin, B. June 1990. Reshaping the Middle East. *Foreign Affairs* 69 (3): 131–146.

6150. Rubin, S. G. 1990. Service Learning: Education for Democracy. *Liberal Education* 76 (3): 12–17.

6151. Rubinson, R., and D. Quinlan. August 1977. Democracy and Social Inequality: A Reanalysis. *American Sociological Review* 42 (4): 611–623.

6152. Rubio, L. 1992. Democracy and Economic Reform in Mexico. *Democratic Institutions* 1: 87–102.

6153. Rubio-Carracedo, J. October 1987. Democracy and Legitimation of Power in Rousseau: Advanced Democracy Versus Political Representation.* *Revista de Estudios Politicos* 58: 215–242.

6154. Rubio-Castro, A. March 1986. Spanish Neo-Corporatism: The Economic and Social Agreement, 1985–1986.* *Revista de Estudios Politicos* 50: 213–239.

6155. Rucinski, D. 1991. The Centrality of Reciprocity to Communication and Democracy. *Critical Studies in Mass Communication* 8 (2): 184–194.

6156. Ruckelshaus, W. D. 1985. Risk, Science, and Democracy. *Issues in Science and Technology* 1 (3): 19–38.

6157. Ruckelshaus, W. D. 1987. Risk, Science, and Democracy. *Chemtech* 17 (12): 738–741.

6158. Rudolph, L. I., and S. H. Rudolph. July 1977. India's Election: Backing into the Future. *Foreign Affairs* 55 (4): 836–853.

6159. Rudolph, S. H. July 1977. *See* Rudolph, L. I. (July 1977).

6160. Rudyk, E. January 1992. The Western Experience of Industrial Democracy and Its Significance for the USSR. *Problems of Economics* 34 (9): 37–47.

6161. Rudyk, E., and J. Vanek. September 1992. Labor and Democracy in the Period of Transition to a Market Economy: Problems in the Selection of Management Systems. *Problems of Economic Transition* 35 (5): 24–41.

6162. Ruel, S. 1988. Dissident China. *Reason* 19: 34–38.

6163. Rueland, J. 1991. Processes of Democratization in Asia. *Aussenpolitik* 42 (3): 281–289.

6164. Rueschemeyer, D. January 1991. Different Methods: Contradictory Results? Research on Development and Democracy. *International Journal of Comparative Sociology* 32 (1–2): 9–38.

6165. Rueschemeyer, D. June 1993. *See* Huber, E. (June 1993).

6166. Ruffieux, R. J. 1985. Meynaud's Discovery of Helvetian Democracy.* *Revue Europeenne des Sciences Sociales* 71: 5–16.

6167. Ruffolo, G. September 1980. Complexity and Democracy: The Role of Information.* *Critica Marxistas* 18 (5): 11–39.

6168. Rufilli, R. March 1988. Constitution and Transformation. *Il Mulino* 316: 239–246.

6169. Rugina, A. N. 1990. The Contemporary Crisis in Democracy and Dictatorship and the Road towards a New Principia-Politica: Final Remarks. *International Journal of Social Economics* 17 (2): 58–64.

6170. Ruiz, C. August 1984. *See* Alvayay, R. (August 1984).

6171. Ruiz, L. E. J. October 1986. Philippine Politics as a Peoples' Quest for Authentic Political Subjecthood. *Alternatives* 11 (4): 505–534.

6172. Ruiz, L. E. J. April 1988. Theology, Politics, and the Discourses of Transformation. *Alternatives* 13 (2): 155–176.

6173. Ruiz, L. E. J. March 1991. After National Democracy: Radical Democratic Politics at the Edge of Modernity (in the Philippines). *Alternatives* 16 (2): 161–200.

6174. Ruiz-Duran, C. January 1989. Pleno Empleo y Bienestar en la Crisis: El Caso de la Socialdemocracia Sueca: Una Reflexion desde el Sur. *Investigacion Economica* 48: 295–316.

6175. Ruiz-Vasquez, J. C. March 1992. *See* Murillo Castano, G. (March 1992).

6176. Ruland, J. May 1991. A Burmese Road to Democracy? The Chances of Political Change in an "Oriental Despotism."* *Internationales Asienforum* 22 (1–2): 87–106.

6177. Rule, W. September 1987. Electoral Systems, Contextual Factors, and Women's

Opportunity for Election to Parliament in Twenty-three Democracies. *Western Political Quarterly* 40 (3): 477–498.

6178. Rule, W. December 1994. Women's Underrepresentation and Electoral Systems. *PS: Political Science & Politics* 27 (4): 689–692.

6179. Rumiantsev, O. June 1992. Our Way to Social Democracy: Reflections before and after the First and Second Conferences of the Social Democratic Party of Russia. *Russian Politics and Law* 31 (1): 90–106.

6180. Rummel, R. J. 1984. On Fostering a Just Peace. *International Journal on World Peace* 1 (1): 4–19.

6181. Rummel, R. J. July 1984. Libertarianism, Violence within States, and the Polarity Principle. *Comparative Politics* 16 (3): 443–462.

6182. Rummel, R. J. November 1989. The Politics of Cold Blood. *Society* 27 (1): 32–40.

6183. Rumpf, H. 1980. The Reason of State in the Democratic Constitutional State.* *Der Staat* 19 (2): 273–292.

6184. Rumyantsev, O. June 1990. Authoritarian Modernization and the Social-Democratic Alternative. *Social Research* 57 (2): 493–529.

6185. Ruoff, K. J. July 1993. Tomino Goes to City Hall: Grassroots Democracy in Zushi City, Japan. *Bulletin of Concerned Asian Scholars* 25 (3): 22–32.

6186. Rupieper, H. J. 1991. Bringing Democracy to the Frauleins: American Policy of Democratization in Germany 1945–1952.* *Geschichte und Gesellschaft* 17 (1): 61–91.

6187. Rus, V. 1984. The Future of Industrial Democracy. *International Social Science Journal* 36 (2): 232–254.

6188. Rusconi, G. E. July 1994. Democracy without Antifascism [in Italy].* *Il Mulino* 354: 623–632.

6189. Rush, M. (ed). October 1994. British Government and Politics since 1945: Changes in Perspective. *Parliamentary Affairs* 47 (4): 497–738. 15 Articles.

6190. Rush, M. E. March 1993. Voters' Rights and the Legal States of American Political Parties. *Journal of Law and Politics* 9 (3): 487–514.

6191. Rush, M. E. December 1994. Gerrymandering: Out of the Political Thicket and into the Quagmire. *PS: Political Science & Politics* 27 (4): 682–685.

6192. Russell, A. T. October 1994. *See* Johnston, R. J. (October 1994).

6193. Russell, R. October 1987. *See* Hirst, M. (October 1987).

6194. Russell, R. May 1987. *See* Carballal, T. (May 1987).

6195. Russett, B. March 1985. The Mysterious Case of Vanishing Hegemony: Or, Is Mark Twain Really Dead? *International Organization* 39 (2): 207–231.

6196. Russett, B. July 1992. *See* Ember, C. R. (July 1992).

6197. Russett, B. 1993. Can a Democratic Peace Be Built. *International Interactions* 18 (3): 277–282.

6198. Russett, B. February 1993. *See* Ember, C. R. (February 1993).

6199. Russett, B. September 1993. *See* Maoz, Z. (September 1993).

6200. Russett, B., and W. Antholis. November 1992. Do Democracies Fight Each Other? Evidence from the Peloponnesian War. *Journal of Peace Research* 29 (4): 415–434.

6201. Rustin, B. 1978. Capitalism, Socialism, and Democracy. *Commentary* 65 (4): 68–69.

6202. Rustow, D. A. March 1985. Turkey's Liberal Revolution. *Middle East Review* 17 (3): 5–11.

6203. Rustow, D. A. November 1985. Elections and Legitimacy in the Middle East. *Annals of the American Academy of Political and Social Science* 482: 122–146.

6204. Rustow, D. A. September 1990. Democracy: A Global Revolution? *Foreign Affairs* 69 (4): 75–91.

6205. Rustow, D. A. December 1992. Democracy: Historic Essentials and Future Prospects. *Harvard International Review* 15 (2): 4–7.

6206. Rutan, G. F. September 1985. The Canadian Security Intelligence Services: Squaring the Demands of National Security with Canadian Democracy. *Conflict Quarterly* 5: 17–30.

6207. Ruth, A. March 1984. The Second New Nation: The Mythology of Modern Sweden. *Daedalus* 113 (2): 53–96.

6208. Rutherford, M. 1974. A Prospect of Germany: Two Societies and Democracies. *Round Table* (255): 277–285.

6209. Rutherford, M. September 1981. Clarence Ayres and the Instrumental Theory of Values. *Journal of Economic Issues* 15 (3): 657–673.

6210. Rutherford, W. T. 1974. Democracy at Work: Or, Only Away from Work. *Atlanta Economic Review* 24 (6): 4–8.

6211. Rutkoff, P. M., and W. B. Scott. March 1983. The French in New York: Resistance and Structure. *Social Research* 50 (1): 185–214.

6212. Rutland, P. 1994. Democracy and Nationalism in Armenia. *Europe-Asia Studies* 46 (5): 839–861.

6213. Ryan, J. J. October 1994. The Impact of Democratization on Revolutionary Movements. *Comparative Politics* 27 (1): 27–44.

6214. Ryan, J. L. December 1993. The Federalist Vision of a Representative Democracy. *Harvard Journal of Law and Public Policy* 16 (1): 33–34.

6215. Ryan, P. March 1991. Market Reforms and Democratization: The Dilemmas of Eastern Europe and the Soviet Union. *Studies in Political Economy* 34: 29–52.

6216. Ryder, J. 1984. Community, Struggle and Democracy: Marxism and Pragmatism. *Studies in Soviet Thought* 27 (2): 107–121.

6217. Saarelainen, T. 1994. *See* Hirttio, K. (1994).

6218. Sabbat-Swidlicka, A. April 2, 1993. Church and State in Poland. *RFE/RL Research Report* 2: 45–53.

6219. Sabbat-Swidlicka, A. November 5, 1993. The Legacy of Poland's "Solidarity" Governments. *RFE/RL Research Reports* 2: 18–22.

6220. Sabel, C. F. 1984. Industrial Reorganization and Social Democracy in Austria. *Industrial Relations* 23 (3): 344–361.

6221. Sachs, A. March 1991. The Constitutional Position of White South Africans in a Democratic South Africa. *Social Justice* 18 (1–2): 1–39.

6222. Sachs, I. 1983. Le Bresil àpres les Elections: Democratie sans Developpement? *Politique Etrangere* 48 (1): 163–179.

6223. Sachs, J. D. 1989. *See* Roubini, N. (1989).

6224. Sachs, J., and D. Lipton. June 1990. Poland's Economic Reform. *Foreign Affairs* 69 (3): 47–66.

6225. Sacken, D. M. 1989. Due Process and Democracy: Participation in School Disciplinary Processes. *Urban Education* 23 (4): 323–347.

6226. Sadlak, J. 1992. *See* Winchester, I. (1992).

6227. Saez, M. A. October 1991. Sobre el Concepto de Paises en Vias de Consolidacion Democratica en America Latina. *Revista de Estudios Politicos* 74: 113–130.

6228. Saffu, Y. February 1988. Papua New Guinea in 1987: Wingti's Coalition in a Disabled System. *Asian Survey* 28 (2): 242–251.

6229. Safran, W. March 1987. Ethnic Mobilization, Modernization, and Ideology: Jacobinism, Marxism, Organicism, and Functionalism. *Journal of Ethnic Studies* 15 (1): 1–31.

6230. Sagues, N. P. October 1991. La Jurisdiccion Constitucional en Costa Rica. *Revista de Estudios Politicos* 74: 471–496.

6231. Sah, K. C. August 1992. On Peaceful Evolution and Anti-Peaceful Evolution [in China]. *Issues and Studies* 28 (8): 32–45.

6232. Saich, T. September 1994. The Search for Civil Society and Democracy in China. *Current History* 93 (584): 260–264.

6233. Said, A. A. January 1979. Precept and Practice of Human Rights in Islam. *Universal Human Rights* 1 (1): 63–79.

6234. Said, A. A., and L. A. Barnitz. December 1990. The Dialogue between Peace and Human Rights. *Peace Review* 2 (1): 9–13.

6235. Saikal, A. April 1992. Afghanistan: A New Approach. *Journal of Democracy* 3 (2): 95–104.

6236. Sainsbury, D. October 1984. Scandinavian Party Politics Re-examined: Social Democracy in Decline? *West European Politics* 7: 67–102.

6237. Sainsbury, D. July 1991. Swedish Social Democracy in Transition: The Party's Record in the 1980s and the Challenge of the 1990s. *West European Politics* 14 (3): 31–57.

6238. Sainsbury, D. January 1993. The Swedish Social Democrats and the Legacy of Continuous Reform: Asset or Dilemma? *West European Politics* 16: 39–61.

6239. Saint-Ouen, F. 1986. Les Partis Politiques Français et l'Europe: Systeme Politique et Fonctionnement du Discours. *Revue Française de Science Politique* 36 (2): 205–226.

6240. Saint-Paul, G., and T. Verdier. December 1993. Education, Democracy and Growth. *Journal of Development Economics* 42 (2): 399–407.

6241. Sakwa, R. June 1989. Commune Democracy and Gorbachev's Reforms. *Political Studies* 37 (2): 224–243.

6242. Sakwa, R. 1993. Christian Democracy in Russia.* *Sotsiologicheskie Issledovaniia* (4): 126–134.

6243. Sakwa, R. March 1994. Democratic Change in Russia and Ukraine. *Democratization* 1 (1): 41–72.

6244. Salame, G. June 1991. On the Causality of a Shortcoming: Why Is the Arab World Not Democratic?* *Revue Française de Science Politique* 41 (3): 307–340.

6245. Salame, K. October 1992. Syrie: Liberalisation Economique Piegée? *Arabies* 40–41.

6246. Salamone, S. D. June 1989. The Dialectics of Turkish National Identity: Ethnic Boundary Maintenance and State Ideology. *East European Quarterly* 23 (2): 225–248.

6247. Salazar Sanchez, M. June 1987. The Present State of the Judicial Defense of Democracy in Chile.* *Estudios Publicos* 25: 227–263.

6248. Salig, K. O. 1990. The Sudan, 1985–1989: The Fading Democracy. *Journal of Modern African Studies* 28 (2): 199–224.

6249. Salkever, S. G. January 1980. Who Knows Whether It's Rational To Vote? *Ethics* 90 (2): 203–217.

6250. Saltman, R. B., and C. Vonotter. 1989. Voice, Choice and the Question of Civil Democracy in the Swedish Welfare-State. *Economic and Industrial Democracy* 10 (2): 195–209.

6251. Salvadori, M. L. 1987. Old and New Subjects of Democracy.* *Teoria Politica* 3 (3): 19–29.

6252. Salwen, M. B. March 1990. *See* Youm, K. H. (March 1990).

6253. Samiuddin, A. 1977. The Genesis of Fascism and Its Threat to Indian Democracy. *Indian Political Science Review* 11 (1): 86–99.

6254. Samiuddin, A. 1982. The Beginning of Parliamentary Democracy in Iraq: A Case Study. *Middle Eastern Studies* 18 (4): 445–448.

6255. Samper, J. A. April 27, 1992. Peru y Venezuela Hacen Temblar a los Democratas. *Cambio* 16: 60–62.

6256. Sampson, E. E. August 1991. The Democratization of Psychology. *Theory and Psychology* 1 (3): 275–298.

6257. Samudavanija, C. A. June 1987. Democracy in Thailand: A Case of a Stable Semi-Democratic Regime. *World Affairs* 150 (1): 31–41.

6258. Samudavanija, C. A. September 1990. Educating Thai Democracy. *Journal of Democracy* 1 (4): 104–115.

6259. Samuels, M. A., and W. A. Douglas. June 1981. Promoting Democracy. *Washington Quarterly* 4 (3): 52–65.

6260. Samuels, M. A., and J. D. Sullivan. June 1986. Democratic Development: A New Role for U.S. Business. *Washington Quarterly* 9 (3): 167–179.

6261. Samuels, R. J. 1984. Public Energy Corporations in the Industrial Democracies: Japan in Comparative Perspective. *Journal of Commonwealth and Comparative Politics* 22 (1): 53–101.

6262. Samuels, S. W. May 28, 1976. Determination of Cancer Risk in a Democracy. *Annals of the New York Academy of Sciences* 271: 421–430.

6263. Sanchez Vazquez, A. November 1983. Marx and Democracy.* *Sistema* 57: 19–30.

6264. Sandberg, A. 1983. Trade Union–Oriented Research for Democratization of Planning in Worklife: Problems and Potentials. *Journal of Occupational Behavior* 4 (1): 59–71.

6265. Sandberger, J. September 1981. *See* Lind, G. (September 1981).

6266. Sandbrook, R. 1988. Liberal Democracy in Africa: A Socialist-Revisionist Perspective. *Canadian Journal of African Studies* 22 (2): 240–267.

6267. Sandbrook, R. September 1990. Taming the African Leviathan. *World Policy Journal* 7 (4): 673–701.

6268. Sanders, A. J. K. January 1990. Mongolia in 1989: Year of Adjustment. *Asian Survey* 30 (1): 59–66.

6269. Sanders, A. J. K. June 1991. Mongolia 1990: A New Dawn? *Asian Affairs (London)* 78 (2): 158–166.

6270. Sanders, A. J. K. June 1992. Mongolia's New Constitution: Blueprint for Democracy. *Asian Survey* 32 (6): 506–520.

6271. Sanders, E. December 1990. The Contribution of Theodore Lowi to the Science of Government. *PS: Political Science & Politics* 23 (4): 574–576.

6272. Sanders, E. December 1990. *See* Ginsberg, B. (December 1990).

6273. Sanders, J. W. March 1991. Retreat from World Order: The Perils of Triumphalism. *World Policy Journal* 8 (2): 227–250.

6274. Sanders, J. W. June 1992. The Prospects for "Democratic Engagement." *World Policy Journal* 9 (3): 367–387.

6275. Sanders, T. G. April 1976. Brazil's Decompression. *Common Ground* 2 (2): 77–86.

6276. Sanders, T. G. 1992. Catolicismo y Democracia en America Latina. *Presencia (El Salvador)* 5 (17): 21–34.

6277. Sandkull, B. 1984. Managing the Democratization Process in Work Cooperatives. *Economic and Industrial Democracy* 5 (3): 359–389.

6278. Sandoz, E. June 1994. Foundations of American Liberty and Rule of Law. *Presidential Studies Quarterly* 24 (3): 605–617.

6279. Sanford, H. D. 1979. *See* Rocha, R. M. (1979).

6280. Sangmpan, S. N. July 1992. The Overpoliticised State and Democratization: A Theoretical Model. *Comparative Politics* 14 (4): 401–417.

6281. Sani, G., and Sartori G. 1978. Fragmentation, Polarization and the Structure of Cleavages: Easy and Difficult Democracies.* *Rivista Italiana di Scienza Politica* 8 (3): 339–361.

6282. Sankowski, A. December 1993. Can the Polish Book Trade Survive Democracy. *Library Acquisitions Practice and Theory* 17 (4): 433–437.

6283. Sankowski, E. January 1982. Freedom, Work and the Scope of Democracy. *Ethics* 91 (2): 228–242.

6284. Santerre, R. E. 1986. Representative Versus Direct Democracy: A Tiebout Test of Relative Performance. *Public Choice* 48 (1): 55–63.

6285. Santerre, R. E. February 1989. Representative vs. Direct Democracy: Are There Any Expenditure Differences? *Public Choice* 60 (2): 145–154.

6286. Santerre, R. E. 1993. Representative Versus Direct Democracy: The Role of the Public Bureaucrat. *Public Choice* 76 (3): 189–198.

6287. Santiago Guervos, J. May 1992. Socialism, Social Democracy and Marxism in the Political Vocabulary of the Spanish Democratic Transition (1975–1982). *Arbor Ciencia Pensamiento y Cultura* 142 (557): 53–67.

6288. Santino, J. December 1993. Uncertain Democracy: Rational Choice Theory and Democratization in Latin America.* *Revue Française de Science Politique* 43 (6): 970–993.

6289. Santoro, E. February 1993. Democratic Theory and Individual Autonomy: An Interpretation of Schumpeter's Doctrine of Democracy. *European Journal of Political Research* 23 (2): 121–143.

6290. Saphire, R. B. 1981. The Search for Legitimacy in Constitutional Theory: What Price Purity. *Ohio State Law Journal* 42 (1): 335–382.

6291. Sarabi, F. December 1994. The Post Khomeini Era in Iran: The Elections of the Fourth Islamic Majlis. *Middle East Journal* 48 (1): 89–107.

6292. Sarangi, P. 1986. Determinants of Policy Change: A Cross-National Analysis. *European Journal of Political Research* 14 (1–2): 23–44.

6293. Sarcinelli, U. August 1993. Constitutional Patriotism and "Citizens" Society or: What Keeps the Democratic Community Together. Orientations for Political Education.* *Aus Politik und Zeitgeschichte* 34: 35–37.

6294. Sarkar, S. 1982. Spain: Return of Social Democracy. *Economic and Political Weekly* 17 (46): 1853–1854.

6295. Sartori, G. 1975. Will Majorities Kill Democracy: Decision-Making by Majorities and by Committees. *Government and Opposition* 10 (2): 131–158.

6296. Sartori, G. 1978. *See* Sani, G. (1978).

6297. Sartori, G. August 1991. Rethinking Democracy: Bad Polity and Bad Politics. *International Social Science Journal* 43 (3): 437–450.

6298. Sarvasy, W. June 1984. J. S. Mill's Theory of Democracy for a Period of Transition between Capitalism and Socialism. *Polity* 16 (4): 567–587.

6299. Sarvasy, W. 1994. From Man and Philanthropic Service to Feminist Social Citizenship. *Social Politics* 1 (3): 306–325.

6300. Sass, R. 1993. The Work-Environment Board and the Limits of Social Democracy in Canada. *International Journal of Health Services* 23 (2): 279–300.

6301. Sass, T. R. August 1991. The Choice of Municipal Government Structure and Public Expenditures. *Public Choice* 71 (1–2): 71–87.

6302. Sass, T. R. December 1992. Constitutional Choice in Representative Democracies. *Public Choice* 74 (4): 405–424.

6303. Sasseen, R. F. June 1990. Liberal Education and the Study of Politics in a Catholic University. *Perspectives on Political Science* 19 (3): 146–152.

6304. Sassoon, D. December 1994. Social Democracy and the Europe of Tomorrow. *Dissent* 41 (1): 94–101.

6305. Sattel, U. 1980. *See* Kissler, L. (1980).

6306. Saul, J. S. 1977. Tanzania's Transition to Socialism? *Canadian Journal of African Studies* 11 (2): 313–341.

6307. Saul, J. S. 1994. Globalism, Socialism, and Democracy in the South African Transition. *Socialist Register* 171–202.

6308. Saul, J. S. March 1994. *See* Leys, C. (March 1994).

6309. Saunierseite, A. 1976. Scientific Liberty and Democracy.* *Mondes en Developpement* 16: 673–677.

6310. Savitskii, V. 1990. Democratization in the USSR: Toward the Freedom of the Individual through Law and Courts. *Criminal Law Reform* 2: 85–110.

6311. Savonnet Guyot, C. 1979. Race and Class in Brazil: Racial Democracy in Question.* *Revue Française de Science Politique* 29 (4–5): 877–894.

6312. Sawada, D. 1987. *See* Chamberlin, C. (1987).

6313. Saward, M. 1993. Direct Democracy Revisited. *Politics* 13 (2): 18–24.

6314. Saward, M. May 1994. Postmodernists, Pragmatists, and the Justification of Democracy. *Economy and Society* 23 (2): 201–216.

6315. Sawyer, J. A., and J. M. Nickens. 1980. Fulfillment of the Democratization Role of the Community College. *College and University* 55 (2): 113–124.

6316. Sawyers, K. April 1993. *See* Purcell, T. W. (April 1993).

6317. Saxonhouse, A. W. September 1993. Athenian Democracy: Modern Mythmakers and Ancient Theorists. *PS: Political Science & Politics* 26 (3): 486–490.

6318. Sayeed, K. B. 1992. The Three Worlds of Democracy in Pakistan. *Contemporary South Asia* 1 (1): 53–66.

6319. Sbarberi, F. January 1994. Liberty and Equality: The Formation of Bobbio's Democratic Theory.* *Archives de Philosophie* 57 (1): 3–31.

6320. Scaff, L. A. May 1981. Max Weber and Robert Michels. *American Journal of Sociology* 86 (6): 1269–1286.

6321. Scalapino, R. A. November 1976. The American Occupation of Japan: Perspectives after Three Decades. *Annals of the American Academy of Political and Social Science* 428: 104–113.

6322. Scalapino, R. A. July 1993. Democratizing Dragons: South Korea and Taiwan. *Journal of Democracy* 4 (3): 70–83.

6323. Scammon, R. M. March 1986. International Election Notes. *World Affairs* 148 (2): 245–246.

6324. Scammon, R. M. September 1986. International Election Notes. *World Affairs* 148 (4): 135–136.

6325. Scarlott, J. 1988. United States Offers Palua Dollars or Democracy. *Bulletin of the Atomic Scientists* 44 (9): 31–35.

6326. Scarpetta, O. December 1991. Political Traditions and the Limits of Democracy in Colombia. *International Journal of Politics, Culture and Society* 5 (2): 143–166.

6327. Scarponi, A. March 1977. Relationship of Democracy and Socialism in the Italian Route to Socialism.* *Argument* 19: 213–222.

6328. Scarritt, J. R. September 1986. The Explanation of African Politics and Society: Toward a Synthesis of Approaches. *Journal of African Studies* 13 (3): 85–93.

6329. Schabas, W. 1978. Management Rights Take Over as Industrial Democracy is Forgotten. *Pulp and Paper Canada* 79 (12): 56.

6330. Schaefer, D. 1978. Yeoman Farmers and Economic Democracy: A Study of Wealth and Economic Mobility in the Western Tobacco Region, 1850 to 1960. *Explorations in Economic History* 15 (4): 421–437.

6331. Schaefer, D. L. 1991. Leo Strauss and American Democracy: A Response to Wood and Holmes. *Review of Politics* 53 (1): 187–199.

6332. Schaefer, D. L., and T. J. Lowi. February 1988. Theodore J. Lowi and the Administrative State. *Administration and Society* 19 (4): 371–421.

6333. Schambra, W. May 1980. Martin Diamond on "Lincoln's Greatness." *Interpretation* 8 (2–3): 26–28.

6334. Scharf, B. June 1988. Teaching about Contemporary Systems. *Teaching Political Science* 15 (4): 147–153.

6335. Scharf, P. 1976. School Democracy: Thoughts and Dilemmas. *Contemporary Education* 48 (1): 29–34.

6336. Schartzman, J. January 1990. Henry George and George Bernard Shaw: Comparison and Contrast: The Two 19th Century Intellectual Leaders Stood for Ethical Democracy vs. Socialist Statism. *American Journal of Economics and Sociology* 49 (1): 113–127.

6337. Schartzman, S. 1979. Science, Technology, Technocracy and Democracy. *Interciencia* 4 (4): 215–219.

6338. Schatzberg, M. G. 1993. Power, Legitimacy, and "Democratization" in Africa. *Africa (London)* 63 (4): 445–461.

6339. Schauer, F. May 1994. Judicial Review of the Devices of Democracy. *Columbia Law Review* 94 (4): 1326–1347.

6340. Schechter, S. L. March 1981. On the Compatibility of Federalism and Intergovernmental Management. *Publius* 11 (2): 127–141.

6341. Scheck, C. L., and G. W. Bohlander. December 1990. The Planning Practices of Labor Organizations: A National Study. *Labor Studies Journal* 15 (4): 69–84.

6342. Scheele, P. E. (ed.). March 1978. Presidential Power and Democratic Constraints. *Presidential Studies Quarterly* 8: 115–214. 8 articles.

6343. Schelder, A. March 1994. The (Stubborn) Communication Structure of Democratic Elections.* *Zeitschrift für Politik* 41 (1): 22–44.

6344. Schell, O. July 1988. Capitalist Birds in a Socialist Bird Cage. *California Business* 23: 34–47.

6345. Schenck, G. V. 1975. Economic Democracy.* *Gewerkschaftliche Monatshefte* 26 (4): 251–259.

6346. Schick, A. March 1986. Macro-Budgetary Adaptations to Fiscal Stress in Industrialized Democracies. *Public Administration Review* 46 (2): 124–134.

6347. Schick, A. January 1988. Micro-Budgetary Adaptations to Fiscal Stress in Industrialized Countries. *Public Administration Review* 48 (1): 523–533.

6348. Schickler, E. December 1994. Democratizing Technology: Hierarchy and Innovation in Public Life. *Polity* 27 (2): 175–200.

6349. Schier, P. September 1989. Chinas Demokratisch Orientierte Intellektuelle Fordern die Freilassung von Wei Jingsheng und Anderen Politischen Haeftlingen. *China Aktuell* 18: 115–119.

6350. Schier, P. September 1993. Vier Jahre Danach: Ein Neuer Chronologischer Ueberblick ueber die Entwicklung und Niederschlagung der Protestbewegung von 1989. *China Aktuell* 22: 894–905.

6351. Schiff, F. 1990. Rewriting the Dirty War: State Terrorism Reinterpreted by the Press in Argentina during the Transition to Democracy. *Terrorism* 13 (4–5): 311–328.

6352. Schiffrin, L. H. September 1981. The Crisis of the Democratic Constitution in Argentina.* *Sistema* 43–44: 199–215.

6353. Schifter, R. December 1990. *See* Horn, G. (December 1990).

6354. Schifter, R. June 1994. Is There a Democratic Gene. *Washington Quarterly* 17 (3): 121–127.

6355. Schiller, B. May 1977. Industrial Democracy in Scandinavia. *Annals of the American Academy of Political and Social Science* 431: 63–73.

6356. Schinderow, B. W. 1976. *See* Sholkowski, K. E. (1976).

6357. Schirmer, D. B. May 1991. Korea and the Philippines: A Century of U.S. Intervention. *Monthly Review* 43: 19–32.

6358. Schlagneck, D. M., and J. L. Walker. April 1992. Democratizing Nations and Terrorism: The Effects of Political Violence on Civil Liberties. *Current World Leaders* 35 (2): 287–309.

6359. Schleicher, H. G. 1992. UNTAG und Der Internationale Faktor im Unabhaengigkeitsprozess Namibias. *Afrika Spectrum* 27 (3): 327–341.

6360. Schlesinger, A. 1978. Capitalism, Socialism, and Democracy. *Commentary* 65 (4): 69–70.

6361. Schlesinger, M. April 1989. Legislative Governing Coalitions in Parliamentary Democracies: The Case of the French Third Republic. *Comparative Political Studies* 22 (1): 33–65.

6362. Schlesinger, P. March 1981. "Terrorism," the Media and the Liberal-Democratic State: A Critique of the Orthodoxy. *Social Research* 48 (1): 74–99.

6363. Schliwa, H. 1977. Freedom and Democracy in Shaping of the Advanced Socialist Society.* *Deutsche Zeitschrift für Philosophie* 25 (11): 1301–1318.

6364. Schlozman, K. L., N. Burns, and S. Verba. November 1994. Gender and the Pathways to Participation: The Role of Resources. *Journal of Politics* 56 (4): 963–990.

6365. Schluchter, W. 1983. Bureaucracy and Democracy: On the Relationship of Political Efficiency and Political Freedom in Max Weber. *Current Perspectives in Social Theory* 4: 313–338.

6366. Schmaltzbruns, R. September 1992. *See* Buchstein, H. (September 1992).

6367. Schmid, A. P. December 1992. Terrorism and Democracy. *Terrorism and Political Violence* 4 (4): 14–25.

6368. Schmid, G. 1994. Reviving Athenian Democracy in California. *Notre Dame Journal of Law, Ethics and Public Policy* 8 (2): 499–527.

6369. Schmidt, A. B. November 1994. *See* Francis, W. L. (November 1994).

6370. Schmidt, H. March 1981. A Policy of Reliable Partnership. *Foreign Policy* 59 (4): 743–755.

6371. Schmidt, M. G. 1983. State and Economy in a Time of Crisis: A Comparison of 23 Industrial Democracies.* *Rivista Italiana di Scienza Politica* 13 (1): 103–137.

6372. Schmidt, M. G. July 1984. The Politics of Unemployment: Rates of Unemployment and Labour Market Policy. *West European Politics* 7: 5–24.

6373. Schmidt, M. G. July 1987. The Politics of Full Employment in Western Democracies. *Annals of the American Academy of Political and Social Science* 492: 171–181.

6374. Schmitt, M. June 1990. *See* Ornstein, N. J. (June 1990).

6375. Schmitter, P. C. December 1983. Democratic Theory and Neocorporatist Practice. *Social Research* 50 (4): 885–928.

6376. Schmitter, P. C. December 1984. Pacts and Transitions: Undemocratic Means for Democratic Ends? *Rivista Italiana di Scienza Politica* 14 (3): 363–382.

6377. Schmitter, P. C. December 1988. Five Reflections on the Future of the Welfare State. *Politics and Society* 16 (4): 503–515.

6378. Schmitter, P. C. January 1989. Idealism, System of Government and Regional Cooperation: Lessons of the Southern Cone of Latin America.* *Estudios Internacionales* 85: 78–130.

6379. Schmitter, P. C. May 1991. *See* Karl, T. L. (May 1991).

6380. Schmitter, P. C. March 1992. The Consolidation of Democracy and Representation of Social Groups. *American Behavioral Scientist* 35 (4–5): 422–449.

6381. Schmitter, P. C. December 1992. The Irony of Modern Democracy and Effort to Improve Its Practice. *Politics and Society* 20 (4): 507–512.

6382. Schmitter, P. C. April 1994. Dangers and Dilemmas of Democracy. *Journal of Democracy* 5 (2): 57–74.

6383. Schmitter, P. C. December 1994. The Proto-Science of Consolidology: Can It Improve the Outcome of Contemporary Efforts at Democratization. *Politikon* 21 (2): 15–27.

6384. Schmitter, P. C. (ed.). April 1977. Corporatism and Policy-Making in Contemporary Western Europe. *Comparative Political Studies* 10: 3–152. 5 articles.

6385. Schmitter, P. C., and T. L. Karl. June 1991. What Democracy Is . . . and Is Not. *Journal of Democracy* 2 (3): 75–88.

6386. Schmitter, P. C., and T. L. Karl. March 1994. The Conceptual Travels of Transitologists and Consolidologists: How Far to the East Should They Attempt to Go? *Slavic Review* 53 (1): 173–185.

6387. Schmitz, J. June 1980. Lateinamerika: "Redemokratisierung" und Systemsicherung im Uebergang zu den 80er Jahren. *Blaetter für Deutsche und Internationale Politik* 25 (6): 685–700.

6388. Schmitz, J. August 1980. "Redemocratisation" in Brazil. *Blaetter für Deutsche und Internationale Politik* 25 (8): 971–981.

6389. Schneck, S. November 1989. Habits of the Head: Tocqueville's America and Jazz. *Political Theory* 17 (4): 638–662.

6390. Schneck, S., W. C. McWilliams, and D. Winthrop. December 1992. New Readings of Tocqueville's "America": Lessons for Democracy. *Polity* 25 (2): 283–313.

6391. Schneider, C. December 1991. Mobilization at the Grassroots: Shantytown and Resistance in Authoritarian Chile. *Latin American Perspectives* 18 (1): 92–112.

6392. Schneider, E. May 1994. The New Parliamentary Elections in Russia, December 1993: An Overview.* *Osteuropa* 44 (5): 442–453.

6393. Schneider, F., and J. Naumann. 1982. Interest Groups in Democracies—How Influential Are They: An Empirical Examination for Switzerland. *Public Choice* 38 (3): 281–303.

6394. Schneider, P. 1988. Utopia between Alternativeness and Conservatism.* *Archiv für Rechts und Sozialphilosophie* 74 (4): 439–451.

6395. Schoenfeld, G. September 1990. *See* Masters, M. F. (September 1990).

6396. Schoenfeld, R. March 1992. Zur Lage in Rumaenien. *Suedosteuropa-Mitteilungen* 32: 203–218.

6397. Schofield, N. June 1976. The Kernel and Payoffs in European Government Coalitions. *Public Choice* 26: 29–49.

6398. Schollmeier, P. June 1988. The Democracy Most in Accordance with Equality. *History of Political Thought* 9 (2): 205–209.

6399. Schonfeld, W. R. 1986. Le RPR et l'UDF a l'Epreuve de l'Opposition. *Revue Française de Science Politique* 36 (1): 14–29.

6400. Schoonmaker, D. March 1982. Novelist and Social Scientist: Contrasting Views of Today's West German Political System. *Polity* 14 (3): 414–440.

6401. Schoonmaker, D. December 1988. The Changing Party Scene in West Germany and the Consequences for Stable Democracy. *Review of Politics* 50 (1): 49–70.

6402. Schopelin, G. April 1991. Post-Communism: Constructing New Democracies in Central Europe. *International Affairs (London)* 67 (2): 235–250.

6403. Schotland, R. A. March 1985. Elective Judges' Campaign Financing: Are State Judges' Robes the Emperor's Clothes of American Democracy? *Journal of Law and Politics* 2: 57–167.

6404. Schott, T. December 1991. The World Scientific Community: Globality and Globalisation. *Minerva* 29: 440–462.

6405. Schraeder, P. J. October 1994. Elites as Facilitators or Impediments to Political Development? Some Lessons from the "Third Wave" of Democratization in Africa. *Journal of Developing Areas* 29 (1): 69–90.

6406. Schram, G. N. May 1980. Progressive and Political Science: The Case of Charles E. Merriam. *Interpretation* 8 (2–3): 174–187.

6407. Schreiber, W. 1975. CDU-CSU and Right-Wing Social Democrats Bourgeois Concepts of Democracy and State.* *IPW Berichte* 4 (7): 20–29.

6408. Schroeder, R. C. December 28, 1986. Pinochet's Chile: What Comes Next? *Editorial Research Reports* 2 (24): 955–972.

6409. Schubert, D. February 1992. Is Gorbachev on the Right Track: Perestroika as a Transitional Process for a Free Market and Democracy. *Osteuropa* 42 (2): 110–120.

6410. Schuck, P. H. September 1989. The Civil Liability of Judges in the United States. *American Journal of Comparative Law* 37 (4): 655–673.

6411. Schudson, M. June 1994. The "Public Sphere" and its Problems: Bringing the State (Back) In. *Notre Dame Journal of Law, Ethics and Public Policy* 8: 529–546.

6412. Schuetz, R. 1983. Dezentralisierung in Spanien, Ein Beitrag zur Stabilisierung der Demokratie? *Demokratie und Recht* 11 (2): 162–173.

6413. Schuller, T. 1981. Common Discourse: The Language of Industrial Democracy. *Economic and Industrial Democracy* 2 (2): 261–291.

6414. Schultz, E. April 1993. Reform Processes and Struggle for Democratization in the Bulgarian Army.* *Osteuropa* 43 (4): 212–224.

6415. Schultze, H. 1983. Social Democracy and History.* *Filosoficky Casopis* 31 (3): 410–417.

6416. Schumacher, E. June 1984. Argentina and Democracy. *Foreign Affairs* 62 (5): 1070–1095.

6417. Schumacher, K. 1982. The Permanent Erosion of Industrial Democracy in West Germany.* *IPW Berichte* 11 (6): 35–40.

6418. Schumaker, P. December 1994. Democratic Ideals and Economic Imperatives in the Resolution of Downtown Redevelopment Issues. *State and Local Government Review* 26 (1): 7–20.

6419. Schuman, H. May 1994. *See* Bischoping, K. (May 1994).

6420. Schumann, M. 1981. Democracy and Socialism: The Dialectics of the Marxist-Leninist Party Democracy and State Power in the Socialist Society.* *Staat und Recht* 30 (10): 866–878.

6421. Schumichin, N. F. 1976. *See* Sholkowski, K. E. (1976).

6422. Schvarzer, J. 1983. Inflacion y Democracia: Los Peligros Latentes. *Realidad Economica* 5: 33–44.

6423. Schwab, S. J. 1992. Union Raids, Union Democracy, and the Market for Union Control. *University of Illinois Law Review* (2): 367–416.

6424. Schwarcz, V. March 1991. No Solace from Lethe: History, Memory, and Cultural Identity in Twentieth-Century China. *Daedalus* 120 (2): 85–112.

6425. Schwartz, B. April 1991. Social Change and Collective Memory: The Democratization of George Washington. *American Sociological Review* 56 (2): 221–236.

6426. Schwartz, D. E. March 1983. Shareholder Democracy: A Reality or Chimera? *California Management Review* 25 (3): 53–67.

6427. Schwartz, J. March 1985. The Penitentiary and Perfectibility in Tocqueville. *Western Political Quarterly* 38 (1): 7–26.

6428. Schwartz, P. June 1981. A Traditional Coup. *Policy Review* 17: 31–35.

6429. Schwartzman, K. 1989. Democratic Instability in Semi-peripheral Countries: The Case of Portugal.* *Dados* 32 (2): 203–224.

6430. Schwarz, G. 1992. Market Economy and Democracy: A Love-Hate Relationship.* *Ordo* 43: 65–90.

6431. Schwarzer, W. W. September 1993. Democracy's Dawn: American Judges and the Rule of Law Abroad. *Judges' Journal* 31: 34–38.

6432. Schweickart, D. March 1992. Economic Democracy: A Worthy Socialism That Would Really Work. *Science and Society* 56 (1): 9–38.

6433. Schweitzer, A. 1990. Democracy and Charisma. *Sociologia Internationalis* 28 (1): 27–41.

6434. Schweller, R. L. January 1992. Domestic Structure and Preventive War: Are Democracies More Pacific? *World Politics* 44 (2): 235–269.

6435. Sciarra, S. 1977. Democrazia Industriale Fra Partecipazione e Contrattazione: Il Rapporto. *Politica del Diritto* 8 (6): 683–696.

6436. Sciortino, J. August 1986. *See* Tidmarch, C. M. (August 1986).

6437. Sciuer, S. E. October 1984. *See* Hutter, J. L. (October 1984).

6438. Sclove, R. 1982. Decision Making in a Democracy. *Bulletin of the Atomic Scientists* 38 (5): 44–49.

6439. Scorza, T. J. May 1980. Comment: The Politics of Martin Diamond's Science. *Interpretation* 8 (2–3): 16–21.

6440. Scott, C. V. March 1992. *See* Cochran, A. B. (March 1992).

6441. Scott, J. V. 1987. *See* Elliott, J. E. (1987).

6442. Scott, W. B. March 1983. *See* Rutkoff, P. M. (March 1983).

6443. Scranton, M. E. March 1992. Panama's Democratic Transition. *Midsouth Political Science Journal* 13: 107–128.

6444. Scully, T. R., and J. S. Valenzuela. December 1993. De la Democracia a la Democracia: Continuidad y Variaciones en las Preferencias del Electorado y en el Sistema de Partidos en Chile. *Estudios Publicos* 51: 195–228.

6445. Scupin, R. December 1980. The Politics of Islamic Reformism in Thailand. *Asian Survey* 20 (12): 1223–1235.

6446. Seaga, E. September 1980. Central America and the Caribbean: The Continuing Crisis. *World Affairs* 143 (2): 136–144.

6447. Sebastian, L. March 1985. Recession, Debts and Counter-Insurgency in Latin America.* *Afers Internacionals* 6: 23–38.

6448. Sederberg, P. C., and M. W. Taylor. March 1981. The Political Economy of No-Growth. *Policy Studies Journal* 9 (5): 735–755.

6449. Sedov, L. November 1992. Russia: The Narrow Road toward Democracy.* *Etudes* 447–458.

6450. Segal, A. March 1985. Caribbean Realities. *Current History* 84 (500): 127–130, 134–135.

6451. Segal, A. December 1988. Caribbean Complexities. *Current History* 87 (533): 413–416, 434–437.

6452. Segal, D. R. March 1994. National Security and Democracy in the United States. *Armed Forces and Society* 20 (3): 375–393.

6453. Segre, D. V., and J. S. Szyliowecz. March 1981. The Islamic Revival. *Washington Quarterly* 4 (2): 126–137.

6454. Segre, S. July 1991. Alternative Concepts of Democracy: Weber and Schumpeter.* *Rassegna Italiana di Sociologia* 22 (3): 313–333.

6455. Seidelman, R. July 1981. Urban Movements and Communist Power in Florence. *Comparative Politics* 13 (4): 437–459.

6456. Seidelman, R. 1989. The Short, Sweet Song of Chinese Democracy. *Dissent* 36 (4): 425–427.

6457. Seidman, L. M. March 1988. Ambivalence and Accountability. *Southern California Law Review* 61: 1571–1600.

6458. Seidman, R. B. June 1979. Development Planning and Legal Order in Black Anglophonic Africa. *Studies in Comparative International Development* 14 (2): 3–27.

6459. Seifert, W. 1988. Some Thoughts on the Problem of Internal Union Democracy in Japan. *Economic and Industrial Democracy* 9 (3): 373–395.

6460. Sejersted, F. 1979. Democracy and the Rule of Law: Some Historical Experiences of Contradictions in the Striving for Good Government. *Social Science Information* 18 (6): 945–966.

6461. Sekun, V. I. 1992. Participative Ruling and Democracy.* *Sotsiologicheskie Issledovaniia* (2): 70–75.

6462. Selassie, A. G. Fall 1992a. Ethnic Identity and Constitutional Design for Africa. *Stanford Journal of International Law* 29: 1–56.

6463. Selassie, A. G. Fall 1992b. Ethiopia: Problems and Prospects for Democracy. *William and Mary Bill of Rights Journal* 1 (2): 205–226.

6464. Selcher, W. A. June 1989. A New Start toward a More Decentralized Federalism in Brazil? *Publius* 19: 167–183.

6465. Seleny, A. 1994. Constructing the Discourse of Transformation: Hungary, 1979–1982. *East European Politics and Societies* 8 (3): 439–466.

6466. Seleznev, M. A. 1980. Democracy and Revolution. *Soviet Studies in Philosophy* 18 (3): 40–62.

6467. Seligson, M. A. January 1983. *See* Caspi, D. (January 1983).

6468. Seligson, M. A. October 1987. *See* Muller, E. N. (October 1987).

6469. Seligson, M. A. September 1994. *See* Muller, E. N. (September 1994).

6470. Seligson, M. A., and E. N. Muller. September 1987. Democratic Stability and Economic Crisis: Costa Rica, 1978–1983. *International Studies Quarterly* 31: 301–326.

6471. Seligson, M. A., and E. N. Muller. 1990. Estabilidad Democratica y Crisis Economica: Costa Rica, 1978–1983. *Anuario de Estudios Centroamericanos* 16–17: 71–92.

6472. Selverstone, R. 1991. Sexuality Education Can Strengthen Democracy. *Educational Leadership* 49 (1): 58–60.

6473. Semetko, H. A. August 1987. *See* Blumler, J. G. (August 1987).

6474. Semi-Bi, Z. October 1986. Genesis of "Ivorian Style Democracy." A Critical Evaluation of Parliamentary Activity in the Ivory Coast during the Sixth Legislature, 1980–1985.* *Le Mois en Afrique* 249–250: 15–32.

6475. Semsay, V. October 1992. The Political Transition in Hungary, 1989–1990.* *Revista de Estudios Politicos* 78: 241–253.

6476. Semyonov, M. June 1979. *See* Tyree, A. (June 1979).

6477. Sen, S. 1991. The Left and Democracy. *Economic and Political Weekly* 26 (46): 2614–2616.

6478. Senese, D. J. September 1986. Factors Blocking Democratic Reform in the PRC. *Journal of Social, Political, and Economic Studies* 11: 289–315.

6479. Seng, M. P. December 1985. Democracy in Nigeria. *Black Law Journal* 9: 113–166.

6480. Sengupta, M. 1974. On a Concept of Representative Democracy. *Theory and Decision* 5 (3): 249–262.

6481. Sengupta, N. 1987. The Philippines: Towards New Democracy. *Economic and Political Weekly* 22 (4): 124–125.

6482. Seong, K. May 1993. *See* Lipset, S. M. (May 1993).

6483. Sepulveda, C. January 1988. The Internationalization of Human Rights: Obstacles to Their Present Progress.* *Boletin Mexicano de Derecho Comparado* 61: 295–316.

6484. Serafino, N. M. March 1988. Dateline Managua: Defining Democracy. *Foreign Policy* (70): 166–182.

6485. Serbinenko, V. V. December 18, 1993. Russian Idea and Prospects for Democracy. *Economic and Political Weekly* 28 (51): 2793+.

6486. Serbinenko, V. V. 1994. On the Prospects of Democracy in Russia.* *Sotsiologicheskie Issledovaniia* (4): 17–29.

6487. Serfaty, M. May 1981. Spanish Democracy: The End of the Transition. *Current History* 80 (466): 213–217, 227–228.

6488. Serlin, R. C. June 1981. *See* Lonky, E. (June 1981).

6489. Serna, M. November 1993. *See* Mallo, S. (November 1993).

6490. Seroka, J. H. February 1979. Legislative Recruitment and Political Change in Yugoslavia. *Legislative Studies Quarterly* 4 (1): 105–120.

6491. Serra, L. March 1991. Wartime and Socialist Crisis Democracy: Reflections Based on the Sandinist Revolution.* *Socialismo y Participacion* 53: 1–33.

6492. Serra, L. March 1993. Democracy in Times of War and Socialist Crisis: Reflections from the Sandinista Revolution. *Latin American Perspectives* 20 (2): 21–44.

6493. Serra, P. July 1993. Metaphysics and Democracy in Augusto del Noce.* *Democrazia e Diritto* 33 (3): 373–382.

6494. Serra Rexach, D. E. December 1987. Spain: Politics and Change. *Washington Quarterly* 10 (1): 23–27.

6495. Sestanovich, S. September 1991. The Hour of the Demagogue. *National Interest* (25): 3–15.

6496. Seth, S. P. October 8, 1994. Australia's Aboriginal Problem. *Economic and Political Weekly* 29 (41): 2661–2663.

6497. Settle, A. K. June 1975. *See* Lutrin, C. E. (June 1975).

6498. Setzer, H. March 1994. Schumpeter's Theory and the Practice of British Democracy.* *Zeitschrift für Politik* 41 (1): 45–74.

6499. Sewart, J. J. October 1981. Alvin Gouldner's Challenge to Sociology and Marxism: The Problem of Bureaucracy. *Pacific Sociological Review* 24 (4): 441–460.

6500. Sewell, J. W., and C. E. Contee. June 1987. Foreign Aid and Gramm-Rudman. *Foreign Affairs* 65 (5): 1015–1036.

6501. Sewell, W. H. March 1992. Some Observations and Reflections on the Role of Women and Minorities in the Democratization of the American Sociological Association, 1905–1990. *American Sociologist* 23 (1): 56–62.

6502. Seyd, P. 1975. Democracy within the Conservative-Party. *Government and Opposition* 10 (2): 219–237.

6503. Seymour, J. D. January 1988. Taiwan in 1987: A Year of Political Bombshells. *Asian Survey* 28 (1): 71–77.

6504. Seymour, J. D. January 1989. Taiwan in 1988: No More Bandits. *Asian Survey* 29 (1): 54–63.

6505. Shabad, G. March 1978. *See* Verba, S. (March 1978).

6506. Shabad, G. July 1980. Strikes in Yugoslavia: Implications for Industrial Democracy. *British Journal of Political Science* 10: 293–315.

6507. Shablinskii, I. G. March 1992. The Workers Question in the Context of Democratization: Reflections on the Sources and Certain Prospects of the Mass Labor Movement in the USSR. *Soviet Law and Government* 30 (4): 5–20.

6508. Shackleton, V. J. 1979. *See* Bass, B. M. (1979).

6509. Shackleton, V. J. 1979. *See* Bass, B. M. (1979).

6510. Shafer, B. E. July 1991. Roberto Michels,Vilfredo Pareto, and Henry Jones Ford: Classical Insights and the Structure of Contemporary American Politics. *International Political Science Review* 12 (3): 185–218.

6511. Shafgat, S. 1990. Political Culture of Pakistan: A Case of Disharmony between Democratic Creed and Autocratic Reality. *South Asia Bulletin* 10 (2): 42–47.

6512. Shafir, M. June 26, 1992. Transylvanian Shadows, Transylvanian Lights. *RFE/RL Research Report* 1: 28–33.

6513. Shahin, E. E., and A. Maghraoui. July 1992. Algeria: Politics and Crisis. *Middle East Insight* 8: 10–26.

6514. Shahin, M., and P. Feuilherade. August 1992. King Hussein Keeps His Balance. *Middle East* 20–21.

6515. Shaikh, F. March 1986. Islam and the Quest for Democracy in Pakistan. *Journal of Commonwealth and Comparative Politics* 24 (1): 74–82.

6516. Shain, Y. January 1991. *See* Berat, L. (January 1991).

6517. Shain, Y. June 1991. *See* Barzilai, G. (June 1991).

6518. Shain, Y., and J. J. Linz. January 1992. The Role of Interim Governments. *Journal of Democracy* 3 (1): 73–89.

6519. Shain, Y., and M. Thompson. January 1990. The Role of Political Exiles in Democratic Transitions: The Case of the Philippines. *Journal of Developing Societies* 6 (1): 71–86.

6520. Shalhope, R. E. April 1992. Republicanism, Liberalism, and Democracy: Political Culture in the Early Republic. *Proceedings of the American Antiquarian Society* 102: 99–152.

6521. Shalin, D. N. June 1990. Sociology for the Glasnost Era: Institutional and Substantive Changes in Recent Soviet Sociology. *Social Forces* 68 (4): 1019–1039.

6522. Shalin, H. J. June 1991. Futility. *Journal of Ethnic Studies* 19 (2): 1–16.

6523. Shamim, C. M. December 1994. Civil-Military Relations and the Future of Democracy in Bangladesh. *Journal of Political and Military Sociology* 22 (2): 351–366.

6524. Shamir, M. 1991. Political Intolerance among Masses and Elites in Israel: A Reevaluation of the Elitist Theory of Democracy. *Journal of Politics* 53 (4): 1018–1043.

6525. Shamir, M. December 1993. *See* Arian, A. (December 1993).

6526. Shamir, M., and J. L. Sullivan. June 1985. Jews and Arabs in Israel: Everybody Hates Somebody, Sometime. *Journal of Conflict Resolution* 29 (2): 283–305.

6527. Shank, G. March 1992. Global Change and Social Justice: An Introduction. *Social Justice* 19 (1): iv-xx.

6528. Shannon, J. B. August 1976. Bicentennial Reflections on Party Government. *Journal of Politics* 38 (3): 128–145.

6529. Shapiro, I. October 1993. Democratic Innovation: South Africa in Comparative Context. *World Politics* 46 (1): 121–150.

6530. Shapiro, I. February 1994. Three Ways to Be a Democrat. *Political Theory* 22 (1): 124–151.

6531. Shapiro, R. Y. March 1994. *See* Jacobs, L. R. (March 1994).

6532. Shaplen, R. April 1975. Southeast Asia: Before and After. *Foreign Affairs* 53 (3): 533–557.

6533. Share, D. 1986. Democratization of Spain. *Center Magazine* 19 (3): 54–59.

6534. Share, D. September 1986. The Franquist Regime and the Dilemma of Succession. *Review of Politics* 48 (4): 549–575.

6535. Share, D. January 1987. Transition to Democracy and Transition through Transaction. *Comparative Political Studies* 19 (4): 525–548.

6536. Share, D. October 1988. Dilemmas of Social Democracy in the 1980s: The Spanish Socialist Workers Party in Comparative Perspective. *Comparative Political Studies* 21 (3): 408–435.

6537. Share, D., and S. Mainwaring. 1986. Transition through Transaction: Democratization in Brazil and Spain.* *Dados* 29 (2): 207–236.

6538. Share, D., and S. Mainwaring. January 1986. Negotiated Transitions: Democratization in Brazil and Spain.* *Revista de Estudios Politicos* 49: 87–135.

6539. Sharkansky, I. March 1989. The Overloaded State. *Public Administration Review* 49 (2): 201–204.

6540. Sharma, S. October 1993. *See* Tamandonfar, M. (October 1993).

6541. Sharma, S. D. September 1986. Democracy in India—Its Ecology. *Journal of Political Studies* 19 (2): 67–80.

6542. Sharma, S. D. December 1994. Indian Democracy and the Crisis of Governability. *The Fletcher Forum of World Affairs* 18: 147–157.

6543. Sharp, E. B. September 1984. Need, Awareness, and the Contacting Propensity: Study of a City with a Central Complaint Unit. *Urban Affairs Quarterly* 20 (1): 22–30.

6544. Sharpe, K. E. June 1982. *See* Bennett, D. C. (June 1982).

6545. Sharpe, K. E. June 1984. *See* Bennett, D. C. (June 1984).

6546. Sharpe, K. E. December 1989. *See* Blachman, M. J. (December 1989).

6547. Sharpe, K. E., and M. Diskin. March 1984. Facing Facts in El Salvador: Reconciliation or War. *World Policy Journal* 1 (3): 517–547.

6548. Sharpe, L. J. July 1988. The Growth and Decentralization of the Modern Democratic State. *European Journal of Political Research* 16 (4): 365–380.

6549. Shatalin, S. December 1992. *See* Alekseev, S. (December 1992).

6550. Shaw, T. M. 1990. Popular Participation in Nongovernmental Structures in Africa: Implications for Democratic Development. *Africa Today* 37 (3): 5–22.

6551. Shayegan, D. 1992. Islam, Modernity, and Democracy.* *Le Trimestre du Monde* 17: 53–60.

6552. Shechtman, Z. September 1993. Education for Democracy: Assessment of an Intervention That Integrates Political and Psychosocial Aims. *Youth and Society* 25 (1): 126–139.

6553. Sheinin, D. December 1993. Making Democracy Safe for the World: The Neo-Liberal Agenda and the New Isolationism in Relations with Latin America. *International Journal* 48 (1): 100–123.

6554. Shelley, F. M. 1984. Spatial Effects on Voting Power in Representative Democracies. *Environment and Planning C: Government and Policy* 16 (3): 401–405.

6555. Shelley, F. M. 1985. *See* Reynolds, D. R. (1985).

6556. Shelley, F. M. 1987. *See* Soloman, B. D. (1987).

6557. Shen, M. C. November 1994. Peking's Report on Women's Position. *Issues and Studies* 30 (11): 125–129.

6558. Shen, T. March 1992. Will China Be Democratic? *World Affairs* 154 (4): 139–154.

6559. Sheng, C. 1981. The Second Sequel to the Fifth Modernization: Democracy and Others. *Issues and Studies* 17 (9): 86–92.

6560. Shepherd, A. May 1992. Is Democracy Good for Business? *African Business:* 12–13.

6561. Shepherd, P. L. September 1984. The Tragic Course and Consequence of U.S. Policy in Honduras. *World Policy Journal* 2 (1): 109–154.

6562. Shepherd, P. L. 1986. Versaeumte Gelegenheiten: Das Problem Formaler Demokratie in Honduras. *Lateinamerika (Hamburg)* (6–7): 45–56.

6563. Sher, G. December 1989. Educating Citizens. *Philosophy and Public Affairs* 18 (1): 68–80.

6564. Sherman, L. W. 1975. Middle Management and Police Democratization: Reply. *Criminology* 12 (4): 363–377.

6565. Sherman, R. R. 1974. Vocational Education and Democracy. *Studies in Philosophy and Education* 8 (3): 205–223.

6566. Sherover, C. M. May 1980. Rousseau's Civil Religion. *Interpretation* 8 (2–3): 114–122.

6567. Sherry, S. 1984. Selective Judicial Activism in the Equal Protection Context: Democracy, Distrust, and Deconstruction. *Georgetown Law Review* 73 (1): 89–125.

6568. Shevtsova, L. September 1994. Russia Facing New Choices: Contradictions of Post-Communist Development. *Security Dialogue* 25 (3): 321–334.

6569. Shi, T. December 1990. The Democratic Movement in China in 1989: Dynamics and Failure. *Asian Survey* 30 (12): 1186–1205.

6570. Shi, T. March 1993. *See* Nathan, A. J. (March 1993).

6571. Shi, Z. T. October 1993. *See* Hage, J. (October 1993).

6572. Shils, E. December 1989. The Modern University and Liberal Democracy. *Minerva* 27 (4): 425–460.

6573. Shils, E. 1992. The Universities, the Social Sciences, and Liberal Democracy. *Interchange* 23 (1–2): 183–223.

6574. Shin, D. C. January 1989. Political Democracy and the Quality of Citizens' Lives: A Cross-National Study. *Journal of Developing Societies* 5 (1): 30–41.

6575. Shin, D. C. October 1994. On the Third Wave of Democratization: A Synthesis and Evaluation of Recent Theory and Research. *World Politics* 47 (1): 135–170.

6576. Shin, D. C., M. Chey, and K. Kim. July 1989. Cultural Origins of Public Support for Democracy in Korea: An Empirical Test of the Douglas-Wildavsky Theory of Culture. *Comparative Political Studies* 22 (2): 217–238.

6577. Shirts, M. March 1989. Socrates, Corinthians, and Democracy. *Wilson Quarterly* 13 (2): 119–123.

6578. Shiu-hing, L. 1992. Taiwan, Business People, Intellectuals, and Democratization. *Pacific Review* 5 (4): 382–389.

6579. Shklar, J. N. November 1990. Emerson and the Inhibitions of Democracy. *Political Theory* 18 (4): 601–614.

6580. Shockley, J. S. May 1985. Direct Democracy, Campaign Finance, and the Courts: Can Corruption, Undue Influence, and Declining Voter Confidence Be Found? *University of Miami Law Review* 39: 377–428.

6581. Sholkowski, K. E., B. W. Schinderow, and N. F. Schumichin. 1976. Contemporary Revolutionary Democracy and Nationalism.* *Sowjetwissenschaft: Gesellschaft Wissenschaftliche Beitrage* 29 (8): 819–825.

6582. Shorett, A. September 1977. *See* Kauffman, K. G. (September 1977).

6583. Shorris, E. 1978. Market Democracy. *Harpers* 257: 93–96.

6584. Shorrock, T. October 1986. The Struggle for Democracy in South Korea in the 1980s and the Rise of Anti-Americanism. *Third World Quarterly* 8 (4): 1195–1218.

6585. Shortridge, R. M. March 1980. Democracy's Golden Age? Voter Turnout in the Midwest, 1840–1872. *Social Science Quarterly* 60 (4): 617–629.

6586. Shraderfrechette, K. March 1992. Science, Democracy, and Public Policy. *Critical Review* 6 (2–3): 255–264.

6587. Shubert, A. June 1984. The Military Threat to Spanish Democracy: A Historical Perspective. *Armed Forces and Society* 10 (4): 529–542.

6588. Shue, V. January 1992. China: Transition Postponed? *Problems of Communism* 41: 157–169.

6589. Shuetsova, O. V. February 1994. *See* Ordeshook, P. C. (February 1994).

6590. Shugart, M. S. December 1987. States, Revolutionary Conflict, and Democracy: El Salvador and Nicaragua in

Comparative Perspective. *Government and Opposition* 22 (1): 13–32.

6591. Shugart, M. S. March 1992. Leaders, Rank and File, and Contituents: Electoral Reform in Colombia and Venezuela. *Electoral Studies* 11: 21–45.

6592. Shugart, M. S., and R. Taagepera. October 1994. Plurality Versus Majority Election of Presidents: A Proposal for a Double Complement Rule. *Comparative Political Studies* 27 (3): 323–348.

6593. Shultz, G. May 1983. Struggle for Democracy in Central America. *Department of State Bulletin* 83: 10–13.

6594. Shultz, G. January 1985. Democracy and the Path to Economic Growth. *Department of State Bulletin* 85: 1–5.

6595. Shultz, G. March 1985. New Realities and New Ways of Thinking. *Foreign Affairs* 63 (4): 705–721.

6596. Shultz, G. April 1986. Nicaragua: Will Democracy Prevail? *Department of State Bulletin* 86: 32–39.

6597. Shultz, G. August 1986. Reform in the Philippines and American Interests: The U.S. Role in Consolidating Democracy. *Department of State Bulletin* 86: 26–30.

6598. Shumer, S. M. February 1979. Machiavelli: Republican Politics and Its Corruption. *Political Theory* 7 (1): 5–34.

6599. Shveitser, V. I. 1987. Social Democracy and the Anti-War Movement in Western Europe. *Soviet Law and Government* 25 (3): 30–52.

6600. Sibiljow, N. G. 1975. Some Problems of Cooperation of Communists and Social Democrats in Struggle for Peace, Democracy and Social Progress.* *Sowjetwissenschaft: Gesellschaft Wissenschaftliche Beitrage* 28 (2): 143–159.

6601. Siccama, J. G. October 1974. Economy and Democracy in the Government of a State: A Critical Reaction.* *Acta Politica* 9 (4): 413–422.

6602. Sicker, M. March 1993. Democracy and Judaism: The Question of Equality. *Jewish Political Studies Review* 5 (1–2): 57–78.

6603. Sid-Ahmed, M. June 1990. Initiatives for Deepening Democracy in the Middle East. *Alternatives* 15 (3): 345–354.

6604. Siddiqi, M. A. 1991. Muslim Media: Present Status and Future Directions. *Gazette* 47 (1): 19–31.

6605. Sidicaro, R. 1986. Trois Années de Democratie en Argentine (1983–1986). *Notes et Etudes Documentaires* 82: 7–26.

6606. Sidjanski, D. 1978. Switzerland: The Power of the Governed, the Power of Prejudices.* *Pouvoirs* 7: 115–119.

6607. Siegelbaum, L. H. April 1980. The Worker's Groups and the War-Industries Committees: Who Used Whom? *Russian Review* 39 (2): 150–180.

6608. Siegle, G. B. June 1977. *See* Bjur, W. E. (June 1977).

6609. Siemers, G. December 10, 1988. Governmental Change in Burma: Change of System?* *Europa Archiv: Zeitschrift für Internationale Politik* 43 (23): 687–696.

6610. Siemers, G. October 3, 1990. Myanmar (Burma) on the Road towards Democracy?* *Aus Politik und Zeitgeschichte* 32: 36–44.

6611. Siemers, G. November 10, 1990. Mongolia on the Road to Democracy?* *Europa Archiv: Zeitschrift für Internationale Politik* 45 (21): 632–638.

6612. Siemineska, R. 1994. Continuity or Change? The Woman's Role in Polish Public Life since the Fall of the Communist Regime. *Social Politics* 1 (3): 326–334.

6613. Sievers, M. July 1985. *See* Dauer, M. J. (July 1985).

6614. Sigel, R. S. February 1979. Students' Comprehension of Democracy and Its Application to Conflict Situations. *In-*

ternational *Journal of Political Education* 2 (1): 47–65.

6615. Sigelman, L., and A. K. Karnig. April 1976. Black Representation in the American States: A Comparison of Bureaucracies and Legislatures. *American Politics Quarterly* 4 (2): 237–246.

6616. Sigelman, L., and N. Y. Syng. October 1978. Left-Right Polarization in National Party Systems: A Cross-National Analysis. *Comparative Political Studies* 11 (3): 355–379.

6617. Sigelman, L., and W. G. Vanderbok. March 1978. The Saving Grace? Bureaucratic Power and American Democracy. *Polity* 10 (3): 440–447.

6618. Sigmund, P. E. January 1985. Latin America: Debt and Democracy. *Freedom at Issue* 82: 25–27.

6619. Sigmund, P. E. January 1986. Revolution, Counterrevolution, and the Catholic Church in Chile. *Annals of the American Academy of Political and Social Science* 483: 25–35.

6620. Sigmund, P. E. September 1987. The Catholic Tradition and Modern Democracy. *Review of Politics* 49 (4): 530–548.

6621. Sigur, G. J. July 1986. Prospects for Continuing Democratization in Korea. *Department of State Bulletin* 86: 46–48.

6622. Sigurdson, R. F. June 1990. Jacob Burckhardt: The Cultural Historian as Political Thinker. *Review of Politics* 52 (3): 417–440.

6623. Siisiainen, M. 1983. On the Theoretical Origins of the Problem of Democracy and Organization Which Have Been Posed by New Social Movements.* *Politiika* 25 (2): 103–117.

6624. Siklova, J. June 1990. The "Gray Zone" and the Future of Dissent in Czechoslovakia. *Social Research* 57 (2): 347–363.

6625. Silant'Ev, A. 1989. Latin America: The Search for a Democratic Idea.* *Mirovaja Ekonomika i Mezdunarodnye Otnosenja* 8: 84–90.

6626. Silva, E. December 1992. Capitalist Regime Loyalties and Redemocratization in Chile. *Journal of Interamerican Studies and World Affairs* 34 (4): 77–117.

6627. Silva, G. R. June 1987. Peru: Crisis and Democracy. *Etudes* 747–758.

6628. Silva, G. R. June 1988. Crisis, Democracy, and the Left in Peru. *Latin American Perspectives* 15 (3): 77–96.

6629. Silver, B. D. July 1990. *See* Bahry, D. (July 1990).

6630. Silver, M. March 1977. Economic Theory of the Constitutional Separation of Powers. *Public Choice* 29: 95–107.

6631. Silverman, M. July 1989. *See* Bradlow, D. A. (July 1989).

6632. Silverstein, J. October 1990. Aung San Suu Kyi: Is She Burma's Woman of Destiny? *Asian Survey* 30 (10): 1007–1019.

6633. Silvert, K. H. 1975. Democracy in Latin America. *New Republic* 172 (12): 19–21.

6634. Sim, B. 1994. Engendering Democracy: Social Citizenship and Political Participation for Women in Scandinavia. *Social Policy* 1 (3): 286–305.

6635. Simecka, M. June 1990. The Restoration of Freedom [in Czechoslovakia]. *Journal of Democracy* 1 (3): 3–12.

6636. Simeon, J. P. 1984. The Individual, Liberty, Equality and Democracy According to Louis Dumont.* *Cahiers Vilfredo Pareto* 22 (68): 95–108.

6637. Simes, D. March 1991. Gorbachev's Time of Troubles. *Foreign Policy* (82): 97–117.

6638. Simkins, C. July 1987. Democracy and Government: A Post-Leninist Perspective. *South Africa International* 18 (1): 19–29.

6639. Simmons, A. J. June 1984. Consent, Free Choice, and Democratic Government. *Georgia Law Review* 18: 791–819.

6640. Simon, A. December 1994. *See* Ansolabehere, S. (December 1994).

6641. Simon, G., and L. Jose. July 1991. La Sociedad Civil en America Latina: Diagnostico y Perspectiva de Organizacion en la Inmediata Posguerra Fria. *Perspectiva Internacional Paraguaya* 3: 123–168.

6642. Simon, M. D., and D. M. Olson. May 1980. Evolution of a Minimal Parliament: Membership and Committee Changes in the Polish Sejm. *Legislative Studies Quarterly* 5 (2): 211–232.

6643. Simonds, A. P. September 1982. On Being Informed. *Theory and Society* 11 (5): 587–616.

6644. Simons, M. June 1981. Guatemala: The Coming Danger. *Foreign Policy* 43: 93–103.

6645. Simpson, M. October 1990. Political Rights and Income Inequality: A Cross-National Test. *American Sociological Review* 55 (5): 682–693.

6646. Sindjoun, L. 1994. Cameroon: The Political System and the Stakes of Democratic Transitions, 1990–1993.* *L'Afrique Politique* 143–165.

6647. Sineau, M. November 1992. Women Never Stormed the Bastille and Political Inequality between the Sexes in European Democracies.* *Histoire* (160): 8–11.

6648. Singal, D. J. October 1984. Beyond Consensus: Richard Hofstadter and American Historiography. *American Historical Review* 89 (4): 976–1004.

6649. Singer, M. September 1990. Militarism and Democracy in El Salvador. *Society* 27 (6): 49–56.

6650. Singer, W. September 1986. *See* Hauser, W. (September 1986).

6651. Singh, B. P. October 1984. India's Fragmented Democracy. *Worldview* 27: 8–10.

6652. Singh, D. S. R. February 1986. Brunei in 1985: Domestic Factors, Political and Economic Externalities. *Asian Survey* 26 (2): 168–173.

6653. Singh, M. P. August 1990. The Crisis of the Indian State: From Quiet Developmentalism to Noisy Democracy. *Asian Survey* 30 (8): 809–819.

6654. Singh, R. November 1993. Nationalism and Progressive Politics In India. *Monthly Review* 45: 11–27.

6655. Singhvi, G. C. July 1979. Towards a Model of Democratic Government. *Administrative Change* 7 (1): 88–95.

6656. Sinopoli, R. C. December 1994. Association Freedom, Equality, and Rights against the State. *Political Research Quarterly* 47 (4): 891–908.

6657. Sirianni, C. 1983. Councils and Parliaments: The Problems of Dual Power and Democracy in Comparative Perspective. *Politics and Society* 12 (1): 83–123.

6658. Sirowy, L., and A. Inkeles. March 1990. The Effects of Democracy on Economic Growth and Inequality: A Review. *Studies in Comparative International Development* 25 (1): 126–157.

6659. Sisk, T. D. March 1992. Divided We Stand? Institutional Choice in Individual Societies: Designs for Democracy. *Southeastern Political Review* 20 (1): 1–27.

6660. Sisk, T. D. January 1993. The Violence Negotiation Nexus: South Africa in Transition and the Politics of Uncertainty. *Negotiation Journal* 9: 77–94.

6661. Sitton, J. F. September 1987. Hannah Arendt's Argument for Council Democracy. *Polity* 20 (1): 80–100.

6662. Sivan, E. March 1987. The Islamic Republic of Egypt. *Orbis* 31 (1): 43–53.

6663. Siverman, M. July 1989. *See* Bradlow, D. A. (July 1989).

6664. Siverson, R. M., and J. Emmons. June 1991. Birds of a Feather: Democratic Political Systems and Alliance Choices in the Twentieth Century. *Journal of Conflict Resolution* 32 (2): 285–306.

6665. Sives, A. October 1993. Elite Behavior and Corruption in the Consolidation of Democracy in Brazil. *Parliamentary Affairs* 46 (4): 549–562.

6666. Skard, T. 1982. Elections to Municipal Councils, Party Rule or Voters Democracy.* *Tidsskrift für Samfunnsforskning* 23 (4): 359–382.

6667. Skillen, J. W. June 1982. Religion and Political Development in 19th-Century Holland. *Publius* 12 (3): 43–64.

6668. Sklar, R. L. October 1987. Developmental Democracy. *Comparative Studies in Society and History* 29 (4): 686–714.

6669. Sklar, R. L., and M. Strege. May 1992. Finding Peace through Democracy in Sahelian Africa. *Current History* 91 (565): 224–229.

6670. Skocpol, T. December 1984. *See* Orloff, A. S. (December 1984).

6671. Skurski, J. April 1991. *See* Coronil, F. (April 1991).

6672. Slabbert, F. v. Z. July 1992. Dilemmas for Democracy in South Africa. *South Africa International* 23: 4–10.

6673. Slater, D. 1987. Socialism, Democracy and the Territorial Imperative: Elements for a Comparison of the Cuban and Nicaraguan Experiences.* *Estudios Sociales Centroamericanos* (44): 20–40.

6674. Slater, P., and W. G. Bennis. 1990. Democracy Is Inevitable. *Harvard Business Review* 68 (5): 167–176.

6675. Slater, R. O. February 1994. Symbolic Educational Leadership and Democracy in America. *Educational Administration Quarterly* 30 (1): 97–101.

6676. Slider, D. December 1990. The Soviet Union. *Electoral Studies* 9 (4): 295–302.

6677. Sloan, J. W. December 1979. Regionalism, Political Parties and Public Policy in Colombia. *Inter-American Economic Affairs* 33 (3): 25–46.

6678. Sloan, J. W. March 1981. Bureaucracy and Public Policy in Latin America. *Inter-American Economic Affairs* 34 (4): 17–47.

6679. Sloan, J. W. 1989. The Policy Capabilities of Democratic Regimes in Latin America. *Latin American Research Review* 24 (2): 113–126.

6680. Slovic, P. December 1993. Perceived Risk, Trust, and Democracy. *Risk Analysis* 13 (6): 675–682.

6681. Smart, P. 1990. "Some Will Be More Equal Than Others": J. S. Mill on Democracy, Freedom and Meritocracy. *Archiv für Rechts und Sozialphilosophie* 76 (3): 308–323.

6682. Smirnov, W. 1991. Domestic and Global Aspects of Democratization in the USSR.* *Sciences Sociales (Moscow)* 84: 89–103.

6683. Smith, A. 1986. History and Liberty: Dilemmas of Loyalty in Western Democracies. *Ethnic and Racial Studies* 9 (1): 43–65.

6684. Smith, A. A. April 1985. Kant's Political Philosophy: Rechtsstaat or Council Democracy? *Review of Politics* 47 (2): 253–280.

6685. Smith, C. June 1994. The Spirit and Democracy: Base Communities, Protestantism, and Democratization in Latin America. *Sociology of Religion* 55 (2): 119–143.

6686. Smith, D. C. December 1983. *See* Stone, W. F. (December 1983).

6687. Smith, G. May 1981. Does West German Democracy Have an "Efficient

Secret." *West European Politics* 4 (2): 167–176.

6688. Smith, G. March 1987. The Changing West German Party System: Consequences of the 1987 Election. *Government and Opposition* 22: 131–144.

6689. Smith, H. September 1977. A New Look at Bullock: Commenting on the Report of the Committee of Inquiry on Industrial Democracy. *Labour Monthly* 59: 403–407.

6690. Smith, K. March 1981. The Representative Role of the President. *Presidential Studies Quarterly* 11 (2): 203–213.

6691. Smith, K. January 1988. The Caribbean Basin: "We Are a Crucible Where a New Civilization Is Taking Place." *Caribbean Affairs* 1 (1): 1–5.

6692. Smith, K. April 1988. President or Puppet? Only Time Will Show Manigat's True Character. *Caribbean Affairs* 1 (2): 1–12.

6693. Smith, K. October 1988. Sooner or Later: Another Bloody Chapter Is Going to Be Written in Haiti. *Caribbean Affairs* 1 (4): 1–5.

6694. Smith, K. July 1989. Disillusionment and Fear as Haitians Battle for Democracy. *Caribbean Affairs* 2 (3): 185–190.

6695. Smith, K. B. December 1994. *See* Meier, K. J. (December 1994).

6696. Smith, M. P. November 1976. Barriers to Organizational Democracy in Public Administration. *Administration and Society* 8 (3): 275–318.

6697. Smith, N. March 1985. *See* Neuhaus, R. J. (March 1985).

6698. Smith, P. H. June 1979. The Wounds of History. *Wilson Quarterly* 3 (3): 130–141.

6699. Smith, P. H. July 1988. On Democracy and Democratization in Latin America: Speculations and Prospects.* *Foro Internacional* 113: 5–29.

6700. Smith, P. H. July 1991. Crisis and Democracy in Latin America. *World Politics* 43 (4): 608–634.

6701. Smith, R. M. September 1993. Beyond Tocqueville, Murdal, and Hartz: The Multiple Traditions in America. *American Political Science Review* 87 (3): 549–566.

6702. Smith, S. J. 1986. Police Accountability and Local Democracy. *Area* 18 (2): 99–107.

6703. Smith, T. 1993. Making the World Safe for Democracy. *Washington Quarterly* 16 (4): 197–214.

6704. Smith, T. W. March 1990. The First Straw? A Study of the Origins of Election Polls. *Public Opinion Quarterly* 54 (1): 21–36.

6705. Smith, W. C. December 1986. The Travail of Brazilian Democracy in the "New Republic." *Journal of Interamerican Studies and World Affairs* 28 (4): 39–73.

6706. Smith, W. C. April 1987. The Birth of Brazilian Democracy.* *Revista Mexicana de Sociologia* 49 (2): 89–126.

6707. Smith, W. C. June 1990. Democracy, Distributional Conflicts and Macroeconomic Policymaking in Argentina, 1983–1989. *Journal of Interamerican Studies and World Affairs* 32 (2): 1–42.

6708. Smith, W. C. December 1991. State, Market, and Neoliberalism in Posttransitional Argentina: The Menen Experiment. *Journal of Interamerican Studies and World Affairs* 33 (4): 45–82.

6709. Smith, W. C. June 1993. Neoliberal Restructuring and Scenarios of Democratic Consolidation in Latin America. *Studies in Comparative International Development* 28 (2): 3–21.

6710. Smolar, A. 1990. Democratic Transition in Poland.* *Pouvoirs* 52: 65–75.

6711. Smolla, R. A., and D. P. Bradberry. September 1992. Introduction: Perspectives on the World's Search for Stable Democracy. *William and Mary Bill of Rights Journal* 1 (2): 177–186.

6712. Smooha, S. 1990. Minority Status in an Ethnic Democracy: The Status of the Arab Minority in Israel. *Ethnic and Racial Studies* 13 (3): 389–413.

6713. Smyser, W. R. December 1994. Dateline Berlin: Germany's New Vision. *Foreign Policy* (97): 140–181.

6714. Snidal, D. 1982. *See* Freeman, J. R. (1982).

6715. Snider, J. H. September 1994. Democracy Online: Tomorrow's Electronic Electorate. *Futurist* 28 (5): 15–19.

6716. So, A. Y., and S. P. Hua. June 1992. Democracy as an Antisystemic Movement in Taiwan, Hong Kong, and China: A World Systems Analysis. *Sociological Perspectives* 35 (2): 385–404.

6717. So, A. Y., and L. Kwitko. 1990. The New Middle Class and the Democratic Movement in Hong Kong. *Journal of Contemporary Asia* 20 (3): 384–398.

6718. So, A. Y., and S. H. May. June 1993. Democratization in East Asia in the Late 1980s: Taiwan Breakthrough, Hong Kong Frustration. *Studies in Comparative International Development* 28 (2): 61–80.

6719. Soares, G. A. D. 1984. The Future of Democracy in Latin America.* *Dados: Revista de Ciencias Sociais* 27 (3): 269–293.

6720. Soares, G. A. D. 1987. Economic Development and Democracy in Latin America.* *Dados: Revista de Ciencias Sociais* 30 (3): 253–274.

6721. Soares, G. A. D., and D. Glaudio. September 1979. Military Authoritarianism and Executive Absolutism in Brazil. *Studies in Comparative International Development* 14 (3–4): 104–126.

6722. Soares, G. A. D., and M. C. D'Araujo. October 1991. Los Mitos de la Prensa y Los Votos en las elecciones de 1990. *Revista de Estudios Politicos* 74: 17–42.

6723. Sobchak, A. A. December 1993. Evolution of Constitutional Ideas and Democratic Ideals in Russia. *Presidential Studies Quarterly* 23 (1): 23–26.

6724. Sobering, B. J. October 1981. Shareholder Democracy: A Description and Critical Analysis of the Proxy System. *North Carolina Law Review* 60: 145–169.

6725. Sobotka, M. 1990. *See* Znoj, M. (1990).

6726. Sodersten, B. 1977. Industrial Democracy: Present and Future. *Scandinavian Review* (2): 70–78.

6727. Soetjatmoko. March 1983. Political Systems and Development in the Third World: New Directions for Social Science Research in Asia. *Alternatives* 8 (4): 483–499.

6728. Sogomonj, G. 1974. Social Democracy in the Federal Republic of Germany: Politics and Ideology.* *Beitrage zur Konfliktforschung* (2): 117–130.

6729. Soh, C. H. S. January 1993. Sexual Equality, Male Superiority, and Korean Women in Politics: Changing Gender Relations in a Patriarchal Democracy. *Sex Roles* 28 (1–2): 73–90.

6730. Soifer, A. 1981. Complacency and Constitutional Law. *Ohio State Law Journal* 42 (1): 383–410.

6731. Sojo, A. 1983. *See* Urrutia, E. R. (1983).

6732. Sokoloff, K. L., and B. Z. Khan. 1990. The Democratization of Invention during Early Industrialization: Evidence from the United States, 1790–1846. *Journal of Economic History* 50 (2): 363–378.

6733. Sola, G. April 1989. Sartori's Democracy Revisited: A Note.* *Rivista Italiana di Scienza Politica* 19 (1): 113–136.

6734. Sola, L. February 1991. Heterodox Shock in Brazil: Technicos, Politicians, and Democracy. *Journal of Latin American Studies* 23 (1): 163–195.

6735. Sola, L. January 1994. Governability, Fiscal Reform and Democratization: Comparative Perspectives on Brazil. *Desarrollo Economico: Revista de Ciencias Sociales* 33 (132): 483–514.

6736. Solano, P. L. 1983. Institutional Explanations of Public Expenditures among High-Income Democracies. *Public Finance* 38 (3): 440–458.

6737. Solarz, S. J. March 1984. Democracy and the Future of Taiwan. *Freedom at Issue* 77: 18–21.

6738. Solarz, S. J. June 1985. Promoting Democracy in the Third World: Lost Cause or Sound Policy? *SAIS Review* 5: 139–153.

6739. Solinger, D. J. September 1989. Democracy with Chinese Characteristics. *World Policy Journal* 6 (4): 621–632.

6740. Soljan, N. N. 1979. Education Needs and the Philosophy of Democratization in Higher Education in Yugoslavia. *Prospects* 9 (1): 58–68.

6741. Soloman, B. D., F. M. Shelley, M. J. Pasqualetti, and G. T. Murauskas. 1987. Radioactive Waste Management Policies in Seven Industrialized Democracies. *Geoforum* 18 (4): 415–431.

6742. Solomon, G. B. H., and D. R. Wolfensberger. June 1994. The Decline of Deliberate Democracy in the House and Proposals for Reform. *Harvard Journal on Legislation* 31 (2): 321–370.

6743. Soltan, K. E. May 1988. Democracy, Dictatorship and Decision Costs. *Public Choice* 57 (2): 155–173.

6744. Solter, A. 1993. Civil Society as a Concept of the Theory of Democracy.* *Jahrbuch für Politik* 3 (1): 145–180.

6745. Solzhenitsyn, A. 1975. Détente and Democracy. *Society* 13 (1): 14–25.

6746. Somerville, K. August 1991. Africa Moves towards Party Pluralism. *World Today* 47 (8–9): 152–155.

6747. Somerville, K. 1993. The Failure of Democratic Reforms in Angola and Zaire. *Survival* 35 (3): 51–77.

6748. Sommer, M. 1987. *See* Baltodano, M. P. (1987).

6749. Somolekae, G. 1989. *See* Holm, J. D. (1989).

6750. Sondrol, P. C. June 1992. The Emerging New Politics of Liberalizing Paraguay: Sustained Civil-Military Control without Democracy. *Journal of Interamerican Studies and World Affairs* 34 (2): 127–163.

6751. Sontheimer, K. 1979. Krisenphaenomene Demokratischer Industriegesellschaften. *Mitarbeit* 28 (2–3): 107–118.

6752. Sorensen, C. December 1993. Social Forces and Changes of Political Regime: The Question of Democratic Development. *Journal of Communist Studies* 9 (4): 37–56.

6753. Sorensen, G. 1989. Democracy and Economic Development: A Case Study of India.* *Politica* 21 (1): 27–44.

6754. Sorensen, G. November 1992. Kant and Processes of Democratization: Consequences for Neorealist Thought. *Journal of Peace Research* 29 (4): 397–414.

6755. Sorensen, K. H. 1985. Technology and Industrial Democracy: An Inquiry into Some Theoretical Issues and Their Social Basis. *Organization Studies* 6 (2): 139–160.

6756. Sorensen, T. C. June 1990. Rethinking National Security. *Foreign Affairs* 69 (3): 1–18.

6757. Sorensen, T. C. 1994. Foreign Policy in a Presidential Democracy. *Political Science Quarterly* 109 (3): 515–528.

6758. Sorge, A. 1976. Evolution of Industrial Democracy in Countries of the European Community. *British Journal of Industrial Relations* 14 (3): 274–294.

6759. Sorge, B. December 6, 1986. The Crisis of the Social State in Italy: From Stalemate Democracy to Mature Democracy.* *Civilta Cattolica* 3275:

6760. Soudan, F. April 24, 1991. Mauritanie: Une Seule Solution, la Democratie. *Jeune Afrique* 31: 53–55.

6761. Soudan, F. June 1992. Mauritanie: Democratie: Ce Qui Reste à Faire. *Jeune Afrique* 32: 33–36+.

6762. Soudan, F., and L. Giraudineau. October 15, 1991. Mauritanie: La Democratie, Oui Mais. *Jeune Afrique* 31: 35+.

6763. Southwell, P. L. 1994. Prenomination Preferences and General [U.S.] Election Voting Behavior. *Social Science Journal* 31 (1): 69–77.

6764. Sovoie, P. November 1994. *See* Bowles, S. (November 1994).

6765. Spain, J. W. March 1983. *See* Ludington, N. S. (March 1983).

6766. Sparks, C. 1988. The Popular Press and Political Democracy. *Media, Culture and Society* 10 (2): 209–223.

6767. Sparks, C. December 1992. The Press, the Market, and Democracy. *Journal of Communication* 42 (1): 36–51.

6768. Sparrow, G. W. 1985. *See* Waste, R. J. (1985).

6769. Spence, J. Junc 1992. *See* Vickers, G. R. (June 1992).

6770. Spence, J. E. 1994. Everybody Has Won So All Must Have Prizes: Reflections on the South African Elections. *Government and Opposition* 29 (4): 431–444.

6771. Spence, J. E. July 1994. Reflections of a First-Time Voter: Comment. *African Affairs* 93 (372): 341–342.

6772. Spencer, M. 1991. Politics beyond Turf: Grass-Roots Democracy in the Helsinki Process. *Bulletin of Peace Proposals* 22 (4): 427–435.

6773. Spieker, M. October 1980. How the Eurocommunists Interpret Democracy. *Review of Politics* 42 (4): 427–464.

6774. Spinner, T. J., Jr. September 1980. The Emperor Burnham Has Lost His Clothes: Guyana's Life in Disarray. *Caribbean Review* 9 (4): 4–8.

6775. Spinrad, W. 1984. Work Democracy: An Overview. *International Social Science Journal* 36 (2): 195–215.

6776. Spiro, D. E. 1994. The Insignificance of the Liberal Peace. *International Security* 19 (2): 50–86.

6777. Spitz, E. 1979. Defining Democracy: Nonecumenical Reply to May. *Political Studies* 27 (1): 126–128.

6778. Spitzer, R. J. December 1990. Liberalism and Juridical Democracy, or What's Interesting about Interest Group Liberalism. *PS: Political Science & Politics* 23 (4): 572–574.

6779. Spoormans, H. April 1991. Changing Perspectives: On Theoretical Explanations of Democratization in the Netherlands. *Netherlands Journal of Social Sciences* 27 (1): 3–16.

6780. Sprake, T. October 1979. Industrial Democracy in the Netherlands. *Employment Gazette* 87: 1008–1010+.

6781. Sprecher, L. 1991. Democracy. *Feminist Studies* 17 (1): 79–84.

6782. Springborg, P. November 1984. Karl Marx on Democracy, Participation, Voting, and Equality. *Political Theory* 12 (4): 537–556.

6783. Springborg, R. March 1991. State Society Relations in Egypt: The Debate

Over Owner-Tenant Relations. *Middle East Journal* 45 (2): 232–249.

6784. Springer, J. F. May 1977. *See* Musolf, L. D. (May 1977).

6785. Sproule Jones, M. December 1984. The Enduring Colony: Political Institutions and Political Science in Canada. *Publius* 14 (1): 93–108.

6786. Squella, A. 1984. Kelsen's Concept of Democracy. *Estudios Publicos* 13: 47–60.

6787. Squella, A. December 1990. Legal Positivism and Democracy in the Twentieth Century. *Ratio Juris* 3: 407–414.

6788. Squire, P., and C. Fastnow. September 1994. Comparing Gubernatorial and Senatorial Elections. *Political Science Quarterly* 47 (3): 705–720.

6789. Srinivasan, M. September 1976. India: The Clear Puzzle, Indira Gandhi and a Tradition of Democracy. *Worldview* 19: 13–17.

6790. Srinivasan, P. 1990. Framing of a Future for South Africa. *Africa Quarterly* 29 (3–4): 68–82.

6791. St. John, R. B. July 1984. Peru: Democracy under Siege. *World Today* 40 (7): 299–306.

6792. St. Peter, L. February 1977. *See* Johnson, D. R. (February 1977).

6793. Staar, R. F. December 1990. Transition in Poland. *Current History* 89 (551): 401–404, 426–427.

6794. Staber, P. 1985. *See* Ebeling, T. (1985).

6795. Stamp, P. May 1991. The Politics of Dissent in Kenya. *Current History* 90 (556): 205–208,227–229.

6796. Stanley, J. February 1977. Equality of Opportunity as Philosophy and Ideology. *Political Theory* 5 (1): 61–74.

6797. Stanley, M. December 1983. The Mystery of the Commons: On the Indis-

pensibility of Civic Rhetoric. *Social Research* 50 (4): 851–883.

6798. Stanley, P. W. 1986. Toward Democracy in the Philippines. *Proceedings of the Academy of Political Science* 36 (1): 129–141.

6799. Stanton, A. 1989. Citizens of Workplace Democracies. *Critical Social Policy* 9: 56–65.

6800. Staravoitov, N. 1978. Along the Path of Development of Democracy. *Soviet Law and Government* 16 (4): 39–43.

6801. Starling, J. D. February 1985. *See* Plumtree, J. P. (February 1985).

6802. Starosta, L. 1980. Oligarchization of the Swedish Political System and Its Assumed Democratic Character. *Studia Nauk Politycznych* 44: 61–75.

6803. Starr, H. June 1991. Democratic Dominoes: Diffusion Approaches to the Spread of Democracy in the International System. *Journal of Conflict Resolution* 35 (2): 356–381.

6804. Starr, H. May 1992. Democracy and War: Choice, Learning and Security Communities. *Journal of Peace Research* 29 (2): 207–213.

6805. Starr, H. December 1992. Why Don't Democracies Fight One Another? Evaluating the Theory-Finding Feedback Loop. *Jerusalem Journal of International Relations* 14 (4): 41–59.

6806. Starr, S. F. March 1988. Soviet Union: A Civil Society. *Foreign Policy* (70): 26–41.

6807. Staub, H. O. June 1980. The Tyranny of Minorities. *Daedalus* 109 (3): 159–168.

6808. Stavenhagen, R. 1980. Disarmament Education as a Democratization Process. *Bulletin of Peace Proposals* 11 (3): 209–210.

6809. Stavenhagen, R. February 1991. Human Rights, Democracy and Development in Latin America. *Economic and Industrial Democracy* 12 (1): 31–41.

6810. Steamer, R. J. September 1977. Contemporary Supreme Court Directions in Civil Liberties. *Political Science Quarterly* 92 (3): 425–442.

6811. Stein, H. June 1981. Economic Problems of the Industrial Democracies: A View from the United States. *American Enterprise Institute Economist:* 8–12.

6812. Stein, N. June 1990. *See* Jonas, S. (June 1990).

6813. Steinbach, U. 1988. Turkey's Third Republic. *Aussenpolitik* 39 (3): 237–255.

6814. Steinberg, A. December 1986. "The Spirit of Litigation": Private Prosecution and Criminal Justice in Nineteenth-Century Philadelphia. *Journal of Social History* 20 (2): 231–249.

6815. Steinberg, D. I. April 1989. Crisis in Burma. *Current History* 88 (537): 185–188, 196–198.

6816. Steinberg, D. I. 1991. Democracy, Power, and the Economy in Myanmar: Donor Dilemmas. *Asian Survey* 31 (8): 729–742.

6817. Steinberg, R. 1983. Elemente Volksunmittelbaren Demokratie im Verwaltungsstaat. *Verwaltung* 16 (4): 465–486.

6818. Steinem, G. May 1987. Humanism and the Second Wave of Feminism: A Four-Point Plan to Carry Humanism and Feminism into the Next Century. *Humanist* 47: 11–15+.

6819. Steiner, J. 1977. *See* Obler, J. (1977).

6820. Steiner, J. April 1981. The Consociational Theory and Beyond. *Comparative Politics* 13 (3): 339–354.

6821. Steiner, J. November 1981. Research Strategies beyond Consociational Theory. *Journal of Politics* 43 (4): 1241–1250.

6822. Steiner, J. January 1985. *See* Germann, R. E. (January 1985).

6823. Steiner, J. April 1987. Consociational Democracy as a Policy Recommendation: The Case of South Africa. *Comparative Politics* 19 (3): 361–372.

6824. Steiner, J. July 1987. *See* Dorff, R. H. (July 1987).

6825. Steiner, J., and R. H. Dorff. March 1985. Structure and Process in Consociationalism and Federalism. *Publius* 15 (2): 49–55.

6826. Steinmo, S. December 1988. Social Democracy vs. Socialism: Goal Adaptation in Social Democratic Sweden. *Politics and Society* 16 (4): 403–446.

6827. Steinmo, S. July 1989. Political Institutions and Tax Policy in the United States, Sweden, and Britain. *World Politics* 41 (4): 500–535.

6828. Stembrowitz, J. 1983. The Problems Connected with the Issue of the State of Emergency in the Bourgeois Democratic State.* *Studia Nauk Politycznych* 63: 7–44.

6829. Stepan, A. March 1992. *See* Linz, J. J. (March 1992).

6830. Stepan, A. 1994. When Democracy and the Nation-State Are Competing Logics: Reflections on Estonia. *Archives Europeennes de Sociologie* 35 (1): 127–141.

6831. Stephen, D. 1984. Argentina and Democracy. *New Society* 67 (1103): 46–48.

6832. Stephens, E. H. September 1989. Capitalist Development and Democracy in South America. *Politics and Society* 17 (3): 281–352.

6833. Stephens, J. D. March 1989. Democratic Transition and Breakdown in Western Europe, 1870–1939: A Test of the Moore Thesis. *American Journal of Sociology* 94 (5): 1019–1077.

6834. Stephens, J. D. 1993. *See* Huber, E. (1993).

6835. Stephens, J. D. June 1993. *See* Huber, E. (June 1993).

6836. Stephens, J. D. November 1993. *See* Huber, E. (November 1993).

6837. Stephenson-Glade, S. June 1991. The Prospects for Democracy in the Southern Cone. *Fletcher Forum of World Affairs* 15 (2): 121–137.

6838. Sterbling, A. 1991. Democratization Problems in Southeastern Europe.* *Suedosteuropa* 40 (6): 307–324.

6839. Steriada, S. December 1993. *See* Campeanu, P. (December 1993).

6840. Sterling, T. D. 1986. Democracy in an Information Society. *Information Society* 4 (1–2): 1–143.

6841. Stern, F. July 1978. Between Repression and Reform: A Stranger's Impression of Argentina and Brazil. *Foreign Affairs* 56 (4): 800–818.

6842. Sternpettersson, M. March 1993. Reading the Project, Global Civilization: Challenges for Sovereignty, Democracy, and Security. *Futures* 25 (2): 123–138.

6843. Stetson, A. March 1992. *See* Fox, D. T. (March 1992).

6844. Steuer, R. M. 1977. Employee Representation on Board: Industrial Democracy or Interlocking Directorate. *Columbia Journal of Transnational Law* 16 (2): 255–296.

6845. Stevens, R. G. June 1990. Liberal Education. *Perspectives on Political Science* 19 (3): 133–135.

6846. Stever, J. A. August 1986. Mary Parker Follett and the Quest for Pragmatic Administration. *Administration and Society* 18 (2): 159–177.

6847. Stewart, A. D. March 1993. New World Ordered: The Asserted Extraterritorial Jurisdiction of the Cuban Democracy Act of 1992. *Louisiana Law Review* 53 (4): 1389–1409.

6848. Steytler, N. March 1991. Democratizing the Criminal Justice System in South Africa. *Social Justice* 18 (1–2): 141–153.

6849. Stiehler, G. 1985. *See* Dittmar, M. L. (1985).

6850. Stiel, N. January 1993. apres Vingt-trois Ans de Dictature, la Presse Renait au Mali. *Mediaspouvoirs* 38–43.

6851. Stimson, J. A. August 1975. Belief Systems: Constraint, Complexity, and the 1972 Election. *Journal of Political Science* 19 (5): 393–417.

6852. Stimson, S. C., and M. Milgate. December 1993. Utility, Property, and Political Participation: James Mill on Democratic Reform. *American Political Science Review* 87 (4): 901–911.

6853. Stivers, C. May 1990. The Public Agency as Polis: Active Citizenship in the Administrative States. *Administration and Society* 22 (1): 86–105.

6854. Stoelting, D. March 1992. The Challenge of UN-Monitored Elections in Independent Nations. *Stanford Journal of International Law* 28: 371–424.

6855. Stojanov, C. December 1988. *See* Wallimann, I. (December 1988).

6856. Stojanovic, S. September 1979. The Possibility of Socialist Democratization in Yugoslavia. *Telos* 41: 76–86.

6857. Stoker, G. March 1985. *See* Campbell, F. G. (March 1985).

6858. Stoker, L. June 1992. Interest and Ethics in Politics. *American Political Science Review* 85 (2): 369–380.

6859. Stokes, W. S. April 1980. Emancipation: The Politics of West German Education. *Review of Politics* 42 (2): 191–215.

6860. Stolovich, L. December 1992. The Paradoxes and Perplexities of an Uncommon Left. *Social Justice* 19 (4): 138–152.

6861. Stolyarenko, A. M. 1989. Psychological Training of a Lawyer and Restructuring of Education and Society Democratization.* *Voprosy Psikhologii* 4: 16–23.

6862. Stone, C. July 1975. Political Determinants of Social Policy Allocations in Latin America. *Comparative Studies in Society and History* 17 (3): 286–308.

6863. Stone, C. 1981. Democracy and Socialism in Jamaica, 1962–1979. *Journal of Commonwealth and Comparative Politics* 19 (2): 115–133.

6864. Stone, W. J., and R. B. Rapport. November 1994. Candidate Perception among Nomination Activists: A New Look at the Moderation Hypothesis. *Journal of Politics* 56 (4): 1034–1052.

6865. Stone, W. F., and D. C. Smith. December 1983. Human Nature in Politics: Graham Wallas and the Fabians. *Political Psychology* 4 (4): 693–712.

6866. Stopsky, F. 1975. School as a Workplace: Extending Democracy to Schools. *International Review of Education* 21 (4): 493–506.

6867. Stormann, W. F. January 1993. The Recreation Profession, Capital, and Democracy. *Leisure Sciences* 15 (1): 49–66.

6868. Strand, D. May 1990. Protest in Beijing: Civil Society and Public Sphere in China. *Problems of Communism* 39 (3): 1–19.

6869. Stras, M. B. March 1992. Forging a New Role for Czechoslovakia. *Federal Bar News and Journal* 39: 468–471.

6870. Stratton, K. 1989. Union Democracy in the International Typographical Union: Thirty Years Later. *Journal of Labor Research* 10 (1): 119–134.

6871. Stratton, W. G. 1988. The Problem of Democracy in Hegel's Philosophy of Law. *Archiv für Rechts und Sozialphilosophie* 74 (1): 33–41.

6872. Straubhaar, T. 1991. *See* Brunetti, A. (1991).

6873. Strawn, J. December 1984. Democracy on the Take: Flick Scandal Shakes West German Politics. *Multinational Monitor* 6: 13–15.

6874. Streeck, W. 1988. Special Issue on Organizational Democracy in Trade Unions: Editorial Introduction. *Economic and Industrial Democracy* 9 (3): 307–318.

6875. Streeck, W. December 1992. Inclusion and Secession: Questions on the Boundaries of Associative Democracy. *Politics and Society* 20 (4): 513–520.

6876. Street, J. 1983. Socialist Arguments for Industrial Democracy. *Economic and Industrial Democracy* 4 (4): 519–539.

6877. Street, J. H. June 1986. Can Mexico Break the Vicious Cycle of "Stop-Go" Policy? An Institutional Overview. *Journal of Economic Issues* 20 (2): 601–612.

6878. Strege, M. May 1992. *See* Sklar, R. M. (May 1992).

6879. Streib, G. March 1992. Ethics and Expertise in the Public Service: Maintaining Democracy in an Era of Professionalism. *Southeastern Political Review* 20: 122–143.

6880. Strike, K. A. June 1993. Professionalism, Democracy, and Discursive Communities: Normative Reflections on Restructuring. *American Educational Research Journal* 30 (2): 255–275.

6881. Stringer, P. 1979. *See* Boaden, N. (1979).

6882. Strom, K. July 1984. Minority Governments in Parliamentary Democracies: The Rationality of Non-Winning Cabinet Solutions. *Comparative Political Studies* 17 (2): 199–227.

6883. Strom, K. August 1985. Minority Governments and Parliamentary Democracies.* *Rivista Italiana di Scienza Politica* 15 (2): 167–204.

6884. Strom, K. September 1985. Party Goals and Government Performance in Parliamentary Democracies. *American Political Science Review* 79 (3): 748–754.

6885. Strom, K. September 1988. Contending Models of Cabinet Stability. *American Political Science Review* 82 (3): 923–929. Rejoinder by Browne, Frendeis and Gleiber, 930–941.

6886. Strom, K. March 1992. Democracy as Political Competition. *American Behavioral Scientist* 35 (4–5): 375–396.

6887. Strom, K., I. Budge, and M. J. Laver. May 1994. Constraints on Cabinet Formation in Parliamentary Democracies. *American Journal of Political Science* 38 (2): 303–335.

6888. Strout, C. February 1980. Tocqueville and Republican Religion: Revisiting the Visitor. *Political Theory* 8 (1): 9–26.

6889. Strubel, M. October 1987. More Direct Democracy? The People's Aspirations and the People's Decisions: An International Comparison. *Aus Politik und Zeitgeschichte* 42: 17–30.

6890. Stryker, R. 1990. *See* Pampel, F. C. (1990).

6891. Stubbe Ostergaard, C. December 1990. Swans Scolding the Tiger? Scandinavian Foreign Policies towards Democratization in China. *Cooperation and Conflict* 25 (4): 171–194.

6892. Stuby, G. 1976. Bemerkungen zum Verfassungsrechtlichen Begriff der "Freiheitlich Demokratischen Grundordnung." *Demokratie und Recht* 4 (2): 143–170. Discussion by Wolfgang Borchers and others.

6893. Studlar, D. T., and R. E. Matland. March 1994. The Growth of Women's Representation in the Canadian House of Commons and the Election of 1984: A Reappraisal. *Canadian Journal of Political Science* 27 (1): 53–79.

6894. Stultz, N. M. December 1982. Bridging the Black-White Gulf in Africa. *Orbis* 25 (4): 881–902.

6895. Sturmthal, A. F. 1977. Bullock and the Aftermath: Main Recommendations of Lord Bullock's Committee of Inquiry on Industrial Democracy in Great Britain. *Industrial Relations (Quebec)* 32 (3): 299–307.

6896. Sturmthal, A. F. May 1977. Unions and Industrial Democracy. *Annals of the American Academy of Political and Social Science* 431: 12–21.

6897. Stuth, R. 1984. Boliviens Widerspruch: Der Weg Zur Entwicklung Heisst Demokratie. *Politische Meinung* 29 (212): 46–51.

6898. Stymne, B. 1986. Industrial Democracy and the Worker. *International Review of Applied Psychology/ Revue Internationale de Psychologie Appliquée* 35 (1): 101–120.

6899. Su, S. June 1992. *See* McCormick, B. L. (June 1992).

6900. Su, T. T., M. S. Kamlet, and D. C. Mowery. February 1993. Modeling United States Budgetary and Fiscal Policy Outcomes: A Disaggregated, System-Wide Perspective. *American Journal of Political Science* 37 (1): 213–245.

6901. Su, Z. June 1988. On Latin America's Process of Democratization. *Latin American Perspectives* 15 (3): 18–25.

6902. Suarez, W. R. September 1994. Economic Development and Democracy in Latin America.* *Civilta Cattolica* 3: 377–390.

6903. Suberu, R. T. May 1994. The Democratic Recession in Nigeria. *Current History* 93 (583): 213–218.

6904. Subrahmanya, K. March 1990. Economic Crisis and the Question of Democratic Transition in Latin America. *Strategic Analysis* 12 (12): 1281–1308.

6905. Sugar, P. F. March 1984. Continuity and Change in Eastern European Authoritarianism: Autocracy, Fascism, and Communism. *East European Quarterly* 18 (1): 1–23.

6906. Suh, M. B. M. May 1993. The Long March toward Democracy: Assessment of the Political Modernization in the Republic of Korea. *Internationales Asienforum* 24 (1–2): 57–74.

6907. Suk, C. H. January 1994. Democracy in South Korea: Foreign Views. *Asian Thought and Society* 55: 49–65.

6908. Sullivan, D. S. July 1993. Effective International Dispute Settlement Mechanisms and the Necessary Condition of Liberal Democracy. *Georgetown Law Journal* 81 (6): 2369–2412.

6909. Sullivan, E. T. March 1991. Democratization and Changing Gender Roles in Egypt. *American-Arab Affairs* 36: 16–17.

6910. Sullivan, J. D. June 1986. *See* Samuels, M. A. (June 1986).

6911. Sullivan, J. D. March 1990. What's on the Table? *National Interest* 19 (1): 87–94.

6912. Sullivan, J. D. March 1992. Democracy and Global Growth. *Washington Quarterly* 15 (2): 175–186.

6913. Sullivan, J. D. October 1994. Democratization and Business Interest. *Journal of Democracy* 5 (4): 146–160.

6914. Sullivan, J. L. June 1985. *See* Shamir, M. (June 1985).

6915. Sullivan, J. L. 1992. *See* Barnum, D. G. (1992).

6916. Sullivan, K. M. December 1992. Religion and Liberal Democracy. *University of Chicago Law Review* 59 (1): 195–223.

6917. Sullivan, L. R. September 1989. The Chinese Democracy Movement of 1989. *Orbis* 33 (4): 561–582.

6918. Sullivan, M. P. January 1991. Panama Revisited: One Year after Operation Just Cause. *Congressional Research Service Review* 12: 22–23.

6919. Sullivan, R. 1989. *Beijing Review* Coverage of the Democracy Movement of Spring 1989. *Political Communication and Persuasion* 6 (3): 169–177.

6920. Sullivan, R. R. June 1982. Authority, Technology, Speech, and Language. *Polity* 14 (4): 585–602.

6921. Sullivan, W. H. December 1983. Living without Marcos. *Foreign Policy* 53: 150–156.

6922. Sully, M. A. April 1978. Austrian Social Democracy: The New Party Programme. *Political Quarterly* 49 (2): 159–170.

6923. Summers, C. W. 1986. The Privatization of Personal Freedoms and Enrichment of Democracy: Some Lessons from Labor Law. *University of Illinois Law Review* (3): 689–723.

6924. Sun, S. L., and G. A. Barnett. July 1994. The International Telephone Network and Democratization. *Journal of the American Society for Information Science* 45 (6): 411–421.

6925. Sun, Y. P. March 1978. The Struggle against the Dictatorship and for National Salvation and Democracy. *Korean Review* 2: 16–29.

6926. Sundhaussen, U. 1991. Democracy and the Middle Classes: Reflections on Political Development. *Australian Journal of Politics and History* 37 (1): 100–117.

6927. Sunkel, G. 1992. La Prensa en la Transicion Chilena. *Estudios Sociales* (2): 155–172.

6928. Sunkel, O. October 1992. Consolidation of Democracy and Development in Chile. *Trimestre Economico* 59 (236): 816–830.

6929. Sunkin, M. 1992. *See* Barnum, D. G. (1992).

6930. Sunshine, C. A. April 20 1987. Haiti: How Far from Democracy? A Year after Baby Doc. *Christianity and Crisis* 47: 136–140.

6931. Sunstein, C. R. December 1991. Preferences and Politics. *Philosophy and Public Affairs* 20 (1): 3–34.

6932. Sunstein, C. R. December 1993. Informing America: Risk, Disclosure, and the First Amendment. *Florida State University Law Review* 20: 653–677.

6933. Sunstein, C. R. September 1994. A New Deal for Speech. *Hastings Communications and Entertainment Law Journal* 17: 137–160.

6934. Sussman, R. 1981. The Rural Community of Appenzeller as an Example of Direct Democracy. *Politische Studien* 32 (259): 541–546.

6935. Sutter, R. G. September 1991. Tianamen's Lingering Fallout on Sino-American Relations. *Current History* 90 (557): 247–250.

6936. Suttmeier, R. P. October 1989. Reform, Modernization, and the Changing Constitution of Science in China. *Asian Survey* 29 (10): 999–1015.

6937. Sutton, F. X. December 1987. The Ford Foundation: The Early Years. *Daedalus* 116 (1): 41–91.

6938. Suvedi, P. S. July 1993. Public Accountability and Public Service Effectiveness. *Public Administration Journal (Kathmandu)* 14: 18–24.

6939. Suvorova, G. F. November 1992. Democratization of the Schools. *Russian Education and Society* 34 (11): 16–22.

6940. Suzuki, B. H. May 1984. Curriculum Transformation for Multicultural Education. *Education and Urban Society* 16 (3): 294–322.

6941. Svanadze, L. N. 1987. The Emergence and Essence of the Tory Concept of "Private Ownership Democracy."* *Voprosy Istorii* 5: 51–68.

6942. Svenson, F. 1979. Liberal Democracy and Group Rights: Legacy of Individualism and Its Impact on American-Indian Tribes. *Political Studies* 27 (3): 421–439.

6943. Swaney, J. A. June 1989. Our Obsolete Technology Mentality. *Journal of Economic Issues* 23 (2): 569–578.

6944. Swank, D. H. January 1983. Between Incrementalism and Revolution: Group Protest and the Growth of the Welfare State. *American Behavioral Scientist* 26: 291–310.

6945. Swank, D. H. April 1984. *See* Hicks, A. (April 1984).

6946. Swank, D. H. December 1984. *See* Hicks, A. (December 1984).

6947. Swank, D. H. November 1988. The Political Economy of Government Domestic Expenditure in the Affluent Democracies, 1960–1980. *American Journal of Political Science* 32 (4): 1120–1150.

6948. Swank, D. H. March 1992. Politics and the Structural Dependence of the State in Democratic Capitalist Nations. *American Political Science Review* 86 (1): 38–54.

6949. Swank, D. H. March 1992. *See* Hicks, A. (March 1992).

6950. Swanson, B. E. 1988. *See* Vogel, R. K. (1988).

6951. Swanson, L. D. June 1980. *See* Hayden, F. G. (June 1980).

6952. Swanton, C. July 1985. On the "Essential Contestedness" of Political Concepts. *Ethics* 95 (4): 811–927.

6953. Sweezy, P. M. 1980. Capitalism and Democracy. *Monthly Review* 32 (2): 27–32.

6954. Sweezy, P. M. 1983. Capitalism and Democracy. *Trimestre Economico* 50 (198): 671–675.

6955. Swenson, P. 1991. Bringing Capital Back In, or Social Democracy Reconsidered: Employer Power, Cross-Class Alliances, and Centralization of Industrial Relations in Denmark and Sweden. *World Politics* 43 (4): 513–544.

6956. Swenson, P. July 1991. Labor and the Limits of the Welfare State: The Politics of Intraclass Conflict and Cross-Class Alliances in Sweden and West Germany. *Comparative Politics* 23 (4): 379–399.

6957. Swianienwicz, P. April 1992. The Polish Experience of Local Democracy: Is Progress Being Made? *Policy and Politics* 20 (2): 87–98.

6958. Syad, A. H. February 1978. Pakistan in 1977: The "Prince" Is under the Law. *Asian Survey* 18 (2): 117–125.

6959. Sylla, L. 1982. The Democratic Management of Social-Political Pluralism in Africa: Competitive Democracy and Consociational Democracy.* *Civilisations* 33 (1): 23–63.

6960. Sylla, L. March 1982. Succession of the Charismatic Leader: The Gordian Knot of African Politics. *Daedalus* 111 (2): 11–28.

6961. Syng, N. Y. October 1978. *See* Sigelman, L. (October 1978).

6962. Szablowski, G. J. July 1993. *See* Derlien, H. (July 1993).

6963. Szabo, K. 1974. Factory Democracy and Political Economy. *Acta Oeconomica* 13 (1): 1–18.

6964. Szabo, M. 1989. The Political Development of Hungary after Kadar (1988–1989): Is It a Return to Parliamentary Democracy and Europe. *Gegenwartskunde: Gesellschaft, Staat, Erziehung* 38 (4): 425–436.

6965. Szabo, M. August 1991. Was There a Strategy? Hungary's Path to Democracy. *IGW (Institute für Gesellschaft und Wissenschaft)* 5: 59–66.

6966. Szabo, M. January 1992. Problems of Democratization in Hungary.* *Aus Politik und Zeitgeschichte* 31 (6): 34–49.

6967. Szabo, M. 1994. The Institutionalization of a Science of Democracy in the Process of Democratization.* *Oesterreichis-che Zeitschrift für Politikwissenschaft* 23 (2): 229–237.

6968. Szabo, M. December 1994. Nation State, Nationalism, and the Prospects for Democratization in East Central Europe. *Communist and Post-Communist Studies* 27 (4): 377–400.

6969. Szabo, S. F. November 1990. Reuniting Germany. *Current History* 89 (550): 357–360, 388–390.

6970. Szabo, T. July 1990. From Party-State to Pluriparty Parliament: Apropos the Political Change in Hungary.* *Il Politico* 55 (3): 515–526.

6971. Szacki, J. December 1991. Polish Democracy: Dreams and Reality. *Social Research* 58 (4): 711–722.

6972. Szamuely, L. 1978. Industrial Democracy in Western Europe: Effects and Contradictions. *Acta Oeconomica (Budapest)* 21 (4): 341–361.

6973. Szarvas, L. April 1993. Transition Periods in Hungary: The Chances for Democracy? *Journal of Theoretical Politics* 5 (2): 267–276.

6974. Szasz, A. December 1992. Progress through Mischief: The Social Movement Alternative to Secondary Associations. *Politics and Society* 20 (4): 521–528.

6975. Szayna, T. S. September 1993. Ultra-nationalism in Central Europe. *Orbis* 37: 527–250.

6976. Szecsko, T. October 1986. Theses on the Democratization of Communication. *International Political Science Review* 7 (4): 435–4422.

6977. Szeftel, M. July 1992. *See* Baylies, C. (July 1992).

6978. Szinai, M. 1990. The Roots of Democratic Change. *New Hungarian Quarterly* 119: 3–9.

6979. Szklarski, B. M. 1991. *See* Mason, D. S. (1991).

6980. Szostak, W. 1980. Analysis of the Possibilities of Cybernetic Applications for Investigating the Society's Political Culture.* *Studia Nauk Politycznych* 43: 159–172.

6981. Szporluk, R. March 1985. *See* Campbell, F. G. (March 1985).

6982. Sztompka, P. September 1991. The Intangibles and Imponderables of the Transition to Democracy. *Studies in Comparative Communism* 24 (3): 295–311.

6983. Szyliowecz, J. S. March 1981. *See* Segre, D. V. (March 1981).

6984. Taagepera, R. December 1990. The Baltic States. *Electoral Studies* 9 (4): 303–311.

6985. Taagepera, R. September 1991. Building Democracy in Estonia. *PS: Political Science & Politics* 24 (3): 478–481.

6986. Taagepera, R. October 1994. *See* Shugart, M. S. (October 1994).

6987. Tabory, E. 1989. Anti-Democratic Legislation in the Service of Democracy: Anti-Racism in Israel. *International Journal of the Sociology of Law* 17 (1): 87.

6988. Taebel, D. 1994. *See* Kisiel, W. (1994).

6989. Taheri, A. 1991. Iran: The Twilight of the Mullahs.* *Politique Internationale* 53: 275–290.

6990. Tahi, M. S. September 1992. The Arduous Democratization Process in Algeria. *Journal of Modern African Studies* 30 (3): 397–419.

6991. Taira, K. 1974. Challenge to Democracy. *Japan Interpreter* 9 (2): 198–209.

6992. Takahashi, K. 1990. Contemporary Democracy in a Parliamentary System. *Law and Contemporary Problems* 53 (1–2): 105–122.

6993. Tamandonfar, M., and S. Sharma. October 1993. India's Democracy: An Analysis of Continuity and Crisis. *Asian Profile* 19 (5): 435–445.

6994. Tamayo, J. O. June 1982. *See* Bohning D. (June 1982).

6995. Tambiah, S. J. November 1990. Reflections on Communal Violence in South Asia. *Journal of Asian Studies* 49 (4): 741–760.

6996. Tamney, J. B. October 1991. Confucianism and Democracy. *Asian Profile* 19 (5): 399–411.

6997. Tanaka, M. September 1993. *See* Chacaltana, J. (September 1993).

6998. Tandon, Y. June 22, 1991. Political Economy of Struggles for Democracy and Human Rights in Africa. *Economic and Political Weekly* 26 (25): 1554–1561.

6999. Tanguiane, A. S. January 1994. Arrows Paradox and Mathematical Theory of Democracy. *Social Choice and Welfare* 11 (1): 1–82.

7000. Tanguiane, S. 1977. Education and the Problem of Its Democratization. *Prospects* 7 (1): 14–31.

7001. Taniguchi, Y. 1988. Japan's Company Law and the Promotion of Corporate Democracy: A Futile Attempt. *Columbia Journal of Transnational Law* 27 (1): 195–241.

7002. Tannenbaum, A. S. 1987. *See* Rosner, M. (1987).

7003. Tanner, L. 1984. *See* Golembiewski, R. T. (1984).

7004. Tanor, B. December 1983. Restructuring Democracy in Turkey. *Review International Commission of Jurists* 31: 75–86.

7005. Tanor, B. July 1992. Fondements des Violations des Droits de l'Homme. *Peuples Mediterraneens* 25–34.

7006. Tarazi, A. M. December 1993. Saudi Arabia's New Basic Laws: The Struggle for Participatory Government. *Harvard International Law Journal* 34: 258–275.

7007. Tarcov, N. September 1983. Philosophy and History: Tradition and Interpretation in the Work of Leo Strauss. *Polity* 16 (1): 5–29.

7008. Tardos, M. 1989. We Must Return to Democracy. *Acta Oeconomica* 40 (3–4): 271–274.

7009. Tate, C. N. 1974. Socioeconomic Development and Democratization in Philippines. *Comparative Political Studies* 7 (1): 47–62.

7010. Tate, C. N. December 1994. *See* Poe, S. C. (December 1994).

7011. Taubenfeld, H. J. September 1990. *See* Taubenfeld, R. F. (September 1990).

7012. Taubenfeld, R. F., and H. J. Taubenfeld. September 1990. Some Thoughts on the Problems of Designing Stable Democracies. *International Lawyer* 24: 689–710.

7013. Tauxe, C. S. March 1993. The Spirit of Christmas: Television and Commodity Hunger in a Brazilian Election. *Public Culture* 5 (3): 593–604.

7014. Tawfic, E. F. January 1979. The Modernizing Individual in a Consociational Democracy: Lebanon as a Case Study. *Indian Journal of Political Studies* 3 (1): 24–46.

7015. Taylor, D. March 1992. Parties, Elections, and Democracy in Pakistan. *Journal of Commonwealth and Comparative Politics* 30 (1): 96–115.

7016. Taylor, I. 1987. Violence and Video: From a Social Democratic Perspective. *Contemporary Crises* 11 (2): 107–127.

7017. Taylor, J. April 1983. *See* Pollack, B. (April 1983).

7018. Taylor, J. B. June 1992. The Supreme Court and Political Eras: A Perspective on Judicial Power in a Democratic Society. *Review of Politics* 54 (3): 345–368.

7019. Taylor, M. K. December 1994. *See* Herrera, R. (December 1994).

7020. Taylor, M. W. March 1981). *See* Sederberg, P. C. (March 1981).

7021. Taylor, N. October 1984. Benevolent Dictatorship to Democracy. *American Bar Association Journal* 70: 126–132.

7022. Taylor, R. 1981. *See* Feldman, R. L. (1981).

7023. Taylor, R. September 1990. South Africa: Consociational or Democracy? *Telos* 85: 17–32.

7024. Tchkhikvadze, V. July 1985. The Genuinely Democratic Character of the Soviet Political System.* *La Vie Internationale* 2: 43–52.

7025. Teasdale, A. L. April 1993. Subsidiary in Post-Maastricht Europe. *Political Quarterly* 64 (2): 187–197.

7026. Tedesco, J. C. 1988. Quality and Democracy in Higher Education: A Possible and Necessary Objective. *Estudios Sociales Centroamericanos* 46: 26–42.

7027. Tedin, K. L. May 1992. *See* Gibson, J. L. (May 1992).

7028. Tedin, K. L. July 1994. Popular Support for Competitive Elections in the Soviet Union. *Comparative Political Studies* 27 (2): 241–271.

7029. Teitel, R. July 1993. A Critique of Religion as Politics in the Public Sphere. *Cornell Law Review* 78 (5): 747–821.

7030. Telo, M. 1987. The Greening of Social Democracy: The SPD Rethinks Economics. *Socialist Review* 91: 83–95.

7031. Tempest, C. September 1993. *See* McSweeney, D. (September 1993).

7032. Templeton, I. 1980. New Zealand's Battle to Retain British Trade Links: Population Drain Could Damage Social Democracy. *Round Table* 277: 53–58.

7033. Terry, S. M. June 1993. Thinking about Post-Communist Transitions: How Difficult Are They? *Slavic Review* 52 (2): 333–337.

7034. Tessler, M. March 1985. The Uses and Limits of Populism: The Political Strategy of King Hassan II of Morocco. *Middle East Review* 17 (3): 44–51.

7035. Tessler, M. May 1985. Tunisia at the Crossroads. *Current History* 84 (502): 217–220, 229–230.

7036. Tessler, M. April 1990. Tunisia's New Beginning. *Current History* 89 (546): 169–172, 182–184.

7037. Teulings, A. W. M. 1987. A Political Bargaining Theory of Co-determination: An Empirical Test for the Dutch System of Organizational Democracy. *Organization Studies* 8 (1): 1–24.

7038. Thakur, R. September 1982. Liberalism, Democracy, and Development: Philosophical Dilemmas in Third-World Politics. *Political Studies* 30 (3): 333–349.

7039. Thakur, R. C. 1976. Fate of India's Parliamentary Democracy. *Pacific Affairs* 49 (2): 263–293.

7040. Thapar, R. 1985. An Uninformed Democracy. *Economic and Political Weekly* 20 (48): 2101.

7041. Theiner, G. December 1984. Whither India? How Free Is the Indian Press and What Is the Future of India's Much Prized Democracy? *Index on Censorship* 13: 3–5.

7042. Theisen, H. 1984. Anxiety about the Future and Democracy.* *Stahl und Eisen* 104 (23): 1195–1198.

7043. Theisen, H. 1991. Can Biotechnology and Genetic Technology Be Reconciled with Democracy.* *Soziale Welt* 42 (1): 109–127.

7044. Therborn, G. May 1977. The Rule of Capital and the Rise of Democracy. *New Left Review* 103: 3–41.

7045. Therborn, G. January 1979. The Travail of Latin American Democracy. *New Left Review* 10: 71–90, 113–114.

7046. Thiam, A. August 26, 1993. Côte d'Ivoire: Les Medias se Democratisent. *Jeune Afrique* 33: 38–40.

7047. Thibaud, P. 1993. Citizenship and Moral Commitment.* *Pouvoirs* 65: 19–30.

7048. Thibaut, B. 1992. *See* Nohlen, D. (1992).

7049. Thibaut, B. April 1993. Presidencialismo, Parlamentarismo y el Problema de la Consolidacion Democratica en America Latina. *Estudios Internacionales* 26: 216–252.

7050. Thiebault, J. November 1980. Le Paradoxe de l'U.D.F.(Union pour la Democratie Française) Cohesion et Conflicts. *Revue Politique et Parlementaire* 82: 52–69.

7051. Thiele, L. P. 1993. Making Democracy Safe for the World: Social Movements and Global Politics. *Alternatives* 18 (3): 273–305.

7052. Thierse, W. April 15, 1994. The 1994 [German] Election: What To Do?* *Aus Politik und Zeitgeschichte* 15: 14–20.

7053. Thigpen, R. B. February 1982. *See* Downing, L. (February 1982).

7054. Thigpen, R. B., and L. Downing. June 1991. Liberty and Community: A Liberal Resolution. *Perspectives on Political Science* 20 (3): 141–147.

7055. Thimm, A. L. December 1979. The False Promise of Employee Codetermination: Employee Codetermination Is More Likely to Destroy Capitalism and Democracy Than to Save Them. *Business and Society Review* 32: 36–41.

7056. Thimme, D. H. 1978. Die Rolle Der Kirche in Einer Wertbestimmten Demokratie. *Mitarbeit* 27 (3): 185–192.

7057. Thomas, A. H. 1975. Danish Social Democracy and European Community. *Journal of Common Market Studies* 13 (4): 454–468.

7058. Thomas, D. 1983. Industria: Democracy at Work. *New Society* 66 (1093): 169.

7059. Thomas, G. 1982. The First Hansard Society Lecture: The Changing Face of Parliamentary Democracy. *Parliamentary Affairs* 35 (4): 348–355.

7060. Thomas, J. J. R. June 1984. Weber and Direct Democracy. *British Journal of Sociology* 35 (2): 216–240.

7061. Thomas, R. D. September 1979. Implementing Federal Programs at the Local Level. *Political Science Quarterly* 94 (3): 419–435.

7062. Thomas, R. D., and V. L. Marando. December 1981. Local Government Reform and Territorial Democracy: The Case of Florida. *Publius* 11 (1): 49–63.

7063. Thomas Woolley, B., and E. J. Keller. September 1994. Majority Rule and Minority Rights: American Federalism and African Experience. *Journal of Modern African Studies* 32 (3): 411–428.

7064. Thomerson, M. J. 1991. German Reunification: The Privatization of Socialist Property on East Germany's Path to Democracy. *Georgia Journal of International and Comparative Law* 21 (1): 123–143.

7065. Thompson, A. W. J. May 1977. New Focus on Industrial Democracy in Britain. *Annals of the American Academy of Political and Social Science* 431: 32–43.

7066. Thompson, B. March 1988. Protecting the Democratic Process. *Public Law* 1988: 18–24.

7067. Thompson, F. J., N. M. Riccucci, and C. Ban. November 1991. Drug Testing in the Federal Workplace: An Instrumental and Symbolic Assessment. *Public Administration Review* 51 (6): 515–525.

7068. Thompson, K. W. April 1979. American Democracy and the Third World: Convergence and Contradictions. *Review of Politics* 41 (2): 256–272.

7069. Thompson, K. W. December 1990. History as End Point or New Beginnings. *Mediterranean Quarterly* 1 (1): 111–126.

7070. Thompson, M. January 1990. *See* Shain, Y. (January 1990).

7071. Thompson, M. R. 1993. The Limits of Democratization in ASEAN. *Third World Quarterly* 14 (3): 469–484.

7072. Thompson, M. R., and I. Roxborough. July 1982. Union Elections and Democracy in Mexico: A Comparative Perspective. *British Journal of Industrial Relations* 20 (2): 201–217.

7073. Thompson, W. R. July 1975. Regime Vulnerability and the Military Coup. *Comparative Politics* 7 (4): 459–487.

7074. Thomson, K. May 1987. Directions for Democracy. *National Civic Review* 76 (3): 199–207.

7075. Thomson, S. D. May 1976. Secondary Schools and the Urban Climate. *Education and Urban Society* 8 (3): 355–374.

7076. Thorburn, H. G. December 1978. Canadian Pluralist Democracy in Crisis: Interest Group Politics and Canadian Ethnic Minorities. *Canadian Journal of Political Science* 11 (4): 723–738.

7077. Thornicroft, K. W. December 1991. "Fair Share" Agency Fees: The Triumph of Individual over Collective Rights? *Labor Studies Journal* 16 (4): 34–47.

7078. Thornton, T. P. June 1989. The New Phase in U.S.-Pakistani Relations. *Foreign Affairs* 68 (3): 142–159.

7079. Thorsrud, E. 1975. Democratization of Labor and Transformation of Organization.* *Sociologie du Travail* 75 (3): 243–265.

7080. Thorsrud, E. July 1977. Democracy at Work: Norwegian Experiences with Non-Bureaucratic Forms of Organization. *Journal of Applied Behavioral Science* 13 (3): 410–421.

7081. Thouez, J. September 1976. Difficult Road to Democracy for Spain after Franco. *International Perspectives* 50–56.

7082. Thouez, J. September 1977. Apprenticeship in Democracy with Spain's "Civilized" Right. *International Perspectives* 35–40.

7083. Thrasher, M. December 1993. *See* Rallings, C. (December 1993).

7084. Thulo, M. D. July 1993. *See* Kolane, J. T. (July 1993).

7085. Tibbetts, G. L. June 1994. *See* Galston, W. A. (June 1994).

7086. Tichomirow, J. A. 1977. Socialist Democracy and the Scientific-Technological Revolution.* *Sowjetwissenschaft: Gesellschafts Wissenschaftliche Beitrage* 30 (3): 239–247.

7087. Tideman, N. May 1994. Capacities and Limits of Democracy. *American Economic Review* 84 (2): 349–352.

7088. Tidmarch, C. M., E. Lonergan, and J. Sciortino. August 1986. Interplay Competition in the U.S. States: Legislative Elections, 1970–1978. *Legislative Studies Quarterly* 11 (3): 353–374.

7089. Tiefenbach, H. June 1981. *See* Weede, E. (June 1981).

7090. Tiemann, H. January 1993. Gewerkschaften und Sozialdemokratie in den Neuen Bundeslaendern: Bestandsaufnahme und Perspektiven nach zwei Jahren Deutscher Einheit. *Deutschland Archiv* 26: 40–51.

7091. Tien, H. July 1989. The Transformation of an Authoritarian Party-State: Taiwan's Developmental Experience. *Issues and Studies* 25 (7): 105–133.

7092. Tierney, W. G. 1989. Advancing Democracy: A Critical Interpretation of Leadership. *Peabody Journal of Education* 66 (3): 157–175.

7093. Tiersky, R. 1988. Declining Fortunes of the French Communist Party. *Problems of Communism* 37 (5): 1–22.

7094. Tietz, U. 1993. Factitiousness, Validity and Democracy: Comments on Habermas Theory of Discourse of the Truth and Establishment of Norms.* *Deutsche Zeitschrift für Philosophie* 41 (2): 333–342.

7095. Tiffany, M. January 1993. Tonga's Call for Democracy. *Pacific Islands Monthly* 63: 16–18.

7096. Tikunnova, L. I. November 1992. Democratization of the Teaching-Upbringing Process in the Primary Link of Instruction. *Russian Education and Society* 34 (11): 23–36.

7097. Tilles, E. A. 1989. Union Receiverships under Rico: A Union Democracy Perspective. *University of Pennsylvania Law Review* 137 (3): 929–966.

7098. Tilly, C. December 1992. Futures of European States. *Social Research* 59 (4): 705–717.

7099. Tilman, R. September 1987. The Neo-Instrumental Theory of Democracy. *Journal of Economic Issues* 21 (3): 1379–1401.

7100. Tilton, T. A. 1974. Social Origins of Liberal Democracy: The Swedish Case. *American Political Science Review* 68 (2): 561–571.

7101. Tilton, T. A. 1979. Swedish Road to Socialism: Ernst Wigforss and the Ideological Foundations of Swedish Social Democracy. *American Political Science Review* 73 (2): 505–520.

7102. Timberland, M., and K. R. Williams. February 1984. Dependence, Political Exclusion, and Government Repression: Some Cross-National Evidence. *American Sociological Review* 49 (1): 141–146.

7103. Timbers, E. December 1990. Legal and Institutional Aspects of the Iran Contra Affair. *Presidential Studies Quarterly* 20 (1): 31–41.

7104. Timmermann, H. March 1985. Democratic Centralism Today: The Debate on Organization Principles and Models of Communist Parties.* *Osteuropa* 35 (3): 169–180.

7105. Timmermann, H. 1990. Reforms of the Communist Party of the Soviet Union and the Left in Western Europe: In Search of Preferential Relations for International Social Democracy. *Beitraege zur Konfliktforschung* 20 (3): 33–60.

7106. Tindigarukayo, J. K. September 1989. The Viability of Federalism and Consociationalism in Cultural Plural Societies of Post-Colonial States: A Theoretical Exploration. *Plural Societies* 19 (1): 41–54.

7107. Tismaneanu, V. November 1989. Civil Society: An Idea That Became the Story. *Deadline* 4 (5): 9–11.

7108. Tismaneanu, V. June 1991. *See* Calinescu, M. (January 1991).

7109. Tismaneanu, V. March 1993. The Quasi-Revolution and Its Discontent: Emerging Pluralism in Post-Ceausescu Romania. *East European Politics and Societies* 7 (2): 309–348.

7110. Tobacyk, J. J. April 1992. Changes in Locus of Control Beliefs in Polish University Students before and after Democratization. *Journal of Social Psychology* 132 (2): 217–222.

7111. Toffler, A. 1976. Prospective Democracy.* *Futuribles* (7): 259–278.

7112. Togeby, L. August 1993. Grassroots Participation in the Nordic Countries. *European Journal of Political Research* 24 (2): 159–175.

7113. Tokei, F. March 1990. Democracy and Socialism in Georg Lukacs' Political Philosophy. *Science and Society* 54 (1): 29–41.

7114. Tokes, R. L. September 1984. Hungarian Reform Imperatives. *Problems of Communism* 33 (5): 1–23.

7115. Tokes, R. L. November 1990. From Post-Communism to Democracy: Politics, Parties, and Elections in Hungary.* *Aus Politik und Zeitgeschichte* 45 (2): 16–33.

7116. Tollefson, S. D. January 1986. *See* Roett, R. (January 1986).

7117. Tollison, R. D. 1975. *See* Amacher, R. C. (1975).

7118. Tollison, R. D. March 1977. Optimum Legislative Sizes and Voting Rules. *Policy Studies Journal* 5 (3): 340–345.

7119. Tollison, R. D. March 1988. *See* Anderson, G. M. (March 1988).

7120. Tolz, V. March 1988. Informal Groups in the USSR. *Washington Quarterly* 11 (2): 137–144.

7121. Tolz, V. March 4, 1994. Problems in Building Democratic Institutions in Russia. *RFE/RL Research Report* 3: 1–7.

7122. Tolz, V., and J. Wishnevsky. April 1, 1994. Election Queries Make Russians Doubt Democratic Process. *RFE/RL Research Report* 3: 1–6.

7123. Tomac, Z. 1988. Party State or Socialist Constitutional State.* *Politicka Misao* 25 (4): 124–133.

7124. Tomlinson, J. D. 1984. Economic and Sociological Theories of the Enterprise and Industrial Democracy. *British Journal of Sociology* 35 (4): 591–605.

7125. Tomlinson, J. D. 1986. Democracy Inside the Black-Box: Neo-Classical Theories of the Firm and Industrial Democracy. *Economy and Society* 15 (2): 220–250.

7126. Tong, J. 1990. Death at the Gate of Heavenly Peace: The Democracy Movement in Beijing, April-June 1989. *Chinese Law and Government* 23 (1): 3–9.

7127. Tong, J., and A. Ma. 1990. Baptism by Fire: The Democracy Movement in Beijing, April-June 1989. *Chinese Law and Government* 23 (2): 9–119.

7128. Tong, Y. April 1994. State, Society, and Political Change in China and Hungary. *Comparative Politics* 26 (3): 333–353.

7129. Tonkin, D. October 1990. The Art of Politics in Thailand. *Asian Affairs (London)* 21: 285–294.

7130. Tonsor, S. J. June 1980. The New Natural Law and the Problem of Equality. *Modern Age* 24 (3): 238–247.

7131. Tooker, E. 1990. Native American Societies and the Evolution of Democracy in America, 1600–1800: Rejoinder. *Ethnohistory* 37 (3): 291–297.

7132. Torgerson, D. August 1993. *See* Dryzek, J. S. (August 1993).

7133. Tornquist, O. 1990. Fighting for Democracy in the Philippines. *Economic and Political Weekly* 25 (26): 1385–1387.

7134. Tornquist, O. 1991a. Communists and Democracy: Two Indian Cases and One Debate. *Bulletin of Concerned Asian Scholars* 23 (2): 63–76.

7135. Tornquist, O. 1991b. Communists and Democracy in the Philippines. *Economic and Political Weekly* 26 (27–2): 1683–1692.

7136. Tornquist, O. 1991c. Communists and Democracy in the Philippines. *Economic and Political Weekly* 26 (29): 1757–1763.

7137. Tornquist, O. 1993. Democratic "Empowerment": Radical Popular Movements and the May 1992 Philippino Elections. *Third World Quarterly* 14 (3): 485–515.

7138. Toropainen, M. 1978. Trade Unionism and Democracy in Business.* *Nordisk Psykologi* 30 (2): 130–131.

7139. Torre, J. C. October 1991. America Latina: El Gobierna de la Democracia en Tiempos Dificiles. *Revista de Estudios Politicos* 74: 145–165.

7140. Torre, J. C. January 1992. Latin America: Democracy and the Test of the Crisis.* *Problemes d'Amerique Latine* 4: 3–18.

7141. Torre, J. C. January 1993. The Politics of Economic Crisis in Latin America. *Journal of Democracy* 4 (1): 104–116.

7142. Torres, J. C. May 1993. *See* Lipset, S. M. (May 1993).

7143. Torres-Rivas, E. October 1991. Centroamerica: La Transicion Autoritaria Lacia la Democracia. *Revista de Estudios Politicos* 74: 431–448.

7144. Toscano, D. J. 1981. Employee Ownership and Democracy in the Workplace. *Social Policy* 12 (1): 16–23.

7145. Toulabor, C. M. 1989. Ten Years of "Democratization" in Togo: Forgers of Democracy.* *Année Africaine* 287–310.

7146. Toulabor, C. M. 1994. Ghana: New Churches and Democratization.* *L'Afrique Politique* 131–142.

7147. Toulabor, C. M. (ed.). October 1993. Intellectuels Africains. *Politique Africaine* 3–120. 8 articles.

7148. Toungara, J. M. September 1986. Political Reform and Economic Change in Ivory Coast: An Update. *Journal of African Studies* 13 (3): 94–101.

7149. Touraine, A. 1986. The Chances of Democracy in Latin America.* *Notes et Etudes Documentaires* 80: 119–133.

7150. Touraine, A. May 1991. What Does Democracy Mean Today? *International Social Science Journal* 43 (2): 259–268.

7151. Tovar, O. 1991. El Sistema Politico Venezuela. *Revista de Derecho Politico* 32: 337–395.

7152. Tovias, A. April 1984. The International Context of Democratic Transition. *West European Politics* 7 (2): 158–171.

7153. Tragardh, L. September 1990. Swedish Model or Swedish Culture? *Critical Review* 4: 569–590.

7154. Transnea, O. January 1983. The Dialectics of the Historical Development of Democracy. *Vittorul Social* 1: 27–35.

7155. Traugott, S. A. September 1976. *See* Bogue, A. G. (September 1976).

7156. Tregurtha, E. J. 1986. *See* Demetrius, F. J. (1986).

7157. Trejos, M. E., and M. Perez. 1990. Decentralization and Economic Democracy within the Framework of Structural Adjustment: The Case of Costa Rica.* *Estudios Sociales Centroamericanos* (52): 53–83.

7158. Trento, A. September 1981. Brazil: The Political System. "The "Opening Process" and the Limits of Democratization. *Politica Internazionale* 8–9: 7–19.

7159. Treskov, V. August 1991. Morality under Conditions of Market Democracy. *Problems of Economics* 34 (4): 85–91.

7160. Treverton, G. F. June 1987. Covert Action and Open Society. *Foreign Affairs* 65 (5): 995–1024.

7161. Triaille, E. April 1994. The Difficult Democratization of Zaire.* *Aggiornamenti Sociali* 45 (4): 291–304.

7162. Triaud, J. September 1992. Au Tchad la Democratie Introuvable: Etat Inexistant, Ingenences Exterieures. *Monde Diplomatique* 39: 18.

7163. Trindade, H. May 1991. Presidential Elections and Political Transition in Latin America. *International Social Science Journal* 43 (2): 301–314.

7164. Trinder, R. B. March 1992. A Springtime in Hungary. *Federal Bar News and Journal* 39: 475–476.

7165. Tripp, A. M. April 1994. Gender, Political Participation, and the Transformation of Associational Life in Uganda and Tanzania. *African Studies Review* 37 (1): 107–132.

7166. Troebst, S. 1992. Nationalismus als Demokratisierungshemmnis in Bulgarien: Von der Vervassungsdiskussion zur Praesidentschaftswahl (Mai 1991-Junuar 1992). *Suedosteuropa* 41 (3–4): 188–227.

7167. Troltsch, K. June 1985. The Code of Conduct for Deputies in the Western Democracies.* *Aus Politik und Zeitgeschichte* 15 (24–25): 3–16.

7168. Troper, M. 1990. Constitutional Justice and Democracy.* *Revue Française de Droit Constitutionnel* 1: 31–48.

7169. Tsai, W. December 1992. New Authoritarianism, Neo-Conservatism and Anti-Peaceful Evolution: Mainland China's Resistance to Political Modernization. *Issues and Studies* 28 (12): 1–22.

7170. Tseng, H. April 1993. Peasant, State, and Democracy: The Chinese Case. *Issues and Studies* 29 (4): 34–50.

7171. Tu, W. March 1992. Intellectual Effervescence in China. *Daedalus* 121 (2): 251–292.

7172. Tugwell, R. G. 1978. Planning and Democracy. *Center Magazine* 11 (5): 59–67.

7173. Tulchin, J. S. March 1988. The United States and Latin America in the 1960s. *Journal of Interamerican Studies and World Affairs* 30 (1): 1–36.

7174. Tullock, G. Spring 1977a. The Demand-Revealing Process as a Welfare Indicator. *Public Choice* 29 (2): 51–64.

7175. Tullock, G. Spring 1977b. Practical Problems and Practical Solutions. *Public Choice* 29 (2): 27–36.

7176. Tullock, G. September 1977. *See* Buchanan, J. M. (September 1977).

7177. Tullock, G. 1981. Why So Much Stability? *Public Choice* 37 (2): 189–202.

7178. Tullock, G. March 1988. *See* Hodgson, G. (March 1988).

7179. Tuma, E. H. January 1979. Agrarian Reform in Historical Perspective Revisited. *Comparative Studies in Society and History* 21 (1): 3–29.

7180. Tumin, J. March 1982. The Theory of Democratic Development: A Critical Revision. *Theory and Society* 11 (2): 143–164.

7181. Tummala, K. March 1986. Democracy Triumphant in India: The Case of Andhra Pradesh. *Asian Survey* 26 (3): 378–395.

7182. Turan, I. January 1980. Attitudinal Correlates of Political Democracy: The Case of South Korea and Turkey. *Orient* 21 (1): 77–78.

7183. Turan, I. October 1987. *See* Muller, E. N. (October 1987).

7184. Turk, H., and L. G. Zucker. June 1985. Structural Bases of Minority Effects on Majority-Supported Change. *Social Science Quarterly* 66 (2): 365–385.

7185. Turner, A. W. October 1993. Postauthoritarian Elections: Testing Expectations about "First" Elections. *Comparative Political Studies* 26 (3): 330–349.

7186. Turner, B. S. March 1993. Talcott Parsons, Universalism and the Education Revolution: Democracy Versus Professionalism. *British Journal of Sociology* 44 (1): 1–24.

7187. Turner, F. C., and M. Carballo de Cilley. May 1993. Equality and Democracy. *International Social Science Journal* 45 (2): 271–283.

7188. Turner, R., and R. Court. 1981. Education for Industrial Democracy: An Evaluation of the Experimental Trade Union Studies Project. *Economic and Industrial Democracy* 2 (3): 371–394.

7189. Turpin, A. 1984. The Philippines: Problems of the Aging New Society. *Conflict Studies* 165: 1–22.

7190. Tushnet, M. V. 1981. The Dilemmas of Liberal Constitutionalism. *Ohio State Law Journal* 42 (1): 411–426.

7191. Tushnet, M. V. 1991. Symposium on Democracy and Distrust: 10 Years Later. *Virginia Law Review* 77 (4): 631–639.

7192. Tushnet, M. V. 1993. Thayer's Target: Judicial Review or Democracy. *Northwestern University Law Review* 88 (1): 9–27.

7193. Twight, C. March 1989. Institutional Underpinnings of Parochialism: The Case of Military Base Closure. *Cato Journal* 9: 73–105.

7194. Tyack, D., and E. Hansot. June 1981. Conflict and Consensus in American Public Education. *Daedalus* 110 (3): 1–25.

7195. Tyler, A. S. June 1990. *See* Grey, R. D. (June 1990).

7196. Tyler, G. May 1984. Democracy Versus Mediacracy. *New Leader* 67: 10–12.

7197. Tymowski, A. W. December 1994. Left Turn in Polish Elections? *New Politics* 4 (4): 99–107.

7198. Tyomkina, A. November 1993. The Problem of Advancing Industrial Democracy in Post-Socialist Society. *Economic and Industrial Democracy* 14 (Supplement) (4): 29–42.

7199. Tyree, A., M. Semyonov, and R. W. Hodge. June 1979. Gaps and Glissandros: Inequality, Economic Development, and Social Mobility in Twenty-Four Countries. *American Sociological Review* 44 (3): 410–424.

7200. Tzschaschel, J. 1993. Algeria Torn between Fundamentalism and Democracy. *Aussenpolitik* 44 (1): 23–34.

7201. Ucakar, K. 1988. Reforming Democracy in Austria.* *Oesterreichische Zeitschrift für Politikwissenschaft* 17 (4): 349–372.

7202. Uchida, M. 1974. Changing Aspects of Spectatorial Democracy in Japan. *Waseda Political Studies* 9: 1–14.

7203. Ucles, M. L. December 1992. Redefining Democracy in El Salvador: New Spaces and New Practices for the 1990s. *Social Justice* 19 (4): 110–125.

7204. Udogu, E. I. September 1992. In Search of Political Stability and Survival: Towards Nigeria's Third Republic. *Scandinavian Journal of Development Alternatives* 11 (3–4): 5–28.

7205. Ugeux, W. November 1980. Juan Carlos 1: Five Years to Build a Democracy.* *Revue Generale* 11: 17–35.

7206. Uhlin, A. 1993a. Transnational Diffusion and Indonesian Democracy Discourses. *Third World Quarterly* 14 (3): 517–544.

7207. Uhlin, A. 1993b. *See* Kinnvall, C. (1993).

7208. Uhr, J. May 1981. Democratic Theory and Consensus: Roots of the Civic Culture. *Politics* 16 (1): 103–118.

7209. Uleri, P. V. August 1985. Forms of Popular Consultation in Democracies: A Typology.* *Rivista Italiana di Scienza Politica* 15 (2): 205–254.

7210. Ulianovskii, R. A. 1985. On Revolutionary Democracy: Its State and Political System. *Soviet Law and Government* 23 (3): 51–67.

7211. Ullrich, H. 1978. Italian Liberals and the Problems of Democratization, 1876–1915.* *Geschichte und Gesellschaft* 4 (1): 49–76.

7212. Um, K. January 1987. *See* Johnson, C. (January 1987).

7213. Unger, A. L. 1991. The Travails of Intra-Party Democracy in the Soviet Union: The Elections to the 19th Conference of the CPSU. *Soviet Studies* 43 (2): 329–354.

7214. Urban, J. December 1991. Nationalism as a Totalitarian Ideology. *Social Research* 58 (4): 775–779.

7215. Urban, M. E. August 1982. Bureaucratic Ideology in the United States and the Soviet Union: Some Empirical Dimensions. *Administration and Society* 14 (2): 139–162.

7216. Urbinati, N. 1993. Loyalty and Dissent: Michael Walzer's Pluralist Democracy.* *Teoria Politica* 9 (3): 111–113.

7217. Urnov, M. I. July 1990. How Ready Are We for Democracy? The Results of a Sociological Study. *Soviet Sociology* 29: 6–31.

7218. Urrutia, E. R., and A. Sojo. 1983. Popular Movement, Social-Conflict and Democracy. *Estudios Sociales Centroamericanos* 12 (36): 165–181.

7219. Ursprung, H. W. 1980. Voting Behavior in a System of Concordant Democracy. *Public Choice* 35 (3): 349–362.

7220. Ursprung, T. March 1994. The Use and Effect of Political Propaganda in Democracies. *Public Choice* 78 (3–4): 259–282.

7221. Useem, M. December 1978. *See* Dimaggio, P. (December 1978).

7222. Utley, J. G. 1976. Diplomacy in a Democracy: United States and Japan, 1937–1941. *World Affairs* 139 (2): 130–140.

7223. Utter, R. F., and D. C. Lundsgaard. 1993. Judicial Review in the New Nations of Central and Eastern Europe: Some Thoughts from a Comparative Perspective. *Ohio State Law Journal* 54 (3): 559–606.

7224. Uwazurike, P. C. March 1990. Confronting Potential Breakdown: The Nigerian Redemocratisation Process in Critical Perspective. *Journal of Modern African Studies* 28 (1): 55–77.

7225. Vail, D. October 1993. The Past and Future of Swedish Social Democracy: A Reply. *Monthly Review* 45 (5): 24–31.

7226. Vajpeyi, D. March 1989. *See* Malik, Y. K. (March 1989).

7227. Vakey, V. P. June 1986. Political Change in Latin America: A Foreign Policy Dilemma for the United States. *Journal of Interamerican Studies and World Affairs* 28 (2): 1–15.

7228. Valen, H. 1994. Norway's Electoral System.* *Statsvetenskaplig Tidskrift* 97 (1): 17–21.

7229. Valentino, N. December 1994. *See* Ansolabehere, S. (December 1994).

7230. Valenzuela, A. 1975. Breakdown of Democracy in Chile. *Rivista Italiana di Scienza Politica* 5 (1): 83–129.

7231. Valenzuela, A. February 1982. Eight Years of Military Rule in Chile. *Current History* 81 (472): 64–68, 88.

7232. Valenzuela, A. February 1985. Prospects for the Pinochet Regime in Chile. *Current History* 84 (499): 77–80, 89–90.

7233. Valenzuela, A. December 1985. Toward Stable Democracy: Chile's Parliamentary Option.* *Revista de Ciencia Politica* 7 (2): 129–140.

7234. Valenzuela, A. December 1989. *See* Constable, P. (December 1989).

7235. Valenzuela, A. March 1990. *See* Constable, P. (March 1990).

7236. Valenzuela, A., and P. Constable. March 1989. The Chilean Plebiscite: Defeat of a Dictator. *Current History* 88 (536): 129–132, 152–153.

7237. Valenzuela, A., and P. Constable. February 1991. Democracy in Chile. *Current History* 90 (553): 53–56, 84–85.

7238. Valenzuela, J. S. July 1989. Labor Movements in Transitions to Democracy: A Framework for Analysis. *Comparative Politics* 21 (4): 445–472.

7239. Valenzuela, J. S. 1990. The Labor Movement in the Transition to Democracy: Conceptual Framework for Its Analysis.* *Desarrollo Economico* 30 (119): 299–332.

7240. Valenzuela, J. S. December 1993. *See* Scully, T. R. (December 1993).

7241. Valenzuela, M. E. September 1990. Gender Issues in Chilean Politics. *Peace Review* 2 (4): 24–27.

7242. Valles, J. M. March 1994. The Spanish General Elections of 1993. *Electoral Studies* 13 (1): 87–91.

7243. Valles, O. 1992. The Programmatic Antecedents of the Punto Fijo Agreement: Project for Democratic Consolidation [in Venezuela] 1946–1948.* *Politeia (Caracas)* 15: 289–302.

7244. Valls-Russell, J. April 5, 1993. Popping Out of the Pyrenees: Andora Loses Its Innocence. *New Leader* 76: 9–10.

7245. Valocchi, S. May 1992. The Origins of the Swedish Welfare-State: A Class Analysis of the State and Welfare Politics. *Social Problems* 39 (2): 189–200.

7246. Valticos, N. 1987. Democracy and Human Rights.* *Annuaire Europeen* 35: 53–68.

7247. Van Amersfoort, H., and H. Van Der Wusten. October 1981. Democratic Stability and Ethnic Parties. *Ethnic and Racial Studies* 4 (4): 476–485.

7248. Van de Walle, N. July 1992. *See* Bratton, M. (July 1992).

7249. Van de Walle, N. July 1994. *See* Bratton, M. (July 1994).

7250. Van Den Doel, J. October 1974. Gains and Sacrifices in the Governmental System.* *Acta Politica* 9 (4): 423–432.

7251. Van Den Poel, H., and T. Grondsmat. November 1979. Income Distribution and the Theory of Public Choice.* *Acta Politica* 14 (4): 433–478.

7252. Van Der Burg, W. 1992. Equality Versus Religious Freedom. *Archiv für Rechts und Sozialphilosophie* 78 (2): 211–218.

7253. Van Der Ross, R. E. December 1981. The Pre-Conditions for a Stable Democracy in South Africa.* *Politikon* 8 (2): 43–56.

7254. Van Der Wusten, H. October 1981. *See* Van Amersfoort, H. (October 1981).

7255. Van Donge, J. K., and A. J. Liviga. July 1990. The Democratization of Zanzibar and the 1985 General Elections. *Journal of Commonwealth and Comparative Politics* 28 (2): 201–218.

7256. Van Hanen, T. 1980. Democracy and the Level of Economic Development.* *Politiika* 22 (1): 125–141.

7257. Van Hanen, T. June 1983. A Study on the Emergence of Democracy. *European Journal of Political Research* 11 (2): 223–227.

7258. Van Hollen, E. February 1987. Pakistan in 1986: Trails of Transition. *Asian Survey* 27 (2): 143–154.

7259. Van Montford, C. J., and D. J. H. M. Van Montford. 1989. Public Information Policy: An Instrument of Democracy or Technology.* *Beleidwetenschap* 3 (1): 40–67.

7260. Van Montford, D. J. H. M. 1989. *See* Van Montford, C. J. (1989).

7261. Van Nieuwkerk, A. January 1994. The Impact of the New [South Africa] Constitution on the Political Process. *Politica Internazionale* 22 (1): 91–105.

7262. Van Praagh, D. October 1992. Bullets and Ballots in Asia. *Freedom Review* 23: 9–12.

7263. Van Praagh, D. December 1993. Thailand's Democracy and Asian Security. *Global Affairs* 8 (1): 73–85.

7264. Van Puyenbrook, R. A. G. July 1985. *See* Letterie, J. W. (July 1985).

7265. Van Roozendaal, P. February 1992. The Effects of Dominant and Central Parties on Cabinet Composition and Durability. *Legislative Studies Quarterly* 17 (1): 5–36.

7266. Van Schendelen, M. P. C. June 1983. Critical Comments on Lijphart's Theory of Consociational Democracy. *Politikon* 10 (1): 6–32.

7267. Van Schendelen, M. P. C. January 1984. The Views of Arend Lijphart and Collected Criticisms. *Acta Politica* 9 (1): 19–55.

7268. Van Schendelen, M. P. C. September 1985. Consociational Democracy: The Views of Arend Lijphart and Collected Criticisms. *Political Science Reviewer* 15: 144–183.

7269. Vanderbok, W. G. March 1978. *See* Sigelman, L. (March 1978).

7270. Vanderbosch, A. May 1979. Brown South Africans and the Proposed New Constitution. *Journal of Politics* 41 (2): 566–588.

7271. Vanderlaan, M. May 1984. The Dual Strategy Myth in Central American Policy. *Journal of Interamerican Studies and World Affairs* 26 (2): 199–224.

7272. Vanek, J. September 1992. *See* Rudyk, E. (September 1992).

7273. Vanhanen, T. 1994. Global Trends of Democratization in the 1990s.* *Politiika* 36 (2): 116–131.

7274. Vankrieken, R. 1981. Participation in Welfare: Democracy or Self-Regulation. *Australian Quarterly* 53 (1): 74–90.

7275. Varas, A. 1985. Democratization, Peace, and Security in Latin America. *Alternatives* 10 (4): 607–623.

7276. Varat, J. D. June 1992. Reflections on the Establishment of Constitutional Government in Eastern Europe. *Constitutional Commentary* 9: 171–187.

7277. Vardys, V. S. July 1989. Lithuanian National Politics. *Problems of Communism* 38 (4): 53–76.

7278. Varga, C. March 1993. Transformation to Rule of Law From No-Law: Societal Contecture of the Democratic Transition in Central and Eastern Europe. *Connecticut Journal of International Law* 8: 487–505.

7279. Vargas, I. 1989. The Road to Democracy in Chile.* *Internasjonal Politikk* 4–6: 241–267.

7280. Vargas Llosa, M. 1985. Latin America: Salvation through Democracy.* *Politique Internationale* 29: 193–214.

7281. Vargas Llosa, M. April 23,1992. Apres le Coup d'Etat au Perou: Non au Fuhrer de Lima. *Nouvel Observateur* 39–40.

7282. Varlack, P. I. June 1977. *See* Harrigan, N. (June 1977).

7283. Varley, P. 1991. Electronic Democracy. *Technology Review* 94 (8): 43–51.

7284. Varn, R. J. March 1993. Electronic Democracy: Jeffersonian Boom or Tera Flop? *Spectrum* 66 (2): 21–25.

7285. Varshney, A. July 1993. Self-Limited Empowerment: Democracy, Economic Development and Rural India. *Journal of Development Studies* 29 (4): 177–215.

7286. Vasconi, T. A. July 1986. Argentina and Brazil: Prospects of Two Processes of Democratic Transition.* *Revista Mexicana de Sociologia* 48 (3): 31–43.

7287. Vasconi, T. A. 1990. Democracy and Socialism in South America. *Latin American Perspectives* 17 (2): 25–38.

7288. Vasconi, T. A., and E. P. Martell. December 1993. Social Democracy and Latin America. *Latin American Perspectives* 20 (1): 99–113.

7289. Vasonic, V. 1979. The Meaning of Collective Decision-Making and Responsibility.* *Sojicalizam* 22 (3): 21–32.

7290. Vasonic, V. July 1989. Democratic Scope and Limits of Political Pluralism (in Eastern Europe). *Socialist Thought and Practice* 29 (7–10): 3–15.

7291. Vasonic, V. August 1989. Democratic Outline and Limits of Political Pluralism. *Teorija in Praksa* 26 (8–9): 1042–1048.

7292. Vaughan, J. H. December 1988. The Greens' Vision of Germany. *Orbis* 32 (1): 83–95.

7293. Vaughn, S., and B. Everson. December 1991. Democracy's Guardians: Hollywood Portrait of Reporters, 1930–1945. *Journalism Quarterly* 68 (4): 829–838.

7294. Veca, S. 1987. Theories of Democracy between Individualism and Pluralism.* *Teoria Politica* 3 (3): 31–41.

7295. Veit, L. A. March 1985. *See* Gwin, C. (March 1985).

7296. Vellinga, M. June 1993. Social Democracy, Development Theory and Political Strategy in Latin America. *Scandinavian Journal of Development Alternatives* 12 (2–3): 197–210.

7297. Vengroff, R. December 1993. Governance and the Transition to Democracy: Political Parties and the Party System in Mali. *Journal of Modern African Studies* 31 (4): 541–562.

7298. Vengroff, R. March 1994. The Impact of the Electoral System on the Transition to Democracy in Africa: The Case of Mali. *Electoral Studies* 13 (1): 29–37.

7299. Venter, A. J. December 1980. Leadership Compliance in Deeply Divided Societies: A Critical Evaluation of Lijphart's Consociational Theory.* *Politikon* 7 (2): 126–148.

7300. Venter, A. J. June 1985. Selected Aspects of Popper's Defense of Liberal Democracy.* *Politikon* 12 (1): 16–29.

7301. Ventriss, C. May 1987. Two Critical Issues of American Public Administration: Reflections of a Sympathetic Participant. *Administration and Society* 19 (1): 25–47.

7302. Venturelli, S. S. December 1993. The Imagined Transnational Public Sphere in the European Community Broadcast Philosophy: Implications for Democracy. *European Journal of Communication* 8 (4): 491–518.

7303. Verba, S. November 1994. *See* Schlozman, K. L. (November 1994).

7304. Verba, S., and G. Shabad. March 1978. Workers' Councils and Political Stratification: The Yugoslav Experience. *American Political Science Review* 72 (1): 80–95.

7305. Verdier, T. December 1993. *See* Saint-Paul, G. (December 1993).

7306. Verduga, C. October 1982. Will the Ecuadorian Democratic Process Be Consolidated? *Revista Mexicana de Sociologia* 44 (4): 1163–1185.

7307. Veron, E. September 1989. Television and Democracy: Concerning the Status of Staging.* *Mots* 20: 75–90.

7308. Veyne, P. October 1983. Did the Greeks Know Democracy?* *Diogene* 124: 3–33.

7309. Vianna, L. W. 1983. The Problem of Citizenship in the Process of Transition to Democracy. *Dados: Revista de Ciencias Sociais* 26 (3): 243–264.

7310. Vichit-Vadakan, J. February 1985. Thailand in 1984: Year of Administering Rumors. *Asian Survey* 25 (2): 232–240.

7311. Vick, D. January 1991. Will a Multiparty Policy Be Good for African Business? *African Business* 10–14.

7312. Vick, D. January 1992. Democratic Tide Turns Africa towards a New Economic Era. *African Business* 10–13.

7313. Vickers, G. R. June 1992. Nicaragua: Is the Revolution Over? *Socialism and Democracy* 16–17: 105–141.

7314. Vickers, G. R., and J. Spence. June 1992. Nicaragua: Two Years after the Fall. *World Policy Journal* 9 (3): 533–562.

7315. Vickery, K. P. 1974. Herrenvolk Democracy and Egalitarianism in South Africa and U.S.-South. *Comparative Studies in Society and History* 16 (3): 309–328.

7316. Vidich, A. J. September 1990. American Democracy in the Late Twentieth Century: Political Rhetoric and Mass Media. *International Journal of Politics, Culture, and Society* 4 (1): 5–29.

7317. Vidojecvic, Z. 1982. Revolutionary Party and Democratic Centralism.* *Questions Actuelles du Socialisme* 32 (8): 47–57.

7318. Vieragallo, J. A. 1982. Documentation and the Democratization of Information. *International Social Science Journal* 34 (4): 737–746.

7319. Viero Schmidt, B. 1994. *See* Dias David, M. (1994).

7320. Vilas, C. M. September 1982. On the Crisis of Bourgeois Democracy in Argentine. *Latin American Perspectives* 9 (4): 5–30.

7321. Vilas, C. M. 1983. Popular Democracy and Workers Participation in the Sandinista Revolution: A Preliminary Analysis. *Estudios Sociales Centroamericanos* 12 (35): 95–138.

7322. Vilas, C. M. 1989. Revolution and Democracy in Latin America. *Socialist Register* 30–46.

7323. Vilas, C. M. December 1992. Latin America: Socialist Perspectives in Times of Cholera (Preliminary Notes for a Necessary Debate). *Social Justice* 19 (4): 74–83.

7324. Villa, M. July 1986. The Fear of the State and the Problem of Contemporary Democracy. *Revista Mexicana de Ciencias Politicas y Sociales* 125: 27–40.

7325. Villadsen, S. March 1993. Another Century for Local Democracy: Decentralization, Deregulation and Participation in Scandinavia in Times of European Integration. *International Journal of Urban and Regional Research* 17 (1): 42–55.

7326. Villalobos, J. March 1989. A Democratic Revolution for El Salvador. *Foreign Policy* 74: 103–122.

7327. Villalon, L. A. April 1993. Democratizing a Quasi-Democracy: The Senegalese Elections of 1993. *African Affairs* 93 (371): 163–193.

7328. Villani, J. May 1993. *See* Ingberman, D. E. (May 1993).

7329. Villanueva, A. B. September 1992. Post-Marcos: The State of Philippine Politics and Democracy during the Aquino Regime, 1986–1992. *Contemporary Southeast Asia* 14: 174–187.

7330. Villegas, B. M. February 1987. The Philippines in 1986: Democratic Reconstruction in the Post-Marcos Era. *Asian Survey* 27 (2): 194–205.

7331. Villegas, M. F. G. October 1993. Liberalism in Modern Times: A Theoretical Perspective.* *Foro Internacional* 134: 684–715.

7332. Villera, H. 1979. Church and the Process of Democratization in Latin America. *Social Compass* 26 (2–3): 261–283.

7333. Vinokurov, J. N. 1993. Intelligentsia and Democratization: Tropical Africa in the 1980s and the 1990s.* *Vostok* 5: 78–85.

7334. Vinton, L. June 1990. *See* Barany, Z. D. (June 1990).

7335. Viola, E. October 1985. *See* Mainwaring, S. (October 1985).

7336. Viola, E., and S. Mainwaring. December 1985. Transitions to Democracy: Brazil and Argentina in the 1980s. *Journal of International Affairs* 38 (2): 193–219.

7337. Violante, L. July 1988. Biology and Democracy.* *Democrazia e Diritto* 28 (4–5): 183–212.

7338. Viou, M. 1982. *See* Brard, Y. (1982).

7339. Visegrady, A. September 1992. Transition to Democracy in Central and Eastern Europe: Experiences of a Model Country, Hungary. *William and Mary Bill of Rights Journal* 1 (2): 245–265.

7340. Vittin, T. E. April 1993. The Weaknesses of Benin's Liberal Model.* *Politica Internazionale* 21 (2): 35–45.

7341. Vittoz, S. December 1993. Confucianism and the Spirit of Democracy in China: The Beijing Uprising of 1989. *International Journal of Politics, Culture, and Society* 7 (2): 329–365.

7342. Vivekananda, F., and I. James. December 1990. Militarism and the Crisis of Democracy in Africa 1980–1985. *Scandinavian Journal of Development Alternatives* 9: 79–94.

7343. Viveret, P. June 1981. Peace and Freedom.* *Esprit* 6: 36–49.

7344. Vlahava, A. S. 1994. Nigeria: From an Authoritarian to a Democratic Pattern of Political System.* *Vostok* (5): 33–44.

7345. Vlastok, G. November 1983. The Historical Socrates and Athenian Democracy. *Political Theory* 11 (4): 495–516. 1 of 2 articles.

7346. Voegeli, W. J. , Jr. October 1981. A Critique of the Pro-Choice Argument. *Review of Politics* 43 (4): 560–571.

7347. Vogel, D. March 1987. The New Political Science of Corporate Power. *Public Interest* 87: 63–79.

7348. Vogel, R. 1977. La Planification Est—Elle Vouée à l'Echec? *Urbanisme* 46 (161): 34–47.

7349. Vogel, R. K., and B. E. Swanson. 1988. Setting Agendas for Community Change: The Community Goal-Setting Strategy. *Journal of Urban Affairs* 10: 41–61.

7350. Vogt, R. June 1981. Property Rights and Employee Decision Making in West Germany. *Journal of Economic Issues* 15 (2): 377–386.

7351. Voinovich, V. 1990. An Exile's Dilemma. *Wilson Quarterly* 14 (4): 114–120.

7352. Voitekhov, M. I. et al. September 1994. Interethnic Contradictions in Russia: The Strategy of Parties and Social Movements (A Roundtable). *Russian Politics and Law* 32: 6–31.

7353. Volard, S. V. April 1978. Project 3P: An Experiment in Industrial Democracy in a Small Firm. *Australian Journal of Management* 3: 91–111.

7354. Volcansek, M. L. January 1994. Political Power and Judicial Review in Italy. *Comparative Political Studies* 26 (4): 492–509.

7355. Volgy, T. J. December 1978. *See* Fenmore, B. (December 1978).

7356. Volgyes, I. December 1990. For Want of Another Horse: Hungary in 1990. *Current History* 89 (551): 421–424, 433–435.

7357. Vollmer, R. J. 1975. Industrial Democracy in German. *Atlantic Papers* (4): 25–33.

7358. Vollrath, E. March 1976. "That All Governments Rest On Opinion." *Social Research* 43 (1): 46–61.

7359. Vollrath, E. June 1993. Elucidation of the Theory of Democracy: Legal and Democratic Theory with Respect to Kant.* *Politische Vierteljahresschrift* 34 (2): 304–305.

7360. Von Alemann, U. March 1981. Party Democracy and Participation of Citizens.* *Revista de Estudios Politicos* 20: 119–135.

7361. Von Beyme, K. 1984. Ungovernability in Western Democracies.* *Leviathan* 12 (1): 39–49.

7362. Von Beyme, K. 1986. The Challenges to Democracy: Corporatism, Social Movement and Interest Groups. *Interdisciplinary Science Reviews* 11 (2): 132–135.

7363. Von Beyme, K. March 1990. Transition to Democracy or Anschluss? The Two Germanies and Europe. *Government and Opposition* 25 (2): 170–190.

7364. Von Beyme, K. April 1991. Architecture and Democracy in the Federal Republic of Germany. *International Political Science Review* 12 (2): 137–147.

7365. Von Beyme, K. 1992. Party Systems in the Process of Democratization in Eastern Europe.* *Geschichte und Gesellschaft* 18 (3): 271–291.

7366. Von Beyme, K. March 1992. The Effects of Reunification on German Democracy: A Preliminary Evaluation of a Great Social Experiment. *Government and Opposition* 27 (2): 158–176.

7367. Von Beyme, K. 1994a. The Theory of Change: A New Sphere of Interdisciplinary Knowledge.* *Gosudarstvo I Pravo* 7: 148–159.

7368. Von Beyme, K. 1994b. A United Germany Preparing for the 1994 Elections. *Government and Opposition* 29 (4): 445–460.

7369. Von Braunmuehl, H. 1977. Die Pancasila-Demokratie in Indonesien: Der Indonesische Weg zu Demokratie und Staatlicher Selbstverwiklichung. *Europa Wehrkunde* 26 (10): 501–526.

7370. Von der Schulenburg, J. M. G. November 1990. *See* Breyer, F. (November 1990).

7371. Von Krockow, C. December 1979. Ethics and Democracy.* *Aus Politik und Zeitgeschichte* 49 (8): 3–22.

7372. Von Krockow, C. August 1980. Faith, Democracy and Political Education: An Answer to Hermann Boventer.* *Aus Politik und Zeitgeschichte* 16 (33–34): 21–27.

7373. Von Metterheim, K. October 1990. The Brazilian Voter in Democratic Transition, 1974–1982. *Comparative Politics* 23 (1): 23–44.

7374. Von Mohrenschildt, D. October 1978. Shchapov: Exponent of Regionalism and the Federal School in Russian History. *Russian Review* 37 (4): 387–404.

7375. Von Voss, R. January 1980. On the Totality of Politics: A Contribution to Political Ethics under Democracy.* *Aus Politik und Zeitgeschichte* 5 (1): 19–31.

7376. Von Weizsacker, R. F. 1992. Public Debt and Democracy.* *Kyklos* 45 (1): 51–67.

7377. Vonotter, C. 1989. *See* Saltman, R. B. (1989).

7378. Vorhies, F. September 1989. *See* Glahe, F. (September 1989).

7379. Vorhies, F., and F. Glahe. September 1989. Liberty and Development in Africa. *South African Journal of Economics* 57: 279–291.

7380. Vowles, J. March 1994. Dealignment and Demobilization: Nonvoting in New Zealand, 1938–1990. *Australian Journal of Political Science* 29 (1): 96–114.

7381. Vredenburgh, D., and Y. Brender. June 1993. The Relevance of Democracy to Organized Management. *Employee Responsibilities and Rights Journal* 6 (2): 99–114.

7382. Vree, D. July 1975. Coalition Politics on the Left in France and Italy. *Review of Politics* 37 (3): 340–356.

7383. Vreg, F. 1991. Prospects of Political Pluralism in Yugoslavia or the "Splendor and Misery" of New Democracies.* *Teorija in Praksa* 28 (1–2): 11–22.

7384. Vujcic, V. 1987. Democracy and Education: A Historical Problematic Approach.* *Politicka Misao* 24 (1): 68–85.

7385. Wade, L. L. April 1982. Politics, Markets and Rationalistic Imbroglios. *Review of Politics* 44 (2): 187–213.

7386. Wade, R. C. 1976. Twenty-five Dollar Democracy. *Nation* 222 (12): 365–366.

7387. Wade, R. C. November 1990. The Enduring Ghetto: Urbanization and the Color Line in American History. *Journal of Urban History* 17 (1): 4–13.

7388. Waegel, W. B., M. D. Ermann, and A. M. Horowitz. December 1981. Organizational Responses to Imputations of Deviance. *Sociological Quarterly* 22 (1): 43–55.

7389. Waelbroeck, J. 1984. Democracy and Redistribution of Revenue: Compatible or Uncompatible.* *Cahiers Economiques de Bruxelles* (103): 409–418.

7390. Wagner, H. 1990. Democracy and Inflation: A Rational Theory of Inflationary Bias in a Democratic Capitalist Economy.* *Jahrbucher für Nationaloekonomie und Statistik* 207 (4): 356–373.

7391. Wagner, M. June 1993. CDC Volunteers Helping to Build Democracies. *PS: Political Science & Politics* 26 (2): 304–305.

7392. Wahid, A. March 1985. *See* Neuhaus, R. J. (March 1985).

7393. Wain, K. September 1993. Strong Poets and Utopia: Rorty Liberalism, Dewey and Democracy. *Political Studies* 41 (3): 394–407.

7394. Wainright, H. 1990. New Forms of Democracy for Socialist Renewal. *Socialist Review* 20 (2): 31–44.

7395. Waisman, C. H. December 1990. The Argentine Paradox. *Journal of Democracy* 1 (1): 91–101.

7396. Waisman, C. H. March 1992. Capitalism, the Market, and Democracy. *American Behavioral Scientist* 35 (4–5): 500–516.

7397. Wald, P. M. 1990. One Nation Indivisible, with Liberty and Justice for All: Lessons from the American Experience for New Democracies. *Fordham Law Review* 59 (2): 283–297.

7398. Waldenberg, M. 1981. Remarks on the Leninist Concept of Socialist Democracy. *Polish Political Science Yearbook* 11: 21–37.

7399. Walder, A. G. September 1989. *See* Dittmer, L. (September 1989).

7400. Waligorski, C. P. April 1984. Conservative Economist Critics of Democracy. *Social Science Journal* 21 (2): 99–116.

7401. Waligorski, C. P. 1994. Keynes and Democracy. *Social Science Journal* 31 (1): 79–91.

7402. Walker, C. March 1988. Political Violence and Democracy in Northern Ireland. *Modern Law Review* 51: 605–622.

7403. Walker, I. June 1987. Socialismo y Democracia: Algunas Experiencias Europeas. *Coleccion Estudios* 14: 23–48.

7404. Walker, I. July 1991. Democratic Socialism in Comparative Perspective. *Comparative Politics* 23 (4): 439–458.

7405. Walker, J. L. April 1992. *See* Schlagneck, D. M. (April 1992).

7406. Walker, K. F. May 1977. Toward the Participatory Enterprise: A European Trend. *Annals of the American Academy of Political and Social Science* 431: 1–11.

7407. Walker, R. B. J. March 1991. On the Spatiotemporal Conditions of Democratic Practice. *Alternatives* 16 (2): 243–261.

7408. Walker, W. E. September 1988. Congressional Resurgence and the Destabilization of U.S. Foreign Policy. *Parameters* 18: 54–67.

7409. Walker, W. E. December 1993. Presidential Transitions and the Entrepreneurial Presidency: Of Lions, Foxes, and Puppy Dogs. *Presidential Studies Quarterly* 23 (1): 57–76.

7410. Wallace, R. 1988. Shaping the Canon: The University Press and the Democratization of American Poetry. *Scholarly Publishing* 19 (3): 144–156.

7411. Wallen, E. January 1993. *See* Lindblad, S. (January 1993).

7412. Wallerstein, M. 1980. The Collapse of Democracy in Brazil: Its Economic Determinants. *Dados: Revista de Ciencias Socialis* 23 (3): 2997–334.

7413. Wallerstein, M. 1980. The Collapse of Democracy in Brazil: Its Economic Determinants. *Latin American Research Review* 15 (3): 3–40. Comments by Werner Baer.

7414. Wallerstein, M. June 1982. *See* Przeworski, A. (June 1982).

7415. Wallerstein, M. 1989. Union Organization in Advanced Industrial Democracies. *American Political Science Review* 83 (2): 481–501.

7416. Wallerstein, M. 1991. Industrial Concentration, Country Size, and Trade Union Membership. *American Political Science Review* 85 (3): 941–953.

7417. Wallimann, I., and C. Stojanov. December 1988. Workplace Democracy in

Bulgaria: From Subordination to Partnership in Industrial Relations. *Industrial Relations Journal* 19: 310–321.

7418. Wallimann, I., and C. Stojanov. 1989. Social and Economic Reform in Bulgaria: Economic Democracy and Problems of Change in Industrial Relations. *Economic and Industrial Democracy* 10 (3): 361–378.

7419. Wallin, E. January 1993. *See* Lindblad, S. (January 1993).

7420. Wallis, V. June 1992. Socialism, Ecology, and Democracy: Toward a Strategy of Conversion. *Monthly Review* 44 (2): 1–22.

7421. Wallis, W. A. December 1975. Unity in the University. *Daedalus* 104 (1): 68–77.

7422. Wallop, M. December 1994. Tyranny in America: Would Alexis de Tocqueville Recognize This Place? *Journal of Legislation* 20: 37–56.

7423. Walsh, E. J. 1983. Three-Mile Island: Meltdown of Democracy. *Bulletin of the Atomic Scientists* 39 (3): 57–60.

7424. Walsh, M. September 1979. The Democratization of Fashion: The Emergence of the Women's Dress Pattern Industry. *Journal of American History* 66 (2): 299–313.

7425. Walter, F. 1991. Saxony, A Traditional Center of Social Democracy. *Politische Vierteljahresschrift* 32 (2): 207–231.

7426. Walter, K., and P. J. Williams. 1993. The Military and Democratization in El Salvador. *Journal of Interamerican Studies and World Affairs* 35 (1): 39–88.

7427. Walton, R. E. July 1977. Work Innovations at Topeka: After Six Years. *Journal of Applied Behavioral Science* 13 (3): 422–433.

7428. Waltz, S. E. January 1982. Antidotes for a Social Malaise: Alienation, Efficacy, and Participation in Tunisia. *Comparative Politics* 14 (2): 127–147.

7429. Walzer, M. 1978. Capitalism, Socialism, and Democracy. *Commentary* 65 (4): 70–71.

7430. Walzer, M. 1981. Primaries Have Ruined Our Politics: Democracy vs. Elections. *New Republic* 184 (1–2): 17–19.

7431. Walzer, M. August 1981. Philosophy and Democracy. *Political Theory* 9 (3): 379–399.

7432. Walzer, M. 1988. Socializing the Welfare State: Democracy in the Distributive Sector. *Dissent* 35 (3): 292–300.

7433. Walzer, M. 1989. *See* Chicoine, D. (1989).

7434. Walzer, M. February 1993. Exclusion, Injustice and the Democratic State.* *MicroMega* 1: 99–113.

7435. Wanandi, J. 1993. Human Rights and Democracy in the ASEAN Nations: The Next 25 Years. *Indonesian Quarterly* 21 (1): 14–24.

7436. Wanbadia, W. 1988. *See* Mandini, M. (1988).

7437. Wanderley Reis, F. September 1985. Political Change in Brazil: Openings, Prospects and Mirages.* *Cadernos de Departamento de Ciencia Politica* 7: 11–36.

7438. Wanderley Reis, F. 1988. Democratic Construction in Brazil: Diagnosis and Prospects.* *Problemes d'Amerique Latine* 90: 3–22.

7439. Wang, S. October 1980. Chinese Communist Democratization and Modernization. *Asian Outlook* 15: 46–50.

7440. Wang, S. 1992. Factors Influencing Cross-National News Treatment of a Critical National Event: A Comparative Study of Six Countries' Media Coverage of the 1989 Chinese Student Demonstrations. *Gazette* 49 (3): 193–214.

7441. Wang, X. Z. 1982. China's Democracy Movement. *New Left Review* (131): 62–70.

7442. Wanker, W. P. 1992. The University and Democracy: Interlocking Learning and Governing. *Interchange* 23 (1–2): 25–40.

7443. Wanna, J. 1982. Urban Planning under Social Democracy: The Case of Monarto, South Australia. *Australian Quarterly* 54 (3): 260–270.

7444. Ward, P. M. 1991. *See* Rodriquez, V. E. (1991).

7445. Ward, P. M. December 1994. *See* Rodriquez, V. E. (December 1994).

7446. Ware, A. April 1981. The Concept of Manipulation: Its Relation to Democracy and Power. *British Journal of Political Science* 11 (2): 163–181.

7447. Ware, A. 1989. Parties, Electoral Competition and Democracy. *Parliamentary Affairs* 42 (1): 1–22.

7448. Ware, A. 1992. Liberal Democracy: One Form or Many? *Political Studies* 40: 130–145. Special issue.

7449. Wariavwalla, B. February 1988. India in 1987: Democracy on Trial. *Asian Survey* 28 (2): 119–125.

7450. Wariavwalla, B. April 1988. Interdependence and Domestic Political Regimes: The Case of the Newly Industrializing Countries. *Alternatives* 13 (2): 253–270.

7451. Warmenhoven, H. J. December 1975. Indonesia and the Changing Order in Asia. *Current History* 69 (411): 236–239, 245, 256.

7452. Warner, M. 1976. Further Thoughts on Experiments in Industrial Democracy and Self-Management. *Human Relations* 29 (5): 401–410.

7453. Warner, M. 1977. *See* Edelstein, J. D. (1977).

7454. Warner, M. March 1985. *See* Campbell, A. (March 1985).

7455. Warner, M. December 1992. Industrial Democracy in Europe Revisited: Summary and Conclusions. *Social Science Information* 31 (4): 773–785.

7456. Warner, M. S. September 1984. Democracy's Hall of Fame: Anti-Communist Heroes of the Third World. *Policy Review* (30): 48–53.

7457. Warren, G. 1991. *See* Gott, M. (1991).

7458. Warren, K. B. 1989. *See* Bourque, S. C. (1989).

7459. Warren, M. March 1988. Max Weber's Liberalism for a Nietzschean World. *American Political Science Review* 82 (1): 31–50.

7460. Warren, M. November 1989. Liberal Constitutionalism as Ideology: Marx and Habermas. *Political Theory* 17 (4): 511–534.

7461. Warren, M. March 1992. Democratic Theory and Self-Transformation. *American Political Science Review* 86 (1): 8–23.

7462. Warren, M. June 1993. Can Participatory Democracy Produce Better Selves? Psychological Dimensions of Habermas's Discursive Model of Democracy. *Political Psychology* 14 (2): 209–234.

7463. Warren, R. December 1994. *See* Moss, M. (December 1994).

7464. Warren, R., M. S. Rosentraub, and K. S. Harlow. June 1984. Coproduction, Equity and the Distribution of Safety. *Urban Affairs Quarterly* 19 (4): 447–464.

7465. Warshkuhn, A. 1991. Political Change in Concordance Democracies.* *Politische Vierteljahresschrift* 32 (1): 11–113.

7466. Warwick, P. 1979. The Durability of Coalition Governments in Parliamentary Democracies. *Comparative Political Studies* 11 (4): 465–498.

7467. Warwick, P. October 1992. Ideological Diversity and Government Survival in Western European Parliamentary Democracies. *Comparative Political Studies* 25 (3): 332–361.

7468. Warwick, P. November 1992. Rising Hazards: An Underlying Dynamic of Parliamentary Government. *American Journal of Political Science* 36 (4): 857–876.

7469. Warwick, P. December 1992. Economic Trends and Government Survival in West European Parliamentary Democracies. *American Political Science Review* 86 (4): 875–887.

7470. Warwick, P., and S. T. Easton. February 1992. The Cabinet Stability Controversy: New Perspectives on a Classic Problem. *American Journal of Political Science* 36 (1): 122–146.

7471. Wasser, H. 1991. Acceptance of Pluralism as Proof of Liberal Democracy in Constitutional Law in German Politics. *Gegenwartskunde: Gesellschaft, Staat, Erziehung* 40 (3): 309–319.

7472. Wasserstrom, J. N. November 1990. *See* Esherick, J. W. (November 1990).

7473. Waste, R. J., and G. W. Sparrow. 1985. Democracy through the Mail. *Social Policy* 15 (4): 58–59.

7474. Waterkamp, R. 1975. Planning Control in Democracy.* *Gegenwartskunde: Gesellschaft, Staat, Erziehung* 24 (4): 413–424.

7475. Waterman, H., and Hao Wang. June 1990. Which Way to Go? Four Strategies for Democratization in Chinese Intellectual Circles. *China Information* 5 (1): 14–33.

7476. Waterman, J. A. December 1994. United States' Involvement in Haiti's Tragedy and the Resolve to Restore Democracy. *New York Law School Journal of International and Comparative Law* 15: 187–215.

7477. Waterman, S. November 1994. The Non-Jewish Vote in Israel in 1992. *Political Geography* 13 (6): 540–558.

7478. Wathall, A. December 1986. Japanese "Gimin": Peasant Martyrs in Popular Memory. *American Historical Review* 91 (5): 1076–1102.

7479. Watkins, E. December 1992. Yemen: Democracy against the Odds. *Middle East* 9–11.

7480. Watson, C. July 1993. Burundi: Un Virage Radical. *La Nouvel Afrique Asie* 16–17.

7481. Watson, C. January 1994. The Death Of Democracy. *Africa Report* 39: 26–31.

7482. Watson, C. May 1994. Uganda: No to Multi-party. *Africa Report* 39 (3): 24–26.

7483. Watson, H. A. October 1988. The 1986 General Election and the Political Economy in Barbados after Barrow. *Caribbean Affairs* 1 (4): 64–83.

7484. Watson, H. L. 1985. Old Hickory's Democracy. *Wilson Quarterly* 9 (4): 101–133.

7485. Watson, P. August 1993. Eastern Europe's Silent Revolution: Gender. *Sociology* 27 (3): 471–487.

7486. Watt, M. July 1991. Entitlements or Empowerment? Famine and Starvation in Africa. *Review of African Political Economy* 18: 9–26.

7487. Wattenberg, M. P. October 1982. Party Identification and Party Images: A Comparison of Britain, Canada, Australia, and the United States. *Comparative Politics* 15 (1): 23–40.

7488. Watts, J. March 1983. The Socialist as Ostrich: The Unwillingness of the Left to Confront Modernity. *Social Research* 50 (1): 3–56.

7489. Watts, R. J. 1990. Democratization of Health Care: Challenges for Nursing. *Advances in Nursing Science* 12 (2): 37–46.

7490. Waylen, G. 1993. Women's Movements and Democratization in Latin America. *Third World Quarterly* 14 (3): 573–587.

7491. Waylen, G. April 1994. Women and Democratization: Conceptualizing Gender Relations in Transition Politics. *World Politics* 46 (3): 327–354.

7492. Weakliem, D. L., and A. F. Heath. April 1994. Rational Choice and Class Voting. *Rationality and Society* 6 (2): 243–270.

7493. Weart, S. R. August 1994. Peace among Democratic and Oligarchic Republics. *Journal of Peace Research* 31 (3): 299–316.

7494. Weatherford, M. S. 1991. Mapping the Ties That Bind: Legitimacy, Representation, and Alienation. *Western Political Quarterly* 44 (2): 251–276.

7495. Weaver, P. E. 1980. Learning about Industrial Democracy Before It Is Too Late.* *Revista Usem* 61: 14–17.

7496. Weber, H. 1990. "You Said Formal."* *Pouvoirs* 52: 23–34.

7497. Weber, M. 1992. On the Bourgeois Democracy in Russia.* *Sotsiologicheskie Issledovaniia* (3): 130–134.

7498. Weber, W. 1984. Demokratie aus Genossenschaftstheoretischer Perspektive. *Zeitschrift Besante Genossenschaftswesen* 34 (1): 78–73.

7499. Webster, D. June 1984. Direct Broadcast Satellites: Proximity, Sovereignty and National Identity. *Foreign Affairs* 62 (5): 1162–1174.

7500. Weck-Hannemann, H. September 1990. Protectionism in Direct Democracy. *Journal of Institutional and Theoretical Economics* 146 (3): 389–418.

7501. Weede, E. June 1980. Beyond Misspecification in Sociological Analysis of Income Inequality. *American Sociological Review* 45 (3): 497–501.

7502. Weede, E. September 1982. The Effects of Democracy and Socialist Strength on the Size Distribution of Income: Some More Evidence. *International Journal of Comparative Sociology* 23 (3–4): 151–165.

7503. Weede, E. 1983. The Impact of Democracy on Economic Growth: Some Evidence from Cross-National Analysis. *Kyklos* 36 (1): 21–38.

7504. Weede, E. 1984. Democracy, Creeping Socialism, and Ideological Socialism. *Public Choice* 44 (2): 349–366.

7505. Weede, E. October 1984. Political Democracy, State Strength, and Economic Growth in LDCs: A Cross-National Analysis. *Review of International Studies* 10 (4): 297–312.

7506. Weede, E. December 1984. Democracy and War Involvement. *Journal of Conflict Resolution* 28 (4): 649–664.

7507. Weede, E. 1986a. Catch-Up, Distributional Coalitions and Government as Determinants of Economic Growth or Decline in Industrialized Democracies. *British Journal of Sociology* 37 (2): 193–220.

7508. Weede, E. 1986b. Sectoral Reallocation, Distributional Coalitions and the Welfare State as Determinants of Economic Growth Rates in Industrialized Democracies. *European Journal of Political Research* 14 (5–6): 501–520.

7509. Weede, E. June 1986. Distributional Coalitions, Government Activity, and Stagnation.* *Politische Vierteljahresschrift* 27 (2): 222–236.

7510. Weede, E. March 1989. Ideas, Ideology and Political Culture of the West.* *Zeitschrift für Politik* 36 (1): 27–43.

7511. Weede, E. November 1992. Some Simple Calculations on Democracy and War Involvement. *Journal of Peace Research* 29 (4): 377–383.

7512. Weede, E. June 1993. The Impact of Democracy or Repressiveness on the Quality-of-Life, Income Distribution and Economic Growth Rates. *International Sociology* 8 (2): 177–195.

7513. Weede, E. March 1994. Determinants of the Avoidance of War during the Cold War and Thereafter: Nuclear Deterrence, Democracy, and Free Trade.* *Politische Vierteljahresschrift* 35 (1): 62–84.

7514. Weede, E., and J. Kummer. 1985. Some Criticism of Recent Work on World System Status, Inequality, and Democracy. *International Journal of Comparative Sociology* 26 (3–4): 135–148.

7515. Weede, E., and H. Tiefenbach. June 1981. Some Recent Explanations of Income Inequality: An Evaluation and Critique. *International Studies Quarterly* 25 (2): 255–282.

7516. Wefford, F. C. May 1993. What Is a "New Democracy"? *International Social Science Journal* 45 (2): 245–256.

7517. Weggel, O. June 1989. Auslaendische Reaktionen auf das Massaker von Beijing. *China Aktuell* 18: 423–427.

7518. Wei, H. 1987. Reform of the Political System and Political Democratization. *Chinese Law and Government* 20 (1): 74–77.

7519. Wei, Y. March 1991. Democratization and Institutionalization: Problems, Prospects, and Political Development in the Republic of China on Taiwan. *Issues and Studies* 27 (3): 29–43.

7520. Weibull, J. W. June 1993. *See* Lindbeck, A. (June 1993).

7521. Weidefeld, W., and M. Huterer. June 1992. The West and the Stabilization of the East European Democracies.* *Europa Archiv: Zeitschrift für Internationale Politik* 47 (12): 325–334.

7522. Weigel, G. 1989. Catholicism and Democracy: The Other Twentieth-Century Revolution. *Washington Quarterly* 12 (4): 5–25.

7523. Weiher, R. L. 1975. Managers Bookshelf: Sources on Industrial Democracy. *Harvard Business Review* 53 (5): 164–168.

7524. Weil, F. D. 1987. Cohorts, Regimes, and the Legitimation of Democracy: West Germany since 1945. *American Sociological Review* 52 (3): 308–324.

7525. Weil, F. D. 1989. The Sources and Structures of Legitimation in Western Democracies: A Consolidating Model Tested with Time-Series Data in Six Countries since World War Two. *American Sociological Review* 54 (5): 682–706.

7526. Weiland, H. 1978. *See* Hanf, T. (1978).

7527. Weiland, H. 1992. Demokratie und Nationale Entwicklung in Namibia: Eine Zwischenbilatz nach Zweieinhalt Jahren Unabhaengigkeit. *Afrika Spectrum* 27 (3): 272–301.

7528. Weiland, M. W. June 1981. *See* Katovich, M. (June 1981).

7529. Weiler, P. C. September 1984. Rights and Judges in a Democracy: A New Canadian Version. *University of Michigan Journal of Law Reform* 18: 51–92.

7530. Weinacht, P. L. 1981. Reconstitution of Party Democracy after 1945.* *Politische Studien* 32 (260): 595–606.

7531. Weinbaum, M. G., and S. P. Cohen. February 1983. Pakistan in 1982: Holding On. *Asian Survey* 23 (2): 123–132.

7532. Weinberg, A. M. March 1990. Technology and Democracy. *Minerva* 28 (1): 81–90.

7533. Weinberg, A. S. 1976. Industrial Democracy in the Netherlands. *Monthly Labor Review* 99 (7): 48–49.

7534. Weinberger, C. September 1985. Peace with Freedom: Why Democracy Is Worth Defending. *Policy Review* 34: 48–49.

7535. Weinberger, O. July 1994. Habermas on Democracy and Justice. Limits of a Sound Conception. *Ratio Juris* 7: 239–253.

7536. Weiner, M. July 1977. The 1977 Parliamentary Elections in India. *Asian Survey* 17 (7): 619–626.

7537. Weiner, M. September 1987. Empirical Democratic Theory and the Transition from Authoritarianism to Democracy. *PS: Political Science & Politics* 20 (4): 861–866.

7538. Weisberg, H. F. October 1994. *See* Mattei, F. (October 1994).

7539. Weiser, P. J. October 1993. Ackerman, Proposal for Popular Constitutional Lawmaking: Can It Realize His Aspirations for Dualist Democracy. *New York University Law Review* 68 (4): 907–959.

7540. Weisfelder, R. F. 1991. Collective Foreign Policy Decision-Making within SADCC: Do Regional Objectives Alter National Policies? *Africa Today* 38 (1): 5–17.

7541. Weiss, A. M. May 1990. Benazir Bhutto and the Future of Woman in Pakistan. *Asian Survey* 30 (5): 433–445.

7542. Weiss, S. March 1980. Israeli Democracy, One Generation Old. *Jewish Frontier* 47: 4–6.

7543. Weissberg, R. May 1975. Political Efficacy and Political Illusion. *Journal of Politics* 37 (2): 469–487.

7544. Weissman, S. March 1985. Dateline South Africa: The Opposition Speaks. *Foreign Policy* 58: 151–170.

7545. Weizssacker, R. October 1982. Crisis and Change of Our Party Democracy.* *Aus Politik und Zeitgeschichte* 42: 3–12.

7546. Welch, C. E. , Jr. September 1991. The Single-Party Phenomenon in Africa. *Transafrica Forum* 8 (3): 85–94.

7547. Welch, P. J. 1977. Inflation and the Destruction of Democracy: The Case of the Weimar Republic: A Reply. *Journal of Economic Issues* 11 (2): 323–326.

7548. Wellens, J. 1977. The Bullock Report on Industrial Democracy: A Summary of Majority Report, with Comment. *Industrial and Commercial Training* 9 (3): 93–100.

7549. Weller, M. October 7, 1994. Democracy through Fire and Sword? *New Law Journal* 144: 1385(2).

7550. Wellington, H. H. 1981. The Importance of Being Elegant. *Ohio State Law Journal* 42 (1): 427–434.

7551. Wells, S. F. , Jr. March 1979. *See* MacIsaacs, D. (March 1979).

7552. Wendt, B. J. April 1992. Politics between Parliamentary Democracy and Presidential Dictatorship: The Bruning Era Reflected in Cabinet Documents.* *Historische Zeitschrift* 254 (2): 383–395.

7553. Werlich, D. P. February 1984. Peru: The Shadow of the Shining Path. *Current History* 83 (490): 78–82, 90.

7554. Werlich, D. P. January 1987. Debt, Democracy, and Terrorism in Peru. *Current History* 86 (516): 29–32, 36–37.

7555. Werlin, H. H. September 1994. A Primary Secondary Democracy Distinction. *PS: Political Science & Politics* 27 (3): 530–534.

7556. Wersebe, I. V. 1978. Democratization by Professionalization: Concept of Functional Participation. *Zeitschrift für Soziologie* 7 (2): 157–174.

7557. Wertheimer, F., and S. W. Manes. May 1994. Campaign Finance Reform: A Key to Restoring the Health of Our Democracy. *Columbia Law Review* 94 (4): 1126–1159.

7558. Werz, N. 1987. Democracy and Forms of Government in South America.* *Verfassung und Recht in Ubersee* 20 (2): 143–176.

7559. Wesolowski, W. June 1990. Transition from Authoritarianism to Democracy. *Social Research* 57 (2): 435–461.

7560. Wessing, R. July 1987. Electing a Lurah in West Java: Stability and Change. *Ethnology* 26 (3): 165–178.

7561. West, D. March 1984. "Happy 1984." *Policy Review* (28): 69–71.

7562. West, D. M. November 1994. Political Advertising and News Coverage in the 1992 California United States Senate

Campaigns. *Journal of Politics* 56 (4): 1053–1074.

7563. Westenholz, A. May 1991. Democracy as "Organized Divorce" and How the Postmodern Democracy Is Stifled by Unity and Majority. *Economic and Industrial Democracy* 12 (2): 173–186.

7564. Western, B. March 1994. Unionization and Labor Market Institutions in Advanced Capitalism, 1950–1985. *American Journal of Sociology* 99 (5): 1314–1341.

7565. Western, B., and S. Jackman. June 1994. Bayesian Inference for Comparative Research. *American Political Science Review* 88 (2): 412–423.

7566. Westin, A. F. November 1977. *See* Baldwin, R. (November 1977).

7567. Westle, B. December 1994. Democracy and Socialism: Political Orientations in Germany between Ideology, Protest, and Nostalgia.* *Kolner Zeitschrift für Soziologie und Sozialpsychologie* 46 (4): 571–596.

7568. Westra, L. June 1993. The Ethics of Environmental Holism and the Democratic State: Are They in Conflict? *Environmental Values* 2 (2): 125–136.

7569. Wettergreen, J. A. April 1992. Constitutional Problems of American Bureaucracy: Beginning with "INS Versus Chadha." *Political Communication* 9 (2): 93–110.

7570. Weyland, K. 1993. The Rise and Fall of President Collor and Its Impact on Brazilian Democracy. *Journal of Interamerican Studies and World Affairs* 35 (1): 1–37.

7571. Whelan, F. G. 1983. Prologue: Democratic Theory and the Boundary Problem. *Nomos* 25: 13–47.

7572. Whelan, J. R. December 1988. Pinochet Revolution: Will Popular Capitalism Lead to Democratization. *Policy Review* 43: 76–79.

7573. Whicker, M. L. June 1986. Direct Democracy Devices: A Computer Simulation Analysis. *Journal of Policy Modeling* 8 (2): 255–271.

7574. Whiddon, B., and P. Y. Martin. 1989. Organizational Democracy and Work Quality in a State Welfare Agency. *Social Science Quarterly* 70 (3): 667–686.

7575. Whistler, D. September 1981. Young Voters and Democracy: An Explanation. *Southeastern Political Review* 9 (2): 153–174.

7576. White, G. January 1994. Democratization and Economic Reform in China. *Australian Journal of Chinese Affairs* 31: 73–92.

7577. White, J. W. October 1981. Civic Attitudes, Political Participation, and System Stability in Japan. *Comparative Political Studies* 14 (3): 371–400.

7578. White, S. December 1990. Democratizing Eastern Europe: The Elections of 1990. *Electoral Studies* 9 (4): 277–287.

7579. White, S. October 1992. Russia Experiment with Democracy. *Current History* 91 (567): 310–313.

7580. White, S. March 1993. Post-Communist Politics (in Russia): Towards Democratic Pluralism. *Journal of Communist Studies* 9 (1): 18–32.

7581. Whitefield, S. October 1993. *See* Evans, G. (October 1993).

7582. Whitefield, S., and G. Evans. January 1994. The Russian Election of 1993: Public Opinion and the Transition Experience. *Post-Soviet Affairs* 10: 38–60.

7583. Whitehead, J. C. June 1987. Securing the Blessings of Liberty. *Presidential Studies Quarterly* 17 (3): 445–451.

7584. Whitehead, J. C. June 1990. The New Freedom in the Soviet Union and Eastern Europe. *Presidential Studies Quarterly* 20 (3): 471–476.

7585. Whitehead, J. C. December 1993. Considerations on the Eve of the 1992

Presidential Election. *Presidential Studies Quarterly* 23 (1): 37–40.

7586. Whitehead, J. S. 1985. The Democratization of Danish Higher Education: Causes, Responses and Adaptations. *Higher Education* 14 (1): 57–73.

7587. Whitehead, L. November 1985. Democratization in Central America and International Factors.* *Politica Internazionale* 13 (11–12): 143–162.

7588. Whitehead, L. 1992. The Alternatives to "Liberal Democracy": A Latin American Perspective. *Political Studies* 40: 146–159. Special issue.

7589. Whitehead, L. August 1993. On "Reform of the State" and "Regulation of the Market." *World Development* 21 (8): 1371–1393.

7590. Whitehead, L. August 1993. Some Insights from Western Social Theory. *World Development* 21 (8): 1245–1261.

7591. Whitehorn, A. 1978. Yugoslav Workers' Self-Management: Blueprint for Industrial Democracy. *Canadian Slavonic Papers* 20 (3): 421–428.

7592. Whitten, G. October 1994. *See* Franklin, M. (October 1994).

7593. Whyte, M. K. May 1992. Prospects for Democratization in China. *Problems of Communism* 41 (3): 58–70.

7594. Wiarda, H. J. March 1978. Democracy and Human Rights in Latin America: Toward a New Conceptualization. *Orbis* 22 (1): 137–160.

7595. Wiarda, H. J. February 1985. United States Policy in South America: A Maturing Relationship. *Current History* 84 (499): 49–52, 86.

7596. Wiarda, H. J. June 1991. The Democratic Breakthrough in Latin America: Challenges, Prospects, and U.S. Policy. *SAIS Review* 11 (2): 21–34.

7597. Wiarda, H. J., and I. S. Wiarda. March 1989. The United States and South America: The Challenge of Fragile Democracy. *Current History* 88 (536): 113–116, 151–152.

7598. Wiarda, I. S. March 1989. *See* Wiarda, H. J. (March 1989).

7599. Wiatr, J. J. 1991. Will Democracy Win in East-Central Europa? *Polish Political Science Yearbook* 21: 17–23.

7600. Wiatr, J. J. 1992. Eastern Europe: The Destiny of the Democracy.* *Sotsiologicheskie Issledovaniia* (1): 6–19.

7601. Wicha, B. 1983. Political Planning and Democracy.* *Zeitgeschichte* 10 (4): 166–180.

7602. Wickham Jones, M. July 1990. *See* King, D. S. (July 1990).

7603. Widmalm, S. 1992. *See* Blomkvist, H. (1992).

7604. Widner, J. April 1994. Two Leadership Styles and Patterns of Political Liberalization. *African Studies Review* 37 (1): 151–174.

7605. Wielhouwer, P. W., and B. Lockerbie. February 1994. Party Contacting and Political Participation, 1952–1990. *American Journal of Political Science* 38 (1): 211–229.

7606. Wienand, P. 1976. Revolutionaries and Revisionists: Youth in Social Democracy before the Turn of the Century.* *Politische Vierteljahresschrift* 17 (2): 208–204.

7607. Wightman, G. December 1990. Czechoslovakia. *Electoral Studies* 9 (4): 319–326.

7608. Wilcox, C., C. W. J. Brown, and L. W. Powell. September 1993. Republican Voting among Democratic [U.S.] Presidential Contributors: A Test of Rival Hypotheses. *Polity* 26 (1): 127–140.

7609. Wildavsky, A. 1985. No War without Dictatorship, No Peace without Democracy. *Social Philosophy and Policy* 3 (1): 176–191.

7610. Wildavsky, A. November 1993. Democracy as a Coalition of Cultures. *Society* 31 (1): 80–83.

7611. Wilde, A., and C. Youngers. December 1990. Latin America: The Challenge of the 1990s. *Peace Review* 2 (1): 25–28.

7612. Will, D. S. June 1986. The Impending Polarization of Israeli Society. *Arab Studies Quarterly* 8: 231–252.

7613. Will, W. M. 1989. Democracy, Elections and Public Policy in the Eastern Caribbean: The Case of Barbados. *Journal of Commonwealth and Comparative Politics* 27 (3): 321–346.

7614. Willborn, S. L. July 1984. Industrial Democracy and the National Labor Relations Act: A Preliminary Inquiry. *Boston College Law Review* 25: 725–742.

7615. Willett, T. D. 1975. *See* Amacher, R. C. (1975).

7616. Williams, A. M. April 1984. *See* Lewis, J. R. (April 1984).

7617. Williams, B. A. July 1988. *See* Matheny, A. R. (July 1988).

7618. Williams, B. A. December 1990. *See* London, B. (December 1990).

7619. Williams, D. C. March 1991. Searching for Governance in Africa: Ethnic Management in Nigeria's Second Republic. *Journal of Ethnic Studies* 19 (1): 21–39.

7620. Williams, D. R. 1994. Environment Law and Democratic Legitimacy. *Duke Environmental Law & Policy Forum* 4: 1–40.

7621. Williams, G. 1987. Policy as Containment within Democracy: The Welsh Language Act. *International Journal of the Sociology of Language* 66: 49–59.

7622. Williams, J. A., Jr. February 1977. *See* Johnson, D. R. (February 1977).

7623. Williams, J. O. March 1991. Democratization and Political Party Development in Post-Tiananmen Hong Kong. *Issues and Studies* 27 (3): 128–137. .

7624. Williams, K. C. April 1994. Sequential Elections and Retrospective Voting: Some Laboratory Experiments. *Journal of Theoretical Politics* 6 (2): 239–255.

7625. Williams, K. R. February 1984. *See* Timberland, M. (February 1984).

7626. Williams, P. J. December 1990. Elections and Democratization in Nicaragua: The 1990 Elections in Perspective. *Journal of Interamerican Studies and World Affairs* 32 (4): 13–34.

7627. Williams, P. J. 1993. *See* Walter, K. (1993).

7628. Williams, P. J. January 1994. Dual Transitions from Authoritarian Rule: Popular and Electoral Democracy in Nicaragua. *Comparative Politics* 26 (2): 169–185.

7629. Williams, R. O. 1976. Democracy, Education, and Social Responsibility: Reflections on Schooling from 1920 to 1970. *Contemporary Education* 47 (3): 172–176.

7630. Williams, S. 1979. The Future of Democracy in Western Europe. *Atlantic Community Quarterly* 17 (1): 20–29.

7631. Williamson, J. August 1993. Democracy and the Washington Consensus. *World Development* 21 (8): 1329–1336.

7632. Williamson, J. B. December 1985. *See* Pampel, F. C. (December 1985).

7633. Williamson, J. B. May 1988. *See* Pampel, F. C. (May 1988).

7634. Williamson, J. B. July 1988. *See* Branco, K. J. (July 1988).

7635. Williamson, J. B. 1990. *See* Pampel, F. C. (1990).

7636. Willis, G. 1981. Democratization of Curriculum Evaluation. *Educational Leadership* 38 (8): 630–632.

7637. Willmott, H. C. 1978. Perceptions of Industrial Democracy: Comment on Dickson. *Personnel Review* 7 (4): 56–57.

7638. Willner, D. March 1980. For Whom the Bell Tolls: Anthropologists Advising on Public Policy. *American Anthropologist* 82 (1): 79–94.

7639. Wilperd, B. March 1978. *See* Dachler, P. H. (March 1978).

7640. Wilson, F. L. April 1979. The Revitalization of French Parties. *Comparative Political Studies* 12 (1): 82–103.

7641. Wilson, F. L. 1991. Democracy at the Workplace: The French Experience. *Politics and Society* 19 (4): 439–462.

7642. Wilson, F. L. May 1992. Communism at the Crossroads: Changing Roles in Western Democracies. *Problems of Communism* 41 (3): 95–106.

7643. Wilson, J. March 1983. Corporatism and the Professionalization of Reform. *Journal of Political and Military Sociology* 11 (1): 53–68.

7644. Wilson, J. L. September 1990. Labor Policy in China: Reform and Retrogression. *Problems of Communism* 39 (5): 44–65.

7645. Wilson, J. Q. December 1990. Juridical Democracy Versus American Democracy. *PS: Political Science & Politics* 23 (4): 570–572.

7646. Wilson, K. June 1993. Democracy on a Shoestring. *Human Rights* 20 (3): 29.

7647. Wimmer, R. 1974. Internal Party Democracy of OVP. *Oesterreichische Zeitschrift für Politikwissenschaft* 3 (1): 25–41.

7648. Win, S. April 1994. Sustaining Burma's Hopes for Freedom. *Journal of Democracy* 5 (2): 150–153.

7649. Winant, H. 1987. South American Letter: Fragile Democracies. *Socialist Review* 93–99: 167–174.

7650. Winchester, I. 1992. Elite and Ordinary: The Essential Tension in the University. *Interchange* 23 (1–2): 91–95.

7651. Winchester, I., G. A. Jones, E. Herbeson, and J. Sadlak. 1992. Special Issue: The University and Democracy. *Interchange* 23 (1–2): 1–225. Introduction and 15 articles.

7652. Windmuller, J. P. May 1977. Industrial Democracy and Industrial Relations. *Annals of the American Academy of Political and Social Science* 431: 22–31.

7653. Windmuller, J. P. (ed.). May 1977. Industrial Democracy in International Perspectives. *Annals of the American Academy of Political and Social Science* 431: 1–140. Selection of articles.

7654. Winfield, R. D. December 1984. The Reason for Democracy. *History of Political Thought* 5 (3): 543–573.

7655. Winkler, H. A. 1982. Class Movement or Popular Party: Program Discussion in Weimar Social Democracy 1920–1925.* *Geschichte und Gesellschaft* 8 (1): 9–54.

7656. Winner, L. September 1992. Citizen Virtues in a Technological Order. *Inquiry* 35 (3–4): 341–361.

7657. Winsor, C. , Jr. September 1986. The Solidarista Movement: Labor Economics for Democracy. *Washington Quarterly* 9 (4): 177–188.

7658. Winter, J. M. March 1988. Socialism, Social Democracy, and Population Questions in Western Europe, 1870–1950. *Population and Development Review* 14: 122–146.

7659. Winthrop, D. December 1978. Aristotle on Participatory Democracy. *Polity* 11 (2): 151–171.

7660. Winthrop, D. May 1986. Tocqueville's American Woman and "The True Conception of Democratic Progress." *Political Theory* 14 (2): 239–261.

7661. Winthrop, D. December 1992. *See* Schneck, S. (December 1992).

7662. Winthrop, N. November 1992. Elite Theory and Neo-Elite Theory Understandings of Democracy: An Analysis and Criticism. *Australian Journal of Political Science* 27 (3): 462–477.

7663. Wirls, D. June 1991. Congress and the Politics of Military Reform. *Armed Forces and Society* 17 (4): 487–512.

7664. Wirth, A. G. 1977. Issues Affecting Education and Work in the 1980s: Efficiency Versus Industrial Democracy, a Historical Perspective. *Teachers College Record* 79 (1): 55–67.

7665. Wirth, R. February 1978. *See* De Ridder, M. (February 1978).

7666. Wiseman, J. 1990. Temples of Democracy. *Canadian Library Journal* 47 (1): 37–39.

7667. Wiseman, J. A. February 1980. Elections and Parliamentary Democracy in Botswana. *World Today* 36 (2): 72–78.

7668. Wiseman, J. A. December 1992. Early Post-Redemocratization Elections in Africa. *Electoral Studies* 11 (4): 279–291.

7669. Wiseman, J. A. 1993. Democracy and the New Political Pluralism in Africa: Causes, Consequences and Significance. *Third World Quarterly* 14 (3): 439–449.

7670. Wishnevsky, J. April 1, 1994. *See* Tolz, V. (April 1, 1994).

7671. Wittman, D. December 1989. Why Democracies Produce Efficient Results. *Journal of Political Economy* 97 (6): 1395–1424.

7672. Wober, J. M. January 1990. Television in the House of Commons: Education for Democracy? *Parliamentary Affairs* 43 (1): 15–26.

7673. Wolchik, S. L. December 1990. Czechoslovakia's "Velvet Revolution." *Current History* 89 (551): 413–416, 435–437.

7674. Wolchok, C. March 1993. The Haitian Struggle for Democracy. *Human Rights* 20 (2): 18–21.

7675. Wold, C. A., and D. J. Zaelke. March 1992. Promoting Sustainable Development and Democracy in Central and Eastern Europe: The Role of the European Bank of Reconstruction and Development. *American University Journal of International Law and Policy* 7: 559–604.

7676. Woldendorp, J., H. Keman, and I. Budge. July 1993. Political Data 1945–1990: Party Government in 20 Democracies. *European Journal of Political Research* 24 (1): 1–119.

7677. Wolf, U. 1987. *See* Mols, M. (1987).

7678. Wolf, W. 1980. Campaigns, Conflicts and Democracy. *Politische Studien* 31 (251): 235–243.

7679. Wolfe, A. 1975. Giving Up on Democracy: Capitalism Shows Its Face. *Nation* 221 (18): 557–563.

7680. Wolfe, A. 1986. Inauthentic Democracy: A Critique of Public Life in Modern Liberal Society. *Studies in Political Economy* 21: 57–81.

7681. Wolfe, D. P. 1978. American Democracy: Its Challenge from Abroad. *Phi Delta Kappan* 60 (3): 159–160.

7682. Wolfe, J. A. 1994. *See* Gurian, P. (1994).

7683. Wolfe, J. D. July 1985. A Defense of Participatory Democracy. *Review of Politics* 47 (3): 370–389.

7684. Wolfe, J. H. March 1988. Cyprus: Federation under International Safeguards. *Publius* 18 (2): 75–89.

7685. Wolfe, J. J. July 1985. Corporatism and Union Democracy: The British Miners and Incomes Policy. *Comparative Politics* 17 (4): 421–436.

7686. Wolfensberger, D. R. June 1994. *See* Solomon, G. B. H. (June 1994).

7687. Wolfenson, G. F. 1987. Argentina: Democracy and International Relations. *PS: Political Science & Politics* 20 (3): 679–684.

7688. Wolf-Rodda, H. A. March 1993. The Support for Eastern European Democracy Act of 1989: A Description and Assessment of Its Responsiveness to the Needs of Poland. *Maryland Journal of International Law and Trade* 17: 107–134.

7689. Wolin, S. S. May 1986. Contract and Birthright. *Political Theory* 14 (2): 179–193.

7690. Wolin, S. S. November 1987. Democracy and the Welfare State: The Political and Theoretical Connections between "Staatsrason" and "Wohlfahrtsstaatrason." *Political Theory* 15 (4): 467–500.

7691. Wolin, S. S. March 1990. Democracy in the Discourse of Postmodernism. *Social Research* 57 (1): 5–30.

7692. Wolin, S. S. August 1993. Democracy, Difference, and Recognition. *Political Theory* 21 (3): 464–483.

7693. Wolin, S. S. September 1993. Democracy: Electoral and Athenian. *PS: Political Science & Politics* 26 (3): 475–477.

7694. Wolin, S. S. April 1994. "Fugitive Democracy." *Constellations* 1 (1): 11–25.

7695. Wolinetz, S. B. January 1993. Reconstructing Dutch Social Democracy. *West European Politics* 16: 97–111.

7696. Woltermann, C. December 1990. Democracy in Pluralistic Societies: The American Ideal Versus Nationalism. *Plural Societies* 20 (3): 1–12.

7697. Womack, B. May 1984. Modernization and Democratic Reform in China. *Journal of Asian Studies* 43 (3): 417–439.

7698. Womack, B. March 1989. Party-State Democracy (in China). *Issues and Studies* 25 (3): 37–57.

7699. Won, G., and I. Oh. October 1983. Grass-Roots Democracy: The Case of the Korean Labor Movement. *Sociological Perspectives* 26 (4): 399–422.

7700. Wong, J. Y. May 1992. The Rule of Law in Hong Kong: Past, Present and Prospects for the Future. *Australian Journal of International Affairs* 46 (1): 81–92.

7701. Wong, K. S. December 1994. The Cuban Democracy Act of 1992: The Extraterritorial Scope of Section-1706(A). *University of Pennsylvania Journal of International Business Law* 14 (4): 651–682.

7702. Woocumings, M. December 1994. The New Authoritarianism in East Asia. *Current History* 93 (587): 413–416.

7703. Wood, D. December 1989. The Senate, Federalism and Democracy. *Melbourne University Law Review* 17: 292–306.

7704. Wood, E. M. 1989. Oligarchic Democracy. *Monthly Review* 41 (3): 42–51.

7705. Wood, E. M., and N. Wood. February 1986. Socrates and Democracy: A Reply to Gregory Vlastos. *Political Theory* 14 (1): 55–82.

7706. Wood, G. H. 1990. Teaching for Democracy. *Educational Leadership* 48 (3): 32–37.

7707. Wood, R. 1981. *See* Feldman, R. L. (1981).

7708. Woodward, B. December 1990. Human Rights and the New Eastern Europe. *Peace Review* 2 (1): 19–22.

7709. Woodward, S. L. 1977. The Freedom of People Is in Its Private Life: Unrevolutionary Implications of Industrial Democracy. *American Behavioral Scientist* 20 (4): 579–596.

7710. Woolf, S. J. May 1981. Prototypes and Terrorists. *Society* 18 (4): 28–29.

7711. Worcester, R. M. December 1987. The Internationalization of Public Opinion Research. *Public Opinion Quarterly* 51 (Supplement): 79–85.

7712. Wrebiak, T. October 1977. The Right to Work, the Right to Manage: Industrial Democracy in Hungary, Problems and Methods. *World Marxist Review* 20: 108–124.

7713. Wright, A. W. 1978. Fabianism and Guild Socialism: Two Views of Democracy. *International Review of Social History* 23 (2): 224–241.

7714. Wright, B. E. June 1990. Pluralism and Vanguardism in the Nicaraguan Revolution. *Latin American Perspectives* 17 (3): 38–54.

7715. Wright, D. S. May 1975. Revenue Sharing and Structural Features of American Federalism. *Annals of the American Academy of Political and Social Science* 419: 100–119.

7716. Wright, E. November 1976. The Revolution and the Constitution: Models of What and for Whom? *Annals of the American Academy of Political and Social Science* 428: 1–21.

7717. Wright, E. O. December 1994. Political Power, Democracy, and Coupon Socialism. *Politics and Society* 22 (4): 535–548.

7718. Wright, J. D. September 1975. Political Socialization Research: The Primary Principle. *Social Forces* 54 (1): 243–255.

7719. Wright, J. J., Jr. December 1992. Thailand's Return to Democracy. *Current History* 91 (569): 418–423.

7720. Wright, R. January 1991. Islam's New Political Face. *Current History* 90 (552): 25–28, 35–36.

7721. Wright, R. June 1992. Islam, Democracy, and the West. *Foreign Affairs* 71 (3): 131–145.

7722. Wrobel, A. February 1988. Democracy and Central Planning.* *Panstwo i Pravo* 43 (2): 53–62.

7723. Wu, J. L. 1982. Some Questions Concerning Socialist Democracy. *Chinese Law and Government* 15 (3–4): 92–99.

7724. Wu, J. X. 1990. The New Authoritarianism: An Express Train toward Democracy by Building Markets. *Chinese Sociology and Anthropology* 23 (2): 36–45.

7725. Wu, J. X., and B. J. Zhang. 1991. Radical Democracy or Stable Democracy. *Chinese Sociology and Anthropology* 23 (3): 7–15.

7726. Wu, Y. April 1989. Marketization of Politics: The Taiwan Experience. *Asian Survey* 29 (4): 382–400.

7727. Wu, Y. January 1990. The Linkage Between Economic and Political Reform in the Socialist Countries: A Supply-Side Explanation. *Annals of the American Academy of Political and Social Science* (507): 91–102.

7728. Wuest, A. M. 1993. Right-Wing Extremism in Germany: Litmus Test for Democracy in the Unified Country. *Migration World* 21 (2–3): 27–31.

7729. Wunsch, J. S. March 1978. Voluntary Association and Structural Development in West Africa Urbanization. *Journal of African Studies* 5 (1): 79–102.

7730. Wur, K. X. 1990. This Is a Democracy and Human Rights Movement. *World Affairs* 152 (3): 151–153.

7731. Wurfel, D. June 1989. The Philippines' Precarious Democracy: Coping with Foreign and Domestic Pressures under Aquino. *International Journal* 44 (3): 676–697.

7732. Wurmser, D. March 1994. Charting a Course Between Real-Politik and Ideology: A Foreign Policy to Sustain the Democratic Community. *Perspectives on Political Science* 23 (2): 96–102.

7733. Wurzbach, P. K. 1978. Freedom of Information and Censor: The Problem of Democracy.* *Beitraege zur Konfliktforschung* 8 (4): 95–104.

7734. Wuthnow, R. 1986. American Democracy and the Democratization of American Religion. *Politics and Society* 15 (2): 223–234.

7735. Wynia, G. W. February 1985. Democracy in Argentina. *Current History* 84 (499): 53–56, 85–86.

7736. Wynia, G. W. January 1987. Readjusting to Democracy in Argentina. *Current History* 86 (516): 5–8, 34.

7737. Wynia, G. W. March 1989. Campaigning for President in Argentina. *Current History* 88 (536): 133–136, 144–145.

7738. Wynia, G. W. January 1990. The Peronists Triumph in Argentina. *Current History* 89 (543): 13–16, 34–35.

7739. Wyrick, T. L. 1982. *See* Arnold, R. A. (1982).

7740. Xian, G. 1989. Political Structural Reform and the Future of Democratization in China. *Journal of Legislation* 16: 47–57.

7741. Xiao, X. June 1992. *See* McCormick, B. L. (June 1992).

7742. Xinshu, Z. October 1990. *See* Jianhua, Z. (October 1990).

7743. Xu, W. June 1981. Advancing the Political Reform of 1980.* *Esprit* 6: 146–152.

7744. Yang, B. K. 1991. Democracy and Authority in the Course of Political Development. *Chinese Sociology and Anthropology* 23 (3): 67–80.

7745. Yang, S. C. March 1994. Where Does South Korean Political Development Stand Now? From Legitimacy Crisis to Democratization Trail. *Korea and World Affairs* 18 (1): 5–22.

7746. Yang, W. L. Y. March 1992. Taiwan since 1988: Democratization, Foreign Policy, and Relations with Peking. *American Asian Review* 10: 42–61.

7747. Yaniv, A., and Y. Yishai. November 1981. Israeli Settlements in the West Bank: The Politics of Intransigence. *Journal of Politics* 43 (4): 1105–1128.

7748. Yao, D. A. 1991. *See* Ingberman, D. E. (1991).

7749. Yarbrough, J. January 1979. Republicanism Reconsidered: Some Thoughts on the Foundation and Preservation of the American Republic. *Review of Politics* 41 (4): 61–95.

7750. Yarbrough, J. March 1979. Representation and Republicanism: Two Views. *Publius* 9 (2): 77–98.

7751. Yarwood, D. L., and D. D. Nimmo. September 1976. Subjective Environments of Bureaucracy: Accuracies and Inaccuracies in Role-Taking among Administrators, Legislators, and Citizens. *Western Political Quarterly* 29 (3): 337–352.

7752. Yasmeen, S. June 1994. Democracy in Pakistan: The Third Dismissal. *Asian Survey* 34 (6): 572–588.

7753. Yates, S. March 1985. More on Democratic Relativism: A Response to Alford. *Inquiry* 28 (1): 113–118.

7754. Yesilada, B. A. December 1988. Problems of Political Development in the Third Turkish Republic. *Polity* 21 (2): 345–372.

7755. Yiftachel, O. 1988. Geopolitical Aspects of Stability in a Biethnic Democracy: The Case of Israel's Policy towards Its Arab Minority. *Politics* 23 (2): 48–56.

7756. Yiftachel, O. January 1992. The Concept of "Ethnic Democracy" and Its Applicability to the Case of Israel. *Ethnic and Racial Studies* 15 (1): 125–136.

7757. Yishai, Y. November 1981. *See* Yaniv, A. (November 1981).

7758. Yishai, Y. June 1992. Interest Groups and Bureaucrats in a Party Democracy: The Case of Israel. *Public Administration* 70 (2): 269–285.

7759. Yishai, Y. January 1993. Public Ideas and Public Policy: Abortion Policy in Four Democracies. *Comparative Politics* 25 (2): 207–228.

7760. Yitri, M. June 1989. The Crisis in Burma: Back from the Heart of Darkness. *Asian Survey* 29 (6): 543–558.

7761. Yongian, Z. 1991. *See* Yue, L. (1991).

7762. Youm, K. H., and M. B. Salwen. March 1990. A Free Press in South Korea: Temporary Phenomenon or Permanent Fixture? *Asian Survey* 30 (3): 312–325.

7763. Young, C. March 1993. Scattered Opposition: Russia's Democracy Movement Has Split over the Pace of Economic Reform. *Reason* 24: 18–24.

7764. Young, I. M. December 1992. Social Groups and Associative Democracy. *Politics and Society* 20 (4): 529–534.

7765. Young, W. D. 1981. The Voices of Democracy: Politics and Communication in Canada. *Canadian Journal of Political Science* 14 (4): 683–700.

7766. Young, W. K. January 1990. South Korea in 1989: Slow Progress toward Democracy. *Asian Survey* 30 (1): 67–73.

7767. Youngers, C. December 1990. *See* Wilde, A. (December 1990).

7768. Yousfi, M. March 1990. Will the Recent Constitutional Reforms in Algeria Lead to a Democratization of Political Life.* *Revue Algerienne des Sciences Juridiques, Economiques et Politiques* 28 (1): 113–144.

7769. Yrarrazaval, J. December 1984. Democracy, Political Parties and Transition.* *Estudios Publicos* 15: 39–56.

7770. Ysmal, C. December 1990. The Electoral Crisis of the UDF and RPR.* *Revue Française de Science Politique* 40 (6): 810–829.

7771. Yue, L., and Z. Yongian. 1991. The New Authoritarianism and Political Democratization. *Chinese Sociology and Anthropology* 23 (4): 31–43.

7772. Yung, W. 1991. Democratization and Institutionalization: Problems, Prospects, and Policy Implications of Political Development in the Republic of China on Taiwan. *Issues and Studies* 27 (3): 29–43.

7773. Yunker, J. A. June 1986. Would Democracy Survive under Market Socialism? *Polity* 18 (4): 678–695.

7774. Z. December 1990. To the Stalin Mausoleum. *Daedalus* 119 (1): 295–344.

7775. Zacher, L. W. 1981. Towards a Democratization of Technological Choices. *Bulletin of Science, Technology and Society* 1 (3): 243–251.

7776. Zaelke, D. J. March 1992. *See* Wold, C. A. (March 1992).

7777. Zaffiro, J. J. 1988. Regional Pressure and the Erosion of Media Freedom in an African Democracy: The Case of Botswana. *Journal of Communication* 38 (3): 108–120.

7778. Zaffiro, J. J. 1989. The Press and Political Opposition in an African Democracy: The Case of Botswana. *Journal of Commonwealth and Comparative Politics* 27 (1): 51–73.

7779. Zafiropoulos, C. November 1994. *See* Chadjipadelis, T. (November 1994).

7780. Zagarri, R. March 1988. Representation and the Removal of State Capitals,

1776–1812. *Journal of American History* 74 (4): 1239–1256.

7781. Zagorski, P. W. March 1988. Civil Military Relations and Argentine Democracy. *Armed Forces and Society* 14 (3): 407–432.

7782. Zagorski, P. W. March 1994. Civil-Military Relations and Argentine Democracy: The Armed Forces under the Menem Government. *Armed Forces and Society* 10 (3): 423–437.

7783. Zaher, L. 1994. The Fall of Communism, What Next? From Totalitarianism to Democracy, or Changing the Paradigm or Social Control.* *Sotsiologicheskie Issledovaniia* (3): 143–149.

7784. Zaimeche, S. E. October 1994. Algeria, Morocco, and Tunisia: Recent Social Change and Future Prospects. *Middle Eastern Studies* 30 (4): 944–955.

7785. Zakorsti, K. December 1994. Hope Factor, Inequality, and Legitimacy of Systemic Transformations: The Case of Poland. *Communist and Post-Communist Studies* 27 (4): 357–376.

7786. Zalaquett, J. 1985. From Dictatorship to Democracy. *New Republic* 193 (25): 17–21.

7787. Zalaquett, J. December 1991. Derechos Humanos y Limitaciones Politicas en las Transiciones Democraticas. *Coleccion Estudios* 18: 147–186.

7788. Zalaquett, J. August 1992. Balancing Ethical Imperatives and Political Constraints: The Dilemma of New Democracies Confronting Past Human Rights Violations. *Hastings Law Journal* 43 (6): 1425–1438.

7789. Zaller, J. October 1983. *See* Chong, D. (October 1983).

7790. Zamosc, L. July 1990. The Political Crisis and the Prospects for Rural Democracy in Colombia. *Journal of Development Studies* 26 (4): 44–78.

7791. Zaninovich, M. G. November 1989. A Prognosis for Yugoslavia. *Current History* 88 (541): 393–396, 404–405.

7792. Zanning, F. 1984. Parliamentary Majority and Popular Majority.* *Problemi Del Socialismo* 3–4: 154–163.

7793. Zapirain, S. October 1976. A Turning Point in the Struggle for Democracy in Spain. *World Marxist Review* 19: 59–64.

7794. Zaret, D. April 1989. Religion and the Rise of Liberal-Democratic Ideology in Seventeenth Century England. *American Sociological Review* 54 (2): 163–179.

7795. Zariski, R. July 1984. Coalition Formation in the Italian Regions: Some Preliminary Findings and Their Significance for Coalition Theory. *Comparative Politics* 16 (4): 403–420.

7796. Zariski, R. March 1986. The Legitimacy of Opposition Parties in Democratic Political Systems: A New Use of an Old Concept. *Western Political Quarterly* 39 (1): 29–47.

7797. Zarkesh, F. 1986. *See* Gould, F. (1986).

7798. Zartman, I. W. November 1992. Democracy and Islam: The Cultural Dialectic. *Annals of the American Academy of Political and Social Science* 524: 181–191.

7799. Zaslavsky, V. March 1992. Nationalism and Democratic Transition in Postcommunism Societies. *Daedalus* 121 (2): 97–121.

7800. Zaslavsky, V. June 1993. Russia and the Problem of Democratic Transition. *Telos* 96: 26–52.

7801. Zaverucha, J. May 1993. The Degree of Military Political Autonomy During the Spanish, Argentine, and Brazilian Transitions. *Journal of Latin American Studies* 25: 283–299.

7802. Zech, C. E. 1986. *See* Kuhn, D. (1986).

7803. Zeichner, K. M. 1991. Contradictions and Tensions in the Professionalization of Teaching and the Democratization of Schools. *Teachers College Record* 92 (3): 363–379.

7804. Zeineddine, A. October 1993. Arabie Saoudite: La Modernisation Tranquille. *Arabies* 24–25.

7805. Zeitlin, J. 1991. *See* Hirst, P. (1991).

7806. Zepp, J. July 1988. *See* Bahro, H. (July 1988).

7807. Zerai, W. October 29,1994. Organising Women within a National Liberation Struggle: Case of Eritrea. *Economic and Political Weekly* 29 (44): WS63-WS68.

7808. Zermeno, S. April 1987. Toward Democracy as Restricted Identity: Society and Politics in Mexico.* *Revista Mexicana de Sociologia* 49 (2): 57–88.

7809. Zeuthen, H. E. 1975. Economic Consequences of Economic Democracy. *Nationalokonomisk Tidsskrift* 113 (1): 4–21.

7810. Zghal, A. 1989. The Concept of Civil Society and the Transition toward Multipartyism. *Annuaire de l'Afrique du Nord* 28: 207–228.

7811. Zhang, B. 1991. *See* Wu, J. X. (1991).

7812. Zhang, B. June 1993. Institutional Aspects of Reforms and the Democratization of Communist Regimes. *Communist and Post-Communist Studies* 26 (2): 165–181.

7813. Zhang, B. April 1994. Corporatism, Totalitarianism, and Transitions to Democracy. *Comparative Political Studies* 27 (1): 108–136.

7814. Zhang, J. 1990. China Spring and the Chinese Alliance for Democracy. *Gazette* 45 (1): 3–17.

7815. Zhao, S. June 1993. A Tragedy of History: The Chinese Search for Democracy in the Twentieth Century. *Journal of Contemporary China* 3: 18–37.

7816. Zhelev, Z. October 1993. Personal Reflections on a Changing Eastern Europe. *Federal Bar News and Journal* 40: 570–572.

7817. Zheng, Y. N. June 1994. Development and Democracy: Are They Compatible in China. *Political Science Quarterly* 109 (2): 235–259.

7818. Zhu, J. H., and S. Rosen. September 1993. From Discontent to Protest: Individual Level Causes of the 1989 Pro-Democracy Movement in China. *International Journal of Public Opinion Research* 5 (3): 234–249.

7819. Zi, M. 1987. Strengthening the Peoples Congress Is the Fundamental Way to Develop Socialist Democracy. *Chinese Law and Government* 20 (1): 84–88.

7820. Zielonka, J. June 1991. East Central Europe: Democracy in Retreat? *Washington Quarterly* 14 (3): 107–120.

7821. Zielonka, J. April 1994. New Institutions in the Old East Bloc. *Journal of Democracy* 5 (2): 87–104.

7822. Ziemer, K. 1992. A False Start for Democracy: Premises, Structure, and Short Comings of the New Political Party System in Poland.* *Geschichte und Gesellschaft* 18 (3): 311–333.

7823. Ziesemer, T. 1990. Public Factors and Democracy in Poverty Analysis. *Oxford Economic Papers New Series* 42 (1): 268–280.

7824. Zimbalist, A. 1980. Economic Democracy: Solution or New Challenge. *Review of Social Economy* 38 (3): 303–311.

7825. Zimbalist, A. September 1993. Dateline Cuba: Hanging On in Havana. *Foreign Policy* 92: 151–152.

7826. Zimmerman, E. 1980. Democracy and Protest.* *Rechts und Sozialphilosophie* 66 (2): 223–238.

7827. Zimmerman, E. 1983. The Comparative Analysis of Political System Crises in the Democratic Industrial Societies: A

Draft Research Project.* *Politische Viertel-jahresschrift* 14: 259–284.

7828. Zimmerman, E. 1993. Mechanism for the Regulation of Violent Conflicts in Liberal Democracies.* *Oesterreichische Zeitschrift für Politikwissenschaft* 22 (2): 221–234.

7829. Zimmerman, J. F. May 1988. Civic Strategies for Community Empowerment. *National Civic Review* 77 (3): 202–212.

7830. Zimmerman, J. F. December 1994. Alternative Voting Systems in Representative Democracy. *PS: Political Science & Politics* 27 (4): 674–677.

7831. Zimmerman, R. F. February 1976. Thailand 1975: Transition to Constitutional Democracy Continues. *Asian Survey* 16 (2): 159–172.

7832. Zimmerman, W. April 1994. Markets, Democracy and Russian Foreign Policy. *Post-Soviet Affairs* 10 (2): 103–126.

7833. Zincone, G. January 1980. For a Wealth-Based Democracy.* *Biblioteca della Liberta* 76: 169–176.

7834. Zingale, A. May 1980. Anti-Terrorist Strategies in the Western Democracy.* *Democrazia e Diritto* 20 (3–4): 467–488.

7835. Zipp, J. F., P. Luebke, and R. Landerman. October 1984. The Social Bases of Support for Workplace Democracy. *Sociological Perspectives* 27 (4): 395–425.

7836. Ziring, L. September 1984. From Islamic Republic to Islamic State in Pakistan. *Asian Survey* 24 (9): 931–946.

7837. Ziring, L. December 1993. The Second Stage in Pakistan Politics: The 1993 Elections. *Asian Survey* 33 (12): 1175–1185.

7838. Zirker, D. September 1986. Civilianization and Authoritarian Nationalism in Brazil: Ideological Opposition within a Military Dictatorship. *Journal of Political and Military Sociology* 14 (2): 263–276.

7839. Zirker, D. 1987. Political Transition and Regionalism in Brazil: A Preliminary Analysis. *Canadian Journal of American and Caribbean Studies* 23 (12): 29–56.

7840. Zirker, D. June 1988. Democracy and the Military in Brazil: Elite Accommodation in Cases of Torture. *Armed Forces and Society* 14 (4): 587–606.

7841. Zirker, D. December 1994. Brazilian Foreign Policy and Subimperialism during the Political Transition of the 1980s: A Review and Reapplication of Martini's Theory. *Latin American Perspectives* 21 (1): 115–131.

7842. Zirker, D., and M. Henberg. December 1994. Amazonia: Democracy, Ecology, and Brazilian Military Prerogatives in the 1990s. *Armed Forces and Society* 20: 259–281.

7843. Zizek, S. 1991. Formal Democracy and Its Discontents. *American Imago* 48 (2): 181–198.

7844. Znoj, M., L. Major, J. Pesek, and M. Sobotka. 1990. Dispute over Democracy at the 17th International Philosophy Congress in Prague in 1934.* *Filosoficky Casopis* 38 (1–2): 87–98.

7845. Zolberg, A. R. June 1992. The Specter of Anarchy: African States Verging on Dissolution. *Dissent* 39 (3): 303–311.

7846. Zolberg, V. L. December 1984. American Art Museum: Sanctuary or Free-For-All? *Social Forces* 63 (2): 377–392.

7847. Zolo, D. November 1986. Evolutionary Risks of Democracy.* *Democrazia e Diritto* 26 (6): 15–38.

7848. Zolo, D., and N. Luhmann. July 1987. An Exchange on "The Future of Democracy."* *Il Mulino* 312: 563–583.

7849. Zoric, J. September 1988. *See* Kelly, E. P. (September 1988).

7850. Zubek, V. March 1992. *See* Gentleman, J. (March 1992).

7851. Zuchert, C. H. July 1983. Reagan and That Unnamed Frenchman (de Tocqueville): On the Rationale for the New (Old) Federalism. *Review of Politics* 45 (3): 421–442.

7852. Zucker, L. G. June 1985. *See* Turk, H. (June 1985).

7853. Zuckerman, A. S. July 1982. New Approaches to Political Cleavage: A Theoretical Introduction. *Comparative Political Studies* 15 (2): 131–144.

7854. Zuckerman, A. S. et al. November 1994. A Structural Theory of Vote Choice: Social and Political Networks and Electoral Flows in Britain and the United States. *Journal of Politics* 56 (4): 1008–1033.

7855. Zuckert, C. April 1981. Not by Preaching: Tocqueville on the Role of Religion in American Democracy. *Review of Politics* 43 (2): 259–280.

7856. Zuckert, C. August 1981. On Reading Classic American Novelists as Political Thinkers. *Journal of Politics* 43 (3): 683–706.

7857. Zuk, G. November 1994. *See* Gryski, G. S. (November 1994).

7858. Zuleeg, M. 1978. Verfassungsgrundsatz der Demokratie und Die Europaieschen Gemeinschaften. *Der Staat* 17 (1): 27–47.

7859. Zulu, G. April 1980. *See* Fincham, R. (April 1980).

7860. Zunes, S. June 1988. Participatory Democracy in the Sahara: A Study of Polisario Self-Government. *Scandinavian Journal of Development Alternatives* 7 (2–3): 141–156.

7861. Zvesper, J. October 1982. The Problem of Liberal Rhetoric. *Review of Politics* 44 (4): 546–558.

7862. Zwaan, T. March 1982. One Step Forward, Two Steps Back: Tumin's Theory of Democratic Development: A Comment. *Theory and Society* 11 (2): 143–164.

7863. Zwane, B. April 1993. Direct Democracy Accepted in Swaziland. *Parliamentarian* 74: 88–91.

7864. Zweig, D. September 1989. Peasants and Politics. *World Policy Journal* 6 (4): 633–645.

Article Collections

(chronologically arranged)

7865. 1970. Sozialreformismus: Theorien, Politik, Widersprueche. *IPW Forschungshefte* 14 (2): 5–159. Introduction & 6 articles.

7866. 1974. Demokratisierung-Gefahr Fuer die Freiheit? *Vorgaenge* 13 (3): 15–127. 13 articles.

7867. November 1974. Inflation in der Demokratie. *Wirtschaftsdienst* 54: 555–568. 3 articles.

7868. 1975. Corporate Democracy and the Corporate Political Contribution. *Iowa Law Review* 61 (2): 545–579.

7869. January 1975. Bedrohte Freiheiten? *Politische Meinung* 20: 5–76.

7870. July 1975. Wird die Schweiz Unregierbar? *Schweizer Monatshefte* 55: 274–298. 3 articles.

7871. October 1980. The Democratic State. *Sistema* 38–39: 3–300.

7872. 1981. Judicial Review Versus Democracy. *Ohio State Law Journal* 42: 1–434. Forward & 15 articles.

7873. April 1981. Democracy in Latin America.* *Revista Mexicana de Sociologia* 43 (2): 535–791. 5 articles.

7874. May 1981. Constitutional Adjudication and Democratic Theory. *New York University Law Review* 56: 259–544. 8 articles.

7875. 1983. Democratizacion y Movimientos Sociales: Ideologias, Objetivos y Organizacion en la Actividad Politica. *Critica y Utopia* (9): 11–123. Conference proceedings.

7876. June 1983. Objective Democracy: Transition in Latin America.* *Politica Internazionale* 6: 41–102.

7877. 1984. Industrial Democracy: Participation, Labour Relations, and Motivation. *International Social Science Journal* 36 (2): 195–366. Collection of articles.

7878. January 1984. Reconstructing the State.* *Pensamiento Iberoamericano* 5a-5b: 1–731.

7879. March 1984. From Authoritarianism to Representative Government in Brazil and Argentina. *Government and Opposition* 19 (2): 152–238. Collection of articles.

7880. June 29,1984. Senegal 1984. *Marches Tropicaux et Mediterraneens* 40: 1671–1673+. 2 articles.

7881. 1985. Record and Prospects of Democracy in the Third World States. *Annuaire du Tiers Monde* 9: 11–356. Special issue.

7882. April 1985. Uruguay in Transition. *Revista Mexicana de Sociologia* 47 (2): 5–248. Whole issue.

7883. April 1986. "Total" (The) State (in India). *Seminar* 320: 12–38. Collection of articles.

7884. June 1986. Divisive Currents (in India). *Seminar* 322: 97–158. Collection of articles.

7885. August 1986. Tropical Africa: The Way Out of the Crisis; Dakar Round Table on "Current Development in Africa and the Problems of Democracy." *World Marxist Review* 29: 54–64. Round table.

7886. September 1986. Dialectics of Democracy in Latin America. *Contemporary Marxism* (14): 1–114. 8 articles.

7887. December 1986. South Korea: Voices for Democracy. *World Policy Journal* 4: 161–178. Interviews.

7888. January 1987. Bases del Regimen Democratico. *Politica.* Special Issue: 5–252. Conference papers.

7889. March 1987. Democracy in Latin America and the Caribbean: The Promise and the Challenge. *Department of State Bulletin* 87: 58–89.

7890. June 1987. Industrial Democracy and Management. *International Studies of Management & Organization* 17: 3–96. 8 articles.

7891. September 1987. The State: The Democratic Requirement. *La Revue Nouvelle* 9: 115–212. Whole issue.

7892. September 1987. Democratic Theory. *Florida State University Law Review* 15: 389–483. 5 articles.

7893. 1988. Parliamentary Democracy. *Human Rights Law Journal* 9 (4): 365–480. Collection of articles.

7894. 1988. Democracy.* *Teoria Politica* 4 (3): 33–89. 4 articles.

7895. June 1988. Between Party and Principle: The Exit and Voice of Fang Lizhi, Liu Binyan, and Wang Ruowing. *Chinese Law and Government* 21 (2): 3–102. Collection of articles.

7896. September 1988. Chile: Camino a la Democracia. *Politica* (17): 5–147. Collection of articles.

7897. December 1988. Symposium on Civil Rights and Civil Liberties in the Workplace. *Harvard Civil Rights-Civil Liberties Law Review* 23: 1–137. Collection of articles.

7898. 1989. Focus: Re-examining the Informal Sector. *Grassroots Development* 13 (1): 3–33. 4 articles.

7899. January 1989. La Democracia Dominicana: Experiencia y Desafios. *Revista de Ciencia y Cultura UNIBE* 1: 1–93. Collection of articles.

7900. June 1989. Conceptions of Democracy: The Case of Voting Rights. *Florida Law Review* 41: 409–657. 9 articles.

7901. October 1989. China: Forty Years of Revolution. *World and I* 4: 22–127. 8 articles.

7902. November 1989. The Electronic Democracy. *Public Management* 71: 2–13. 5 articles.

7903. November 1989. Socialist Pluralism: Roundtable Discussion of the Novosti Press Agency and the Editorial Board of Sotsiologischeskie Issledovaniia. *Soviet Sociology* 28: 6–41.

7904. 1990. Reforming the Canada Elections Act. *Canadian Parliamentary Review* 13: 2–14. 5 articles.

7905. 1990. Democratie et Democratisation dans le Monde Arabe. *Egypte Monde Arabe* (4): 5–140. 5 articles.

7906. 1990. Chile. *Canadian Journal of Latin American and Caribbean Studies* 30: 7–322. 10 articles.

7907. January 1990. Summary Report of the 35th Commonwealth Parliamentary Conference: Threats to Democracy; The Commonwealth Response: The 1990s and Beyond. *Parliamentarian* 71: 7–57.

7908. March 1990. The European Revolutions. *Dissent* 37: 159–236. 17 articles.

7909. March 1990. Iglesia Catolica, Crisis y Democratizacion en Centro America. *Panorama Centroamericano: Temas y Documentos de Debate* 13–539. Documents from various episcopal conferences, 1976–1990.

7910. May 1990. Building a Democratic Eastern Europe. *World and I* 5: 20–59. 5 articles.

7911. June 1990. The Future of the USSR. *Telos* 3–154. Collection of articles.

7912. July 1990. Democracy (the) Movement in the (Chinese) Provinces. *Australian Journal of Chinese Affairs* 24: 181–314. Collection of articles.

7913. August 1990. Special Report: Perestroika in Black Africa. *World and I* 5: 20–47. 3 articles.

7914. September 1990. Democracy in the New Europe.* *Cadmos* 5: 9–99. Collection of articles.

7915. October 1990. Chiles Weg Zur Demokratie. *Lateinamerika (Hamburg):* 5–29+. 6 articles.

7916. November 1990. El Proceso de Paz y Democratizacion de Centro America. *Panorama Centroamericano: Temas y Documentos de Debate:* 3–674. Collection of documents, 1989–1990.

7917. November 1990. La Dimensione Politica Della Comunita Europea. *Europa Forum:* 9–57. Collection of articles.

7918. 1991. Focus: NGOs Face the Challenges of a New Decade. *Grassroots Development* 15 (2): 1–37. 4 articles.

7919. March 1991. Approaching Democracy: A New Legal Order for Eastern Europe. *University of Chicago Law Review* 58: 823–869. 8 articles.

7920. April 1991. India: Tradition and Democracy. *Parliamentarian* 72: 120–137. 6 articles.

7921. May 1991. Afrique: La Voie Etroite de l'Ouverture. *Jeune Afrique Economie* 112–137. 7 articles.

7922. June 1991. Quelle Democratie pour Quel Citoyen? *Cosmopolitiques:* 5–174. Proceedings of colloquium.

7923. June 1991. International Reform in Higher Education. *Survey of Business* 27: 2–27. 8 articles.

7924. July 1991. India: Culture and Democracy. *Parliamentarian* 72: 187–191+. 16 articles.

7925. July 1991. Democrazia e Sviluppo in Africa. *Politica Internazionale* 19: 41–93+. 13 articles.

7926. July 1991. Benin: The Democratic Model. *Courier:* 18–28. 5 articles.

7927. September 1991. Tonga: A Kingdom in Search of Greater Democracy. *Courier* 22–33. Articles & interviews.

7928. October 1991. Democratie et Developpement dans le Tiers Monde. *Economie et Humanisme:* 11–70. 10 articles.

7929. November 1991. Le Retout de l'Afrique. *Monde Diplomatique* 38: 22–25. 7 articles.

7930. November 1991. Kenya: Democracy; Winning the Hearts and Minds of Wananchi. *Courier:* 11–29. 6 articles & 1 interview.

7931. December 1991. Constitucion 1991: Nuevo Pais. *Revista Foro* 20: 9–118. 9 articles.

7932. December 1991. La France Face à l'Afrique. *Relations Internationales et Strategiques:* 81–126. 7 articles.

7933. 1992. Industria Electoral y Communcacion Politica. *Estado y Sociedad* 8: 1–119. Conference papers presented by Facultad Latinoamericana de Ciencias Sociales, September 1991.

7934. 1992. Strukturanpassung und Demokratie: Die Quadratur des Kreises? Das Beispiel Venezuela. *Lateinamerika (Hamburg)* (21): 5–121. 6 articles.

7935. 1992. L'Imperatif Democratique dans les Relations Internationales. *Trimestre du Monde* (1): 21–35. 10 articles.

7936. 1992. Zaire: Troubled Past, Uncertain Future. *Africa Today* 39 (3): 5–66. 3 articles.

7937. March 1992. Senegal: La Democratie à l'Epreuve. *Politique Africaine:* 2–99. 6 articles; English summaries 177–178.

7938. April 1992. Parliamentary Profile: Cayman Islands. *Parliamentarian* 73: 113–117+. 5 articles.

7939. April 1992. Burkina Faso: Democratie. *Jeune Afrique Economie* supplement: 46–75. 5 articles and interviews.

7940. April 1992. Demokratisierung und Demokratisierungshilfe. *Entwicklung und Zusammenarbeit (E & Z)* 33: 8–16. 7 articles.

7941. May 1992. Country Reports: Côte d'Ivoire. *Courier:* 5–25. 8 articles.

7942. May 1992. Questions Africaines. *Defense Nationale* 48: 21–33. 3 articles.

7943. May 1992. The Challenge of Freedom: Fostering Market Enterprise in the Developing Democracies. *Economic Education Bulletin* 32: 1–48. Conference proceedings of Progress Foundation; Prague, September 24, 1991.

7944. June 1992. Quelle Democratie pour l'Europe. *Politique Internationale.* 109-page supplement.

7945. July 1992. Capitalism, Socialism and Democracy. *Journal of Democracy* 3 (3): 3–137. Whole issue.

7946. July 1992. Country Reports: Seychelles. *Courier* 31–45. 5 articles.

7947. September 1992. Country Reports: Guinea. *Courier* 8–22. Special report.

7948. September 1992. Democracy after the Nation-State. *New Perspectives Quarterly* 9: 4–53. 14 articles.

7949. October 2, 1992. The Media. *RFE/RL Research Report* 1: 1–91. 19 articles.

7950. October 9, 1992. L'Afrique Martyre. *L'Express:* 20–31. 4 articles and 1 interview.

7951. November 1992. Country Studies: Senegal. *Courier:* 24–41. 6 articles.

7952. November 1992. Islam: The State and Democracy. *Middle East Report* 22: 2–32. 4 articles and 2 interviews.

7953. December 1992. Les Problemes Institutionnels de la Transition en Europe Centrale et Orientale. *Revue d'Etudes Comparatives Est-Ouest* 23: 4–181. 10 articles; English summaries 185–190.

7954. January 1993. Country Report: Mauritania. *Courier:* 17–44. 5 articles & 3 interviews.

7955. March 1993. Zambia: The Score So Far: Democracy 2, Economic Recovery 1. *Courier:* 31–54. 10 articles.

7956. July 1993. Political Islam. *Middle East Report* 23: 2–12. 5 articles.

7957. July 1993. Political Data 1945–1990. Party Government in 20 Democracies. *European Journal of Political Research* 24 (1): 1–119. Collection of articles.

7958. July 1993. Cyprus: Constitutional Democracy in the European Tradition. *Parliamentarian* 74: 156+ (35-page section). 7 articles.

7959. July 1993. Le Incognite della Transizione nel Corno d'Africa. *Politica Internazionale* 20: 7–23+. 6 articles.

7960. September 1993. Political Economy in Post-Communist Eastern Europe: Voices from Within. *International Journal of Politics, Culture and Society* 7: 5–74. 4 articles.

7961. October 22, 1993. The Crisis in Russia. *RFE/RL Research Report* 2: 1–15. 2 articles.

7962. November 1993. Country Report: The Gambia. *Courier:* 13–31. 2 articles and 4 interviews.

7963. November 1993. Country Report: Tanzania. *Courier:* 32–47. 2 articles & 3 interviews.

7964. November 1993. Gobernabilidad? Sueno de la Democracia? *Nueva Sociedad* 128: 49–157. 7 articles.

7965. December 1993. Teledemocrazia e Partecipazione. *Problemi dell'Informazione* 18: 377–413. 4 articles.

7966. January 1994. Country Report: Niger Winning the Economic Battle, a Very Long Shot. *Courier:* 12–37. 3 articles and 3 interviews.

7967. March 1994. Democracy or Civil War. *World Press Review* 41: 10–15. 6 articles.

7968. March 1994. Venezuela: Rethinking Capitalist Democracy. *Report on the Americas* 27: 15–43. Special section.

7969. March 1994. Diplomacy's Focus on Business. *Foreign Policy Journal* 71: 32–41. 4 articles.

7970. March 1994. Country Report: Ghana. *Courier:* 20–45. 6 articles and 4 interviews.

7971. March 1994. National Security and Democracy: A Symposium. *Armed Forces and Society* 20 (3): 353–472. 6 articles.

7972. April 1994. Central Asia. *Current History* 93: 145–186. 9 articles.

7973. April 1994. Symposium on Bruce Ackerman's *We the People. Ethics* 104 (3): 446–535. 5 articles.

7974. May 1994. Country Report: Ethiopia. *Courier:* 16–40. 7 articles & 2 interviews.

7975. May 1994. La Question Constitutionnelle. *Revue Politique et Parlementaire* 94: 2–41. 7 articles.

7976. June 1994. A New South Africa? *Third World Quarterly* 15: 187–217+. 5 articles.

7977. July 1994. Information Resources and Democracy. *Journal of the American Society for Information Science* 45: 350–421. 7 articles.

7978. December 1994. Germany in Transition. *Daedalus* 123: 1–284. 14 articles.

Index

trade union newspapers, freedom of speech, 1919
trade union reform movement, 5236
trade unions, 577, 5236
  anti-democracy, 565
  armed forces, 1432
  attitude survey, 4570
  bargaining (1971–1981), 2161
  clientelism, 566
  collective bargaining, 3221
  Labor Management Reporting and Disclosure Act, 3313
  planning, 6341
  tax funds misuse, 564
  workplace democracy, 496
transition to democracy, foreign aid, 3251
treaty-making power, 2976
two-party system, bicentennial, 6528
United Automobile Workers, 4452
urban government, 492, 2813
  elite perceptions, 2816
urban politics, 1290
U.S.S.R., 2219
values (18th century), 2661
voter fatigue, direct democracy, 800
voter rights, Supreme Court, 6190
voter turnout, 217, 515
  comparative study, 5698
  Midwest (1841–1872), 6585
voters, students, 7575
voting behavior, 1367, 2234, 3855, 7854
  congressional, 1138
  elections, presidential (1988), 6763
voting rights, 184
Voting Rights Act, 1992
  homeless persons, 2837
  Supreme Court, 2715
voting, Democratic Party, 5784
war
  covert action, 2213
  election results, 1437
war making powers, president, 2802
war on poverty, local government, 3589
war powers, judicial review, 3596
Washington, George, 6425
water management, decision making, participation, 3510
Watergate, 3822
  crisis, 4562
welfare, equal protection, 4241
welfare state (1881–1920), 5319
welfare state policies, 5
White House Conference on Families, participatory democracy, 5258
women, 184
  De Tocqueville, 7660
  democratization, 728
  interest groups, 2422

representation, 4010
  workplace democracy, 4097
women's rights, 1912
  (1821–1840), 2565
  Equal Rights Amendment, 750
  policy, Germany (F.R.) (1941–1952), 6186
  pro-choice, 7346
workplace cooperation, 409
workplace democracy, 159, 3774, 3827, 6283, 7897
  clerks, 2118
  federal bureaucracy, 1488
  support, 7835
  Topeka, 7427
  trade unions, 496
  women, 4097
yeoman farmers, economic democracy, 6330
zoning politics, group homes, 1311
REPUBLICANISM, 4361
  liberalism, 5571
  U.S.A., 7749
REQUISITES, 4204, 7891
  China, cultural, public opinion survey, 5093
  liberal democracy, 4937
  participatory democracy, 3909
RESEARCH
  consociational democracy, strategy, 6821
  democracy-war hypothesis, future, 1180
  democratization, 2597
  future, democracy-war hypothesis, 1180
  strategy, consociational democracy, 6821
  transition to democracy, 2612
  work, 103
RESISTANCE POLITICS, 1792
RESOURCE ALLOCATION
  direct democracy, 6066
RESOURCES
  gender, participation, 6364
RESPONSIBILITY, 3765
RESURGENCE, 4019
RETAIL
  U.S.A., 921
RETIREMENT
  U.S.A., Congress (102nd), 2692
RETURNED SCHOLARS
  democracy movement, China, 2920
REUNIFICATION
  China and Hong Kong, 2633
  China and Taiwan, democratization, 4900
  democratization, Germany (F.R.), 302, 1557, 7363
  elections, Germany (F.R.) (1990), 3317
    (1994), 7368
  Germany (F.R.), 302, 632, 1557, 2415, 4752, 5139, 6969, 7366, 7978
    Common Constitution Commission, 5139

democratization, 7363
  elections, 3961
  elections (1990), 3317
  elections (1994), 7368
  national archival system, 3431
  property rights, 7064
  Social Democratic Party, 7090
  trade unions, 7090
  North Korea, policy, 3643
  South Korea, 4006
REVENUE SHARING
  U.S.A., federalism, 7715
REVISIONISM
  liberal democracy, Africa, 6266
REVOLUTION, 6466
  democratization, 1412, 1413
  Latin America, democratization, 7322
  Luxemburg, Rosa, 4030
  Nicaragua, 1412, 1413
    pluralism, 7714
  U.S.S.R. (1917), citizens' rights and freedoms, 3272
REVOLUTIONARY DEMOCRACY, 7210
  library service, 3066
  nationalism, 6581
  Thomas, C. V., 4700
REVOLUTIONARY MOVEMENT
  Latin America, democratization, 6213
  social democracy, Russia, 2080
REVOLUTIONARY VALUES
  U.S.A., 3554
RIGHT OF PROPERTY
  Philippines, 6120
RIGHT TO LIFE MOVEMENT
  Roe v. Wade, U.S.A., judiciary, 4173
RIGHT WING DEMOCRACY
  Reagan Doctrine, U.S.A., 2001
RIGHTS
  economic, 5082
RIGHTS OF MAN
  Paine, Thomas, 3501
RIKER, WILLIAM
  epistemology, 1335
RIOTS
  democratization, Algeria (1988), 1883
RISK, 3971, 6156
  analysis, 5911
  management
    trust, 6680
    U.S.A., 4287
  India, 653
  Latin America, 4873
ROBOTS
  technology, 4905
ROE V. WADE
  right to life movement, U.S.A., judiciary, 4173
ROGERS, LINDSAY
  presidential emergency powers, U.S.A., 1291
ROMAN CATHOLIC CHURCH, 1550, 4927
  Africa, democratization, 747

⧼⧽